ONWARD

ONWARD

The King's Own Calgary Regiment
in Peace and War, 1910–1960

PATRICK H. BRENNAN

© 2025 Patrick H. Brennan

University of Calgary Press
2500 University Drive NW
Calgary, Alberta
Canada T2N 1N4
press.ucalgary.ca

All rights reserved

No part of this book may be reproduced in any format whatsoever without prior written permission from the publisher, except for brief excerpts quoted in scholarship or review.

This book is available in a digital format which is licensed under a Creative Commons license. The publisher should be contacted for any commercial use which falls outside the terms of that license.

LIBRARY AND ARCHIVES CANADA CATALOGUING IN PUBLICATION

Title: Onward : the King's Own Calgary Regiment in peace and war, 1910-1960 / Patrick H. Brennan.
Other titles: King's Own Calgary Regiment in peace and war, 1910-1960
Names: Brennan, Patrick H., author
Description: Includes bibliographical references and index.
Identifiers: Canadiana (print) 2025010119X | Canadiana (ebook) 20250101270 | ISBN 9781773856001 (jacket hardcover offset) | ISBN 9781773856377 (case laminate hardcover POD) | ISBN 9781773856018 (softcover) | ISBN 9781773856032 (PDF) | ISBN 9781773856025 (Open Access PDF) | ISBN 9781773856049 (EPUB)
Subjects: LCSH: Canada. Canadian Army. King's Own Calgary Regiment—History—20th century. | LCSH: World War, 1914-1918—Regimental histories—Canada. | LCSH: World War, 1939-1945—Regimental histories—Canada. | LCSH: Cold War—Regimental histories—Canada. | LCSH: Canada—History, Military—20th century.
Classification: LCC UA602.K56 B74 2025 | DDC 358.1/80971—dc23

The University of Calgary Press acknowledges the support of the Government of Alberta through the Alberta Media Fund for our publications. We acknowledge the financial support of the Government of Canada. We acknowledge the financial support of the Canada Council for the Arts for our publishing program.

Copyediting by Peter Midgley
Cover image: The King's Own Calgary Regiment's guidon, photograph courtesy of
  The King's Own Calgary Regiment (RCAC); Colourbox 34181353
Cover design, page design, and typesetting by Melina Cusano

For Major Lester Webster and Corporal Nathan Hornburg

CONTENTS

List of Illustrations	IX
List of Maps	XV
Acknowledgements	XVII
List of Abbreviations	XIX
Introduction—Fifty Years of Peace and War	1
Chapter 1—From Calgary to Vimy Ridge	11
Chapter 2—From Vimy Ridge to Amiens	35
Chapter 3—The Hundred Days and Home	71
Chapter 4—A Short Peace and a Second War	111
Chapter 5—From Mobilization to Dieppe	141
Chapter 6—From Dieppe to Ortona	171
Chapter 7—From the Gari to the Arno	215
Chapter 8—From the Arno to Holland and Home	263
Chapter 9—Neither Peace nor War	303
Conclusion—In the Service of Their Country	325
Notes	329
Bibliography	411
Index	419

LIST OF ILLUSTRATIONS

Forging the 50th Battalion

1.1 "103rd Regiment (Calgary Regiment) marching in Calgary Exhibition and Stampede Parade, Calgary, Alberta," 1912, nc-78-72. Glenbow Library and Archives Collection, Library and Cultural Resources, University of Calgary. — 7

1.2 "Sarcee Army Camp, Calgary, Alberta," 1915, na-989-1, Glenbow Library and Archives Collection, Library and Cultural Resources, University of Calgary. — 7

1.3 "Regimental ball, Calgary, Alberta," 1912, na-3232-69, Glenbow Library and Archives Collection, Library and Cultural Resources, University of Calgary. — 8

1.4 "50th Battalion and 31st Battalion, Canadian Expeditionary Force, marching up 9th Street SW hill in winter, Calgary, Alberta," 1915, nc-44-39, Glenbow Library and Archives Collection, Library and Cultural Resources, University of Calgary. — 9

1.5 "Major-General Sam Steele inspecting soldiers of the 50th Battalion, Calgary, Alberta," 1915, na-3419-2, Glenbow Library and Archives Collection, Library and Cultural Resources, University of Calgary. — 9

1.6 "Troops on train en route for overseas service, probably including the 103rd Calgary Rifles leaving Calgary, Alberta," 1914, na-4355-38, Glenbow Library and Archives Collection, Library and Cultural Resources, University of Calgary. — 10

1.7 "137th Battalion, Canadian Expeditionary Force leaving by train, Calgary, Alberta," 14 August 1916, na-1617-5, Glenbow Library and Archives Collection, Library and Cultural Resources, University of Calgary. — 10

The 50th Battalion at War

2.1 "Mud bespattered Canadian heroes returning from the trenches," November 1916, 19920085-154, Canadian War Museum. — 60

2.2 "Photographs taken during the Battle of Vimy Ridge - Canadians searching captured German trenches for hiding Huns," 1917, 19920085-914, Canadian War Museum. — 60

2.3 "Studio Portrait of LCOL E. G. Mason – 50th BN – Photo by Hess, Calgary," c. 1915, P-200-10-0133, King's Own Calgary Regiment Archives. — 61

2.4	"Lieutenant Colonel William C. G. Armstrong," April 1916, na-2362-2, Glenbow Library and Archives Collection, Library and Cultural Resources, University of Calgary.	61
2.5	Emmeline (Mae) and David Argo on their wedding day, n.d., P-200-10-0150, King's Own Calgary Regiment Archives.	61
2.6	"Famous Central Electric Generating Station on the banks of the Souchez River," August 1917, 19920085-695, Canadian War Museum.	62
2.7	"Captain Robert Pearson of the Y.M.C.A., umpiring behind the plate at a baseball match held in the Canadian lines," September 1917, 19920085-807, Canadian War Museum.	62
2.8	"Alberta elections - 5th Battalion recording their votes near the shelling area," August 1917, 19920085-632, Canadian War Museum.	63
2.9	"Battle of Passchendaele - Mud and Boche wire through which the Canadians had to advance," November 1917, 19930013-512, Canadian War Museum.	63
2.10	"Private John George Pattison, VC," n.d., 19940079-083, Canadian War Museum.	64
2.11	"Lens - Canadians resting in a trench," September 1917, 19930013-947, Canadian War Museum.	64
2.12	"Machine gun section of the 50th Battalion, Canadian Expeditionary Force," c. 1917–18, na-4025-24, Glenbow Library and Archives Collection, Library and Cultural Resources, University of Calgary.	64
2.13	"Canadian troops on their way up the line," January 1918, 19930013-667, Canadian War Museum.	65
2.14	"Canadians filling their water bottles, etc.," August 1918, 19930012-495, Canadian War Museum.	65
2.15	"Battle of Amiens, August 1918 - Wounded arrive at a Canadian Field Dressing Station," 1918, 19930012-399, Canadian War Museum.	66
2.16	"Canadian Corps Heavy Artillery in Action," 1918, 19930012-646, Canadian War Museum.	66
2.17	"Canadians moving forward into attack on Cambrai," 1918, 19930012-742, Canadian War Museum.	67
2.18	"Arras Front – Mouvres [sic]," April 1919, 19920044-925, Canadian War Museum.	67
2.19	"Demobilization, Bramshott and Whitby, April, 1919," April 1919, 19940003-473, Canadian War Museum.	68
2.20	"Welcome home parade for 50th Battalion of the Canadian Expeditionary Force, Calgary, Alberta," 9 June 1919, na-3965-8, Glenbow Library and Archives Collection, Library and Cultural Resources, University of Calgary.	68

2.21	"Soldiers from the 50th Battalion, Canadian Expeditionary Force, with family at Overyssche, Belgium," 1918, na-4025-25, Glenbow Library and Archives Collection, Library and Cultural Resources, University of Calgary.	69
2.22	"Brig.-Gen. Hayter, 10th Infantry Brigade, and his Battalion Commanders," November 1918, PA-003414, Library and Archives Canada.	69
2.23	"Lt.-Col. L.F. Page, D.S.O. and two Bars," December 1918, PA-007705, Library and Archives Canada.	70

Surviving the Peace and Preparing for War

3.1	"Unveiling war memorial at Central Park, Calgary, Alberta," 23 May 1924, na-2742-4, Glenbow Library and Archives Collection, Library and Cultural Resources, University of Calgary.	107
3.2	"Studio Portrait of COL. D.G.L. Cunnington, MC - Photo by Benninhams Courtland Studio – Calgary," c. 1930, P-300-10-0015, King's Own Calgary Regiment Archives.	108
3.3	"Portrait of LCOL L.O. Svenson," c. 1930, P-300-10-0049, King's Own Calgary Regiment Archives.	108
3.4	"Portrait of LCOL F.L. Shouldice," c. 1930, P-300-10-0050, King's Own Calgary Regiment Archives.	108
3.5	"Calgary Regiment Parade Along 4th Street SW Calgary - Rememberance Day? [sic] - Central Park Centograph Visible at Far Right Edge of Photo," Remembrance Day, 1935, P-300-10-0003, King's Own Calgary Regiment Archives.	109
3.6	"Group Photo - Camp Sarcee - Identified: Capt J. Begg (ADJ); LCOL L.A. Cavanaugh (OC); Maj W.K. Jull MC VD (2nd in Command)," 1935, P-300-10-0060, King's Own Calgary Regiment Archives.	109
3.7	"Calgary Regiment (Tank) Going Into Camp at Camp Sarcee in 1939 with Their First "Tanks,"" 1939, P-300-10-0021, King's Own Calgary Regiment Archives.	110
3.8	"Photo Postcard - Regiment Marches in the Calgary Stampede Parade," July 1941, P-300-10-0068, King's Own Calgary Regiment Archives.	110

Tragedy at Dieppe and the Regiment Reborn

4.1	"Camp Borden - Unidentified Soldier in Renault Tank," spring 1941, P-400-10-0170, King's Own Calgary Regiment Archives.	133
4.2	"Calgary Regiment Entrains Departing Camp Borden for "Somewhere,"" 18 June 1941, P-500-10-0089, King's Own Calgary Regiment Archives.	133

4.3	"Group Photo of Five Tank Members in Front of Their Tank – "Taken in England Not Long Before We Left" -England to Italy," 1942, P-400-10-0208, King's Own Calgary Regiment Archives.	134
4.4	"Group Photo - Seaford- Identified L to R: Back Row - Stoney Richardson; D.C. Taylor; John Begg; Bruce De Trotter; Pim Watkins; Bill Hunt; Doug McIndoe - Front Row - Bill Payne; Doc Alexander; Dave Clapperton; Chester McDonald; Bob Taylor," 1942, P-400-10-0214, King's Own Calgary Regiment Archives.	134
4.5	"The Lord Mayor of Birmingham meeting officers of the 1st Canadian Army Tank Brigade, Birmingham, England," 17 July 1941, PA-196826, Library and Archives Canada.	135
4.6	"W.C. Love (Left) and H. Knodel (Right) in Worthing," 1942, P-400-10-0253, King's Own Calgary Regiment Archives.	135
4.7	"L to R in front of Churchill Tank - Seaford - Frank Bevan; Ed Bennett; Archie Anderson; Bill Stannard; Bobby Cornellsen [sic]," April 1942, P-400-10-0101, King's Own Calgary Regiment Archives.	136
4.8	"Bodies of Canadian soldiers lying among damaged landing craft and 'Churchill' tanks of the Calgary Regiment following Operation 'Jubilee,'" 19 August 1942, C-014160, Library and Archives Canada.	136
4.9	"German troops examining "Churchill" tank of the Calgary Regiment abandoned during the raid on Dieppe," 1942, C-029878, Library and Archives Canada.	137
4.10	"Group Photo - Calgary Regiment Prisoners of War - Dieppe Raid - Identified L to R: Front (Kneeling/Sitting): Cunningham; McArthur; Doda - Front (Seated): Cote; Anderson; Brownlee; Cordner; Menzies; Johnson; Halase; Hunchuk; Lee - Second Row (Standing): Mcbride; Johnston; Skinner; Dunsmore; Bell; Gilbert; Schnieder; Clifton; McIntyre; Heard? - Third Row (Standing): Porter; Taylor; Anderson; Watson; Storvold; Johnstone; Holden; Bereton; Nash," c. 1942–44, P-400-20-0051, King's Own Calgary Regiment Archives.	137
4.11	"A/LCpl Gus A. Nelson Portrait - Ref #: M27156," n.d, P-400-20-0029, King's Own Calgary Regiment Archives.	138
4.12	"Capt Tony Kingsmill, MC, RCOC/RCEME OC 61 LAD," c. 1943–44, P-400-30-0220, King's Own Calgary Regiment Archives.	138
4.13	"Portrait of Captain George Thring," c. 1944, P-400-30-0038, King's Own Calgary Regiment.	139
4.14	"Dorothy Thring," c. 1941, P-400-10-0315, King's Own Calgary Regiment Archives.	139
4.15	"King George VI visits Calgary Tanks, England," 23 March 1943, pa-1599-385b-15, Glenbow Library and Archives Collection, Library and Cultural Resources, University of Calgary.	140

4.16 "Photo of Laurence G. (Doc) Alexander (L) and LCOL John Begg (R) - Buckingham Palace," 1942, P-400-10-0265, King's Own Calgary Regiment Archives.   140

4.17 ""Spartan Scheme" - England - Group," March 1943, P-400-10-0311, King's Own Calgary Regiment Archives.   140

Victory—The Italian Campaign and Holland

5.1 "Infantrymen of the West Nova Scotia Regiment riding on a Sherman tank of the Calgary Regiment during the advance from Villapiano to Potenza, Italy," 18 September 1943, PA-177155, Library and Archives Canada.   207

5.2 "Group of Indian Div. officers of the Frontier Force Rifles who worked with the Canadian Tank Brigade on the crossing of the Gari River," 1944, PA-132798, Library and Archives Canada.   208

5.3 "A Sherman tank of "A" Squadron, Ontario Regiment, crossing a stream near Colle d'Anchise, Italy," 26 October 1943, PA-204149, Library and Archives Canada.   208

5.4 "Infantrymen of the 1st Battalion, 5th Mahratta Regiment jumping from a Sherman tank of the Calgary Regiment during a tank-infantry training course, Florence, Italy," 28 August 1944, PA-141747, Library and Archives Canada.   209

5.5 "Canadian forces advancing from the Gustav Line to the Hitler Line," 1944, PA-140208, Library and Archives Canada.   209

5.6 "'Sherman' tank of the Ontario Regiment entering San Pancrazio" 1944, PA-160448, Library and Archives Canada.   210

5.7 "Canadian Tanks in Italy (1st Canadian Armour)," May 1944, 20020045-2721, Canadian War Museum.   210

5.8 "Brigadier Murphy, 1st Canadian Armoured Brigade, visiting the Forward Headquarters of the Calgary Regiment to make rush plans to cut off German paratroops withdrawing from Aquino, Italy," 23 May 1944, PA-204305, Library and Archives Canada.   211

5.9 "Technical Quartermaster O.T. Hanson of the Calgary Regiment checking tank parts as the regiment re-equips with Sherman Vc Firefly tanks, Dottignies, Belgium," 22 March 1945, PA-144121, Library and Archives Canada.   211

5.10 "Capt J.W. Quinn and Lt R. Dan Spittal - Holland," c. 1945, P-400-40-0075, King's Own Calgary Regiment Archives.   212

5.11 "Liberation of Ede, Holland," 17 April 1945, P-400-40-0079, King's Own Calgary Regiment Archives.   212

List of Illustrations   *xiii*

5.12	"Group Photo of the M5A1 Stuart ('Honey') Tank RECCE Troop Personnel," June 1945, P-400-40-0106, King's Own Calgary Regiment Archives.	213
5.13	""A" SQN Group Photo - Driebergen Holland," 18 June 1945, P-400-40-0092, King's Own Calgary Regiment Archives.	213
5.14	"Calgary Tanks celebrate Christmas," c. 1944, pa-1599-385b-20, Glenbow Library and Archives Collection, Library and Cultural Resources, University of Calgary.	214
5.15	Calgary Regiment homecoming parade, 1 December 1945, pa-1599-618-64, Glenbow Library and Archives Collection, Library and Cultural Resources, University of Calgary.	214

The Cold War Years

6.1	"Sherman Tank and Crew - KOCR - Summer Camp Wainwright," 1956, P-600-10-0013, King's Own Calgary Regiment Archives.	298
6.2	"Troop of Six KOCR Sherman Tanks with Crews "Wainwright 1948-1949 Winter Camp"," 1948–49, P-600-10-0049, King's Own Calgary Regiment Archives.	299
6.3	"Soldiers Training in Rescue Techniques - Camp Sarcee "Gregsville" [sic]," c. 1965, P-600-10-0136, King's Own Calgary Regiment Archives.	300
6.4	"KOCR on Parade with Guidon / Guidon Party - RSM Cunningham 1/c Guidon Party - Mewata Armoury," c. 1960, P-600-10-0008, King's Own Calgary Regiment Archives.	301
6.5	"Mewata Armouries, Calgary, Alberta," c. 1940-45, pa-3538-24, Glenbow Library and Archives Collection, Library and Cultural Resources, University of Calgary.	301
6.6	"Cpl. Nathan Hornburg (2007), killed in action in Afghanistan," 2007, King's Own Calgary Regiment Archives.	302

LIST OF MAPS
Maps by Jennifer Arthur-Lackenbauer

Map 1.	Canadian Operations in France and Belgium, 1915–1917.	16
Map 2.	Vimy Ridge, 9–12 April 1917.	29
Map 3	Lens, 21–25 August 1917.	36
Map 4.	Canadian Operations in France and Belgium, 1918.	72
Map 5.	Amiens, 9–18 August 1918.	76
Map 6.	Drocourt-Quéant Line, 2–5 September 1918.	84
Map 7.	Canal du Nord, 27 September – 11 October 1918.	89
Map 8.	Canadian Operations in Southern Italy, July 1943 – June 1944.	180
Map 9.	Crossing the Moro and the Battle for Ortona, 6–28 December 1943.	193
Map 10.	Breaking the Gustav Line, 11–15 May 1944.	228
Map 11.	Canadian Operations in Northern Italy, June 1944 – February 1945.	248
Map 12.	The Advance to the Arno, 21 June – 5 August 1944.	258
Map 13.	The Gothic Line and the Advance on Bologna, 25 August – 30 December 1944.	268

ACKNOWLEDGEMENTS

Unquestionably one of the most pleasant tasks authors face is acknowledging the organizations and individuals who made vital contributions behind the scenes. First and foremost among these is the Regimental Foundation which, by financing publication costs and much of the research, made the book possible. Two individuals, both former senior regimental officers, did yeoman work liaising with the author. Joe Howard's appreciation of the requirements of scholarly work was especially helpful, as was the commitment of his successor in the role, Jay Milne. The fact that the Foundation held to its commitment to honour the author's editorial independence was the right course, but nevertheless much appreciated. I also wish to thank those present and former members of the regiment who agreed to interviews. The KOCR archives was a valuable research source, particularly of personal memorabilia and memoirs. Al Judson deserves much credit for expertly organizing the bulk of this material during his tenure as regimental archivist, while Roy Boehli proved a master of the photographic collection.

Three of my former graduate students—Chelsea Clark, Michael Swanberg and Dr. Geoff Jackson—served as research assistants. The latter, an accomplished Great War scholar, also accompanied me on research trips to the Western Front and Italy which were invaluable in providing an appreciation of "the lay of the land" where the regiment fought. It goes without saying that the many archivists who shared their time and knowledge of their document collections—too many to name—advanced my research immeasurably. My gratitude also goes to Jennifer Arthur-Lackenbauer, the accomplished cartographer who created the maps based on those in G. W. L. Nicholson's *Canadian Expeditionary Force, 1914-1919* (Ottawa: Queen's Printer, 1964) and *The Canadians in Italy: 1943-1945* (Ottawa: Queen's Printer, 1967). And I would be remiss not to express my gratitude for the encouragement, patience and good humour lavished on the author by various staff members at the University of Calgary Press including Brian Scrivener, Helen Hajnoczky, Alison Cobra, Melina Cusano and my accomplished copy editor, Peter Midgley. The book was so much better for their involvement. Finally, I want to acknowledge the thoughtful improvements suggested by my two anonymous peer reviewers.

xvii

Those offering ongoing personal support seldom realize what a salvation it is. Dr Jackson shared his considerable knowledge of the Great War operations by the armies of the British Empire during "strategy" sessions at pubs in Calgary and overseas. Tamara Sherwin generously shared her extensive knowledge of the Canadian reserves post–1945 and regularly inquired into the progress being made on *das Buch*. Dr. Meig McCrae dispatched endless encouragement from her outpost "Down Under" at the Coral Bell School of Asia Pacific Affairs, Australian National University. Thank you all so very much. Finally, I thank my wife Clare for her faith in the author and his book, and for never failing to keep the former grounded. Of course any errors or omissions here are the sole responsibility of the author.

LIST OF ABBREVIATIONS

A/Cpl.	acting corporal
A/Sgt.	acting sergeant
BEF	British Expeditionary Force
Brig.-Gen.	brigadier general (oftentimes simply brigadier, or Brig.)
CASF	Canadian Active Service Force
Capt.	captain
CEF	Canadian Expeditionary Force
CO	commanding officer
Cpl.	corporal
DND	Department of National Defence
DCM	Distinguished Conduct Medal
DHH	Directorate of History and Heritage (Department of National Defence)
DND	Department of National Defence
DSO	Distinguished Service Order
D-Q Line	Drocourt–Quéant Line
Gen	general
GHQ	General Headquarters (of the BEF)
GSO 1	general staff officer grade 1
GA	Glenbow Archives (University of Calgary)
IWM	Imperial War Museum
KOCR	The King's Own Calgary Regiment
KOCRA	The King's Own Calgary Regiment Archives
KORR (Lancaster)	King's Own Royal Regiment (Lancaster)
LAC	Library and Archives Canada
L/Cpl.	lance corporal
L/Sgt.	lance sergeant
LOB	left out of battle
LST	landing ship tank
Lt.	lieutenant
Lt.-Col.	lieutenant colonel
Lt.-Gen.	lieutenant general
Maj.	major

Maj.-Gen.	major general
MC	Military Cross
MD	military district
MM	Military Medal
NPAM	Non-Permanent Active Militia
Pvt.	private
RCAC	Royal Canadian Armoured Corps
Sgt.	sergeant
Sgt.-Maj.	sergeant major
TLC	tank landing craft
TNA	The National Archives
Tpr.	trooper
VC	Victoria Cross
WD	war diary
WO	(British) War Office

INTRODUCTION

Fifty Years of Peace and War

This book recounts the first fifty years of the history of what is now The King's Own Calgary Regiment—the period 1910 through 1960. The regiment was established during the last years of collective innocence before the outbreak of the Great War, a period characterized throughout British Canada by the imperialist euphoria and the culture of manliness and militarism that pervaded the British World during the late 19th and early 20th centuries. For the Anglo-Celtic Canadian majority, the Great War demanded an unprecedented sacrifice of blood and treasure. The 50th Overseas Battalion, raised and subsequently reinforced from Calgary and the surrounding area, was a tangible manifestation of this sacrifice. Over 4,000 men volunteered (and by 1918, were conscripted) into its ranks. The 50th reached the trenches in mid-1916 as part of the 4th Canadian Division, and served through most of the remaining twenty-six months as part of the Canadian Corps. Although Canadian units had been engaged since April 1915, the 50th Battalion still arrived in time to participate in virtually all of the savage attritional battles whose names would later be inscribed on cenotaphs across the country, starting with the Battle of the Somme and continuing through Vimy Ridge, Hill 70/Lens, Passchendaele, Amiens, the Drocourt–Quéant Line, the Canal du Nord and Valenciennes. By the time the fighting ended on 11 November 1918, just over 650 of its men had been killed in action and hundreds more wounded, many maimed for life in body or mind. As this study will show in considerable detail, the soldiers of the 50th quickly mastered their twin tasks of surviving and killing and performed every bit as well in battle as their sister units. It was a remarkable achievement since only a minority of those serving had pre-war experience part-time soldiering. Courage and grim determination were possessed in abundance, as any glance at the honour roll confirms—one VC, six DSOs (with two bars, that is second awards to the same individual), 32 MCs (with four bars), 22 DCMs and 215 MMs (with 22 bars).[1]

The war ended with a victory to which the 50th had contributed its fair share. There was pride in the young Dominion's military achievement, but

1

aching grief at the human cost. Homecoming and a speedy return to a civilian life many hardly recognized followed. Neither veteran nor civilian seemed to doubt the necessity of the war, but both wanted to move on. Few thought of the Great War as something that ever would (or should) be repeated.

The immediate post-war years saw the militia re-established in Calgary. The whole concept of part-time military service struck most, for the reasons just outlined, as an abstraction (many would have said absurdity). Moreover, most Canadians noted that the vast majority who'd served in the Canadian Corps had no pre-war military training at all, adding another reason to question the need for an organized militia. Having a credible purpose would have helped justify the militia's role (and modest cost), but during all but the last few interwar years Canadians happily (and understandably) believed they lived in the proverbial fire-proof house, far from flammable materials.[2]

The 1920s saw the Calgary Regiment split into separate organizations, both of which remain in place today, the Calgary Highlanders and the second incarnation of the Calgary Regiment from which The King's Own Calgary Regiment can trace its lineage. The 1920s also saw the emergence of a pattern which would repeat itself after the Second War—a difficult relationship with Canada's modest professional army and the lack of basic resources with which to train. The problems worsened during the Great Depression, which plunged much of Canada, and certainly Alberta, into desperate poverty. Starved of modern equipment and even parade pay, the Calgary Regiment barely managed to survive. Only when war clouds gathered over Europe did Canadian attitudes toward military matters start becoming more realistic.

In September 1939, Canada was again staring over the precipice, committed, after some understandable questioning, to a second major expeditionary force to fight our own and the British Empire's battles. Only a few years earlier, as part of a series of paper reforms of the military, the regiment had chosen to convert to the armoured role, a serendipitous decision as it turned out. But despite the efforts of all ranks to turn themselves into tankers during the few years they had, it proved challenging without actual tanks. Canada having managed the almost impossible feat of being more poorly prepared militarily than in 1914, it is no exaggeration to say that in September 1939 the men's most modern piece of equipment was their black armoured corps berets. Fortunately, the war would unfold in such a way that Canada did not need much of an army for several years—since it took that long to assemble, train and equip a proper force, there was really no choice. When parliament officially declared war on 10 September 1939, the Calgary Regiment, which after a flurry of name changes would emerge mid-war as the 14th Canadian Armoured Regiment, existed only in the minds of optimists, which fortunately included its own officers and men. Eager to see their regiment mobilized for overseas service, they put heart and soul into such training as they could conjure up from a still threadbare arsenal. In early 1941, the Calgary Regiment was at last mobilized, at any rate those members who met the age, physical and technical standards of the armoured corps. In short order they were despatched to Camp Borden for the few months of limited instruction available there, which included seeing their first actual tanks, and then shipped out for the United Kingdom.

It was in England, beginning in July 1941, where one could say the regiment's officers and men finally had a chance to begin proper training. This was none too soon for thirteen months later they would see action at Dieppe, where most of the men landed to support two brigades of infantry were taken prisoner, and every tank put ashore was lost. Effectively about half of the regiment's fighting strength had to be replaced. And while a nucleus remained and the replacements were forthcoming quickly enough, a collective identity had to be rebuilt almost from scratch. In a little over a year that had been accomplished. Despatched to the Mediterranean Theatre, the regiment spent almost all of its fighting war in Italy with the rest of the "D-Day Dodgers," mostly in the infantry support role, serving as self-propelled artillery. Though far from glamorous, it was essential work, and they became very good at it. During the majority of their time in Italy, they found themselves attached to British and Indian divisions. They thus suffered a double historical blow—ignored both for serving in a secondary theatre and, after 1943, for not fighting alongside the rest of their countrymen. The Italian enterprise ended miserably, stuck in the frozen Apennines north of Florence and basically sentenced by weather, geography and logistics to serve an increasingly limited military role. Their extraction and transfer to the North West Europe Campaign occurred too late for the regiment to play more than a modest role in the liberation of the Netherlands. As in 1918, they had the reward of freeing conquered (and grateful) people, which took some of the sting out of the loss of comrades. At least as an armoured unit those losses, while bad enough, were much lower than their infantry forebears had suffered a generation earlier—just under 100 killed in action or dying of wounds, with several more succumbing in accidents.[3] As had been the case with the 50th Battalion, heroism and sacrifice had been on regular display, and their skill at making war matched anything achieved by their peers.[4]

The soldiers came home in 1945, among them nearly 160 *kriegies* who had suffered much deprivation and mistreatment during their thirty-two months of captivity, and passed back into civilian life, raising families, building careers, and coping with what they had seen and done in the private way of veterans. By all accounts most of them did so successfully. Although few put on a uniform again, as was the case in 1919, the option of part-time soldiering was re-established in the reserves. The KOCR promptly reverted to this role. But circumstances had changed fundamentally. In a nuclear war only armies-in-being would matter—there would be no need for large expeditionary forces because there would be no time to train them. But in that case, what meaningful role could part-time units play? The failure of both Ottawa and the army to answer that question boded ill for the reserves' future.

While conditions from 1945 to the early 1960s were fundamentally different than during the interwar decades, the result was remarkably similar—atrophy of the part-time military. During both periods, a mix of veterans and newcomers, motivated by a desire to serve their country and maintain proud military traditions, had managed to keep such soldiering alive in Canada, though it was a constant struggle. Certainly the efforts of The KOCR post-1945, and of the Calgary Regiment post-1919, illustrate what could be accomplished by tireless dedication in the face of a broadly unsupportive public and regular military. In both instances, mere survival as a functioning institution constituted success.

Objectives, Parameters, Constraints

Portraying the history of a Canadian regiment during the first half of the 20th century raises an obvious difficulty. How does one integrate the experiences of the war years, when the regiment operated as a highly trained combat formation, with those of the extended periods of peace when the regiment struggled to survive as a part-time force? One could make the case that the crucial periods were the two wars, and they should be recounted at the expense of downplaying the interwar and post–World War II periods when little of importance happened. This book explores the war years in depth, but the peacetime story of Canada's part-time army during the first half of the 20th century has been little covered by military historians, and certainly not from the perspective of the militia/reserve forces. This deserved to be addressed.

Exploring the wartime periods raises another problem—maintaining too narrow a focus and producing what military historians dismiss as "stovepipe" history. The King's Own Calgary Regiment exists uniquely within the broader context of Canada's army, and much of what follows explores its unique experience. But without losing sight of the fact that this is the study of one regiment and its community, that study benefits from being situating squarely within that larger Canadian, and when appropriate, Allied context. After all, in neither war did the regiment fight isolated from its brigade mates, supporting artillery and engineers, and so forth, so that adhering to a narrow perspective obscures how the regiment actually experienced combat.

Historians have to conceptualize the audience for whom they are writing. As a scholarly account, the author anticipates Canadian and other military historians will read it and incorporate it into their own work. It was also the author's goal to provide a more complete story of The KOCR's exploits than has heretofore been available to its past, current and future members. But more than anything, the book was framed to provide the descendants of the men who went to war in the 50th Battalion or 14th Armoured Regiment with a thorough understanding of what their forebears experienced. Thus, to the degree research sources have permitted, the book reveals what soldiering entailed psychologically and emotionally as well as how the soldiers' war affected loved ones back home.

Too many regimental histories focus not only on the war periods but almost exclusively on operations. The men are at the front when the account begins, and when the fighting stops, so does the story. But such an approach fails to tell us where the soldiers came from, and for those fortunate enough to have survived, what they came home to—in other words, how Canada's citizen soldiers were made and unmade? An operational preoccupation also tells us little about what soldiering was like during the soldier's time in uniform. During their respective two-plus years in action, both the 50th Battalion and 14th Armoured Regiment actually fought for only a few weeks. And even the majority of that time was spent preparing for combat, waiting for combat, or recovering from combat. "Hurry-up-and-wait" aptly described their lot, which is why this story flows rather than jumps from battle to battle.

Ensuring this was a scholarly account—one that had been thoroughly researched from the available archival sources and rigorously analyzed and argued to the standards of academic military history—will open scholars' eyes, in and outside of Canada, to the wartime achievements of The KOCR. It is lamentable that the 50th Battalion's and 14th Armoured Regiment's exploits have been far less visible than they should have been within the broader sweep of Canadian military history because no authoritative account existed. Whether for the military historian or interested layperson, the regiment's involvement in World War II shouldn't begin and end with the Dieppe raid. Or in the Great War, with Vimy Ridge. But as the author has absorbed from the work of some of the leading lights of Canadian and World War I military history, high standards of research and rigorous analysis are perfectly compatible with storytelling and human interest.

As much as the author has tried to reveal the perspective of the ordinary soldier, a great deal of the regiment's story is conveyed from the perspective of commanders and other officers. Partly this is a function of the manner in which contemporary sources—war diaries, after-action reports, and so forth were compiled—and partly it is a recognition that armies are inherently hierarchical institutions with commanders playing a disproportionately important role in preparing, executing, and absorbing lessons from operations. Contemporaneous institutional records, for all their biases and gaps, remain the most solid account of what happened as it was seen at the time, and are indispensable to any reconstruction of those events. In the hope of humanizing the regiment's experience, much effort has been invested in telling the story of the many by teasing out the story of the few. Whenever possible, personal accounts and subsequent recollections were used to balance the perceptions from on high. Like all historical sources, recollections have their weaknesses—nostalgia being one—yet they can be measured against official documentation for factual accuracy and often provide insights into matters otherwise unrecorded. The experience of the Dieppe prisoners of war could not otherwise have been told.

Lastly, one of the weaknesses that has bedevilled too much Canadian military history has been its excessive focus on matters Canadian.[5] Naturally, Canadians would want to know their own story, but in both wars the Canadian Army operated as part of a much larger British-led coalition, practically speaking a single army. The implications were particularly visible during the assignment of the 1st Canadian Armoured Brigade to a British Corps for most of 1944, the period which coincided with the regiment's most important fighting during the Italian Campaign. Focusing too narrowly on Canadian military achievements has tended to distort their overall significance. And the same can be said of embracing Canadian military myths, appealing though they might be. Both weaknesses plague too many regimental histories. For its part, *Onward* makes no attempt to laud The King's Own Calgary Regiment—but rather to ensure it receives proper recognition for its role in Canadian military history.

Finally, *Onward* will not recast the major elements of what we know about how either war was fought. Units the size of an infantry battalion or an armoured regiment can have input into but do not depart from the larger tactical consensus established at the higher levels of command. British army practice, which the Canadian Army emulated, aimed for a standardized way of war, so the various fighting components would be interchangeable, and wisely so. Groundbreaking innovation did not come from individual lieutenant colonels and their commands. But if the hope is to tell the soldier's story, then it is the story of a regiment—at times mundane, heroic and tragic—which offers the greatest promise.

1.1 The 103rd Regiment (Calgary Rifles) marching smartly in the Calgary Exhibition and Stampede Parade, 1912. (Glenbow Archives, nc-78-72)

1.2 Adjacent to Calgary, Sarcee Camp, seen here in 1915, was quickly transformed into a major training facility for the thousands of Alberta volunteers flocking to fight for King and Country. (Glenbow Archives, na-989-1)

1.3 A ball held by the 103rd Regiment (Calgary Rifles) in 1912. Established only two years earlier, the militia regiment had quickly become an integral part of the city's life. (Glenbow Archives, na-3232-69)

1.4 Soldiers of the 50th and 31st Battalions march through Calgary on a snowy day in early 1915. Serving in the 2nd Division, the men in the 31st would reach the trenches some eleven months earlier than their comrades. (Glenbow Archives, nc-44-39)

1.5 Maj.-Gen. Sam Steele, accompanied by Lt.-Col. Edward Mason, inspects the 50th Battalion in 1915. That a hero of the Klondike Gold Rush and Boer War in his late sixties played a leading role in assembling and training the Canadian Expeditionary Force during the first half of the war spoke volumes about Canada's lack of preparedness. (Glenbow Archives, na-3419-2)

Forging the 50th Battalion   9

1.6 The 103rd Regiment (Calgary Rifles) depart for Valcartier Camp in late August 1914. As the core of the Canadian Expeditionary Force's 10th Battalion, they first saw action at Ypres in April 1915. Few of them would see Calgary again. (Glenbow Archives, na-4355-38)

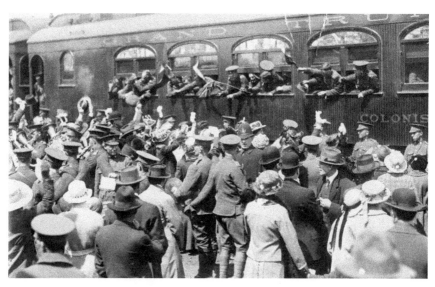

1.7 The 137th Battalion departs Calgary on 14 August 1916. Like the bulk of the units reaching England after the spring of 1916, it was broken up for reinforcements. Most of its men, including Pvt. John Pattison VC, would go on to serve in the trenches with the 50th Battalion. (Glenbow Archives, na-1617-5)

1

From Calgary to Vimy Ridge

Learning by Doing and Dying

When the 50th Battalion successfully assaulted its Vimy Ridge objectives in April 1917, it was already a battle-tested formation. Somehow in barely two years a throng of enthusiastic amateurs had been transformed into first-class fighting troops. It is a remarkable story, one which can be traced back to the pre-war Canadian militia.

Prairie Roots

In the aftermath of the Boer War, Canada's first experience of raising expeditionary forces in defence of the Empire, budgets for both the training and equipping of the militia increased substantially. By 1914, the force numbered 70,000 officers and men. Enhanced by a romanticized version of military service linked intimately to manly qualities, part-time soldiering was widely respected, especially among the Anglo-Canadian majority for whom imperialist sentiments were at their apex. Nowhere was the latter more apparent than in the militia's wholehearted embrace of British military traditions.[1]

Chafing that their burgeoning community of 60,000 souls lacked a major militia presence, on 1 April 1910 a group of local business and professional men established the 103rd Regiment (Calgary Rifles), with Lt.-Col. W. C. G. Armstrong as commanding officer and Maj. E. G. Mason, a respected local physician, his second-in-command. R. B. Bennett, a lion of the city's legal and commercial elite, agreed to serve as honorary colonel. In the few remaining years of peace, the "Saturday soldiers" trained at the Victoria Barracks (located in present-day Stampede Park) and became a central feature of the city's public life.[2]

For King and Empire

Contrary to popular belief, the outbreak of war in the summer of 1914 was not greeted with enthusiasm in Canada. However, there is no question that those of British descent strongly supported London's decision to declare war for the Empire and fully expected the Dominion to do its duty. The existing plan to raise armed forces for Imperial defence called for the orderly mobilization of militia units. Instead, the minister responsible for military matters, the energetic but erratic Sam Hughes, simply telegraphed authorizations to existing militia units to assemble at an incomplete training camp near Quebec City where under his dynamic leadership they would be miraculously transformed into the Canadian Expeditionary Force. Lt.-Col. Armstrong was promptly authorized to mobilize the 103rd to its war strength, a task soon accomplished, and by month's end officers and men had entrained for Valcartier. After some perfunctory training, the First Contingent of the Canadian Expeditionary Force set sail for England in October. While militia units provided most of its 31,000 soldiers, the thousand-strong infantry battalions were merely numbered, creating a new military identity. The 103rd's fate was to be split up, 846 of them being merged with others from Winnipeg's 106th Regiment to form the 10th (North-West) Battalion that would serve from April 1915 onward as part of the 1st Canadian Division.[3]

A second contingent soon followed, and recruiting efforts continued unabated. Hughes authorized new battalions and generally relied on prominent local individuals, often with a militia background, to find the volunteers. In Calgary, the skeleton of the 103rd Regiment would serve as a recruiting agent and provide rudimentary training for five more of Hughes' numbered battalions. The first authorized was the 50th on 14 December 1914. Maj. Mason accepted command and remaining officers and other ranks from the 103rd joined as well, providing a semi-trained nucleus.[4] Imperial passions (and a sharp economic downturn on the Prairies) ensured a steady stream of volunteers, mostly Calgary men. The initial attestee was Leo Ricks, who claimed service number 434001.[5] During that first winter, training was carried out at the cramped Victoria Barracks and in rented horse barns, but with the arrival of spring, Sarcee Camp could be used.[6] Despite dire shortages of every piece of military equipment, including rifles, and a dearth of competent instructors, the 50th Battalion was making steady progress.[7] The Second Battle of Ypres brought the first heavy casualties for the Canadians, and Mason was ordered to assemble a reinforcement draft of five junior officers, fifteen NCOs and 236 other ranks.[8] A few months later, the 50th was stripped of a second reinforcement draft (255 officers and men). Eager recruits quickly filled the gaps.

In late summer 1915 word reached Mason that his command would be part of the next wave of battalions proceeding to England. They entrained on October 20, and typical of those heady days, friends, family and ordinary Calgarians gave them a rousing send off. Cheering citizens dotted the marching route of "Mason's Man-Eaters" from Sarcee Camp.⁹ At the Canadian Northern station east of the downtown, a throng of 12,000 more had gathered. Planned speeches were wisely cancelled to allow the soldiers and their loved ones a few more precious minutes for goodbyes before the former clambered aboard their two troop trains.¹⁰

For most of the passengers the trip was an adventure. There seemed to be crowds on every platform thrusting chocolates and tobacco into soldiers' outstretched hands. "On the whole we have had a fine trip," Sgt. David Argo confided to his wife as they steamed eastward along the shores of the St. Lawrence. "Service and meals ..., I don't think it could be beat."¹¹ A few who had qualms quietly deserted, their places taken by others eager to go overseas. In Ottawa, the men paraded to Parliament Hill where with traditional British army ceremony they received their first regimental colours, embroidered by the sister of one of their officers, Maj. Joshua Wright. Once in Halifax the 41 officers and 1,036 other ranks—fully 836 of whom were British-born¹²—filed aboard the HMT *Orduña* which slipped out of the harbour on October 27. The nine-day crossing to Plymouth was blessed with decent weather and otherwise uneventful. Their convoy quietly docked on November 4, and the battalion immediately boarded a train bound for Bramshott in Hampshire, close by a major Canadian assembly and training ground.¹³ In the dark and pelted by rain, the officers and men marched the final few kilometres to what would be their home for the next nine months.

Bramshott Camp

When the 50th Battalion left Calgary, the soldiers had mastered parade ground drill and completed plenty of route marches. Simply being together had nurtured comradeship, and certainly morale was high. The officers and NCOs had gained experience commanding their men in basic military tasks, and had generally won their confidence. But in most respects the battalion remained a work in progress, far from ready to face the challenges of trench warfare. That gap would have to be closed or they would be slaughtered in their first action. The broad outlines and most of the details of the training regimen at Bramshott Camp reflected contemporary British army practice, which was constantly evolving as lessons drawn from combat were incorporated. But even the training of Kitchener's New Army suffered from various shortcomings, starting with a chronic shortage of capable instructors.¹⁴ However, the Canadian situation was considerably worse.¹⁵ Sam Hughes had set up a series of competing fiefdoms operating all but independently under civilian and military leaders who were a mix of well-intentioned amateurs and militia cronies. The inevitable result was that much of the training time was wasted.¹⁶ Nonetheless, for the battalions steadily arriving from Canada there were at least opportunities to master basic weaponry, and for their officers and non-commissioned officers to gain some experience directing platoon, company and battalion-scale exercises. The 50th Battalion would do its best with the instructional staff they inherited, but one has to bear in mind that Lt.-Col. Mason, his second-in-command (Maj. J. R. L. Parry), and his four company commanders (Capts. Lester Webster, Robert Eaton, Charles McKittrick and Herbert Keegan) had nothing more than militia experience themselves or, in Keegan's case, its British equivalent. Only Eaton had ever soldiered in the field—and that was during the South African War. While three-quarters of the officers had spent some time as part-time soldiers, among the other ranks the figure fell to one-third. Overall, close to seven of every ten men in the battalion had no military experience save what they had picked up in 1915.[17]

"Mason's Man-Eaters" found themselves amid a sea of Canadian battalions—eighteen in all. There were also "hundreds of wounded and crippled soldiers," a daily reminder to the new arrivals of the war's butcher bill.[18] Training commenced immediately, often under the instruction of soldiers from other units who had simply been there a bit longer. This kept everyone busy, focusing their minds on thoughts other than home and separation.[19] Unit cohesion and the benefits of such training as was accomplished were abruptly undone by the constant demand to make good losses at the front. In turn, battalions providing drafts were reinforced by cannibalizing other training battalions or units recently arrived from Canada. The 50th Battalion sent substantial reinforcements to front-line Alberta battalions after the battles of the St. Eloi Craters in April and Mount Sorrel in June, receiving replacements from the 56th and 89th Battalions, both recruited from elsewhere in Alberta, as well as the 71st and 74th raised in Ontario.[20] No one knew whether their battalion would actually reach the front lines intact—as recruits had been led to believe when they enlisted—or be arbitrarily disbanded. That said, many men were chafing to reach the front, even with another battalion, and were crestfallen when they were not selected as reinforcements.[21]

In the spring of 1916, after a few false starts, Maj.-Gen. David Watson was picked to command the 4th, the final Canadian division sent to the front. A reasonably experienced and capable brigade commander, Watson was even more effective at navigating the warren of back channels in the army and government.[22] He immediately placed the dozens of training battalions on notice that his inspections would fix their fate. Ottawa was keen on having regional balance, which included cobbling together another Western brigade, a decision from which the 50th stood to benefit. In the end, they appear to have been better trained than many of their competitors, a tribute to Lt.-Col. Mason and his officers and NCOs who had imparted what military expertise they had.[23] With a collective sigh of relief, "Mason's Man-Eaters" learned they would get to test their mettle against The Hun.

Having picked his battalions, Watson focused on hardening their training to improve battlefield readiness (which he considered far from adequate) and combat the restlessness of men tired of being stuck in Bramshott.[24] By early August, as the Battle of the Somme entered its second month, it was clear the division would soon be crossing the Channel, and the 50th was awash in rumours.[25] "The whole Division seems keyed up to try and do their utmost," Watson confided, and "I foresee the very highest results."[26]

Commit These Gallant Sons of the Empire

On Sunday, August 13, surrounded by local parishioners, the battalion assembled in Bramshott church to deposit their colours in a ceremony "charged with significance and deep sentiment to those who witnessed it," as signaller Victor Wheeler remembered. The vicar's words were brief but heartfelt: "Commit these gallant sons of the Empire to God's gracious mercy and protection."[27]

At last, the day arrived. As his men stood in ranks, Lt.-Col. Mason spoke a few words reminding them of their duty. Major Parry followed with a rather more hellfire speech, ending with a stern warning: "I don't want any angels in my battalion … and I don't want you to take any prisoners! I hope you understand!"[28] With that to steel them, the battalion in full kit marched to the nearby station bound for Southampton where they boarded HMT *La Marguerite* for the overnight crossing. Forty-six officers and 1,013 other ranks disembarked at La Havre late on the following afternoon.[29]

British practice had newly arrived formations introduced to the trenches by experienced units, in this case the 2nd Canadian Division's 20th Battalion. Each company spent 48 hours in the line. In their turn, columns of anxious men stumbled forward in the dark, neither smoking nor talking, yet keen to finally see the *Boches*. One lesson was quickly absorbed: Unable to resist peering over the parapet into no man's land, A Company's commander, Maj. L. O. Webster, promptly had his head split open by a sniper's round, the 50th's first fatal casualty of the war.[30] They then crossed into Belgium to relieve their sister 47th Battalion on the western flank of the infamous Ypres Salient, spending the rest of the month alternating periods in and out of the front line.[31] Day and night, Mason made a point of plodding up and down the trenches, and it cheered his men.[32] The 50th then crossed back into France with the rest of the 10th Brigade, marching for three solid days to new billets near St. Omer.[33] One thing was certain—during these few weeks in the line "all the touted glamour of soldiering had perished."[34]

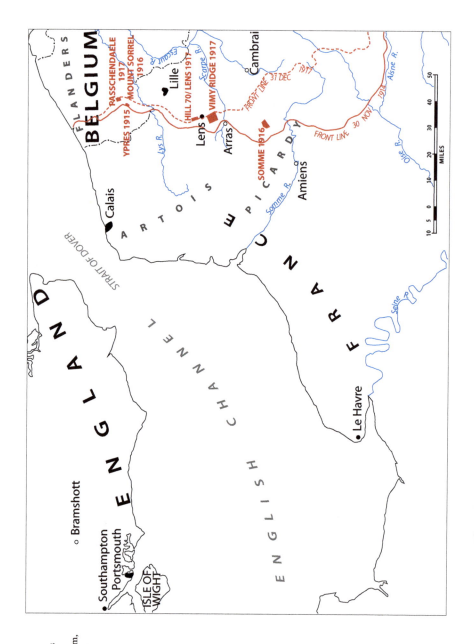

MAP 1: Canadian Operations in France and Belgium, 1915–1917.

The Somme

The battle raging north of Paris along the meandering Somme River during the summer and autumn of 1916 was the first sustained action for hundreds of thousands of soldiers in Kitchener's New Army. British artillery set out to tear huge gaps in the German line and the infantry would then pour through to overwhelm any surviving defenders, inflicting a crushing defeat. But the plan came unstuck, degenerating into merciless "wearing down" battles (to use Field Marshall Douglas Haig's phrase) designed to bleed the German Army, regardless of the casualties incurred.[35] In mid-September, eleven weeks on, Canadians entered the fray with the 2nd Division's successful attack on Courcelette. The 1st and 3rd Canadian Divisions soon followed.

By early October the 50th was on the move again, bringing them ever closer to the Somme battlefield. As Victor Wheeler vividly remembered:

> "We were herded into cattle cars steaming with animal dung .... The sweat from the unwashed men turned our stomachs. The darkness, relieved by a guttering candle stub, providentially hid much of the unsanitary mess [as we lay] crammed together, head-to-head and feet-to-feet, with only sodden, evil-smelling straw between us."[36]

On October 5 the commander of the Canadian Corps, Lt.-Gen. Julian Byng, inspected the battalion, a sure sign they were would soon see action.

Nine days later they relieved the 44th Battalion in the front-line trenches. Men who had spontaneously cheered when told they were Somme-bound were now jeered for their cockiness as they passed the beaten-down remnant of another Canadian battalion. It was now cold and raining steadily. Soldiers stood in fire trenches or rather the remnants of these trenches, sometimes knee-deep in water and slime, while being shelled day and night. Simply holding the line over the next ninety-six hours cost them one killed and forty-four wounded.[37] The frequent reliefs were especially onerous "as the mud is knee deep [in the communications trenches] and takes all the strength out of us before we get there."[38] The worst, as Sgt. Argo confided to his wife, choosing his words carefully, was "some of the things we see here [which] make one get down."[39]

Ancre Heights

At the start of October, the Canadians were given the objective of securing Regina Trench as a jumping-off point for a larger British attack to follow. Regina Trench was a heavily wired German defensive position, well manned and shrewdly dug to lie just beyond the crest of a spur and therefore difficult for British or Canadian artillery to get at. The initial attacks either enjoyed little success or were outright failures, all of them incurring very heavy losses. On October 21, a major assault on the largely obliterated Regina Trench included the 11th Brigade. By day's end, one-half of what was now reduced to little more than a series of waterlogged, interconnected shell craters and bits of crumbling ditch was finally in British and Canadian hands. With the 50th in brigade reserve, an attempt by the 4th Division to capture the remainder four days later failed utterly.[40] Mason's men were promptly ordered forward to relieve the 44th Battalion. Numbers of them volunteered to help evacuate the Manitobans' casualties (which numbered close to 200), an unselfish act which cost Pvts. Cole and Westlake their lives and left three others wounded.[41]

Desire Support Trench ... And a New Commanding Officer

During the first two weeks of November, as the Battle of the Somme neared its overdue end, the 50th Battalion was in and out of the Canadian line, a "shredded ribbon of hell," but not involved in any attacks.[42] On November 11, however, Mason, suffering from "severe strain of overwork" and accumulated medical problems, was removed from his command. He returned to England and served out the remainder of the war as a doctor at Shorncliffe camp. It is not clear how much the change Watson recommended was due to Mason's breakdown and how much to failings in the field. Most of the wartime and post-war assessments from his men stressed his personal courage, sense of duty and compassion. While militia officers provided outstanding command talent to the Canadian Corps, some thrust into leadership in 1914–15 weren't up to the job once reaching the front, trench warfare being a cruel judge of commanding officers' abilities.[43] Maj. Robert Eaton, who was much respected in the battalion, temporarily assumed command.[44]

The physical conditions steadily deteriorated. A half-century later, a battalion veteran offered a brutal assessment—the only firm ground in some trenches was offered by unburied corpses.[45] All ranks endured it stoically, though the 50th's first cases of shell shock were now appearing.[46] Having personally reconnoitred the front lines, Watson had no illusions as to what his men faced.[47] But Field Marshall Haig's plans called for a continuation of pressure. Thus, on the 17th, Eaton received orders for half of his battalion to attack on the following morning, with a company of the 46th joining in on their right and four battalions from the 11th and 12th Brigades on their left. The immediate objective was Desire Support Trench which lay from 300 (in the case of the 50th's position) to 800 m distant from the various jumping-off points. Having cleared it, the survivors were to press on another 100–150 m and establish a new line from which a further exploitation to Grandcourt Trench, some 500 m beyond their initial objective, might be possible. This was of course wildly optimistic.

By the standards of the Somme, there would be substantial—if not necessarily sufficient—artillery support, with a standing barrage on the main objective and simultaneously with the creeping barrage escorting the four waves of infantry, an extensive smoke screen. Sadly, the weather was unco-operative. The season's first snowfall turned to blinding sleet by the launch of the attack at 0600 and then heavy rain, compromising any follow-up artillery support while ensuring the infantry would be crossing slippery, sodden ground and would likely lose direction in a snow-covered and unfamiliar landscape. While the 11th Brigade still managed to reach most of its objectives, capturing hundreds of German troops in the process, the same could not be said of the 50th and 46th Battalions.[48] The single company from the 46th was stopped in its tracks by small arms fire and had to fall back. Meanwhile, the 50th Battalion's two companies reached Desire Support Trench against relatively light resistance and consolidated their position, but the smoke barrage caused them to lose contact with the 75th Battalion on their left, leaving a 200-m stretch of trench in German hands. What remained of the two companies did press on to capture a smaller trench lying some 200 m inside the German position, but with two open flanks, and the enemy still holding ground behind them, they came under intense enfilade machine-gun fire. As casualties quickly mounted, the decision was wisely made to fall back and root the enemy out of their bit of the Desire Support Trench. This accomplished, German artillery began relentlessly shelling their still-exposed position. The only choice was to retreat to Regina Trench, evacuating as many wounded as could be managed, along with the more than 100 prisoners, the first the battalion had managed to capture. Close to 350 men had gone "over the bags," and although wounded had been evacuated continually, the final party that fought its way back to the start lines numbered a single officer—Lt. W. R. Elliot—and 60 other ranks. Eaton's initial count of the casualties compiled in the confusion of the day—he was wounded himself—listed two officers killed and three more, including A Company's commanding officer, Maj. J. S. Wright, missing and (correctly) presumed killed, along with seven wounded. Twenty-nine other ranks were either known or thought to have been killed, and a further 83 were missing. Ninety-one more had made it back to their lines wounded, some grievously. "Baptism of fire" is an awful phrase, and while not an excessive butcher's bill for attacks on the Somme, the 50th's first major engagement was tragic enough.[49] In the hopes of consolidating his men's gains, Watson was prepared to press on the next day, but in light of the overall situation and deteriorating weather, the British Corps commander prudently overruled him.[50] Instead, British Expeditionary Force (BEF) Headquarters officially declared the Battle of the Somme over.

During the night of November 19–20, the badly shaken battalion withdrew to their old haunts outside Albert. Burials in a nearby cemetery continued apace. Among those killed in the attack had been Sgt. David Argo, whose stream of letters to his wife Mae had chronicled the 50th's short history. The correspondence, while remarkably expressive and intimate, nonetheless bore the mark of a man who knew his letters would be censored and was self-censoring so as not to unduly alarm loved ones. Thus Argo's admonishments to his wife that "it [was] no use worrying ... [but to] get along the best you can and look on the bright side."[51] The sergeant's letters had been infrequent in November, but he had taken pains to reassure her that it only reflected the terrible conditions of mud and shelling that he and his comrades were enduring. Once the promotion to sergeant became official, he reminded her, there would be more money deducted from his monthly pay for her and their boys. In his final note, penned on November 15, he suggested that it might not be wise to write so often "as you will be looking for [letters] all the time."[52]

Loss and Coping

We know little of the impact on next of kin of the devastating news that a husband or son had been killed in action, though it would be repeated too many times in the 50th Battalion's case during the course of the war. Cpl. C. T. Hodge, who had been befriended by the Argos in Calgary and was completing his own training in England, wrote Mae as soon as he learned of her husband's death:

> All I can say is that you have my deepest sympathy. It is hard to express oneself. I was glad to know that Mrs. Hodge [his wife] was with you and hope she did the best she could in helping you. I do hope you and your children are keeping well. I am sure your kind friends will be doing what good they can for you. No doubt Mrs. Hodge will pay you a visit now and again.[53]

We do know a bit more about the widow of L/Cpl. Sydney Nightingale. Part of a reinforcement draft from the 56th Battalion, Nightingale was killed in action on November 18. His wife Jessie was 34 years old with two young children. "My dear little Pete," he had written in April 1916 on the back of a postcard showing his troop ship, the White Star liner SS *Baltic*, "when I get to England I am going to send you something nice, so be a good boy to your mother and don't forget your daddy, with fondest love and kisses."[54] On 1 March 1917, Mrs. Nightingale was granted a yearly widow's pension of $384 which would cease if she remarried. In addition, there was $6 monthly for each of her children, Florence and Peter, ages 8 and 7, respectively, until they reached their sixteenth birthdays. She also received a burial report thirteen months after her husband's death, but of course this proved a temporary interment and in June 1920 she received a notice of his reburial "with every measure of care and reverence" in one of the new military cemeteries being constructed amid the old battlefields by the Imperial War Graves Commission.[55]

Those of the battalion's soldiers who had survived the Somme unscathed or with minor wounds—the majority—faced their own coming to terms. Some did it privately—others with mates in their section or platoon who, like veterans of combat throughout history, would understand without having to be told. On leave in England, where it was easier to confide in letters, Pvt. Andrew Munro, a battalion runner during the battle, minced no words:

> That was an awful day Dad. I was not a bit nervous during it all, even when I went through German barrage three times, but after I got back to billets my nerves could stand it no longer, and I collapsed. Guess the strain had been too great.... There are pictures in my mind that I shall never forget as long as I live.[56]

Munro was deeply religious, and concluded divine intervention, spurred by his parents' prayers, had spared him. Like Munro, Cpl. Victor Wheeler was emotionally overwhelmed by the losses. His battalion, a close-knit family only days before, now seemed hardly recognizable to the originals.[57]

Reinforcements

Within days the first reinforcements arrived, 152 other ranks stripped mostly from the 56th and 137th Battalions.[58] The 50th also accepted a few dozen Japanese-Canadian soldiers who had originally tried to enlist in British Columbia but had been turned away repeatedly despite Japan being an ally of the Empire and the Japanese having a stellar martial reputation. They had eventually found their way into several Alberta battalions, particularly Medicine Hat's 175th. The times were racist and most Canadians believed it was a white man's war. Maj.-Gen. Watson inherited them all and offered a platoon to any battalion that would accept them. The 50th already had a few First Nations soldiers, and for whatever reason (or reasons), they accepted his offer. Few of the newcomers spoke English well enough to be trained or fight in that language, and there were no bilingual white officers. Consequently any Japanese-Canadian soldier who spoke even passable English was immediately made an NCO. For the same reasons the men also had to be kept together. But the other soldiers in Lt. Roberts' D Company, where the Japanese-Canadians were slotted, apparently thought highly of their fighting ability and courage. Since reinforcements could not be had, the Japanese component ultimately had to be broken up, with the remnant reassigned as batmen or cooks.[59]

By month's end, the battalion, with the rest of the 4th Division, had withdrawn well to the west of the Somme battlefield and settled into a camp in the Divion area, about 25 kms northwest of Arras, where they commenced an intensive period of training. On December 13, word came from division headquarters that Lt. Lowes had been awarded the MC and Pvts. Rosenthal, Bowen, Jenkins and McCallum the MM (the equivalent for other ranks), all earned for acts of gallantry in the attack on Desire Support Trench.[60] A few days before Christmas, the battalion marched to new quarters at Villers-au-Bois, the silhouette of Vimy Ridge dominating the eastern horizon. Only the senior command of the Canadian Corps knew its future significance. A lone 50th soldier was killed on Christmas Day during a relief, the last to die in 1916.

A New CO—and More Gallantry Awards

The first days of 1917 brought a second change of commanding officer. Maj. R. B. Eaton departed to attend the three-month senior officers' course at Aldershot, for which only particularly promising British and Dominion officers were usually recommended.[61] Eaton's temporary replacement was Lt.-Col. Charles Worsnop, who had come over from the 102nd Battalion. He left little imprint on the 50th, and only two months later was gone to another command, and then to England and a training role. But his appointment indicated none of the battalion's majors were deemed experienced enough to take on the role.[62] By mid-month, GHQ had approved a second round of gallantry awards for November's fighting on the Somme, an MC for Lt. Elliot and MMs for Sgt. Santell, Cpls. Grant and Cusack, and Pvts. Fahy and Hodgkins.[63] There was little else to cheer—the winter weather was unseasonably cold, hampering the training program and making basic living conditions miserable.[64]

A Spring Offensive

The major Anglo-French operations of 1916, namely the attacks on the Somme and the defence and subsequent counterattacks at Verdun, had been attritional "victories" given the grievous losses suffered by the German Army. Plans took shape during the winter calling for major British operations in the general area of Arras and advancing toward the Hindenburg Line and the vital rail junction at Cambrai. This offensive would be launched in support of a powerful French attack farther south at Chemin des Dames ridge. Under these dual blows, the German front would collapse and the road to victory finally be in sight. As part of Gen. Henry Horne's First Army, the Canadian Corps' role would be to capture and hold Vimy Ridge, the crucial high ground on the left shoulder of the British axis of attack. To confuse the enemy, the British assault would commence on April 9, a week before the French attack. The Canadian Corps' commander learned the full outline of his men's task on 19 January 1917.[65] Thereafter Lt.-Gen. Byng and his able staff and command team single-mindedly focused entirely on preparations for seizing Vimy Ridge.

Bite-and-hold

Disappointment with the BEF's overall performance on the Somme had led to a general questioning of accepted attack doctrine that had assumed heavy preliminary bombardments would neutralize the fixed defences the assaulting infantry would confront. But the German defences were too extensive and the artillery resources insufficiently powerful, resulting in prohibitive casualties among the attackers. Drawing on these hard lessons, British commanders and their staff, with significant input from their Dominion colleagues, set about recasting the BEF's attack doctrine. Henceforth, the artillery would suppress what it could not obliterate. The latter required a great deal of additional heavy and medium artillery manned by crews trained to fire far more accurately so that bunkers, ammunition dumps and the enemy's own artillery could reliably be hit. The former would require masses of lighter field artillery to execute creeping barrages, a curtain of explosions and shrapnel advancing across the battlefield immediately in front of the infantry, forcing surviving defenders to shelter instead of rushing to man their weapons. Simply put, the objective now was to seize the objective primarily with artillery and consolidate with men. But how the infantry would fight was significantly altered as well. On the Somme, infantry plans had been inflexible, a recognition that most of the battalions (and their commanders) were unproven in battle. Primitive communications technology had rendered command and control of troops struggling forward all but impossible, and when the infantry encountered unexpectedly strong resistance, they had usually foundered. The only practical solution was to accept any attack was bound to come unstuck, and train company and platoon officers and NCOs and even ordinary soldiers to exercise initiative, quickly adapting, no matter the circumstances. Byng and his chief of staff, Brig.-Gen. Percy Radcliffe, enthusiastically embraced the new "bite-and-hold" doctrine, as did most of their subordinates, ensuring that over the next few months the four Canadian divisions practised the new schemes until they became second nature. The Battle of Arras would be the critical test—could militarily significant victories be gained without punishing casualties?[66]

A New Brigadier

When Maj.-Gen. David Watson accepted command of the 4th Canadian Division in the spring of 1916, he had expected full autonomy in selecting key subordinates "on merit alone."[67] But Watson had been forced to accept the minister of militia and defence's younger brother, William St. Pierre Hughes, as commander of the 50th Battalion's 10th Brigade. When the "Mad Mullah" was finally dropped from the cabinet in November 1916, Watson argued that the brigade's mediocre performance on the Somme was the doing of the incumbent and staff officers personally selected by him. The affair dragged on into January when the sheer weight of Watson's case and the 10th Brigade's lack of improvement persuaded Byng to act. Hughes was sacked, and Watson got the man he had wanted all along, Lt.-Col. Edward Hilliam.[68] The 46-year-old had served in the British Army before immigrating to Canada, and his record in action from Second Ypres onward, including as a battalion commander at The Somme, was sterling.

Trench Raiding

Throughout the war the British high command embraced the idea that long periods merely holding the line would dull troops' aggressive spirit. But stretches of relative inactivity were inevitable in what amounted to mutual siege warfare. To avert that malaise, provide necessary combat experience to the multitude of raw recruits, and gain intelligence on the enemy's defences and the morale of their garrisons, GHQ had authorized "minor operations"—trench raiding. "Dash and slash" was the most common format—small groups of volunteers crossing no man's land in the dead of night, relying on stealth to wreak havoc, nab a few prisoners and documents, and quickly withdraw to their own lines. No element of the BEF embraced the raiding cult more than the Canadian Corps. By 1917, raids could involve dozens or even hundreds of soldiers, with dedicated training and ample artillery support, and on occasion be carried out in broad daylight.

The real utility of raiding could be questioned—forward defences were easily repaired and reorganized, and aerial photography could reveal much more. Furthermore, raiding losses were not always light, and tended to be concentrated among the most enterprising and aggressive soldiers. Though the German response to raiding was usually retaliatory shelling of the attackers' trenches, Canadian soldiers took great pride in their raiding prowess, or so their senior officers claimed.[69]

In late January, in conjunction with the 44th Battalion, Lt.-Col. Worsnop was told to prepare a major raid on a 225-m stretch of German trench lying in front of the rubble of Souchez village immediately opposite his lines. It was the first raid of any size the 50th Battalion undertook.[70] It commenced at 2100 on February 3, with a total of six parties from the 50th leaping into action, six officers and 100 other ranks under Maj. Keegan's overall command, plus seventy-seven officers and men from the 44th. Along with their personal weapons, the raiders were carrying a mix of hand grenades and explosive charges as well the wooden handles of their shovels for close-quarter work.[71] During the four minutes it took to cross no man's land, Canadian field artillery blasted the German front line, then immediately shifted to their rear to prevent any counterattack. During the brief stay in the German trenches—the entire operation lasted only 20 minutes—the raiding party went about their work with brutal efficiency. Worsnop later estimated his men had killed or wounded one hundred of the enemy and destroyed numerous defensive works, though the fact that German artillery chose to shell their own position obviously added to the enemy's losses. The Canadians also managed to make off with seven terrified prisoners. Despite a forty percent casualty rate—one officer and four soldiers missing and presumed killed, and three more officers and thirty-four other ranks wounded—the raid was branded a complete success.[72]

As part of the Canadian effort to maintain pressure on the Germans in the Vimy sector, 10th Brigade authorized a major raid drawing on all four battalions for the early morning of February 13. On this occasion the 50th's contribution was a full company plus support troops, five officers and two hundred other ranks under the command of Lt. Henderson. The objective was to take control of a section of enemy defences on the flank of The Pimple at the far western end of Vimy Ridge, and the general goal was "kill and capture."[73] On the 11th, two mock assaults involving all 800-odd participants were held on a marked course mimicking the objective, an attention to detail now typifying the seriousness of operational preparations throughout the BEF. [74]

The following night the entire force, under the overall command of the 44th Battalion's Lt.-Col. R. D. Davies, silently slipped into the 50th Battalion's trenches from where the attack was launched at 0400. Furious artillery and mortar fire promptly shattered the German front line, before establishing a box barrage sealing off the entire area from counterattacks. Meanwhile the raiding force, passing through gaps in the German barbed wire blown with Bangalore torpedoes, dashed forward in three waves and were soon into the enemy's first line. The 50th Battalion assault temporarily came unstuck when Henderson and several other officers and NCOs were wounded, and Lt. J. W. Swinton killed. But the men rallied and small groups from all four battalions, including one led by the 50th's Lt. Morgan (who would be severely wounded during the withdrawal), pressed forward into the second trench where they overcame stubborn resistance with bombs and bayonets.[75] An organized withdrawal commenced at 0435, with all of the raiders back inside their own lines by 0510, having brought with them many of their own wounded plus fifty-two prisoners including a German officer, a prize indeed. Enemy casualties were estimated at 160, with a great many dugouts and other defensive positions (the claim, no doubt exaggerated, was forty-one) blown up.[76] The total Canadian losses were twenty-six killed and 113 wounded, of which the 50th suffered a disproportionate fourteen and thirty-five, respectively.[77]

The 10th Brigade's opponents were the recently formed 16th Bavarian Infantry Division, specifically four companies of its 11th Regiment. Their evaluation was guarded, acknowledging that the raiders "had succeeded in penetrating the forward positions in several places but, after a lengthy battle with many casualties, they were driven out."[78] German intelligence officers had five prisoners of their own to interrogate, including two from the 50th Battalion.[79] Prisoners of war frequently told their captors what it seemed they wanted to hear, and the German report emphasized the lack of preparation for the raid, which was anything but the case.[80]

Watson's division had suffered considerable attrition from their intensive raiding around The Pimple, having launched twenty-three raids by the end of February. But the assessment of Crown Prince Rupprecht's headquarters, which was in overall control of the Vimy Ridge sector, confirmed that these attacks, and even more so, the continual shelling of German lines along with the grim winter weather that greatly hindered repair work, had significantly degraded their defences facing the Canadians.[81] Furthermore most German units in the Vimy sector were seriously understrength, with little prospect of receiving reinforcements.[82] Surmising that such intense activity must presage something, the Germans had drawn the obvious conclusion—that "an attack against Vimy Ridge is ... probable."[83]

A New Commanding Officer

On March 10, Lt.-Col. Worsnop left to take over command the 75th Battalion, their CO having been killed in action days before during a disastrous operation in the Hill 145 sector.[84] The new CO was 42-year-old Lt.-Col. Lionel Page, a British immigrant who had settled in the Red Deer area, where he had served eight years in the local militia, rising from trooper to lieutenant. Page immediately enlisted in 1914 and was posted to the 5th Battalion, where he distinguished himself during the Ypres gas attack, and by year's end was second-in-command. There had been talk he would be sent back to Alberta to assist in recruiting and training another battalion, but fortunately these plans were scrapped. The better battalion commanders earned the respect of their officers and men by willingly facing the same risks they did, and displaying level-headedness and competence in action, and not spending their lives pointlessly—all qualities Lionel Page possessed. To be sure, he was strict and rather straitlaced, enjoining his men to take a teetotalling friend along when venturing into *estaminets*, and forbidding the singing of the ribald "Mademoiselle from Armentières" on the march. But he cared for his men in small ways that meant a lot to the ordinary soldier and was consistently fair in his personal dealings with them.[85] Page wasted no time putting his stamp on the battalion by appointing four new company commanders—Majs. John Costigan and Lionel Casewell and Capts. Wesley Eveleigh and Olaf Svendsen. As events would prove, these were all sound selections.[86]

The Final Days

Throughout March, preparations for the forthcoming attack intensified. For the 50th Battalion that meant familiarizing companies and platoons with the new infantry tactics over courses that replicated the terrain and known enemy dispositions.[87] Commencing April 1 the battalion engaged in five days of training focused on familiarizing them with their specific assignments in the looming battle. Nevertheless, given all the replacements and their uneven levels of training, time had to be devoted to even the most basic matters.[88] It was welcome news when both Eaton and Keegan returned to active duty, and to augment his pool of combat-experienced lieutenants, he promoted five of his best NCOs. At the last minute, the battalion also took on strength nearly a hundred more reinforcements, meaning about one in seven of the 50th's men "going over the bags" at Vimy Ridge would have barely had time to introduce themselves to their new comrades, let alone train with them.[89] On the morning of April 6, Maj.-Gen. Watson, who had harboured concerns about training and leadership shortcomings in several of the 10th's battalions during the preceding weeks,[90] inspected the brigade one last time.[91] No doubt in hopes of breaking the tension, the men were treated to a brigade-wide sports meet that afternoon.

The assault scheduled for Easter Monday, April 9, called for the 50th Battalion to support the 11th and 12th Brigades only if needed. Their turn would come in the ensuing days. At 1900 on the 8th, 26 officers and 675 other ranks moved forward to take up their assigned positions in the Quarries area.[92] The platoons, well separated so as not fall victim to random German shelling, slowly snaked their way forward, following their assigned guides. Burdened down with weapons, extra ammunition and grenades, and engineer supplies for building improvised defences, the soldiers were glad for their heavy great coats in the cold, wet conditions. Lt.-Col. Page and his headquarters staff set up their temporary command post in the Souchez tunnel. Without having incurred a single casualty, assembly was completed just before midnight.[93] Now, only the waiting remained. Whether facing your first action was an advantage when it came to one's nerves only those who had already been through the ritual could say. A "when your number's up" fatalism was common but certainly not universal. Once settled in a shattered bit of diggings or shell crater, those who could sleep did so; others just tried to keep warm. They knew their tasks and believed in the plan. But would they be found wanting? That, after all, was every soldier's dread. Would the wound be clean or death be quick? Would they ever see loved ones again? The thoughts of a soldier on the cusp of battle.

The Enemy Perspective

On March 18, a conference held at the headquarters of the 1st Bavarian Corps mulled over options in the sector. General von Fasbender, Corps commander responsible for the ridge's immediate defence, led the presentation in front of General Ludendorff, the de facto head of all German forces on the Western Front, as well as senior staff officers from Army Group Crown Prince Rupprecht and the Sixth Army. Von Fasbender emphasized the weakness of the German position, that geography had precluded the construction of the normal defence in depth while such defences as had been built were badly degraded by the incessant artillery bombardment, and there were serious shortages of men and weapons. "Initial enemy success," he opined, would be "extraordinarily difficult to rectify."[94] All agreed the Vimy position was far from impregnable.

April 9 … The Attack

At 0530, in the faint light of dawn, as hundreds of field and medium artillery pieces erupted with one deafening crash and the sky filled with dazzling flares to alert the waiting infantry, elements of all four divisions of the Canadian Corps commenced their epic attack on Vimy Ridge. It was the first operation that could rightly be called a Canadian battle,[95] and that day Canadians met with almost complete success. The task of the 4th Division, on the far left of the attack, was to overrun Hill 145, the ridge's high point. The assault battalions of the 11th and 12th Brigades were able to form up in the darkness within 150 m of the forward German outposts at the ridge's base. With each reinforced by a battalion from the 10th, the brigades were to swiftly overwhelm the two principal defensive lines on the forward slope as well as two more surrounding the summit, then immediately prepare to repel counterattacks by German troops, who were assumed to be sheltering in deep bunkers dug into the reverse slope.[96] The plan went badly awry. The right flank of the 11th Brigade's assault was initially successful, capturing the summit of Hill 145. But the left flank incurred appalling casualties and made barely any progress at all. The open

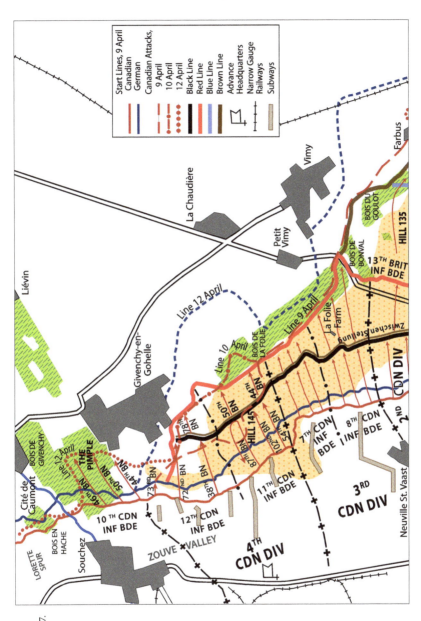

MAP 2:
Vimy Ridge,
9–12 April 1917.

1 | From Calgary to Vimy Ridge 29

flank compelled the Canadians on the summit to fall back. A confused mêlée raged all day, until just before dark a final push by what was left of the infantry saw the 11th Brigade's portion of Hill 145 seized for good, with all German counterattacks that night being repulsed. Meanwhile, the 12th Brigade attack on their left had come under intense enfilade fire from German machine guns on The Pimple (a lesser summit to the north) and had suffered heavy losses. As light faded, the spent remnants of the assault battalions had still not captured their section of Hill 145. Since the 4th Division's objectives beyond Hill 145 could not be attacked until the entire summit was secured, Watson and his staff decided around 1800 that there was no alternative now save committing the rest of the 10th Brigade—the 44th and 50th Battalions—even though both had been training to attack The Pimple.[97]

April 10 ... Hill 145

The 50th Battalion had stayed put throughout the 9th, awaiting orders and watching the depressing stream of ambulances and walking wounded coming off the ridge.[98] But around 2230 Lt.-Col. Page received orders to move his unit forward to a support line where they spent an uneasy night. Early the following morning he personally reconnoitred the slopes over which his men would attack. Orders were then issued to the two assault companies, Capt. Costigan's A Company on the left and Capt. Svendsen's C Company on the right. B Company (Capt. Eveleigh) and D Company (Capt. Casewell) would serve in left and right support, respectively. At noon, officers and men set off through a warren of communications trenches to the assembly area, reaching their designated start lines well to the north of the summit of Hill 145 just minutes before their zero hour of 1515. Their 44th Battalion comrades were deployed immediately to their right. It was cold, with snow flurries driven by a biting wind. Once the artillery barrage erupted, it was a mad dash downhill over open ground, muddy and pitted with shell craters, against "strong resistance" from elements of both the 261st and 18th (German) Regiments. Nevertheless, within 30 minutes the lead platoons had overrun their objective, the northern tip of the Bois de la Folie, and consolidation was well underway. The backbone of German resistance on Hill 145 had finally been broken, but at a terrible cost. "The sight of our decimated ranks ... almost tore the hearts out of us as we, who were still standing, looked around for our buddies and brothers—and saw them not," signaller Victor Wheeler recounted in his memoir.[99] Pvt. Robert Forrest, a runner, was the only one of the eighteen originals from the Okotoks area to come out alive. Losses among platoon and company officers had been particularly severe, with Maj. Costigan and five lieutenants killed, and Capt. Eveleigh and another five lieutenants, all platoon commanders, wounded. Apart from these, Page unofficially tallied 57 killed, 130 wounded and 31 unaccounted for—a total of 230 men.[100] At 2300 the battalion was relieved, retiring with their ambulatory wounded and 125 German prisoners to Music Hall support line, a two-hour trek to the rear.[101]

Pvt. John Pattison, VC

As the badly cut-up platoons, some led by non-commissioned officers or even privates, had pressed home their attack, there had been much valour on display. In one incident, 42-year-old Pvt. John Pattison, who had enlisted in Calgary's 137th Battalion so he could watch out for his teenage son, Henry, silenced an enemy machine-gun nest pinning down his men. Working his way from shell hole to shell hole, he managed to get within 30 m of the MG 08. A well-placed Mills bomb silenced its crew, whereupon he rushed forward and bayonetted five more German soldiers before any could cut him down. Pattison won the Victoria Cross for his extraordinary display of courage, one of four earned on Vimy Ridge and the sole VC awarded to a member of The King's Own Calgary Regiment.[102]

April 12 ... The Pimple

For the 50th Battalion, the Battle of Vimy Ridge was not quite over. It remained for a joint British-Canadian assault to overrun the far northern end of the ridge dominated by The Pimple, a rise only slightly lower than Hill 145. Despite the 10th Brigade's already heavy losses, this task fell to its 44th, 46th and 50th Battalions, which were given a single day to collect themselves. Page used April 11 to reorganize his remaining manpower into two ad hoc companies, each about 150 strong, one under Capt. Svendsen and the other Maj. Casewell. Around 1600, orders reached him outlining the plan for their attack.

Dawn on April 12 came with a blinding snowstorm driven by gale force winds at the Canadians' backs. This at least made visibility even worse for the enemy. Having relieved the decimated Bavarians, the 5th Prussian Grenadier Guards Regiment had endured 24 hours shivering in shell craters filled with icy water while under remorseless artillery fire.[103] Nonetheless, getting at their positions would not be easy. In places the mud was waist deep, and the cratered landscape was strewn with the detritus of war, including numerous dismembered corpses. Nor had the attackers had much rest, having spent most of the night struggling forward to their jump-off positions. At 0500, after a brief but savage preliminary bombardment, the officers and men of the two companies stumbled forward into no man's land along with their Prairie compatriots, "hugging" a well-executed creeping barrage. The attack was aided by the numerous gaps between enemy outposts, which the infantry exploited to liquidate German positions from the flanks and rear. The 50th's war diary credited the defenders with "a good fight" while recording that "a great many of the enemy were bombed and bayonetted."[104] Much of the fighting was of the savage, close-quarter variety, with the Albertans taking a mere fifteen prisoners. As Wheeler recalled, almost matter-of-factly, "more and more *Boches* were emerging from their ... underground hideouts, unarmed and nervously trudging toward our advancing line, hoping to be taken alive [but] many of them were not."[105] The combat was intimate, and all the more savage for it. The men's blood was up—it wasn't just hatred of the German militarism and aggression spurred by propaganda, but of the individual enemy soldier.[106] Recent instances of treachery—hurling grenades at Canadian stretcher bearers and the wounded they were tending—outraged even Maj.-Gen. Watson and screamed for revenge.[107] With the Canadian attack undermanned to start with and the wounded steadily accumulating, there were no men to guard prisoners on a battlefield littered with abandoned weapons. Finally some officers—certainly in the 50th—had actively discouraged their men from accepting surrenders this time. Mercifully, the battle was over quickly, all objectives having been seized within 45 minutes.

It fell to the exhausted victors to hold the line through the night until relieved. Only a handful of the reinforcements managed to reach the 50th Battalion's improvised defensive line, and most lost their way in the awful conditions. Despite some alarms, which were promptly met with flares and bursts of Lewis-gun fire, there were no counterattacks, though snipers and artillery remained a constant menace. Considering what had been achieved, the overall casualties were modest, Page attributing this chiefly to the severe weather that had blinded defenders until his men were practically on top of them. Amazingly, only four from his command were known to have been killed in the attack, with another forty-two wounded and seven more missing. Late on the afternoon of April 13, the 50th advanced another 1,000 m without encountering any opposition. A British battalion finally relieved them that evening. The column that wended its way to the rear was hardly recognizable from the one that had moved into its attack positions mere days earlier. Those who had managed to get through it were proud of what they'd achieved, but utterly spent. After wolfing down a hot meal, sleep in their muddy, blood-stained clothing came quickly.[108]

Aftermath

During the ensuing days officers and men alike collected their thoughts and coped with the effects of what we would now diagnose as PTSD. For most, sweeping the enemy off Vimy Ridge did not equate with feeling the war was being won.[109] The evidence of death and destruction was everywhere. Most of Canadian dead had quickly been removed for burial, but clearing the enemy corpses was more roughly handled. Wheeler saw:

> hundreds of [dead Germans], piled like cordwood ... being cremated, and nauseating smoke [rising] from these funeral pyres with only the wind to scatter the ashes. The pungent, offensive smell of the exposed, decomposing human corpses, beings horribly devoured by Vimy's rats and insects, and the loathsome odour of slowly burning human tissue, from which spindles of grey-white smoke ascended, was overpowering.[110]

Reorganizing the battalion, now at little more than half-strength, took three full days. Before long, however, it was providing large work parties, and some training had resumed.[111] On April 21, as part of his visit to all of the units in his division, Watson addressed the officers and men of the 50th. Most soldiers had long since tired of the boot and button polishing required "for inspections by some 'big guns' who let out lots of hot air," but attendance was never optional.[112] Watson used more judgment than most on these occasions, keeping his remarks brief and confining them to praise. It was certainly merited. Two days later the first reinforcements arrived—eighty-three other ranks—and over the next two weeks there would be 150 more. Most had been combed out of the 10th Brigade's transport lines, such was the Corps' shortage of trained replacements.[113]

The Larger Meaning of the Battle

Gen. Sir Henry Horne, who had overseen the Vimy Ridge operation as commander of the BEF's First Army, had immediately issued a congratulatory statement to be read to all Canadian and British troops involved. Heaping praise on officers and men, he attributed their resounding success to "soundness of plan, thoroughness of preparation, dash and determination in execution, and devotion to duty on the part of all concerned"[114] Although the first few days of the larger British offensive to the south had started out very well, it soon petered out as infantry were pushed beyond the artillery support pivotal to successful bite-and-hold attacks. The French breakthrough at Chemins des Dames on the Aisne, which the Battle of Arras was intended to support,[115] failed disastrously, severely weakening the French Army's morale. This in turn compelled the British to renew their offensive, transforming it into still another battle of attrition with no larger strategic purpose.[116]

As a result, the major Anglo-Canadian success on April 9–12 glowed all the more brightly. Vimy Ridge unquestionably vindicated the BEF's embrace of bite-and-hold attack doctrine. While hard experience would lead to modifications, all future BEF offensives would follow this pattern. As for the Canadians, they had thrived under the mentorship of Byng and able British staff officers. The elimination of political interference in senior appointments and the empowerment of those who'd shown merit infused the Canadian Corps with an ethos of military professionalism, transforming it into a first-rate fighting formation. Vimy Ridge was by far the most complete victory the Canadians had won up until that time, and their collective pride soared (as did British respect for Canadian arms).[117] These were the foremost achievements of those three bloody days in April 1917—not the myth of a national birth embraced by so many decades later.

The First Two Years

In 1913 no one could have foreseen the transition from peaceful foothill and Prairie country to Vimy Ridge. But well over a thousand men, most of them Calgarians, had made that awful journey from soldiering for fun (as well as duty) to killing and being killed on the Western Front. Raised in 1915 and drawing on a nucleus of militiamen from Calgary's 103rd Regiment, but to all intents amateur warriors all, the men of the 50th (Overseas) Battalion of the Canadian Expeditionary Force had become, like the rest of the Canadian Corps, excellent fighting soldiers. But that knowledge had been dearly bought. Vimy was a notable military victory, but the war would grind on for another nineteen months and severe trials lay ahead.

2

From Vimy Ridge to Amiens

Grim Months

For the 50th Battalion and the rest of the Canadian Corps, the remaining months of 1917 would be the bleakest period of the war. Tough fighting and heavy casualties would seem to bring the Canadians little closer to victory. And save for the greenest reinforcements, which made up a large part of the Corps by late April, the novelty of war had worn very thin.

"Quiet Times"... Or So They Say

On the night of the April 24–25, the 50th was back in the front line near Liévin on the southwest outskirts of Lens, and only a few kilometres north of Vimy Ridge. Given their line was a railway embankment, lacking both trenches and dugouts, digging in was the priority. But under Watson's command, there would be aggressive patrolling to prod the enemy, too. Leading one of the first patrols, Lt. John Ladler was badly wounded and became one of the handful of 50th men taken prisoner during the war.[1] The enemy's nighttime forays had to be repelled, too. Their artillery and trench mortars steadily bombarded Canadian positions, and the Canadian artillery retaliated in kind, sometimes sparking "shoots" that lasted for hours. Gas shelling added to the misery. Such was life at the front during so-called quiet periods, when regardless of the reason, the infantry took the beating.[2]

Henry "Ducky" Norwest

On April 28, the 50th's war diary noted proudly that "sniper Norwest got three Boches."[3] This was the first mention of one of the deadliest marksmen in the BEF, Henry Louis Norwest. Although he was in his early thirties and supporting a wife and three children, the Alberta-born Métis man had enlisted in the 3rd Canadian Mounted Rifles in January 1915, only to be dismissed three months later for insobriety. In September he tried again, this time joining the 50th Battalion. It was a challenge for Natives or Métis to gain full acceptance from

35

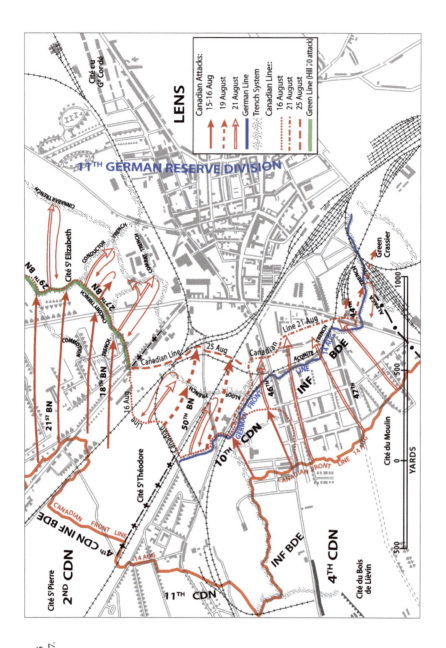

MAP 3:
Lens, 21–25
August 1917.

white soldiers, and the 50th was overwhelmingly white. However, Norwest's quiet, uncomplaining temperament ultimately won over most of his comrades, as did his bravery and the marksmanship skills, which all of them recognized could save their lives. One of his closest friends in the 50th remembered him simply "as one man who fought for his country and his buddies' sake." But in a way that sadly reflected the racism of those times, for that same comrade maintained years later that while "his colour may have been dark ..., his heart was white, and also his mind all the way through."[4] The sniper's job entailed a very personal form of killing, first stalking and then, with a single aimed shot, usually to the head, slaying an enemy whose features he could clearly make out. "Ducky" Norwest was one of the many Indigenous Canadians who filled the CEF's sniper ranks[5]—Indigenous soldiers accounted for the Corps' six most proficient snipers. By Vimy Ridge, Norwest had slain nearly sixty unwary Germans from blinds meticulously constructed within Canadian lines or natural hideaways in no man's land. His exceptional performance picking off officers and machine-gun crews during and after the assault on The Pimple earned him the MM, and a bar (second award) would follow for comparable work during the Battle of Amiens, shortly before he was himself cut down by a German sniper's round.[6]

The Advance on Lens

The next objective for Horne's First Army had begun to take shape—an advance northward to the coal-mining centre of Lens. For the 4th Division, this would first entail clearing a number of defended positions blocking their route along the main Arras–Lens highway.[7] On May 29, Page was alerted that his battalion would soon be thrown into action to clear and hold open ground between the Souchez River and the highway which included an abandoned power station and beyond it Callons Trench. The 44th Battalion would simultaneously attack on the right flank, pushing the Germans back beyond the highway and capturing the village of La Coulotte and a nearby brewery complex. The entire area had been heavily fortified with numerous well-concealed strong points and underground shelters for their garrisons. Page and Hilliam were careful to reconnoitre the ground, with scouts undertaking follow-up reconnaissance two days later to make sure nothing vital had changed.[8]

The Electric Generating Station

The plan was to launch the operation at midnight on June 2–3. Lt.-Col. Page decided on a two-company attack—Capt. Svendsen's C Company on the right and Lt. P. G. Leadley's A Company on the left, with B Company (Capt. Allen) and D Company (Maj. Dawson) in support, respectively. Given that the power station was already a ruin, thus offering plenty of opportunities for improvised strongpoints, the preliminary bombardment was made solely with gas, which proved very effective. June 2 was spent preparing for battle: checking weapons, ammunition and other gear, and ensuring they had adequate water, since over mostly open ground resupply of anything would be difficult.[9] All officers met at noon for a final conference.[10] Then it was just a matter of waiting for zero hour as the men filtered forward into their jumping-off positions, a shallow "trench" hardly recognizable as such after days of German bombardment. Victor Wheeler painted a vivid picture of these last hours:

> It was a time of sobering reflection. Men became edgy and jaws clamped as zero-hour approached; their thoughts turned to safety and home, to life itself. [They] grew quiet and serious, and unashamedly puffed on their Woodbine Willies with an unaccustomed introspection, as Eternity tapped on [their] shoulders and enquired, *"Are you ready?"* [11]

At precisely midnight, a mix of heavy and field artillery, trench mortars and machine guns rudely shattered the silence. And with that, fifteen officers and 435 other ranks from the 50th moved off to their fate. The initial German counter-barrage was desultory, though men remembered "[we] caught it all."[12] Regardless, German artillery would dominate the day. The advancing infantry almost immediately encountered stubborn resistance, and everything started breaking down.

Back at battalion headquarters, the situation was obscure since communications with the forward troops, as was inevitable in trench warfare, all but completely broke down. The lack of information was excruciating, but finally at 0235 word came from Capt. Allen that B Company had seized its objectives and was in touch with elements of both the 44th Battalion on its right and A Company on its left. Subsequent reports (delivered by courageous runners) from C and D Companies were less reassuring—Capt. Leadley, A Company's commanding officer, had been killed in the initial advance. While the 44th Battalion had taken its objectives, it could not hold them against fierce German fire, and at 0520 Page learned that the Manitobans had fallen back all the way to their start line. Daylight did not clarify matters, and he went forward to gauge the situation himself. It was not good. Troops had occupied the ruins of the generating station and sections of Callons Trench, while others had managed to improvise shallow defensive positions in the rock-hard soil wherever they found themselves. But this was little help against the pinpoint salvoes from German artillery and the trench mortars that were directed without interference from

Hill 65 on the far side of the Souchez. Added to this was devastating sniper and machine-gun fire, including from the open flank exposed by the 44th Battalion's retreat. To make matters worse, German reserves were streaming forward and infiltrating the gaps between the scattered Canadian positions. They were soon launching localized counterattacks from what seemed like every direction.[13] An isolated party of A Company men was trapped far forward, and a plan was improvised to relieve them. But this would have been suicide given the murderous German fire, and Page called off the attempt. By 1500, Lieut. Barge, the only officer left with D Company, reported his men had suffered 75 percent casualties and their position was untenable.[14] A decision was now made to launch a limited counterattack with what remained of B Company to keep open a line of withdrawal for the other three companies. Reserves were also allotted from Brigade headquarters to reinforce both A and D Companies, but they arrived well into the evening, far too late to be used. At 1800, Page received a message from a wounded Capt. Svendsen that ammunition was running low and there were great numbers of wounded. Without immediate reinforcement and resupply, they would be overrun. It took forever to get messages authorizing withdrawal to any of the embattled groups, and forty-five minutes later a hurricane bombardment from the German field guns signalled a powerful counterattack against all remaining Canadian positions. The men resisted heroically, driving off the enemy until they ran out of grenades. Then, pooling their ammunition and abandoning what little cover they had, the survivors somehow managed to extract themselves from the battlefield, some bearing the wounded while the rest formed a rear guard, keeping their pursuers at bay with short bursts of rifle and Lewis-gun fire. Nineteen hellish hours after setting off, the survivors collapsed into the shell craters and bits of trench where they'd started the attack.[15]

Wheeler called the fighting their hardest yet, and overall casualties had been very heavy. The Germans, too, had suffered steep losses, with the garrisons of several of their strongpoints reportedly wiped out in hand-to-hand fighting or incinerated by the liberal use of phosphorous bombs.[16] The further from the blood and gore, the more positive the assessment of such operations tended to be. Maj.-Gen. Watson had stayed up through the night to keep apprised of his brigade's progress, later noting approvingly in his diary that "90 prisoners taken and a great number of casualties inflicted. Canadian losses 700 [and] congratulations received from the higher ups."[17] But for the participants, there was no attempt to disguise the operation as anything but a disaster. Page identified the chief causes: unrestricted German observation of the battlefield from Hill 65, the inability to interdict German reinforcements, the unfortunate (if unavoidable) withdrawal of the 44th Battalion that left their right flank hanging, and the difficulty of digging any protective cover in such compacted soil.[18]

The practical purpose of this and most of the other attacks staged by the 4th Division during this period was to draw out (and kill) German reserves while identifying the routes feeding them forward so these could be shelled when future counterattacks seemed imminent.[19] Worthy goals in attritional warfare, but it hardly seemed worth the price paid here. And for the 50th Battalion, the butcher's bill, including a junior officer listed as missing, came to 201 of the 450 men committed, or two-thirds of the officers and close to half of the overall force.[20] The following day a brief truce permitted both sides to clear their wounded. For good reason, soldiers were always suspicious the enemy would fail to honour such an arrangement and open fire. The Canadians fixed bayonets, tied strips of bandage to the blades, then slung their Lee-Enfield rifles over their shoulders so that the white cloth would clearly show their intentions as they moved out into no man's land.[21]

A Posthumous Victoria Cross

Among those killed on June 3 was Pvt. John Pattison, who'd been recommended for the Victoria Cross at Vimy. Having suffered a minor foot wound there, he had only just returned to the battalion. Given his age and the buzz about a pending award, Page had been willing to keep him behind the lines, but soaring casualties meant sending everyone forward. By noon Pattison and five others, having become separated, were holding out in a crater in the Callons Trench system, the 50th's final objective. Unable to advance or retreat, sometime in the early afternoon a direct hit from a German howitzer had killed them all. On August 4 Lt.-Col. Page wrote Sophia Pattison confirming her husband's Victoria Cross, and offering some hope that he might be a prisoner. It was not until August 18 when a British advance swept through the area and found some crude wooden crosses, one of them with Pattison's identity discs attached, that he was confirmed as killed in action. German soldiers had buried his remains.[22] In early October his widow received a formal letter signed by the king. It said simply: "It is a matter of sincere regret to me that the death of ... Private J. G. Pattison, 50th Canadian Infantry Battalion, deprived me of the pride of personally conferring upon him the Victoria Cross, the greatest of all rewards for valour and devotion to duty."[23] Doubtless it was some consolation. On the evening before the attack, Pattison had penned a letter to his son Henry who, having just turned eighteen, was now old enough to be put in a reinforcement draft:

> I was pleased to hear that you [were] quite well and I am pleased to say it leaves me the same at present but I don't know for how long as we take another trip pretty soon. I will write to you as soon as possible when we get through. That is if I'm able ... I have

been in quite a few places out here but everything is about the same—nothing but war. I wish it was all over. I hope you succeed in staying over there some time yet. I have not got that decoration yet but the captain said it had gone through to England and he thought it would be Jake ... Dear Hen I hope I have the same luck as last time and come through safe. Remember me to all friends. I don't think I can say anymore this time. Hoping to see you soon I remain your loving father.[24]

Aftermath

In light of the June 3 debacle, Arthur Currie, who was soon to be appointed Byng's successor as Corps commander,[25] suggested to Gen. Horne that in future such attacks should be conceived as large raids, inflicting maximum pain but making no attempt to hold the ground, since German artillery was too strong. The First Army commander and his staff required little persuading.[26] For men pondering their good fortune to be alive, there was the welcome news that relief was imminent. It was a "honey sweet" word, second only to "blighty" in the trench soldiers' lexicon.[27] On their first day out of the line, Page saw to it that only "rest" was on the schedule. The following day, save for a muster to get an accurate count of men on strength (necessary for "company reorganization"), he wisely set aside for soccer and baseball games.[28]

The first significant body of reinforcements, thirty-one other ranks, reached the battalion on the June 11, with another 273 following five days later.[29] Unfortunately there were few officers, and the serious shortfall had to be made good from men returning from courses or leave, but mostly with field promotions from the ranks. The latter men at least had combat experience, which was no small advantage. Toward the end of the month, Brig. Hilliam gave a lecture to all of his officers on recent operations entitled "How we did it and how it should have been done." No record of his analysis survives. In what was surely more entertaining if not more informative, that evening the other ranks enjoyed a performance by the visiting *Blighty* entertainment troupe.[30]

Future Plans ... And Preparations

In late June, First Army had been ordered by GHQ to tie down German reserves so they could not be shifted to Flanders where a major offensive—ultimately the Battle of Passchendaele—was being prepared. It was assumed that any attack on the major coal-mining district around Lens would threaten Lille as well, forcing the Germans to stand and fight. How these plans unfolded would define the Canadian Corps' operations over the next two months.[31]

Tactical training intensified as July wore on. This usually saw the infantry and specialist arms training on their own under their own officers, but also included a couple of successful full-battalion exercises. There were also plenty of lectures, mostly focusing on practical subjects like "Platoon Organization in the Attack" or "Tactical Handling of the Lewis gun." Page's own favoured subject was "Discipline." And a number of officers and NCOs were always detached on courses at the various British or Canadian training schools.[32] But it was not all smooth sailing. Inspecting the battalion on July 20, Currie had found it "in a shocking state," whereupon Watson went down with Hilliam the next day "and gave them another going over." It is not clear what was shocking—appearance (spit and polish), discipline, or something else, and though it was no consolation, Watson had considered the 47th Battalion almost as bad after inspecting them. Regardless, there is no indication that Page's reputation suffered any permanent damage. And when the divisional commander next inspected the battalion, Currie was pleased to find "a great improvement."[33] With the pace and complexity of training increasing, and with Page and Hilliam regularly monitoring its progress, a return to action seemed imminent.[34] On August 11, the 4th Division formally marked the anniversary of its arrival in France. No doubt the originals pondered the implications of their much-thinned ranks after only twelve months in the field. But there was little time to dwell on that.

The Battle of Hill 70

On August 15, as dawn broke, a thunderous artillery barrage heralded the start of an assault on Hill 70, a height of land immediately north of Lens that dominated the city. Both Horne and Currie and their staffs had concluded that Canadian possession of it would compel the enemy to fight hard to retake it. The men of the 1st and 2nd Divisions had to overcome stiff opposition and several battalions were badly cut up, but success marked the day.[35] Simultaneous with the main assault, the 10th's sister brigade, the 12th, launched a feint from the south which ended up drawing more German artillery fire than the main attack itself. Four hours later, the 11th Brigade pushed strong patrols toward the centre of Lens, again to draw German attention (and reserves) from the real objective. Although Brig. Odlum's men were beaten back, the 4th Division's diversions on August 15 "had proved [their] worth."[36]

During the ensuring four days the Canadians poured pre-arranged artillery and machine-gun fire into the German lines to break up what they incorrectly took to be the anticipated German counterattacks. Nevertheless, Canadian arms, in what was Currie's first operation as Corps commander, had won an unquestioned victory.[37]

The Scorching Furnace

So far, the 4th Division had been no more than an intermittent participant on the 2nd Division's southern flank, edging closer to the outskirts of Lens and its miner-cottage suburbs to the west. Now, Watson's men would carry the burden of the battle. First Army was determined to make the Germans fight hard for Lens so any reserves could not be transferred to the Ypres Salient where the Battle of Passchendaele was now well underway.[38] After Lt.-Col. Page and his scout officer, Lt. A. W. Scott, had carefully reconnoitred it, the 50th completed an uneventful occupation of their new frontage on the division's far left flank near the Béthune–Lens road and nearby rail line during the night of August 17–18.[39] The following day, Page received orders from Brig. Hilliam spelling out his immediate plans—a two-brigade attack into Lens with the 46th and 27th Battalions on the 50th's flanks. This would entail seizing and occupying a 2,700m stretch of the enemy's front line, including Aloof, Aconite and Alpaca Trenches. There would be ample artillery support including three heavy artillery groups.[40] All of the battalion's resources would be committed. B Company (on the right) and D Company (on the left) would lead the assault, each deploying two platoons in two waves, for a total of eight, while A and C Companies would both provide two platoons equipped with special bunker-busting explosive charges for mopping up. The remaining four platoons would be held back at battalion headquarters as a ready reserve. Given that bombing was matchless in annihilating enemy garrisons during the mêlée of trench fighting, everyone would carry extra grenades. Zero hour was set for first light on August 21.

Barely twenty-four hours before the planned attack, Page received a 2nd Division intelligence report claiming that the Germans appeared to be abandoning Aloof Trench. As its capture "would materially assist my attack the following morning," he requested and received Hilliam's permission to seize it immediately. A daylight attack without the benefit of either artillery preparation or support meant total reliance on surprise. Immediately, platoon-sized parties from B Company under Lts. J. H. Colville and J. M. Taylor moved off via old communications trenches to Aloof and commenced the relentless task of bombing their way in from either end. But the intelligence was faulty, and the attackers were driven back with heavy losses. To make a bad situation worse, the Germans then bombarded the battalion's forward positions. Overall, there were about fifty casualties to no purpose.[41] Since the planned operation was still going ahead, the night was spent assembling the various units in their jumping-off positions. Page concluded that he had to reverse A and B Companies' original roles, the latter's recent losses outweighing the confusion last-minute changes were bound to cause. Meanwhile the Germans, now alerted, battered the Canadian positions with high explosive and gas shells, causing another sixty-odd casualties.[42]

Fair weather greeted the Canadians on the August 21, but little else went right. The 50th Battalion advanced over open ground on a 650-m frontage, over-running Aloof Trench and continuing on to the junction of the Béthune and La Bassée roads, their final objective. Aided by an excellent barrage, that advance started well, but German artillery carpeted Aloof Trench as the Canadians arrived, causing numerous casualties, and withering machine-gun fire picked off more. Pressing on with marked courage but steadily thinning numbers, only small parties—Lt. John Weir's twenty-odd men was the largest—managed to reach their final objectives where, unable to link up, they held on for dear life. Eventually, Weir attempted to lead his men back to their own lines. A fair number managed to make it, but tragically Weir was not one of them.

At 0600, when Lt.-Col. Page went forward to ascertain the situation for himself, he could locate only 138 men. Recognizing the danger, he immediately summoned forty-eight men from his reserve platoons to close the battalion's open right flank. There were only two officers to lead them, one of whom was promptly wounded while the other had only been taken on strength forty-eight hours earlier. Facing an intense barrage, the effort had no chance.

By midday, Page had submitted two plans for a co-ordinated second attack on Aloof Trench, with Hilliam adopting the one requiring the least artillery support, since little would be available. At 1800, the assault force—now just remnants of platoons—attempted to bomb their way into and down Aloof from three directions, using ruined German communications trenches to avoid a suicidal overland approach. In the event, only the attack from the southern end led by Lt. Hodges gained much ground, and it was too weak to repel counter-attacks. The other two parties were forced back under fire, though they managed the remarkable feat of evacuating all their wounded. The day's assaults were greatly hindered by the ground. This was a built-up area—not the usual farmland. Beyond including a warren of badly damaged but still serviceable communication trenches (which were ideal avenues for enemy infiltration), there were countless demolished houses and other buildings, many of which had been transformed into machine-gun-equipped strong points or snipers' blinds. None of the infantry had trained to operate in this alien landscape.[43]

At least with darkness, the scattered groups of infantry still holding forward positions could finally begin clearing the many wounded, receive desperately needed ammunition and water, and strengthen their improvised positions, for to live one simply had to find cover. It was a disheartening for those who had successfully retreated only to find themselves back at their start lines after such terrible sacrifices.⁴⁴ To all intents a battalion had not fought that day—rather handfuls of courageous but terrified men in isolated, disconnected groups had.

When the 50th's attack was blunted, it exposed the flanks of both its neighbouring battalions. Such gains as the 6th Brigade's units managed on its left exacted a heavy price and by day's end were only tenuously held. On its right, the attacks by the 46th and 47th Battalions managed to reach—and barely hold— their objectives, but they, too, suffered severe casualties. Overall, Canadian efforts that day had been a disaster, repulsed by the robustness of the defences, German firepower and well-planned counterattacks almost everywhere. The six battalions committed suffered 1,154 casualties, 346 of them fatal.⁴⁵ That only 200 German soldiers, many of them wounded, were taken prisoner points to both the ferocity of the fighting—much of it hand-to-hand in the case of the 50th Battalion—and the fact that for most of the day, Canadians were engaged in desperate defensive actions or falling back.

There was no further action on August 22 though both sides continued to shell the area heavily. As the war diary recorded, "the men [were] very fatigued and they were rested as much as possible." ⁴⁶ Page managed to cobble together a preliminary casualty list covering known losses over the previous 36 hours, but it considerably understated the dead given the enemy retained the battlefield, and his list included no missing in action. Still, they were bad enough: eleven killed and 188 wounded (including many gassed).⁴⁷ The following evening, August 23, Maj. Parry reached the front line with what reinforcements could be scraped together, ninety men mostly drawn from the 50th's transport lines. Their appearance permitted Lt.-Col. Page to dispatch an equal number "showing signs of weakness and strain" to the rear.⁴⁸

The final act in the Lens tragedy fell to the 50th Battalion. On August 24, plans for another attack on Aloof Trench were cobbled together. Page improvised three understrength companies and a small reserve from the infantry at hand. In place of the usual supporting artillery barrage, the assault force would rely on an intense barrage of mortar bombs and rifle grenades, which in the event did suppress most German fire. Carrying parties bringing ammunition and other stores forward suffered twenty casualties from shelling, but all was ready by zero hour, 0200 on August 25. The goal of the three parties, together about 120 men, was to fix blocks at either end of a section of Aloof Trench several hundred metres long, cutting off any possibility of reinforcement (or escape) and slaughtering the garrison. On time to the second, Canadian and British heavy batteries commenced smashing German rear areas, while a storm of mortar bombs and rifle grenades pummelled the ground the assault parties would have to cross as well as Aloof Trench itself. The latter abruptly stopped after four minutes, with the infantry on their objectives. This operation went almost flawlessly, with only seven wounded. Despite intelligence reports, there were few German defenders as many of them had fled. By 0345, Aloof Trench—which like the rest of the Lens battlefield reeked from the nauseating stench of rotting corpses—was at last in Canadian hands.[49]

On the night of August 25–26, the 50th Battalion was relieved. The men who snaked to the rear were physically spent, and one can only guess at their mental state. In his memoir, Wheeler described their time in Lens as "this scorching furnace," notably refusing to condemn those among his comrades who had wounded themselves to escape from it.[50] Writing to his hometown newspaper a few days later, Pvt. William Orritt simply summed up their six days trying to capture Aloof Trench as "pure slaughter," noting wryly that "our battalion has done its bit, for we came out awful short of men."[51]

The operations undertaken after Hill 70 were a test of commanders as well as the courage and determination of ordinary soldiers. Generally, historians have been critical of the command judgments of Brig. Hilliam, Maj.-Gen. Watson, and the division's senior staff officer, Lt.-Col. William Ironside.[52] There is no doubt that at this stage of the war the latter pair believed there was no substitute for aggression, and Hilliam fit that mould as well. In fairness, the boundary between rashness and calculated risk is hard to measure in combat. Overall, the plans to press on into the outskirts of Lens were driven by the Corps commander and his staff, and larger British considerations at the Army level and above. Senior 4th Division officers were given a task that the ruined urban terrain, the strength of the German defences, and the loss of surprise rendered problematic. After the success at Hill 70, continued attacks predictably degenerated into attritional fighting but did succeed in executing Horne's and Currie's strategy of preventing German units from being shifted to the Ypres Salient, where a far more important offensive was underway. In the words of General Hermann von Kuhl, "the fighting at [Hill 70 and Lens] cost us ... the expenditure of considerable numbers of troops who had to be replaced [and] the whole previously worked out plan for relieving the fought-out troops in Flanders had been wrecked."[53]

As for Lt.-Col. Page, Lens was his second major operation. A battalion commander executed plans in which he often had little or no input. His recommendation to Hilliam to attack Aloof Trench a day early when intelligence indicated the German garrison had been withdrawn illustrated his aggressiveness. Had the intelligence been correct, it would have been a coup for the brigade, and saved many lives on August 21. Criticism that this attack was rash, giving away Canadian plans, cannot be sustained, since the Germans, after being shoved off Hill 70 only days before, must have suspected a major push into Lens might well follow. Once the battle for Aloof Trench commenced, the battalion's resilience under quite awful combat conditions reflected well on Page's commitment to the training of his officers and men, not to mention the respect in which they clearly held him. His competence, steel nerves and personal courage were on ample display during those five days. As one veteran put it, "by his personal example, [he] was able to influence the example of every man in the battalion."[54] More than anyone, he held the battalion together. And not for the last time.

Out of the line, Page could finally determine an accurate casualty count. It made bleak reading: three officers and fifty-four other ranks killed or died of their wounds, twelve officers and 268 men wounded or gassed, and thirty-three other ranks missing—altogether 370, or a loss rate of over fifty percent.[55] The following day the men bathed, and those needing new boots and clothing received them. There was also the thankless but necessary task of completing the reorganization of decimated platoons and companies. By month's end, the first 118 replacements were in hand, soon followed by another 177, including fourteen freshly-minted lieutenants. Rebuilding the battalion meant bringing the newcomers up to speed, for their training in England always left gaps.[56] But it also meant imbuing the new men with the *esprit de corps* and fighting culture old-timers had forged under fire and which the reinforcements needed to absorb as quickly as possible.

As September passed, the battalion quickly fell into the usual routine of periods out of the line or holding quiet sectors. Casualties for the entire month numbered only five killed and nineteen wounded. As for training, platoon, company, and even full-battalion exercises, over-the-tapes were the norm now, providing the element of tactical realism that had proved invaluable when introduced for Vimy.[57] After inspecting Page's battalion, Maj.-Gen. Watson left most impressed.[58] Word also filtered down confirming the first batch of gallantry awards for actions at Lens. Among those acknowledged was L/Cpl. F. A. Brown with a DCM.[59] Brown's actions were typical of the sort of individual initiative and courage the fighting around Aloof Trench had required:

> When driven back with his section from their final objective he returned to the position which was swept by machine-gun fire and snipers, in search of his platoon commander. At his second attempt he was severely wounded, but this did not prevent him from again returning until he eventually found his officer, who was dead. He brought back with him a wounded man whom he had found in a shell hole, and a great deal of extremely valuable information. His self-sacrifice and devotion throughout the whole

of this operation were a magnificent example to all who witnessed his conduct.[60]

Passchendaele

Plans for a major BEF offensive in Flanders had been gestating for many months. The one finally adopted called for a breakout from the Ypres Salient, both to end the general trench stalemate on the Western Front, but also to recover the Belgian channel coast and the ports from which the U-boat menace was threatening to strangle Britain's seaborne commerce.[61] The collapse of morale in much of the French field army after the disastrous Chemin des Dames offensive in the spring meant fighting just to keep the Germans distracted also became a justification for a major push. As it finally took shape, Haig's scheme combined the old optimism of victory through decisive breakthrough and the pragmatism of victory through relentless attrition. The shaping of major operations was beyond the purview of Canadian commanders but suffice to say the Corps would be inevitably drawn into the literal and figurative morass that was Passchendaele.

The great offensive was launched at dawn on July 31, but all hope of a breakthrough vanished in the first few days. It didn't help that the heavens soon opened, turning the farmland, with its drainage destroyed by relentless shelling, into a swamp. Regardless, the battle—attritional warfare at its grimmest—ground on, steadily drawing in fresh divisions, German as well as British, to replace the spent ones. By September, drier weather (and ground), coupled with the shift of the main thrust to Second Army (which was commanded by Hubert Plumer, a committed practitioner of bite-and-hold tactics), delivered more hopeful results. But the rains returned in early October onward—"our most effective ally," as Crown Prince Rupprecht, the Canadians' old adversary from the Vimy Ridge sector, candidly noted in his diary.[62] Both Plumer and other senior commanders recommended calling off the offensive before conditions became impossible, but Haig was not persuaded. Instead, the BEF would press on to capture Passchendaele Ridge and the eponymous nearby village before calling it a day. By October 12 a herculean effort by Anzac troops got within striking distance of that objective but could go no further. It would now be the Canadian Corps' turn.[63]

On October 13, four days after the Corps was transferred to Plumer's Second Army, Currie and his able staff were told to prepare a plan to capture Passchendaele Ridge and what was left of the namesake village. The Canadians relieved II Anzac Corps five days later and got to see first-hand the desolate sea of mud across which they would attack. "[The] battlefield looks bad," Currie noted with understatement in his diary.[64] Logistical preparations, particularly the assembly of overwhelming artillery superiority, took priority since without adequate supplies and the firepower to blast out the defenders, infantry assaults would be doomed. The final directives called for a methodical series of limited attacks supported by crushing barrages, with the infantry quickly replaced by fresh units before the mud exhausted them.[65]

German Defences

The German defences faced by the 50th Battalion and the rest of 4th Division at Passchendaele were dictated by considerations of terrain and manpower. Given that a spade could barely be put into the ground before flooding occurred, sophisticated trench systems and underground bunkers were out of the question. One solution—though in the event not one the 50th Battalion would face until the autumn of 1918—were pill boxes, reinforced concrete structures built at ground level in which soldiers could shelter from a bombardment before moving outside to fight their weapons from the cover of nearby shell craters. At least when it could be applied, German doctrine now called for a series of defensive zones that would mostly rely on mutually supporting machine guns to wear down the attack until it ran out of momentum and could be successfully counterattacked by fresh units. The Germans' own artillery would buttress these machine-gun defences. Spreading the defences out in zones (rather than concentrating them in lines) would reduce the impact of the attackers' own artillery, the element of bite-and-hold doctrine the enemy most feared.[66] In practice, however, the limited depth of BEF attacks during the preceding weeks and the Germans' heavy infantry losses meant this integrated defensive plan was reduced to a lone defensive zone and reserves adequate for only limited counterattacks. German soldiers who found themselves in the attackers' path would be expected to die where they stood.[67]

Back into Belgium

On October 7, Lt.-Col. Page returned from sick leave (more accurately an enforced rest) and re-assumed command. Two days later, the battalion received orders to prepare to move north with the rest of the 4th Division. General Horne's inspection of the 10th Brigade as it left his command fell victim to a downpour, but he saw to it that his brief congratulatory message was still read to all officers and men: "I have formed the highest opinion of your soldierly qualities. Your record speaks better for your fighting qualities than I can. Good luck with you."[68]

Heading to Passchendaele they would surely need it. After three days, first by bus and train and ending with a gruelling six-hour march in the rain—"many sore feet" the war diary lamented—they finally reached their new billets about 5 kms west of Hazebrouck, close by the Belgian border, where they would remain for a week.[69] The few days were not wasted. Page started by lecturing his platoon and company commanders on German defensive practices and BEF attack methods employed so far, including how to deal with pill boxes. The following day company-level tactical training commenced, with the CO's promise of a bottle of Belgian ale to every man no doubt spurring enthusiasm.[70] It's worth noting how impressed the Germans were with the infantry tactics employed by British Empire troops at Passchendaele. *British Offensive Procedures*, a thorough assessment drawn up by senior staff and circulated throughout the German Army in late October, is worth citing:

> In the overwhelming majority of instances the infantry attack is prepared with the utmost care …. [The infantry] advances immediately behind its own artillery fire…. One wave is allocated a particular objective in advance. The waves in rear leapfrog the forward waves in turn. The objectives are generally set close together; so the amount of ground gained each time is slight. Having taken its objective, each wave organises itself immediately for hasty defence …. Whenever necessary, the troops prepare their attacks on specially designed exercise areas. The role of each man in the attack is laid down exactly. [71]

Still, the enemy recognized that it was the skillful employment and prodigious scale of their artillery that was carrying British assaults to success.[72]

On October 18, all four of the brigade's battalion commanders reconnoitred the new front line, and the following day thirty officers and senior NCOs bused to Poperinghe to study a ground plan. On October 21 officers from all four of the 10th Brigade's battalions were addressed by General Currie. A shy man not known for inspirational eloquence, at least in front of large groups, most of his observations didn't seem to strike the war diarist as worth recording.[73] The 50th's other ranks, who attended a church service, may have benefited more. Early the next morning the battalion were transported to Poperinghe, where they formed up and marched through the remains of Ypres to Potijze on its eastern outskirts to take up their reserve position.[74] For the newer men, Ypres' charred and rubble-choked ruins must have swept away any illusions about the destructive power of artillery.

The 4th Division's Plan of Attack

The Canadian Corps planned to carry out their assault in four stages spread over a fortnight, with the 3rd and 4th Divisions responsible for the first two. Stage 1 would see Maj.-Gen. Lipsett's 3rd Division attack on a broader and deeper front, advancing 1,100 m to their Red Line objective. Meanwhile, on their right, Watson's men, initially just the 46th Battalion, with the rest of the 10th Brigade, including the 50th, in support, would attack on a smaller section of frontage and advance only about 500 m. The most heavily defended obstacle was Decline Copse, a wooded area that straddled the Ypres–Roulers Railway on the far right flank of 4th Division's sector (which was shared with the 1st Australian Division). After enduring heavy shelling, Decline Copse had been reduced to a tangled landscape of shattered stumps bisected by a deep railway cutting. The latter provided the depleted ranks of the 11th Bavarian Division a rarity in the Ypres Salient—the opportunity for defenders to dig in and fortify their positions. Having reached the Red Line and cleared Decline Copse, the 4th Division would briefly regroup, then renew its attack with the 12th Brigade to capture the Blue Line, with the 3rd Division paralleling their advance. The Blue Line would provide a base from which the fresh 1st and 2nd Canadian Divisions could complete the final two stages by seizing Passchendaele Ridge and village.[75]

Mud and Guts

As any veteran of the Ypres Salient would have maintained until his dying day, it never stopped raining. "Ground bad going," the 50th's war diary noted on their first day in the line.[76] The Canadian gunners' ceaseless bombardment earned the inevitable retaliation, which made the situation of the men who were sheltering in caved-in ditches up to their knees in cold, fetid water or lying in the open, wrapped in their groundsheets, even more miserable that it already was. Considerable energy was expended to repair the trenches but it proved a Sisyphean task owing to the rain and shelling. Amidst all this, Brig. Hilliam and Lt.-Col. Ironside visited battalion headquarters to discuss the attack scheduled for October 26 with Page and his senior officers.[77]

Shortly after dusk on October 25, the 46th Battalion crept forward through the muck and took up their assembly positions immediately behind the two platoons holding the 50th's outpost line. Their attack was set for 0540. The 50th's C and D Companies would constitute the reserve, and the battalion was under orders to help mask the 46th's assembly by aggressively patrolling throughout the night.[78] Most of the two-man outposts also edged as near to the enemy as they could.

At 0500, having suffered four straight days of shelling, the Bavarians now endured its forty-minute crescendo.[79] That over, the Saskatchewan boys then staggered forward, hugging their creeping barrage which unfortunately included many "shorts."[80] The objective, Decline Copse, was well defended, and the intervening 600 metres was a sea of mud. At 0940, D Company moved forward so they could respond more quickly if called upon. In the early afternoon, Lt.-Col. Page went to the 46th Battalion headquarters to consult with Lt.-Col. Dawson at the latter's request, and thereafter acted as the operation's unofficial second-in-command.[81] In fact, the 46th's assault had gone miraculously well, for despite cruel losses they had cleared most of their objective.[82] But under continuous German shelling, the survivors struggled to consolidate their gains. Late in the afternoon, the enemy vigorously counterattacked, a crisis made worse when the defenders' mud-caked rifles and Lewis guns and even the Vickers machine guns that had been manhandled forward to provide additional firepower started jamming. Flares fired to call in artillery support brought no response for twenty minutes—an eternity for the desperate infantry.[83] With both flanks hanging, enabling the Germans to attack on three sides, the 46th's position was precarious. Fearful they would be cut off, Capt. Reid managed to rally the mostly isolated groups of men who were often without officers or senior NCOs to steady them, and slowly fall back, carrying their wounded with them.[84] As invariably happens during fighting withdrawals, some soldiers appeared to be drifting back rather further than intended, past the 50th's outpost line, and only the timely intervention of D Company's Lts. Albert Thorne, William Gordon, and Walter Burgess, along with some of the 46th's own officers, checked what seemed might have become a much more serious episode.[85] Page, who had witnessed the actions of the three lieutenants, was understandably proud that all the D Company men had held their ground, but seems to have judged the 46th Battalion's performance rather too harshly.[86]

The 46th's front finally stabilized immediately in front of the outpost line and the remainder of the 50th Battalion were ordered forward to support them, though in reality they hardly had to move at all. Two non-commissioned officers, A/Sgt. C. Rattray and A/Cpl. E. J. Clarke, earned DCMs for their initiative and sterling leadership during the fierce fighting that had ensued.[87] The German counterattack spent itself, and apart from the continual shelling of the Canadian lines, which would have taken many more lives had so many German shells not been duds, the action died down. Apart from D Company's involvement (three platoons had joined the assault) and the fire support from the 50th Battalion's machine gunners throughout the afternoon, the battalion was not directly involved in the fighting until later in the day when it reinforced the 46th Battalion's fall-back line. Both battalions were relieved that night by the 47th, which was promptly ordered to regain the ground taken and then lost by the 46th, but their improvised effort failed to make any headway. After a brief rest and some food, parties of Page's men were sent back out to retrieve the many dead and wounded, an exceedingly dangerous assignment given the relentless shelling.[88] Among the many who participated, Pvt. Morrill, a battalion stretcher bearer (medic), was singled out for recognition. The citation for his DCM bears repeating:

> He went forward [during the 46th's attack] dressing and attending to the wounded throughout the day under heavy shell and machine gun fire. Though wounded, he remained in "No Man's Land" during the night searching for and bringing in wounded. His example of fearlessness and devotion to duty was an inspiration to all ranks.[89]

This first round of attacks by the Canadian Corps continued for two more days, with the 50th Battalion standing to both nights in case they were needed.[90] By late on October 27, all 10th Brigade objectives had been consolidated, including Decline Copse, and twenty-four hours later, the second phase of the 4th Division advance was complete.[91] Three days of heavy fighting had gained a secure jump-off line for the next phase of the attack, which culminated in the capture of Passchendaele Ridge (and village) on November 10.[92] And with that, the Battle of Passchendaele was over. On the evening of October 28, the 50th trudged back to Potijze, and then by train on to Brandhoek the following day where hot meals, recreation, and concert entertainments filled the remainder of the month. Casualties over their seven days in the line amounted to 194 killed, wounded and missing.[93] Given that most of these casualties occurred among members of the battalion who had not been engaged in any offensive action, the figures testify to the steady toll exacted when living under almost constant shellfire. While the 50th had been spared the worst of Passchendaele, it had suffered.[94] The poignant words of a young Bavarian *leutnant* who faced the Canadians in late October, and who had found himself in the same predicament as Page's men—serving as part of a front-line reserve force that was not committed—eloquently describe their shared experience:

> On October 29th, we who had been in reserve moved forward into the front line itself, where, split into groups of six or eight men, we occupied water-filled shell holes. In the event we were not involved in a battle, but having to sit it out, enduring these awful

conditions, had a far worse effect on morale and spirit than even the most difficult fighting.[95]

A New Brigadier

The relationship between Watson and two of his brigadiers—Victor Odlum and James MacBrien—was professionally, and in the case of Odlum, personally, close. Both held their commands from the division's arrival at the front through to the armistice. The 10th Brigade proved a different matter. Politics and personal favour had forced Watson to accept his third brigade commander, but after a poor performance on the Somme, he had successfully worked to get Brig. Hughes sent home. His replacement, the English-born Edward Hilliam, had been something of a Watson protégé, but the latter's enthusiasm for his new brigadier faded. At both Lens and Passchendaele, Hilliam had pressed attacks too far, and he displayed an authoritarian streak in dealings with subordinates and even Watson's own staff. Commanding in the "English style," as it was derisively called, alienated Canadian officers. But as a pre-war regular, the British were more than willing to take him, and Watson and Currie were just as willing to let him go.[96] The 10th Brigade's new commander would be Ross Hayter. Canadian-born and a graduate of RMC, he had pursued a career in the British Army. In 1914, the latter had assigned him to the Canadian Expeditionary Force, where he had performed ably in senior staff positions.[97] Hayter proved an inspired selection, displaying flare, competence and a common touch in executing his responsibilities until he left the brigade mere weeks before the armistice.

November brought the start of a slow move back to the Vimy Ridge/Lens area where the most intensive regime yet of classroom and field training was soon in full swing.[98] The steady diet of infantry and specialized-arms work ensured the platoon and company assault tactics outlined in the latest BEF manuals would become second nature as well as prepare all ranks to lead if their officers became casualties.[99] As usual, Page was on hand to encourage and cajole, and their new brigadier was also a regular observer.[100]

Thanks to the passage of the Military Voters' Act, 845 soldiers on the battlefield would be able to make their voices heard in the Canadian federal election. Voting was slated to start on December 10, so on December 9 all officers and men, two companies at a time so as not to interfere with the day's training schedule, were lectured by their commanding officer and a senior staff officer from brigade on the issues at stake.[101]

Even the heavy snowfalls in the latter part of the month did not interrupt the pace of training, though at least it made their surroundings seem more

Christmassy. In an army of civilians far from home, the season tugged at soldiers' hearts, and being out of the line, carolling was permitted. On Christmas day, most attended either the Anglican or Catholic morning services, though doing so was voluntary. A concert followed, but the highlight was a Christmas dinner "declared to be excellent by everyone."[102] There were four servings during the day so as to accommodate the entire battalion in some comfort. Page attended them all, extending his personal best wishes and reading aloud the various greetings from King George V and Queen Mary and a string of senior commanders.

After a sixty-four-day hiatus, the 50th found itself back in the front line holding a section of trenches extending from the Souchez River to the Arras–Lens railway line, ironically the very spot where many comrades had been killed seven months earlier. The war diary's entry for December 30 offered a reassuring "a quiet day throughout. Little activity on either side. No casualties."[103] In fact, the battalion had not suffered a single casualty that month. Nonetheless, it had been a year of trials for the battalion. In the eight months since Vimy Ridge, it had suffered 153 killed and 830 wounded, plus seventy-seven gassed, and a further eighty still listed as missing.[104] Those spending that penultimate day of 1917 carrying out the mundane tasks of trench warfare—buttressing trench walls, repairing barbed wire and the like—surely pondered what 1918 would hold, and when the war might finally end. Only the most optimistic could have thought anytime soon.

The Final Year

By the middle of January, the weather conspired to turn the trenches and ground in general into a quagmire—with B Company nearly flooded out at one point. Conditions were so bad that raiding was even called off, but the work of resupply, salvage, and repair had to proceed and the exhausted soldiers kept at it.[105] The ceaseless demand for work parties remained a drain on the men's time and energy and could (and did) frustrate the best laid training plans.[106]

Fortunately, March brought a stretch of fine spring weather and the return of more intensive training, with most of the work focused on the company, platoon, and section in combat, emphasizing the use of their various weapons in combination and manoeuvring on the battlefield.[107] To harden the men physically, route marches in full packs became commonplace. And in a harbinger of things to come, Lt.-Col. Page, Maj. Parry and Maj. Keegan and eight other 50th Battalion officers attended a day-long lecture where British experts discussed the new art of infantry-tank co-operation.[108] This was followed up with two days of practical field demonstrations for all ranks by members of the 7th Brigade Tank Corps.[109] Everyone had seemed attentive—in a matter of months, some of the things they had learned would save their lives. Page pushed his men hard, knowing energy expended on training now would pay big dividends in combat soon enough. But training could be tedious, so he often turned the training into platoon-on-platoon competitions, drawing on his soldiers' competitive natures and unit pride. Company soccer matches—where significantly, officers and men played together—achieved the same goals. "Battalion holidays," granted after especially productive rounds of training, were another Page innovation, one eagerly embraced by officers and men alike.[110]

The Kaiserslacht

By March 23, the 50th was back occupying a portion of the front line in the Loos sector immediately north of what was left of Lens. Here things were relatively quiet, but the same could not be said of the Third and Fifth Army fronts further south, where on the morning of March 21 all hell had broken loose. The Germans had unleashed an offensive of overwhelming ferocity designed to rip open the hinge between the two British Armies near St. Quentin and roll up the remainder of the BEF—including First Army and its Canadian Corps—against the channel coast. Employing their best (and by this stage of the war, irreplaceable) infantry units, particularly the elite *stosstruppen*,[111] the Germans hoped to deal a war-winning blow before the flood of American "doughboys" tipped the military scales irrevocably in the Allies' favour.[112] The onslaught would wreak terrible damage on the BEF, but it still stopped short of sparking the outright panic the German high command had counted on. And the attackers suffered grievous losses themselves. Follow-up attacks in April also started well but facing bitter resistance and crippled by faltering logistics, these too petered out.[113] Thereafter, the Germans' attention shifted to the French front, but with no more success, their effort to seize Paris and destroy the Grand Army of the Republic culminating in a decisive French victory at the Second Battle of the Marne in July.[114]

Learning How to Defend ... All Over Again

For the BEF, an army that had not had to seriously defend ground since the spring of 1915 and had frankly become careless, preparing to absorb and defeat a surprise attack now assumed priority. During most of the spring, the Canadian Corps, along with the rest of the BEF, toiled to improve their defensive positions and put much effort into developing a more effective defensive doctrine and suitable tactics to implement it. Elastic defence coupled with powerful counterattacks became the broad plan. For a unit unfortunate enough to be in the front line this meant fending for—and if need be, expending—themselves. As the 50th's *Plan of Defence and Action in Case of Attack* spelled out, "All ground occupied by [companies] must be fought for and there is to be no voluntary retirement [even if outflanked]."[115] The hard lessons of March and April were absorbed (even if, ironically, they would not be needed). But as the focus returned to preparations for offensive operations, the Allied commands would continue to exaggerate the German Army's fighting strength right up until the armistice.[116]

Waiting for the War

Throughout this period, from March through July, when the fate of the Allies' cause hung in the balance, the Canadian Corps saw no major action—in this, they were almost alone among the units of the BEF. For a variety of reasons, Currie felt it best to keep the Corps together rather than parcelling out individual divisions as "fire brigades," and Borden's government supported this position. The British were disappointed (to put it mildly) and pointed to the willing co-operation of the comparable Australian Imperial Force in staunching the bleeding. Realistically, of course, the smaller, nimbler British and Australian divisions were more effectively employed under the prevailing operational conditions than an oversized corps of over 100,000 men. The Canadian contribution came in defending an ever-expanding frontage—eventually half as much again as they had held in mid-March—freeing up British and other Empire forces to do the fighting.[117] For its part, the 50th Battalion suffered minuscule casualties in April—four killed and thirty-one wounded[118]—a month of otherwise fierce fighting for the BEF. It meant, however, that when the opportunity for counterattacking a much-weakened enemy arrived later in the year, the Canadian Corps, alone among the formations of the BEF, would be well rested and at full strength.[119]

The waiting, training and digging continued into June.[120] Methods of infantry-tank co-operation were now a regular part of training, though for the most part without actual tanks. The battalion was finally able to rectify this toward the end of the month with an ambitious exercise calling for the 50th, flanked by phantom British battalions, and with six real tanks in support, to evict the Germans from a ridge they had just captured.[121] While this would provide the platoons and companies the opportunity to employ everything they'd learned about leapfrogging and sectional rushes, smoke screens, dealing with open flanks, and maintaining communications, the centrepiece was getting close-up experience with tanks. The exercise was completed twice, with tank officers leading a debriefing session between the two. As an obviously frustrated Maj. Parry summed up the day,[122] "the show started well, but owing to the well-intentioned 'butting-in' of brigade staff, was not an unqualified success [although] many lessons were learned."[123]

2 | From Vimy Ridge to Amiens

Gas

One of the most disturbing passages in Victor Wheeler's memoir describes him watching the death throes of a friend and fellow original. Although his comrade had also been severely wounded, it is the gassing that obsesses Wheeler:

> The wheezing and frothing from [Cpl. Tom's] mouth like that of a horribly bloated bullfrog, the dilated eyeballs, the pond scum-green discoloration of face and the gurgling sound issuing from his throat ... Green gas suds bubbled up, ran down his chin and trickled inside his khaki tunic.[124]

By 1918 gas warfare was widely used by both sides. No longer merely blown by the prevailing wind, the chemicals were loaded as pressurized liquids into artillery shells that could be delivered accurately onto their targets regardless of weather conditions. In 1918, mastering the ability to fight in a gas environment was one of the Canadian Corps' highest priorities. Coping with gas was a necessity not just for the infantry but for all the arms who had to venture into the killing zone, including stretcher bearers. The impact of poison gas on combat operations is often understated, and sometimes even dismissed, mostly because it directly killed relatively few soldiers. But gases, all of which sank into low-lying areas, natural places of refuge for wounded men, undoubtedly killed many whose cause of death was attributed to their initial wounds. And even if soldiers were not killed, treating gas casualties helped overwhelm the field medical services, especially during offensives. While the British Empire forces were equipped with an excellent gas mask—the small box respirator (SBR)—it was designed for normal exertion, not the demands of combat. Having to dash about, carry heavy loads, or feed shells into a howitzer for hours on end while wearing an SBR taxed even the fittest men, greatly reducing their battlefield efficiency. Mustard gas rarely killed, but it severely disabled men by blistering any moist surface, from lungs to eyes and sweat-drenched skin. Other gases came in devilish cocktails—a lachrymatory or nausea-inducing gas to make the soldier rip off his SBR mixed with a poison gas that could then fill his lungs. Right to the end of the war ordinary trench soldiers considered gas the most insidious of weapons, and the psychological toll alone cannot be underestimated. The fact that the Canadian Corps developed effective anti-gas practices did not alter that.[125] Nor should it be forgotten that as much as gas warfare interfered with soldiers on the battlefield, it crippled logistics, horses being far harder to protect than men.

The End of the Beginning ... The Beginning of the End

From April 1917 through the early summer of 1918, the Canadians had endured long periods of inactivity, at least when it came to sustained combat. This was particularly true for the 50th Battalion, which had played only a modest role at Passchendaele. Of course the time had not been wasted since training had been intensive. Confident and at full strength, Currie's command was now the most powerful corps available to the BEF, and the 50th Battalion was an integral part of this exceptional fighting machine. As "Bomb-Proof" Andy Munro had put it in a letter home written some months earlier: "Yes, the Canadians have a record that is second to none, and our unit has a record too, that is not surpassed, but equaled by others. The boys all know it. They do not boast of it or feel vain, but they feel proud of it just the same."[126]

Preparations were well underway for British troops to relieve the 4th Division along with the rest of the Canadian Corps. On the morning of August 1, Page's men trekked back to billets at Neuville St.-Vaast.[127] The veterans especially could feel something very big was in the works. From March through July, luck had been on their side, the battalion suffering a mere seven killed and sixty-eight wounded.[128] But their long absence from battle would end in the rolling grain fields southeast of Amiens. What came to be called The Hundred Days was about to start. For the Canadian Corps it would bring their hardest sustained fighting of the war—three battles on the scale of Vimy Ridge fought in just over nine weeks. Past achievements faded—what mattered now was conquering this challenge. Though none in the battalion would have dared dream it, the end was finally in sight.

2.1 Exhausted 46th Battalion infantrymen come out of the line in the Ancre Heights sector, November 1916. Fighting side by side in the 10th Brigade, their 50th Battalion comrades endured the same travails. (Canadian War Museum, 19920085-154)

2.2 Groups of Canadian soldiers cautiously sweep captured German trenches on Vimy Ridge, alert for survivors—or holdouts. Little mercy was shown the latter. (Canadian War Museum, 19920085-914)

2.3 Lt.-Col. Edward G. Mason, commanding officer of the 50th Battalion, in 1915. A dedicated commander who was much respected by his officers and men, he led them during their first serious fighting in October and November 1916 but was then replaced. (KOCRA, P-200-10-0133)

2.4 Lt.-Col. William C. G. Armstrong, commanding officer of the 56th Battalion as well as the pre-war 103rd Regiment (Calgary Rifles), April 1916. After training his men in England, his (and their) hopes of going to the trenches as an intact unit were dashed. Hundreds of them reinforced the 50th Battalion. (Glenbow Archive, na-2362-2)

2.5 Emmeline (Mae) and David Argo on their wedding day. His tragic death in the Somme mud on 18 November 1916 left her one of the first of the 50th Battalion's war widows, and their sons fatherless. (KOCRA, P-200-10-0150)

The 50th Battalion at War   61

2.6 Wreckage of the electrical generating station nearby the Souchez River, August 1917. Devoid of shelter and under constant bombardment throughout their attack on 1 June 1917, the 50th suffered very heavy losses and were ultimately driven back to their start line. (Canadian War Museum, 19920085-695)

2.7 Soldiers cheer on their comrades at a baseball game behind Canadian lines, September 1917. Like the majority of his peers, Lt.-Col. Page encouraged competitive sports to raise morale and build teamwork. (Canadian War Museum, 19920085-807)

2.8 Alberta soldiers in the 5th Battalion cast their votes in the August 1917 provincial election. Lt.-Col. Page was a candidate for one of two seats set aside for overseas military voters, finishing fifth. (Canadian War Museum, 19920085-632)

2.9 The Canadian front at Passchendaele, November 1917. Most who were there considered the conditions the worst they faced during the entire war. (Canadian War Museum, 19930013-512)

The 50th Battalion at War   63

2.10 Having enlisted in the 137th Battalion, Pvt. John Pattison subsequently joined the 50th as a replacement. Confirmation of his Victoria Cross, awarded for his heroism at Vimy Ridge, came two months after he was killed in the ill-fated attack of 3 June 1917. (Canadian War Museum, 19940079-083)

2.11 A month after the battle, Canadian soldiers rest in a trench somewhere in Lens. Shelled into rubble by both sides, the landscape of urban combat greatly favoured the defender, as the officers and men of the 50th battalion had learned only too well. (Canadian War Museum, 19930013-947)

2.12 A 50th Battalion Lewis gun section in France during the last year of the war. Back row (L-R) Davy Dean, Arthur Foulds, Hugh Mackenzie and Edward Ede—front row (L-R) W. R. Edgar and Hugh Everest. All six men seem to have survived the war. The Lewis greatly increased infantry fire power and by 1918 every Canadian platoon had two. Apart from the gunner and his loader, the others simply packed as many 47-round magazines as they could carry. (Glenbow Archives, na-4025-24)

2.13 An unidentified Canadian battalion moves "up the line" to relieve a sister unit, January 1918. The last winter of the war was defined by the rhythms of training and reliefs, and a lot of "hurry up and wait." Few Canadian soldiers saw the war ending anytime soon. (Canadian War Museum, 19930013-667)

2.14 Although ordered not to do so, summer heat during the Battle of Amiens forced Canadian soldiers to quench their thirst with ditch water. Not surprisingly dysentery became rife, adding to their misery. (Canadian War Museum, 19930012-495)

2.15 Wounded arrive at a Canadian forward dressing station during the Battle of Amiens. The operation's unprecedented success was bought at a heavy price. German POWs in the background may have been wounded themselves, but more likely volunteered to evacuate badly injured Canadians. A willingness to do so likely spared many of their lives. (Canadian War Museum, 19930012-399)

2.16 A Canadian 6-inch howitzer in action during the Battle of Amiens. The domination of British (and Dominion) artillery during The Hundred Days campaign obliterated defensive positions, sapped defenders' morale, and spared the lives of Canadian infantry in equal measure. (Canadian War Museum, 19930012-646)

2.17 Canadian infantry advance beyond the Canal du Nord, October 1918. The generally open country and resulting lack of cover unnerved Canadian soldiers. This was a war-weary army, and no one wanted to die in a war that was won but not yet over. (Canadian War Museum, 19930012-742)

2.18 The ruins of Mœuvres, April 1919. The 10th Brigade launched its assault across the Canal du Nord and on to the Marquion Line from jump-off positions immediately north of the town. (Canadian War Museum, 19920044-925)

The 50th Battalion at War   67

2.19 Soldiers of the Canadian Corps are processed for demobilization at Bramshott Camp, April 1919. Given it was a necessary step before embarking for home, few complained about the poking and prodding. (Canadian War Museum, 19940003-473)

2.20 Calgarians welcome home their heroes, 9 June 1919. Only a fraction of those parading had fought at Vimy Ridge, and far fewer still were "434-originals" from 1915. (Glenbow Archives, na-3965-8)

2.21 Four unidentified 50th Battalion soldiers who had been billeted with a Belgian family in Overyssche (now Overijse) after the armistice. Desperate to get home, these were frustrating months for most soldiers, though seeing the gratitude of ordinary Belgians first hand made things a bit more bearable. (Glenbow Archives, na-4025-25)

2.22 The commanders of the 10th Brigade during the greater part of The Hundred Days campaign. Brig. Ross Hayter (centre), and flanking him (L-R) Lt.-Cols. Lionel Page (50th Battalion), Herbert Dawson (46th Battalion), Herbert Keegan (47th Battalion) and Reginald Davies (44th Battalion). Keegan had originally served with the 50th. (LAC, PA-003414)

The 50th Battalion at War 69

2.23 Lt.-Col. L. F. Page, his wife Rose and two of their nieces in London, December 1918. The occasion was the award of a second bar to his D.S.O., given for his sterling leadership of the 50th Battalion during the Battle of Amiens. (LAC, PA-007705)

70   ONWARD

3

The Hundred Days and Home

Tout le monde à la bataille

On July 18, Gen. Charles Mangin's troops launched a powerful counterattack on the German salient between Soissons and Reims, ground only recently seized by the Germans. Achieving complete surprise, the French and American troops won a stunning victory. For Marshall Ferdinand Foch, the Allied Supreme Commander, Soissons confirmed that the German Army, despite its stunning spring advances, was dangerously overextended and vulnerable. Now was the time to launch a succession of short, sharp offensives aimed at strategically vital objectives the German Army would have to defend, continually bleeding its manpower until, with any luck, it would collapse.[1] In was in these operations that the Canadian Corps and 50th Battalion would play a central role.

Setting the Table for Amiens

As the fierce struggle around Soissons entered its third day, far to the north Lt.-Gen. Currie was confidentially briefed on immediate plans for his forces. Only on July 29 did he inform his senior subordinates that the Corps would immediately shift south to participate in "a *real* big show," as an excited Maj.-Gen. Watson noted in his diary that evening.[2] Commencing on August 8, General Henry Rawlinson's Fourth Army would attack east and southeast of Amiens (a crucial logistical hub for the entire BEF) in the general direction of Roye, driving the Germans back from the vital Paris–Amiens railway line. From north to south, Rawlinson would deploy the British III Corps, the Australian Corps and the Canadian Corps, with Gén. Debeney's French First Army protecting the latter's southern flank. The other troops were already in the area, but the challenge would be shifting Currie's more than 100,000-strong force and its arms and supplies undetected from Arras to their assembly area immediately southwest of Amiens—some 75 kms—without alerting the enemy. While the logistical challenges were resolved, various wireless and other deceptions persuaded German Army intelligence that the Canadians had stayed put. Secrecy

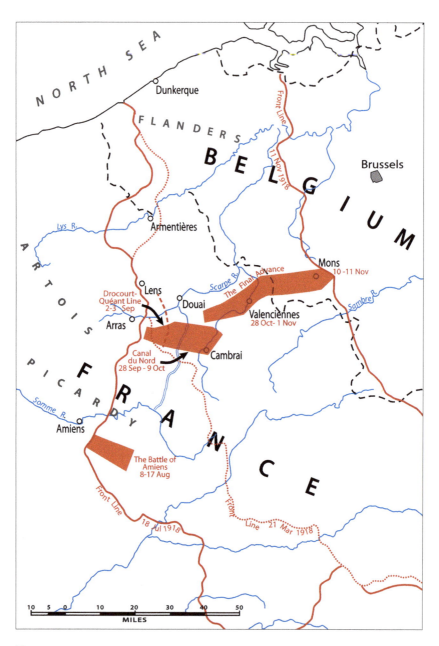

Map 4:
Canadian Operations in France and Belgium, 1918.

ensured surprise, reduced casualties, and heightened prospects of success, but there were risks. As one Canadian brigadier later fumed, battalion and company commanders hardly had time to look at their maps.[3]

After Currie's army reached the general area west of Amiens, the various units began marching—always at night—to assembly points behind the frontline positions they would take over from the Australians. Fortunately much of the area was treed, enabling men and machines to remain under cover during the daytime. Moving up munitions and artillery was more difficult, the few roads getting hopelessly congested with horse-drawn and motorized transport. The RAF generally swept the skies clear of German reconnaissance aircraft, while low-flying planes tried to drown out the din made by over 500 tanks.[4] Having no chance to register their pieces, gunners would rely on firing off-the-map. As usual, the British provided much of the field and the bulk of the heavy artillery for the Dominion corps as well as their own. Some 2,000 guns of all calibres had been allocated to either barrage work or counter-battery fire. In the event, Currie's men did not take over their attacking positions until the night of August 7–8, only a few hours before zero hour, scheduled for 0400. Successful completion of the preparatory phrase for a major battle in barely a week was an extraordinary accomplishment by staffs who worked under stringent time constraints and oppressive secrecy. The outcome now rested with the courage and skill of the infantry.[5]

The 50th Moves Up

The transfer of the 50th Battalion into position commenced on August 1 and took a week, some of it by bus and train, but much by night marches that disrupted their sleep, leaving them "a very tired battalion."[6] During the days, the men checked their weapons and other gear, honed their bayonets, and generally completed the timeless rituals of soldiers preparing for action. After a few days, Page visited each company in turn, reminding them all in the most general way about the "possibility of active operations in the near future."[7] On the morning of August 5 most of the 50th's transport, which had come by road the entire way, rejoined the battalion. Another night march took them south of Amiens to Pissy. Private Charles Oke remembered the ruined villages they passed though that night, the constant and ominous rumbling of artillery fire to the east, and the searchlight beams magically dancing above Amiens—the latter entrancing his comrades. They were served their breakfast at 0100 and told to "have a good rest until noon," as welcome an order as they could have heard.[8]

Early in the afternoon of August 6, Brig. Hayter and his chief of staff, Lt.-Col. Édouard Panet, were finally able to brief the dozen battalion commanders on the forthcoming attack and their specific assignments.[9] But secrecy still precluded Page from sharing what he knew with any of his officers.[10] One final overnight route march took them to Dury,[11] only a few kilometres south of Amiens. Page spent the early afternoon reconnoitring their assembly area. Upon returning, he was at last able to reveal to his men that the attack would commence around dawn the next morning, and outline their specific roles. Charles Oke particularly remembered the colonel reminding them that much was expected of the Canadians, and that while the 4th Division would be in support to start, "[we all] would be expected to do our full share before the battle is over."[12] Around 2100, after a brief delay to let another battalion pass, the 50th headed off for their assembly positions immediately north of Gentelles Wood. Unlike the other nights, the pace was modest, so as not to wear everyone out. The routes were crowded with long processions of men silent save for the rhythmic sounds of their loose gear and boots on the gravel. The columns frequently had to give way to horse teams pulling supply wagons and field artillery, and of course for the tanks, their roaring engines and clanking tracks all but drowning out the snorting and whinnying—and the teamsters' cursing. "All ranks very cheery," the war diary recorded, though one wonders whether cheery was the most appropriate descriptor.[13] By 0230 the battalion was in place, most just sprawling on the wet grass. Page had ensured the field kitchens were brought forward so his men could at least have a mug of hot tea.

The Sound of the Guns

Promptly at zero hour, the 45-minute hurricane bombardment erupted, deafening, murderous—and to the Canadian infantry huddled in shallow pits, reassuring. Soon, in the dim light of dawn, the visibility further reduced by a thick ground fog, they could see swarms of scout (fighter) and spotting planes speeding toward the enemy lines. At 0630, an hour after the 11th and 12th Brigades had set off, the 50th Battalion began to move, crossing the Luce at midday. After pausing east of Hangard, they reached Peronne Wood by late afternoon, where they dug in for the night. They had not suffered a single casualty, but the baking summer heat and shortage of drinking water had taken quite a toll.[14]

The 4th Division's objective on the opening day of their attack was the southern half of the Blue Dotted Line that ran just beyond the villages of Harbonnières (in the Australian zone), Caix, and Le Quesnel. The 12th Brigade gained its section of the objective that day, but the 11th Brigade encountered much tougher going and had to resume their assault the next day. The 50th moved forward to the Blue Dotted Line that same afternoon to relieve the 12th Brigade's 85th Battalion on the outskirts of Caix, where they spent the night. Once again the battalion had emerged all but unscathed, with only a single man wounded.[15]

While the Canadian Corps continued to make spectacular gains on the second day of the battle, overall German resistance—and Canadian casualties—steadily mounted. German reinforcements were being rushed forward to plug the many gaps torn in their defences. While they found no prepared positions, they did inherit something almost as valuable, "a belt three miles wide pitted with shell-holes and befouled with tangles of barbed wire and the remains of old trenches overgrown with long concealing grass," the remains of the Allied and German front lines from the late winter of 1917.[16] It would be their killing ground. The fighting on the 10th, when Hayter's brigade would be fully committed, promised much harder going.[17]

Facing the Enemy

Late on August 9, 10th Brigade received orders to launch their assault the following morning at 0800. The details were immediately passed on to battalion, but there was obviously little time to prepare. Page's men spent a poor night trying to catch some sleep surrounded by the carcasses and stench of numerous dead horses. Desperate for water, quite a few had slaked their thirst from a well or ditch and dysentery was now racing through the ranks.[18] The battalion fell in at 0600 and hastily marched to its assembly position abutting the Vrély–Warvillers road, just south of the former and about 2 kms west of the larger village of Méharicourt. Currie's plan called for MacBrien's 12th Brigade to attack eastward along the railway embankment that constituted the boundary between the Canadian and Australian battle zones, with the 10th Brigade attacking on its right. Hayter's battalions would advance in pairs, with the 46th on the left (and the 50th in support) and the 44th on the right (with the 47th in support). Once the lead battalions reached the Maucourt–Fouquescourt road and captured the latter village, the support battalions would leapfrog and press the attack all the way to the shallow embankment of the Hallu–Hattencourt rail line, the brigade's final objective. The sixteen tanks allotted to the 10th Brigade would precede the infantry, and two field artillery brigades, one of them Australian, would fire a rolling barrage to further shield the infantry as they advanced over open ground. The gunners were rushed, with only an hour to prepare,[19] and when the assigned tanks were late arriving,[20] divisional headquarters delayed the attack until 1015. When it did finally commence, the 50th encountered no serious opposition, save some sporadic shelling, until they were about to pass through the 46th Battalion, whereupon "heavy machine gun fire was encountered from Fouquescourt and the wood to the rear which made it impossible for us to advance until the [44th Battalion] had cleared up the situation on their front."[21] In fact, the MG 08s tore through the Albertans like scythes. Among the great many casualties were three company commanders,

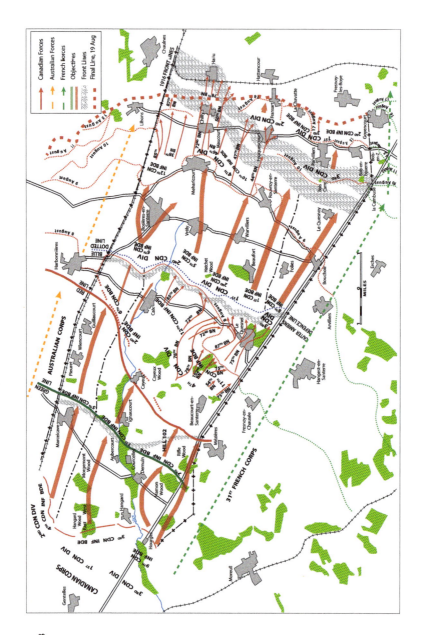

MAP 5:
Amiens, 9–18
August 1918.

two of whom were wounded—Maj. W. J. Eveleigh and Capt. J. B. Corley—and the other killed, Capt. Thomas M. Tweed, who had been cut down while trying to direct one of the tanks.[22] The twenty-six-tonne behemoths were supposed to silence machine-gun nests and crush uncut wire, but with their limited manoeuvrability and modest speed further compromised by the many broad remnant trenches in the area, they proved easy targets for German field guns hauled forward for the purpose.

The entire 10th Brigade advance depended on the 44th Battalion evicting the German garrison from Fouquescourt. By midday, Page still believed everything was going well, and assumed his companies had already advanced through the 46th Battalion. Nevertheless, with all communication cut, he decided to go forward himself, whereupon he soon grasped that Fouquescourt was still in German hands and that his own infantry were well short of their objectives, stuck in the open, and being shelled, machine-gunned and even strafed. He hurried to the brigade command post to consult with Brig. Hayter, who confirmed his assessment—the brigade's operations were stalled until the village was taken. Offers by the commanders of the two field artillery brigades to push forward a few of their guns to provide neutralizing fire were accepted by Maj.-Gen. Watson, and a pair of tanks miraculously showed up as well. By late afternoon, the bloodied 44th Battalion had finally cleared the Fouquescourt, opening the way for the resumption of the advance by the 47th and 50th Battalions.[23]

Hallu

To cover the 1½ kms to their objective, the 50th faced very bad ground, riven with wire and old trenches (and with no suitable maps to navigate them). They faced fresh German troops, manning improvised but formidable defences, and they would face them without artillery or tank support.[24] At 1940, in the face of withering machine-gun and rifle fusillades and a 77-mm battery firing over open sights from nearby Hallu Wood, the infantry set off. With three of his four companies now commanded by lieutenants, Page personally led his men to a point just south of the village of Hallu where those who made it quickly dug in. While lasting barely an hour, the advance must have seemed an eternity. Although the 78th Battalion (12th Brigade) had matched the 50th's progress on their left flank, the 47th, commanded by Page's former adjutant, Lt.-Col. Herbert Keegan (a 50th original), had fallen well behind, leaving the 50th's right flank hanging dangerously in the air. Page only managed to seal that off by committing his last reserves.[25] Brig. Hayter acknowledged the courage and tenacity of all his officers and men, particularly singling out the 44th Battalion, which had faced the worst of the action. The open warfare training undergone in May, June and July, he enthused, had enabled them to carry the day.[26] But the fighting on August 10 had not exactly been open warfare. All four battalions had been engaged in trench warfare in its crudest form, mercilessly clearing the enemy with bayonet and bomb. Training had been invaluable, but ultimately the day had been carried by hundreds of terrified clerks, labourers and farm boys—officers, NCOs and men—who had summoned the fortitude and endurance to do it.

The war diary included a full page of names nominated for gallantry awards and brief descriptions of their actions. Some of these entries bear repeating. Lt. William Oliver, despite being wounded, led his men to their final objective. When a second wound left him with a broken arm, he refused evacuation until the gains had been consolidated. Three other subalterns, Lts. James Taylor, Percy Brown, and W. S. Grant, were also cited for exceptional leadership. Taylor won an MC, but though put forward, the other two did not.[27] Brown already held the MM, a reminder that the heavy casualties among lieutenants were increasingly filled by promotions from the ranks. Not surprisingly, many of the platoons lost all their officers, and leadership fell to NCOs. Sgt. A. B. Dixon was one such. Despite being wounded in the arm, he continued to lead his comrades forward until a second wound—in the stomach—ended his battle. His leadership earned Dixon a DCM.[28] L/Cpl. W. G. Watson, the war diary adding the by now redundant "with conspicuous gallantry," had repeatedly exposed himself to fire while repairing communications lines, and along with two comrades even found time to storm a machine-gun nest, taking the entire eight-man crew prisoner. He, too, won the DCM,[29] as did Pvt. R. A. Harrop who neutralized an enemy machine gun and then under heavy fire carried his grievously wounded platoon commander to an aid post.[30] Also most deserving of note were the stretcher bearers from the 13th Field Ambulance under Capt. Walsh who were tireless in performing their duties, as was the battalion chaplain, Capt. the Rev. W. L. Murray, who was constantly seen tending to the wounded.[31]

For leading the attack on Hallu and repeatedly rallying his men, Page won a bar to his DSO. The many acts of heroism and leadership that day by officers and men all mattered, but those of the commanding officer were singularly vital. Before the attack was even launched, he had lost three of his company commanders, and during the course of the next few hours, a total of ten officers. BEF tactical doctrine had come to rely on the leadership abilities of company and platoon officers and senior NCOs, with each the proverbial next man up, trained to carry out his superior's role as well as his own. Under the chaotic circumstances Page faced he had to be—and was—everywhere on the battlefield, constantly exposing himself to enemy fire as he directed, steadied and encouraged his men. It was a superb performance by a superb battalion commander.[32]

The Canadian Corps won a major victory at Amiens, arguably the greatest so far, and the 50th Battalion had fully shared in that victory. But it had been costly, with the 4th Division alone suffering 585 officers and other ranks killed and 1,623 wounded. The battalion's own preliminary casualty report listed three officers killed and seven wounded; among the other ranks, the figures were twenty-nine killed and 159 wounded, with twenty more missing in action. This represented slightly more than a third of the strength committed.[33] Of the stress casualties we know nothing, as its impact was seldom acknowledged unless the man was too far gone to function as a soldier. Losing 218 officers and men reflected the price inevitably paid for what amounted to an unsupported infantry attack against stout trench defences, and a sad reminder of the norm earlier in the war.[34] It was mainly such infantry fighting that was sustaining the Amiens offensive now, and none of the senior commanders, Field Marshall Haig included, saw merit in continuing to press such attacks. Before the day ended, after consulting with GHQ, Gen. Rawlinson communicated to his corps commanders that Fourth Army's offensive would be discontinued for now, leaving it to their "discretion ... to make local improvements in the line which they were then holding."[35] Unfortunately, the 50th Battalion was going to face further hard fighting before its battle was over.

Gegenangriff

Efforts to bring up supplies and evacuate the wounded on the night of August 10–11 were stymied by the near impossibility of navigating through the old trenches and wire in the darkness. With the battalion so short of men, signaller Charles Oke found himself manning a parapet for the first time. "Peering into the darkness and watching the flares and star shells and the gun flashes," he was struck by the awful beauty of it all and pondered "the thousands who had been doing this, night after night for years."[36]

Daylight brought some respite from the random shelling, but the machine-gun fire was relentless, and that, along with the ubiquitous sniping, made daytime movement a precarious project, too. This was a serious matter given the men were now running very short of the staples of trench defence—rifle ammunition, Lewis-gun magazines, and Mills bombs, not to mention iron rations and water. As we have already seen, shortages of potable water were a constant during the Amiens operation, and especially hard on the wounded lying in the hot sun. The summer weather had been glorious, but the heat—temperatures exceeded 30°C—and the long hours of daylight at basically the same latitude as Calgary took their toll.[37] Showing great initiative, Sgt. Swanson organized a party from battalion headquarters staff and at least managed to get sufficient ammunition forward. And it was none too soon, for while inspecting his positions that morning, Lt.-Col. Page witnessed the obliteration of Hallu, which compelled the 78th Battalion to fall back. Drawing the obvious conclusion, Page hurriedly readied his men to repulse a counterattack. Occupying a miniature salient protruding well ahead of the rest of the 10th and 12th Brigade line, their position was precarious. It wasn't long before everyone could see German infantry forming up in front of Hallu Wood. Flares fired requesting a barrage in front of their position went unanswered because brigade were unsure exactly where the 78th was and feared friendly fire casualties.[38] The CO scrambled from position to position, ordering his company commanders to "contest every inch of ground" before returning to his temporary command post some distance from their forward positions to establish contact with brigade headquarters.[39]

At 1030 the German infantry surged forward in densely packed waves but quickly lost momentum as Lewis-gun and rifle fire ripped bloody gaps in their ranks.[40] Unsurprisingly, the counterattack found more success on the open flanks. Fearing they might be cut off, Capt. Moore, the senior officer forward, ordered a fighting withdrawal to a more tenable position.[41] Mustering as much covering fire as they could (and finally benefiting from artillery support), they managed to extricate themselves, taking great pains to leave no wounded behind. In his after-action report, Page was quick to acknowledge the vital efforts of the 46th Battalion dug in immediately behind them in keeping the enemy at bay.[42] By late morning the counterattack had withered away, though the Germans continued to shell the surrounding area for hours. Given what they had endured, the casualties were remarkably light—seven killed and ten wounded.[43]

From Lt.-Col. Page's perspective, much had been learned at Amiens, particularly noting that "our recent training ... and the lessons learned during that time were of great value." Still, there were things to be mastered. Liaison between battalions had broken down during leapfrogging operations. Furthermore, in this sort of fighting with its broad frontages and thinning manpower, holding a common axis of advance rather than drifting apart was crucial, and had to be impressed on junior officers. Finally, the fighting had placed a greater premium than ever on NCO training, for "much depended on them [and their] casualties ... were very heavy."[44]

What was left of the battalion was relieved on the evening of August 12, reaching Rosières-en-Santerre, about 6 kms behind the Canadian line, by 0300 where they were promptly fed and told to sleep. If signaller Oke's experience was typical, most of them had hardly slept in five days.[45] The following evening they moved on to Le Quesnel to rest and refit, while tentative plans were drawn up to move the 4th Division back into the line and resume the attack.

Indeed, by nightfall on August 16 the 50th had reoccupied positions near Fouquescourt. But wiser heads prevailed, and instead the Corps rejoined First Army in the Arras area where preparations to attack the formidable German defences guarding Cambrai were already in motion.[46]

On August 13, in his order of the day, the Corps Commander had attributed the Canadians' impressive success to their professionalism: "your training was good, your discipline was good [and] your leadership was good."[47] Currie's comments aptly summed up the 50th Battalion's performance. But for the rank and file there was one obvious difference about Amiens. While they had won battles before, the haggard columns trudging west toward prisoner of war cages made it possible to think they were winning the war.[48]

When Your Number's Up

The 50th Battalion's brief period back in the line near Fouquescourt was unmemorable save for the shocking death on August 18 of their peerless marksman, Henry Norwest. Norwest had been shot through the head shortly after he and his spotter (Oliver Payne) had set up in their "hunting blind" to start the day's work. As soon as he heard, Lt.-Col. Page ordered a couple of soldiers to find the exact spot where Norwest had fallen so it could be appropriately commemorated, a rare honour for an enlisted man. He also assembled the officers from his headquarters to salute the body as it was carried in. Canadian artillery even put a crash shoot on Dead Wood from where the fatal sniper shot had been fired. At least one soldier, Herbert Hogg, remembered the normally jovial Norwest being sad when he had gone up to the front line two days earlier, as if he had a premonition. Ironically, Norwest had been temporarily assigned rear duty to rest, but hearing German sniper activity was menacing their forward positions, he'd insisted on returning, managing five more kills to bring his confirmed total to 115.[49] The battalion was soon taken out of the line, but the joy of moving rearward was tempered by having to take their dysentery with them. By nightfall on August 28 the battalion was encamped on the southern outskirts of Arras, some 60 kms to the north.[50]

MSA Men

A little over four weeks hence, in the gruelling attack on the Marquion Line, Pvt. David Muirhead would be killed—as is so often the case, it is not clear exactly how. What is known is that on 20 October 1917 the twenty-four-year-old unmarried labourer had been called before a draft board in Welland, ON under the terms of the Military Service Act (MSA), briefly interviewed, given a medical examination, and accepted for military service in the Canadian Expeditionary Force. He reported on 10 January 1918 and embarked for

England a month later. After completing the bulk of his infantry training there, he was despatched to France as a reinforcement and taken on strength by the 50th Battalion on August 26. Supposedly a reluctant warrior, young Muirhead left a widowed mother—and no doubt others—to grieve.[51]

Three days after Muirhead joined the battalion, and just before the men were served supper, Lt.-Col. Page took time to address the 181 reinforcements who had arrived that day, welcoming them to their new family.[52] The battalion war diary consistently mentions the arrival of reinforcements, but never clarifies whether they were returned wounded, part of the last trickle volunteers from 1917, or others who had enlisted earlier but had only recently been assigned to front-line service, or whether, like David Muirhead, they had been conscripted under the MSA. In fact, conscripts are never identified as such even when they earned gallantry awards. Prejudice against MSA men was most pronounced among senior officers, whereas assessments were generally favourable among the junior officers, NCOs and ordinary riflemen who had led and fought alongside them. Victor Wheeler effusively praised the conscripts he encountered in the 50th Battalion during 1918:

> Draftees' loyalty was never in question; their willingness to fight and sacrifice, once in khaki, was certain; and their prowess as first-rate infantrymen and front-line soldiers was equal to that of [the volunteers]. No differentiation was ever made between "volunteers" and "draftees" [in the 50th Battalion]—neither should there have been![53]

But it speaks volumes that the commanding officers of nineteen of the Corps' forty-eight infantry battalions refused to nominate a single conscript among the scores of men they put forward for the Military Medal from the Battle of Amiens onward. To his credit, Lionel Page was not one of these—seven of the 50th Battalion's MSA men were awarded the MM for bravery in the field, the most for any Canadian battalion. What is clear is that conscripts fought well. A cross-section of reports on their service from officers who had commanded them in action prompted the Militia Department to conclude that "the recruits obtained under the Military Service Act are a fine body of men, physically and mentally—the equal of the best sent over since the war began."[54] Equally clear is that the 25,000-odd who reached combat after Amiens were the largest portion of the reinforcements received, likely constituting one-quarter of active infantry strength during the last three months of the fighting. As such, they were central to the Canadian Corps' success during the campaign that did so much to shape its historical reputation. Simply put, the Military Service Act meant that the Corps did not have to be particularly worried about reinforcements and could keep up the hard-pounding style of attack used so successfully against the exhausted German forces they faced. Yet beginning in the months following the armistice and continuing through the interwar years, with Sir Arthur Currie in the vanguard, the wartime commanders of the Canadian Corps never ceased besmirching the conscripts' reputation as fighting men and understating their role in the common victory.[55]

The Drocourt–Quéant Line

Unlike the attacks launched earlier in the war by the Canadian Corps, this time there would be only a few weeks for units to recover, upgrade the training of their reinforcements, and rebuild a sense of teamwork before everyone was thrown into a new offensive.[56] On the morning of 31 August 1918, Page attended a conference at brigade headquarters where plans drawn up by Watson and his senior field and staff officers only the day before were discussed. He immediately briefed his company commanders on the 50th's role in the forthcoming operation.[57]

In the aftermath of the stunning success at Amiens, Foch's strategy of mounting successive offensives to draw off and wear down the enemy's reserves was given free rein. Virtually the entire BEF, including the two powerful Dominion Corps, would be committed, and French and American forces would follow suit in their sectors of the front.[58] All but the AEF were worn-out armies, but their opponent, as the coming weeks would confirm, was in even worse shape.

The task set for Gen. Horne's First Army was breaching the formidable defensive complex of the Drocourt–Quéant Line (D–Q Line) and Buissy Switch east of Arras, a particularly robust section of the extensive *Siegfriedstellung*[59] (or to the British, the Hindenburg Line) fortifications, then fight their way across the Canal du Nord to liberate the major logistical junction of Cambrai. The operation would be carried out in two stages just over three weeks apart. In order to gain more favourable positions from which the 1st and 4th Divisions could attack the D–Q Line proper, the 2nd and 3rd Divisions would have to overrun the intervening Fresnes–Rouvroy Line, which they completed by August 28 after two days of very bitter fighting.[60] The main attack was set for September 2. The nemesis facing the 4th Division, and their 1st Division comrades on their right,

> Consisted of a front and a support line, both abundantly provided with concrete shelters and machine-gun posts and protected by dense masses of barbed wire. The Buissy Switch, connecting the

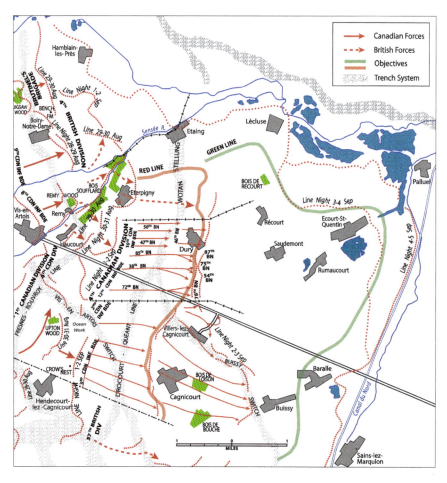

Map 6:
Drocourt-Quéant Line, 2–5 September 1918.

D–Q Line with the Hindenburg support system, was constructed along the same solid principles .... In general, the front [of the] D–Q Line was sited either on a crest or a forward slope in order to provide a good field of fire—the support system being on the reverse slope.[61]

The final plan called for the 12th Brigade, supported by the 11th, to sweep up and over the D–Q Line dominated in that section by Mont Dury, while simultaneously Hayter's brigade, along with the 4th British Division, would attack to the north, advancing through the village of Dury that formed an integral part of the overall defence line. All three brigades would then press their attacks eastward to clear the enemy all the way to the Canal du Nord. The 50th Battalion, with the 47th on its right, would attack and seize the first four defensive lines in the Dury sector, with the 46th then leapfrogging both to overrun the village itself. The 44th would then pass through the 46th to continue the brigade attack.[62] Six tanks and two British field artillery brigades (thirty-six 18-pounders and a dozen 4.5-inch howitzers) would support the assault. After being briefed at Currie's headquarters on August 29, Watson confided in his diary that "it is a very ambitious programme, and I doubt if it can be carried through to the extent they have laid down."[63] But optimism reigned at the highest levels of the Corps, and if he voiced his concerns they were not accepted. The only alteration to the original plan was a last-minute reduction in the British 4th Division's role. Currie had little option since the latter had been decimated in recent fighting. The additional burden fell to Hayter's men.[64]

The 50th Battalion's move to their assembly point had to be carried out at night, the ground being under direct observation and—when anything moved—heavily shelled. Maj. James Parry led the men on an onerous 15 km march which got them into position by 0245 on September 2. For the attack, Page decided to have two companies up, and two in support, each with their four platoons lined up one behind the other. From the outset there were bad omens. There were the last-minute modifications to the assault plan, in addition to which their British predecessors had been unable to clear out a nest of machine guns, forcing the assembly position back 200 m. On top of that, bombs for the trench mortars, which were a key support for the attack, failed to arrive. The C Company lost its commanding officer, who was wounded and gassed before they even set off for the assembly positions, necessitating Lt. J. R. Harris assume command. Officially, "the men were in good spirits and the many new recruits were eager for their first show."[65] Given the Germans had bombarded the assembly areas with high explosives and gas all night long, this might have been a tad optimistic. For Pvt. Charles Oke, it was his worst experience waiting for zero hour. Surely surprise had been lost, which was always a depressing thought.

Dawn brought fine weather, and at 0500 "promptly on the second every gun for miles on either side opened fire and furnished the heaviest and most effective barrage ever experienced by our troops."[66] Having only received their fire plans at midnight, it was an extraordinary performance by the British gunners. The ferocity of the barrage stunned the defenders, and in short order infantry were able to overrun the problem machine guns. The first wave of infantry, much aided by smoke screens (but not the tanks, which were late), stormed the 500 m to the German forward line so quickly they actually had to stop and wait for their own creeping barrage to lift before they could leap into the trench and commence their grim butchery with grenades and bayonets. Within a minute all was calm, with "every Hun ... accounted for." The enemy machine gunners—generally select troops now—fought their weapons to the end but the garrisons in bunkers "showed a willingness to surrender."[67] The few hundred prisoners, many of them wounded, were shepherded to the rear under minimal guard. Upraised arms and plaintive cries of "mercy kamerad, mercy kamerad" spared most of them from anything worse than rough handling and the theft of "souvenirs," but no doubt some were simply gunned down in the mayhem by men who were as frightened of dying as they were or seeking revenge. As succeeding platoons surged forward, they encountered wire uncut by the barrage, but the tanks had finally showed up, and with their help the attackers managed to overrun the remaining trenches in short order. Just as the barrage lifted from the furthest zone of the D–Q Line, the last dugouts and tunnels had been cleared. The whole enterprise—"the most brilliant attack ever made by the battalion"—had taken barely two hours.[68] The 47th Battalion had been equally successful, permitting the 46th to pass through both units and carry the fight into the ruins of Dury and the 44th to start moving forward so it could continue the assault as soon as that objective was cleared. Dury had been cleared by 0825, though the 46th had faced much harder going. Brigade ordered Page and Keegan to reorganize their battalions and prepare to move forward immediately, if ordered.[69] The marked decline in their opponent's capabilities and battlefield good fortune that fell disproportionately to the victors underpinned much of the day's success. But apart from the deserved praise for his men's courage, initiative and esprit de corps, Brig. Hayter correctly identified preparation, specifically small unit training, as key factors in the successful execution.[70] This was true, but Charles Oke's perspective as an ordinary soldier was telling—infantry could only get through such tough defences if the way was paved by "an avalanche of shell fire."[71] By the summer of 1918, Canadian infantry were thoroughly trained in a tactical attack doctrine in which they had confidence. Supported by a powerful artillery arm, they could break into any position, even if well defended, and at Dury they had.

Foremost among the leaders that morning had been D Company's commanding officer, Lt. A. J. Slade, "who seemed to be everywhere at once, encouraging and directing his men and urging them on to even greater efforts," deservedly earning a DSO.[72] But remarkable acts of courage and initiative under fire were commonplace that day. Sgt. J. H. Dowler, a signaller, had repeatedly risked his life to maintain the telephone lines linking the fighting companies and battalion headquarters. When Sgt. R. N. Tufts' platoon had been pinned down by a machine gun, he silenced it single-handedly, bayonetting the entire crew of eight. Dowler's and Tufts' were among the thirty MMs (five of them second awards) for particularly noteworthy actions by non-commissioned officers and privates. Among his several feats of valour, Pvt. Charles Davis had attacked another machine-gun position with grenades, killing the crew and taking fifty prisoners, for which he was awarded the DCM. Cruelly, the battalion also lost two of its company commanders—Capts. A. R. Batson and S. A. Moore—ironically killed by the same shell burst as they crouched behind cover discussing consolidation plans.[73]

Casualties were amazingly light during the attack itself but as consolidation got underway in the trenches immediately in front of Dury, German artillery began firing high explosive and gas shells into the position, killing and wounding many. Counter-battery fire couldn't be summoned, as Hayter's communications with division had been severed and remained so until evening despite the heroic efforts of signallers and runners who both suffered heavy losses.[74] The day's work had yielded over 1,000 prisoners and 90 German machine guns, the former hinting at declining German morale and the latter pointing to the growing reliance the enemy were now forced to place on the machine gun to hollow out infantry attacks.[75] Under the circumstances, the 50th's own losses were not considered severe—thirty-one killed and 183 wounded.[76]

Unfortunately, while the morning's operation was unfolding according to plan for the 10th Brigade, the fate of their sister brigades remained uncertain. As they grimly fought their way up the slopes of Mont Dury, the 12th's battalions were raked by machine-gun fire, and once cresting the ridge they were immediately pinned down. In an attempt to save the situation, Watson ordered Odlum's men forward, only to have them meet a similar fate.[77] Casualties—MacBrien's brigade suffered nearly 50 percent losses—were appalling. It was one of the worst setbacks inflicted on the Canadian Corps during the war. The hoped-for hard push up to the Canal du Nord had failed, a combination of bad luck but mostly bad planning by Currie and Brig.-Gen. Norman "Ox" Webber, his chief of staff. No doubt it was small consolation to Watson that his suspicion about the plan expecting too much from soldiers and underestimating German resistance was borne out. A chastened Corps ordered the attack resumed at 0500 the next morning when the situation would be clearer and units reorganized (and reinforced), and critically when tank support and a robust barrage—both absent in the original plan for Mont Dury—could be guaranteed. With his communications down, none of this reached Brig. Hayter before he had already gone ahead on his own authority and cancelled any further advance, sparing his men from what would likely have been heavy losses.[78] For his part, Lt.-Col. Page was understandably very pleased with the performance of his officers and men. Their only sin was not holding back when it might have been prudent to pause, but he was hardly going to fault anyone for being too keen.[79] Quite properly, the week's fighting to breach the Drocourt-Quéant Line was considered a major victory, with Field Marshall Haig stopping by to congratulate Currie on his Corps' fine effort even as the luckless infantry of the 11th and 12th Brigades were fighting for their lives on the far slopes of Mont Dury.[80]

With first light on September 3, reconnaissance patrols were able to confirm that the enemy had retreated.[81] During the next two days the 1st and 4th Divisions followed cautiously until they had secured the western approaches to the Canal du Nord. And so the situation would remain for almost three weeks.[82]

The Canal du Nord and Cambrai

Now in reserve, Page's command spent their time attempting to train, but good intentions initially were frustrated by rainy weather, muddy ground, and a shortage of facilities for classroom work.[83] Only once the weather turned for the better could proper training resume. Reinforcements, including returned wounded, were welcomed (or welcomed back). No fewer than seventeen lieutenants had been taken on strength since Amiens, most of them green as the proverbial grass, so that considerable time was specifically devoted to upgrading their skills, with the CO himself frequently taking a hand.[84]

On September 18, Brig. Hayter summoned his battalion commanders to discuss forthcoming operations, with Page briefing his own officers in turn that evening.[85] The CO wasted no time readying his men, for the following day the entire battalion practised quickly clearing and consolidating trenches, with two companies assaulting the mock front-line trench and the other two leapfrogging them to take the support trench, all of this carried out within the strict time constraints of a mock rolling barrage.[86] The battalion completed its move into the support line just before midnight on September 25. The fixing of the "Left out of Battle" and burial detail nominal lists earlier in the day were sure signs an attack was imminent. On the 26th everyone was allowed to rest, and many of the soldiers spent their time lying in the grass in the fine weather,

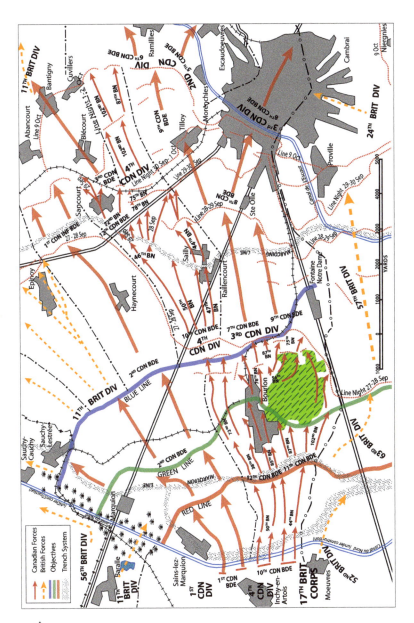

MAP 7: Canal du Nord, 27 September – 11 October 1918.

3 | The Hundred Days and Home 89

taking in the spectacle of dogfights over the German lines.[87] Meanwhile, the heavy artillery commenced blasting lanes through the wire, which infantry patrols later confirmed had been cleared. Brig. Hayter briefed his four battalion commanders one last time during the afternoon. Now, like everyone else in the 50th Battalion, Lionel Page had nothing left to do but wait, though unlike the former, he bore life-or-death responsibilities for hundreds. His decision to have the kitchens brought up before dawn and again after dark so his men could enjoy some hot food was no doubt much appreciated.[88] Across the Corps nothing seemed to have been left undone—thorough preparation would not guarantee success, but everyone recognized it was the necessary precondition.

The Overall Plan

The BEF planned to launch near-simultaneous offensives in late September, an attack by Horne's First Army (which included the Canadian Corps) toward Cambrai, and another by Byng's Third Army toward St. Quentin. The former would puncture the defensive positions in front of the vital rail centre of Cambrai, envelop the city, and immediately press on toward the Belgian border so the Germans would have no opportunity to re-establish any sort of formal defensive position. But there were daunting challenges. Cutting across their axis of advance was the partially constructed canal. A marshy area, which the enemy had further flooded, extending north from Sains-les-Marquion almost to the Canal de la Sensée would be impassable to major units. But from Sains-les-Marquion southward for 4 kms to Mœuvres, the canal bed and ground on either side of it were dry. Any large-scale crossing would have to occur here. Numerous machine guns and extensive wiring constituted the main obstacle the attackers would face immediately beyond the canal, but a kilometre further on lay the Marquion Line and the dominating feature of Bourlon Wood, and 5 kms beyond that, the Marcoing Line. The plan put together by Currie and his staff called for a two-stage assault. The first step entailed crossing the canal, then breaking through the Marquion Line and seizing Bourlon Wood and the high ground between it and the Arras–Cambrai highway. The second would send reserves pouring through this bridgehead and fanning out to the north and northeast, crushing the Marcoing Line and sweeping past Cambrai all the way to the Canal de l'Escaut. First Army's other two corps, the British XXII and XVII, would advance on the Canadians' flanks. But the main thrust, upon which overall success depended, would fall to the powerful Canadian Corps, which made up more than half of Horne's force.

The offensive was scheduled to start on September 27 with a set-piece attack executed by two brigades from 1st Division and, in front of the village of Inchy-en-Artois, by Watson's 10th Brigade. Brigadier Hayter's infantry would carry the attack as far the Marquion (or on Canadian battle maps, Red) Line, then consolidate. The 11th and 12th Brigades would then pass through their position to reach first the Green and then Blue Lines, the latter to capture Bourlon Wood and the former to seize Bourlon village and brooding high ground immediately to the northeast. The 46th and 44th Battalions would lead the 10th Brigade's assault, forcing the canal and then neutralizing the defences immediately beyond. As soon as practicable, the 50th and 47th would leapfrog them and press on to the Marquion Line. To maintain critical momentum, the entire brigade would effectively move forward as one.[89] For his part, Page chose to attack with his A and D Companies abreast,[90] while B and C Companies, with specific consolidation and mopping-up responsibilities, would follow close behind.[91]

The Attack

Dawn on September 27 promised another fine autumn day with warm (but not hot) temperatures, excellent visibility for both ground observers and reconnaissance aircraft, and dry footing for the men as well as the horse teams drawing supply wagons and field artillery forward, and towing ambulances to the rear. It was a good day to attack—and hopefully survive. As soon as darkness had fallen the previous night, battalion scouts had set out to complete their crucial tasks, laying tapes marking the 50th's assembly positions and the routes leading to these, and then leading the silent lines of their comrades forward. That night Pvt. J. E. Fox earned a DCM for executing these very responsibilities.[92] The trek had been made more difficult by constant German shelling, including gas shells that forced everyone to wear their restrictive respirators, but at least the men had been held back as long as possible so as to limit their time under fire. At least attacking infantry were no longer the beasts of burden they had been at the Somme or Vimy. Full battle kit now meant only gear that would help them kill Germans—anything else was left behind. The only exception was scaling ladders to get everyone up and over the far side of the steeply sloped canal wall. Predictably, the bombardment knocked out all the telephone lines forward from brigade headquarters, which meant the start of another arduous day for battalion signallers who would need to locate the breaks and (repeatedly) repair them. Snipers knew full well how critical this work was, making them prime targets.[93]

The Marquion Line

Unbeknownst to the Canadians, the German command was so confident in their defences in this sector of the canal that they had dismissed the possibility of an attack. But an attack it would be for the troops who had reached their jump-off positions by 0330. There they waited in silence under a steady drizzle for the better part of two hours. "A nasty, miserable night," Oak recalled. Many of the men relied on cups of rum-laced tea to keep from getting too stiff.[94] Despite personally disapproving of "drink," Page knew that the double-ration of "liquid courage" traditionally doled out before an attack was a godsend for officers and men alike, so rum it would be this night.[95]

Then, precisely at 0520, the wait was over, shattered by the deafening thunderclap from hundreds of artillery barrels firing high explosive, shrapnel and, to blind German machine gunners, smoke shells. The din led the old-timers to claim it even put the Vimy barrage to shame. In addition, the brigade benefited from the supporting fire of five Vickers machine-gun batteries as well as the two trench mortars that would advance with the men.[96] German artillery barely responded, which allowed the men to get well away from their jump-off positions relatively unscathed. But not entirely, as Capt. D. Fraser was cut down as D Company crested the far side of the canal. All four of the company commanders from August 8 were now gone, with three of them killed. With Fraser dead and every other D Company officer wounded within minutes of leaving the start line, Sgt. Maj. A. L. Watkin successfully led them to their objective, single-handedly subduing a machine-gun nest along the way. For his courage and leadership, he was awarded the DCM.[97] Overall, the 50th advanced rapidly, following close behind the 46th. Having strictly adhered to the artillery barrage tables, the latter were on their objective in just over two hours, whereupon their Alberta comrades pressed on through their position.

Prisoners started flowing back almost immediately—a bedraggled lot, mainly cavalrymen sent into the line despite having no infantry training. Stunned by the opening barrage's ferocity, few had put up much resistance. In contrast, German machine gunners kept firing their weapons until the bitter end, inflicting many casualties during the early stages of the advance. Despite a "heavy and accurate" barrage, machine-gun positions were almost impossible to identify beforehand and generally only hit by luck, and there were still plenty in action.[98] By 0730 the engineers had completed the first bridges over the canal, enabling some of the 4th Division's field artillery batteries to get forward, and with that, the German machine guns could be silenced one by one. But before the gunners could assist, it had chiefly been an infantry battle, with the sections and platoons having to root out enemy strongpoints using the fire-and-movement techniques mastered in training.[99] Once the 50th gained the Red Line, the men, protected by a 45-minute standing barrage immediately laid down in front of their position, put their entrenching tools to work with gusto. Right on schedule, the battalions of the 12th Brigade leapfrogged them and kept moving forward.

During the afternoon, Page received word by runner that he should prepare to renew the attack come morning. A preliminary casualty list showed fourteen killed and 122 wounded. As was usually the case, officer losses had been especially heavy, with two of them killed and nine wounded, and Page ordered replacements forward from among the supernumerary officers who had been retained on strength for just this eventuality. Even with one company having been merged into the remaining three, their commanders were now looking at fewer than 70 men on average, and were forced to reorganize their units by reducing the number of platoons to three or even two.[100] Late in the afternoon, a conference was held at brigade headquarters where Hayter encouraged—and got—a frank discussion of the next day's attack and the barrage to support it. Just after midnight his battalions received their final orders.[101]

The Marcoing Line

There was little time to prepare and none at all to sleep.[102] All four battalions assembled during early morning hours, with the 50th reaching its jump-off point by 0550, barely ten minutes before zero hour.[103] The brigade plan placed the 50th Battalion on the left flank of the attack, once again with two companies up and two in support, each with three platoons abreast and a fourth in close support. This was purely aspirational given the "consolidation" of companies and platoons necessitated by the first day's losses. The 46th would follow up, while on the right flank the 47th Battalion would lead with the 44th in support. This arrangement would carry the attack as far as the Marcoing Line, running northeast from Raillencourt (on the Arras–Cambrai highway) toward Sancourt, whereupon the two support battalions were to leapfrog and continue pressing forward as far as the Cambrai–Douai highway running just to the west of Sancourt. Rather than digging in, the 50th and 47th would follow some 300 m behind them.[104] Despite their losses so far, the 50th's morale remained high.

When the attack went in, Page's men encountered little opposition until they had advanced about a kilometre up to the outskirts of Raillencourt where they were raked by heavy machine-gun fire from positions in the village and along the Marcoing Line itself, the latter fronted by dense swaths uncut wire. One by one, the German machine guns were dealt with using the tactics that were now habit, with Capt. Alfred Hodges' A Company doing most of the work. The 50th's ruthless neutralization of the Marcoing Line was much aided by the bravery and enterprise of Lt. Henry A. Sharpe, a former NCO who already wore the MM ribbon on his tunic. Sharpe managed to find a way through the wire, enabling his platoon to outflank and then enfilade a section of the main trench, wiping out practically the whole garrison (at least eighty bodies were subsequently counted) and forcing the rest to pull back, decisively shifting the tide of the battle and sparing many Canadian lives. Sharpe earned an MC for his "conspicuous gallantry and initiative" while Hodges got the same award for "exemplary tactical leadership and gallantry."[105] Still, it was not always individual heroism that carried the day, but sometimes steadiness under trying conditions. Page later took pains to highlight the case of Lt. F. L. Clouse, who, although he had only been with the battalion for 18 days, and whose combat experience was measured in minutes, had had to assume command of C Company in the midst of the attack and rose to the occasion.[106]

The 47th and 50th Battalions completed the capture of the Marcoing Line by 0900, enabling the 44th and 46th Battalions to sweep forward. But murderous machine-gun fire from both flanks and the railway embankment beyond the Douai–Cambrai road forced them to fall back almost to their starting positions where they dug in as best they could. Sustained artillery fire and the constant machine gunning inflicted heavy casualties on all four battalions as the day wore on. Likely, only the close proximity of the 12th Brigade dug in southeast of Sancourt spared them from German counterattacks. Of great assistance, too, were standing barrages put down by field batteries valiantly attempting to keep up with the infantry's advance (and much praised in the 50th Battalion's war diary for doing so).[107] Meritorious service did not automatically entail fighting, as the case of Capt. (the Hon.) William Murray, the 50th's padre, made clear. He had volunteered to join the attack that morning so he could help with the wounded. Then, seeing a greater need, he offered to accompany the 46th Battalion as it leapfrogged his own unit. When their medical officer was seriously wounded, Murray dressed his wounds and carried him back to safety, after which he "continued advancing with [the 46th Battalion], who had lost all their medical staff except one, dressing wounded in the open, [and showing] splendid devotion to duty under heavy fire." Padre Murray deservedly won a second MC. [108]

Late in the afternoon, around 1700, just after telephone communications had been restored with all four of his battalions, Hayter informed Page and the others that 4th Division had ordered them to make another push to seize the Douai–Cambrai road, with zero hour set for 1915. By this time the 50th Battalion was a shadow of itself, having been reorganized yet again by merging what remained of the four companies into two under Lts. Hodges and Dyde.[109] Given the approaches to the road were heavily wired, the field artillery promised to pound the position for 45 minutes. The objective was taken in a short, sharp action, opening a route to the fortified railway embankment just to the east, which the 12th Brigade successfully overran the following day.[110] Efforts to consolidate 50th's gains during the evening and into the night required the last reserve of energy from officers and men who were exhausted, physically and emotionally. In fact, their position was parlous—ranks so thinned that it was impossible to maintain a continuous line, which left them vulnerable to infiltration, let alone counterattack. All four of the 10th Brigade's battalions resorted to offensive patrolling in the hope of conveying a semblance of strength.[111]

It had been another long and arduous day of combat, with not only a successful advance to point to but also 450 prisoners and considerable battlefield booty that included sixty machine guns and a pair of 15-cm howitzers.[112] Their casualties were a further eighteen killed (a third of them conscripts) and 114 wounded, raising the total to thirty-two killed and 236 wounded, close to 40 percent of their initial strength. But there was relief at the high proportion of wounded-to-killed and the fact that so many of the wounded were suffering from bullet wounds rather than the far more dangerous shrapnel wounds.[113] In his after-action report to Brig. Hayter, Lt.-Col. Page praised his officers and men for their "keenness and determination in the attack, their cheerfulness in the face of hardships, [and] their willingness to respond to all orders." And in a special order, he told them their efforts had given "me the greatest pride and confidence in the battalion."[114] He was also quick to acknowledge the unstinting co-operation of the entire 10th Brigade, highlighting in particular the 46th and 47th Battalions without whose timely support the 50th's own success would have been in jeopardy. As was always the case, it had been a brigade attack even if made by battalions. Hayter's assessment of the actions the 50th Battalion had fought was straightforward: "There were no particularly new features in the way of lessons brought out during these operations [; rather] the lessons learned in previous battles were put in practice and proved invaluable."[115] In essence, the bite-and-hold tactics of 1917 had been successfully applied to the new environment of semi-open warfare. Still, the cost was heavy. While the German Army's undeniable decline helped the Corps succeed at the Canal du Nord, the Canadian infantry paid a hefty butcher's bill.[116]

As soon as the 12th Brigade had passed through its lines on the morning of September 29, the 50th Battalion (along with the rest of the 10th Brigade) withdrew about 5 kms to divisional reserve just north of Bourlon, taking over "organized shell holes" that, ironically, many of the men they'd just killed had only recently occupied. The last day of September—the cruellest month of the war for the 50th Battalion—saw the usual post-action routine unfold—inspecting gear for repair and replacement and mustering the survivors to enumerate the casualties, but mostly resting and coming to terms with private horrors.[117] Two lieutenants and thirty-six other ranks joined the battalion on October 2, its last reinforcements of the war.[118] A day earlier, Gen. Horne, recognizing the attack was losing steam and that the troops were played out, ordered Currie to consolidate his gains. With that, the rest of the 4th Division were relieved.

On a cheerier note, word came the same day that Lt. D. G. L. Cunnington, a popular officer everyone believed had been killed at Amiens and buried by the enemy, was alive and well in a German prisoner of war camp.[119] A few days later Watson inspected the 10th Brigade, now just over 2,000 strong, or about half-strength. The general, who was always brief on such occasions—a trait the men appreciated—expressed his gratitude to all for their grit and determination. But he was furious over reports of fraternization with captured Germans, and admonished the troops to "impress upon the enemy in the most forcible manner that we were at war."[120] During the next few weeks, the great majority of Page's men would take that injunction to heart.

End Game

By early October, BEF attacks had ripped open the Hindenburg Line along almost its entire length. The German Army was now in permanent retreat, utterly beaten but still capable of inflicting pain on its pursuers. On October 14, Hayter's brigade left reserve, the 50th Battalion being assigned a section of line abutting the Canal de la Sensée. Elements of First Army, including the Canadian Corps, were ordered to closely pursue the retreating Germans toward Valenciennes and the Franco-Belgian border. If the enemy could be brought to battle, all the better, but it was critical to prevent them from regrouping or improvising a proper defensive line. The German scorched-earth tactics, especially the destruction of bridges and crossroads, combined with the ever-increasingly distance from railheads, strained logistics. And with every advance the troops marched past lines of refugees who "have lost all and are in a pitiful condition."[121]

Victims and Executioners

As the German Army's discipline broke down, militarily justifiable destruction blended seamlessly into wanton destruction that the Canadian soldiers could see with their own eyes every day as they marched northeastward. What they witnessed made more credible the accounts of a heartless occupation freely related to them by the civilians who often billeted the soldiers at night. Atrocity stories, particularly the spate of rapes and cold-blooded killings committed during the withdrawals, matched the worst propaganda the men had been fed about the brutish Hun, and hardened hearts.[122] Not every soldier saw evidence of an atrocity first-hand, but in the cold and wet of a bleak French autumn, they all faced the danger of a random shell or burst of machine-gun fire. No one wanted to die with the end so close. And after the appalling slaughter of the past few weeks,[123] many had scores to settle, too. For all of these reasons, many soldiers gave little quarter as the war's final weeks played out.[124] Increasingly, those among the enemy who offered more than token resistance fared badly. As Currie bluntly confided to his diary: "I know that it was not the intention of our fellows to take many German prisoners as, since they have lived amongst and talked to the French people here, they have become more bitter than ever against the Boche[s]."[125] It is common to see front-line soldiers in the First World War as universal victims, but they were executioners, too, and the moral line separating a soldier's duty to kill an armed opponent from the choice to kill an unarmed one was definitely blurring.

Liberators

In the final weeks of The Hundred Days, the Canadians were a bone-tired, wet and cold lot, and save for the few fresh reinforcements, the very definition of "war weary."[126] Yet they did find cheer in their role as liberators. Heretofore it had been rare to see civilians in battle zones—now it was common. "In each town we went through the women were at the front doors inviting us to have coffee," one 50th man remembered, "and the people were out with flags ... everybody had a French flag ... and couldn't do enough for us."[127] On October 19, Charles Oke's diary records that as he and his comrades were "feeling our way forward" near Denain, "we liberated [our] first civilians. They were delirious with joy [and] wanted to kiss everyone."[128] Even their very proper commanding officer could not escape the patriotic attentions of *les mesdemoiselles et madames*, much to his men's amusement.

Onward ... One Last Time

Prisoner interrogations convinced First Army that the Germans would not defend the Canal de la Sensée. On the 17th, in dense fog, which in the absence of German resistance ironically did more to hinder the crossing than aid it, Capt. A. J. Slade managed to get his own D Company and one other, plus two more from the 54th Battalion, across on a bridge improvised from spare lumber and abandoned wagons.[129] By dawn, the entire battalion was across and patrols had gotten as far as Fressain. But just after noon, as the lead platoons approached Émerchicourt, about 5 kms beyond the canal, machine-gun fire and shelling forced the battalion to wait for their own artillery which, upon arriving, quickly reduced Émerchicourt to rubble.[130] The infantry then attacked, though it took the better part of a day to clear the place, at the cost of four killed and twenty-two wounded. The 50th was soon advancing again. Many villages they would pass through had been forcibly depopulated—even livestock and dogs had vanished—and "everywhere there was abundant evidence of wanton and senseless destruction by the enemy, the contents of the houses being smashed up and thrown in all directions, nothing being left intact that it was possible to destroy."[131] Rœulx, their next objective, was an exception but thankfully they were able to take it without a fight. Its 900 inhabitants were understandably overjoyed.[132] Advancing through this new, largely natural, landscape proved a terrible strain. For a man used to fighting in almost obscene surroundings, pretty woodlands filled with bird songs were "sinister asylums for [German machine gunners]—and in those woods every movement or sound in the foliage—the scurrying of a hare, the caw of a crow, the chirp of a cricket, the dancing of dappled light in the shadow—startled him."[133]

The 10th Brigade was relieved during the night of October 22–23. On October 27, two days after Brig. Hayter had left to take over as Currie's senior staff officer,[134] the battalion formed part of the honour guard lining the streets of Denain through which Currie, Watson and the Prince of Wales passed on their way to a memorial service at the cathedral.[135] Valenciennes, a major pre-war steel-making and industrial centre, and the largest French city still occupied, lay barely 10 kms to the northeast. On the evening of the 29th, Lt.-Col. Page briefed his senior officers on its capture.[136]

The Plan

Taking Valenciennes would be a formidable challenge. To the west and north, the city hugged the eastern bank of the Canal de l'Escaut. The bank was thickly wired with numerous machine-gun nests hidden in the houses, factories and warehouses overlooking the waterway. Further constraining any assault, most ground southwest, west and north of the city had been purposely flooded. Although rising less than 20 m above its surroundings, wooded Mont Houy with its defensive works and artillery emplacements dominated the approach from the south and southeast. Finally, with so many civilians sheltering in the city, artillery could not automatically employ their usual annihilating bombardments.[137] Judging by the numbers of troops thought to be garrisoning the city, the enemy intended to make a stand.[138]

The original plan of attack hinged on a British division overrunning Mont Houy and 4th Canadian Division's 10th Brigade extending that assault as far as the southern outskirts of Valenciennes the following day. Then, after a short pause to reorganize the artillery, the 4th Division would outflank the city from the east, enabling the rest of the Corps to cross the Canal de l'Escaut and complete the envelopment from the west.[139] This plan came unstuck when the Scottish battalion that had fought its way onto Mont Houy failed to hold it against a German counterattack. A revised plan now called for Valenciennes' capture in a single powerful thrust, with 10th Brigade overrunning Mont Houy and immediately pressing on into the southern outskirts of the city, while Odlum's men, in conjunction with British formations on their right, would sweep along the city's eastern flank. That left MacBrien's brigade to force the canal and mop up Valenciennes proper. To minimize infantry casualties, the assault on Mont Houy would rely on a crushing artillery bombardment. It would prove Brig. Andrew McNaughton's tour de force, employing no fewer than eight field and six heavy artillery brigades (well over 300 barrels) and what amounted to an inexhaustible stock of shells for an attack by barely 1,200 infantry.[140]

The Last Attack

As zero hour approached, the 50th's sergeants distributed the double tots of rum, ensuring "all men were then in good shape for the work in hand."[141] The assault went in at 0515, with no preliminary barrage in order to maximize the effect of McNaughton's maelstrom. The 44th and 47th Battalions quickly swept over Mont Houy, and the surviving garrison surrendered in a daze. 50th Battalion's assembly positions had been heavily shelled with both gas and high explosive, though the effects of the former were not felt until hours later. While the 50th was serving as brigade reserve, Capt. A. J. Slade's D Company had been assigned a mopping-up role for the 47th Battalion. They encountered tough fighting, especially in the built-up area along the Escaut River where German machine gunners often waited until the range was point-blank before opening fire. Slade's men took numerous prisoners. "It was impossible to avoid taking so many," the war diarist acknowledged almost apologetically, before adding "but some very useful killing was also achieved."[142] In his own summary report written after the battle, the 10th's new commanding officer, Brig. John Ross, brusquely noted that "the miserable enemy could expect and certainly received no quarter."[143] Slade's personal courage and leadership was acknowledged with the award of an MC.[144]

As the attack unfolded, the battalion's three remaining companies, which were keeping pace with advance, increasingly found themselves drawn into the fighting. Early on, when Sgt. William Mayson's platoon ran up against heavy shelling and machine-gun fire, the soldiers wavered. But Mayson managed "by personal coolness and his exceptional bravery" to rally them and continue moving forward. Later in the day, with his men holding a series of shell craters atop Mont Houy and once more under relentless fire, he calmly crept from post to post, raising their spirits and keeping them focused on the fight. For the many such displays of "conspicuous gallantry and good leadership," Mayson earned a bar to his earlier MM.[145]

Once the outskirts of Valenciennes had been reached, stiffening resistance pinned the two attacking battalions down. This was particularly true on the right flank in front of Marly where, around dusk, the British brigade across the La Rhonelle fell back in the face of a sharp counterattack, exposing the Canadian flank.[146] It fell to two of the 50th's companies to hurry forward and repair the damage.

The overall operation had been a remarkable achievement for the 50th Battalion (and the rest of the brigade). In their mopping-up role, D Company alone had killed 200 of the enemy and taken 450-odd prisoners, and when called upon, the reserve companies had fought very effectively, too. Losses in action were surprisingly modest, just five killed and thirty-five wounded.[147] Only late in the day were the serious effects of the much earlier gas bombardment apparent, with a total of eighty-five soldiers, including Lt.-Col. Page and Capt. T. H. Prescott, his adjutant, having to be evacuated. Although all of them were suffering from breathing problems and nausea, and temporarily blinded, the majority were able to return to duty in a matter of days.[148] The following day the 11th and 12th Brigades finished the 4th Division's job by clearing the city itself. Valenciennes had been almost entirely a Canadian victory, but when Gen. Horne chose to downplay that, Currie, Watson and many of their subordinates were furious, resulting in the official liberation ceremony on November 7 turning into a rather testy affair.[149]

Some Good Homemade Apple Pie

After marching into Valenciennes on November 5, the 50th Battalion was billeted by rank, the officers in private homes and the men in a rather less posh pre-war French Army barracks. And there they would stay. "What glorious news," Watson recorded in his diary the following day, having received word of the pending armistice. Early on Monday, November 11, the general took a telephone call from Corps headquarters confirming hostilities would officially cease at 1100. When the hour arrived, the assembled bands of the 10th Brigade played "La Marseillaise," the mayor raising the tricolour in the city square as a remarkably sombre throng looked on.[150] Members of the 50th Battalion had had no sense the end was so close. One soldier recalled hearing the news from civilians as he and his comrades walked to the square for the formal ceremony. Another heard about it around 0900, and had it confirmed by his officers about an hour later.[151] Division issued an order that officers were to maintain strict discipline in marking the event—in other words, no untoward celebrating by the other ranks—and that there be no fraternization with German prisoners. Untoward celebrating or not, among the Canadians the sense of relief was palpable. A letter written a day earlier by Pvt. Earl Doxsee to his mother in Alberta surely reflected the immediate thoughts of many:

> Next year at this time I hope that I am at home. It will not take a great deal to feed me ... and I don't think I will turn my nose up at anything, as I used to before I came out here, but one thing I shall want and lots of it is some good home-made apple pie, my mouth waters for some now, and let us hope mother it will not be long before I can have some.[152]

Victor Wheeler, a man of acute insights into his comrades' feelings, also observed "a depressing languor ... we were tired and inexplicably drained of purpose and spirit." Somehow they had managed to survive. In the reasonably near future they would return home, and with any luck die of old age, albeit pursued by memories—many comforting and others terrifying. Literally overnight, the great unknown that with difficulty they had come to terms with had been supplanted by another. Drawing on soldierly metaphors, Wheeler wrote eloquently about this:

> Our scarred minds and hearts, where barbarism and savagery, fear and hatred, had so long lodged, wondered what lay beyond the peaceful western horizon. The future for us was but another No Man's Land—and we were reluctant to go Over the Top into the treacherous unknown.[153]

A Winter of Waiting

Only the 1st and 2nd Canadian Divisions participated in the occupation of the Rhine bridgeheads that winter. Instead, the 4th Division would spend the better part of the next six months guarding Belgium and waiting for shipping to take its men home. During the two months following the armistice, the battalion moved several times, until finally reaching Overyssche near Brussels in early January, where they remained for the remainder of their time in Belgium.[154] No matter how busy the officers kept everyone, it was not long before morale began to suffer, the men grumbling mostly about the snail-like pace of repatriation. They were civilians again, or certainly felt they were, "an army of homesick civilians, cold, restless [and] fed up."[155]

At long last, on April 15 the battalion entrained for the Canadian Embarkation Camp at Le Havre where, after more waiting, they finally boarded an overnight ferry for England. Early the following afternoon, on April 28, they reached Bramshott Camp, tired but no doubt pleased. It had been thirty-one months and eighteen days since the battalion had left there for the front. For the relative handful of originals remaining, it must have been an emotional moment. Preparations for demobilization were now in full swing, with everyone having to endure the rigours of documentation and medical boards.[156] Page's battalion seemed unaffected by the turmoil festering among some of the Canadian units at the English camps, undoubtedly at least in part because they arrived so late and were there so briefly. Apart from an honour party of four officers and 125 other ranks selected to participate in the great victory parade held in London, everyone was kept in camp until May 4 when thirty officers and 300 other ranks set off on an eight-day leave, with the remainder the battalion quickly following suit.[157] With so many of the soldiers having friends and family in Britain, the leaves were a great morale-raiser.

Homeward Bound

The men began streaming back into camp on May 20, and six days later orders confirmed their embarkation on the SS *Empress of Britain* two days hence. The 50th was the last of the Corps four Alberta battalions to leave England. Final arrangements hurriedly completed, the officers and men assembled at 0200 on the night of May 27–28 and marched out of Bramshott Camp, proudly carrying the battalion colours they had left for safekeeping at a nearby church in 1916. Arriving in their train at the Liverpool docks just after 1 pm, they immediately boarded the liner and were soon steaming past Merseyside, bound for the open sea and Canada.[158] What their individual futures held must have been on many minds—rebuilding civilian lives, including marriages and families, would be a daunting task for some. But at least they had a future, which could not be said of their comrades who would lie forever in the soil of France and Belgium.

The crossing was uneventful and the coast of Newfoundland was sighted on the evening of June 2. After stopping briefly at Halifax, the *Empress* proceeded on to Quebec City, with its superior railway connections, docking late on 4 June. There, Lt.-Col. Page received a telegram from R. C. Marshall, the mayor of Calgary: "Calgary rejoices in your homecoming. You have covered yourselves with glory in the service of your king and country. We are proud of you. Welcome home."[159]

The following morning they boarded a troop train bound for Calgary.[160] Batches of soldiers from the battalion, mostly seriously wounded men, had already been repatriated, some as early as December, and the large crowds that had braved vile winter weather to welcome these heroes home spoke volumes about how ordinary citizens felt.[161]

Having already welcomed the 10th and 31st Battalions back, the city could hardly wait for the arrival of the main body of the 50th. From the moment they reached Quebec City, the local newspapers had published daily updates on their progress across the Dominion. After years of censorship that had masked the true nature of the 50th Battalion's war, the *Herald* began publishing unvarnished accounts of all their battles.[162] In October 1915, forty-one officers and 1,036 other ranks had left Calgary—the contingent now steaming across Canada numbered thirty officers, including Lt.-Col. Page, and 438 other ranks. Only one officer, Maj. Eveleigh, and about seventy other ranks were originals.[163]

Finally the great day arrived—Monday, June 9. Three days earlier, the 50th Club and The Great War Veterans Association had finalized arrangements for a grand reception to complement what city officials had already planned.[164] It was mid-morning when the train slowly pulled in with its precious cargo, bands serenading everyone with refrains of "Home, Sweet Home." The open areas of the station were jammed and large crowds waited outside, undeterred by drenching rain. The soldiers in one of the cars had chalked on its side "From Calgary to Hell and back, via the Somme, Vimy, Passchendaele, Amiens, Arras, Canal du Nord, Cambrai, Valenciennes." Accompanied by his English war bride and their daughter, Lt.-Col. Page climbed down first to be immediately hugged by his mother who had travelled from Red Deer for the moment. This touching scene completed, some of his men hoisted him on their shoulders and carried him the length of the platform to loud cheers. Then it became utter chaos as the remaining soldiers rushed from their cars to meet the crowd of friends and loved ones surging forward. It took some time to reassemble the battalion, whereupon, led by their own band, they marched out of the station, down Centre Street to 8th (Stephen) Avenue and on to the armouries. Large crowds lined the route and the drill hall was crammed with well-wishers. Standing in ranks on the parade floor, their colours proudly displayed, a hush fell as Page spoke to his men. The *Herald's* summary, like Page's speech, was brief: "He told the boys he was proud of them and thanked them all for the way in which they had responded to every call [and] on their endurance and bravery since he had been in command of them ... [then wished] them good-bye and Godspeed."[165] Spontaneously, he was hoisted in the air again to loud cheers from what were truly *his* troops. A bouquet of roses was presented to John Pattison's widow and a few other dignitaries added their words, and it was over. But as the crowds exited the armoury, the paperwork of formal demobilization commenced. It wasn't finished until mid-afternoon. Wheeler remembered the latter as rather an anti-climax after the "deeply emotional" reception. The army at least thought to provide a "tasty lunch" for the waiting lines, with members of the Great War Veterans Association Ladies Aid serving.[166] The day ended with a smoker held jointly for veterans of the 50th and 31st Battalions and doubtless uncounted private parties. Some of the men probably had nowhere to go, and others were already aboard trains dispersing them across Alberta.

Moving On

While the demobilization of the 50th was completed the day it returned to Calgary, the battalion itself was not officially dissolved until 15 September 1920. But only one more significant event in its history remained. On Sunday, July 27, before a large contingent of battalion veterans, the original colours received in Ottawa in 1915 as they proceeded overseas, were deposited in Central Methodist (now United) Church. It was a moving ceremony, blending the religious with the patriotic, from a stirring sermon simply entitled *The British Flag* to the enthusiastic singing of "Onward Christian Soldiers" and "Land of Hope and Glory."[167]

Soon enough, however, the celebratory tone that marked the men's homecoming petered out. There is no doubt that most members of the community deeply respected the returned men, but the values embraced at the time, not least by the veterans themselves, held that citizen soldiers were not supposed to be defined by their military service, which they had taken on as a duty. Having returned to civilian life, they should make their own way. Moreover, upper class Canadians as well as the great majority of the middle class had viewed the war as a fight to preserve the social and economic status quo, not to empower supposed "radical" reforms, no matter how badly large swathes of the population wanted (and needed) them. The 50th Battalion had returned to the city at the height of the Winnipeg General Strike, and sympathy strikes in other parts of the West, including Calgary. Some leading lights openly warned the demobilized men that Bolshevism was the greatest threat facing the country—one prominent clergyman in the city had dismissed returned soldiers as putty in the hands of Red agitators. This was too much for Page, who publicly refuted such extreme talk, insisting that soldiers who'd served overseas had surely proven their loyalty to Canada.[168] Demobilization benefits were slender and oftentimes impractical, and the pension system, while probably the most comprehensive and generous among the Allies, fell well short of meeting the needs of physically disabled veterans, and did next to nothing for the psychologically wounded. As best they could, most veterans looked to return to the farm or factory or business they had left when they enlisted—for the younger men, who had not left anything, there was the need to find a career. Both groups would have to integrate into peacetime Canada in the midst of a severe recession that dragged on through 1921.[169]

Some closest to the 50th Battalion saw the difficulties hampering many of the veterans and set about assisting them. In July 1919 a group of wives, widows, mothers and sisters of former members founded the 50th Battalion Ladies Auxiliary under the leadership of Mrs. Katherine Mason, the wife of its first commanding officer. Whether visiting the sick or those suffering from war wounds, comforting the lonely, or simply helping those in general need, the Auxiliary did sterling work. Mrs. Mason remained its driving force until 1949 when old age and ill-health compelled her to step down.[170] The veterans themselves soon formed the 50th Battalion Veterans Association, which helped veterans cope with wartime memories only they shared simply by keeping former comrades in contact with each other.

The 50th Battalion at War

When the 50th Battalion assembled prior to marching out of Sarcee Camp in October 1915, Col. Paul Weatherbee solemnly addressed them: "I know ... that the men of the 50th will do their duty and will be a credit to Alberta and your country, and in wishing you good-bye and good luck I hope that many of you will return."[171] Given the optimism of such send-offs during the early years of the war, his closing observation was a remarkably frank assessment of their prospects. The number of men who served in action with the battalion will never be known precisely, but from the date it reached France through the armistice the total for other ranks alone reached 4,227. In total, twenty-nine officers and 623 other ranks were killed in or as a result of battle, and another 127 and 2,562, respectively, were wounded.[172] These are disheartening totals for the twenty-five months the 50th was deployed on the Western Front and they speak to both the extensive action it saw and the attritional nature of the fighting. But at the same time, the colonel's confidence that they would do their duty and be a credit to Alberta and Canada had proven well placed. The great majority of the men serving in the battalion had no prior military experience. Their training got steadily better, but mostly they learned to fight by fighting. And probably one-quarter of them were facing combat for the first time in each battle. Courage and spirit where never enough by themselves, though the awarding of five DSOs (plus two bars), thirty-two MCs (plus four bars), twenty-two DCMs, 215 MMs (plus twenty-two bars) and a Victoria Cross are ample evidence of exceptional leadership and bravery under fire.[173] All who served in the battalion benefited from the steady improvement in the firepower, staff work, and tactics at the disposal of the Canadian Corps, which matured into arguably the best fighting formation of its size in the BEF. In Lt.-Col. Page, they had a first-rate commanding officer with all the advantages accruing from that. And they faced an enemy that, not the least as a result of their own efforts, was steadily worn down even if it remained dangerous to the end. As one of the last battalions in the last Canadian division to be sent into action, the 50th and their 4th Division comrades quickly matched their predecessors' proficiency on the battlefield.[174] This was a crucial factor in their success, for they never fought in isolation but side by side with other elements of the 4th Division, and especially their three sister battalions in the 10th Brigade. Overall, the 50th Battalion was not exceptional but it was certainly good. And it performed at its best when it mattered most—during the Hundred Days when the Canadian Corps was a battering ram in the most decisive military campaign Canadians soldiers have ever fought. The officers and men had indeed done Alberta and Canada proud.

3.1 Unveiling the Great War soldiers' memorial in Calgary's Central Park, 23 May 1924. (Glenbow Archives, na-2742-4)

3.2 Lt.-Col. Douglas Cunnington, c. 1930. Cunnington had been severely wounded during the 50th's fierce fighting near Hallu on 11 August 1918 and thought dead until miraculously turning up on a prisoner of war list. During the late 1920s, he served as the postwar militia regiment's commanding officer, tirelessly promoting their British connections. (KOCRA, P-300-10-0015)

3.3 Lt.-Col. Louis Olaf Svenson served with the 50th Battalion, rising to Major and for a time commanding a company. Like other COs during the interwar years, he struggled against long odds to keep the Calgary Regiment afloat. (KOCRA, P-300-10-0049)

3.4 Lt.-Col. Frederick L. Shouldice served with the PPCLI, earning a MC for the exemplary leadership of his company during the Canal du Nord attack. His tireless efforts on behalf of the Calgary Regiment during the 1920s, including a stint as commanding officer, won him much respect in militia circles. (KOCRA, P-300-10-0050)

3.5 Lt.-Col. Water Jull (L) and Capt. John Begg lead the Calgary Regiment past the Cenotaph on Remembrance Day 1935. Participation in such annual rituals helped to keep the militia in the public eye during the difficult interwar years. (KOCRA, P-300-10-0003)

3.6 (L-R) Capt. John Begg, Lt.-Col. L. A. Cavanagh and Maj. Walter Jull assist with the supervision of militia training at Sarcee Camp during the summer of 1935. (KOCRA, P-300-10-0060)

Surviving the Peace and Preparing for War   109

3.7 Improvised armour for an armoured regiment without tanks. "Snow White" and the "Six Dwarfs" arrive at Sarcee Camp for summer training in 1939. (KOCRA, P-300-10-0021)

3.8 The 14th Reserve Army Tank Battalion (The Calgary Regiment) marching in the Stampede Parade, July 1941. It did yeoman work during the 1941–1945 period, providing the initial training for over 1,500 young men who went on to serve in the Army, RCAF and RCN, many of them overseas. (KOCRA, P-300-10-0068)

4

A Short Peace and a Second War

The Militia and Hard Times

The Canadian militia had thrived during the years immediately prior to 1914. Senior militia officers viewed their units, not the small regular army, as the backbone of Canada's defence, and if need be, its contribution to Imperial defence. The militia units of 1914, and particularly their cadre of officers, played a significant role in both the formation of the Canadian Expeditionary Force and the subsequent operation of its fighting arm, the Canadian Corps. But by the Great War's end, even Anglo-Canadians, the community that had been most supportive of Canada's intervention, had paid most of the cost in blood, and had believed the military effort had been noble, were hard-pressed to see any threat on the horizon. Soon, many Canadians would question the need for the militia or, indeed, defence of any kind, with the result that the part-time military would be forced to operate in survival mode during the two decades of peace the Great War bought. Isolationism, the belief that the combination of favourable geography and friends with powerful navies could shelter us from troubles abroad, became widespread. And why not hope for peace, given the suffering the Dominion had just endured? Only in the late 1930s did any Canadians begin to question isolationism's viability as a national defence strategy. The irony of isolationism was that the dominant Anglo-Canadian community never questioned Canada's duty to rally to the defence of the "mother country." With no such prospect on the horizon in 1919, or for years thereafter, the question of exactly what we would rally with could be safely ignored. But world events have a way of intervening, and allowing the militia to whither for twenty years looked like a very poor choice in September 1939. Having barely survived the lean years, the officers and men of the Calgary Regiment scrambled to prepare for another war. They had little time—within two years they would be overseas.

111

The Militia Reborn

Despite the conviction that foreign entanglements were unlikely, Ottawa did turn to the question of how to constitute and maintain the regular army and militia in the post-war world. When Permanent Force officers put forward the idea of a full-time force of 30,000—a real army—supported by a substantial conscript militia, it was dismissed out of hand. Instead, Canada entered the 1920s with a more modest professional army numbering around 5,000 officers and men. But what of the militia (officially the Non-Permanent Active Militia) that had modestly more support in the country and came much cheaper? The reorganization of 1919–20 attempted to graft the wartime organization of numbered battalions onto the pre-war militia structure.[1] Before the 50th Battalion had even left England, Lt.-Col. Page had pressed the idea that its record should be perpetuated in a militia unit bearing the same designation, as such units "would have more real value than they had before the war for they would have all their old traditions [as well as the] history in France to look back to and live up to."[2] While Australia adopted this template, Canada would not. Instead, after considerable debate, battle honours won by the numbered battalions of the Canadian Corps would be assigned to a militia regiment. Enough of the latter would be created—or in many instances revived—to satisfy the many veterans who felt preserving the achievements of their wartime (numbered) battalions was sacrosanct. But it would also satisfy militia supporters who were determined that pre-war regimental identities also survive. In practice, the compromise meant militia regiments that had supplied a substantial portion of recruits to a numbered battalion would simply inherit its battle honours and thereafter commemorate that unit.[3]

The Calgary Regiment

On 15 March 1920, as part of this post-war militia reorganization, the 103rd Regiment (Calgary Rifles) became the Calgary Regiment. An ensuing reorganization designated that the 1st Battalion of the Calgary Regiment (1/Calgary Regiment) would commemorate the Canadian Corps' 10th Battalion and the 2nd Battalion (2/Calgary Regiment) the Corps' 50th Battalion.[4] Three more battalions of the Calgary Regiment were authorized to commemorate the CEF's 56th, 82nd and 137th Battalions but never recruited personnel. All trophies, mess equipment and the cash reserve of the 103rd Regiment were divided between the 1st and 2nd Battalions.[5] Splitting the silverware was one thing; splitting the honorary colonel quite another. R. B. Bennett chose the 1/Calgary Regiment, leaving the 2/Calgary Regiment to locate a replacement with sufficient standing in the local business and professional community. They were fortunate to persuade Senator Pat Burns to take on the responsibility. Lt.-Col. R. B. Eaton, briefly commander of the 50th in 1917, became the 2nd Battalion's first commanding officer, with Maj. L. O. Svendsen, another veteran of the 50th, as second-in-command. Almost all of the initial group of officers and men had overseas experience, and by early 1921, evening parades were drawing an average of thirty officers and fifty-one other ranks.[6] The 50th Battalion's dissolution in September 1920 also saw its colours officially retired. A month earlier, the armoury had been jammed with 50th veterans and guests as Brig. A. H. Bell presented the officers and men of the 2/Calgary Regiment with their new colours.[7]

1st Battalion/Calgary Regiment

The dual identities and traditions of the Calgary Regiment as formed in 1920 confused everyone outside militia circles and satisfied no one within. A second reorganization resolved this in May 1924. Henceforth the 1/Calgary Regiment became the Calgary Highlanders and the 2/Calgary Regiment become 1/Calgary Regiment.[8] For the remainder of the interwar period, these two regiments dominated the militia world in Calgary.[9]

During the early 1920s it had been enough that the new militia structure simply take root in the community and survive. Officers soon realized that the days when militia units had found it easy to recruit were over and, short of a war, unlikely to return. Managing to maintain a strength of 125 to 150, which the army considered barely acceptable, proved elusive, with numbers bottoming out at ninety in 1923.[10] And turnover was stubbornly high. Annual inspections consistently praised the enthusiasm and training proficiency of the battalion's officers but acknowledged that the unit was no more than "an efficient skeleton organization."[11]

The great majority of the part-time soldiers who stuck at it during the 1920s were overseas veterans of the Great War, the militia likely supplying the military camaraderie they missed as civilians. But age, changing family situations and career demands inevitably led many of even these men to drift away. What would motivate younger men—men with no military background—to take their places? While Lt.-Col. Page had admitted in 1919 that "this is the last war most of us will see," he still believed there had to be a measure of military preparedness, and "the discipline that is gained from military training is undoubtedly a big asset to the nation."[12] Not many Calgarians seemed to agree. It certainly did not help matters that the militia myth had not survived the war. The great majority of the men who served overseas had lacked any military experience when they joined up, and yet performed just as well as their militia comrades. Once one embraced the idea that the nation's defence could (indeed, should) rest on the shoulders of such citizen soldiers, it was easy to dismiss the militia's worth.[13]

Sheer Survival

Keeping in the public eye was a constant priority; building regimental spirit another. Opportunities to perform in the community achieved both objectives. The two obvious opportunities came during the annual victory commemoration, usually held in August or September, and the more sombre remembrance ceremony that followed in November.[14] Viscount Byng of Vimy's participation in the former in 1922 drew throngs of Calgarians, with the twenty-six officers and eighty-five other ranks of the then 2/Calgary Regiment providing a guard of honour.[15] On 23 May 1924, the now 1/Calgary Regiment provided part of the honour guard for the dedication of the Soldiers' Monument in front of the city library.[16] And when Calgary's cenotaph was solemnly dedicated in Memorial Park before 10,000 citizens on Armistice Day, 1928, the 1/Calgary Regiment and Calgary Highlanders each contributed fifty men for the ceremony.[17] But it was the regiment's "very active brass band," which played concerts in Central Park throughout the summer months, that likely garnered it the most attention during these years.[18]

Of course, a great deal of the regiment's life revolved around its own social activities. Among these were a variety of annual events—the picnic on St. George's Island, the regimental smoker commemorating Vimy, the Christmas party, and the Brides Dinner honouring the wives of officers or men married during the previous year. But there was no end to initiatives on the social front, since any open to the public—dances were especially popular—could double as fundraisers. Most of these were organized and catered by the Ladies Auxiliary, "which added a great deal to the [regiment's] success."[19]

Training During the 1920s

"The record of the Battalion's fourth training year contains few items of outstanding interest," Lt.-Col. Svendsen's annual report to Ottawa for 1923–24 concluded, "but is nevertheless a record of continued progress."[20] Ironically, both statements were true. Throughout the decade, training followed a pattern constrained by the limited facilities of Mewata Armoury and even more by the limited funding allocated by Parliament. With tongue firmly in cheek, the 1927 annual report outlined the weekly routine: "Each Thursday night [from 2000 till 2200] a more or less numerous band of lawyers, accountants, mechanics, grocers, bond salesmen, men drawn from every phase of the city's multitudinous activities, don the King's uniform and take their places as members of the 1st Bn Calgary Regiment." The men drilled by company and platoon and alternately filled the basement firing range. "The 'sirs' mostly come naturally on parade," the author noted, with "only a smattering of Fred's and Tom's uttered."[21] Some sort of lecture on the military arts would follow at 2115, and the evening's activities ended with a welcome round of competitive sports.

By the mid-1920s the regiment comprised a headquarters, four rifle companies, and a signals platoon. Weaponry was mostly Great War-vintage .303 Lee-Enfield rifles and Lewis light machine guns. The promised attachment of regular force members to assist with training had begun and ended with a single officer from the Princess Patricia's Canadian Light infantry (PPCLI) during the winter of 1920–21. For most officers and men, summer training with other militia units under canvass at nearby Sarcee Camp was the yearly highlight. Otherwise, militiamen got July and August off. But in 1923 tightened finances led Military District 13 to cancel the camp, a major loss to the militia because so much of the indoor training focused on being able to apply the lessons learned to outdoor exercises, no matter how modestly. A short training camp resumed at Sarcee in 1927—all of four days—but it allowed the new commanding officer, Lt.-Col. D. G. L. Cunnington, to direct a weekend tactical scheme. About sixty members of the regiment, mostly officers and NCOs, participated, and "all ranks felt it was at least a beginning."[22] Thereafter the duration of summer camp gradually lengthened—the most promising development on an otherwise bleak training front.[23]

Money, Money, Money

"In peacetime the success of a [militia] regiment depends to a large extent on its finances."[24] So opined Lt.-Col. Cunnington in 1929. In fact money—specifically not having much of it—underpinned every aspect of the Calgary Regiment's existence during the 1920s and 1930s. So-called local training one evening per week for ten months considerably exceeded the funding available, which varied with the annual militia budget but averaged about enough for eight days a year. For summer camp, pay was allotted by the day, with the training periods varying from four days to two weeks, depending on the militia budget. But this was misleading because only a limited number of men were ever funded. For most of these years other ranks drew no local pay, though during the latter 1930s they drew half their local pay. At no time did officers draw any pay (nor receive a uniform allowance), all their pay being voluntarily transferred for regimental purposes, which included buying boots for the men since Ottawa did not budget for any. Every year, officers also contributed out of their own pockets for various regimental purposes. In addition to their regular parades, NCOs and officers who attended "schools" at the armouries did so without pay.[25] It is in this light that one must view the endless fundraising efforts undertaken by the regiment and the Ladies Auxiliary as well as acknowledge the generosity of the honorary colonel, for Senator Burns repeatedly came to the regiment's financial rescue.[26]

The hand-to-mouth existence typical of the militia—and in fairness, of the Permanent Force as well—put enormous stress on senior militia officers. During the winter of 1926–27 Colonel Redman (a Non-Permanent Active Militia [NPAM] officer commanding the 24th Brigade, the umbrella organization for militia units in the southern half of the military district),[27] criticized the sad state of both Calgary units. It was particularly infuriating that he lectured them about the need to arrange more outdoor training, given the benefits to their men. A clearly frustrated Lt.-Col. Ritchie (the Highlanders' CO) could hardly contain himself, reminding Redman that apart from the interminable financial saga, "it was found impossible to get both officers and men to turn out owing to their being unable to leave their business or work."[28]

The post-war decade had been a trying time for the Calgary Regiment. Its own assessment of what had been achieved bears repeating: "In spite of the small allowance and a considerable amount of public indifference and even opposition the unit in common with others in the [military] district maintained its organization and efficiency owing to the determination and enthusiasm of its members."[29]

Indeed, dedication had been the only resource not in short supply. Unfortunately, the regiment's officers and men, like the rest of the Canadian militia, would soon face even more daunting trials.

An Allied Regiment

Amidst a sea of troubles, the regiment took a step during the 1920s that would have a lasting impact on its identity. After the end of the war, the British War Office, in co-operation with the Department of Overseas Settlement, conceived of an emigration scheme whereby British regiments would be formally linked to Canadian militia units, the hope being that this would lead to the settlement of the former's expired (retired) men in Canada. Though the scheme never achieved much by way of resettlement, the opportunity to ally with established British regiments was enthusiastically embraced in Canadian militia circles, for whom any British link gave added lustre. The Calgary Regiment's first suggestion was stillborn, but Ottawa's follow-up recommendation bore fruit. The result was a formal alliance with The King's Own Royal Regiment (Lancaster), approved by King George V in the autumn of 1927, which remains in place today. The Calgary Regiment's interest was straightforward.[30] As its annual report for 1927 enthused, a unit that could only trace its roots to 1910, and whose only real soldiering was the 50th Battalion's twenty-six months on the Western Front, "now has a background and a tradition second to none in the history of British arms."[31] The adoption of the alliance led to the anointing of St. George's Day as the Calgary Regiment's own annual celebratory date. Cunnington's enthusiastic support for the latter was crucial. He was one of those adult immigrants whose outlook remained thoroughly English despite crossing the Atlantic, and for years he'd expressed dismay that his adopted city had no suitable commemoration of England's patron saint. Now Alberta's grand British heritage and their allied regiment (whose regimental day it was) could be honoured simultaneously. Despite some flickering of a national identity in the overseas forces during the latter stages of the First World War, it had not taken long in the post-war years for the great majority of the senior ranks in the Canadian military—regulars and part-timers alike—to regress into a state of near total deference to all things British. Cunnington encountered no opposition in getting St. George's Day, April 24 adopted and its predecessor—Vimy Ridge Day, April 9—peremptorily dropped.[32]

Battle Honours

It was only toward the end of the 1920s the matter of battle honours was sorted out between individual militia units and the Department of National Defence. In the case of the Calgary Regiment this meant the honours earned by the 50th Battalion as well as the 89th and 137th. Ottawa provided an official list of seventeen, with the option of choosing up to ten of them. The committee struck in late 1927 included Lt.-Cols. Page, Mason, Cunnington, and Svendsen.[33] In the year-long deliberations, Cunnington and Page seem to have played the leading roles, with the committee finally settling on Ypres 1915, 1917; Festubert 1915; Ancre 1916; Vimy 1917; Arras 1917, 1918; Passchendaele; Amiens; Drocourt–Quéant ; Canal du Nord; and Valenciennes. Noticeably absent was Hill 70, which was intended to include Lens as well. Ypres 1915 (the Second Battle of Ypres) and Festubert, engagements fought more than a year before the 50th Battalion even reached the front, were included out of respect for the 846 men from the 103rd Regiment who were part of the 10th Battalion when it was mobilized in the autumn of 1914. Because 250 recruits drawn from the 50th before it left Calgary had reinforced several of the participating battalions, Mount Sorrel (June 1916) had also been put forward. But unable to prove that any of them had actually fought there, Ottawa refused.[34] It's hard not to conclude that the Calgary Regiments' officers were self-conscious about the 50th Battalion and the rest of the 4th Division being last to the dance, and determined somehow to match the 1915 and 1916 battle honours of their city rivals, the Calgary Highlanders, whose predecessor 10th Battalion had been in the thick of the fighting from the start. But Ypres 1915 was fully deserved—had they not pressed the matter, ordinary citizens would have remained blissfully unaware that the Calgary Regiment's claim to that battle honour was every bit the equal of the Highlanders'.

Militia Rivals

The militia occupied a small world in Calgary and given both the Calgary Regiment and Calgary Highlanders struggled to be noticed, a rivalry was inevitable. The roots went back to the war itself, when the 10th Battalion had outshone the 50th in public estimation despite the latter having the greater claim by local enlistment numbers for the title "Calgary's Own." The formal split in 1924 was driven in no small part by the desire to cease being Calgary's "other regiment." However, the problem did not go away, for "ordinary infantry dressed in regular khaki" could never compete with the glamour of kilts, sporrans and Glengarry bonnets.[35] Throughout the remainder of the interwar years, it grated officers and men that their regiment earned insufficient respect from the community. As the commanding officer lamented in 1935, in a thinly veiled reference to the Highlanders, "[our] standard of excellence would be appreciated by those able to look beneath the surface, [but] to the majority of our people it has no significance, and as we have left the flag-waving and drum beats to others, to them has gone the appreciation and remembrance of the people in general."[36]

The Dirty Thirties

By 1930, Calgary and southern Alberta had entered a sharp recession, marked by steep declines in agricultural prices, construction and investment and ominous rises in unemployment and bankruptcies. Within a year it had become the Great Depression, which would drag on until the outbreak of World War II. Added to the suffering were periods of severe drought that gave the decade its cruel name on the Prairies.[37] A decade of hard times and despair would certainly not make the militia's lot easier.

King's Own Royal Regiment, Calgary?

When King George V officially authorized the association with The King's Own Royal Regiment (Lancaster), the Calgary Regiment's officers had debated whether to procure new colours and incorporate "King's Own Royal" in their own title, a step the allied regiment strongly encouraged. A request duly went forward to the Department of National Defence. At the time (1930), there was no militia regiment with the designation "Royal" west of the Lakehead, and it would also be the first regiment from the 4th Division of the Canadian Corps so honoured, so receiving the title would be quite a coup. Moreover, as Lt.-Col

E. R. Knight, Cunnington's successor, emphasized, it would help to further distinguish the two principal militia regiments in Calgary in the public mind.[38] Knight's correspondence that spring with his opposite number in England neatly summarizes his and his brother officers' views about the indispensable role Britishness played in their regimental identity:

> To the average Canadian ... loyalty to His Majesty the King, faith in British institutions and pride in upholding the British tradition grows stronger .... The [regimental] alliance therefore, means a great deal to us in many ways. It is one more tie with England, it gives us a [military] background which we otherwise would lack and ... an incentive in these days of small appropriations from Parliament, of talk of universal peace, of apathy to the Militia from the great bulk of our own people, to make of the Calgary Regiment something of which our Allied Regiment need not be ashamed.[39]

For reasons that are not entirely clear, the issue of renaming faded away, only to be revived after World War II.[40]

From Infantry to Machine Gunners

As part of broader militia reforms, 1930 saw one of the Calgaries' infantry companies converted to a machine-gun company and to all intents the regiment became a hybrid infantry/machine-gun battalion. In the spring of 1936, when the city's 13th Machine Gun Battalion was wound up in still another round of militia reform (which invariably meant dissolution during the 1930s), its sole company was shifted to the Calgary Regiment. This entailed a complete reorganization of the latter, whereby all four companies of the erstwhile infantry battalion emerged as machine-gun companies equipped with the water-cooled Vickers.[41] The transformation would prove short-lived—even more dramatic changes were only months away.

Tough Times

In 1931, for the first time since pre-war days, summer training at Sarcee Camp extended beyond four days. Although everyone agreed camp training gave the best return on money spent, being the costliest it also placed a great strain on the regimental purse. Officers' pay for the entire year was absorbed just in messing expenses for the 120-odd members planning to participate. Just when it seemed an extended summer training period might become the norm, a militia budget already considered "meagre and wholly inadequate" underwent the first of its Depression-era cuts. With the regiment running a deficit of close to $600 that year, further economies were hard to find. As was often the case, the honorary colonel's generosity made the difference between survival and disbandment.[42]

The nadir of the Depression in Canada was 1932, and funding for anything to do with the military was the lowest priority of all. Fearing there would be no militia training grant at all and recognizing that prolonged breaks from parade accelerated turnover among the men, Lt.-Col. Knight and his officers hatched a plan. If the other ranks agreed to train for the first half of the year without pay, the officers would find a way to finance a three-day camp at Sarcee. Most accepted the offer, even those whose jobs would keep them from attending. In the end, some funding from Ottawa miraculously appeared, and that, along with the men's pledge, ensured everyone who wanted to attend the training camp could.[43] In 1933, summer camp was extended to eight days. The regular Thursday evening training tried to avoid square bashing, instead focusing on tactical exercises, lectures and the firing range. Regular officers from the Calgary garrison also volunteered to prepare their militia comrades for the annual round of classification tests. When Knight stepped down as CO in 1934, the regiment's annual report stressed that he had "battled years of financial stringency more daunting than any which had been seen before and managed to keep the regiment afloat."[44] He was especially remembered for the effort he put into selecting and grooming a cadre of young officers. Though passing unnoticed at the time, his success, and that of his militia peers across the country, would make possible the rapid expansion of the Canadian Army when war broke out.[45]

Warmongering

The new commanding officer, Lt.-Col. L. A. Cavanagh, immediately faced a major crisis. In 1933, with the Depression dragging into its fourth year, the Bennett government had launched a national public works program. With the Permanent Force garrison, and nearly 900 militiamen, 180 of whom belonged to the Calgary Regiment, relying on its facilities, Mewata Armoury was bursting at the seams. Word filtered down that the Calgary project would comprise barracks and other facilities to accommodate the Permanent Force units in the city, thus freeing the armoury for its original purpose—militia training.[46] Cavanagh was a leading figure in the business community and worked hard to mobilize his associates to persuade council to accept Ottawa's largesse. Had it been a post office or customs building, opposition would have been nil. But it was a military base, and that ran head-on into vocal opposition from women's peace groups, assorted idealists, and very vocal left-wing working-class groups like the Workers' Ex-Service Men's League.[47] Still, it was the anti-military sentiments found among the general public which were the real obstacle.[48] Not the least through Cavanaugh's tireless efforts, initial opposition on the council was eventually won over and the project to construct Currie Barracks and an adjacent military airfield went ahead.

The 1936 Militia Reorganization

The restructuring of the Non-Permanent Active Militia in 1936 had a lasting impact on the Calgary Regiment. Recent international disarmament and arms limitations conferences suggested a reassessment of the Dominion's defence needs. Clearly, protecting Canadian territory or providing a modest expeditionary force for Empire defence were the only justifications for land forces, and if budgetary savings could be had, all the better. Obviously, Canada required considerably fewer forces than the militia's nominal 123 infantry battalions, fourteen machine-gun battalions and thirty-five cavalry regiments, even if many of those were close to inactive and the majority of the rest were oversized companies training 30 days a year with World War I equipment. Detailed planning by DND on how to cut back on the militia had been in the works for several years and there had even been some discussion, not always harmonious, with militia leaders.[49] When changes were finally implemented in 1936, Military District 13 emerged in better shape than many, its six infantry battalions being only reduced to three, with a fourth accepting conversion to a tank battalion.[50] The changes were inevitable, but that hardly reduced their negative impact on the morale of the country's "Saturday soldiers" who felt it was just another case of their contributions being disregarded.[51] In reality, militia reorganization mattered little when Canadian defence plans now had the army and its militia reserve pulling up the rear. As one historian caustically put it, with these priorities the re-equipping of the army and militia would occur "as soon as resources permitted—that is, never."[52] This didn't bode well for the six new tank battalions that had been authorized, one of which was the Calgary Regiment.

Saying Goodbye to the PBI

No record survives of the consultation between DND, MD 13, and the Calgary Regiment that led to the latter's conversion from infantry/machine gun to armour. Lt.-Col. Cavanagh and his officers had the foresight to see the idea's possibilities, given the army was keen to embrace mechanization, and seized the opportunity.[53] On 14 December 1936 the Calgary Regiment officially disbanded, to be reconstituted the next day as the Calgary Regiment (Tank), technically making it the first armoured regiment in the Canadian Army. "We have said good bye to the P. B. I. [Poor Bloody Infantry]," the year-end report announced with fanfare, and "all ranks looking forward to annual training in 1937 when we hope to go into camp with some sort of equipment resembling tanks and trying to find out how it [sic] works and why."[54] Better they were optimists—none of them would see an actual tank until they reached Camp Borden in the spring of 1941, and most of those would be Great War-vintage relics.

A Funeral and a Coronation

Early in 1937 the regiment suffered a grievous loss when Senator Pat Burns, their long-time honorary colonel, passed away. Fortunately, John Burns was willing to assume his father's role, thus averting what could have been a major crisis. The Coronation of King George VI followed in May. There had been great excitement when it was learned that MD 13 would be able to send three officers and eight other ranks as part of the Canadian contingent, and equal disappointment when none of the regiment's nominees were accepted. The news was doubly disappointing since Lt.-Col. J. Packard, the commanding officer of the 2/King's Own Royal Regiment (Lancaster), had generously offered any of the Calgary officers attending the coronation the opportunity to observe the battalion's training and manoeuvres and "see all we have to show them."[55] Lt.-Col. Cavanagh had planned to pay his own way if any of his officers and men had been chosen to go to London, and watching a real army train would have cheered his spirits. His initial enthusiasm about the shift to armour was undergoing its harsh confrontation with Canadian military reality. "We do not know when we will receive a tank, if ever," he confided to his British opposite number, "so that our training will be pretty much theoretical with the exception of our musketry and Vickers work."[56]

The Last Years of Peace

Despite the worsening international situation in 1937, few Calgarians, including those in the militia, believed war was imminent. Yet as the troops, among them 140 uniformed members of the regiment, marched back to Mewata Armouries from Victoria Park and their part in the city's coronation ceremonies earlier that afternoon on May 12, it lay a mere twenty-eight months away.[57] Cavanagh knew that for now preparing his men meant continuing to train as an infantry/machine gun unit along Great War lines. As for tank work, a handful of pamphlets had arrived from Ottawa, and they would improvise.[58] No matter how comical some of these improvisations seem in retrospect, at least an effort was being made. In one drill, for example, each crew (the new name for section) pretended to be a vehicle and made wheels instead of turns. Having mastered this, the platoons (now troops) followed suit.[59] At Sarcee Camp in early July the regiment had been authorized to make use of civilian vehicles—in lieu of actual tanks these would at least be more mechanical and add some realism to their training. Albeit slowly, the tank-oriented component of their training improved. The men were exposed to various types of crew exercises to foster teamwork and studied tank signalling (with flags) and basic armoured tactics. For those who could find the extra time—always the militiaman's bane—there were courses at Currie Barracks in motor mechanics and welding. Still, the greater part of their parade nights continued to focus on infantry skills.[60]

Lt.-Col. Walter Jull, who had spent fifteen years with the regiment, assumed command in March 1938. After serving overseas in the 31st Battalion—where he had risen from the ranks to the level of captain, had been wounded three times, and had won an MC—Jull chose to pursue a law career, articling in R. B. Bennett's firm.[61] Only a month earlier the entire regiment had enrolled in a six-week course taught by an officer from the Armoured Fighting Vehicles School at Camp Borden. Summer camp was supposed to practise these would-be tankers' skills but once again marauding thunderstorms and a lack of suitable equipment frustrated their best intentions. Later that summer a group of officers and men who could manage time off work (five of the twenty-five slots went unfilled) set off for Camp Borden to complete the practical portion of the earlier course.[62] The highlight of the year, certainly on the morale front, came when the men were issued their new regimental shoulder flashes and tankers' signature black berets.[63] "This change from the regulation infantry cap at least designated the Regiment as a tank unit," the annual report noted with more than a little sarcasm, "as there is still some doubt in [our] minds … whether or not we actually are."[64]

Indeed, it was hard to be tankers without tanks, and the enterprise shown in overcoming this shortcoming was impressive. During the winter of 1938–39 some of the mechanically inclined members cobbled together the regiment's first stand-in tanks, basically motorcycles around which frames covered in burlap had been rigged, and armed with a light machine-gun firing blanks. The contraptions were deemed safe enough to operate on the armoury parade floor, and soon sparked the idea of more capable dummy tanks for outdoor training. The solution was ingenious:

> Six old Chevrolet cars were bought, stripped to their chassis and the engines overhauled [in the local RCMP detachment's garage]. A frame of angle-iron was welded on and sheet metal was bolted to the angle-iron [to give them a tank-like appearance]. In all of the vehicles a machine gun was mounted. The work was all done

by members of the unit, and cars and material bought ... without any expense to the government.⁶⁵

Some of the men had worked three or more nights a week through the spring to get them ready for summer camp, where they added some realism to the training and combined operations exercises. The regiment also managed to acquire an old Caterpillar tractor, loaned by a local business, which they armed with a machine gun. Nicknamed "Snow White"—to go with the Chevy conversions, the "Six Dwarfs"—it gave the crews some experience operating a tracked vehicle.

A Royal Visit on the Cusp of War

The royal tour of Canada undertaken by King George VI and Queen Elizabeth in the late spring of 1939 was an opportunity for Canadians to see their new monarchs but, even more, for ordinary citizens to come together in the face of now-certain war. The royal couple passed through Calgary on May 26 and practically the entire population turned out to cheer them. All of the NPAM and regular units from southern Alberta provided honour guards along the parade route. The band of the Calgary Regiment (Tank) were given the honour of playing "O Canada" as their highnesses stopped at city hall, while the rest of the regiment lined 7th Avenue as far west as 1st Street East.⁶⁶

Once Again

It was hard to imagine a country more unprepared for war than Canada had been in 1914, but somehow in 1939 Canadians had managed it. The army numbered barely 10,000 officers and men, and although armoured units had been established three years earlier, none possessed a single modern tank. While the regulars would constitute the nucleus of the inevitable expeditionary force, Canada would depend on the militia's 40,000-odd "Saturday soldiers,"⁶⁷ not to mention many tens of thousands more volunteers with no military training whatsoever, to fill its ranks.⁶⁸ Obviously it would be several years before this force would threaten anybody. There were no illusions during those warm days of early September about what war would mean for the country or its families—the Great War had put paid to illusions. Faith in the justice of the cause, coupled with a grim determination to see it through, would need to suffice now.

Despite selfless efforts by members of the Calgary Regiment (Tank) during its three-year existence, little useful armoured training had been possible, and nothing much changed during the first months of the war. Yet the tone of everything that mattered had changed fundamentally. The same day Britain declared war, the Mackenzie King government proclaimed a state of apprehension. From the militia's point of view, Canada *was* at war—waiting a week for the parliamentary declaration was a formality, though an important one for national unity's sake.[69] In fact the Calgary Regiment (Tank) had actually been put on active service on August 26 in order to guard Mewata Armoury and some facilities at Sarcee Camp, even though the regiment was not parading (that is, active) during the summer. Majs. Purdy and Begg had actually driven around the city in their own cars to alert their comrades. By September 8, most of the officers were on duty (though still unpaid). The regiment soon took over responsibility for guarding the Seebe internment camp, and the men not called to active service resumed weekly training.

Initially hopes were high that the regiment would be designated part of the Canadian Active Service Force (the overseas army).[70] But once it became clear that this would be delayed, officers openly encouraged their men to enlist elsewhere. Many did exactly that, many of the younger officers joining them, so that within a few months, ten of them along with 150 other ranks had "gone active," including quite a number of the training personnel. As the economy quickly improved, others found better jobs but had to give up part-time soldiering. And numbers of the older men joined the Veterans Home Guard.[71] For now, the regiment was not allowed to recruit above its peacetime establishment, which for NCOs and especially other ranks was well below "active" strength.[72] There was no way to mask the disappointing start to the regiment's war, and it grated that both the Calgary Highlanders and Edmonton Regiment had been included in the first wave of mobilization. The lone consolation during those early months was Ottawa's pledge that when (or if) the regiment was mobilized it would be as a tank unit.

Limited Liabilities ... Then Total War

Initially, Ottawa had no intention of raising an expeditionary force on the scale of the Great War, preferring to emphasize economic production (which had the added benefit of putting the unemployed back to work) and a sizable commitment of air power. Keeping the overseas army small(er) promised lower casualties, which might spare the country another conscription crisis. At the time, this policy of "limited liabilities" was sensible and initially popular. Of course events—specifically the fall of France in the spring of 1940, which left Britain standing alone with only meagre help from a neutral United States, the Dominions, and the Empire—led the Mackenzie King government to accept total war. This meant a much-expanded economic effort and, by 1941, a much larger overseas army (of which the Calgary Regiment [Tank] would be a part). But all that lay in the future.

Gearing Up

In June 1940, the mobilization of the South Alberta Regiment siphoned off five more officers and 179 other ranks.[73] A month later, orders came to reorganize the regiment as a Reserve unit of the Canadian Army and to recruit to war establishment (though Ottawa still couldn't guarantee every recruit would be issued a uniform). Jull was ecstatic, but given that the Army, RCAF, and RCN had already recruited pretty intensively in Calgary, finding the men would be easier said than done. The farms and small centres of Central Alberta were a largely untapped source, and Jull and others in the regiment were convinced that many of them would possess the mechanical skills tank units required. He pressed the army to let him decentralize his recruiting, and they quickly agreed. Henceforth, the Calgary Regiment (Tank)'s Headquarters Squadron would be based in Calgary, with A, B, and C Squadrons operating out of Red Deer, Stettler, and Olds, respectively. The CO's hunch would be vindicated, as waves of volunteers from the new locales stepped forward to enlist.[74]

A substantially increased budget for NPAM (now Reserve) units and sheer demand turned September 1940's Sarcee Camp into the biggest training event in MD 13's history, involving some 5,500 men over two fifteen-day sessions. Officers and NCOs still had to work around serious equipment shortages, but even the men forced to train in their civvies showed plenty of enthusiasm. The Calgary Regiment (Tank) sent 477 all ranks, including 110 from Stettler, forty from Red Deer and seventy from Olds, "a very good showing ... considering the numbers in the regiment who were [occupied in harvest] operations at that time of year."[75] The honorary colonel gave the regiment a large cheque, a goodly part of which went toward a wind-up party in the officers' mess, while A. E. Cross entertained the NCOs at his brewery.[76] In just five months, the majority of those sweating under the prairie sun, trying to master the basics of tank warfare sans tanks, would "go active" with their regiment. Without formal announcement, their great adventure had begun that September, for the friendships forged at the 1940 camp would carry them through Dieppe and beyond, to Italy and the Low Countries.[77]

The Last Months of Part-time Soldiering

Through the autumn and into the winter of 1940–41 training proceeded apace at Mewata Armoury and the regiment's various small-town outposts. Though the bulk of the training evenings were still unpaid, C Squadron regularly saw as many as 200 men turn out for the twice-weekly parades at Olds. There were remarkable stories of dedication—men managing to get to Sundre by horseback or car, then riding into Olds in the back of an open truck. Invariably, those who lived close by passed the hat to pay for their gas and a meal. Even the onset of a prairie winter barely put a dent in the turnout. Many of the instructors had to commute from Calgary. Maj. Begg, the second-in-command, not only ran a school for officers and NCOs in the city that autumn, but offered a compressed version in Olds, Stettler, and Red Deer as well.[78] What could be achieved by way of training was still pretty limited, but there was no lack of enthusiasm. As one man proudly put it, "we train to become efficient in the use of arms for the defence of our country, and previously have not restricted our training to the number of nights for which the government have been able to provide funds."[79]

The Big Army Plan

The ditching of "limited liability" after the fall of France transformed the army's role in the national war effort. When the so-called "big army plan" was finalized late in 1941, Canada had committed itself to an expeditionary force of three infantry divisions, two armoured divisions, and two additional tank brigades[80]—altogether twelve armoured regiments instead of the three originally planned.[81] This would have all but guaranteed the eventual mobilization of the Calgary Regiment, but in fact the decision came much earlier.

Mobilization

Regimental myth tells us that Brig. Frank Worthington, the father of the Canadian Armoured Corps and commanding officer of the 1st Army Tank Brigade, asked a number of reserve tank units how quickly they could form an active unit. Instead of responding with questions or vague assurances, Lt.-Col. Jull's telegram read simply: "When do you wish me to report?"[82] Not only did Worthington immediately order them to Camp Borden, but he retained a soft spot in his heart for the Calgary Regiment thereafter. Reality was a bit more prosaic—when the brigade came into being at Camp Borden on February 4, Worthington promptly incorporated the two tank units already training there—the 11th (Ontario) and the 12th (Three Rivers) Regiments. Likely, the Calgary Regiment was simply rated the best-prepared of the rest, while also providing a desirable geographical balance. Regardless of how it happened, authorization to mobilize the 14th Army Tank Battalion (The Calgary Regiment) followed nine days later.

When the headquarters squadron, which was drawn from the city as well as the nearby High River and Okotoks districts, paraded on the evening of the 15th, Jull announced the news. Amid rousing cheers, twenty-nine men volunteered on the spot.[83] Given the army intended to move the regiment to Camp Borden around March 7, there was no time to waste in bringing numbers up to the establishment of thirty-two officers and 625 other ranks.[84] And there was an additional hurdle—beyond the army's universal age, fitness, and educational requirements, all ranks in armoured units were expected to possess "technical aptitude."[85] With his adjutant, the MD 13 recruiting officer and a medical board in tow, the CO immediately set off to visit the outlying units, starting with Olds. Drawing mostly from the reserve unit (C Squadron), sixty-two men, including the town's entire senior hockey team, enlisted within the week.[86] By February 23 they had managed to recruit a further 157 men from the Red Deer and Stettler districts (home of A and B Squadrons, respectively), and successful forays had been made to the Nanton, High River, Brooks, and Bassano areas, too. Within a fortnight an impressive sixteen officers and 400 other ranks from the reserve unit had gone active, while other members tried, but either failed the medical or were over-age.[87]

On February 25, Worthington appointed Maj. Gerard Bradbrooke, a decorated Great War veteran and army regular, to replace Lt.-Col. Jull. The latter's loss of an eye during a training accident at one of the summer camps precluded his going overseas.[88] Bradbrooke's first task required him to interview all the current officers, turning down any he deemed "deficient in mechanical aptitude or temperamentally unsuitable."[89] They volunteered to a man, and many were crushed when he selected just thirteen.[90] To make up the remaining manpower shortfall, the regiment chose officers and NCOs from training facilities in Calgary, Red Deer, Camrose, and Edmonton, including 120 from the Seaforth Highlanders of Canada who were completing their infantry training at Currie Barracks.[91]

By the first week of March, all personnel were concentrated in Calgary preparatory to setting out for the East. The now Lt.-Col. Bradbrooke addressed his command for the first time on March 4.[92] Two days later, the majority of officers and other ranks were granted a 96-hour embarkation leave. Upon their return, various inspections and formal social events helped fill the remaining time.[93]

On the afternoon of the 17th, all ranks got word they would be heading east in a matter of hours. At 1800, they formed up in full kit and marched the short distance from the armoury to a siding on the main line between 11th and 14th Streets along 9th Avenue where their CPR troop train, and nearly 3,000 well-wishers, were waiting expectantly. The 14th Reserve Army Tank Battalion, many of them old comrades, provided an honour guard. Only after they had boarded were family and friends permitted to approach the train for last goodbyes. The locomotive, pulling eighteen passenger cars, steamed out of the city just before 1900, the soulful sound of its whistle a familiar—and haunting—sound to anyone raised on the Prairies.[94] Including the advance party already at Camp Borden, the 14th was still thirty-eight men understrength, and a small recruiting detachment remained behind to deal with this shortfall.[95]

The Calgary Regiment That Was Left Behind

On the evening of 3 July 1942, an invading force advancing from Cochrane overwhelmed the city's defenders after a sharp fight and captured Mewata Armoury. The victorious assault, complete with smoke screens, rifle fire and thunder flashes mimicking artillery, was spearheaded by the reconnaissance squadron of the Calgary Regiment, riding in universal carriers borrowed from Currie Barracks. Throngs of city residents gathered along the route to watch the battle unfold, listening to the running commentary provided by a mobile public address system.[96] Such actions draw a wry smile now, but publicizing the war effort by trying to give ordinary citizens a taste of what absent fathers, sons and husbands overseas would soon risk their lives doing was one of the very public faces of the reserve forces during wartime.

Few today are aware that the 2nd Battalion of the Calgary Regiment remained active throughout the war. The former militia unit, most of whose men had quickly enlisted in the 14th Army Tank Battalion (The Calgary Regiment), was redesignated the 14th Reserve Army Tank Battalion (The Calgary Regiment) on March 22, with Jull, its commanding officer through the remainder of the war, immediately told to bring his unit up to strength.[97] Reorganization was the first priority. Red Deer had been so depleted that it was no longer possible to base a squadron there. Olds and district (which now included the shrunken Red Deer detachment) became A Squadron, while Stettler and the surrounding area manned B Squadron and C Squadron was formed around newly established detachments in the communities of Coronation, Consort, Veteran, and Alliance. These new arrangements were in place in time for the 1941 summer camp where 400 officers and men from the regiment participated, overwhelmingly new recruits, and with just under half of them from the city.[98]

In the following months, Jull and his senior officers scoured the province for recruits, knowing full well many they found would soon move on to active service. By year's end, the reserve battalion numbered twenty-five officers and 521 other ranks, including a large veterans' detachment.[99] In the summer of 1942 the 14th Reserve Army Tank Battalion, along with the other reserve tank units, began training as a reconnaissance regiment. Surging war production enabled them to acquire a few of their own universal carriers, 6-pounder anti-tank guns and Bren guns along with some radio sets and other basic equipment which raised the training standard substantially.[100] The major purpose of reserve units was to provide trained men to other Alberta formations in the Active Army. It is worth noting that during the course of the war, Jull's unit funnelled more men into the regular army than any other reserve battalion in Military District 13. Beginning in 1943, recruiting began to concentrate on high school students, while maintaining enough older officers and other ranks to ensure continuity. Anyone fit and young enough to go active was strongly encouraged to do so, with many enlisting as soon as they reached eighteen. Altogether, seventy-seven officers and over 1,500 other ranks passed through the regiment's reserve battalion into the three active services during the war years, a praiseworthy record, indeed.[101]

Camp Borden

In the censored obfuscation of contemporary press releases, the Calgary Regiment had departed "for an armoured vehicles training centre in Eastern Canada."[102] The train ride east from Calgary, surely the longest journey many of the men had ever made, went uneventfully. Mostly they spent their time sleeping, making the acquaintance of new comrades, and just staring out the windows at the countryside for whose occupants they had volunteered to give their lives. Sixty-two hours after pulling out of Calgary, they detrained at Camp Borden, their home for the next three months. Deemed "very fit and of [a] good type" by welcoming brigade officers, the new arrivals marched to their assigned complex of officers', sergeants', and men's quarters, messes, storage facilities, offices, and lecture halls adjacent to the training area of the Ontarios.[103]

With a well-deserved reputation as a taskmaster, Brig. Frank Worthington wasted no time outlining to the new officers precisely what he expected of them—getting their unit combat-ready as quickly as possible.[104] Within eight days of arriving, the men received their first training tanks—fifteen obsolete M-1917s.[105] With only a two-man crew and a top speed of barely 5 mph, these 6-ton tankettes offered limited potential for tactical training, but at least one could learn the basics of driving and maintaining a tracked vehicle and gain some gunnery experience.[106] Training was soon humming, with select groups being tabbed for more specialized instruction at other army schools in Ontario, or in one instance, England.[107] When they paraded for inspection on April 23, officers and other ranks beamed with pride as they wore their pale blue shoulder flashes bearing the inscription *Canada—The Calgary Regiment* for the first time.[108] As April wound down, the first Valentine tank arrived at Camp Borden. This was a modern infantry (i.e., heavy) tank of the type the British were actually using in North Africa. Such a precious training commodity required parcelling out, each squadron having the use of it for a few days at a time.[109] That same day, Lt. F. T. Ward returned from leave, having used the opportunity to marry his nurse sweetheart, Miss Ivy Dunlap, appropriately enough on St. George's Day.[110] He was the third member of the battalion to wed since mobilization, a reassuring sign that even amidst the uncertainties of war, love, and faith in a shared future prevailed.

In May, the training intensified, albeit with every sort of equipment still in depressingly short supply. A three-day convoy and harbouring exercise through the heart of Ontario's cottage country was carried out by the whole brigade.[111] Lt.-Col. Bradbrooke managed to assemble almost two-thirds of his wheeled vehicle establishment, though only by scrounging from other units. Trucks had to serve in lieu of tanks which, save for the training specimens, still had to be imagined. Worthington's staff pulled no punches. Very poor use had been made of cover when stopped. Furthermore marching discipline was "appalling." At momentary halts men "dismounted at free will, lit cigarettes, ate their rations, drank from water bottles, relieved themselves, then scrambled wildly for their vehicles as the column moved on—very much like a troop of boy scouts on a day's outing." As for the officers, many had clearly failed to grasp "that in a very few months, they will be playing 'for keeps' and that they are responsible for the lives of their men."[112] In fairness, the scheme was too ambitious, but that's how lessons are learned.[113]

Officers and men had just begun the laborious process of moving out of their barracks and under canvas for the summer when on May 29 the news came that everyone was desperate to hear—they were heading overseas.[114] Embarkation leaves commenced the following morning, and by day's end, their encampment was more or less a ghost town.[115] To ensure that those without plans did not stray into the fleshpots of Toronto, the army promptly declared ten hotels and another ten restaurants, the latter all in "Chinatown," off limits.[116]

Keeping the Faith

Keeping the military spirit and institutions alive during the interwar years was no easy task. A country that had fought the Great War did not expect to repeat the experience ever, let alone within a generation. Furthermore, it was almost universally felt that that war had been won by an army of citizen soldiers, men with the requisite qualities of courage, duty and self-sacrifice but no military background at all. Even most veterans felt that way. Under such circumstances, what was the point in playing soldier? Post-war, a revived militia faced long odds merely to survive, let alone thrive. That the Calgary Regiment managed to make it through the post-war decade and the Great Depression years was an achievement.

When war came, survival was small consolation. Like the rest of the militia units the country looked to in September 1939, the Calgary Regiment could offer a few hundred men who possessed only modest military skills, but an abundance of grit, determination, and courage. While no army in being, they were assuredly a potential army if circumstances provided them with the time and resources consistently denied them in peacetime.

Good intentions may have been in abundant supply over the next two years, but little else was. When the 14th Army Tank Battalion headed overseas in June 1941, it was an armoured unit in name only. Still, the human capital of a regiment had been assembled. Once in England, they would have no choice but to learn quickly, and they would prove quick learners. In a little more than a year, the men would find themselves in deadly combat on the shores of France. The Dieppe raid would be a disaster for the Canadians in every way one could measure. For the Calgary Regiment, it would mean the loss of their commanding officer and nearly half of their fighting personnel, mostly to prisoner of war camps, in a matter of a few hours.

4.1 An unidentified member of the Calgary Regiment explores his first tank at Camp Borden, April 1941. The 20-year-old American variant of the WWI Renault light tank was totally obsolete but Canada's tank crews had to start somewhere. (KOCRA, P-400-10-0170)

4.2 The great adventure begins. Soldiers of the Calgary Regiment entrain at Camp Borden bound for "an eastern Canadian port" and thence overseas, 18 June 1941. (KOCRA, P-500-10-0089)

Tragedy at Dieppe and the Regiment Reborn   *133*

4.3 The unidentified crew of a Churchill tank taking a break, probably while on a training exercise. As is evident in this picture taken in 1942 (but before the Dieppe raid), parade-ground spit and polish was neither a priority (nor a possibility) for tank crews on the move. (KOCRA, P-400-10-0208)

4.4 Standing (L-R) Stoney Richardson (CO 1944-45), Don Taylor, John Begg (CO 1942–43), Debruce Trotter (killed at Motta Montecorvino), Pim Watkins, Bill Hunt and Doug McIndoe, and kneeling (L-R) Bill Payne, Laurence "Doc" Alexander, Dave Clapperton, Chester McDonald and Bob Taylor. Seaford, 1942. (KOCRA, P-400-10-0214)

134   ONWARD

4.5 The Lord Mayor greets a party of the Calgary Regiment in Birmingham, 17 July 1941. In their semi-trained state the men were hardly a "dagger pointed at the heart of Berlin," but the Canadian Corps' sterling Great War reputation preceded them. British authorities felt such public appearances by the latest wave of Canadians would give a welcome morale boost to soldiers and civilians alike, and they were right. (LAC, PA-196826)

4.6 W.C. Love (L) and Herb Knodel walking along a residential street in Worthing, 1942. During the "long wait," first in Seaford and then Worthing, members of the regiment got to mix with the locals, in the process cementing warm relationships with the British people. (KOCRA, P-400-10-0253)

4.7 (L-R) Frank Bevan, Ed Bennett, Archie Anderson, Bill Stannard and Bobby Cornelssen pose in front of their Churchill, April 1942. Lt. Bennett's crew, with L. Storvold having replaced Bevan, landed at Dieppe in "Bellicose" where Cornelssen was killed and the rest taken prisoner. (KOCRA, P-400-10-0101)

4.8 Death and devastation—"Blossom" and TLC 5 that ferried it along with "Buttercup" and "Bluebell" to the beach at Dieppe. "Blossom" was commanded by Lt. Marcel Lambert who, with his entire crew, was captured. (LAC, C-014160)

4.9 Immobilized on the promenade beyond the sea wall after losing a track, "Bert" receives a thorough examination from German soldiers keen to gather intelligence on the newest British tank. Its crew of Squadron Sgt.-Maj. G. M. Menzies and Tprs. N. A. McArthur, T. A. Dunsmore, W. G. Stewart and F. H. Noel were all taken prisoner. (LAC, C-029878)

4.10 This photograph was taken in 1943 or 1944 at Stalag VIII-B, either by the Germans or representatives of the Swiss Red Cross. It shows (mostly) Calgary Regiment prisoners, easily distinguishable in their black tanker berets. No doubt, camp guards would have preferred more smiling. (KOCRA, P-400-20-0051)

4.11 L/Cpl. Gus Nelson was held at Stalag II D in July 1944 when he slipped away from a work detail and escaped to Sweden. Nelson had been the driver of Lt.-Col. Andrews' tank "Regiment" at Dieppe. (KOCRA, P-400-20-0029)

4.12 Capt. Tony Kingsmill c. 1943–44. An engineer and CO of the 61st Light Aid Detachment attached to the Calgary Regiment, he developed a novel method to quickly get a fully assembled Bailey bridge pushed across the Gari River and speed the tanks into action. (KOCRA, P-400-30-0220)

4.13 George Thring arrived as a reinforcement just prior to Motta Montecorvino and served with the Calgary Regiment through the end of the war, rising in rank from sergeant to captain. His transformation from civilian to soldier, repeated by many thousands of his countrymen, was the key to creating a formidable Canadian army during both World Wars. (KOCRA, P-400-30-0038)

4.14 Mrs. Dorothy Thring in 1941. Engaged in the autumn of 1939, they were married in December 1941 during George's Christmas leave. Sixteen months later he went overseas, and they were only reunited in December 1945. The common thread of their married life had been separation, an underappreciated sacrifice a great many married (or engaged) couples made for their country during both wars. (KOCRA, P-400-10-0315)

4.15 H.M. King George VI reviewing the Calgary Regiment, 23 March 1943. Flanking him (L-R) are Vincent Massey (Canadian High Commissioner, behind the others), Brig. Robert Wyman, Lt.-Gen. Andrew McNaughton, Maj.-Gen. J. H. "Ham" Roberts and Lt.-Col. John Begg. Being reviewed by the king was a signal honour, but the 'spit and polish' preparations required were onerous. (Glenbow Archives, pa-1599-385b-15)

4.16 Capt. "Doc" Alexander (L) and Lt.-Col. John Begg pose outside Buckingham Palace in late 1942 after both received the Military Cross. The king had told Laurence "it was a dirty thing" and he was right about Dieppe. (KOCRA, P-400-10-0265)

4.17 Rebuilding the regiment after the losses of the Dieppe raid required a great deal of determination and a lot of work. An unidentified crew enjoy a welcome break from the exertions of Exercise Spartan, March 1943. (KOCRA, P-400-10-0311)

140   ONWARD

5

From Mobilization to Dieppe

Training and Disaster

The excitement of heading overseas could not mask the daunting task that lay ahead of the regiment. When they had been mobilized in February 1941, Lt. Dick Wallace had not been exaggerating when he recalled that "none of us knew anything about [tank warfare], not even the officers."[1] The few weeks of training at Camp Borden had improved matters marginally at best. Once in England, the learning curve would be steep, with no guarantee they would have enough time to master armoured warfare before being sent into action.

Overseas

As the majority of the officers and men returned from their embarkation leaves, packing gear and cleaning up the camp for those coming to take their place absorbed most of their remaining time at Camp Borden. On June 16, an advance party of just over one hundred of all ranks left for what wartime newspapers discreetly referred to as "an Eastern Canadian port." Two days later, after being served a fine lunch by the Perth Regiment, the remainder of the regiment set off on the great adventure.[2] Their troop train had hardly come to a stop in Halifax when the officers and men tumbled off, formed up in column, and marched away. Their destination was Pier 21 and the converted French liner, HMTS *Pasteur*. Necessary documentation and berthing cards checked and issued, up the gang plank they clambered.[3] The 11th Tank Battalion (The Ontarios) had already boarded, and the rest of the day saw still more men and their gear loaded, including Les Fusiliers Mont-Royal, until the *Pasteur*, built to carry 750 first-class passengers on the South Atlantic run was crammed with 3,400 Canadian soldiers.[4]

At noon the following morning she steamed out of the harbour with the rest of her convoy—five converted liners plus a heavy escort of two capital ships to beat off any surface attack and three destroyers to provide an anti-submarine screen.[5] Apart from a steady diet of PT and inspections and periodic lifeboat

141

drills, there would be little to do. Officers, warrant officers and NCOs, and enlisted men all had their segregated areas, with the officers having exclusive use of the shipboard tennis courts and elevators. Smoking was strictly restricted and gambling forbidden, the latter to keep the *Pasteur's* crew from fleecing the unwary.[6] Five days into the crossing some men spotted an overturned lifeboat and debris drifting past, a grim reminder that they were in a war zone. Save for the powerful battlecruiser HMS *Renown*, the escort slipped away to Iceland at mid-crossing, and was replaced by five destroyers and a Dutch cruiser. As the convoy neared its goal, with the first of the Hebrides in sight, "all the boys [were] in good spirits," but as to be expected, "kind of bored,"[7] and *mal de mer* had claimed plenty of victims. At 0815 on the 30th, the *Pasteur* dropped anchor in the Firth of Clyde off Gourock, just west of Glasgow.[8] Unhappily for the many who would have gladly swum ashore, administrative snarls kept everyone stuck onboard for the rest of the day.

The First Steps

On Dominion Day morning tenders began ferrying the units ashore where they were welcomed by a pipe band and enthusiastic townsfolk. By evening the regiment, split between two trains, was England-bound. Until darkness fell, the young Canadians spent most of their time gazing at the countryside, driven by sheer curiosity.[9] Whereas the great majority of the 50th's soldiers had been British immigrants, only a handful of these men weren't Canadian-born. England was a foreign country to them, albeit one for which most felt a deep attachment.

By late the following evening, bone weary but excited, they reached Lavington Camp on the Salisbury Plain, where they bivouacked under canvas close by their two sister tank battalions.[10] Officers and men looked forward to their forthcoming six-day landing leave, especially those fortunate enough to be assigned billets with English and Scottish families. Brig. Worthington took this opportunity to hammer home the necessity of their behaving themselves.[11] Just as the men were temporarily absenting themselves, equipment began to trickle in, including trucks, tracked carriers, and the first Matilda IIA* tanks.[12] The Canadians had been rushed to England with that very factor in mind— British industry could do what Canada's could not, which was supply them with sufficient modern equipment to commence proper armoured training.

As the men began returning to camp, Worthington briefed all his officers about the training that was about to start. Four maxims would guide his brigade: discipline, fighting efficiency, maintenance efficiency, and care of the men.[13] From July 15 onward, the regimen was intensive, interrupted only by inclement weather, which was not infrequent, England being England. Apart from the opportunity to train with reasonably modern tanks—although by month's end there were still only six Matildas on hand[14]—plenty of time was devoted to practical skills like camouflaging, and groups were continually sent to the appropriate British Army schools for specialized instruction or to observe the tactical demonstrations at nearby British camps. Even Lt.-Col. Bradbrooke was absent for nearly four weeks attending the Royal Armoured Corps Tactical School.[15] On July 26, 250 other ranks and several officers were invited to a garden party at the vicarage in West Lavington. It served as a useful lesson in the culinary challenges of British wartime rationing, with the war diary lamenting that "those who attended in anticipation of a hearty meal were sadly disappointed."[16] By month's end "all members of the unit [had] a much more up-to-date and … much wider knowledge of the equipment and role of an Army Tank Battalion."[17] Events would show this to be a tad optimistic, for there was much more to learn, but the process that would transform them into a combat-ready unit had started.

By early August training was deemed sufficiently advanced for the battalion to participate in an infantry-tank scheme to root out German parachutists. Normally troops only had their proper allotment of tanks one day per week, but enough were scraped together to equip a full squadron, leaving the remaining crews to participate as infantry. Ironically, all the infantry training carried out in Calgary in 1939 and 1940—when there were no tanks to be had—now paid some dividends.[18] The first brigade exercise, Operation Ajax, entailed eliminating still more of the ubiquitous German parachutists, played in this instance by the Ontario Regiment.[19] Worthington's assessment of the 14th's performance was scathing, from Lt.-Col. Bradbrooke on down the chain of command. Among the umpire's more telling criticisms:

> Time factor almost entirely neglected …. Lack of tactical knowledge shown by *all leaders*. Even most elementary fundamentals such as protection, use of ground, etc., entirely neglected. Misuse of troops, i.e. … men [unnecessarily] exposed to enemy fire …. General lack of imagination and knowledge of what was required [and] the importance of hitting hard and hitting fast seemed furthest from the minds of all concerned.[20]

In fairness, Worthington acknowledged that when the 14th left Canada it had completed only the most basic training, and "it follows that [they] would be some distance behind the others."[21] There was a lot of catching up to do, and attitudes became noticeably more serious.[22]

Anglo-Canadian Relations

The sense that they were finally making real progress in becoming a combat-capable armoured unit did wonders for morale, and the ambitious training program kept everyone busy and focused. But turning civilians into soldiers remained a work in progress, which was reflected in the disciplinary records for August. Most offences were minor, with failing to appear for parade or fatigues like kitchen duty the most common, but there were a few cases of insolence or in one case, calling a sergeant an "obscene name." Some of the farm boys found the abundant rabbit population irresistible, though local landowners were less than amused.[23] Bradbrooke showed judgment, with most offences earning reprimands or short periods confined to base.[24] Because they involved civilians and tarnished the image of the whole Canadian Army, incidents in Lavington or other nearby towns were dealt with the most sternly.

Post-war nostalgia portrays relations between English civilians and Canadian soldiers during World War II as a mutual admiration society, and overall they were good, and became progressively better as time went on. But in the early stages of the war this was not always the case. Censorship of the other ranks' letters revealed considerable tension. Everything was in short supply in England, and a group of soldiers, unused to pub culture and the very limited weekly supplies of beer, could drink an establishment dry in a single visit, not exactly endearing themselves to the locals. Nor did being boisterous help. As one weekly intelligence report put it, "the people of Devizes are still wondering whether they had another air raid the other night ... or whether it was just another night with the Canadians."[25] When such complaints from local village officials occurred too often for the army's taste, the Provost Corps would turn out in force. But of course contact with young women was *the* major source of friction. Even British soldiers, and there were many in the nearby training camps, resented the Canadians swanning around with their higher pay and a young lady on their arm. For their part, Canadians often mistook English reserve for standoffishness or worse. Soldiers' complaints about the British way of life, a term covering a lot of ground, including the weather, were a constant theme in letters during the initial years.[26] The winter of 1941–42, the Calgary Regiment's first in England, is taken as marking the low point of Anglo-Canadian relations, with boredom and discontent rife on the Canadian bases and depressing war news on every front. A British newspaper offered sympathetically that the Canadian Army's inactivity had to be "a galling situation for men of high mettle and indomitable spirit."[27] Being derisively referred to by some civilians as the "home guard" definitely didn't help. Even Lord Haw-Haw's propaganda broadcasts openly alluded to the festering problems. The mutual ill will never disappeared entirely, but once the flood of GIs began arriving, the Canadians' sins didn't look quite so dark, and the outpouring of British hospitality eventually overwhelmed the Canadians.[28] It took time for Canadian soldiers and British civilians to appreciate one another, but the former would have lots of time—most of them would have argued rather too much.

Becoming Tank Men

In September the tank crews, using their own Matildas, were finally allotted an 8-day slot at the armoured fighting vehicle ranges near Castle Martin on the Welsh coast. For three days, gunners and spare gunners were able to fire their 2-pounder main armament and hull-mounted machine guns from both stationary and moving positions at fixed, moving, and surprise targets. It was their first experience with live-fire training. After a maintenance day, crews devoted the remainder of their stay to battle practice by complete troops.[29] Meanwhile, the rest of the battalion had completed the move to new winter quarters at Headley (near Aldershot). In what was a real perk to morale, the residents threw out the welcome mat to the newcomers, staging regular dances and opening their village hall to the 14th's enlisted men in the evenings for reading, writing, games, and free weekly movies.[30] Meanwhile, the regular training regimen quickly resumed, facilitated by generally fair weather. For the first time, a portion now focused on the vital skills of infantry-armour co-operation.[31] And there continued to be plenty of opportunities to watch practical demonstrations at other camps, with a tank-hunting exercise staged by an infantry anti-tank platoon leaving an especially deep impression.[32] On October 16, an inspection by the "top brass" filled the day, the visitors including J. L. Ralston, the minister of national defence; Lt.-Gen. Andrew McNaughton, the Corps commander; Maj.-Gen. Henry Crerar, the chief of the Canadian general staff; and Brig. Worthington. On the vehicle front, things continued to look up. With forty-seven Matilda Mk IIs in hand, the regiment was now only nine below war establishment, ensuring that each troop had at least one tank to train on full-time.[33] And matters were steadily improving when it came to trucks and universal carriers, too. Unfortunately, it was common for one-third of their vehicles, whether tracked or wheeled, to be out of service on any day.[34]

On November 7, the battalion participated in its most demanding tank-infantry scheme to date. The crews had to assemble their machines on a pitch-black moonless night, which they completed in good order. The assault commenced the following morning, the squadrons advancing line abreast with the infantry of the Canadian Scottish in support. Their purpose was to get the Canscots onto their second objective, held by an anti-tank regiment and imaginary infantry, then pull back. Lt.-Col. Bradbrooke was clearly pleased with the performance of both units.[35] Other more demanding exercises followed.

The 12th and 14th Tank Battalions soon had to start focusing on the arrival of their first Churchill Mk IVs, the newest British infantry tank.[36] This was going to necessitate a major reorganization of personnel to accommodate a fifth crewman. Otherwise, Bradbrooke had been told to expect the conversion to the new tank to proceed quickly. But until sufficient numbers arrived, the negative impact on training would be obvious.[37]

Seaford Bound, and a Change of Command

Further changes were afoot. On November 20 Lt.-Col. Bradbrooke informed his officers that within ten days the battalion would decamp to the general area of Brighton on the Channel Coast. Two days later, he announced his own departure. Tabbed for higher command, he was to spend several months in the Middle East observing armoured operations close-up. He had been their commanding officer since mobilization, and as (then) Lt. C. A. "Stoney" Richardson summed it up, he "was certainly a wonderful CO to put everything together from the start."[38] His officers and men had come a long way, and he deserved a great deal of the credit. There was a going-away party at a Headley pub, and Bradbrooke took time from that to visit a sergeants' dance in order to break the news to them personally. It was an emotional evening.

A New Commanding Officer

On December 8, Lt.-Col. J. G. (Johnny) Andrews assumed command. The thirty-two-year-old was as close to a star as the Canadian Army's undertrained, -manned and -equipped armoured force possessed. After a brief stint in the militia, he had joined the PPCLI in 1930. When Worthington set up the Canadian Tank School in 1936, Andrews was one of five young officers he hand-picked to join him. In 1939, he followed his mentor to the Canadian Army Fighting Vehicles School at Camp Borden, and from 1940 onward served there as Worthington's principal staff officer. Andrews proved an inspired choice as the 14th's CO, and immediately threw himself into his new responsibilities, starting with getting to know his officers (and they him).[39]

On December 12 an advance party set off for the new camp at Seaford where so many Canadians had trained during the Great War, with the remainder following soon after.[40] Seaford Camp offered a spectrum of accommodations, from former guest houses and cottages to the pre-war Seaford Ladies College (with some irony now the other ranks' quarters), several schools, and a large vehicle garage (converted into a workshop). The onerous tasks of unpacking gear and familiarizing themselves with their new surroundings completed, there was a surge in pride among all ranks knowing they were now part of the front-line defences expected to hold southeastern England against a German invasion.

And a New Brigadier

Word came late in January that Brig. Worthington would be taking command of the 4th Armoured Division now forming in Canada. He had been the driving force behind the formation and subsequent training of the 1st Army Tank Brigade, and it would be hard to imagine the formation without him. Brig. R. A. Wyman, just shy of his thirty-eighth birthday and a gunner by background, who had most recently served in the 5th Armoured Division, would replace him. Richardson remembered him "[coming] with a great deal of ambition for things that had to be done and … very well received by our regiment in particular."[41] Being an Albertan no doubt helped with the latter.

Exercises and More Exercises

In the first months after transferring to Seaford, much of the training focused on repelling a German invasion. Exercises usually involved individual squadron schemes intended to replicate tactics they would employ in action. As Lt.-Col. Andrews spelled out:

> [As] near battle conditions as possible [will be] represented. [But] their success rests largely in the thoroughness of previous troop and squadron training and the training of headquarters personnel. Full value can be gained only if every commander is untiring in his efforts to keep his subordinates in the picture and maintain interest. [These] exercises … should not be attempted until the lessons which it is intended to teach have been firmly established in troop and squadron training and in model and skeleton exercises for commands.[42]

Apparently the CO's obsession with realism was enough to fool some of the locals. When A Squadron rumbled through the port of Newhaven on one such sortie, the nervous inhabitants feared an invasion was actually underway. Fortunately, when the chief constable phoned battalion headquarters, Andrews managed to reassure him that the forces were entirely friendly.[43]

Intensifying training made plenty of sense, but the challenges of actually carrying it out in a country without the wide-open spaces of Canada were daunting. For instance, the battalion grounds lacked a thousand-yard range where gunners could acquire the rather useful skill of firing at moving targets.[44]

And the Churchills' teething problems persisted. As of mid-March, a frustrated Wyman reported to his superiors in Canada that close to a third of his brigade's tanks were non-runners at any given time, and spare parts shortages were chronic.[45] Wyman had confidence in the Churchill as a design, but little at all in the tank's manufacturers, and let them know it.[46]

Commencing in March, the battalion faced the prospect of participating in a trio of advanced tactical exercises which would see them in the field for days on end.[47] The participants in Beaver III, the first of these and set to commence of March 19, were the 1st Tank Brigade and 6th Infantry Brigade. For the first four days, the battalion practised navigating from harbour (encampment) to harbour, all the while maintaining tight convoy discipline, circumventing obstacles like imaginary blown bridges and roadblocks, and carrying out necessary maintenance on their temperamental Churchills.[48] But late in the afternoon of the 23rd, as the battalion was refuelling, Andrews was ordered to mount an attack against "enemy" armoured forces 11 kms away. Within ten minutes the lead tanks were underway. As the 14th's war diary enthused:

> Much to the surprise of the umpires, the unit arrived on time and the "enemy" were taken completely by surprise. As a result, the Calgary Regiment was awarded the battle. This proved to be the highlight of the exercise for with the winning of the attack came the completion of the exercise [two days early].[49]

It was a tired but happy group who returned to Seaford.[50] Overall, the CO was pleased with his battalion's performance. Indeed, his major criticisms focused on the lack of independence of action allowed by higher command.[51] The chief umpire's overall verdict was especially cheering. Across the board, officers and men had showed initiative, a willingness to learn, and high morale, and "the way the tanks were driven, kept going, repaired and brought on was worthy of the highest praise."[52] Indeed it was, given "the tendency of the Churchill to 'die' at the wrong moment."[53]

Early on the afternoon of May 9, the battalion once again departed Seaford Camp, heading for their assembly area and the launch of Beaver IV. It was an impressive sight—stretched out along the narrow English roads in combat formation, the column took an hour to pass. From midnight on May 10–11 Andrews' men were under orders to move on short notice. But while moving repeatedly over the next few days, they were only involved in a single mock infantry-tank attack, which they carried off successfully. That accomplished, their role in Beaver IV was over.[54]

However, with the launch of Exercise Tiger, the largest war game involving Canadian troops yet attempted, looming, there would be little time to rest. But Tiger was not to be, at least not for the 14th Tank Battalion. Instead, they were abruptly ordered to an as yet unknown location where "advanced training with other arms of the service will be carried out."[55]

Simmer

Participation in Simmer, the code name given to this training, was restricted to the tank crews plus a few other specialists.[56] As their medical officer, Capt. "Doc" Alexander, noted in his diary, those selected could hardly contain their excitement and rumours abounded.[57] Why the 14th was chosen ahead of its two sister battalions has never been definitively answered. Their superior performance in Beaver III would have impressed, but not as much as Gen. Montgomery's appraisal of Wyman's command in early May where he'd rated Andrews' battalion first class and the best of the lot.[58] One suspects that Worthington's admiration for his protégé also played its part. Late on the evening of May 20 the Churchills and their crews had reached the temporary camp near Osborne Bay on the Isle of Wight, where most of the training would take place. Using specialized tank landing craft, Simmer commenced the next morning at dawn with the crews driving their now waterproofed tanks off and then back onto beached landing craft. The training continued without let-up, save for Sundays, which were devoted to maintenance and perfecting waterproofing techniques. The initial skills mastered, the squadrons shifted to landing tanks and infantry simultaneously "with the object of securing a beach head."[59] On the 30th, Exercise Suvla, a practice landing employing three landing craft and subsequent advance inland by the nine tanks, was unsuccessful, but a reprise a week later met all objectives.[60] Finally, on June 12 Yukon, a full-scale mock attack with accompanying infantry, was carried out on the nearby Dorset coast. The exercise began shortly after dawn and by mid-afternoon, all tanks and infantry had safely re-embarked.[61] Nonetheless, Yukon revealed serious flaws of execution—tank landing craft arriving over an hour late and some of the infantry being put ashore miles from their designated landing points.[62] The following evening, Andrews briefed his officers on the purpose of their training—a major raid on the French coast. The reaction was electric. As Capt. Alexander scribbled in his diary that night—"We are all very enthusiastic and certain that we can carry it out."[63]

Rutter Is On!

Planners scheduled a virtual repetition of Yukon (called Yukon II) for June 22–23. One of the drivers, who had dismissed Yukon as "a schmozzle," thought this time "it was a helluva lot better."[64] More to the point, the senior command considered it sufficiently successful to proceed with the real thing.[65] Preparations for what everyone was led to believe would be the final trial run—Exercise Klondike—were well underway at month's end. By 0300 on July 3, all members of the unit assigned to Klondike and their tanks were aboard their landing craft in Newhaven harbour. With security assured, they were told what their commanding officer learned six days earlier—Klondike was Rutter, the real thing. After a year in England waiting for action, they were finally going to war.[66] But after poor weather forced a cancellation, delay followed delay. Apart from cleaning weapons, checking gear, and going over maps for the umpteenth time, there was nothing for the men to do but wait.[67]

It's Off

Finally, about mid-afternoon on the July 7, word filtered down that the operation had been cancelled. They were back at Osborne Bay the following morning, where they and their infantry comrades were addressed by Lt.-Col. Andrews and then Maj.-Gen. Hamilton Roberts, the 2nd Division's CO. The disappointment was palpable, and both speeches were more pep talk than anything.[68] Within a week, everyone was back at Seaford. Anyone who'd participated in the aborted raid had been granted eight days' leave.[69] With thousands of Canadian soldiers knowing full well they had trained to raid Dieppe, maintaining security was hopeless, a predicament that led Montgomery to wisely recommend "that the operation be off for all time."[70]

Rutter Revived: Operation Jubilee

The decision to resurrect Rutter emanated from Adm. Louis Mountbatten and his Combined Operations Headquarters but had the support of the Combined Chiefs of Staff who reapproved a raid on Dieppe, now code-named Jubilee, on July 10. Senior Canadian commanders were fully onside. While it was recognized the enemy might have caught wind of Rutter after its cancellation, commanders felt strict security around Jubilee and the last-minute movement of the force to their embarkation points would secure surprise. The soldiers themselves were told that preparations merely presaged another exercise. More than ever, the outcome of the raid would depend on surprise and sheer good luck. By the end of July, the battalion had resumed its regular routine of infantry-tank training, though tank crews continued practising beach landings alongside combat engineers from the 2nd Canadian Division.[71]

On August 12, Andrews received instructions that his unit would be taking part in a combined operations exercise within the next week, and preparations were soon in full swing. One of the officers temporarily attached to the Calgary Regiment for the forthcoming raid, Lt. J. H. B. MacDonald of the Ontarios, later compiled a report on his experiences during those days. Having arrived at Seaford on August 13, he was present to hear Lt.-Col. Andrews reveal to his senior officers that the exercise would in fact be Rutter redux. As befit his role and the circumstances, the CO's presentation was upbeat.[72] But as Lt. Ed Bennett recalled:

> After the briefing we all had apprehension. But there were hardly any questions …. We were all in shock. I thought that we in the tanks might be ok, but remembering the film *Next of Kin*, when the troops on a raid were slaughtered, I thought it might happen to some of the infantry.[73]

On August 16, Andrews addressed all participating personnel on the critical importance of secrecy, reminding them about two of their comrades who had recently been court-martialed and sentenced to two years' imprisonment for violating an order of secrecy. A visibly angry Andrews sternly reminded his audience that security breaches would cost lives, and that it was their duty as soldiers to turn such men in.[74]

On Their Way

The fighting personnel and their vehicles departed for Newhaven (and some for Gosport) late on August 17. The loading of the tanks and other vehicles, ammunition, and other supplies, and of course the men aboard their allotted tank landing craft (TLC), an intricate and time-consuming ritual, went on through the night.[75] The following afternoon, all remaining personnel were informed they would be raiding Dieppe. In a way impossible for civilians to comprehend, and difficult for a historian to describe, once everyone knew the attack was on, they were keen to get going, doubts or not. Lt.-Col. Andrews was stoic and did his duty, visiting every one of his landing craft. But Maj. Allan Glenn, commanding C Squadron, remembered his CO staring him in the eye and clasping his hand: "'Well, Al, this is it, I guess. Be seeing you, I hope.' But he was a sad boy. He didn't think the plan would work."[76]

The hours dragged on intolerably, but at last the diesel engines of the transports rumbled to life in Newhaven and the several other ports of embarkation along the south Channel Coast used by the attacking force. By 2330, a mere two hours after the first TLCs sallied from Newhaven, the harbour was empty. The weather augured well—clear with only gentle swells. As the coast disappeared, "personnel, after adjusting their life belts, retired to their hammocks to await the coming of dawn."[77] Apart from stars and a first quarter moon,

5 | England and Dieppe

all that could be made out were the faint red stern lights of the ship ahead of you. Lt. MacDonald, who had expected the men would spend a fitful night, instead remembered most sleeping soundly. But Tpr. Tom Pinder's recollections were quite the opposite and ring more true: "We tried to get some sleep, but we couldn't get any ... we were all so excited."[78] It didn't help that smoking was forbidden. The chaplain held a brief service aboard his landing craft, with those who chose to attend gathering under a tarpaulin overhanging the front of the lead tank. As a soldier held a small flashlight over his bible, the padre read from St. Paul's Letter to the Ephesians, then spoke briefly about their bringing a sign of deliverance to the captive peoples of Europe and ended with a short prayer.[79] It was not long before the various groups of ships, plus their naval escort, formed up in convoy, and set a course for Dieppe. All told, the landing force totalled about 6,100 men, of whom just under 5,000 were Canadian, including 417 officers and other ranks from the Calgary Regiment.

Jubilee—the Plan

Four flank attacks set for 0450, at first light to hinder the defenders, were intended to silence coastal batteries (British commandos) or seize the headlands (Canadian infantry) that dominated the main beach at Dieppe itself. At 0520 two battalions of the Canadian infantry, along with the first nine tanks, would come ashore in front of Dieppe, with about half of the other fifty-odd tanks following in short order. The remainder would be held back until Dieppe was secured. Simultaneously with the main assault, a second infantry battalion would land to the west of Dieppe and advance inland to meet up with a tank force that would have broken through the town, their joint objective being a *Luftwaffe* airfield and supposed divisional headquarters. That achieved, they would withdraw to the coast and evacuate. A reserve infantry battalion would hover offshore until landed to consolidate the main beach area and act as a rearguard during the subsequent evacuation of the main force. As much destruction as possible would be done to the harbour and other infrastructure, but intelligence gathering—including the evacuation of prisoners—was also a high priority.[80] To preserve surprise, there would be no preliminary bombardment from the sea or air, and relatively little fire support thereafter.[81] Everything would depend on surprise, the élan of the attackers, and weak German defences. But as history has made clear, hope is not a strategy.

The responsibility for defending the Dieppe sector fell to the 302nd Infantry Division, which the Germans considered a second-rate formation because many of its men had not completed their training and large numbers were ethnically Polish and hence deemed "unreliable." The defenders confronted in the immediate area of Dieppe amounted to one of the 302nd's two regiments, meaning the strength of the forces were roughly equal, though the Germans could bring additional reserves to bear. Overall, the defences of Dieppe were neither stronger nor weaker than those generally found along the French Channel Coast at the time. Nor were the defenders on heightened alert, apart from what was dictated by the weather and tides and a general conviction that the British were going to raid somewhere during the good summer weather. A firefight between patrolling *Kriegsmarine* vessels and part of the convoy that night did alert the Germans, but in no way affected their readiness at Dieppe. Finally, the intelligence available to the attacking forces, despite a few errors, was generally sound.[82] The problem was more one of underrating potential difficulties, or not acting on the intelligence at all.

Jubilee—the Attack

This account will focus on the Calgary Regiment's role in the assault on Dieppe proper, and so provide only a brief overview of what befell the rest of the raiding force.[83] The British commandos' assaults on the major seaward-facing batteries produced mixed results, but nonetheless proved the most successful elements of the raid. The landing on the eastern flank (Puy) was late, losing the cover of darkness. A few dozen German soldiers atop the cliffs that hemmed in the landing area were sufficient to all but wipe out the Royal Regiment, leaving the critical eastern headlands overlooking Dieppe firmly in German hands.

On the western flank (Pourville), the South Saskatchewans managed to get ashore on schedule and unopposed, but landed some distance west of where they should have been, an error enabling the defenders to pin them down well short of their objective, the headlands overlooking the Dieppe beach from the west. The Cameron Highlanders, who landed an hour after the SSRs (and half an hour late), managed to press inland until stopped by stiffening resistance. Both battalions had to conduct fighting withdrawals to re-embark, with only about 60 percent of the men who'd landed making it back to England.

With the headlands and their ample defences remaining firmly in German hands, the main attack on Dieppe proper was doomed. Both the Essex Scottish and Royal Hamilton Light Infantry (RHLI) were put ashore almost exactly on time and in the midst of a short-lived attack by RAF fighter-bombers. Unfortunately, the first group of nine tanks were delayed a crucial 10 to 15 minutes, and as the army's official historian concluded, "the impetus of the [infantry] attack ebbed quickly away, and by the time the tanks arrived the psychological moment was past."[84] Withering German mortar, machine-gun and artillery fire resumed as soon as RAF departed. Although suffering very heavy losses, the RHLI managed to advance beyond the sea wall and clear the partially demolished casino perched on the promenade by shortly after

0700. But only a few scattered groups managed to get into the town proper. Meanwhile, hardly any of the Essex Scottish got beyond the sea wall, and within half an hour of landing, the battalion had ceased organized fighting. Poor communication led Maj.-Gen. Roberts, the force commander, to misjudge the progress ashore—of which there was effectively none. He tragically ordered the Fusiliers Mont-Royal into the cauldron around 0700, where they would meet the same fate as the others. By 1100 an evacuation from the main beach was underway, though under appalling conditions. Miraculously, perhaps 400 men, many of them wounded, were extricated. The courageous efforts by the RAF to cover the withdrawal were hardly noticed. Under unrelenting bombardment, few soldiers were inclined to stare skyward. Isolated groups scattered across the breadth of the beach and beyond the sea wall, including the Calgary Regiment's tankers who had displayed such heroism during the attack and then covered the re-embarkation, began surrendering in the early afternoon. By 1400 all the rescue efforts were terminated, and those hundreds still alive would spend the rest of their war as *kriegies*. The infantry losses in front of Dieppe were very heavy, less than a quarter of the force put ashore managing to get off.[85]

The Calgary Regiment at Dieppe

The participation of Calgary Regiment in the raid marked the first time a unit of the Canadian Armoured Corps had gone into battle as well as the first employment of both the Churchill tank and the specialized tank landing craft. Sadly, it was memorable for little else save the painful lessons learned. The armour came shoreward in three waves. All of the landing craft were smothered by artillery, mortar, machine gun, and small arms fire as soon as they came within range, and being slow and all but unarmoured, suffered heavy damage and severe casualties among their naval crews. The TLCs basically had to beach or all but beach themselves to disgorge their cargo, leaving them sitting ducks, and several were soon blazing torches littering the shoreline or adrift offshore. Fewer than half of them managed to make their way back to England. The first wave arrived no more than 15 minutes late but nonetheless it represented a crucial breakdown in the raid's precise timing. The second arrived shortly after the first, or almost on time, and the third (made up of four TLCs instead of three, and the only group benefiting from a smokescreen) beached about half an hour later, again basically on schedule. TLC 8, part of this final grouping, carried the headquarters troop, which included Lt.-Col. Andrews' tank. Altogether two Churchills drowned as they debouched, but twenty-seven made it onto the beach. A dozen of the latter became immobilized there, but the remaining fifteen got over the seawall, mostly at either end of the beach where the climb was more manageable. Once onto the open promenade they engaged enemy strong points in support of those groups of infantry who were still attacking. Getting off the promenade into Dieppe (and beyond) was impossible, as any potential exit had been blocked. Parties of combat engineers were supposed to blow up the barriers (along with parts of the seawall), but despite their gallantry in the face of murderous fire, none were.[86] As it became clear to the tank crews that there was no useful fighting to be done on the promenade, they, along with the infantry they were supporting, fell back to the beach area, the tanks specifically to cover the evacuation. There they manoeuvred as best they could, drawing disproportionate enemy fire and in so doing, saving many Canadian lives. Throughout the fighting, the robust armour of the Churchill served its crews well, as not a single tank was penetrated by a German anti-tank round. However, one by one they had either bellied, suffered immobilizing track damage from the beach stones, or lost a track to artillery fire, some suffering such a fate immediately after landing and others, hours later. And there were mechanical breakdowns, too. Regardless of how the Churchills became immobilized, they continued to fight on to the last as pill boxes, providing fire support with their cannons and machine guns until they exhausted their ammunition or their weapons jammed, and using their bulk to shelter the wounded on the exposed beach.[87]

Baptism of Fire

One only really grasps the tankers' experience by relying on personal accounts—some given back in England, some provided by prisoners, and some recalled years later during interviews or in memoirs. Maj. C. E. Page, who commanded B Squadron, landed in the second echelon, his tank *Burns* coming ashore directly in front of their objective, the Tobacco Factory.[88] Crawling up the rather steep beach, they ran straight into an anti-tank ditch hidden in front of the central section of the sea wall. Steering hard right to avoid becoming stuck, a shell explosion shattered a track and wrecked the radio. Now unable to command, Page quickly passed control to C Squadron's Maj. Allan Glenn. That accomplished, he and his crew took their personal weapons, abandoned *Burns* and sought cover behind the sea wall. Astonishingly, they found themselves completely alone until a small party of Essex Scottish joined them. Both of the other Churchills in his troop, along with quite a few others that had landed toward the centre of the beach, were similarly disabled—feeling their way along the face of the ditch/sea wall to find a crossing point. Page and the others stayed put until around noon, when word somehow filtered through that they should withdraw.

Tpr. Roy Johnston served as co-driver/ hull machine gunner in *Confident*, part of a C Squadron troop. During the last few hundred metres of their run into the beach, a forest of geysers from shell explosions surrounded their TLC. Having run that gauntlet for what seemed like forever, the order was finally given to warm up the engines and when the ramp fell, out rumbled the lead Churchill. As *Confident* quickly moved forward onto the ramp, the explosion of a mortar round stalled the engine, though driver Pat Patterson was able to restart it. Amid the deafening noise, the crew could hardly make out one another on the intercom, but he did hear Cpl. Ralph Dowling, who had a better view from the commander's position, tell Patterson to try to avoid driving over the wounded soldiers strewn in their path. As *Confident* lurched forward, Johnston's first views of the beach gave him "a sick, helpless feeling," with dead and wounded lying everywhere, and burning landing craft on both sides of their own TLC. [89] Even the rolling surf was tinged bright crimson. They immediately made for a low section of the sea wall that had already crumbled under the 40-ton weight of a few earlier Churchills, but as they crested it, *Confident* was shaken by an ear-shattering explosion, reared up and then crashed down, wrecking the steering. Having then reversed back to the water's edge, Patterson clambered out to inspect the damage, which was obviously bad. After a brief conference back inside *Confident*, they crept back up to the sea wall and succeeded in taking out the gun that had gotten them. From then on, they spent the battle methodically obliterating machine-gun nests lurking in the upper storeys of buildings beyond the promenade.

Lt. Bryce Douglas' *Calgary* had been the last to exit Maj. Glenn's TLC 1. The sappers who were supposed to blow a gap in the sea wall for the three Churchills were cut down by a burst of machine-gun fire as they disembarked, and *Calgary* threw a track on the shingle before even reaching the obstacle. With German machine gunners raking the tank, Douglas refused the request of his driver, Cpl. Hank McCann, to climb outside and try to fix it. Although they were hit many times by large calibre rounds, nothing penetrated, and the tanks' electrical system continued to work, meaning they could traverse the turret and communicate. Douglas kept gunner Ken Smethurst firing at anything they could draw a bead on.[90] Smethurst hesitated only once—when they saw horse-drawn artillery moving up behind the casino. He could not bear killing horses. Conditions inside immobilized tanks like *Calgary* were appalling. Men suffered concussions and burns and were badly cut by spalling—the tiny shards of metal launched off the interior plating when a shell hit. Ventilation in any tank is poor, and crews were soon suffocating from the cordite fumes and, in the runners, extreme heat from the engine. Al Wagstaff passed out more than once in *Calgary*, and everyone was vomiting at some point. With their intact radio link, Douglas and his crew knew full well the raid was falling apart. Those with periscopes could see their TLC had been sunk behind them, as had several others nearby. A few of them burned furiously. Dead dotted the beach in every direction, with wounded sheltering behind the sea wall or beside tanks or any beached landing craft not yet afire.[91] Had the infantry and tankers been better able to communicate, the tanks would have been much more effective. But short of hand signals or an aimed Bren gun burst, the crews had no way of knowing what the soldiers pinned down all around them needed. During his debriefing in England, a grateful Maj. Denis Whitaker, the highest ranking RHLI officer to get off the beach, attested to numerous occasions when the tanks had responded to just such prompts.[92]

Part of the third wave, TLC 8 carried Lt.-Col. Andrews and his staff, including Maj. John Begg, the second-in-command. As soon as they had grounded on Red Beach near the jetty, Capt. A. G. Stanton's lead tank *Ringer* exited, bellying on the loose shingle and blocking the ramp. TLC 8 managed to pull away and stood offshore for about 90 minutes while Maj. Glenn directed all the tanks ashore. Glenn opposed landing any more Churchills until beach congestion cleared, and Andrews, who could follow it all on the radio net, agreed. But when it became clear that many tanks were being held up at the sea wall, it was decided to make another attempt to land TLC 8 with its considerable store of demolition charges and the combat engineers to do the blasting. Witnesses' accounts also confirm that the worse the situation ashore became, the more the CO wanted to be with his men. As Lieut. Dick Wallace, already ashore in *Backer*, put it:

> He was so full of vim and vigour. I can understand his attitude of "I am coming in to help you fellas out." Johnny was that kind of man. He wanted to get into the fight and get in with the tanks he had sent. He knew we were in trouble and he was going to come in to help.[93]

Around 0800, TLC 8 made its second landing attempt, this time on White Beach in front of the casino. To speed the exit of the remaining pair of Churchills, the crewmen left the ramp partially down, but as they closed on the shore the ramp's supporting chains were blown away, causing it to plunge into the water where it dug into the mud. Almost immediately, a second explosion blew the ramp itself askew. In the confusion, a sailor signalled Andrews' tank *Regiment* to drive off and it promptly drowned in over two metres of water. The crew scrambled out and were pulled into a small boat, only to have it hit and burst into flames, forcing rescuers and rescued alike to swim for their lives. All made it, save Andrews. Cpl. T. L. Carnie, who was *Regiment's* co-driver, thought he saw him reach the shoreline, while fellow crewman Sgt. C. Reinhart was certain he had seen his CO's body washing back and forth in the surf just short of it. Lt.-Col. Andrews' remains were never recovered.[94]

Under the most unpromising circumstances imaginable, Begg immediately had to take overall command. The ship was raked by German fire of every calibre, and soon floated helplessly broadside to the beach. The carnage on TLC 8 was horrific, and conditions got a lot worse as wounded from the beach were brought aboard. Over the next few hours, Capt. "Doc" Alexander tended to the wounded, many grotesquely mutilated or burned, with other members of the headquarters staff like L/Cpl. Calvin Helmer assisting as best they could.[95] In a letter to his father, which appeared on the front page of the *Herald* in early September, Sgt. A. H. Rutledge credited their medical officer for getting him and his comrades through the ordeal: "He is a master psychologist and can buck you up with just a smile or a wink ... With shells dropping all around us, he kept going without any thought of his own safety, bandaging his wounded and spreading cheering remarks to each of them."[96]

Aboard TLC 10, which was lingering far enough offshore to be out of range of German guns, Capt. Waldo Smith, the chaplain, was listening in on the communications from the tanks, astonished at the calmness of the radio operators as they called out targets to their comrades.[97] Large, slab-sided, and virtually unarmoured, TLCs were too vulnerable to close on the beach and participate in the rescue effort. This fell to infantry landing craft, which were faster and more nimble and presented a smaller target. Finally, at 1045, TLC 10 received orders to head for home. For the next 90 minutes the padre listened to the fading communications from Maj. Glenn and the other officers he knew so well. "I cannot find words for the pathos of it," he later recalled.[98] About 1130 he heard reports of infantry stampeding toward rescue boats, and just before noon another that the incoming launches were being picked off one by one as they tried to reach the beach. Thinking it might be important, he had scribbled an informal log of these communications, but in French so as not to alarm the soldiers peering over his shoulder, desperate for any news of their friends' fate.

Evacuation

About 1100, acting on Begg's order, Glenn radioed the tanks that were still mobile to fall back to the beach and cover the evacuation as best they could—six radios responded in the affirmative. About an hour later, he ordered crews to abandon their tanks if further infantry landing craft approached. And at 1225 he gave the terse order "unload crews from tanks," though by then the evacuation was all but finished. Only the final gasps of resistance remained to play out.

Throughout the morning, three troops of C Squadron and the entirety of A Squadron, including Lt. MacDonald's TLC, lay offshore waiting for orders to land that never came. The "men of A Squadron were badly depressed at having been helpless to assist their comrades," he recorded in his notes. "One of the last radio calls, in which a member of a tank crew asked if there was any sign of barges coming in to take them off at about 1430 hours when the convoy was well under way [for home], affected everyone rather badly."[99]

By the time Maj. Begg was authorized to withdraw, TLC 8 was barely afloat and the dead and dying lay everywhere. An improvised crew of the two unwounded naval ratings and some willing tankers manned the wheel and managed to get the engine started, and after a false start, got her turned seaward and pulling away, ever so slowly, all the while attracting the attention of what seemed like every German gun in France. Before long she was dead in the water, but miraculously, a distress message had been picked up by a Royal Navy gunboat, which managed to come alongside, lash herself to the crippled landing craft, and slowly crawl out of range of German fire. By late evening, they were safely back in Newhaven harbour.[100]

Surrender

"I don't think the average guy who went on [the] Dieppe [raid] had any conception of having to face surrender," recalled Sgt. Tommy Cunningham, who commanded *Bolster*, and with the rest of his crew was taken prisoner. "You're too young. You think you're well trained. You're going to do this thing and do it well, and it was an adventure. And all of a sudden, the balloon bursts."[101] For compassionate reasons, Lt. Dick Wallace, who commanded *Backer*, made a personal decision to cease firing:

> Corporal [J. O.] Cote, who was my wireless operator, when I gave the orders to stop firing, he said what are you doing that for sir? I said we've got all sorts of infantrymen trying to crawl under our tank for protection ... [and] I [couldn't] see any reason why we should kill innocent soldiers anymore.[102]

Tpr. Tom Pinder, who had escaped drowning in *Ringer*, never forgot the sound of surrender after enduring "seven hours of hell"[103] on the beach:

> All the firing seemed to ... stop at once. Just this great silence fell and we could hear some shouting and through our periscopes we could see the Germans coming and a white flag here or there. And very shortly after there was a German outside the tank saying "Raus." So I opened the escape hatch and Johnny Mayhew and I

got out and there was this Jerry there with his rifle. The wrong end of a rifle sure looks big.[104]

For Tpr. Denis Scott in *Calgary*, the end came quickly after they'd received Glenn's order to get out of their tanks and destroy them. As he stood up and looked around the view was surreal: "The carnage was worse than I thought. We were stunned, without emotion. We were alive standing amidst dozens of dead and wounded comrades."[105]

Tpr. Roy Johnston and his crewmates had received the order to evacuate somewhat earlier. Abandoning *Confident* where she lay at the sea wall, they crawled away to find some better protection, but not before arming a demolition charge inside her, a sad moment for any tanker. The five of them spent the final part of the battle huddled with several dozen Essex Scottish and some engineers against one of the wave breakers extending toward the shore from the sea wall. The beach reminded those who had seen one back home of an abattoir. As close as they were to the water, any thoughts of making a dash for it and then wading or swimming out to a rescue launch evaporated as soon as they saw the bursts of machine-gun fire slicing through the ranks of those desperate enough to try. Around 1330, Johnston remembered the few remaining boats hovering offshore out of range of the mortars turning and then disappearing over the horizon. Many in his group burst into tears. As the firing began to die down, a few talked about somehow holding out till nightfall before trying to slip away. But as other parties scattered across the beach began struggling to their feet with hands raised, and it became clear how many wounded needed medical help, Johnston's group, without a word being said, stood up and surrendered, too.[106]

Together they walked toward the promenade where, meeting their first armed Germans, they were roughly searched.[107] Then, in a ragged line, they were marched through largely empty streets, burning buildings lining the route. Upon reaching the hospital grounds, everyone was searched a second time, Johnston losing everything that might have remotely qualified as a souvenir from the vanquished Tommy, though a German NCO at least retrieved the pictures of his wife and son.[108] Eventually everyone who could walk had been assembled at the hospital grounds, including those who had stayed behind on the beach to help the medics—Canadian and German—treat the casualties or carry the badly wounded up to the sea wall so they wouldn't drown. It was a broiling summer day and as the men waited, they received a single ladle of water but nothing to eat. The lucky among the walking wounded received some treatment, but in fairness there were far worse cases to attend to. Finally, late in the afternoon, the prisoners formed up in a long column, three abreast, a sorry looking lot, many only half dressed and a few, who had presumably stripped down to swim out to a rescue boat, wearing only underpants, and marched out of Dieppe, "to where, no one knew."[109] The prisoners barely spoke to one another, "our minds dim and throbbing from the catastrophe of it all."[110] It was a gravel road, and it tore up the feet of any who had discarded or otherwise lost their boots.[111] Several accounts mention passing a wedding party where the best man, who took off his own shoes and threw them to a passing Canadian, was roughed up to make an example.[112] The German guards could be cruel or not, as the mood suited. Some of the wounded men were soon struggling to keep up and were roughly pummelled with rifle butts. And as Tpr. Harry Ganshirt recalled, "food [was] knocked out of our hands or of the hands that tried to give it to us along the way (and) water knocked or poured away in [the] same manner."[113]

At Envermeu, about 15 kms east of Dieppe, the officers were separated from the men, permanently as it turned out, with the latter trudging on a while longer until they reached the hamlet of St. Nicholas d'Aiermont around 2130. Utterly exhausted, dehydrated and ravenous, they were herded inside the walls of a brickyard and cement works.[114] For supper, the Germans poured water into their helmets and handed out some rock-hard *schwarzbrot*,[115] though most of the men simply collapsed from fatigue and were soon asleep on the concrete floor. The next morning they were roused early and given ersatz coffee or tea and more *schwarzbrot* with a thin glaze of dubious-looking jam.[116] French civilians gathered outside the compound and tried to hurl food inside but were chased away by the guards.

The next day they marched to a rail siding where they were packed into boxcars stencilled with the notional capacity—*Quarante Hommes ou Huit Chevaux*. By now they were constantly hungry and the smokers dying for a cigarette. Vern Richardson remembered seeing men fight for water.[117] The train took them to a transit camp at Verneulles, about 30 kms west of Paris, where sleeping arrangements and hygiene were rudimentary.[118] Here they were sorted by unit and camp destination, as well as interrogated—the other ranks rather casually but the NCOs more vigorously. After about a week, the guards crammed them into another train, so tightly that they had to sleep head to foot on the straw-covered floors. Bathroom facilities consisted of a couple of buckets emptied when the Germans felt like it, and all save one of the ventilation ports were locked shut. In the suffocating heat, conditions were intolerable, with the worst-off being the "lightly" injured who lay in agony while their wounds festered. Thirst was constant, and the daily ration for fifty-odd men was a single loaf. For the tank crewmen, the trip took five days, during which they were never allowed off the train, though the doors were opened at every stop so German soldiers could poke fun at the *kriegsgefangene*. To add to their misery, dysentery broke out. When the POWs finally arrived at Lamsdorf (now Łambinowice) in Silesia, the men clambered out "dirty, unshaven and foul-smelling," but still relieved they were there—wherever there was.[119] A final march brought them to the gates of their home for the foreseeable future—Stalag VIII-B.

Aftermath

The damaged ships as well as any others carrying wounded had begun arriving at Newhaven by early evening, while the rest sailed on to Gosport, which they reached the following morning. Throughout the 20th, vehicles arrived at Seaford, singly and in small groups, returning members of the battalion until by early evening everyone but the tank crews and wounded were home. Apart from medical treatment for the wounded, the priority was confirming the losses, which in the confusion took time. Maj. Begg issued an order of the day reminding everyone that "by the magnificent stand made by those who met the enemy, we have a high place to maintain."[120] It was heartfelt, and what else could he say. Padre Smith had immediately set off to visit the B Squadron area of the camp where he found only a handful of cooks and truck drivers "sitting around benumbed—the billets were empty—it was eerie."[121] It was only two days before the first replacements arrived from the armoured reinforcement units, seven officers and fifty-eight other ranks.

The 23rd was a Sunday and everyone assembled at Seaford Parish Church for a service. They were all still in a state of shock. Their ranks had been filled with men who had been together for almost two-and-a-half years, only to have a third of them disappear in a matter of hours. That there would be no confirmation for weeks on the fates of the "missing" made it all the harder.[122] The padre rose to the moment. His congregation sang Psalm 23, even the shy men joining in. Smith's sermon—it was more a sharing of feelings than instruction—focused on reminding the assembly why they were there. "We give ... our grateful thanks for those fine men, who we have known as comrades. In the presence of their sacrifice we can only bow our heads in reverence." After praying for the wounded, he turned to the prisoners of war—"In what for them is defeat wilt Thou give to them confidence and hope [and] deliver them from bitterness." Then, thinking not just of the officers and men in front of him but the many loved ones back home, "give to those who mourn ... the comfort God has promised [and] may anxious hearts soon be set at rest." He concluded with the hope that God would "keep in us that hunger and thirst after righteousness."[123]

When he'd got back to Seaford, a despairing "Doc" Alexander had scribbled in his diary—"Terrible here today—all these men gone, for what purpose?"[124] Yet within a few days he could see some positives. While not denying that "the days following the return were full of gloom," he was relieved "the spirit of the men was not dampened."[125] In fact, army censorship reports, gleaned from the letters written to Canada by men from all of the participating units, were reassuringly positive, in spite of the losses.[126] There was also a notably more realistic view of what it would take to win the war. As Brig. Wyman put it in a report to Lt.-Gen. Crerar, "the war has now become a very personal matter to every officer and man in [the Calgary Regiment]."[127] Even British civilians took note that almost overnight the Canadians were a far more serious lot.

Autopsy

The autopsy of Jubilee began almost immediately, and one might add by both sides. The German command was shocked by the scale of the raid, which they had neither expected nor detected forming up. And they were impressed by the depth of the intelligence on the area's defences. On the other hand, they were well satisfied with their own defensive preparations and the fighting prowess of their garrison. As for the plan and execution of the attack, the assessment of the 15th Army Headquarters was blunt. Among its most telling points, that "the Englishman [sic] had underestimated the strength of the defences, and therefore, at most of his landing places ... found himself in a hopeless position as soon as he came ashore."[128] Beyond this, they questioned numerous elements of the plan, not least the sacrifice of dozens of the most modern British tanks when both topography and the character of the anti-tank defences ensured they could not be used to advantage.[129] None of their post-raid analysis dwelt much on the actual operation of the tanks, but given the impossibility of the task, they took pains to note "the tank crews did not lack spirit."[130] The speedy dismissal of Maj.-Gen. Roberts from his 2nd Division command was unfair, designed mostly to cover up the deficiencies of Canadians farther up the chain of command. But the post-mortem conducted by British and Canadian staffs acknowledged the raid had failed utterly, and consequently learned much that proved useful.[131]

As for the tanks' role, the analysis spent little time discussing this. Tanks were used at Dieppe mostly because they were available, but only in "an enthusiastic plan based on too much faith" would they have been deployed in a "theater of operations ... considered ... most unsuitable for tank warfare."[132] A clear appreciation of how the Calgary Regiment had performed only became available when the senior officer captured, Maj. C. E. Page, B Squadron's CO, was medically repatriated fourteen months later. Having interviewed every other officer POW while they were ensconced at Oflag VII-B, he returned with detailed information on what the tanks had achieved. Both RAF reconnaissance and German propaganda films showed virtually all of the Churchills somewhere on the beach or partially submerged by the rising tide, which reinforced the view that the great majority had only advanced a short distance before being immobilized—in other words they'd made a minimal contribution to the fighting. Page knew that at least a dozen and maybe as many as fifteen had gotten over the seawall and onto the promenade where they had manoeuvred about and furiously engaged the enemy, in some cases for hours.[133] The concentration of tanks on the beach at the end of the fighting—only five remained on the promenade, all disabled—was a consequence of all the "runners" being recalled to reinforce a defensive perimeter for the evacuation. Page also reported that enemy fire had eventually immobilized eighteen tanks and another four had lost a track to the infamous shingle. Moreover, no crewman had suffered more than minor wounds while inside his tank, no tank had had its armour penetrated, and none had caught fire and burned out, a tribute to the Churchill's robust protection. With good reason, Page and the other officer prisoners felt strongly that the presence of tanks, including the disabled ones, and their continual firing until they ran out of ammunition or joined in the general surrender, dissuaded the Germans from rushing the beach during the evacuation.[134]

It is hard to talk about any "good fortune" at Dieppe but ironically the tank crews that landed, while trapped on the promenade by the anti-tank obstacles blocking street exits, were also probably saved by them. A battery of 75-mm anti-tank guns—lethal for a Churchill's side armour—had been brought up by mid-morning only to find their view of what would have otherwise been open-sight targets blocked by the massive slabs of concrete.[135] And as frustrating as milling around was, crews knew they were far better off inside their Churchills than huddled in the open like most of their countrymen. Overall, only a dozen members were killed, with another dying of his wounds in captivity, and a further twenty-three were wounded, four of whom were evacuated.[136] Conversely, their role as an improvised rearguard that fought till the bitter end to make possible the evacuation of many others made them part of Roberts' "abandoned," ensuring most of the men who landed were taken prisoner, 157 all told, or about 90 percent.[137] Nor should it be forgotten that the decision to continue fighting their tanks, rather than abandon them as soon as the evacuation was authorized *for all troops*, was a decision made by tank commanders. The Calgary Regiment had fought valiantly and maintained a remarkable level of cohesion throughout the raid. When the need for individual initiative was thrust on them, they seized it. But they had had little opportunity to show the capabilities of armour.

As the Canadian Army's chief historian Charles Stacey concluded a quarter century later, "an assault operation of this type [was] obviously not a suitable introduction to battle for troops who [had] never fought."[138] That said, more experience or even more training—and by the standards of 1944 neither the armour nor infantry were close to being adequately trained—would have made little and probably no difference because the plan was so terribly flawed. Jubilee represented the best in Allied thinking about landing on the French coast in mid-1942. That it did not in 1943 and 1944, when the detailed planning for D-Day was carried out, speaks tellingly about the Dieppe raid's legacy. Finally, when lamenting the awful losses we must remember that there would have been no Dieppe in 1942 without Canadians playing the largest role, such was the determination of Canadian soldiers and their commanders to test their mettle, and of the Canadian government and people to have them try.

Home and Heartache

"Canadian civilians, particularly those who had lost relatives, saw only the casualty lists and the failure," wrote army historian C. P. Stacey in the official history, "[and] the public mind continued to dwell upon it for months, and comment, frequently very ill-informed, continued in the press and elsewhere."[139] His assessment was certainly insensitive to the feelings of Albertans or the home communities of the other units sacrificed in the raid. Glancing through the *Calgary Herald* in the months preceding Dieppe, one sees plenty of death notices, usually accompanied by the smiling picture of a young airman. But it was the sheer scale of the Dieppe losses—over 900 Canadians killed in a single day—that shocked the nation. For days, and in some cases weeks, the fate of those from the 14th Army Tank Battalion taken prisoner—even whether they were prisoners, and not dead—remained unknown. Moreover, because of the geographical pattern of the unit's recruitment in February 1941, the anxiety in some smaller Alberta communities was especially acute.

As one would expect, the first news of Jubilee was vague—the *Herald* simply reporting that unnamed Canadian units had been involved in a successful commando raid on Dieppe, but that losses were expected to be heavy.[140] The following day a banner headline proclaimed "Calgary Tanks at Dieppe Carry Brunt of Attack," with the story again alluding to apparent success but "severe" casualties.[141] On August 21, the newspaper carried a British report about flag-waving crowds cheering the returning members of the Calgary Regiment as they drove into Seaford, offering them beer, meat pies, and cigarettes. Apparently, so the rosy account claimed, smiling troopers had reassured the locals they had given the Germans "something to think about."[142] But the tone changed abruptly once Ottawa began to release casualty lists, although the first two included only a lone member of the Calgary Regiment—Lt.-Col. Andrews—as missing in action. Five days after the raid, the *Herald* headlined

"More Alberta Soldiers Missing After Dieppe—Calgary Regiment Loss Mounts in New List."[143] Knowing their neighbours were desperate for solid information, next of kin had begun contacting the newspaper with their private news as personal telegrams from England began reaching the city and surrounding communities. Capts. George Valentine and T. A. Turney and Tpr. Jim Horne were now officially missing in action. But the families of Lt. Dave Clapperton and Capt. "Doc" Alexander had been similarly notified, yet both had sent off personal cables confirming they were back in England and unwounded.[144] Capt. Bill Payne's wife shared word she'd received from another wife that both her husband and Maj. Robert Taylor were safe. Dr. Alexander's wife permitted his first letter to be published, containing as it did mostly stories about brother officers now missing and their state of mind before the attack, the sort of thing that would reassure loved ones. Other families just shared what they knew from official sources—well-known Olds baseball player L/Cpl. Frank Howe had been reported badly wounded, according to his family there, and Tpr. Michael McIntyre, his Drumheller parents advised the *Herald*, was officially missing.[145] So while official releases continued to push the heroism-but-heavy-losses version, mostly thanks to a steady flow of information volunteered by families and friends, the *Herald*'s focus was plainly on the fate of individuals.

Given that the enemy knew full well what had happened, the only people being kept in the dark by the official media coverage were Canadians. It didn't help that the Canadian Army had given over control of media publicity to Combined Operations Headquarters—the British command that masterminded raiding operations. Their plan was to portray Dieppe as a successful dress rehearsal for bigger things, and in the event of a setback, there would just be extra emphasis on the soldiers' heroism. The result was that:

> The Canadian public ... faced a smokescreen when it was told about Dieppe. Stories of heroism, claims of success, and the lack of a timely overview of the raid obscured the reality of the disaster .... For weeks they had to guess at what had transpired .... Those who had lost family, who had to suffer for months waiting to hear the fate of the missing, certainly deserved a more open and honest explanation of what had happened and why.[146]

The willingness of the *Herald*, and no doubt other newspapers across the country, to accept and publish uncensored information from friends and relatives, helped counterbalance this to some degree.

By early September, more detailed accounts from soldiers who had survived the operation began to reach Albertans. One of the first was forwarded from RSM. Norman Kirkham's family in Red Deer, a grim account of how strong the defences had been and how the men had fought until they ran out of ammunition or were forced to abandon disabled tanks. Kirkham, who had not landed himself, did not mince words:

> Wednesday, August 19, will be a very sadly remembered day in Central Alberta ... We who are left are very sick about the grand boys whom we left in France, but we are very, very proud of them and they were magnificent. They fought to the very last shell. The best that we can hope for is that many of them are prisoners of war, but we know that there are many who died fighting for their King and Country.[147]

In a letter to his aunt, a Stettler boy, Tpr. Dick Freeman, glumly acknowledged that he had "just been looking at the nominal roll of those listed as missing in 'B' Squadron and I don't feel particularly cheered." Only twenty-two out of 117 had gotten back to England, and neither the Sgt.-Maj. nor any of the officers were among them. "Things were not what they were supposed to be on the beach," he added, "there being a great deal more opposition than was expected."[148] By mid-month the full casualty story was finally public, at least the raw totals, and while very few from the Calgary Regiment had been confirmed as killed in action, nine officers and 136 other ranks were still listed as missing. Tpr. Roy Gilbert, the loader/radio operator in *Beefy* (and a POW), remembered being told after the war that "the worst feeling [in Stettler] was ... when they found out that we were missing and presumed dead."[149] To deal with her own anguish, his mother had thrown herself into the work of the local "good cheer club" set up to help maintain the spirits of the families of other soldiers serving overseas. It was only toward the end of the year that Gilbert's status could be clarified and officially changed to prisoner of war, thus relieving—though not eliminating—the worry at home.[150]

The painfully slow process by which next of kin learned the fate of their loved ones is best illustrated with specific examples. In the case of the Calgary Regiment, hardly anyone who knew anything made it back to England, while those who did were prisoners of war. Correspondence from the latter only began to arrive in late 1942 and early 1943 and was heavily self-censored so the German authorities would not restrict mailing privileges, while communication between the German and Canadian governments was shunted through the International Red Cross, a time-consuming process. Tpr. V. F. Olliffe went ashore as driver of one of the regiment's scout cars. On August 24 his mother was notified by telegram that he was missing in action. Some weeks later, she and her husband were visited by Cpl. Helmer, who had been awarded the MM for his selfless actions assisting Dr. Alexander and was home on leave. He told them their son was dead. She heard nothing more until November when a letter arrived from Padre Smith:

> I am very sorry to have to inform you that your lad, Freddie, died in the action at Dieppe. We have been forbidden to send word about lads being killed except where official notice has come to the regiment. In this case I wrote to [L/Cpl.] Frank Howe, who was with Freddie in the scout car. Frank himself was at death's door for a considerable time and when I saw him it would have been criminal to have harrowed him by questions about the other lads. Frank has just written to me as best he could. A shell pierced their scout car and struck your lad so that he died instantly. He never knew what happened to him .... It will be a sad Christmas for you, to have this word. There are many empty hearts this Christmas.[151]

After four months with no news from the army, an understandably upset Hilda Olliffe wrote to the Office of Records, inquiring why her son was still listed as missing despite the fact that "we have received proof of his death from members of his regiment ... Why does it take so long for parents to be informed of the truth?"[152] In fact, unbeknownst to her, the process to declare him deceased was already underway. Given that she knew her son had died, the telegram that arrived on April 15 likely brought relief instead of the usual heartache: "Regret deeply M60232 Trooper Victor Frederick Olliffe previously reported missing now officially reported killed in action nineteeth August 1942 authority German official death list."[153]

A fuller text of official condolences was mailed a week later, soon followed by the standard royal condolences. On 3 June 1943 Ottawa issued the death certificate necessary for accessing veterans' benefits and the life insurance policy soldiers frequently purchased for their next of kin. Later that month she was further notified that the Canadian Army had received word through the veterans department of the Vichy government that her son's remains had been interred in the village cemetery at Hautot-sur-Mer, just west of Dieppe.[154] Olliffe's mother continued to receive correspondence from the various bureaucracies responsible for assisting the next of kin. Though always considerate and informative, they were also a constant reminder of loss. The last came on 4 September 1945, a list of personal effects recovered by the Red Cross from Victor's body—one photo and a burnt pay book. After the war, his remains were reinterred in the Dieppe Commonwealth War Graves Cemetery, also in Hautot-sur-Mer.

L/Cpl. Dwight Welch, a twenty-three-year-old from Erskine, Alberta, who had been assigned to one of the beach parties from B Squadron, was severely wounded by machine-gun fire. Transported to the Reserve Hospital for Prisoners of War in Obermassfeld, he was twice operated on but died on the 31st. With a British padre conducting the service, Welch was buried in the nearby Meiningen town cemetery. A German firing party attended, along with three British officers, including his surgeon, Maj. G. M. Hadley, and an honour guard of POW orderlies and patients. Dr. Hadley wrote a report to the Swiss legation in Berlin hoping it could be forwarded to the British Red Cross, with portions of it intended to assure the next of kin in Canada that "everything that could be done for him [was] and that he was not allowed to suffer."[155] A summary reached Welch's father in November, a couple of weeks after Ottawa had issued the formal death certificate. The telegram changing his son's status from "missing" to "died of wounds" had arrived on September 21.[156]

Thirty-one-years-old and unmarried, Tpr. Bobby Cornelssen had lived in Stettler his whole life before enlisting in the regiment during the recruiting wave of February 1941. At Dieppe he was serving as the driver of *Bellicose*. Like so many, he was initially declared missing in action. His mother Rose learned of his fate from letters sent by prisoners of war to other residents in the town. The first news came in the early autumn from Lt. Ed Bennett, who had commanded *Bellicose* and was now a POW. "My driver Bobby Cornelssen was killed after we returned to the beach when he went out into the water to rescue a chap who was floundering around," Bennett wrote, "I was blind from my burns … but my radio operator (Tpr. A. F. Anderson) told me."[157] Tpr. Al Johnson, a crewman in *Bob*, wrote his mother in late September from Stalag VIII-B, and as with so many of the early letters, he mentioned the fate of everyone he could think of from his home area, knowing his parents would circulate the news. Johnson ended his enumeration with "Bobby Cornelssen is the only one from home I know for sure that got it."[158] Tpr. Michael McIntyre (*Beefy*), also imprisoned in the camp, wrote a Stettler friend around the same time, confiding to her "I found out this morning that … poor Bobby Cornelssen got it too."[159] By December the army was able to confirm Cornelssen's fate and so informed his mother a week before Christmas, painful timing that could not be avoided.

Conclusions

All elements of the 14th Army Tank Battalion's first action save one—the men themselves—had been found wanting. The unit had lost the better part of half of its fighting strength in a matter of hours, and with that, much of the thirteen months' work to transform the men into an effective armoured force was thrown away. Losing the intimate bonds of trust and the teamwork that only sustained training can forge, and which underpin any successful combat unit, was especially devastating. The missing ranks could—and were—swiftly replaced. But the challenge would be rebuilding the regiment *as a regiment*. The war would not allow much time to carry out these tasks, one requiring leadership of the first order, not just at the command level but throughout the ranks. In this, the survival of a sizable cadre of experienced men would prove a huge asset. And rebuilt the regiment would be—to play its full part in achieving the final victory.

6

From Dieppe to Ortona

Up from the Ashes

The raid on Dieppe was a disaster, the tanks crews, like the infantry, having been defeated before they landed. Quickly rebuilding the 14th Canadian Armoured Regiment (as it would soon be renamed) was a high priority for the army, one it carried out successfully. Within a year, the 14th's officers and men would be fighting and winning on a grim, blood-soaked ridge none could have put on a map in 1942.

At Dieppe the officer contingent had suffered especially heavy losses—fourteen just from the tank crews, either killed or taken prisoner, and seventeen out of thirty-three overall.[1] Apart from Begg's elevation to commanding officer, there were changes almost across the board. Maj. R. R. Taylor (formerly commanding A Squadron) took over as second-in-command with Lt. D. H. McIndoe becoming intelligence officer, while Capt. D. F. Cameron returned from his brigade appointment to serve as adjutant. Capt. F. T. Jenner was reassigned from a staff training position to assume command of A Squadron, while Maj. R. B. Purves took over B Squadron with Capt. Debruce G. Trotter replacing him as second-in-command. Finally Maj. A. J. Miller assumed command of C Squadron with Capt I. A. Allison as second-in-command. Replacement officers and men soon filled the gaps, with the army's reinforcement system providing good men and providing them quickly.

By the beginning of September, the tank crews were at the Minehead firing range. Given the flood of replacements, this was the first time many had operated the Churchill's armament or repaired the tank in the field. Gunnery training had to proceed methodically, starting with the basics of stationary firing at fixed and then moving targets, and then from a moving tank. There was no lack of enthusiasm, and the new crews made rapid progress.[2] A detachment from the British 11th Armoured Division School assisted with more technical crew training, staying at Seaford for two months.[3] For a time, Wyman exempted the regiment from any tactical schemes or exercises that required squadrons to be away from camp so as not to interrupt basic instruction.[4] Unlike human reinforcements, replacement Churchills were initially slow to arrive, and still plagued by reliability issues, the brigade commander's vigorous complaining notwithstanding.[5] The month closed with some cheering news as Lt.-Col. Begg received confirmation of the awards for exemplary courage and leadership earned at Dieppe. These included his own DSO as well as MCs for Capts. Alexander and Eldred and MMs for L/Cpls. George Greenwell and Calvin Helmer and Tpr. Archie Anderson.[6] As was inevitable, others equally deserving were passed over.[7]

By late October basic training and coursework had advanced to the point where the squadrons were able to commence elementary tactical manoeuvres.[8] The battalion was also effectively at full strength—thirty-nine officers and 596 other ranks including attached personnel—and the same could be said of its vehicle strength, including fifty-seven Churchill tanks, though some were older models suitable only for training.[9] With so many untested men on hand, and perhaps feeling he needed to establish his own distinctive style of command, Begg had been continually emphasizing the need for his soldiers to show discipline in everything they did, particularly in things that might strike some of them as the minor transgressions of citizen soldiers. For instance he launched a crackdown on bartering or selling food to civilians. Given wartime Britain's severe rationing, nothing save problems with women would tarnish the Canadians' reputation more. Carrying civilian (invariably younger female) passengers in army vehicles was also strictly prohibited. And casual or slovenly dress in public, even when off duty, now brought serious consequences. Basically no breaches of military order were deemed minor now, but "a direct reflection [on the offender's] unit" that wouldn't be tolerated.[10]

For reasons never explained, the brigade's three armoured regiments exchanged camps in late November, with the 14th moving to the Ontarios' former camp in Worthing, about 40 kms to the west on the other side of Brighton.[11] But there was no pause in training. Indeed, the excellent progress made during the previous three months meant the emphasis could shift to the "practical" work necessary to get the battalion—and hence the brigade—up to a combat-ready state. The difficulty of carrying out large-scale mechanized training in the cramped confines of rural England is underappreciated. With few official training grounds, tank squadrons had no option but to pick their way along narrow country lanes. No matter what it looked like, southern England was not an occupied country, and local farmers were quick to claim damages for demolished stone fences and gates, rutted fields, and injured livestock. And accident or not, a 36-tonne tank made short work of a bicycle or car, or in rare cases, their drivers or passengers. "It is recognized that as one cannot make omelettes without breaking eggs, so one cannot train large bodies of troops without doing *some* damage," the 14th's war diary lamented.[12] Unfortunately, some of the practices adopted to spare the farmers and avoid the courts—particularly the tendency to stick to the shoulders of roads rather than venturing farther afield—led to a dangerous tendency by British and Canadian tank crews alike, which the Germans would be quick to exploit.

Irate farmers and bicyclists aside, Worthing and the surrounding area proved welcoming. There was such a good turnout for the first couple of regimental dances that the CO made them a regular Saturday evening event. Most of the associations between Canadian soldiers and the civilian population in Worthing were positive ones, but the incidence of venereal disease infection continued to be a problem. In December, the medical personnel started distributing prophylactics without asking the recipients to identify themselves, which it was hoped would encourage men to seek help. And an American Army instructional film, *Sex Hygiene*, was reshown, with the adjutant sternly recommending that "attendance will be [as] strong as possible."[13] But as Brig. Wyman lamented, nearby Brighton "with its obvious distractions does not lend itself to furthering the welfare of the troops along desired lines."[14] The onset of colder weather also launched the Canadian Army's much anticipated schedule of winter sports. Having grown up in a place where open-air rinks usually sufficed, the army managed to book skating time at the only nearby arena, saving the hockey season. The season was a sensation for the regiment's team, capped with a 5-0 thrashing of the Three Rivers Regiment in the brigade championship. Hopes were high, then, when they played in the I Corps championship game at the Brighton arena, cheered on by 160 of their mates, but unfortunately the Alberta boys ended up on the short end of a 4-2 score.[15]

Christmas 1942 and Thoughts of Home

On Christmas Eve, 1942, in what had quickly become a tradition at Canadian camps, the regiment held parties for over 300 English children from the Worthing area whose fathers were either away on active service or prisoners of war. Each of the children had received a personalized invitation from Lt.-Col. Begg. Several of the responses, in laboured handwriting or carefully printed, with a hovering mother obviously helping with spelling, were included in the regiment's war diary. Six-year-old Leila Rothstein's sweet, if rather formal, note was typical: "Dear Sir, Thank you very much for the invitation to your party. I shall be delighted to come. Yours sincerely, Miss Leila Rothstein." The entertainment—a mix of games played with the soldiers, a Punch & Judy show, and reels of cartoons—was a terrific hit, as was the formal tea with cookies, cakes and a gift for each child. Eyes popped when they opened the latter—two chocolate bars donated from the soldiers' own parcels from home.[16] It was an emotional time, with not a few tears among the officers and men, many of whom had either younger siblings or their own children, none of whom they'd seen for at least a year and a half.

The 25th dawned mild and clear. It was the regiment's second and, as it turned out, last Christmas in England. After the Protestant and Catholic services, the men were paraded for their Christmas dinner, the menu consisting of roast turkey and roast pork, Brussels sprouts, potatoes, dressing, plum pudding, and mince pies. Though the turkey was in short supply, every soldier got a portion. Following British Army tradition, officers and senior NCOs served the ranks beer. Brig. Wyman stopped by briefly to wish everyone a Merry Christmas.[17] A somewhat delayed, but most welcome, Christmas present arrived on December 28 when Canadian Army pay rates were raised.[18] The year, which had brought such tragedy, ended with a renewed sense of purpose.

Still More Training

Plans had been formulated to carry out intensive tank-infantry training throughout First Canadian Army during January and February. By its completion, all troop leaders and platoon commanders would have practised minor tactical situations of the sort they would encounter in mobile operations, as would all squadron leaders and company commanders. The 1st Army Tank Brigade would provide the armour. That the 14th was included confirms how far its own training had progressed in the four months since the Dieppe raid. The exercises began immediately after New Year's, with some of the tankers' time also spent on the Dorset coast working with landing craft.[19] The latter exercises culminated in a dawn attack on a beach west of Cowes on the Isle of Wight, an eerie reminder of the preparations for Operation Rutter a mere seven months earlier. As February drew down, all the tank crews, accompanied by a dozen Churchills, spent a priceless day at the Beach Head gunnery range, their first firing practice on a proper gunnery range in five months.[20]

Exercise Spartan

On February 22, Lt.-Col. Begg gave a briefing to his squadron leaders on the forthcoming Exercise Spartan, an unprecedented war game involving the bulk of the Canadian Army in England along with numerous British formations, altogether ten divisions plus ancillary units. It was particularly significant for the Canadians, as it marked the first time McNaughton's First Canadian Army took the field under his command. Things went fairly well at first, but soon unravelled in a cascade of command and control errors by McNaughton and his staff. By the time these problems were sorted out, Spartan had been terminated.[21] The British considered Spartan a poor show, and their critique of McNaughton's performance was especially harsh. Before the year was out he was ignominiously ousted by a Canadian government (and Army command) broadly in sympathy with the British assessment.[22] For its part, the Calgary Regiment had ended up playing only a modest operational role in the exercise. Over eight days, commencing March 4, they had driven their Churchills a gruelling 250 kms, from the concentration area west of Portsmouth to well north of Reading, impressively losing only a single tank to mechanical breakdown. Despite preparing to launch several attacks, they were stood down every time—to the great disappointment of both officers and men.[23] In a matter of days all the men who had been involved in Spartan as well as their vehicles were back in Worthing.[24] By the second half of March regular training was back in full swing, and so was the post-mortem of Spartan. The battalion's contribution was a report compiled by Maj. Purves largely based on Begg's canvass of his officers. There was broad agreement on two points—the need for an adequate (that is, not road-bound) reconnaissance vehicle so the tanks wouldn't be blind half the time, and an end to planners' zeal for stand-to (prepare to attack) orders, which interfered with everything, not least the hours of daily maintenance required to keep the Churchills moving.[25]

A Brief Ram Experiment

Shortly after the termination of Spartan, word filtered down that all three tank battalions would be re-equipping with the Canadian-built and -designed Ram tank.[26] Between the Churchills' demonstrated imperviousness to German anti-tank fire, and the fact that most of the mechanical bugs had now been sorted out, most crews were "pretty disgusted" at the prospect.[27] Unfortunately this was viewed as the usual army grumbling, and as more and more Rams arrived, crews were resigned to putting their Churchills in first-class running order and packing them off to some lucky British regiment.[28] For a time training had to be interrupted as everyone struggled to master their new equipment.[29]

A New Commanding Officer

Post-Spartan training had barely resumed when the army announced that Lt.-Col. Cyril H. Neroutsos would take over as commanding officer. Begg's roots in the regiment ran deep, and he was well liked (and respected). Deservedly, he had received much of the credit for rebuilding the 14th after Dieppe, but field command was increasingly viewed as a younger man's game. Neroutsos was already quite familiar with the battalion from his time with them during Spartan when he had temporarily replaced an "injured" Begg. But the transition and his ensuing fourteen-month tenure as CO (before stepping down for medical reasons) never went smoothly. Many of the 14th's officers viewed Neroutsos as an outsider, and more than a few thought there were perfectly qualified men in the regiment who could have been chosen, or that there should have been no change at all.[30] Neroutsos displayed an aggressive streak in action, and was a loner by nature, but he was a capable tank officer and never lost the support of his superiors.

To Scotland Again

On April 27 word came the regiment would shortly be moving, and five days later the squadrons marched through Worthing for the last time, bound for "somewhere in Scotland."[31] Apart from training in a new locale, more than a few hoped they might finally be headed for action. In fact, they were commencing the final preparations for their transfer to the Mediterranean Theatre—in ten weeks less a day, their tanks would roll ashore in Sicily. The battalion's new camp was a lodge (the other ranks would make do with Nissen huts) situated in the picturesque Scottish border country, just north of the village of Langholm. Here, the officers were able to celebrate a delayed St. George's Day anniversary and in some style. As a sombre Dr. Alexander scanned the room, he counted only seven men who had been at their first dinner overseas only two years earlier.[32]

The Sherman Tank

Primarily because of ready access to the American logistical chain in the Mediterranean, the 1st Army Tank Brigade was going to be equipped with the American-built Sherman M4, the basic tank they would fight in for the remainder of the war.[33] In its many versions, the Sherman was the principal (and frequently most maligned) Allied tank of World War II. Derived from the M3, its design facilitated mass production (50,000 were built) and ease of shipment by sea. As contemporary tanks went, the Sherman had much to recommend it. It was mechanically reliable and easy to repair, with a spacious interior for the five-man crew, a good turn of speed, and solid cross-country capability. But they were also slab-sided and too high, making their profile an easier target for enemy gunners. The Sherman's most infamous flaw was a supposed propensity to catch fire when hit, but this was a universal problem with tanks, and in the case of the Sherman pretty much resolved later in the war by design improvements in ammunition stowage. Well supplied with escape hatches, it was also (relatively) easy to bail out of, so survivability was high, endearing it to crews. Standard armament was a 75-mm gun with adequate armour-piercing capability, at least until 1944. Furthermore, the gun had an excellent high explosive (HE) round for bombardment purposes and general infantry support, which is what the regiment would mostly be called upon to do. A pair of .30-calibre Browning machine guns rounded out the armament. Though it was approaching obsolescence by 1944, the M4, with some helpful improvements, continued to be deployed to the end, swamping the German Army with sheer numbers. It was the Mark V (a British designation), with a slightly more complicated power plant and extra maintenance requirements that found its way to allies via Lend-Lease.[34] First impressions of their new tank were positive, and it certainly helped that while some crews still pined for their Churchills, no one wanted to keep the Ram.[35]

Mediterranean Plans

In April 1943 the chief of the imperial general staff, Field Marshall Alan Brooke, had shared with his Canadian opposite number forthcoming plans for the Mediterranean Theatre, and specifically whether a Canadian infantry division and tank brigade might be made available. Apart from Dieppe, the substantial Canadian Army stationed in Britain had seen no action. While national pride had once seemed a valid justification for keeping the overseas army together until it could strike a decisive blow, its continued absence from the battlefield had become an intolerable situation—for the officers and men, senior commanders, the government, and a majority of Canadians at home. Consequently the offer was quickly accepted, with the 1st Infantry Division and the 1st Army Tank Brigade being assigned to the Anglo-American force intending to invade Sicily.[36] On May 8, as his command completed their move to Scotland, Brig. Wyman confided to his unit commanders and brigade staff that their next move would involve "a long sea voyage and a tropical climate."[37]

Working-up in Scotland

The move to Scotland made it possible to train in much more rugged terrain, a big plus considering what was coming. New Shermans continued to arrive and with those on hand basic familiarization commenced under the direction of the 148th Battalion Royal Tank Regiment. Though the Sherman and Ram shared many similarities, there remained a lot to master and not much time to do it. Experienced hands loaned from a British unit that had already converted to the Sherman helped immeasurably.[38] Initially, as much time as possible was spent on the Kirkcudbright range honing firing skills and building critical crew teamwork.[39] Another two weeks was spent in waterproofing vehicles, all of which, tanks included, had been replaced with brand new models. It was a time-consuming, onerous process that had to be done with great care if it was going to produce the desired result.[40] Everything now pointed to a deployment though no one spoke openly about it. Reinforcing the suspicions, Lt.-Col.

Neroutsos assembled his entire command in the local cinema to watch two security movies: *Name, Rank and Number* and the rather ominously entitled *Next of Kin*.[41] Save for a bit of poaching, discipline was not much of a problem in rural Scotland, the isolation from temptation being almost complete.[42] However, maintaining a smart appearance remained a high priority—one might say, an obsession—and in the view of their commanding officer, "still far below [the] standard demanded." Of special concern were their black berets, which were to "be worn ONE INCH ABOVE THE EYEBROWS, level on the forehead with the top pulled straight over to the right side, badge directly above the left eye."[43] Violators were promptly put on report. Fortunately, the tankers would soon have something more useful to shoot at than Scottish deer or rabbits.

To War Again

By the second week of June, preparations were completed, and all personnel were granted four-day embarkation leaves. Advance parties then proceeded to the embarkation ports to assist in the complicated process of loading supplies and equipment. All personnel had been poked and prodded, endured rounds of shots, and been issued summer kit, which certainly pointed to "The Med." Promptly at 0800 on the morning of June 20, most of the remaining personnel (some would stay behind to prepare the camp for its new occupants), formed up by squadrons and led by Lt.-Col. Neroutsos, marched to Langholm station. Accompanied by the Ontarios, they were soon steaming northward to the Clyde. As was the custom with troop trains, villagers paused to waive and shout encouragement to the Canadian soldiers as they steamed by. Upon reaching Greenock later in the afternoon, they detrained and, shouldering their kit bags, marched to temporary billets. Two days later, boarding commenced in a steady rain, until by the 25th the entirety of the 1st Brigade's tank arm, along with fuel, ammunition and other supplies, had been safely stowed shipboard.[44] Before long, the LSTs—three of which carried the Calgary Regiment—had dropped anchor, formed up with their escort, and were slowly gliding down the Firth of Clyde toward the open sea. The rest of the battalion's (and brigade's) personnel sailed a few days later in a separate convoy aboard the HMT *Cameronia*. The previous day, all ranks had assembled on the main deck for a brief Dominion Day service where Wyman reminded them how proud he was to command men who "would prove, in the coming action ... that this was the best brigade in the Canadian Army."[45]

Apart from lifeboat and fire drills, and aircraft and submarine watches, there was little of a warlike nature to interrupt the daily routine aboard ship for either group as they steamed to Gibraltar and into the Mediterranean.[46] Sea sickness stalked those aboard the large American-built LSTs (Landing Ship

Tank), which rolled and pitched at the slightest opportunity. Such "training" as could be fit in focused on militarily useful bits of Italian, familiarizing with first aid, hygiene and tropical diseases, and of course plenty of PT.[47] After two years in blacked-out England, the men in the LSTs were enthralled by the lights of Tangier glittering in the night as they slipped by neutral Spanish Morocco.[48] Being faster, the troop ships had passed the LSTs and docked in Algiers on July 10, the day of the Sicily landings. Three days later the men aboard the LSTs put into Siracusa (Syracuse), which the British had captured two days earlier.[49] Late in the afternoon, the LSTs beached and began disgorging their cargo which, amidst inevitable chaos, formed up and headed off to their planned harbouring area at Cassabile, 20 kms to the south. Reaching it around 0200, the tired crews spent most of the few remaining hours of darkness camouflaging their vehicles and digging slit trenches.[50] On the same day the *Cameronia*, carrying the rest of Neroutsos' command, had dropped anchor off Malta.

Operation Husky ... The Plan

Operation Husky went through several iterations before the adoption of a definitive plan in early May. Seaborne assaults by American, British and Canadian troops, supported by airborne landings, would be made along the southern and eastern coasts, stretching from Siracusa to Licata. After quickly seizing several ports to consolidate the landing area, breakouts—their exact nature to be determined by events—would overrun the remainder of the island. The British Eighth Army, which included the Canadians, made up the Allies' right flank, and the American Seventh Army the left.[51]

Disappointing Times

After having gotten little if any sleep, the men were roused at 0530. After Lt.-Col. Neroutsos and his senior officers received their first briefing on the regiment's (and brigade's) role, the CO, accompanied by his intelligence officer (Lt. C. G. Elliott) set off to familiarize themselves with the front line.[52] The rest of the personnel and vehicles put ashore around mid-morning on July 17, finally reuniting the battalion. It wasn't long before they had their first encounter with the enemy when a patrol encountered eight Italian artillerymen near the camp who happily surrendered. Mostly everyone was waiting for orders to advance. In the sweltering heat, at least being close to the sea provided ample opportunity to swim. Finally, in the early morning of the 21st, the battalion set out on a twelve-hour drive replete with numberless twists and turns to Vignali where, after a brief respite, they were to continue on to an assembly area overlooking the Catania plain. Refuelling tanks was dangerous work. Possibly due to careless smoking, during such a stop one of the Shermans caught fire and

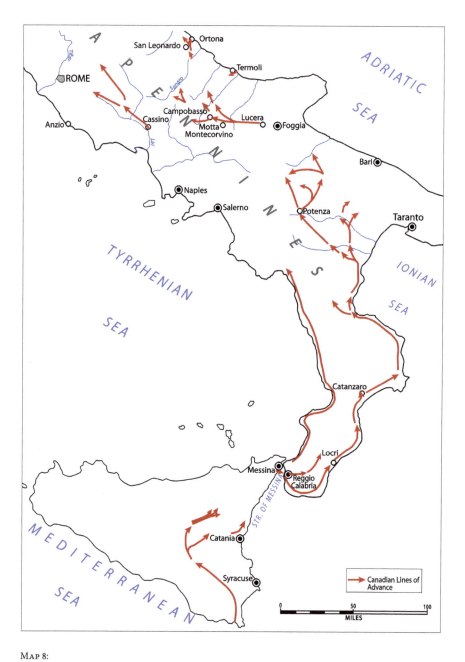

Map 8:
Canadian Operations in Southern Italy, July 1943 – June 1944.

exploded, badly burning Maj. R. R. Taylor, the CO of B Squadron, and Capt. J. W. Singleton, his second-in-command, as well as the driver, Tpr. J. L. Monz.[53] The column wasn't able to set off again until midnight, and what should have been a short leg turned into a nightmare when the Ontario's tanks ahead of them nearly collapsed a bridge, necessitating an exhausting cross-country detour. The day offered the first of many lessons on the perils of manoeuvring through hilly country on poor Italian roads.[54]

Generally, first impressions of Italy were not good. "Doc" Alexander, admittedly a man of strong opinions, dismissed the country and its people alike:

> The heat was terrific, the dust very bad and the whole country, with the exception of [irrigated] garden plots, were dry and parched. The hills were bare and nothing of natural beauty could be seen ... The small towns ... are unbelievably filthy—row on row of dirty stone houses, in which lived people, donkeys, pigs, hens etc.—with no attempt at sanitation.

As for the Sicilians:

> [They] were very swarthy, the women in particular were dirty and unkempt—the children were terrible—the men showed a certain semblance to civilized folk, but were a sly underhanded looking bunch.[55]

While the Calgary and Ontario Regiments had been slowly working their way northward unopposed, British forces advancing ahead of them and along the coast toward Catania had encountered determined German (though not Italian) resistance. Meanwhile 1st Canadian Division, supported by the Three Rivers Regiment, had fought their way inland toward Enna, which they bypassed, and were now battling their way eastward, successfully evicting the enemy from Leonforte and Assoro on the same day the 14th's tanks had reached their new assembly area (Scordia). During the next few days, the 14th stayed put, though they were on alert to deal with any German armour attacking nearby British positions.[56] On July 26, Field Marshall Montgomery dropped by to give a Monty-style pep talk, reminding his audience that he had reviewed them in Sussex and how pleased he was to command Canadians again. For that he was roundly cheered, though as the tankers crowded around his staff car, pranksters discreetly lifted all four hubcaps as souvenirs.[57]

Two days later, the day Canadian infantry fought their way into Agira, unhinging German defences southwest of Mt. Etna, word came down that the brigade would pass to the XIII British Corps which, as part of the ponderous

British advance toward Messina, was engaged in bitter fighting. Finally they faced the prospect of action, but it was not to be. Along with the Ontarios, their role was to block a German counterattack that never came.[58] Canadian combat operations had all but ended on August 6 when the 1st Division went into reserve. As evidenced by the start of the brigade baseball league on August 9, normalcy was returning.[59]

The Luck of the Draw

The proverbial luck of the draw had denied the Calgary Regiment its chance at combat in Sicily. It had been mostly an infantry-artillery war, with reduced opportunities for tanks. Stoney Richardson later recalled that Sicily "had [been] almost a rest."[60] And thanks to the abundance of fresh fruit and vegetables, whether bought from local peasants or "liberated" from empty orchards and fields, the fare was a noticeable improvement from England. As usual, letters home often made their way into local newspapers. The first from Sicily published by the *Herald* was from Lt. D. W. Clapperton, reassuring his parents that (on July 14) he was passing his time on "a quiet beach, sitting in the sun ...," and not to worry.[61] A report from the field penned by veteran war correspondent Ross Munro followed a little over a month later, and gave *Herald* readers their first clear account of the Sicily fighting. Under the headline "Calgary Tanks Invaded Sicily—Alberta Soldiers Disappointed At Lack of Fight in Campaign," Munro didn't try to hide the truth, and was presumably allowed to do so because the tone—soldiers keen to get at the enemy—would have pleased the military and was perfectly true.[62] Still, the failure to see some real action frustrated officers and men alike, and definitely undermined morale.

At a brigade conference on August 11, everyone's attention was focused on the presentation by the commanding officer of the 12th Army Tank Battalion, Lt.-Col. E. L. Booth, as he discussed useful lessons learned from their recent fighting.[63] Almost exclusively, the latter had entailed the classic "infantry tank" role of fire support for the infantry, serving as mobile artillery to supress or obliterate defensive strongpoints, with their enemy usually being anti-tank weapons, including mines, and rarely other tanks.[64] The extensive training along these very lines they had been put through in England had obviously paid dividends.

For the Allies, Sicily had to be deemed a success. Casualties were not excessive,[65] and the embarrassing evacuation of the bulk of the German garrison along with their equipment to the mainland where they would have to be defeated a second time was merely a disappointing ending. Both American and Canadian troops acquitted themselves well, as did their British opposite numbers, who had considerably more combat experience.

Where Next?

The question of what might be done after Sicily had been overrun was hotly debated. The compromise—a landing in strength in southern Italy, with objectives rather vague beyond that—crystallized in early June. The royalist military putsch deposing Mussolini and his Fascist government in late July led to a final plan calling for British forces to land at the tip of Calabria in early September, with a follow-up landing by British and American forces at Salerno farther up the coast shortly thereafter. As part of XIII British Corps, the Canadians were to participate in the earlier operation. The great unknown was how far south in Italy would the enemy mount any serious resistance. In fact, the German Army fully intended to defend as much of Italy as it could, making the Allies bleed for every kilometre.[66] Hitler's determination that his troops hold their ground proved a godsend for Allied strategic planners, but cursed the soldiers who would have to root those troops out.

A Brief Interregnum

The 1st Army Tank Brigade would have about three weeks before being committed to battle again. The heat continued unabated, but at least movies resumed. The first screening was a Dagwood and Blondie comedy that offered pin-up queen Rita Hayworth in a supporting (but undoubtedly the most watched) role. A full program of squadron training also resumed, and the sergeants' humbling of the officers 14-7 on the ball diamond was especially well received—by the sergeants. On the evening of the 19th, the first anniversary of the Dieppe raid, memorial services honoured lost comrades. Germans weren't the only threat the liberators faced—malaria was endemic in southern Italy, and the heat combined with the shortage of potable water and the consumption of unwashed fruits and vegetables saw dysentery soar. The threat had been appreciated, and medical staffs had done their best to educate the men. If not a losing battle, it was a constant one, and by late August both illnesses were exacting a steady toll.[67] Lt.-Col. Neroutsos along with some of his headquarters staff spent the last day of the month consulting with the officers of A Squadron as well as meeting others from the 2nd and 3rd Canadian Infantry Brigades. Upon his return, he assembled all of his remaining officers and briefed them on the looming Operation Baytown.[68] On September 1, A Squadron proceeded to Augusta to be loaded onto their LST. By the next evening they were lying offshore, waiting to sail for the enemy coast. Pre-invasion rituals—and the tension that accompanied them—never became old hat.[69]

Operation Baytown

Canadian troops landed just north of Reggio Calabria in the early morning of September 3, mercifully unopposed, and over the next few days managed to seize all of their initial objectives. A Squadron landed on D-Day in support, with B Squadron joining them late the following day. Meanwhile, German units were offering only token resistance as they withdrew into the interior.[70] The population of Reggio Calabria had turned out in their thousands to see the newcomers, "neither cheering nor looking very downcast."[71] As the Canadians began to advance inland into the rugged Aspromonte plateau, Lt.-Col. Neroutsos was sent to reconnoitre the suitability of the terrain for tanks. Seeing the poor state of the roads, the extensive forest, and German demolition efforts first-hand, he reported in the negative. That accomplished, he checked out the coastal road toward Locri, which he reported seemed to be open.[72] Needing confirmation, Maj.-Gen. Guy Simmonds ordered him to seize and hold Locri. Three troops of B Squadron Shermans accompanied by two truck-borne companies of the Carleton and Yorks headed off that very afternoon. They harboured at Melito overnight, then at first light they pushed on up the coastal highway, encountering a number of road and bridge demolitions and the occasional glimpse of German rearguards melting away into the hills. The local Italians, who at first seemed merely "curious," soon became "really overjoyed to see us."[73] By nightfall on September 7, the lead part of the column had managed to reach what remained of Locri, having advanced nearly 100 kms in less than 30 hours.[74] Leaving modest numbers to consolidate, the remainder of Neroutsos' force (which now included the entirety of B Squadron) pressed on in an attempt to thwart more demolitions, reaching Monasterace by evening, just as word reached them Italy had surrendered. The local inhabitants were beyond ecstatic at this turn of events. "Doc" Alexander described their arrival (and several days thereafter) as one long celebration, people waving British and American flags (to go with the large white flag fluttering atop the town halls), cheering and throwing the Canadians flowers and grapes. Crowds of Italian soldiers in uniform swarmed them as well, shaking their hands, shouting choruses of "bravo" and pressing bottles of wine on any who would take them.[75]

The Difficulties of Liberating an Enemy

Despite the outpourings of jubilation seen during the early days, Italian civilians, particularly in the southern half of the country, rarely gave the Allies the sort of heroic welcome their comrades would consistently receive in France and the Low Countries. Apart from families grieving loved ones lost in faraway battles, impoverished rural Italy experienced the war first-hand only when the

Allies arrived. The Germans had not occupied these areas long enough to alienate the population the way they did in central and northern Italy. Destruction, whether the result of land operations or bombing, or merely from trying to squeeze lumbering tanks through narrow streets, tearing the fronts off homes and shops in the process,[76] was mostly the liberators' doing. Individual Italians could be helpful, but overall the population south of Rome struck ordinary Allied soldiers as sullen and ungrateful, "a very poor class of people" who could not be trusted, as the medical officer was soon dismissing them in his diary.[77] This only served to strengthen the troops' view that switching sides was simply opportunism, and reinforce anti-Italian prejudice, especially among British and Canadian troops. After having gazed for days at throngs of Italian soldiers drunkenly celebrating along the roadsides, Alexander's observation that "the war is over for them—but not for us" was telling.[78]

Pressing On

With the weather still baking hot, turning the tanks into ovens, the pursuit continued, slowed only by the numerous demolitions. By September 10, they had reached Catanzaro, astride the neck of the Italian boot, where thanks to Montgomery pausing to give his fighting units a breather and consolidate his logistics, B and A Squadrons were finally reunited. Having advanced some 200 kms in six days, the tanks and other vehicles were badly in need of repairs, and everything, including the men, needed cleaning. At least the beaches on the Gulf of Squillace offered ample opportunity for the latter.[79]

It wasn't long, however, before the Calgary Regiment was again in action. As part of the Anglo-Canadian effort to reduce pressure on the Salerno bridgehead, a mixed force under the command of Lt.-Col. M. P. Bogert (CO of the West Nova Scotia Regiment), which included A Squadron in the lead, pressed north into the Apennines to capture Potenza. Merely reaching the hilltop town was difficult enough, as the route was narrow, winding and hilly, and strewn with numerous anti-tank mines, and of course every bridge had been blown up. But reach it they did, thanks to the heroic work of their sappers. After the initial attack during the night of September 19–20 was stymied, a second, spearheaded by a troop of Maj. Trotter's Shermans, carried the day. The Potenza operation was brilliantly executed and a tribute to all participating units, not the least Trotter's armour.[80] War correspondent Ross Munro penned a story highlighting the Calgary Regiment's key role in capturing "an Italian town," and although it was held back by army censors for nine days, it became the first *Herald* account that did more than hint at what the local boys had been up to.[81]

Motta Montecorvino

On September 28, Lt.-Col. Neroutsos was informed that his tankers would be forming part of the vanguard of another major advance northward, this time to seize and hold Campobasso, some 85 kms northeast of Naples. By late afternoon on September 30, all three squadrons, A Squadron having worked its way cross-country from Potenza, had assembled near their jump-off line close by Foggia.[82] At 0400 the following morning they set off, an impressive column under Neroutsos' overall command, led by its reconnaissance element, the Royal Canadian Dragoons, followed by its armoured fist—the tanks of the Calgary Regiment—and their vital infantry support (the Royal Canadian Regiment). Then came the engineers, a battery of towed anti-tank guns, field and medium artillery regiments, and two more infantry battalions. The 2nd Infantry Brigade would provide flank protection, while the 3rd would constitute a ready reserve. The Eighth Army had grown confident the Germans wouldn't make a stand before they were well north of Rome, and among the officers and men of the fighting units, the belief they had "Jerry on the run" was virtually universal.[83] They would soon learn otherwise.

By 0800, the main portion of the drawn-out column was edging westward along National Route 17, searching for indications of the enemy. Initially the landscape was gently rolling, the highway dotted with signs warning drivers that "Rita Hayworth has curves—so has this road!"[84] But after passing Lucera, with its dominating thirteenth-century fortress, the terrain was transformed into lines of formidable ridges, hills and low mountains across their path offering an excellent view of the advance and ideal positions from which to harry it. Atop the first of these ridges perched the village of Motta Montecorvino. As the recce screen—which included a squadron of tanks—neared, the mood became more apprehensive.[85] Initially, the plan was to organize a full-scale infantry-tank attack supported by all available artillery to seize Motta, but traffic control failures kilometres to the rear eliminated the artillery. Assembling his own and the various other commanders present, Neroutsos made it clear he favoured pressing home the attack with what they had, substituting a "shoot" from C Squadron's Shermans for the absent artillery. But effectively, the infantry and armour would have to go in alone. According to "Doc" Alexander, who was no longer part of the regiment but whose field ambulance unit was supporting his former regiment, "these orders did not meet with general approval."[86] Neroutsos had canvassed for opinions and got them. Lt.-Col. Dan Spry, CO of the Royal Canadian Regiment (RCR), was alarmed over his rifle companies having to rely on improvised fire support. And the senior artillery officer present called flat out for delay until he could get his guns up, arguing that without their suppressing fire the Germans would easily separate the infantry from the tanks, likely a fatal development for both. Maj. R. J. R. (Bob) Donabie, commanding C Squadron, deemed his orders unclear and the task, given the tanks' guns lacked sufficient elevation to fire at targets well above them, probably beyond their capacity. Neroutsos weighed the advice, then ordered the assault to go in at 1600. In fairness, the intelligence supplied proved woefully misleading—the ridge was supposed to be defended by machine guns and mortars, not anti-tank guns. As the orders group broke up Maj. Trotter muttered to Alexander that it was "bloody suicide."[87] Starting at 1600 meant the tanks, some of which were running low on fuel, would not be able to top up. Worse still, it would be dark within two hours, probably about the time they entered Motta.

The Shermans of A and B Squadrons rumbled past the start line right on schedule, followed by the RCR in trucks. Trotter's A Squadron was tasked with attacking the centre of Motta while also encircling it from the left, with Maj. Ritchie's B Squadron encircling it from the right. After dismounting, the RCR companies would follow immediately behind the tanks on foot. In their first major action, the troops of tanks rolled forward with great dash, but machine-gun and mortar fire quickly drove most of the infantry to ground, leaving the tankers to press on alone in the face, ominously, of sporadic anti-tank fire.[88] Spry knew his infantry would be slaughtered if they continued advancing in daylight, and no one disagreed, but calling back the armour was dismissed as well. Things started off badly when a shell hit the Sherman carrying Maj. Robert Purves, who was in overall command, severely concussing him. The two squadron leaders, along with the troop leaders and their crews, were soon plunged into a life-or-death action. The lead troop of B Squadron, commanded by Lt. A. J. Charbonneau, manoeuvred up the hairpin switchbacks leading to the crest and the village. Out of nowhere, an anti-tank round howled past just beneath his Sherman. The driver, Cpl. Ted Court, instinctively reversed behind a low hill as in quick succession two more shells screamed by. After quickly radioing he was under anti-tank fire, Charbonneau headed off cross-country, hoping to get a clear shot at his opponent. Just as *Amos* crested the ridge he caught sight of an 88 and gunner Tpr. Jack Haase quickly got a round off. Knowing their fate at such close range, the German crew spiked their gun and scrambled to safety.[89] As this excitement had been playing out, Sgt. Curly Lynch's Sherman had just slowed to pull around the same corner when it was hit, killing Lynch and badly wounding the rest of his crew. Trotter was following close behind with the rest of his troop, his head and shoulders protruding through the turret hatch so as to better see what was going on, when a mortar round stuck the roof, killing him instantly.

Capt. Don Taylor had immediately taken over command of the squadron but in the chaos its attack became more mêlée than organized assault. Even had it been possible to order a piecemeal withdrawal, many of the tanks would have surely been picked off as they slowly backed away.[90] Within an hour, a troop from A Squadron had reached the centre of Motta and other surviving tanks had nearly surrounded it. But without infantry to protect them from enemy tank-hunting squads, they would be sitting ducks. In the fading light, a withdrawal plan drawn up by the regiment's acting second-in-command, Maj. Stoney Richardson, was put in motion and within an hour all the "runners" had withdrawn 7 kms to the rear.[91] Capt. Alexander, who with a handful of his medical staff, had braved fire to get forward and using his flashlight check each tank for wounded, patching the less serious cases up and evacuating those in bad shape. The dead were left in the tanks, to be removed later.[92] Once darkness had fallen, a well-planned and executed operation carried Spry's infantry to the outskirts of the village at the cost of a single casualty, only to be subsequently evicted.[93]

Ironically, in the chaos of the firefight, *Amos* regained the road and managed to make it to Motta where it was rocked by a shattering explosion, undoubtedly a mine. Mercifully, the tracks were intact and *Amos* was able to limp on toward the centre of Motta. Nearing the square, they sighted a 37-mm anti-tank gun immediately ahead of them, sprayed it with machine-gun fire, and simply ran over it, but bellied on the wreckage. Throughout this perilous adventure, *Andy* and *Archie,* the other tanks in Charbonneau's troop, had been trailing close behind. *Andy* was hit by another 37-mm, killing the co-driver, Tpr. V. T. M. Palsson, and wounding two other crewmen. Now ordered to retreat, *Andy* somehow managed to extricate itself and along with *Archie* slowly withdraw back to the start line.[94] This left Charbonneau and his crew on their own. Stuck in a narrow street, he and his four comrades fought *Amos* as a pill box for close to four hours, fending off attacks from German infantry, who repeatedly tried to destroy the Sherman with sticky bombs and mines, on occasion swarming on top of it only to be knocked off by abrupt traverses of its powered turret. During one brief lull, Capt. Taylor's tank miraculously appeared out of the gloom and following a brief discussion, managed to push *Amos* off the rubble and back onto its tracks before withdrawing. But it was a false hope—as soon as they managed to get the engine started and in forward gear, one of the tracks snapped. Their miniature war within a war resumed, only ending when one of the dozen shaped-charges their besiegers had managed to detonate on the rear deck above the fuel tanks penetrated the plating and *Amos* burst into flames. Fortunately for the crew, the fact that the fuel tanks were almost empty meant it was a fire, not an inferno, giving them all a few extra seconds to get out.

Suspecting that some of the enemy were likely lurking near the front of the tank to despatch survivors, Tpr. Duke Ross expended an entire 250-round belt from the hull machine gun to discourage them. Charbonneau, Reimer, Court and Hasse promptly bailed out through the floor hatch, with Ross right behind. Miraculously all five men managed to slip away in the darkness.[95] It had been an extraordinary fight, with Charbonneau earning an MC for his day's work. With the RCR some distance back, it was left to the 2nd Field Regiment, which had come up during the night, to "literally blow the enemy out."[96] This the gunners set about doing, dropping 240 shells into the luckless village in 10 minutes. An hour later, around 0400, Spry reported his men were in possession of what remained.

Motta had been the first full-scale attack carried out by the regiment in Italy, and really of the war. Combat casualties—the first of the campaign—were three killed and nine wounded. A trio of tanks were write-offs, with several more badly damaged but salvageable. The assault had come badly unstuck, with the lack of combat experience from top to bottom clearly on display. But men and machines had responded well in the heat of action, and Lt.-Col. Neroutsos had shown the aggression his superiors prized if not necessarily the best judgment. The most important lesson had been absorbed—underestimating your opponents was fatal.

Motta and Beyond

Some hours later, with operational command having passed to Brig. H. D. Graham of the 1st Canadian Infantry Brigade, the advance resumed, with C Squadron having replaced A and B Squadrons in the vanguard with the infantry. Struggling to see through heavy rain, the two lead troops had barely progressed beyond Motta when they came under heavy anti-tank fire. Five tanks were hit in quick succession, and the advance ground to a halt.[97] The Sherman of Sgt. Frank Underhill, who commanded the lead troop, was hit twice and caught fire. He and his radio operator/loader managed to get out, with Underhill assisting his wounded gunner. Once they had reached cover, Underhill made his way back to the tank through a maelstrom of mortar and machine-gun fire to aid the driver and co-driver but found both men dead. Desperate to get morphine for his wounded comrade, he managed to crawl to several of the other tanks, only to be driven back by the heat and flames. He finally managed to find an artillery-spotting detachment, and with his assistance, they directed a couple of salvoes onto the German guns, effectively silencing them. For his heroism and initiative, Underhill was awarded the MM. [98] In a fierce assault that lasted the entire day, the rest of C Squadron and their supporting infantry, with strong artillery support, managed to push the enemy back to the Volturara. But casualties among the tankers were heavy—another ten killed and five wounded.[99]

When it came to confronting the enemy, the two days of heavy fighting around Motta set the tone for the next few months, and to all intents for the rest of the regiment's time in Italy. Orders issued to the German forces south of Rome in late September had been clear: "Within the limits of the delaying action, every opportunity is to be taken of destroying enemy forces that have pushed ahead incautiously, and of inflicting heavy losses."[100] Sgt. George Thring, who had reached the regiment just in time for the fighting on October 2 and was promptly thrown into action as a crew replacement, surely echoed the feelings of many of his new mates when he offered: "I knew we had a lot to learn about tank warfare ... The Germans had made us look like idiots."[101]

On October 3 the 2nd Canadian Infantry Brigade pressed on without armoured support, the terrain being deemed too rugged for tanks. This allowed a party of men, including Dr. Alexander, to recover the bodies of those killed the previous day and give them a proper burial in the small cemetery the regiment had established on the outskirts of Motta.[102] Clearing burned-out tanks was unpleasant work. "They are burned beyond recognition," the doctor sombrely noted in his journal, "but I find eight and am able to recognize them by their [crew] positions."[103]

A flanking advance by tanks the following day intended to gain some high ground was called off, Maj. Donabie having reported that the approach road itself was targeted by 88s (an 8.8 cm anti-aircraft gun also employed against armour with devastating effect), and mortar and machine-gun fire had thwarted any attempts to reconnoitre alternatives. In his assessment, proceeding would have been suicide, and his superiors agreed.[104] Over the next few days there was some further fighting, but it only occasionally employed armour and then mostly to buck up the morale of worn-out infantry. The overall push to Campobasso resumed on October 9, this time with B Squadron supporting the 3rd Infantry Brigade, at least when the terrain permitted, which was infrequently, while close by to the south C Squadron continued its own slow advance with the 2nd Infantry Brigade.[105]

A Welcome Lull

Campobasso fell to Canadian infantry on October 14, the day after Italy formally declared war on Germany. Word came down that the Calgary Regiment would be replaced by the Ontarios and move into reserve at Jelsi. Most of the men had not had a hot bath in over three weeks, so personal hygiene along with cleaning and repairing kit, and vehicle maintenance would come first, and then training could resume.[106] There were opportunities for leave in

Campobasso—the first chance for "town leave" since Scotland. The army had done its best to provide a wholesome experience there, setting up three movie houses and opening a Beaver Club where those so inclined could read or write and have a meal. The Canadian Legion, YMCA, Salvation Army and Knights of Columbus had all established a presence. Of course, the military police were always about to ensure no one wandered.[107] With Italy's co-belligerency, it had to be impressed on soldiers that civilians were no longer the enemy, and now "as far as possible we must obtain what we need for our operations through friendly cooperation …."[108] In practice, little changed since officers generally tolerated what amounted to looting, and attitudes toward the Italian civilian population remained broadly dismissive.

Lessons Learned

It is hard to underestimate the impact of the shared experience of combat in the bonding of a unit, and in turn its impact on future combat effectiveness. They were no longer just a well-trained tank battalion, but a battle-tested one, and that made a world of difference. Attention turned to drawing lessons from what they had just come through, and how tactics and training might benefit from applying these. Neroutsos' exchanges with his squadron commanders were frank, the only sort which served the purpose. There was agreement that the greatest problem was inadequate tank-infantry co-ordination, which the CO believed required infantry commanders to accept "that they can command much better from [inside] a Sherman tank than from a hole in the ground."[109] Maj. Amy bluntly observed that "the infantry still do not understand the tank or tank men … [and] this [is] due to only one thing—lack of co-ordination of training in England."[110] In keeping with his studious approach to most matters, Richardson submitted three closely-typed pages, which almost entirely focused on minimizing the threat of anti-tank defences. Whenever possible, he argued, tanks had to keep off the roads and use the available ground for cover, for it was far better to lose a tank to a mine than three or four to pre-sited anti-tank fire. Nor should tanks bunch together, but instead constantly cover one another at a distance, and when under fire, keep moving. For the tank commander, Richardson stressed, prudence and aggressiveness were both indispensable.[111] All of them agreed that these lessons needed to be front and centre in training, whether in England or Italy, and that the armoured unit's tactical flexibility was tactical unpredictability from the enemy's perspective and this always had to be encouraged.[112]

For most of November, I Canadian Corps enjoyed a well-earned reprieve from action. The hot, sunny days of summer were now a distant memory, the weather having been steadily deteriorating with frequent rain and much colder temperatures. And of course there was plenty of mud. It was hard to stay warm and dry, even out of the line, and colds were rampant. More ominously, the increased difficulty in keeping both the men and their clothing clean (and lice-free) raised the spectre of typhus, despite a thorough vaccination program. At least the malaria season was over.[113]

The State of the Italian Campaign

Italy's defence had to be situated within Germany's larger strategy in late 1943. Military manpower and material were stretched very thin, and priority had to be given to fending off the Red Army in the East, preserving access to Romanian oil and other Balkan resources, and building up sufficient strength to repel the expected Allied invasion in the West. As for Italy, enough of it had to be held to block any Allied intervention in the Balkans and keep Anglo-American strategic air power from bombing southern Germany and central Europe. The re-establishment of a Fascist regime in the northern half of Italy meant the Germans could employ their military resources south of Rome, where an improvised defensive line across the peninsula and grim winter weather could stall the Allied advance for months. The Anglo-American response to the Germans' decision to remain in Italy was to continually engage them. But the priority of the cross-channel invasion meant their margin of superiority would be slender. Italy would remain a secondary theatre, where except for tying the enemy down, there would be little chance (or even intention) of gaining complete victory.[114]

North of the Sangro

The 14th Armoured Regiment received relocation orders on November 21.[115] The following morning, with their fifty-one Shermans borne on transporters to save wear and tear on their running gear (not to mention the notoriously fragile Italian roads), they set off on a two-day trek to Petacciato. On the morning of November 24, Lt.-Col. Neroutsos gathered his senior officers and informed them that the 1st Armoured Brigade, with the 14th Armoured in the lead, would be supporting the 1st Canadian Infantry Division's imminent assault north of the Sangro River.[116] Apart from vehicle maintenance, now much complicated by chronic shortages of spares, there little to do but wait "in the mud and disagreeable weather." Despite everything, morale remained high.[117] They didn't have long to wait, for within a matter of days Wyman's brigade received orders to move to the San Vito Chietino area abutting the Adriatic and take up positions alongside the 1st Canadian Infantry Division.[118]

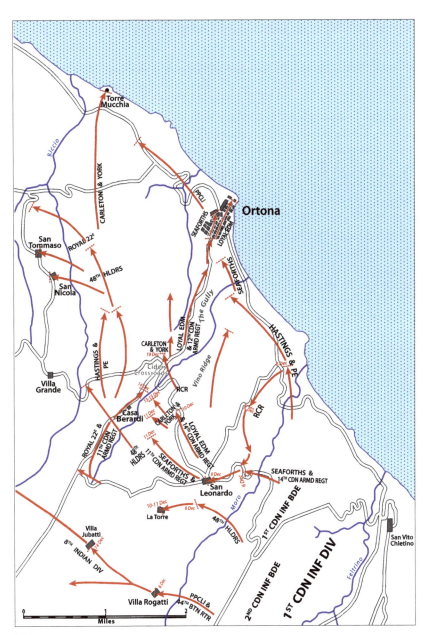

MAP 9:
Crossing the Moro and the Battle for Ortona, 6–28 December 1943.

A Canadian Plan to Force the Moro River

The successful attack across the Sangro River at the end of November by Indian, British and New Zealand troops had completely unhinged the enemy, and Montgomery was determined to build on that momentum by pushing on to Ortona and then Pescara. Canadian infantry and armour would spearhead this operation under Maj.-Gen. Christopher Vokes' overall command. They faced rugged terrain riven by numerous ravines and ridges and cut by three rivers that had carved steep-sided valleys that in many locations were gorges in all but name. Much of the tillable land was covered with olive groves and vineyards, which had a nasty habit of obscuring the already restricted view from tanks. The highway serving as the Canadians' axis of advance ran northwest from San Vito and on past San Leonardo before turning northeast toward Ortona. It was decent enough by Italian standards; that is, it could cope with reasonably heavy traffic assuming the weather co-operated and engineers could make frequent repairs. But it was sinuous in the extreme—the distance from San Vito to Ortona was 8 kms as the crow flies but more than three times that to drive.

The Canadians commenced their attack during the night of December 5–6, making several successful crossings of the Moro, save near San Leonardo where the attempt was repulsed, forcing Vokes to quickly cobble together a second attempt, this time with ample tank and artillery support. On December 8, infantry of the 1st Brigade were to seize and hold the far side of the valley, with a second attack across their right flank crushing the defenders in a pincer and a third near the coast drawing off reserves. A mixed tank and infantry force would then cross over to capture San Leonardo itself. In the event the assault at the foot of San Leonardo was hemmed in at the base of the heights and had to be withdrawn, while the flanking attack was stopped well short of its objectives. Only the more distant coastal attack succeeded. Everything now depended on the last phase of the operation.[119]

San Leonardo

At first light on December 9, the enemy held San Leonardo and dominated the river valley below. It was critical that tanks be gotten across the Moro. The bridge and both approaches had suffered heavy damage, but during the night Canadian sappers had managed to complete some repairs to the structure and bulldoze alternate routes across both riverbanks. Brig. Wyman had given A Squadron's commander, Maj. E. A. C. (Ned) Amy, who would earn a MC that day, the briefest order he ever received: "They haven't secured a bridgehead—you do it now."[120] Just before 0700, the dozen tanks available rumbled past their start line to marry up with D Company of the Seaforth Highlanders of Canada and were off.[121] The start was inauspicious—two of the Shermans, failing to negotiate a sharp turn along the steep, twisting road, tumbled down a 10-m cliff.[122] The remaining tanks, with the Seaforths clinging to the engine decks, pressed on. When the column reached the river, German mortars opened up, forcing the infantry to clamber off, but they and the tanks still managed to get across.

Advancing up the steep road exiting the valley, Lt. R. E. Hyde's lead Sherman had a track blown off, which at least alerted everyone that the road was mined.[123] Amy's own tank had broken down, but he commandeered Sgt. Ole Anderson's and wasted no time ordering Lt. C. A. Charbonneau's troop to work around the disabled tanks and then head off cross-country through a warren of vineyards and olive groves. Sgt. A. J. Harrison was on point, followed by Cpl. D. Morgan, with Charbonneau, as was normal practice for troop leaders trailing as "ass-end Charlie." Anderson's Sherman, with Amy squeezed into the turret, followed behind with the remaining tanks. Amy's initiative was fraught with risks, for such terrain constituted an anti-tank obstacle in its own right. One never knew what lurked behind and beneath olive thickets, and the heavy wires draped between concrete pillars that held the grape vines could bring tanks to a dead stop by snagging drive sprockets.[124] But as their infantry surged ahead, what choice was there?[125] All but the first four Shermans, plus one other, bogged down, but those five stumbled onto a side road and pressed on, with Charbonneau swinging past Harrison to take over lead. Anticipating heavy action, all crews had stowed extra machine-gun belts and cannon rounds aboard, a providential move.

Around 1000, supported by a timely artillery barrage, the remaining Seaforths—the one hundred men in an understrength company had been reduced to thirty-nine effectives—attacked German strongpoints on the outskirts of San Leonardo. Charbonneau's troop edged toward the square, having lost communication with Morgan when the latter's radio stopped working. Having apparently failed to get the message to hold back in a covering position, Harrison soon found himself about 100 m in front. Standing in his open hatch to get a better view, he was shot dead. Another German soldier planted a mine against the Sherman, which blew a hole through the side armour, severing the arm of the driver, Tpr. C. W. Moncrief. Even though also badly wounded, the co-driver, Tpr. C. A. Childress, somehow managed to extricate himself, and was lying against the front of the tank when another German darted out and shot him point-blank in the chest. Charbonneau's tank moved up, cleared the enemy with bursts of machine-gun fire, and managed to rescue the two remaining crewmen, both of whom were wounded. He then withdrew to the edge of the town, where they happened upon three tanks motionless under some tree cover. The gunner, Tpr. M. Knodel, thought they might be Canadian and failed to fire when ordered to. But Charbonneau immediately recognized one of them was a short-barrelled Panzer IV, and sharply ordered the driver to get them out of there. Crews invariably kept an armour-piercing (AP) round in the breach, so Knodel managed to get off a kill shot over the rear deck. Fortunately, they found a location close to some buildings which offered cover. It was none too soon, either. In a matter of minutes Charbonneau caught sight of another Mark IV edging out of a side lane, perhaps 40 m away. An excruciating wait allowed the panzer to completely expose his flank, and with Tpr. J. Beaton slamming rounds into the breach, Knodel pumped five shells into the hapless German tank, which erupted in a thunderous explosion.[126]

For Charbonneau and his crew, the capture and consolidation of San Leonardo and defeat of the initial counterattack pretty much unfolded as one unbroken action.[127] But for most of it they were carrying out Amy's plan to organize his handful of infantry and tanks so as to guard the most likely approaches, knowing full well that they would be hit hard and often. Given the Seaforths hadn't been able to bring up any of their 6-pounder anti-tank guns, the Shermans would have to deal with the German armour.[128] In short order, German infantry and a dozen Panzer IVs from the 90th Panzer Grenadier Division obliged, hurling themselves at the Canadians. Tank gunners destroyed two of the Mk IVs and damaged a third during a string of firefights.[129] The one knocked out at point-blank range belonged to Herb Knodel.[130]

Fortunately, the worst of the crisis was over by noon as the main road had been swept for mines, allowing two troops from B Squadron and the remaining companies of the Seaforths to reinforce Amy's exhausted force. He deployed the tank reinforcements on his flanks, losing a Sherman from each troop to German tank fire as they manoeuvred into position. Shortly after, the balance of Maj. F. N. Ritchie's B Squadron plus Maj. G. F. Gray's C Squadron and the regimental headquarters reached the town. Lt.-Col. Neroutsos, who had been co-ordinating operations over the radio net, now set up his headquarters and quickly assembled his senior officers to draw up a further defensive plan.[131] Weaker attacks continued throughout the afternoon, until San Leonardo was finally deemed secure by 1740. All formations then hunkered down for a fitful night, a fusillade of mortar and artillery shells from the town's recent occupants ensuring that the troops got little sleep. In a serious miscalculation, the enemy had deployed the bulk of his resources against the Hasting and Prince Edward Regiment's lodgement along the coast road and the isolated RCR position on the plateau immediately northeast of the town; even so, capturing and then holding San Leonardo had still been a close-run thing.[132]

The fighting on December 9 had been savage, with the Seaforths' losses being especially heavy. But as their commander in situ, Lt. J. F. McLean, later argued, "[my men] would have been massacred without the tanks."[133] The Calgary Regiment's casualties were lighter—six killed and ten wounded, plus five tanks knocked out, all of them recoverable.[134] It is worth noting that that this was the first time the regiment had engaged German tanks.

Cider Crossroads, the Gully, and Vino Ridge

The next stage of the advance called for infantry, supported by tanks, to break out of San Leonardo, advance up the road about 3 kms to an intersection (nicknamed Cider Crossroads) from which the main road to Ortona split off. Paralleling the latter to the south lay a deep ravine, nicknamed The Gully, now the main German defence line. In miserable conditions the following morning, A and B Squadrons supported a pair of Seaforth attacks that succeeded in clearing the way for C Squadron, supporting infantry from the Edmonton Regiment, to proceed up the road to their crossroads objective. As the column advanced north on high ground along a rise overlooking The Gully from the south (soon to be nicknamed Vino Ridge), it met fierce resistance, losing three tanks in short order. They withdrew.

Sgt. George Thring commanded the point tank in the lead troop, with the other two Shermans trailing on each flank about 40 metres apart. Thring heard on the radio net that Sgt. Johnny Johnson's Sherman on the right had been struck by anti-tank fire, severing his leg. Thring closed in to help and failed to see a group of Panzer IVs creeping up behind some farm buildings. A loud crash signalled his own tank had been hit, instantly bursting into flames. "We had practised bailout drill," he noted laconically, "and it certainly worked."[135] Thring was able to lead his comrades to safety but then returned to see if he could help Johnson and his crew. Later that day his nerves went and he asked for an hour's "rest," which it was their CO's policy to grant in such situations, no questions asked.[136] Neroutsos had cobbled together a plan to have B Squadron and the PPCLI set off to reinforce the embattled C Squadron and Seaforths, but the deteriorating condition of the ground caused him to put the plan on hold.[137]

On December 11, the third day of the battle, conditions had improved sufficiently to proceed with the assault. B Squadron's handful of remaining Shermans—the entire regiment had been reduced to twenty-four battle-worthy tanks—and the PPCLI pushed off at noon, sticking to the reverse slope of Vino Ridge.[138] As they slowly made their way through more tangled olive groves and vineyards, all heavily mined and booby-trapped, the infantry and tanks silenced numerous machine guns. By late afternoon, they held a position about 2 kms northeast of San Leonardo. During the night, the 90th *Panzergrenadier*

Division launched several determined but unsuccessful attacks to dislodge the Canadians. Both sides were exhausted, and December 12 proved a relatively quiet day, figuratively if not literally.[139]

Determined to keep the pressure on, Maj.-Gen. Vokes drew up plans early the next morning calling for the 48th Highlanders to advance beyond C Squadron's flank, with the Carleton and Yorks then passing through the position. A single troop of C Squadron under Lt. R. W. Butler would assist the infantry it they got held up. Prior to the attack, A and C Squadrons were merged, their numbers no longer tactically justifying having two separate squadrons. In deteriorating weather, the assault went in at 0930, and almost immediately one company of the Carleton and Yorks radioed for support. Butler's three tanks crept forward, passing through the New Brunswickers, his Sherman in the lead and the others trailing at a safe distance to offer covering fire. In short order, Butler's tank was hit and promptly "brewed up." Both the driver and co-driver[140] had been killed instantly, but Butler and his two mates managed to exit their burning vehicle, and under withering machine-gun fire crawled through the mud the 50-odd metres back to their own lines. The two surviving Shermans then cautiously withdrew, leaving the Carleton and Yorks to dig in where they were.

December 14 proved another grim day. The German infantry counterattacked the Carleton and York position furiously, with both sides suffering substantial losses, but the timely intervention of B Squadron helped repel each onslaught.[141] Being continuously on call, day and night, not to mention under frequent shelling, kept the crews "buttoned up" inside their tanks, and sleep was impossible. Utterly exhausted, they finally started to be rotated.[142] Still, ammunition and fuel resupply were becoming most critical. After beating off still more counterattacks on December 15, they were down to their last rounds, man-handling them from tank to tank just to keep all the guns ready to fire. And there wasn't enough fuel even to consider withdrawing. With the tracks under constant bombardment and otherwise impassable, resupply by pack mules seemed the only recourse. Maj. Schmidlin managed to get this organized for that night, the muleteers and mules being loaned by the 8th Indian Division. The task of leading the party forward fell to B Squadron's Sgt.-Maj. Charles Halstead; his bravery and initiative earned him an MM.[143] Fewer than half of the forty pack mules with their precious cargo of 75-mm ammo and jerry cans of fuel got through, but it was enough to keep the tanks fighting for another day.[144] Schmidlin also saw to it that an extra rum ration was included with the next resupply.[145]

After another uneasy night, December 16 brought no lessening of the artillery and mortar bombardment. Whatever the enemy's predicament, it did not seem he was running short on shells. On B Squadron's front, a company of the PPCLI and two troops of Shermans sortied to attack a house on the ridge top. The Germans responded by unleashing a torrent of fire, making the position untenable for the infantry and forcing both to withdraw. The Patricias' losses were heavy, and two tanks were blown up on mines, though mercifully both crews were unscathed and managed to get back to their own lines. Tank crews faced their own share of mortal risks in combat, but they all knew that inside an armoured box their chances were a lot better than those the infantry faced. Powerless to intervene, Tpr. David Ewart witnessed a heart-rending scene during that action which graphically illustrated this. A wounded Patricia had

> crept within a few yards of our tank and I presumed he had a red rag tied around his waist, but realized it was his guts hanging out. He managed to get his pack off and fell into a deep track made by one of the tanks in the mud. In the coolness one could see his breath getting weaker and weaker until he died—about 8 minutes. [It] sure made me respect the ... infantry.[146]

Since the initial push into San Leonardo and onto Vino Ridge there had been only small-scale advances intended to occupy the enemy's attention and wear him down. Finally, on the night of December 18, the Three Rivers Regiment moved up to relieve the Calgary Regiment, save its B Squadron which, because of its more exposed position, could not be extricated for another 48 hours.[147] A few days more of hard fighting saw Cider Crossroads and The Gully beyond Vino Ridge cleared of the enemy, finally opening the road to Ortona.[148]

The Canadian Army had paid a terrible price, especially its infantry battalions, but the Calgary Regiment had been in the thick of the fight with its officers and men repeatedly displaying courage and tactical skill. Fifteen had been killed in action, and another fifty-eight wounded, two of whom subsequently died. Infantry-tank co-ordination continued to fall short of the ideal, as infantry commanders persisted in underestimating the teamwork required to make it work. In fact, it was not until the major attack wresting Cider Crossroads from the enemy that one saw the kind of thorough preparation armoured commanders like Neroutsos had long been advocating.[149]

A Time for Introspection

Over the next two weeks of December, other Canadian formations, including the two other regiments in the 1st Armoured Brigade, engaged in relentless, no-quarter combat to clear the Germans out of Ortona and the surrounding area to the west and north.[150] The Calgary Regiment had done its share of fighting, and welcomed a well-earned period in reserve. It was a chance to attend to the backlog of maintenance, of course, but bathing, grooming and laundry consumed much of the men's spare time, as did catching up on correspondence with family and friends back home.[151] Realizing his men needed rest more than anything, the CO kept work to a minimum during this stint out of the line.

For an introspective commander like Lt.-Col. Neroutsos, a period out of action granted some time to reflect on what recent experience could add to the army's collective knowledge. In compiling a lengthy report of over forty pages, he focused on two major elements—the performance of his own tank crews and the recurring problems of tank-infantry co-ordination. His men had been through the most intensive, sustained fighting they had experienced thus far, and he was pleased with their overall performance. The many reinforcements had learned quickly, "action, after all [being] the ultimate teacher."[152] He emphasized that his squadron and troop officers were confident that tanks, properly employed, would get the infantry through to their objectives every time, even in Italy's difficult terrain. But this would require very close co-ordination between the two, and "[close co-ordination] only exists where a Squadron has been working and fighting for a considerable period of time with the same infantry regiment, commanded by a commander who thinks of and has a knowledge of tanks, and imbibes this spirit of co-operation and confidence into his Company Commanders."[153] The San Leonardo operations were a reminder that in the Italian Theatre armour was usually employed in what tank zealots dismissed as piecemeal fashion, a squadron at most and usually only one or two troops, whether they were shooting the infantry onto their objective or breaking up a threatening counterattack. To Neroutsos, their actions had vindicated the *raison d'être* of the independent tank regiment—subordinating themselves to the infantry's needs rather than carrying out breakthroughs. Although often ignored in the grand sweep of a campaign, it bears remembering that the appearance of even a handful of tanks raised infantrymen's morale by orders of magnitude and carried many an operation to success that would otherwise have stalled or failed outright—the capture of San Leonardo being a prime illustration.[154]

Another Christmas Far from Home

Being in reserve also made it possible to apply some serious thought to the matter of Christmas preparations. There were no turkeys available, but there was plenty of pork and together with acquisitions from the countryside and some extra rum, this gave promise of a "bang-up" dinner.[155] At least as welcome were the cigarettes sent from home by the regiment's Ladies Auxiliary and the

Calgary Brewing Company, plus the generous Christmas issue of chewing gum, candy, beer, whiskey and still more cigarettes from NAAFI.[156] And as the war diarist noted, rather tongue in cheek, "large supplies of local 'vino' have been found in vacated houses in the Regimental area!"[157] As December ended, word came that their second-in-command, Maj. Schmidlin, would be leaving. Although only with them for two months, he'd proven a talented administrator and was well liked. It helped that his replacement, Maj. Stoney Richardson, one of the originals from 1941 and a pre-war member of the NPAM unit, was highly regarded by everyone.

The last days of 1943 were miserably cold and wet, and mail delivery, after briefly picking up over Christmas, dropped off to a trickle with most of the cherished parcels from home long overdue. Apart from drinking up the remainder of their "liberated" vino, nothing special was planned for New Year's. But the fate of comrades, including the twenty-five who'd lost their lives so far in Italy, was surely on many minds.[158]

Waiting at Home

For every soldier missing his home in Canada, there were parents, siblings, wives, children and close friends who missed him every bit as much. Wartime separation, and its risks, exacted its toll from a great many people.[159] Writing his wife fifteen months after he had left Calgary, Sgt. Lyman Slifka expressed the sentiments of most soldiers: "God I'm home sick today … no fooling it brings tears to your eyes when you open [parcels] up and you know who packed them. It makes you feel so darn far away."[160]

Just before the regiment was blooded at Motta Montecorvino, Sgt. Elly Raskin received a letter from his wife. She had used one of the special *airgraphs* set aside for the use of servicemen (and women) overseas and next of kin in Canada. Printed on it was a picture of the four-month-old son he had never seen:

> My dearest. Well, honey, what do you think of this airgraph? Say I am not giving you much chance to forget us sending you all these photos. I hope you are getting them ok, sweet. Don't you think Keith's growing up … he wouldn't smile, hope you like it anyway. He was 3½ months when it was taken … I love you darling and keep hoping it won't be long till I see you again, sometimes I think it won't, miss you awfully honey … Wish you could really see him … Mother and dad send their love … Say hello to the boys for me. Take care of yourself, darling. God bless you. All my love and kisses, yours always, Marjorie.[161]

Life went on at home. On top of taking care of their children alone in a time of growing shortages and restrictions, a lot of wives had taken jobs, some for the first time in their lives. Many couples had been married for only a few years before their lives had been interrupted by the war. Would their partnership survive? Would two people being transformed by their separate war experiences still be in love when they were reunited? Would their husbands be faithful? And on every wife's (or fiancée's) mind, would their husband (or hoped-for husband) survive to come home? In the case of the Calgary Regiment, many couples faced more than four years of separation.

News was scarce during the war. Letters were always the principal vehicle of communication, and the army gave high priority to mail, knowing how central it was to maintaining morale. That letters from home were almost always found among the personal effects of a deceased soldier speaks volumes. Thousands of letters were travelling back and forth on any day, vulnerable to the vagaries of enemy action and logistical breakdowns. Soldiers' letters were censored by military authorities, but letters going either way were invariably self-censored, each party wishing to spare the other worry. There were odd snippets on CBC radio, where you might actually hear your son's or husband's or brother's voice. And army-produced newsreels were devoured in the hopes of simply seeing a face. A few soldiers came back to Alberta, mostly men who had been seriously wounded or those on leave after returning to take up Canadian postings. When Lt.-Col. Begg was sent back from England to become an instructor at Camp Borden in the spring of 1943, he managed to spend a few weeks in Calgary. As his train rolled into Union Station on April 19, a crowd of friends and loved ones lined the platform to greet him, but it was his ten-year-old son Billy who captured the moment with his spontaneous cry of "there's dad!"[162] Later that month, when a film about the Canadian Army's activities in England was shown at St. Stephen's Anglican Church, the families and friends of Calgary soldiers packed the hall. As the 14th Canadian Tank Regiment paraded past in one segment, there were tears and smiles on many faces in the audience, and small children ran up to touch their fathers' flickering images on the screen.[163]

The children's story is a particularly touching one, having to cope, as they did, without fully grasping why the separation was happening. In his diaries, Capt. Laurence Alexander, the regiment's medical officer for over two years, left a candid account of the war he experienced. He had been married since the 1920s and had four sons. Donnie (Donald) Alexander was in grade 2 when his father, feeling it was his duty despite already having seen plenty of war in the CEF after enlisting underage, joined the Calgary Regiment in 1939. And he was in grade 9 when his father returned in 1945. When the regiment paraded the short block and a half from the armoury to board their troop train for Camp

Borden, the police had kept the crowds of well-wishers well back but the youngster had slipped through and walked proudly alongside his dad, until "Doc" turned to him and said softly "go back to your mom now." The youngster remembered breakfast being interrupted one morning by an almost unheard-of event—a long-distance telephone call—which turned out to be from his father in Halifax. It quickly dawned on them all that their father and his comrades were about to board a troop ship. Young Donnie was late for school that morning, and when his grade 4 teacher asked him why, he told her, then burst into tears. She was so upset she left the room, and none of his classmates teased him for crying. Dieppe scared all of the Alexander kids, but miraculously their father had managed to send a telegram confirming he was safe before the ominous missing-in-action telegram reached their mother. Try as she might to shield them, he could always tell his mother was worried sick about their father's fate. She was Donnie's hero, and the centre of his wartime life. Donnie and his father wrote to one another but it was very hard having an absent father. When the decorated Major Alexander came home at war's end, the family followed the ritual of waiting expectantly on the platform as the train steamed in. Donnie remembered being worried he would not recognize his father, though of course he did. Within days, they were all off to Banff, their first family holiday ever, but it was a holiday, he remembered in his eighties, with a stranger. As was typical for very young children, Donnie's younger brother clung to his mother in this strange world, taking a considerable time to get used to having his father around. Emotionally it was hard for Donnie, too; for a time, seeing everyone shake the hand of the returning hero, he tried not to feel angry, silently asking "where were you when I needed you, when we all needed you?"[164] Of course the Alexanders' was a loving home, and such feelings soon passed, but they should remind us of how hard it was to grow up a soldier's youngster during wartime, and of the sacrifices made by their fathers and mothers.

Soldiers' wives banded together to support their husbands overseas. Communities had a way of caring in fits and starts—the crowds at the station cheering the troop trains faded away with time, literally and figuratively. Churches, neighbours, even relatives simply could not be there as much as servicemen's families needed. Oftentimes the greatest support for soldiers' wives came from others in the same position. The Ladies Auxiliary of the Calgary Regiment (LACR) was formed shortly after the unit left for Camp Borden. From the outset, the wives of present (and past) officers dominated the group's leadership, though the wives of John Burns and brewer A. E. Cross were also very active, and a great asset in the work.[165] The Dieppe raid, with the fate of the many prisoners providing a second focus, galvanized the Auxiliary into greater action. A second group soon formed in Red Deer, where so many from the regiment had been recruited. There was nothing surprising about the bulk of the LACR's activities—whether POWs or serving in the field, the men were all well provided with knit goods, shaving needs, candy, over-the-counter medicines, and of course cigarettes by the thousands, and news clippings and snapshots from home were stuffed in all the packets. With Cross Brewing donating all the mailing cartons, teas, dances, and bake sales raised enough funds to keep the parcels flowing. And privately members solicited donations from individuals and businesses. During the first ten months of 1943, the women raised $1,000 for prisoners of war alone. There is no question the soldiers were quite overwhelmed by the Auxiliary's efforts. It was hard not to be grateful to people you did not know and in all likelihood would never meet, yet who worked selflessly just so you would have gifts from home.[166] Singly or in small groups, LACR members also regularly checked in on other soldiers' wives or parents to provide moral and practical support (such as assistance with mailing problems, which was a constant frustration for POW families). And they never failed to contact those who had recently lost someone—the most emotional visits of all. Finally, the Auxiliary held an annual Christmas party for the wives and children of all members of the regiment who had gone overseas.[167] While the principal beneficiaries of the work were the men overseas, one shouldn't underestimate how much these joint endeavours with other women helped these ladies cope with their own anxieties and loneliness too.

War Brides

As the months slipped by, more and more Canadian servicemen agreed that "Britain was no longer a strange and forbidding place with awful weather, deplorable living conditions, and cold people," but a second home.[168] And it had, to use the term of the day, "girls." The majority of the Canadian servicemen were unmarried and love, as the saying goes, is as perennial as the grass, perhaps even more so during wartime. The results were predictable—couples met and fell in love. Initially, the Canadian Army neither wanted marriages, with all their complications, nor thought the men would be in England long enough for these situations to become commonplace. However, the combination of the Canadian Army seemingly becoming a permanent fixture in places like Seaford and Worthing and the negative publicity associated with illegitimate pregnancies, led to the adoption of a more realistic marriage policy.[169]

Mildred Clark and A/Cpl. Percy Scott of the Calgary Regiment were one such couple. Scott had left school after grade 9 so he could help out full-time on the family farm in the Kneehill Valley district. He had enlisted in Red Deer in February 1941 immediately after completing the then one-month of mandatory training under the National Resources Mobilization (home defence conscription) Act. Mildred Clark was solidly middle class, born and raised just outside London. Having earned a degree in psychology from Cambridge, she was a sergeant in the WAAF. They had begun courting in June 1942, and it had obviously blossomed, for eight months later he formally applied for permission to marry. It usually fell to chaplains to assess matters, with the commanding officer making the final decision. Capt. (Hon.) N. E. L. Smith's report noted the twenty-five-year-old Scott was an experienced farmer and would take over his father's operation, complete with "good machinery, paid for," when the war ended. The family seemed to have ability, Smith noted approvingly—a younger son running the farm (but intending to go to university), one daughter married, another working in Calgary and a third serving as a nurse in the RCAF, with a third son serving in an RAF bomber squadron. Miss Clark was "a girl of quiet tastes [and] presumably ... equipped to recognize the type of man she would prefer to marry." Religion was not going to be a problem as they were both Anglicans, and they would have their own house on the farm, minimizing the potential for parental interference. The chaplain was pleased to hear that Scott had "told her about conditions in Canada—isolation, cold, hard work." Overall, Scott seemed "to be taking it all conscientiously."[170] And last, but by no means least, the couple had decided not to start a family until after the war. Lt.-Col. Neroutsos approved the request four days after he received the chaplain's report, and Philip and Mildred wed on 31 May 1943 while the regiment was completing its final training in Scotland before it set out for the Mediterranean.

Barely six months later, during the attack on San Leonardo, A/Cpl. Philip Scott lost his life when his tank was hit and burst into flames. That such tragedies were common enough in Mildred's circle will have brought sympathy but won't have made bearing the news any easier. The official condolences—Canadian and royal—reached her early in 1944. When she inquired as to when she might receive her husband's personal effects, items that would have meant the most to her, like photographs, his wedding band, and watch, she was informed that "all personal effects of your late husband were destroyed by enemy action at the time of his death."[171] No doubt she realized exactly what such phrasing meant. Though a widow, Mildred Scott chose to come to Canada with the thousands of other war brides. She reached the farm in February 1945, but stayed only briefly, following her mother- and father-in-law to Calgary when they had decided to retire. Her plan was to stay with them for a year before setting out on her own. Like other war widows, in the midst of her grief she had to deal with all of the time-consuming bureaucratic burdens such as the disposition of her late husband's estate, his post-war reburial, and the phrase she wished to have inscribed on his permanent gravestone. In 1946, Philip Scott was reinterred in the Moro River Canadian War Cemetery with full honours, and his marker bears the inscription she thoughtfully chose: "For Ever Dearly Remembered—Wife, Mother and Dad, Brothers and Sisters."[172] In Calgary, Mildred busied herself in the Red Cross work she had done in England, her supervisor reporting that "she is very happy in her new home."[173] Like many next of kin, she wrote to the authorities in Ottawa about the possibility of visiting her husband's grave if the opportunity arose. The last correspondence that survives is a letter to the Department of Veterans Affairs written in July 1949, informing them that she had remarried and requesting that all information pertaining to her late husband and in particular the promised photograph of his grave be forwarded to her. "I will appreciate it very much if you will take note of this request."[174]

No End in Sight

In the late summer of 1942 there had been little time to dwell on the disaster at Dieppe. Rebuilding the regiment was the only priority, and efforts to this end proceeded apace under the leadership of Lt.-Cols. Begg and Neroutsos. In this task, they were ably assisted by the cadre of officers and men of the old regiment. By the late spring of 1943, a new regiment was ready for battle. The despatch of sizable forces, including the 1st Army Tank Brigade, to the Mediterranean Theatre was meant to be a temporary separation from the rest of the Canadian Army; however, it became all but permanent, which meant the Calgary Regiment's war would be defined by the Italian Campaign. Beginning in early October, combat became the norm for the tankers as they supported the infantry in their gruelling advance northward. Early engagements at Motta Montecorvino and San Leonardo were victories but the regiment suffered a bloody nose in both operations, confirming that officers and men still had plenty to learn about fighting an experienced, determined, and at times, fanatical enemy on ground that greatly favoured defence. But these engagements also showed the Canadians had plenty of courage and determination of their own.

There was a disheartening sameness about the Italian Campaign that was readily apparent even in the early days. Save for the changing weather—it was always another ridge, another river, another strongpoint, another casualty, another pair of identity discs carefully slipped from around a comrade's neck. In the absence of any possibility of sweeping advances, most of the actions were small but brutal, and the Calgary Regiment had suffered through their share in 1943. There seemed to be no end in sight, and 1944 simply promised more of the same.

5.1 Infantry from the West Nova Scotia Regiment hitch a ride on a Calgary Regiment (A Squadron) Sherman during their joint advance from Villapiano to Potenza, 18 September 1943. (LAC, PA-177155)

5.2 British and Indian officers serving in the 6/13 Royal Frontier Force Rifles pose in a Jeep. They and their men had fought alongside the Calgary Regiment during Operation Honker. (LAC, PA-132798)

5.3 A Sherman tank of the Ontario Regiment crossing a stream near Campobasso, 26 October 1943. Obvious fords and their approaches would invariably be mined, and possibly in the sights of German anti-tank guns, so this was far from a straightforward matter. (LAC, PA-204149)

5.4 Riflemen of the 1/5 Mahratta Regiment dismount from a Calgary Regiment Sherman during a joint training exercise in late August 1944. The effectiveness of tank-infantry cooperation on the battlefield was determined by the thoroughness of such training. A month later both regiments had crossed the Arno and were pressing northward toward the Gothic Line. (LAC, PA-141747)

5.5 Canadian units attempting to advance from the Gustav to the Hitler Line, late May 1944. Such traffic snarls were the bane of the regiment as it shifted toward the Aquino sector of the front. (LAC, PA-140208)

5.6 A Sherman of the Ontario Regiment, entering the ruins of San Pancrazio on 16 July 1944, not long after B Squadron of the Calgary Regiment and its accompanying infantry from the 2/Royal Fusiliers had cleared it of the enemy. From time to time the Germans would resist fiercely before resuming their retreat. Rooting them out devastated these unlucky Italian communities. (LAC, PA-160448)

5.7 A massed column of heavily camouflaged Sherman tanks from a Calgary or Ontario Regiment squadron wait east of the Gari River on May 10 or 11, 1944, immediately prior to the launch of Operation Honker. The danger was being detected by German artillery spotters, hence the extensive camouflage. Fortunately *Luftwaffe* reconnaissance (or activity of any kind) was almost non-existent by this stage of the Italian campaign. (Canadian War Museum, 20020045-2721)

5.8 Brig. William "Spud" Murphy (far R) briefs Lt.-Col. Neroutsos (standing, centre) and other Calgary Regiment officers during a brief lull in British operations near Aquino, 23 May 1944. (LAC, PA-204305)

5.9 Checking through parts as the Calgary Regiment re-equips with the more powerfully armed Sherman Firefly in Dottignies, 22 March 1945. (LAC, PA-144121)

Victory—The Italian Campaign and Holland   *211*

5.10 Capts. Jim Quinn and R. D. Spittal mixing with the locals somewhere in Holland, likely after VE Day. (KOCRA, P-400-40-0075)

5.11 Citizens of Ede celebrate with their Canadian and Scottish liberators, 17 April 1945. The Ede operation was the last serious fighting for the Calgary Regiment, the war ending (in Holland) seventeen days later. None too soon for the brave young men who had made it through. (KOCRA, P-400-40-0079)

5.12 Personnel of the Reconnaissance Troop pose beside one of their M5 Stuart light tanks, June 1945. The otherwise obsolescent Stuart proved invaluable in this role, as well as in transporting fuel, ammunition and other supplies to forward areas during combat. In Italy the turrets had often been removed to lower the vehicle's profile. (KOCRA, P-400-40-0106)

5.13 Officers and men of the Calgary Regiment's A Squadron assembled in Driebergen, 18 June 1945. With almost daily departures for early repatriation or service in the expected invasion of Japan, the regiment was rapidly being dismantled. It was an emotional time, with the sadness addressed to a degree by the many good-bye parties. (KOCRA, P-400-40-0092)

Victory—The Italian Campaign and Holland   213

5.14 Maj. Bob Taylor, then commander of A Squadron, celebrates Christmas in the sergeants' mess, San Martino in Gattara (north of Marradi), 1944. The joviality, and Taylor's presence as an officer, speak volumes about the camaraderie in a tank unit where rank distinctions certainly mattered, but nonetheless inevitably became blurred. (Glenbow Archives, pa-1599-385b-20)

5.15 Officers and men of the Calgary Regiment march through downtown Calgary in their homecoming parade, 1 December 1945. A point system instituted to make demobilization fairer than in 1919 meant many veterans had already returned. And soldiers from other units had been temporarily incorporated into their ranks simply to facilitate getting the men back to Alberta. But the core of the regiment from 1944 was there to be honoured. (Glenbow Archives, pa-1599-618-64)

7

From the Gari to the Arno

Onward

The spring of 1944 would see the Calgary Regiment shift west to the Gari River/Cassino area south of Rome, where in May they would play a key role in breaking the Gustav and Adolf Hitler Lines—Operation Honker. This operation would be the regiment's singular achievement of the war. At the same time they would leave I Canadian Corps and pass under British and Indian Army command, and in the process all but disappear from Canadian military history.[1] After Honker and the follow-up Liri Valley operations, the regiment, along with the rest of 1st Army Tank Brigade, continued their relentless pursuit of the retreating German forces until by mid-summer they had reached the Arno River. Never had the Calgary Regiment's motto—*Onward*—seemed more appropriate.

Where the Allies Stood

The Ortona operations brought an end to the Eighth Army's winter offensive. While German losses had been heavy, the Allies had suffered too. Unforgiving terrain and foul weather had limited opportunities for their superior tank and air forces to intervene, forcing the infantry, artillery and engineers to bear the brunt of the fighting. Every Canadian rifle company had suffered at least 50 percent casualties in these operations, and it was especially worrying that almost half of the wounded were "battle exhaustion" cases. Logistics were fraying, especially the vital supply of artillery ammunition, and German defences, though badly battered, remained formidable. To make matters worse, the Italian front was suffering (and would continue to suffer) from the diversion of all manner of resources to Britain as part of the build-up for D-Day. Clearly a period of rest and consolidation was in order.

Ironically, when Canadian forces had been assigned to the Sicilian invasion it had been (naively) assumed they would take their combat experience back to First Canadian Army in time to participate in the Normandy invasion and subsequent North West European Campaign. But they stayed put, to be joined, ironically, by a further 40,000 Canadian soldiers who would replace British units that had been withdrawn for D-Day.[2] It was now likely the Calgary Regiment would spend most—and perhaps all—of the remainder of the war in Italy.

A New Year

The regiment welcomed in the New Year shivering in sodden blankets, having been battered by the worst storm they'd yet experienced in "Sunny Italy." They were at least at full strength (thirty-four officers and 670 other ranks), with an additional three officers and forty-one other ranks attached. Tank strength stood at fifty-one machines.[3] During an inspection on January 7, General Crerar, soon to depart for the Normandy build-up himself, praised the officers and men for the fighting prowess they'd displayed so far and predicted "more good hunting" and victory in 1944.[4] For now, however, the Eighth Army mostly assumed a static role along its entire front. The only military activities were periodic holding actions where they were called on to provide fire support for small-scale probing attacks, the purpose of which was to prevent German withdrawals to more threatened sectors. Soldiers roundly disliked these, the gains always seeming less apparent than the casualties. The loss of Lt. G. A. Richardson during a two-day action by three troops from B Squadron in support of a Hastings and Prince Edward Regiment foray made the point only too tragically.[5] January's highlight undoubtedly occurred on the 19th when, one squadron at a time, all personnel were trucked to San Leonardo to enjoy the rare luxury of a hot shower.

A New Brigadier

Toward the end of the February, word filtered down that Brig. R. A. Wyman was joining the exodus for England. As a fellow Albertan, and a superior officer who had fought doggedly for their interests, the regiment held him in high regard. His replacement was Brig. W. C. "Spud" Murphy, a former infantry officer but most recently the senior staff officer of the 5th Canadian Armoured Division.[6] Like a great many commanders of Canadian armoured units at the time, Murphy lacked hands-on tank experience but he was bright and seemed to get along well with everybody, which was no small asset. The lack of hands-on experience hardly mattered since in the British system copied by Canadians an army tank brigade was primarily involved in infantry support, where it fought as individual regiments and even squadrons—and to all intents directly under the control of the infantry division or brigade to which these were temporarily attached. This left the army tank brigade commander a much-reduced operational role save for transmitting orders and consulting. His normal responsibilities were largely confined to training and administration, which was certainly vital work. Only the British employed this awkward system; the others, whether Allied or enemy, had concluded it offered no advantage. About the same time, Maj. R. R. Taylor returned from a long stint in hospital, where he had been recovering from his injuries in Sicily, and took over as A Squadron's CO from the departing Maj. Amy.[7]

As the seemingly endless Italian winter dragged on into March, morale was clearly suffering. The men were getting bored, and in danger of losing their fighting edge. Even in leave areas the decline in discipline among Canadian soldiers was showing. But the weather gradually began to improve in the second half of the month, and with it everything else.[8]

Into the Caldron

At a brigade conference on March 23, Neroutsos received word that his regiment would be relieved in a matter of days, and shortly thereafter men, tanks and other vehicles would entrain for the Cassino area where fierce fighting was already raging. As incomprehensible as it might seem to civilians, nothing raised soldiers' morale like the prospect of action. Their immediate destination was the Venafro area in the Volturno Valley, which served as the Eighth Army's principal mountain warfare training site.[9] And there was also some other welcome news from brigade—all three regiments would be re-equipping their reconnaissance units with American M5 Stuart light tanks, a long overdue upgrade.[10]

Kriegsgefangene

Nineteen months had passed since the Dieppe raid, during which the regiment had been rebuilt, deployed to the Mediterranean Theatre, where they engaged and outfought a determined enemy. During those same nineteen months nearly 200 members of the regiment captured at Dieppe had endured punishments, hunger, cold, boredom, loneliness and for all too many, depression. They remained proud soldiers, but their war was the war of the *Kriegsgefangene*—prisoners of war.

A New Home, Far from Home

When their Churchill lumbered onto the fire-swept beach at Dieppe, Tpr. J. D. White turned to his crewmate Elmer Cole and uttered the memorable lines, "Elmer, I don't think we'll be home for dinner tonight!"[11] He could have hardly imagined the truth of it. Thirteen days later, as the exhausted column of soldiers captured that day passed through the gates of Stalag VIII-B, British

7 | From the Gari to the Arno   217

POWs saluted them as they walked by. The Dieppe men were immediately rushed through delousing and showering stations, which reminded many of the arrangements for cattle back home, and then given perfunctory medicals. The showers may have been rude, but after two weeks without bathing, no one complained. Three weeks crammed into the quarantine compound followed, with the neediest receiving some Red Cross clothing or a blanket. Their quarantine over, they marched under armed guard into their permanent accommodations, where other prisoners besieged them with queries about the war, showered them with cigarettes, and shared soup they'd saved from Red Cross parcels—the first decent meal any of the Dieppe captives had eaten since they'd left England.[12]

Stalag VIII-B was a sprawling affair with a prisoner population, including absent work parties, of about 30,000, all of them other ranks from the army. The Dieppe prisoners were assigned to a group of barracks comprising the Canadian section, an area of about 180 m by 135 m which held about 2,000 men, including the new arrivals. Each of the barracks consisted of two long, narrow huts built of brick and straw and plastered on the inside. Beds and tables each occupied half the hut. In theory these quarters could be heated, but shortages of coal and peat meant they rarely were, even during the coldest months. The pair of huts were connected by a combination laundry and shower facility, with urinals and wash basins. There was no pretence of heating this area and having any hot water for laundry was a cause for celebration. Each barracks initially held ninety men but eventually 120 were crammed in. The latrine building—home of the forty-holer—was separate, and shared by all the prisoners, its permanent stench hanging over the compound.[13]

Prisoners appointed two of their number, usually NCOs, as the hut commander and his assistant. They interacted with the Germans, but also ensured the prisoners remained an organized group, distributing rations and administering discipline for things like the theft of food. It was a thankless (but necessary) job—as Tpr. Denis Scott noted, it was not easy to divide a loaf of bread among twelve hungry men and have it appear fair.[14] While roll calls defined the prisoners' day, the guards otherwise besieged the men with innumerable rules, most of which seemed little more than harassment. Regardless, they were strictly enforced, with often-arbitrary punishments imposed on the entire barracks (one of the cruellest being forcing prisoners to open all the containers in their food parcels so most of the contents would spoil before they could be consumed).[15] Searches were random but frequent. Among the "goons," as prisoners disparagingly referred to the guards, some showed more enthusiasm for their work than others. A few, like Stalag VIII-B's "Spitfire," were downright sadistic. As for the surroundings, they were meant to be intimidating—a goal they attained with much barbed wire and machine-gun-equipped guard towers. Each compound was demarcated by less ominous fencing, but between 0800 and 1900 men were allowed to circulate between them and socialize with the other POWs, unless of course they were under lockdown.[16]

The biggest concern for prisoners was always food. Mornings began with roll call at 0600, followed an hour later by breakfast—ersatz coffee (burned barley) laced with chicory or a sort of mint tea which, as one wag put it, was best used for shaving—and one-sixth of a normal-sized loaf of almost indigestible black bread, whose true contents became the subject of endless speculation. In addition to this, prisoners received 30 g of spread (typically margarine, plain fat or some sort of "jam"). Lunch followed at noon—a half-litre of vegetable soup, mostly cabbage with lumps of turnip, and any leftover black bread. At 1700, supper offered the most surprises, but was usually some variation on vegetable stew, three or four potatoes and occasionally pieces of horse meat or fish. The notorious "fish cheese" was also frequent fare. Constant hunger pangs ensured the prisoners ate everything they were given, except the "fish cheese," which was hard to keep down.[17]

The Germans placed officers and men in different camps. The handful of captured Calgary officers were first sent to Oflag VII-B near Eichstadt in Bavaria. From individual space to the food, camp conditions for officers, while still austere, were definitely superior.[18]

POWs, the Third Reich, and the Geneva Convention

The International Committee of the Red Cross handled the affairs of British and Commonwealth POWs, and by 1941 was interacting with the Canadian government directly and not just through London. With prisoners of the Western Allies, Berlin broadly adhered to the Geneva Convention and other international agreements spelling out expected standards of treatment, and the swelling numbers of German POWs guaranteed it would remain so. This ensured officers would not be made to work, that other ranks would not have to work at tasks directly benefiting the German war effort, and that both would be fed a diet approximating what German civilians in the same locale enjoyed. Within Canada, responsibility for prisoner of war matters overlapped between government and various volunteer organizations, but among the latter the Canadian Red Cross came to dominate, Ottawa having given it close to total control over food parcels—a responsibility it carried out impressively.[19]

God Bless the Red Cross ... And the Ladies Auxiliary

Had they depended entirely on German rations, Allied prisoners of war would have starved. "We owe our lives to the Red Cross," Trooper Archie Anderson offered years later, and he spoke for every Canadian POW.[20] The five-kilogram parcels were supposed to reach the prisoners weekly and provide the recipient with 2,070 calories per day. The standard fare included whole milk powder, butter, cheese, corned beef, pork luncheon meat, salmon, sardines, dried apples, dried prunes, sugar, jam, biscuits and chocolate, along with some tea and salt.[21] Problematic wartime transportation, especially within Germany, combined with the periodic withholding of the parcels as punishment, meant the weekly schedule was rarely met. But when they did arrive, well, "who wouldn't be a *gefangener* on parcel days," Tpr. Tom Pinder quipped in his diary.[22] Parcels were invariably shared so that every prisoner got something, making them the morale booster *par excellence*.

The Red Cross efforts were sustained by public donations supplemented by Ottawa, and all the packing was done by women's groups.[23] The Canadian Prisoner of War Relatives Association were permitted to send large food parcels quarterly as well as one-time "relief" shipments, but families were prevented from mailing food to their POW loved ones (though this could be circumvented by routing them through the United States). Families in Canada could send clothing, books and like goods, and the Calgary men were particularly fortunate because the Ladies Auxiliary faithfully sent knitted items, cookies, "and most blessed of all, cigarettes" by the thousands.[24] Both the Women's Auxiliary and the reserve regiment channelled money from their fundraisers to any next of kin who couldn't otherwise have afforded to send their own parcels.[25] Finally, other volunteer groups and organizations like the YMCA made sure hockey and baseball gear, musical instruments, and reading material reached the camps.

Settling in for the Long Haul

As the months became years, prison camp life exacted a toll. Apart from food, boredom was the overriding problem, and depression was common, especially, it seemed, among married men with families. It was critically important to keep busy—at practically anything. Reading, classes on virtually every subject including correspondence courses offered by British and later Canadian universities, musical and drama performances, and sports helped keep spirits up. Card playing offered the added attraction of gambling. And there was certainly plenty of time to walk circuits around their own compound, or others when it was permitted.[26] The entrepreneurial hawked items from personal or Red Cross parcels while others carried on a stealthy trade (cigarettes for food) with guards.[27]

Kriegsgelangenenpost

If food was the top morale booster, writing letters and even more so receiving them was close behind. "First letter from home," Tpr. Tom Pinder enthused when a letter finally reached him after three months, and "feel 100% better."[28] *Kriegsgelangenenpost*—the postal service for prisoners of war—allowed men to send brief letters or cards once a week at best, and they knew even remotely interesting content would be censored.[29] Early letters invariably followed the "I am fine, and X and Y are alive, too" template, but were eagerly circulated among prisoners' loved ones back home.[30] Canadian and German authorities strictly vetted the responses, too, sometimes leaving the disappointed prisoners with little more than redactions.[31] Most prisoner correspondence in 1943 and 1944 focused on reassuring the recipient that they were healthy, well fed and contented with their lot, or requests for cigarettes (the currency of camps), pictures of loved ones (everything had been left in England), and personal items. And of course inquiries about how family, friends and neighbours back home were doing.[32] Delivery times both ways were usually measured in months, but it was tangible contact with places and people they longed to return to.

Shackling

Certainly the most notorious aspect of the Dieppe prisoners' treatment was their shackling, which the Germans commenced with self-righteous fanfare in October 1942 and terminated quietly thirteen months later. Although much of the shackling was perfunctory, at other times the Canadian POWs suffered harshly. The Germans had captured of a copy of the Dieppe operational plan in which it was recommended that "whenever possible the hands of the [German] prisoners are to be bound, so that they may not destroy their papers." In early October, hoping to score some diplomatic points and embarrass Britain, Berlin ordered the hands of the Dieppe prisoners bound.[33] Initially this was strictly enforced from 0800 till 2000. Even going to the bathroom was humiliating, and having their wrists tightly secured behind their backs with binder twine for hours on end caused painful chafing sores. When mail and Red Cross parcels were withheld as well, morale plummeted (though regular delivery of both were soon resumed). Shackling was temporarily suspended for Christmas, the camp commandant even issuing some beer to fuel the spirit of the season. In January 1943, Red Cross officials told the Germans to use a more humane method, which led to the introduction of handcuff shackles linked by foot-long chains. Ingenious prisoners learned to pick the locks and doff the new hardware, which was followed by a mad scramble to put it on again if lookouts spotted a guard approaching the barracks.[34] As the months passed, all but the most fanatic guards simply turned the other way, and by November 1943, when Berlin let the shackling affair drop, wearing them was only being required during roll calls.[35]

Work Parties

Enlisted prisoners could volunteer for work details that took them outside the camp confines, and many did so. The food was generally better (or at least there was more of it), there was the chance to get some exercise, and it kept one occupied. Tpr. J. D. White worked with about twenty other POWs on farms where they slept in the barns until they returned to the main camp for Sundays. It was hard work and the food certainly failed to live up to the promises—a bowl of soup a day, a loaf of black bread shared seven ways, and potatoes they dug from the fields supplemented by their carefully rationed Red Cross supplies. The six-day work week was eventually raised to six-and-a-half "for the good of the German people." White and his comrades thought the extra half day violated the Geneva Convention but an officer grimly informed them they'd be shot if they refused. As White observed, "the Geneva Convention is a long ways away when you are a prisoner of war."[36] Along with forty others, Don Craigie worked on the same farm for a year, starting in the summer of 1943, thereafter unloading food from trains.[37] Vern Richardson did forestry work, everything from felling to reforestation, as well as rail line, bridge, and tunnel repairs.[38] Lunch breaks created plenty of opportunities to barter with their German co-workers or the guards, the ready access to cigarettes lubricating commerce.

Escapes

Escapes have long been standard fare in war movies, but in reality there was no military requirement or expectation that prisoners would try to escape (even though most POWs believed there was). Of course in all camps, including the Canadian section of Stalag VIII-B, escape committees were soon established, and serious plans hatched. But few got beyond that stage, not least because the Germans were every bit as ingenious in thwarting escapes as prisoners were in trying to pull them off. The vast majority could see that the odds of successfully escaping, unless you were German-speaking or could at least pass yourself off as a foreign labourer, were slim—and next to hopeless from a camp only 200 kms closer to London than Moscow. After the tragic "Great Escape" from Stalag Luft III in late March 1944, where fifty of the seventy-six escapees were executed after their recapture, Allied POWs were no longer deemed exempt from the Bullet Decree, all but putting paid to group escape attempts.[39]

Despite the formidable obstacles, some escapes—at least, the spur of the moment variety—were successful. Having volunteered for a work party, the Calgary Regiment's Cpl. Gus Nelson made a dash for freedom with a friend from the Camerons, Sgt. Red McMullen. The two of them somehow managed to reach the port of Stettin, fortuitously entering during the chaos of an air raid, where they slipped into a French work detail in the midst of changing shifts and managed to reach the docks. There, with the help of a sympathetic Swedish sailor (Nelson spoke Swedish), they stowed away on a badly damaged freighter that was set to depart under tow for Sweden. To avoid detection by the German troops and their dogs sweeping the ship, the two hid in a fuel bunker, then spent the rest of their sixteen-day crossing secreted in the engine room and expecting the vessel to founder at any time. But miraculously it stayed afloat, appropriately arriving in neutral Sweden on Dominion Day. Nelson snuck ashore and phoned the British consul, who promptly collected them. Four months later he was flown back to England, debriefed, and awarded a MM.[40]

The Beginning of the End

During January and February 1944 most of the Dieppe prisoners had been moved from Lamsdorf to Stalag II-D just outside the town of Stargard, about 30 km east of Stettin (now Szczecin, Poland). Prisoners sensed a more congenial live-and-let-live attitude on the part of their guards, though officially there was no moderation of harsh policies. Travelling to and from their workplaces allowed them to witness some appalling sights, the most shocking being slave labourers of every nationality, both male and female. Among them were wraith-like Soviet POWs, their ribs showing, limbs like sticks, dressed in rags. Still, every new wave of arrivals—American other ranks captured during the Battle of the Bulge were the last to do so—brought news of Allied advances, and most nights there was the drone of bomber engines or the distant crump of Red Army artillery to confirm that news. What turned out to be the last Christmas of the war was celebrated with enthusiasm in Stalag II-D. They had been scrupulously saving items from food parcels to ensure an appetizing dinner, and decorated their barracks with whatever could be improvised or else scrounged from the guards. On December 25, a blustery, cold day, the commandant even cancelled morning roll call. Just before supper was served, one of the guards came into Roy Johnston's barracks to take the usual head count. As he departed, he waved his hand and offered a cheery *Frohliche Weinachten zu alles*.[41]

Returning to camp from a work detail on 2 February 1945, Tpr. Archie Anderson was handed a letter from his wife. It was more poetry than prose, and captured beautifully what the couple both wanted from their war:

> Two letters lie before me, many times I've read them through—
> They bring me hope for future days, when our dreams will all come true—Fleecy clouds will go a-sailing in a sky of clearest

blue, on that day when I'll wade again—Through autumn leaves with you.[42]

Having barely recovered from a botched hernia surgery that kept him in hospital for half a year, Anderson had survived almost thirty months of German captivity. Now, on the very cusp of freedom, the next few weeks would bring by far the worst conditions he and his comrades endured as prisoners of war. In the midst of a frigid winter and the dying paroxysms of Hitler's regime, tens of thousands of Allied POWs would be force-marched west to keep them as negotiating pawns and prevent their liberation by rapidly advancing Soviet forces.

Allied Plans for a Spring Offensive

Initial plans for 1944 were predicated on simultaneous landings in Normandy (Overlord) and Southern France (Anvil) in May, with the Italian Campaign, having succeeded in pushing the Germans well north of Rome, merely conducting holding operations. But the Germans were still entrenched south of Rome in early 1944. There was no choice but to postpone Anvil and mount an all-out offensive to capture Rome and compel the German Army to withdraw northward. To accomplish this, the weight of the British Eighth Army would shift from the Adriatic Coast to the immediate right of the American Fifth Army. Once having broken through the Cassino area, the valley of the Liri River offered a corridor to press on to Rome. Eighth Army's XIII British Corps would occupy a key portion of the front abutting the Liri River and Cassino, with about half of its armour support coming from the 1st Canadian Armoured Brigade. The attack—Operation Honker—was tentatively set for May 10. As was so often the case during the Italian Campaign, the German high command failed to divine Allied intentions. Nonetheless, their defences were formidable, starting with the Gustav Line dominated by mountains (including Monte Cassino itself) and protected to the south and east by fast flowing rivers, including the Gari. Beyond it lay a second stretch of defences, the Adolf Hitler Line. Even achieving surprise would not guarantee victory here.[43]

Preparing for Battle

With the greater part of Eighth Army in motion, the regiment's move to its new encampment area near Presenzano in the XIII British Corps zone was time-consuming, but they were in place and their base up and running before the end of the first week of April.[44] Given their brigade would likely stay put for the remainder of the month, there was an opportunity to carry out further tank-infantry training. This was a high priority for Lt.-Gen. S. C. Kirkman, XIII British Corps' commander, who at a meeting with all his senior officers, including Lt.-Cols. Neroutsos, Purves, Caron and Brig. Murphy, emphasized that they would be facing an opposed river crossing for the first time.[45] The infantry would have to secure bridgeheads for the tanks and neutralize the anti-tank defences, while the tanks would be indispensable in suppressing the machine-gun defences and keeping infantry casualties manageable. Close co-operation between the two arms was going to be essential. Once they'd broken through, armour would be best employed in the close support and mopping-up roles where "their presence is most detrimental to enemy morale" rather than being assigned "impossible tasks." The general wrapped up by emphasizing that every step in the assault, including the time allotted for securing objectives, must accommodate the speed of the infantry's advance and the defenders' determination to hold on. In plain English, slow and successful was to be preferred over fast and failed. At the same time, he didn't expect slavish adherence to the plan—plans invariably unravelled in battle, and his tank commanders still needed to seize any opportunities to deal a fatal blow to the enemy.[46] It was a sound assessment.

During this period, two of Murphy's regiments did participate in an intensive regimen of infantry-armour training with the 8th Indian Division to bring everyone up to speed and build familiarity and confidence between units which would be fighting alongside one other.[47] There had been off-and-on co-operation between the Indians and Canadians since January, and the 8th's CO, Maj.-Gen. Dudley Russell, had specifically requested that his men again be paired with Murphy's tanks.[48] When drawing up a training plan, Kirkman had sought input from his Canadians officers, and the resultant syllabus was very much a joint product. The practical exercises, which culminated in a mock attack with live ammunition, were followed by debriefings among the infantry and tank officers where they could grasp one another's problems and settle on workable solutions. Battlefield communication was probably the most critical problem. Infantry-tank radio networks invariably frayed in action, and it was agreed that the most foolproof method was for infantry to point their weapons in the direction of the enemy fire or, at least when they were English-speaking, use the telephone sets being installed on the rear of the Shermans.[49] The four-day training programs were repeated with several of the Indian battalions. As much as the Canadian tankers liked to joke that they found it every bit as hard to fathom the brogue of the highlanders as they did the mysteries of Urdu, the language barrier was a serious complication for the Indian soldiers in both training and in action.[50] Everyone just coped as best they could. The benefits of their training with the 19th Indian Brigade in particular, abbreviated though it was, would soon be evident.

The training was brief because the 8th Indian Division battalions, which were still taking their turns in the line, had to concentrate on mastering opposed river crossings.[51] Although forcing the river was planned as a joint operation, Maj.-Gen. Russell rightly argued that "the success of the whole operation is ... dependent on getting tanks forward early."[52] Yet inexplicably none of the Canadian tank units participated in any of this training, an absence that troubled at least one of the 8th Indian Division's brigadiers.

By month's end, with the attack less than two weeks away, tension was clearly mounting. Lt.-Col. Neroutsos and Maj. Richardson were attending meetings discussing this or that aspect of Honker with other senior officers almost daily. A preliminary reconnaissance of the likely area of their assault along the Gari had been completed by Lts. J. S. Hunter and J. L. Whitton, the regiment's intelligence and recce officers, respectively. And XIII British Corps had begun dispensing unit call signs, always a harbinger of imminent action.[53]

As the calendar rolled over, the pace of meetings and other preparations only increased.[54] Finally, on the morning of May 7, Neroutsos gathered his squadron commanders and other senior officers to outline the operation in full detail, with tank crews briefed in turn the following day.[55] After darkness fell on the 9th, the Shermans moved up to their jumping-off positions. The same night the last of the boats that would ferry the 19th Indian Brigade's two assault battalions were transported to their staging area a few hundred metres from the river. Once in place, the tank crews were excused from their duties to give them a chance to rest. A 1st Armoured Brigade war diary entry summed things up: "last minute details ... were very few, all matters having been so completely covered at planning conferences and during order groups."[56] There was nothing to do but wait. "Everyone is all keyed-up anticipating the action to come very shortly ... and the morale is very high," the regiment's own war diary calmly recorded.[57] The penultimate day dawned warm and sunny. The tanks were well camouflaged and no tents had been pitched in an attempt to mask the build-up from *Luftwaffe* reconnaissance flights, which were purposely left alone so as not to alert the enemy.[58] Officers briefed their men on a few last-minute changes, and the commanding officer held a final orders group late in the afternoon. That evening Lt. Hunter attended a last intelligence briefing while Lt.-Col. Neroutsos ate supper at Brig. Murphy's headquarters with Lt.-Cols. Caron and Purves, returning around 2230.[59]

An Awful Lesson Remembered

Three months earlier, the American Army had attempted to attack across the Garigliano River in the same general area that Canadian and Indian troops were now planning to assault. On January 20, two regiments (equivalent to Anglo-Canadian brigades) of the 36th Infantry Division managed to cross what Americans called the Rapido River in boats but were repelled.[60] A follow-up assault the next day gained a tenuous foothold, but German shelling prevented the construction of pontoon bridges. Reinforcement was thus impossible, most critically by tanks. Under continual shelling and facing repeated counterattacks, the bridgehead was soon abandoned. The Texans suffered over 1,300 killed and wounded, with another 800-odd taken prisoner. The failed assault naturally loomed large in British planning for Honker.[61]

The Attack Plan

The Eighth Army would rely on XIII British Corps to cross the Gari south of Cassino and by frontal attack breach first the Gustav and then the Hitler Line. On its right flank, II Polish Corps would sweep around Cassino and its dominating namesake mountain before joining XIII Corps' advance further up the Liri. The *Corps Expéditionaire Française* of the Free French forces, made up primarily of North and West African colonial units, would protect the left flank. While I Canadian Corps would start in reserve, it would be used to reinforce XIII British Corps' breakthrough.[62] 1st Canadian Armoured Brigade fell under the command of Lt.-Gen. Kirkman and so would be involved in the attack from the outset, supporting the 8th Indian Division's assault across the Gari, its far bank constituting the forward zone of the Gustav Line defences. The Calgary Regiment would serve alongside Brig. T. S. Dobree's 19th Indian Infantry Brigade, helping them consolidate their bridgeheads before rolling up the remaining forward German defences.[63] Intelligence on the defence the Canadian tankers would face was hardly reassuring. Enemy doctrine relied on towed and self-propelled anti-tank weapons—not tanks—to neutralize attacking armour, so no one expected much tank-on-tank action. There was every expectation that the anti-tank defences would be sited to cover the roads and tracks the British and Canadian tanks would likely have to use. The Sherman's only advantage was the propensity of nervous German crews to engage at long range, revealing their positions and leaving them vulnerable to well-placed high explosive rounds.[64] In the event, the biggest danger the tanks confronted was bogging down in the muddy flats that extended along the Gari's western bank. In hindsight, the enemy had relied on the river to block tanks, and never established a proper anti-tank gun defence.[65]

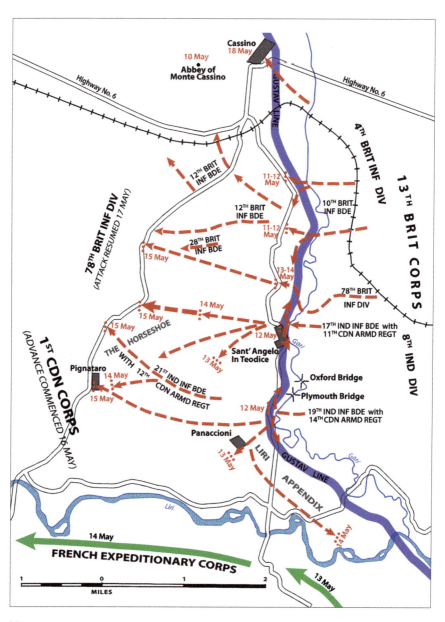

MAP 10:
Breaking the Gustav Line, 11–15 May 1944.

Battle Engaged, May 12

A half hour after Neroutsos had returned from his dinner, a deafening crash shattered the quiet all along the front. Over 1,000 guns of the XIII British and II Polish Corps—400 on the 8th Indian Division's frontage alone—lit up the sky and shook the ground through early morning, obliterating all known German mortar and artillery emplacements. Honker had commenced. Struggling to convey the barrage's ferocity, CBC war correspondent Peter Stursberg breathlessly spoke of "sheets of flame and balls of fire ... leaping back and forth across the valley as battery after battery fire salvoes. It's an amazing and terrifying sight yet thrilling."[66] Then he turned his microphone to the sky and recorded the deafening symphony. A Squadron was hidden close to several British heavy batteries, and the guns' rhythmic roar "ensured we were awake and our adrenalin going," Capt. Jim Quinn recalled.[67] At 0100, the Shermans of C and the HQ Squadrons roared to life and headed out along Speedy Express, the track assigned to the Indians. They reached their forward assembly area about 2 kms from the east bank of the Gari in just 45 minutes, with the others moving to their assembly points in turn.

Their immediate obstacle was the Gari and getting across it. It was in full spring flood and flowing fast. As much as 20 m wide in places and 3 m deep, it was impossible for tanks to ford. The flats on the east side were extensive, about 700 m deep, but much shallower on the German side, extending at most 250 m away from the water. Beyond that the terrain rose to a false ridgeline about a kilometre distant and then to a main ridge, with lateral roads about 500 m further on. The river flats on both sides were boggy and thick with tall marsh grass. Beyond, as the ground rose on the enemy side, extensive groves of olive and fig trees had been shattered during previous fighting or cut down by the Germans to make clear fields for fire and observation.[68] So as not to alert the enemy, there had been no patrolling on the enemy side at all. It may have preserved tactical surprise, but it left the attackers ignorant of critical features of the terrain and the nature of the defences. For the tank units, the extent of the swathe of muddy ground they'd need to traverse in order to reach higher (and drier) ground beyond the river would come as a cruel surprise.[69]

The initial assault by the 8th Indian Division would fall to two battalions from each of the 17th and 19th Indian Brigades, supported by the 11th and 14th Armoured Regiments, respectively.[70] The infantry would be on their own until the tanks could get across, and that depended on when the bridges were in place (the expectation/hope being 0400). The tank crews knew it was crucial to join up with their infantry as soon as possible. Unfortunately circumstances prevented that, and the rifle companies paid dearly.

Rapido Redux?

The main German defensive position stretching back (and gradually upward) from the river several hundred metres consisted of minefields (anti-personnel and anti-tank) covered by numerous machine guns and mortars, together with a screen of anti-tank guns, thickets of barbed wire to channel infantry into killing zones, and deep bunkers to protect the weapons' crews from the inevitable bombardment. The enemy were understandably confident that any attack would meet the Americans' fate, and indeed the whole area along the river was strewn with the decomposing corpses of GIs, a grisly warning to the Canadian, Indian and British soldiers.[71]

The assault infantry of the 8th Indian Division—the 3/8 Punjabs and 1/Argyle and Sutherland Highlanders—and to the north of them, from the 4th British Division, began crossing at 2345. It was clear from the initial German reaction, or lack of it, that surprise had been achieved. But it was about all that went right. Between the darkness and dense smokescreen, tracer had to be used to guide the boats to their landing zones.[72] Having made it across, the first wave found little immediate cover and the Argyll and Sutherland Highlanders suffered the added misfortune of debouching into a minefield.[73] Casualties rapidly mounted, breaking the companies up into isolated groups struggling to reorganize and press on. As succeeding platoons were ferried across, more and more boats were sunk or swept away in the current. By 0230 both battalions had only been able to put two companies ashore. The 3/8 Punjabs managed to advance between 200 to 300 m from the riverbank before being pinned down by intact German strong points and wire. Poor communications rendered artillery support only marginally effective. During the course of the night, one company was all but wiped out, with the remnant surrendering at dawn, their ammunition exhausted. A second managed to gain its initial objectives but was reduced to thirty men. The third was continually pinned down by machine-gun nests that had to be silenced by heroic individual actions like that of nineteen-year-old Sepoy Kamal Ram, who won a VC in his first action. Russell's battle log rightly noted that the infantry had been left on their own because of the painfully slow progress getting the bridges operating and the tanks across. By 0600, when sunlight had begun to filter through the murk, the Punjabs managed to ferry their last men across and more critically, a 6-pounder anti-tank gun and a jeep to pull it, which was quickly followed by several more, soon putting paid to the German pill boxes.

The 1/Argyll and Sutherlands endured an even worse time of it. Only one company and two platoons from a second had managed to get over before all their boats and rafts had been lost. After three hours of heavy fighting, the commanding officer had assembled fewer than half of his shattered force. Chaos and the tenuous bridgehead meant only a feeble stream of reinforcements had reached them. With Russell's approval, around 1500 Dobree finally decided to abandon the bridgehead (though isolated pockets of men remained) and attempt to recross later in the day closer to where the Punjabs were enjoying at least some success.[74] That the Indian and British infantry managed to hold on, and in the case of the former consolidate their fragile bridgehead, before Canadian armour finally reached them in the afternoon was a tribute to their remarkable tenacity and enterprise.[75]

A King of a Bridge

Normally, engineers could not throw a bridge across a river like the Gari without the infantry first securing a sufficient bridgehead on the far side. Lt.-Col. Neroutsos had become convinced that only an extra bridge could reasonably guarantee their getting two regiments of tanks across as quickly as required.[76] Maj.-Gen. Russell agreed, but it took persistence by him, his staff, and Neroutsos to persuade the corps commander. Once authorized, the Calgary Regiment's CO chose a site for *Plymouth* about 500 m south of *Oxford*. It fell to the regiment's engineering officer, Capt. Tony Kingsmill, to conjure up a way of doing it.[77]

He soon came up with a novel solution that would make it possible to lay a conventional prefabricated Bailey bridge structure in a fraction of the normal time. It was tried out a few times at the Volturno training area—with irregular success, but the results were promising enough to proceed. Kingsmill's brainstorm involved placing a 30m length of bridge atop two tanks, the lead one having had its turret removed and rollers attached to the top of the hull so the bridge could move forward, while the rear end of the bridge sat on a bracket mounted on the front of the second tank's hull. The lead tank would drive a short distance into the water while the rear tank pushed the bridge forward until it grounded on the far bank. Three hours after the infantry had launched their assault, while Indian sappers were wrestling with the construction of *Oxford* (the Ontario Regiment's bridge) under heavy fire, the bridging tanks reported that they were making their way forward with *Plymouth*, and by 0500, work on Kingsmill's gamble had commenced, with an estimate it would be operational by 0800.

Dawn broke around 0530, with a heavy mist thickened by all the smoke from the barrage reducing visibility to 45 m. C Squadron and the other tanks could only cool their heels. Just before 0900 word came that *Oxford* was finally open and the Ontarios had gotten one of their squadrons across. Maj.-Gen.

Russell's had earlier instructed that if *Oxford* was ready first, part of the Calgary Regiment force should make for it and double back to their planned marrying-up point with the 3/8 Punjabs. Traffic congestion slowed C Squadron but it still managed to reach *Oxford*, and once across, tanks that avoided bogging down in the mud or hitting mines hastened to try to find their infantry and link-up.[78]

Meanwhile, in the face of heavy machine-gun and mortar fire, *Plymouth* was finally being pushed into place. So far the luck had all been bad. The carrier tank had drifted off line and had bogged down, and it took nearly three hours to free it, assemble the bridge components, hoist them onto the carrier, and then get the ungainly contraption ready to move out from cover toward the river. By the time they were ready to go it was light. But go they did, though excruciatingly slowly, Kingsmill walking alongside with a telephone connection to the two-man carrier crew, Tprs. George McLean and Ian Seymour, whose jobs Neroutsos considered suicidal given their turretless Sherman was bound to drown. It was several hundred metres to the Gari's eastern bank, where Kingsmill paused his creation to ensure it was precisely lined up with the far bank. Then, at 0930, he gave the signal for the pusher tank to proceed. Once it was certain the end of the bridge had extended a safe distance beyond the far bank, he ordered the carrier tank into the river to lower *Plymouth* into its final position. MacLean and Seymour managed to bob to the surface and swim ashore after decoupling from their load. An overjoyed Tony Kingsmill messaged the good news to regimental headquarters.[79] After all the delays, the critical emplacement had only taken 15 minutes.

Lined up nose-to-tail awaiting orders, the tankers had been in their forward assembly areas for hours, and sensed things were not going well. Kingsmill's message was enough for Lt.-Col. Neroutsos, who ordered A Squadron to get across on *Plymouth* and rescue what was left of 19th Brigade's assault force. Of course the bridge itself was vulnerable, and Kingsmill pressed for an annihilating barrage on the far shore perimeter and more smoke. The howitzers of the British 98th Field Regiment (Self-Propelled) happily obliged.[80] The lead unit of Maj. Bob Taylor's A Squadron, Lt. Al Wells' troop, arrived first and wasted no time crossing, with Lt. Jim Quinn's Sherman right behind. But as soon as Quinn crossed, a German shell shattered the far ramp and caved in the supporting bank, rendering *Plymouth* temporarily unusable.[81] At least the four A Squadron tanks that had made it were able to rake everything in sight with 75-mm and machine-gun fire, finally securing a safe perimeter for bridge repairs to proceed. Meanwhile, the remainder of A Squadron had no choice but to divert to *Oxford*, costing them more time.[82]

Tanks to the Rescue

The first troop from C Squadron to reach *Oxford* had been Lt. Al Cawsey's. Cpl. Bill McWithy's lead Sherman had bogged down just short of the ramp, blocking the narrow approach, forcing Cawsey to navigate around him over unswept ground so he could extricate McWithy from the mire.[83] With visibility near zero and the area under heavy machine-gun and mortar fire, one of the crew walked in front trying to pick out any mines. They were lucky, as they had straddled three mines but failed to detonate any of them. As it turned out, the ground on the far side was too soft to support the 30-ton Shermans, and most crossing that morning bogged down in the mud—from the first wave, Cawsey's and McWithy's were actually the only ones to get clear.[84] Only minutes later they encountered a small party of Punjabs whose wounded officer informed Cawsey the tanks would have to proceed on their own. When Cawsey managed to contact his CO, Maj. Don Taylor,[85] whose own tank was among those stuck back at the river, Taylor told him to use his judgment— music to any troop commander's ears. He and McWithy decided to press on to the village of Panaccioni, one of the squadron's first-day objectives, and see what happened. They had hardly got moving when McWithy glimpsed a *StuG* assault gun manoeuvring to get a shot away. Cawsey's gunner knocked it out with his first round, McWithy machine-gunning the crew when they bailed out. Over the next few hours, as they traversed the countryside in search of the main force of the 3/8 Punjabs, they destroyed a Panzer Mk. III, a second *StuG*, and a 75-mm anti-tank gun, as well as blew up several stone farm buildings they suspected were strong points or headquarters. When they finally reached a crossroads just north of Panaccioni, Taylor radioed Cawsey to conserve his ammunition and instead direct the fire from field artillery batteries across the river, which he did for several hours, until the first tanks from A Squadron finally appeared.[86]

As Cawsey's and McWithy's adventure was unfolding, Lt. Jim Quinn was advancing parallel to the river trying to cause mayhem and hoping to make contact with the Argyll and Sutherlands. The only infantry he and his men caught sight of were counterattacking units from the 115th *Panzergrenadier* Regiment seeking to plug (the many) gaps in the German line. Wisely concluding it was far too risky to continue marauding without infantry support, Quinn headed inland, finally reaching a rise just east of Panaccioni not far from their C Squadron mates. Carefully camouflaging the tanks alongside a hedgerow, they, too, hunkered down to observe enemy activity and call in artillery shoots. A German patrol eventually passed close by, first waving at the Canadian tanks but then opening fire. Quinn's small force responded with everything they had, and German artillery and mortars soon had their range. Without infantry for perimeter defence, they and their tanks were living on borrowed time. Finally around 1700, the separate groups of Shermans, along with a few more that had joined them, were ordered to fall back to the main lateral road west of the river where they joined up with some sepoys and hunkered down in an improvised harbour. Fearing that tank-killing teams of German infantry would try to infiltrate their position during the night, they arranged to call in artillery fire on their own position, though fortunately this didn't prove necessary. Instead, the only visitors were more small groups of Indian soldiers and Recce Squadron Stuarts bringing badly needed fuel and ammunition. Still, it was the only night during the war Al Cawsey slept inside his tank.[87] Jim Quinn probably summed it up best: "On reflection it was probably just as well that we did not know ... how very exposed we were that first day and night!"[88]

The persistent difficulties the armour encountered in marrying up with their infantry until well into the afternoon left the fate of the attack in jeopardy.[89] However, Lt.-Gen. Kirkman's instructions had made it clear that "the tankers had to be prepared to push forward without the infantry ... in order to prevent the reeling Germans from reorganizing, and to maintain contact [with them]."[90] That's precisely what the two groups had done. By late afternoon, A Squadron's remaining troops had taken up positions just southwest of Panaccioni, while two depleted companies of the 3/8 Punjabs had finally managed to link up with Taylor's tanks. The bridgehead was now deemed reasonably secure. Still, it was obvious that opportunities for tactical exploitation were lost throughout the day as the tanks fruitlessly searched for their infantry. Brig. Murphy's conclusion—that in future opposed river crossings tanks should break out of the bridgehead with fresh infantry rather than those engaged in the initial assault—certainly had merit.[91] Nevertheless, marauding tanks in their rear areas had unbalanced the enemy, causing him to husband his few armoured reserves instead of throwing them into immediate counterattacks against Brig. Dobree's fragile enclaves.[92]

Assessing the First Day

It would be easy to say that in the 8th Indian Division's sector, the results had fallen well short of the plan, with the infantry being very badly cut up.[93] On the other hand, facing bitter resistance from both the enemy and the terrain, two infantry brigades and five armoured squadrons had managed to cross the Gari and secure a firm, if still discontinuous, bridgehead on its far side, giving the enemy a hard whack from which he was unable to recover.[94] By day's end the 4th British Infantry Division's bridgehead to the north was only precariously held, and II Polish Corps had been unable to penetrate the defences north of Cassino. As the Indian Army official history proudly claimed, "it was the initial success gained by the 8th Indian Division in seizing and holding a firm bridgehead at Sant' Angelo [immediately north of 19th Indian Brigade's sector] which paved the way for the final victory."[95] And, one might add, an operation carried out with the notable assistance of the Ontario Regiment of the 1st Canadian Armoured Brigade.[96] While matters had not gone nearly as well for the 19th Brigade and Calgary Regiment, it had been no Rapido, either. Only a few days earlier, Maj.-Gen. Russell had enjoined his command that "full advantage can only be reaped from success or surprise if calculated risks are taken and action is speedy."[97] The tankers of the Calgary Regiment had done their best to carry out those instructions.

Battle Resumed, May 13

The tanks that had gotten across the Gari on the first day encountered a landscape they would face during the remainder of the battle. Mostly it was gently rolling farmland interspersed with vineyards and fig and olive groves and crossed with numerous gullies— perfect country for masking defensive positions, and by 1944 the Germans had become masters of that art. Moving cross-country was seldom realistic, so both the Indian and British infantry and the Canadian tankers supporting them mostly stuck to the roads and tracks linking the scattered communities.[98]

The 13th dawned with very good news—during the night Indian and Canadian sappers had managed to repair *Plymouth* bridge and recovery crews had been successful in getting most of the Shermans stuck in the mud flats along the Gari moving again. At 0700, as their crews ate breakfast, squadron leaders were given the day's objectives. With the fresh 6/13 Royal Frontier Force Rifles supported by two troops of B Squadron protecting their right flank, the 3/8 Punjabs, supported by C Squadron, would take the crossroads near Panaccioni. Then the flanking force would clear the village. Finally, the remainder of B Squadron and a batch of reinforcement tanks would cross *Plymouth* and hold a blocking position along the Sant' Angelo road. With the 1/Argyll and Sutherland Highlanders finally across the river to stay during the night, A Squadron (in reserve) finally had their own infantry. It would fall to the Ontario Regiment and 17th Indian Brigade infantry to eject the Germans from Sant' Angelo itself, which in Maj.-Gen. Russell's mind was the key to cracking open his division's section of the Gustav Line.

Although German artillery now enjoyed better visibility, they were unable to knock out either *Plymouth* or *Oxford*, their principal goal.[99] By mid-morning, the various advances were underway, and by 1400 C Squadron and the Punjabs were pressing into the crossroads area against stiff resistance. Tank fire had already killed two *StuGs* when a lethal round from another slammed into Lt. Al

Abram's lead Sherman, killing him and Tpr. A. A. Coloumbe. The remainder of the force manoeuvred onto high ground immediately north of the village. Meanwhile around 1600 two of the companies from the 6/13 Royal Frontier Force Rifles and the two troops of B Squadron Shermans with the welcome support of a ten-minute barrage from seventy-two 25-pounders, commenced their attack on Panaccioni. By 1730 the village had been cleared. It proved the last stand of the 2/576 *Panzergrenadiers*, which the 19th Brigade and Calgary Regiment had wiped out over the past two days.[100] A scratch German force that was assembling in Pignataro for a counterattack was shattered by calling in another barrage. The arrival of more tanks (from A Squadron) scattered the remnants of the assembling force.

Everywhere along the 8th Indian Division's sector on May 13 attacks had been crowned with success. Most of the engagements were textbook demonstrations of thorough infantry-armour training, and a tribute to Murphy's and Russell's commitment to same during the preceding weeks.[101] The successes pointed to the enemy's growing weakness, too, for the Germans had few reserves remaining. Those were being thrown in piecemeal to deal with local crises, usually with little armour support, and they had no answer for the tanks that accompanied every attack. In essence, the Germans had been shocked by the sheer weight and speed of the offensive, and never recovered.[102] That evening, with his forces having driven back the enemy line some 1,500 m on a 2,700 m front, Russell proudly declared the Gari bridgehead secure. The night was spent carrying out needed resupply while the tank crews completed pressing maintenance and then sought what rest they could.[103] Morale was high, for everyone grasped that the enemy had lost the day and likely the battle.

The Battle Won, May 14–16

Plans for May 14 called for the fresh 21st Indian Brigade, supported by the Three Rivers Regiment's tanks, to pass through the Calgary Regiment's and 19th Indian Brigade's position and press on toward Pignataro, about 4 km northwest of Panaccioni. Only A Squadron would be in action, assisting the 1/Argyll and Sutherlands in clearing the Liri Appendix, a wedge-shaped feature bounded by the Liri and Gari Rivers. Supported by the combined fire of a regiment each of medium and field artillery, this modest infantry-tank force completed the task by noon. By now, even intermittent German shelling had practically ceased, enabling officers and men to bed down early and enjoy their first good sleep in days.[104]

The forecast for May 15 promised fine weather. Later that morning Brig. Murphy paid a visit to Lt.-Col. Neroutsos, praising the performance of the latter's men and passing on the hearty congratulations of Gen. Oliver Leese, the

Eighth Army commander. Shortly after noon, Neroutsos returned from Brig. Dobree's headquarters with plans they had jointly drawn up for the assault on Pignataro, plans that called for B Squadron to support the 6/13 Royal Frontier Force Rifles, with A Squadron and the 1/Argyll and Sutherland Highlanders providing flank protection.[105] Setting out around 1330, the combined force found the going easy until they neared their objective. First machine-gun fire pinned down a company of the Scots, which Lt. Quinn's troop quickly silenced. In short order, a second company was forced to ground and as Lt. Wells manoeuvred his three Shermans to deal with the problem, a shell fired from a well-camouflaged *StuG* sliced through his turret, killing both Wells and his loader, Cpl. Lauzon, and seriously wounding the gunner, Tpr. Tony Szeler. Almost immediately, Sgt. Rolly Marchant's tank was hit by the same self-propelled gun, mortally wounding him. When Lt. Quinn's Sherman then bogged down, the situation became "very serious," forcing the infantry to hunker down around the tanks, as it turned out, for the night.

Meanwhile, the assault force bound for Pignataro slowly made its way toward its objective. By late afternoon, the 6/13 RFFRs had approached within 200 m of the outskirts when they came under sharp mortar and machine-gun fire from inside the village. Field artillery and the guns of B Squadron's Shermans firing high explosive rounds soon obliterated these positions. At last light, with the aid of a smoke screen also provided by the tanks, two rifle companies infiltrated Pignataro, and in the deepening gloom, overran the German garrison house by house, taking very few prisoners. By midnight, the village was deemed clear. A counterattack three hours later was obliterated by yet another artillery shoot called in by radio.[106] In their own assessment of the last few days' fighting, German commanders had drawn one pre-eminent lesson—the tanks supporting infantry, if not dealt with at the outset, rendered those infantry advances unstoppable.[107]

Out of the Line

The series of assaults by the 8th Indian Division in conjunction with the 1st Canadian Armoured Brigade had torn a gaping hole in the Gustav Line. While that success was not quite matched by the assaults of the British and Polish forces further north, the Germans had no choice but to order a staged withdrawal to the prepared defences of the Adolf Hitler (or Dora) Line. To keep up pressure on the enemy, Gen. Leese ordered the fresh I Canadian Corps to relieve the Russell's weary force and continue the attack. The relief commenced overnight and by late afternoon on May 16, the Calgary Regiment was safely in harbour 15 kms to the rear.[108]

The Adolf Hitler Line

During the next week, the Allied advance continued until the Canadian, British, Polish and Free French forces were within sight of the Adolf Hitler Line. Respite for the Calgary Regiment was all too brief. Brig. Murphy almost immediately informed both the 14th and 11th Armoured Regiments that they would be adding some punch to the 78th British Division's assault on Aquino which, if successful, would open the way for a breakout by British armour. The decision to rush the attack was rooted in faulty British reconnaissance indicating that the area around Aquino and adjacent sections of the Adolf Hitler Line were thinly held and that the defenders were on the verge of withdrawing.[109] On the 18th, the first British attack was stopped cold. The two Canadian armoured regiments were to join up with the British infantry and try again the following day, which necessitated their moving overland during the night to jumping-off points near the Aquino airport. Unfortunately numerous other units were making the same trek. Amidst a warren of what were more tracks than roads—narrow, twisting, heavily cratered in places and boggy everywhere, and with most of them incorrectly plotted on maps—traffic control broke down. During the 8-hour ordeal the two tank regiments at least managed to avoid stumbling into any mine fields.[110]

The Canadian armour now faced having to assault the Adolf Hitler Line head-on. Less formidable than the Gustav Line, not the least because it didn't incorporate a river, it was still a significant obstacle. The anti-tank defences (*Pantherturm*) comprised a number of turrets stripped from Panther tanks and mounted on concrete pill boxes. Their long-barrelled 75-mm guns proved lethal against Shermans at even medium ranges. Each of these positions was covered by several *StuGs* in well-camouflaged positions. This group of defensive nodes was protected by an extensive anti-tank ditch and approaches thickly sown with both anti-tank and anti-personnel mines—the intent being to separate the tanks from their infantry, to the detriment of both. There were plenty of machine guns and mortars, too, and the whole area was extensively wired. Fortunately, there had been neither the time nor labour to complete everything, so there was little depth to the defences. Even the Germans felt their handiwork would merely delay, not stop, a serious attack.[111]

Aquino

The 19th dawned foggy, with visibility reduced to 100 m. Both armoured regiments were told they would attack as soon as the British infantry brigades they were accompanying ordered them to do so. Ominously, when he consulted with British officers, A Squadron's Jim Quinn found the tactical situation "to say the least very confused."[112] Word came down to prepare to advance by 1000. But due to confusion at the various British headquarters, only the Ontario Regiment received the order to move out. By noon, as pre-emptive German shelling intensified, the Calgary squadrons still had received no formal attack order, so they waited. Around 1500 they received news that the Ontarios' attack had been crushed. Forced to go ahead of their infantry, which had been pinned down by withering machine-gun and mortar fire, the tankers had made good progress until, as the protective morning mist lifted, they fell under the sights of an anti-tank screen consisting of several of the aforementioned *Pantherturm* strongpoints and some towed anti-tank guns. In short order, German gunners coolly picked off thirteen Shermans. "This cooled the ardour for our [own] effort," Quinn noted caustically.[113] Murphy spent the evening consulting with the Maj.-Gen. Keightley's staff and brigade commanders about the 78th's plans for an immediate follow-up. After waiting all the next day for the go-ahead, around 1830 Murphy personally delivered the word to Lt.-Col. Neroutsos that the Eighth Army had vetoed the operation, Leese having wisely concluded that the Aquino defences were too strong for brigade-sized assaults supported by a few dozen tanks to have any chance. No doubt Neroutsos and his squadron commanders heaved a collective sigh of relief.[114]

Late the following day the high command hatched another scheme, this time a diversionary attack on Aquino employing elements of A and B Squadrons in support of two British infantry battalions. The purpose was to draw attention away from I Canadian Corps' push immediately to the south, which now constituted Eighth Army's principal effort.[115] If it turned out the Aquino garrison had withdrawn, the modest force would occupy the town, which British artillery had already reduced to little more than a rubble pile. Maj. Bob Taylor and Capt. Fred Ritchie spent much of the day discussing operational details with their infantry opposite numbers. The go-ahead order reached the regiment during the night of May 23–24. At first light, two troops from A Squadron crept forward with two companies of the 2/Lancashires to ascertain enemy strength. As they neared the outskirts of Aquino, heavy machine-gun fire pinned down the infantry who had mistakenly gone past their stop line. Lt. Beresford selflessly led his troop forward to relieve the pressure—and into the sights of four anti-tank guns. His tank and Sgt. Allison's were immediately hit, killing both men. The guns' attention immediately shifted to Lt. Lamb's troop, knocking out his Sherman and taking his life. During the entire action, which had lasted only two minutes, six Calgary tanks suffered at least two penetrating hits, with four of them brewing up.[116] Both lieutenants had only just been made troop commanders.[117] At least the enemy now had every reason to believe a full-scale attack was intended, which greatly assisted the 5th Canadian Armoured

Division's attack that carried them to the banks of the Melfa River by day's end. But the Calgary Regiment had paid an awful price for a diversion—seventeen casualties—and no men who witnessed the Germans repeatedly firing on the ambulance jeeps attempting to evacuate their wounded comrades from the battlefield would forget—or forgive.[118]

Early the following morning B and C Squadrons escorted British infantry into Aquino. As the majority of the defending garrison, mostly *Fallschirmjägers* of the 1st Parachute Division, had begun withdrawing during the night, active opposition was desultory. Anti-tank mines and booby traps were another story—they seemed to be everywhere, at times slowing the armour literally to a crawl but only costing the regiment a single tank. B Squadron scored a coup by capturing the withdrawal plans of the 1st Parachute Division's artillery regiment—valuable intelligence indeed. Eighth Army Headquarters commended Neroutsos for his men's initiative, pointing out that it was the first time they had received such orders before the enemy had fully carried them out. By mid-afternoon all three squadrons had passed through Aquino and were advancing westward along National Route 6, A and B Squadrons on either side of the road and C Squadron trailing close behind with the footsore British infantry happily catching rides. By late afternoon they had reached the banks of the Melfa just beyond Roccasecca station, but a crossing point proved elusive and enemy resistance had once again stiffened alarmingly. Prudence dictated hunkering down, and at a safe distance from the Melfa, too. It was a very tense night, everyone fearing infiltration, and even the *Luftwaffe* paid a rare visit. Fortunately, sleep was the only casualty, and by dawn "Jerry" had quieted down considerably.[119]

On May 26, the British 6th Armoured Division (part of XIII British Corps) passed through the Aquino area, crossed the Melfa, and headed northwest along the main highway to exploit the rupture in the German defences. Now caught in the open, and without many anti-tank weapons, the German infantry suffered heavy losses.[120] Around midday, new orders from Maj.-Gen. Keightley via Brig. Murphy's headquarters outlined a follow-up advance by 78th Division infantry, which the Calgary and Ontario Regiments would support. In the event, only the Ontarios were called out, Neroutsos getting word they'd be relieved. That evening, courtesy of NAAFI, the officers and senior NCOs celebrated their good news with spirits and the others with rum. Next morning the first item to address would be a sad but necessary one—setting up a promotions board where the senior officers tabbed men from the ranks to replace the many NCO casualties suffered in the recent fighting. In the way of war, however, a sense of normalcy quickly descended on the camp, marked by the resumption of sports and other entertainments, the appearance of appetizing food, and proper rest.[121]

Paying the Price

Later in the day the regiment's chaplain, Capt. (Hon.) A. E. Larke, and his driver returned to the Aquino airport area, their jeep loaded down with wooden crosses. Performing a proper service at the burial of comrades killed only days earlier was another sad but necessary task. May's victories had been won dearly. For the rest of his days, Stoney Richardson adamantly maintained it was the toughest fighting the regiment endured during the Italian Campaign, and no one who had been there would have argued the point. It had taken eighteen lives (a third of them officers), and wounded another 45, the heaviest unit losses in the brigade and the regiment's worst month of the war.[122] Tank casualties had also been heavy. Twenty Shermans had either been destroyed outright (including five brew-ups) or damaged beyond repair, six of them by mines and twelve by AP rounds from *StuGs* or towed anti-tank guns. Another fifteen had been lost to mechanical breakdown and thirteen had bogged, but all twenty-eight were quickly recovered, repaired and sent back into action. Eight Stuart recce tanks were also temporarily lost, though only one of them to enemy action. In a tribute to American industry, Allied logistics, and the stalwart work of the 25th Canadian Armoured Delivery Regiment, the Calgary Regiment had taken delivery of twenty-two new Sherman Vs and four new Stuarts while the fighting was still going on. Mechanical breakdowns had been excessive, but the tank workshops attributed this to the weeks of training preceding Honker, when there had been little time for even regular maintenance. It was also clear that anything more than three weeks of sustained fighting simply wore out the Shermans. Weary crews and overworked workshops couldn't perform miracles, and regardless of their efforts, stocks of spare parts ran out by then. Finally, many of the regiment's Shermans were already worn-out machines when they reached Venafro.[123] Ammunition expenditure confirmed that most of their action had been in the infantry support role. Out of over 9,000 75-mm rounds fired, high explosive had exceeded armoured piercing by a ratio of more than five to one.[124]

Band of Brothers in a Steel Box

Though they shared with other soldiers the waiting and the bursts of violence, tank crews fought a peculiar war. More than the other arms, they fought alone, separated even from their own regimental mates. During the periods of combat, but even during the long gaps separating those, the crewman of a Sherman Mk V operated in his world unto himself, a world of one tank and four other men. There was an intimacy between and dependency on one another that only came close to being matched by the closeness among the crew of a heavy bomber. From the execution of battlefield tactics to tank maintenance, success could only be achieved as a team. Despite all the talk of armour protection and muzzle velocity, the foremost determinant in surviving an encounter with a German tank, *StuG*, or anti-tank gun was who got off the first shot, usually in just a matter of seconds from the first awareness. This required the crew to work as one or suffer the immediate consequences. By tank standards, the Sherman was comfortable, some thought having been given to crew ergonomics. But the crew still worked in cramped, exhausting conditions. In action, they were virtually blind, and hence largely unaware of the "bigger picture" outside. Crew communication, easily overwhelmed by engine and battle noise, could be reduced to a slap on the shoulder or kick in the behind. And they were assailed by the stench of gasoline fumes and sweat—it got worse the longer they were confined to their beast. At least inside the tank, maintaining the formal hierarchy between officer, NCO, and trooper was difficult, even counter-productive. The greatest bulwark of tankers' morale was success on the battlefield, and a belief that no one—from the squadron commander to the lieutenant, sergeant, or corporal commanding a tank—would give or be given impossible or pointless orders. But combat, which was the focus of their service, was a rare occurrence, and it is easy to forget how essential it was to keep the crews engaged during the long periods of waiting between action, when frustration and boredom could take hold—the same periods that were filled with essential tasks like maintenance and training. Finally, faith in the weapon on which your life depended was critical, too, and despite the rough ride the Sherman is frequently given in military histories, the officers and men of the Calgary Regiment respected it every bit as much as they had the Churchill.[125] Jim Quinn, who served through the period detailed in this chapter, would later sum up the unique elements of tank crew morale from his own experience:

> Unless one has served as part of a tactical combat unit it is difficult to understand the feeling of trust, respect and spiritual attachment that exists. Serving together during the most critical times in our lives, sharing the good and the bad, along with the personal feelings of fear, of joy, of pride in each other's individual and collective accomplishments cannot be duplicated in any other collective experience.[126]

These elements gave them their best chance to keep going—and to survive.

The Worm of Fear

In his reminiscences, Maj. Fred Ritchie wrote eloquently about the impact of accumulated strain on tankers. Generally tank crews never stopped to assist with the recovery or burial of other tankers. Of course they were usually too busy to attend to either, but it was also an unwritten rule, particularly when it came to recovering bodies. "As more of your comrades are killed," he observed, "you become aware that your own time may be running out [and] the worm of fear grows in your gut." Like all soldiers they suffered what we now diagnose as PTSD—"battle exhaustion" in contemporary army parlance. But unless you were completely overwhelmed by symptoms, you were expected to tough it out. Ritchie recounts an incident during the Liri Valley fighting where a crewman shot himself in the foot to escape the unbearable strain. There were times when entire crews refused to get out of their tanks, so fearful were they of mortar fire. And he recalled an officer "who had seen a great deal of action cracking up and feeling ashamed, but his nerve was gone."[127] There was an understanding among most armoured commanders that even the bravest had their limits, and as we have seen, they would try to arrange a few hours or even days out of the line for those who had clearly reached them. That respite, coupled with loyalty to comrades, and the fear of letting them down, usually enabled most to return to action, until "the worm of fear" took hold again.

Brewing Up

Being inside a tank was much safer than being one of the "poor bloody infantry" outside, and tank crewmen knew it. But anyone passing through a battlefield could see thick black smoke pouring from knocked-out tanks and knew full well the likely fate of at least some of the crew. Statistically speaking, Shermans burned no more readily than the best German tanks, but in 1943 two-thirds of them still caught fire when suffering a penetrating hit. Once ammunition stowage was altered to include wet jackets and armoured shell bins, this fell to 15 percent. But it was not so much how likely fire was—the risk was definitely exaggerated—as what happened if there was a fire. Many crews kept the twin front hatches ajar even in action so they could get out more quickly if their tank brewed up, and British or Canadian tank crews were never criticized for abandoning their tank after it had been hit—but before it caught fire. Radio connections between Allied tanks were excellent, greatly facilitating fluid battle tactics. But it also let nearby crews hear the last agonies of comrades burning to death. Few soldiers, even among the recovery crews, wanted to look inside a burned-out tank. Standard practice was simply to haul them back to workshops, spray the interiors with creosote, and after a suitable period, climb inside and remove any human remains. It was a gruesome task.[128] On May 24, Lt. Wilfred Beresford's Sherman, *Confident*, was hit by an 88-mm round only seconds after his lead tank had suffered the same fate. Both Shermans burst into flame. Three of his crew—Tprs. J. W. McMullin (the driver), W. L. Evans (the co-driver), and R. C. Langley (the loader/radio operator) managed to clamber out. Under withering German small arms fire, they only just managed to escape. A few hours later, when it was safe to approach the burned-out wreck, a cursory look inside and a search of the surrounding ground provided no evidence of the fate of Beresford or his gunner, Tpr. H. N. Elmes, so both were listed as "missing in action, presumed killed." Subsequently, a more careful examination of the tank's interior located the remains of one or perhaps both of them—so awful was the fire damage that it wasn't clear. Later in the day the remains were buried in a common grave. An inquiry ordered by Lt.-Col. Neroutsos concluded that an ammunition detonation would have killed them both instantly, though no one could ever be sure.[129]

Reflection

Reflecting on the tactical lessons learned in May and the preceding months, Brig. Murphy had concluded that armoured commanders had to rethink traditional ideas about what constituted "tank country," namely wide-open spaces where armour could be massed. His critique—entitled *What is tank country?*—was widely circulated through his command, and one presumes beyond. Even handfuls of tanks had proven invaluable in the infantry support role, he pointed out, especially when the enemy didn't expect them. Such surprise could almost be guaranteed "by [executing] the unexpected or seemingly impossible." In essence he was arguing that "the more difficult the tank going, the better the tank country," and that the impossible terrain of Italy "need hold no … terrors for the tank [as long as] it is co-operating with infantry schooled in the [proven] lessons of infantry-cum-tank warfare."[130] The brigadier's ideas were not without merit, but only up to a point—actually trying to implement them would be a severe test of men and machines. As one of his lowly troop leaders put it, "when the Good Lord created Italy, he did everything possible to make it difficult if not impossible to use tanks."[131]

Overall, the Gari and Aquino operations were clearly successful, and Lt.-Col. Neroutsos concluded his own after-action report with a resounding endorsement of the brigade and its support arms as a "perfect smooth working machine which was what one always dreamt that the army ought to be like but never was, until now." Still, he saw deficiencies that needed addressing. He particularly disapproved of the repeated instances where he had been ordered to move his squadrons "on short notice with little or no information about

[the] enemy, [our] own [infantry] or [the] commander's intention." Could anyone have described the Aquino operations any better? Such attacks invariably stumbled, he continued, and left his tanks "in a precarious and dangerous position."[132] It was an assessment which he knew his squadron leaders were in wholehearted agreement since he had polled them. As was to be expected, Maj.-Gen. Russell took a broader perspective, focusing on Honker's success and the manifest abilities of his men to overcome the adversity even the best planned attacks present. More than anything, it was "the time that was available for preparation and training [that ensured] those who were to fight together got to know each other" that had decided the outcome.[133]

An Opportunity Lost

Amidst all this useful reflection, and as British forces relentlessly pursued the beaten enemy northward toward Rome, Field Marshall Alexander made the decision that Gen. Mark Clark's US Fifth Army would have the prize of liberating Rome, which they accomplished on June 4. Unfortunately Clark's obsession with doing so, and the employment of all his troops to do it, ran contrary to Alexander's clear intention to complete the destruction of the enemy south of Rome first. Instead, Clark's strategic blunder enabled the badly mauled enemy to escape northward to the prepared defences of the Trasimene Line, and in effect to execute a fighting withdrawal all the way to the Po Valley.[134]

Forgotten Canadians ... And British Praise

Canada's 1st Armoured Brigade had played a stellar role in the Eighth Army's May victory, but under Indian and British, not Canadian command, so not for the first time in 1944 they were forgotten by Ottawa when formal congratulations were handed out to the rest of the Canadian forces. Still, in a note penned to Murphy in late March as his brigade was readying to shift to the Cassino front, Lt.-Gen. Charles Allfrey, commander of V British Corps, had confided that over recent months, "word went around that the Canadian Tanks were full of guts.... You have now established the fact that you will see any infantry through a fight. It is a great thing to have established, and you can be proud of it."[135] The men *were* proud of it, and by their actions in May had further burnished that reputation.

A Well-earned (but All-too-short) Break

A normal—and welcome—routine re-emerged during the period in reserve near Castrociello, just north of Aquino. The days filled with the usual mix of training, maintenance and sports. Movies, when available, proved almost as popular as baseball, and a performance by a touring entertainment troupe—especially a Canadian one, as they'd just been treated to—even more so. Brig. Murphy brought down the house with his thank-you speech to the Canadian Women's Army Corps performers by noting that after looking over the Gustav and Adolf Hitler Lines, and a lot of other lines, "it was a pleasure to look at curves."[136] A few false alarms about imminent moves northward geared everyone up, only to disappoint. But the exciting news on June 6, ironically received courtesy German Armed Forces radio, was a cause of celebration for with the successful landing in Normandy, the end of the war seemed a little nearer. Back home, however, it doomed the Italian Campaign to fade ever further from the public eye.

A New Commanding Officer

Lt.-Col. Neroutsos' painful right knee had been plaguing him since before the Gari River crossing and made it difficult to carry out his duties. On June 11 he announced, first to his senior officers and then to the remainder of his men, that he faced hospitalization in England, and Maj. Richardson would assume command with Maj. Ritchie becoming the new second-in-command. "It was a departure met with surprise, and a very deep and genuine regret, throughout the regiment," the war diary opined diplomatically. Stern, aloof and lacking the common touch so helpful to those possessing it, Neroutsos was not unpopular, per se. What was unquestionable—and duly noted by Murphy—was that during his fourteen months in command he had raised the regiment "to a high state of fighting fitness through his untiring planning and control."[137] Richardson's elevation was an instance of the regimental system working at its best—a successor groomed within the unit who was already widely respected by his fellows and who had the self-reliance and confidence to make the transition from equal to uncontested boss. "It was a delight to take command," he noted years later, "as we had gone through a lot of very difficult fighting and I had been with [them] through [it] all."[138] It was a delight to everyone else, too. They had found their Page.

Roma

Plans now took shape quickly. The regiment would be moving to a new encampment north of Rome. As the war diary enthused, "quiet jubilation reigned throughout the camp at the prospect of escape from the spit and polish of static life, the probability of seeing Rome ... and the certain excitement of the forward area."[139] The tanks were soon rolling toward Pontecorvo where they would meet up with their transporters, kicking up great clouds of the choking, fine-grained Italian dust that had been their companion for weeks. The remaining personnel stayed put for a bit longer, waiting for their own departure time, "reading beneath trees, standing in unsettled groups, or listening to a versatile accordion (acquired after the mysterious fashion of accordions …) playing jazz, cowboy tunes and Lily Marleine [sic]."[140] With supply convoys and fighting units pressing northward along the few available Italian highways, the traffic congestion was beyond description. Thankfully Allied air superiority was total. Just after sunrise, the second column passed through Rome, "a city apart from the Italy seen thus far; magnificent buildings, altogether not a city of war."[141] The two convoys reunited to cover the last few kilometres to their new harbour area about 25 kms north of the capital, close by to where the British 4th Infantry Division, to which they were now attached, was encamped. The regiment was actually not far from the banks of the Tiber River which "for all its historic grandeur," the war diary noted disappointingly, "resembled the Moose Jaw Creek at its barest points."[142]

But they were soon on the move again, this time a day-long 100-km grind snaking overland through picturesque hillside villages to a new harbour near Montefiascone, just southeast of Lake Bolsena. Though Rome was now all but out of bounds for leaves, Richardson did his best to arrange for a few dozen men at a time to visit the eternal city. With his friend Perry Millar, Fred Ritchie was among the lucky. The Sistine Chapel left him awestruck:

> It was open, but empty of people, with only a Swiss guard at the entrance. We were exhausted and got sore necks gawking at the magnificent ceiling so we lay down on our backs and gazed and gazed. There was so much beauty to behold and no one to interrupt us …[143]

The Trasimene Line

Dust and heat were soon but a memory, replaced by rain and the atrocious local gumbo. On days they moved, it was through "terrible country," the CO lamented, where "we did a lot of towing of the infantry [i.e., their vehicles], we had infantry riding on our tanks, we were pulling one tank with another out of the mud."[144] The awful state of the ground was also providing the Germans with precious time to cobble together a string of defensive positions east and west of Lake Trasimene, the so-called Trasimene (or Albert–Frieda) Line. Field Marshall Kesselring had intended to make only perfunctory stands before reaching the Gothic Line north of the Arno River in order to ensure that what remained of his army would actually survive to fight there. But outraged by the strategy, Hitler ordered Kesselring to stand fast at the Trasimene Line. Almost overnight the Germans managed to throw together a string of well-sited

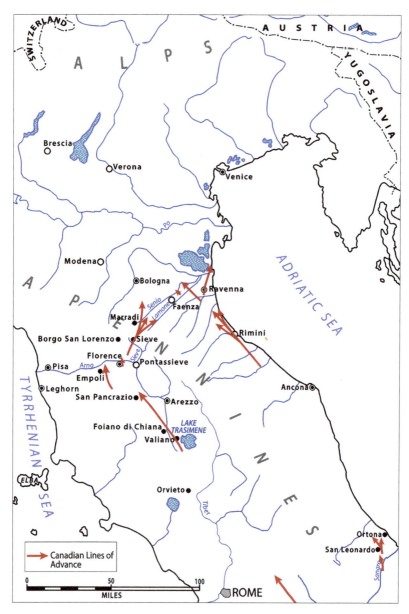

MAP 11:
Canadian Operations in Northern Italy, June 1944 – February 1945.

defensive positions astride the British line of advance.¹⁴⁵ That was a godsend for the enemy because the German Tenth Army formations that XIII British Corps and its Canadian armour faced remained woefully understrength. Between them, the 334th and 356th Infantry Divisions, 1st Parachute Division, and Herman Göring Panzer Division numbered fewer than 10,000 men with only a handful of *panzers* and *StuGs*.¹⁴⁶ But these remnants were battle-hardened and determined to fight. Believing the reinforcement woes of "English Divisions" (by which they meant British as well as Indian and Dominion forces) ensured "[they] cannot stand large sacrifices of blood," German commanders intended to make their pursuers bleed for every kilometre.¹⁴⁷

On June 22 the regiment received word that stiff resistance had been encountered along the Trasimene Line. The Ontarios were already engaged, and the Calgary Regiment's commitment seemed imminent. With no transporters available, their tanks had to make it forward on their own tracks, which was never desirable. Most of their Shermans were originals, and with over 1,500 kms on the odometers, pretty well worn out. To make matters worse, there were severe shortages of spares, particularly the rubber elements of the tanks' running gear, which were literally burning up in the summer heat.¹⁴⁸ Their 80-km move to Città del Pieve, about 10 kms south of the battle zone, took five hours and cost them fifteen Shermans, most of them disabled by burned-out bogies. Lt.-Col. Richardson spent his evening consulting with Murphy and Brig. Algernon Heber-Percy, the commanding officer of the 12th British Infantry Brigade, and their staffs, only returning around midnight. The regiment was immediately placed on full readiness and everyone was keyed up to go, but a series of postponements followed. This time, the fighting had fallen to others.¹⁴⁹

The Arezzo Line

Once the Trasimene Line had been broken, it was known the enemy would fall back about 40 kms to the Arezzo area.¹⁵⁰ The considered view of the intelligence staff was that once the Arezzo Line had been breached the Germans "may well" fall back all the way to the Gothic Line not far north of Florence, leaving only "scattered rearguards" to sweep aside, though this turned out to be optimism bordering on fantasy. The misconceptions aside, infantry, armour, and artillery alike were warned that once they advanced into the Apennine foothills, movement would be restricted to roads all the way to the Arno. It would be a major advantage to the defenders whom Kesselring had ordered to carry out every manner of demolition "with sadistic imagination."¹⁵¹

The Eighth Army plan to drive on Arezzo and then Florence placed Kirkman's XIII British Corps in the central role, with his 4th British Infantry Division, supported by Murphy's tanks on the left, and the 6th British Armoured

Division on the right. On the morning of June 28, orders were issued that the Calgary Regiment, along with two infantry battalions from Heber-Percy's brigade and a regiment of self-propelled howitzers, would join the fighting in 24 hours.[152] It was likely they'd encounter their old opponents from Aquino, the *Fallschirmjäger* of the 1st Parachute Division, who had a well-earned reputation for fanaticism.[153] While an unpleasant prospect, it was also taken as something of an honour—the best against the best. C Squadron and half of A Squadron, along with the eleven Stuarts of the reconnaissance troop, set off that afternoon to occupy their jumping-off point, with B Squadron following a few hours later. At dawn on June 29, Richardson and Maj. D. C. Taylor slipped away to reconnoitre the attack route. The plan's final iteration called for a narrower thrust led by C Squadron and accompanied by 1/Royal West Kents, with B Squadron and the 2/Royal Fusiliers trailing some distance behind. Delayed by a heavy mist, when Taylor's tanks were finally able to advance it proved uneventful. As the British rifle companies cautiously infiltrated Laviano around mid-afternoon, the inhabitants confirmed that the German rearguard had melted away only an hour earlier.[154] With a lot of daylight left, it was decided to break with the plan and press on a further 4 km to Valiano. After two hours the force had only managed a kilometre. The tanks had found navigating around a succession of gullies difficult. At the same time, sniper fire took its toll of crewmen who ventured outside to speak with the infantry, or in the case of commanders, stood in an open hatch to better direct operations—a calculated risk that cost Lt. V. J. St. Martin his life. When the infantry tried to proceed on their own, they had no better luck. C Squadron caught up with them 1½ kms short of the village, the 14-km advance having cost the squadron three tanks, two of them to mines. It was obvious that rooting the Germans out of Valiano was going to require a prepared attack.

By 2000 A and B Squadrons and their infantry had made harbour just northeast of Laviano. One of the Shermans had arrived with a pig sticking out of the co-driver's hatch and a few of the others were veritable grocery delivery vans, carrying geese and sacks of vegetables and fruit supposedly acquired from farmers en route and that provided a welcome supplement to the thin army rations on hand as the campaign's logistical train unravelled.[155] At midnight both forces radioed regimental headquarters that they would hold in place until the operational situation had been clarified.[156]

At first light, patrols reported that the enemy had dug in in strength on the low ridge along which the route linking Valiano and Petrignano ran and would definitely have to be evicted. This would require using both infantry battalions, each supported by a squadron of tanks. C Squadron and their infantry would assault Valiano once B Squadron and the 1/Royal West Kents had outflanked it and headed on toward Petrignano, about 3 kms to the east. Simultaneously, the 4th Division's 10th Brigade, supported by tanks of the Three Rivers Regiment, would move directly on Petrignano from the south. The attacks on both villages ran into a host of difficulties—battlefield confusion, poor intelligence, the usual demolitions and mines, fierce resistance, and difficult terrain for tanks and infantry to operate in, let alone co-operate. Both armoured regiments shared the blame for liaison so poor they were unaware where the other was, but neither took any responsibility.[157] The confusion forced the artillery to call off barrages so as to avoid friendly fire.[158] Desperate to block the advance, the Germans threw a number of tanks, *StuGs* and anti-tank guns into the fray. At least one Panther was crippled, and a Mark IV probably disabled, by Calgary tank fire, though Richardson's men took the worst of it.[159] Covering the 3 kms to Petrignano took hours, and when the last German paratroopers slipped away around 2000, B Squadron had still not managed to reach the village. Brigade typically urged continued pursuit, but fearing a counterattack, and with C Squadron well behind and still trying to clear Valiano, consolidation was the prudent course. "Superficially, the day was not a marked success," the war diary truthfully recorded, "but we had inflicted casualties, and seen the enemy once more retreat, and higher command was very happy over the regiment's performance."[160] Mostly they'd been reminded that Kesselring's army was no spent force.[161]

Dominion Day passed unnoticed. Aware only hot pursuit would forestall demolitions, the regiment was ready to start out for Petrignano by 0530. But B Squadron had barely gotten underway when mines blew the tracks off two Shermans, requiring engineers and a bulldozer to come up and clear a path. The advance was repeatedly delayed by mines, demolitions and the steep terrain, and the tanks frequently lost contact with the infantry. Meanwhile C Squadron and the 1/Royal West Kents advanced into Valiano with the recce troop probing along the east side of the Maestro della Chiana canal.

During the early afternoon, in sweltering temperatures, both forces continued to press northeastward. Bent on Gabbiano, B Squadron managed to link up again with the Royal Fusiliers, who with tank support "advanced more willingly."[162] By late afternoon, A Squadron and the Black Watch Battalion passed through C Squadron's sector but soon encountered a blown bridge. Sappers hurriedly laid a replacement under the Shermans' covering fire. The column finally reached their objective just west of Gabbiano around 2230. An hour and a half earlier, in fading light, B Squadron and a company of Royal Fusiliers had attacked Gabbiano, though they were unable to clear it completely and had withdrawn to safer ground for the night. Overall, the day had been "a classic example of pursuit fighting," the 14th's war diary enthused, requiring "aggressive thinking and action on everyone's part."[163] But more than anything, it was Brig. Heber-Percy's steady hand and mastery of infantry-tank operations, that had carried the day and kept losses light. Still, as darkness fell near Gabbiano, Sgt. Tweedy had been killed and three of his crew wounded when a *StuG* knocked out their Sherman, and in earlier action, a shell burst had killed Maj. Alex Leslie as he stood in his turret consulting with some infantry officers.

Just after 0400, as dawn broke the following morning, engines coughed to life and all three squadrons headed off on divergent routes. Within four hours, by the usual circuitous traverse of the Italian hill country, C Squadron had advanced a good 20 kms and was overlooking the large town of Foiano della Chiana from across the canal. In an extraordinary turn of luck married to enterprise, the recce troop, which had already watched German engineers blow one bridge crossing the canal, saw A/Cpl. Lionel Kreger and a handful of comrades drive another demolition party off the main span, then hold it until reinforcements arrived. Brig. Heber-Percy rightly praised the recce troop's "gallant and invaluable work,"[164] for without a bridge suitable for 30-ton Shermans, the advance would have been stymied for days. Tanks and infantry were soon across the canal, and with South African armour closing in from the southwest, Foiano fell in short order. But sustaining the pace of pursuit was becoming more and more challenging. Between combat losses and breakdowns, by the end of most days the three squadrons were lucky to have thirty-five or forty "runners" between them, though often several more were being repaired by the attached Light Aid Detachment personnel. Here, the sterling work of the Light Aid Detachment fitters led by Sgt. Tom Curtin who slipped forward most nights to effect emergency repairs on abandoned Shermans deserve particular acknowledgement.[165] Finally, with supply dumps now as much as 120 kms to the rear over suspect roads, resupply—or rather the inadequacy of supplies—was adversely impacting every aspect of armoured operations.[166] Of course no matter how strained Allied logistics became, the enemy's situation was infinitely worse.

Into the Mountains

The recent advances had been through relatively open, undulating country, but they were now entering a more heavily treed landscape of steep hills. The sole route was a winding, narrow road, frequently enclosed by those same hills, where, in the frank assessment of Heber-Percy's staff, "demolitions would become a more serious problem and … the employment of our tanks seriously curtailed."[167]

Despite the now very tired state of the 12th Infantry Brigade and their tankers, Maj.-Gen. Ward, the CO of the 4th British Infantry Division, concluded he had no option but to keep pushing them. The next objective for A and C Squadron and their infantry was Badicorte, a mere 17 kms southwest of Arezzo. As they jointly neared the village, a German counterattack that was forming up was smashed by artillery, but after probing attacks by the British infantry had been repelled, it was clear that capturing Badicorte would be best left for the following day. A plan drawn up overnight called for B Squadron and the 2/Royal Fusiliers to attack Badicorte at first light, while two-and-a-half hours later, A Squadron and the 6/Black Watch would head toward Ciggiano. Tank strength was down to thirty-three, with C Squadron by far the worst off, forcing Richardson to place it in reserve. The Germans, of course, had abandoned Badicorte, and so the tank-infantry force pressed on, reaching Oliveto, about 3 kms distant, in *only* 4 hours, the slow pace being attributed to the deteriorating terrain, not German resistance. A Squadron and their infantry made similarly depressing progress. North of Oliveto the tankers ran into a defender's dream, outright mountainous country "in the strongest sense of the word."[168] By early afternoon, B Squadron and the 2/Royal Fusiliers had covered an impressive 22 kms on what might only euphemistically be described as roads. But hopes of reaching the tiny hilltop hamlet of Gebbia, some 5 kms to the north for a crow but for tanks rather farther, had faded, and they harboured where they were, the infantry utterly spent from the heat. A Squadron's route encountered the practised handiwork of the enemy's own sappers—deeply cratered roads and every last bridge blown. They and their infantry called it a day at Verniana, about 5 kms to the southwest.[169]

Dawn on the July 5 found the enemy hanging onto their positions rather than withdrawing. Nonetheless, A Squadron and the 6/Black Watch, with bulldozers to help clear the way, managed to seize Monte Altuzzo, hopefully opening the way for C Squadron and the 1/Royal West Kents to press on to San Pancrazio along a twisting route that was vital because it was the 4th British Infantry Division's main avenue of advance. Forward movement was painfully slow, with the rifle companies becoming separated from the tanks every time the latter were held up by demolitions. For operations such as these, a single bulldozer was worth a troop of Shermans. But at least they were making progress, at any rate until their advance ground to a halt in mid-afternoon, whereas B Squadron and the 2/Royal Fusiliers were stopped cold as they resumed their advance on Gebbia. The German paratroopers, who were liberally equipped with *panzerfausts* and *panzerschrecks*, lethal close-range anti-tank weapons, proved too stubborn to overcome.[170] One breakthrough attempt faltered when a *panzerschreck* destroyed Lt. P. V. Knibbs' tank, leaving him badly wounded and two of his crew, Tprs. D. B. Scott and B. A. Reynolds, dead. The squadron spent most of the day pinned down at its starting position, firing high-explosive rounds at various distant targets and perhaps hitting some. It had been an equally exhausting day for the 28th British Infantry Brigade and the Ontario Regiment on their flank.[171]

The following day's plan assigned A Squadron and their infantry to batter their way into San Pancrazio, while the B Squadron force would stay put but hopefully distract the enemy from the main thrust. Getting close to San Pancrazio was one thing, taking it another. The Germans had dug in on the slopes the British infantry and Canadian tanks would have to cross, and neither artillery nor the Shermans' own guns could dislodge them. By late afternoon accurate fire from anti-tank guns and *StuGs* forced A Squadron to fall back until they had dealt with this threat, temporarily abandoning the 6/Black Watch. Darkness finally put an end to the slugfest when the entire attacking force withdrew. As the regiment's war diary bluntly summed the day, July 6 "was distinguished by an almost complete absence of progress."[172] But this gloom was not found in the 12th British Infantry Brigade's assessment, which noted appreciatively that "somehow the t[an]ks of the 14 CAR forced or bludgeoned their way up to the inf[antry], no doubt considerably surprising the Germans who might have thought their chosen country impassable to AFVs [i.e., armour]."[173]

Continuous pressure harried the enemy's efforts to carry out an organized retreat, and given the Allies' relative advantage in resources, it was the appropriate strategy, but it rapidly wore down the pursuers, too. Road-bound in such rugged terrain, their ability to advance generally depended on the speed with which sappers could construct detours and fill in craters. And in the process the infantry frequently found themselves without their crucial tank support. When the German commanders were ordered to stand and fight, as on July 5 and 6, the combat was brutal and stalemate inevitable.

Temporary Stalemate

Faced with the imperative of holding onto the Arezzo–Florence highway in order to extricate as many units and their equipment as possible, the *Heer* continued to resist any advances by XIII British Corps. As the regimental war diary summed up the state of things, the "enemy's tenacity was too apparent to press the attack,"[174] and Corps headquarters agreed. Lt.-Col. Richardson promptly implemented 8-hour reliefs to give his crews some respite, while officers from the Calgary Regiment and their British colleagues set about improvising shared facilities for their men in San Savino, a nearby village spared by the fighting. These included an officers' club, a movie theatre for the other ranks, and a bakery to supply doughnuts and cookies (Maj. Ritchie's inspired idea). Everyone deemed it a major improvement over leaving worn-out soldiers "parked in orchards and left without entertainment."[175]

A Different Italy

The changes in the countryside were not all topographic. As CBC war correspondent Peter Stursberg reported, the tankers found Umbria and Tuscany "a friendlier sort of country" like England, with villages that were not "dirty and evil smelling and ... crumbling away." And the people were nicer, too, they told him, not "greedy" and "dirty" like in the south.[176] Finally they were seeing people who seemed grateful for their liberation. Partisan bands were more common the farther north one went, and their invaluable intelligence helped to overcome prejudices as well.[177] Having occupied these localities significantly longer, the German Army had more opportunity to alienate peasants and villagers with their harsh reprisals, confiscations of property and forced labour.[178] Still, the liberators suspected many Italians remained sympathetic to the Fascist cause (which of course an element did), and this certainly worked against more favourable impressions of Italians generally.

The Push Resumes

During the night of July 14–15, the 6th British Armoured Division launched a major assault to crack open the Arezzo Line defences and break the stalemate. The attack, and a simultaneous one by the 2nd New Zealand Infantry Division, met with success. Exploiting this opportunity would fall to the 4th British Infantry Division.[179] Facing them across the hills, and determined to prevent the withdrawal from degenerating into a rout, were a motley assortment of German infantry, paratroop and armoured units.

Early on July 16, watched by a "crowd of doleful peasants," Brig. Heber-Percy and Lt.-Col. Richardson drove through the rubble of San Pancrazio only an hour or so after B Squadron and 2/Royal Fusiliers had cleared it and moved on. On their right flank were A Squadron and the 6/Black Watch—their joint objective being Capannole, about 20 kms due west of the city of Arezzo (which the New Zealanders would capture the same day). Thanks to the German proclivity for mining roads, periodic fierce artillery and mortar barrages, and numerous machine gun nests that pinned down the infantry until they were eliminated by the tanks, both advances were painfully slow. To minimize casualties, resistance was dealt with by overwhelming artillery firepower, and a mere report of an 88 hidden in a village was enough to get the unfortunate place levelled by British gunners in a matter of minutes. German soldiers were more demoralized by Allied artillery barrages than anything else thrown at them, but the potent high explosive rounds fired by the Shermans came a close second. The roads/tracks were steep and twisting, and any attempt to move off them necessitated crossing through orchards, in and out of gullies, and up exposed ridges and hills "that were never meant to be ... climbed [by tanks]," not to mention being exceedingly dangerous for the crews. But advance they did, reaching the outskirts of Capannole by early that evening.[180]

The battle—really a series of battles—to break the Arezzo Line lasted a fortnight and officially ended on July 18. The official historian of the Canadian Army's role in the Italian Campaign would later write that "the prolonged battle for Arezzo had given Kesselring ... ten extra days ... to complete the defences of the Gothic Line."[181] However, G. W. L. Nicholson's assessment was unfair because it was misleading, for interrogation of German prisoners and captured enemy documents both made clear that the German Army had been ordered to hold the Arezzo Line until the middle of August. Constant Allied pressure and unsustainable casualties prevented them from complying.[182] Reducing the Arezzo defences was a victory—not wrapped in bows—but a victory nonetheless.

A Partnership Renewed

The Calgary Regiment had stood down on July 17 and was anticipating being relieved. There was the usual backlog of maintenance to attend to, and no one turned down the opportunity to bathe in a nearby stream, their first clean-up in many days. But as it always seemed when things quieted down, the respite would prove short-lived. In fact, on the evening of July 18 Murphy informed Richardson that the brigade would probably be shifted back to the 8th Indian Division. Richardson passed on the news to his officers that very night, promising them he would press for their re-assignment to 19th Indian Brigade, their Honker comrades. Maj.-Gen. Russell, "The Pasha" as his soldiers affectionately nicknamed him, had already spelled out his own thoughts on the matter:

> In the fighting in Italy ... this Infantry Division ... has been supported at various times by five different Armoured Brigades with the resulting difficulties of getting to know new friends ... Armour will always be required ... [so] we must be prepared to work with any. Every endeavour should, however, be made to place under command armour with which the infantry have previously fought or trained successfully.[183]

With the Calgary and Ontario Regiments available, Russell was happy to oblige them.[184] Parting with the 4th British Infantry Division was not easy, however.[185] With not a little emotion, the war diary recorded the prevailing mood:

Brigadier Heber-Percy and members of his staff made a farewell visit to our mess tent. On both sides there was a most genuine reluctance to part, an adversity in which we were only sustained by gin and rum cocktails. Col[onel] Richardson and the Brigadier spoke words of mutual appreciation, the latter relating, how, on the previous day, the [Black Watch] had spontaneously cheered the tanks for two minutes. No eloquence could have meant as much as this simple statement. On our side the memory of 12th [British Infantry Brigade] will remain one of achievement, tuition, vigour, all seasoned with robust humour.[186]

The senior officers of the 98th (Self-Propelled) Field Artillery Regiment had also attended this goodbye. The British gunners had been fighting alongside the 1st Canadian Armoured Brigade almost continually since Sicily, and later both Lt.-Col. Richardson and Maj. Ritchie adjourned to the 98th's mess to hoist a few more toasts. "I've got his back, he's got mine" forged iron bonds, soldier to soldier.

On to the Arno

On July 16, Lt.-Gen. Kirkman's XIII British Corps launched a full-scale attack to seize all the Arno River crossings west of Florence. Spearheading the advance was the 6th South African and 6th British Armoured Divisions, with the 4th British Infantry Division between them and the 8th Indian Division in reserve.[187] Moving forward with the latter four days later, the Calgary Regiment was under orders not to press too hard and save their tanks for later. The column moved north from Capannole, making for the historic hilltop town of Sienna and then Poggibonsi. The circuitous 60-km route at least promised easier going. Unfortunately, the easier going ended at Sienna where they were swallowed up in an almighty traffic jam. By late afternoon, the squadrons reached their new harbours and, along with the Indian troops, were preparing to relieve Free French units worn out by their own weeks of hard fighting and now being withdrawn to participate in the forthcoming invasion of southern France. The tankers slept that night a mere 40 kms from Florence and the Arno River.

As it entered the line, the 8th Indian Division placed two of its brigades, the 19th and 21st, forward, with the former (and the Calgary Regiment) on the left, and an American division on their flank. The 8th's axis of advance lay generally north-northwest in the direction of the large town of Empoli on the Arno's southern bank. Brig. Dobree temporarily delayed the start of any concerted action so as to give the French more time to extricate themselves, but was open to the acquisition of better positions from which to launch such

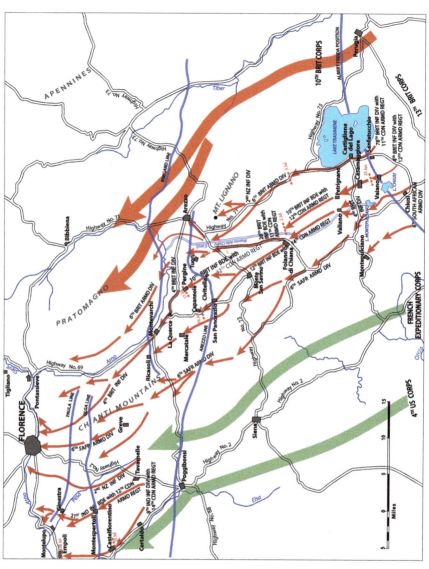

MAP 12:
The Advance to the Arno, 21 June – 5 August 1944.

"concerted action."[188] In the process of doing so, some German prisoners taken in C Squadron's sector revealed very welcome news—while the enemy were aware of the Indians' presence, they had no idea the 1st Armoured Brigade was in the area.[189]

On July 23, A Squadron and the 1/Argyle and Sutherlands went on the attack, advancing north toward their standing objective, Castelfiorentina, which was known to be strongly held. As they closed in, troops of tanks fanned out to support the infantry companies by "dusting up" targets of opportunity and providing counter-battery fire. The intent was to envelope the town, and in the process force the Germans to abandon the ridge dominating the area, which was accomplished by last light. Meanwhile, in the 21st Indian Brigade's sector some 15 kms to the southeast, C Squadron was temporarily supporting operations by the 1/5 Mahrattas. Save for having to navigate heavily mined roads, it had been relatively easy going until, as the column edged closer to Marcialla, intense fire from German artillery and *StuGs* put paid to any thoughts of advancing further. Maj.-Gen. Russell had made it clear to his subordinates that at this stage of the campaign their advances had to be carried out, when at all possible, without casualties, such was the reinforcement situation, but steady losses among engineers and infantry couldn't be avoided.[190]

July 24 dawned sunny and hot, soon to be hotter, which was pretty much all anyone could remember weather-wise over the preceding weeks. C Squadron and the 1/5 Mahrattas moved late, as was often the case because they had to await results elsewhere, and now found Marcialla clear. Labouring on they were repeatedly held up by demolitions and repeatedly warned by helpful locals that the *soldati tedeschi* were everywhere and mining everything. Forewarned, the snail-like advance continued, until by suppertime the tanks and infantry had managed to get within a kilometre of Lucardo, where they came under fire from a hidden detachment of *StuGs* and took the wise option—consolidate and await the morrow. Further west, A Squadron had even less to show for their efforts, having spent the day firing at uncertain targets, shooting a company of infantry across the Elsa River, and getting into position to push some of their tanks across it the following morning when a suitable ford had been located. German sappers, with their usual thoroughness, had blown up all the bridges.

The rapid advance over the previous weeks had now all but severed XIII British Corps' logistics, with shortages of artillery ammunition reducing many field guns and mediums to fifteen rounds per day. This meant the lead tank-infantry forces could no longer rely on the gunners to obliterate any opposition they encountered. Food was also running short, with the war diary lamenting sardonically that "war is war, and dehydrated potatoes are dehydrated potatoes."[191] But mostly it was the usual constellation of factors that were slowing the advance—very difficult terrain, demolitions, and the seemingly numberless anti-personnel and anti-tank mines.

On July 25, C Squadron advanced slowly, passing through Lucardo but then stopping for the rest of the day as they waited for New Zealand success on their flank. To the west, A Squadron was still waiting to cross the Elsa, while B Squadron, now very spread out, continued to claw its way in the general direction of Montespertoli. By evening, the Highlanders had occupied Castelfiorentino and two troops of Shermans had managed to follow them into the town to assist with consolidation. The place proved to be one big booby trap, exacting its toll for days after it had been officially liberated.[192]

July 26 brought the 8th Indian Division and their Canadian tanks, as well as the New Zealanders and South Africans on their right, up against the Olga Line, an improvised but formidable position stretching about 15 kms from Montespertoli to San Casciano. It was manned by *Fallschirmjägers*, amply supported by *StuGs*, field artillery and a few tanks, including a handful of Tigers.[193] As A and B Squadrons and their accompanying rifle companies edged forward, they encountered the usual German welcome—all manner of mines and booby traps to complement mortar barrages and shelling. It was grim and dangerous work for the infantry and engineers, but tankers faced their own threats. Far worse befell the 2nd New Zealand Division who were hammered by a powerful German counterattack and suffered heavy losses. As was so often the German plan, their troops melted away with the ridge-top Olga Line "fad[ing] overnight like the morning mists."[194]

Il Fiume Alla Fine

Mercifully, both July 27 and 28 brought easy advances, a strong indication the enemy was hastily withdrawing to the Arno River and probably beyond. At long last the terrain began to slope downward, though the open country made the tanks sitting ducks and initially they were wisely held back. By late afternoon on the 28th, as 1/Argyll and Sutherland patrols cautiously infiltrated Empoli, they encountered a thin rearguard from the 3rd *Panzergrenadier* Division and delirious civilians bursting with intelligence about German defences on the far side of the Arno, some of it actually useful. Over the next few days, the Canadian armour participated in mopping-up operations all along the south bank of the river.[195] At first, enemy patrols crossed the river nightly, and while there were fierce skirmishes, "many were captured without great show of disappointment."[196] But the nightly forays petered out, leaving only random shelling to harass the Canadian, British and Indian troops. Only the 8th Indian Division's 21st Brigade and the Ontario Regiment were involved in any sustained action. It fell to the New Zealanders and South Africans on the right flank of the XIII British Corps to mount the final thrust toward Florence in the opening days of August.

Calm Before the Storm

Having reached the Arno, early August saw most units shifting positions as part of a tried Eighth Army strategy to confuse the Germans and hopefully gain tactical surprise when the assault across the Arno was launched. As soon as the 8th Indian Division and 1st Canadian Armoured Brigade had handed over the Empoli sector, the regiment, divided into separate wheeled and tracked columns, set off on separate routes south and then east leading to a new camp south of Florence. For the tank crews, this meant 35 kms of twists, turns and switchbacks. The remaining vehicles followed a longer route with better grades, but traffic clogged both roads, stirring up the usual choking clouds of dust. To preserve secrecy, all unit identifiers had been removed or obscured, radio silence was maintained, and only rearward movements permitted during daylight hours. The reward for all this toil was inheriting a proper officers' mess with four walls and a roof. After a flurry "of voluntary homemaking, sweeping, picture-hanging, wine-hunting, fly-screening, radio-installing, furniture-moving [and] rug-laying, everyone slumped into chairs to view the magic scene."[197] Not to be outdone, the sergeants quickly laid claim to another building and proved equally energetic renovators. Nightly movie screenings and day-long leaves to Sienna helped lighten the routine of repair work and laundry. And following the wartime tradition, there was an end-of-campaign regimental dinner plus individual squadron dinners. Preparations for the former were chaotic, and when the promised pig failed to materialize, vegetables proved scarce and all a "procurement" party managed to return with was a jeep-load of pears, the situation looked grim. But at the last minute the mess secretary, Lt. Pat Patterson, wrought a miracle, and no one questioned how he had managed it. Both the commanding officer and squadron leaders kept their speeches witty and brief and the well-lubricated revelry continuing into the wee hours. Suffice to say the celebrations and rest soon re-energized the regiment. Otherwise, there was little to do but wait.

Scoring the Regiment

The Calgary Regiment's performance in the XIII British Corps' pursuit north of Rome, first breaking through the Arezzo Line and then harrying the retreating German Army to the Arno River, had been first-rate. As with everywhere else their brigade had fought in Italy, topography gave the resourceful and determined defender a notable advantage, which made the achievements of all three tank regiments even more impressive. Casualties had been bearable, certainly when compared to the heavy losses suffered by the infantry they were there to support. That said, the tanks' repeated intervention in firefights had kept those losses from being much worse.

July had seen the 14th Armoured Regiment advance nearly 120 kms "with greater or less opposition the whole way" and all of it on tracks.[198] Stoney Richardson thought this an extraordinary achievement for armour—not just his men's adaptability to new operational demands, but also their dedication to the mundanities of maintenance—and he was right. These weeks had seen the first sustained operations under his command, and his overall management of the regiment both during and between actions had ensured that when the time came to fight it was ready. That said, most his officers and NCOs—indeed the new CO himself—were already a battle-experienced team which was a tribute to Richardson's predecessor.

The role of a regiment in an independent armoured brigade was more to execute than create operational plans—Richardson's most substantial contribution was preparing his officers and men to fight, and when fighting, to deal with the inevitable crises on their own. The CO intervened when appropriate. Most of the regiment's actions were fought by individual squadrons or even troops working in close conjunction with their infantry partner, and usually were only loosely linked to any larger regimental plan. For the most part, tank-infantry co-operation had been textbook, with all three of the brigade's regiments deserving their solid reputations. Thorough training reinforced by experience had convinced the 14th's officers and NCOs that practising the doctrine on the battlefield was, if not a guarantor of success, then certainly a prerequisite. Despite the seemingly endless grind of overcoming roadblocks, demolitions, mines, and ambushes, not to mention the constant threat of anti-tank rounds turning ones Sherman or Stuart into an inferno, their morale had held.[199] Being cautious was inevitable, for while Canada's volunteers were prepared to give their lives for the cause, they were not seeking opportunities to do so. Nonetheless, courage and initiative had been amply displayed.

8

From the Arno to Holland and Home

The Final Year

There was a sense of foreboding gazing at the Arno River. To the north lay Kesselring's Gothic Line, which over the previous months had assumed mythic proportions. Everyone in the regiment knew that it was only a matter of time before they headed north to help smash through it and liberate the remainder of Italy. When the time came, their German nemesis would prove as tough as ever, but the terrain and weather would be the more fearsome opponent in what degenerated into a trial of endurance and will. They would endure tough times until finally in early 1945 all Canadian Army units were withdrawn from Italy and reunited with First Canadian Army in the Low Countries for the war's final months.

Waiting

As they tried to cope with the sweltering August heat, Allied forces were hopeful that the enemy was too weak to contest the river itself.[1] The Germans withdrew from Florence on the night of August 10–11, allowing the Allies to deliver food and water to the city's desperate civilian population, now swollen with refugees. Thereafter, except for desultory shelling, there was an ominous quiet. Lt.-Col. Richardson was aware that sometime around mid-month the brigade would once more come under Lt.-Gen. Kirkman's command, with their own regiment rejoining the 8th Indian Division. On August 17, Richardson was able to pass on a clearer picture of the situation to his officers. Basically, the enemy remained dug in on the low hills immediately north of the river, and it was felt most likely that after offering token resistance they'd fall back. But what if they didn't? The Arno was a major obstacle, several hundred metres across and with steep banks. Furthermore, the water level was high for mid-summer, the current swift, and the riverbed mostly a mix of boulders and mud. Anything less than a full-scale attack supported by tanks and artillery—basically a repetition of the Gari operation—seemed too risky. As assault plans were drawn up, the 8th Indian Division's front stretched from the town of Pontassieve 5 kms west to Sieci. On the right C Squadron would support 17th Indian Brigade, and on the left A Squadron the 19th Indian Brigade, with B Squadron and the 21st Indian Brigade in reserve. The recce officer, Lt. Cawsey, joined patrols of Indian engineers reconnoitring potential approach and crossing points. Fortunately, elements of the 356th and 715th German Infantry Divisions holding the area showed no interest in contesting these, even when they were carried out in broad daylight.[2] It became clear that the enemy saw the river as a mere nuisance to their foes. At best, they undertook token patrolling and the town of Pontassieve was not defended at all. But of the hill country beyond, not much was known.

Preparations paused briefly on August 20 to permit the new chaplain, Capt. (Hon.) G. E. Darroch, to hold a Dieppe commemoration service. So great had the personnel turnover been in 24 months that few men attending had participated in those grim events—Lt.-Col. Richardson being an obvious exception. Immediately afterward, all personnel save those like the tank crews who were essential to completing preparations for the attack assembled with the rest of the brigade to see Prime Minister Churchill. He arrived "wearing a sun helmet and Palm Beach suit ... and looking perhaps older and more tired than we had expected," the war diarist noted. The soldiers had gathered on a long hillside with Shermans from the Ontario and Three Rivers Regiments, their guns raised, silhouetted against a cobalt Italian sky. His speech was brief and no tub-thumper, but everyone cheered.[3]

Two days later A and C Squadrons had taken up temporary positions close to their jumping-off points, only 1,500 m from the riverbank. Indian sappers had managed to open the sluice gates downstream, dropping the river's depth by almost a metre, and had also located a fording point that eliminated the need for bridging.[4] To provide extra punch, the tanks would be accompanied by a battery of M10 tank destroyers and two batteries of Priests (self-propelled 25-pounders). Supply dumps were filled with fuel and ammunition, and the decision was made to have all resupply carried out by the regiment's modified Stuart recce tanks, with the extra units loaned to them by the Three Rivers Regiment. Secondary theatre or not, the scale of Allied material superiority was impressive. The final reconnaissance was carried out by the COs of the two squadrons who went aloft in a spotter plane so as to get a bird's eye view of their battlefield.[5]

Jumping the Queue

On the night of August 23–24 the 1st British Infantry Division had come under heavy artillery fire as it approached its jumping-off points, a bombardment that continued throughout the day. Alarmed, Corps headquarters ordered the 8th Indian Division on the 1st's right flank to stay put. But in less than 24 hours Lt.-Gen. Kirkman changed his mind. He ordered Maj.-Gen. Russell to lean into the German defences in his sector by sending his 17th and 19th Brigades across the river immediately west of Pontassieve, with the Calgary Regiment's C and A Squadrons following as soon as the assault companies of the 1/5 Gurkha Rifles and 1/Royal Fusiliers had secured a bridgehead.[6] By 1030, using foot bridges erected by Indian engineers, both battalions' assault companies had made it across, and within half an hour, C Squadron was on the far shore as well. Fearing congestion in the bridgehead, Maj. Gray's tanks were held back at the last minute. Only when it was too late to interfere with the crossing did German artillery finally open up, and then with little effect. By late afternoon, some of the infantry had advanced 2 km inland, whereas others had achieved considerably less. C Squadron had failed to take its first-day objective—the hilltop Villa Tassinato, though two of its Shermans had thrown tracks trying to get there. With no reason to be reckless, the overall attack had been executed cautiously. Until a vehicle bridge could be built across the river, lack of supplies would limit exploitation. Priority was given to consolidation, which included ordering A Squadron to cross the following morning. Everyone was waiting for the enemy's response.[7]

Beyond the Arno

The following day brought some clarification, and a modest advance. It was clear that the German forces—basically the 735th Regiment of the 356th Infantry Division—had withdrawn onto the higher ground around Tigliano and the still higher summits of Monte Cerrone, Calvana and Giovi—rugged country separating the valley of the Sieve from the Arno.[8] As the war diary put it, their opponents "were stubborn rather than aggressive and relied on shelling rather than counterattack" to hold their positions. British and Indian artillery responded by pounding German positions with high-explosive rounds on what one officer dryly termed "a reasonable scale."[9] For now the tanks confined their aggression to joining in the artillery bombardment. The truth is the terrain was unforgiving country for armour, the worst yet encountered, and "reduced [them] to secondary roles."[10] But it was the lack of progress by the British infantry (supported by the Ontarios) on the attack's left that was the major impediment. By month's end, both tank regiments had become entrapped in what amounted to static warfare. As the Calgary Regiment's war diarist aptly summarized the situation eight days into the offensive:

> Mountain warfare is one of heavy infantry patrolling, light shell ing, considerable sniping, much recceing of tank routes, cautious encroaching from hill to gully, small scale but sudden and sharp engagements, [and] heavy patrolling once more. Tanks may and do sit inactive for three or four days.[11]

Kesselring's Confusion—Alexander's Dilemma

The German command was thoroughly confused as to where along the Allied front their opponents would strike, since the US Fifth Army, including Kirkman's corps, occupied the western and central portions, and the British Eighth Army the eastern. Unknown to Kesselring, Alexander had ceded nearly one-quarter of his forces for Operation Dragoon, the landings in southern France. A thrust through the Apennines offered the most direct route to Bologna and the northern Italian plains, but guaranteed the most difficult mountain fighting yet encountered. Pushing along the Adriatic Coast faced its own litany of river and ridge obstacles. In the end, he decided to attempt both.[12]

To the Sieve

As September opened, intelligence, a good deal of it from partisan bands,[13] pointed to a thinning out of the German line. Increasingly frustrated by the deadlock that had stymied XIII British Corps' advance, Maj.-Gen. Russell was determined to sweep the enemy off their dominating positions. It was clear, however, that only a full-scale attack supported by ample armour could eject the German Army from the two principal defended summits, Monte Calvana and Monte Giovi. Preparations to assault the latter—the Americans had been given responsibility for the former—were literally bogged down by wet weather that kept artillery spotter planes grounded and prevented sufficient numbers of tanks from getting forward. The disappointment was short-lived, however, for patrols found the summits abandoned, and with the Americans not yet in position, "The Pasha" had his infantry occupy both positions the following night (September 8–9) without having to fire a shot. The Germans were again falling back, and by September 10, the 8th Indian Division (and the Americans on their left) had reached—and in some instances crossed—the Sieve River.[14] Since crossing the Arno the Calgary Regiment had advanced fewer than 20 kms, though an optimist might have pointed out they were now only 60 kms from Bologna. But modest though the gains had been, reaching the Sieve was symbolic. At long last, the Gothic Line was in sight, but getting there was going to be a challenge. When Richardson reconnoitred potential routes immediately north of the river, he found the slopes "precipitous" and the roads little more than "wagon tracks [and] goat paths," dolefully concluding that what he could see would be "utterly impassable to tanks."[15]

The Attack on the Gothic Line

While Eighth Army's efforts to press north along the Adriatic Coast was facing fierce resistance, Gen. Mark Clark was confident that his Fifth Army could break through. As part of his command, the XIII British Corps' role "was merely to keep the enemy under pressure."[16]

Clark's forces would have to fight their way through unforgiving terrain, altogether "a confusion of jagged peaks and broken ridges interspersed with deep pocket-like valleys, which provided the enemy with a series of excellent ready-made defensive positions."[17] Only a handful of proper highways crossed from south to north through the Apennines by more or less direct routes. In XIII British Corps' sector, there were four. The two best were National Route (NR) 67, which connected Pontassieve to Forli, and NR 65, the main road linking Florence to Bologna, which traversed Futa Pass and had the advantage of decent grades, a major consideration for tanks. Lying between these were two other routes heading northeast from the valley of the Sieve that would be "usable" by mechanized units—from Borgo San Lorenzo across Casaglia Pass and then down the valley of the Lamone River to Faenza, and from San Piero a Sieve over Il Giogo Pass and via the valley of the Santerno River to Imola. A determined defence of these gateways to the plains of northern Italy was the centrepiece of Kesselring's strategy to grind down the Allies. The deep defensive zone in front of each pass comprised a warren of "concrete pillboxes, anti-tank walls and ditches, artillery bunkers and machine-gun posts" sited and camouflaged to minimize their vulnerability to the Allies' two trump cards—overwhelming artillery and air power.[18] Fortunately, with the Germans convinced that the infantry and armour for a major assault couldn't be assembled in such terrain, the Gothic Line proved much less formidable than feared. It wasn't just overconfidence, however—unrelenting Allied bombing of the Germans' tenuous supply lines left their garrisons chronically short of everything from weapons and ammunition to food.

On September 8, Alexander unleashed Clark. After nearly a week of severe fighting, II US Corps broke through Il Giogo Pass, with follow-up attacks by the Americans tearing the breach wide open. The secondary attack by the XIII British Corps toward Casaglia Pass proved less spectacular. It fell to the 8th Indian Division, with the Calgary Regiment under command, to advance

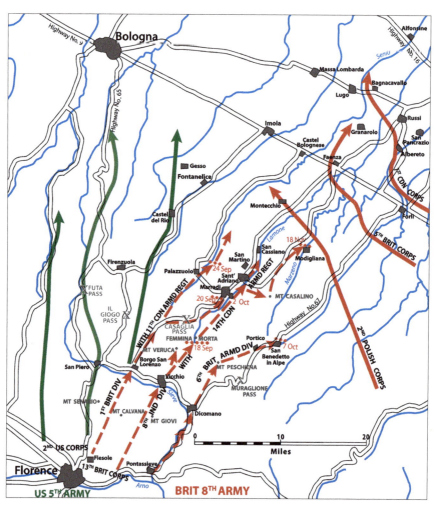

Map 13:
The Gothic Line and the Advance on Bologna, 25 August – 30 December 1944.

from Vicchio across the intervening watershed to outflank the German forces guarding the pass. Russell's force had been allotted the worst terrain. Even by Apennine standards the country was rugged and the roads few and unlikely to support heavy usage, so resupply would be on a shoestring. Of course, armoured forces would greatly strain that shoestring. On the other hand, the sector's apparent inaccessibility hopefully meant it would be more lightly defended.[19]

Orders called for the rest of Maj.-Gen. Russell's men to cross the Sieve early on September 12 and seize Vicchio, employing a single brigade (the 21st) supported by B Squadron, with the remaining tanks following closely enough behind to serve as self-propelled artillery. The crossing was almost an anti-climax. Not until mid-afternoon did the Indian infantry encounter any resistance, which B Squadron helped sweep aside. It was late in the day before A and C Squadrons managed to extricate themselves from the horrendous traffic congestion on the south side of the river—every bridge was down—and get across.[20]

Femmina Morta

The 8th Indian Division's goal was to capture Femmina Morta, a 1,100-m massif dominating Casaglia Pass from the southeast. But the immediate objective was ejecting the enemy from three intervening heights. On the 13th, the 1/5 Mahrattas attacked Monte Veruca. Late the previous evening, Maj. W. G. James had managed to get a troop of his Shermans up a precipitous track to within 1,500 m of the objective. When the platoons of the 1/5 Mahrattas went in, accurate tank fire blanketed enemy strong points immediately ahead of them. The support was a godsend, and the "Indian troops once again showed their touching and even astonishing faith in Canadian tanks by advancing without hesitation ... behind our fire even though the inevitable stray shot felt short." By late evening, the summit was safely in Indian hands, with the defenders having taken much the worst of the casualties.[21]

Still, as Capt. R. T. Currelly of the Army's Historical Branch succinctly put it in a subsequent report, "it was becoming increasingly difficult to move tanks ... and they gradually faded out of the picture."[22] Henceforward, the infantry's success would be more dependent on German withdrawals, artillery support, and winning the war of supply so that positions taken could be held with firepower alone. As the war diary of the 17th Indian Brigade bluntly summed it up, "the problem was now one of [road] maintenance."[23] Or in the words of Kirkman's staff, "the difficulty is to maintain our forces and get forward supporting arms."[24] Their extensive training in mountain warfare would prove the 8th Indian Division's salvation, but in many of these operations, as the Calgary

Regiment's war diary frankly acknowledged, "[our] tanks were clearly impotent, if not utterly immobile."[25] The Indian brigades' reports confirmed this, usually mentioning only the role field artillery was playing in their advances, though there were certainly exceptions when some tanks could be gotten into position and made critical contributions. The situation did not keep Russell from pressing to get some armour brought forward, knowing they were invaluable in repelling counterattacks and useful as infantry support whenever they could be employed. For his part, given the conspiracy of circumstances confronting his tankers, Richardson knew their prospects of seeing much action in the immediate future were not promising.[26]

During the next few days the infantry probed more than attacked the 715th Infantry Division's outposts. Having gone weeks without any reinforcement, and short of everything including food, the morale of the latter's soldiers was thought to be low. Whatever their morale, the German units were methodically falling back into higher terrain, until their pursuers had to be supplied with ammunition, food and water by mule trains, since their jeeps were no longer up to the task. By September 17, the heights in front of Femmina Morta had been cleared and on the following day the 1/5 Gurkhas (17th Brigade) overran the summit in five-hour battle. Three days later the 1st British Infantry Division occupied Casaglia Pass unopposed.[27] Having broken through the Gothic Line, the victors were disheartened to see terrain spread out below them was just as unsuitable for mechanized warfare as what they had just battled through.

A Sapper's War

Any possibility of road-bound tanks advancing, let alone catching up to infantry, depended on the herculean efforts of exhausted engineers. The extent of the road demolitions gave a new meaning to the term thorough. German engineers had of course destroyed every bridge, but in many instances, even long stretches of their approaches had been blown clean off the cliff side.[28] Booby traps were being left now whose sole purpose was to blow up bulldozers and kill or maim their drivers. And when you added heavy rains that frequently swept away repairs as soon as they were finished, the Indian Army sappers faced a Sisyphean task.

Into Reserve

On September 17, word had reached the Calgary Regiment that save for one squadron kept forward to meet any contingencies, they would go into reserve on seventy-two-hour recall. Within twenty-four hours Richardson was bidding bon voyage "with a warning as to behaviour" to eighteen trucks crammed with sixteen officers and 300 other ranks, all grinning at the prospect of a week in

Rome.[29] Apart from the usual routine of repairing equipment, there wasn't much else to do for those in harbour but rest. Everyone was still amazed (and relieved) the Gothic Line had turned out to be a sort of paper tiger. Nevertheless, their opponent continued to display a disheartening "ability to withdraw rather than collapse."[30]

The Advance Resumed

Any significant advance by XIII British Corps awaited the capture of Marradi and San Benedetto. With this achieved by September 25, tanks and supplies could be brought forward and the 14th Armoured "could once more tackle ground which would begin, but only begin, to be tankable once more."[31] On the 28th, 17th Indian Brigade supported by A Squadron were to set off down the main road through the Lamone Valley toward Faenza, some 35 kms distant, but snarled transport stretching all the way back to Borgo San Lorenzo dictated otherwise, and all units stood down. Two days of torrential rain then ended any thoughts of action, forcing jeeps to use chains, and trucks to be winched up and down the steepest grades. It even made some of the mule tracks impassable to mules! For the wretched infantry, even patrolling had become exhausting. While there was nothing to be done about the weather, it was doubly frustrating because the Americans on XIII British Corps' left flank had managed to make significant progress. When the rain finally let up, A Squadron, with a handful of Ontario tanks temporarily under command, were told to be ready to move on the first of the month.

Once More into the Breach

During the past two weeks Clark's Fifth Army had mounted a series of localized probing attacks to keep pressure on the Germans and at least prevented the front from congealing into static warfare. But Clark now intended to renew the offensive, with American troops mounting the main push on Bologna. To accommodate this, the XIII British Corps would temporarily suspend its own advance toward Faenza and simply occupy the Germans on the Americans' right flank.[32] In this role, the 8th Indian Division's first objective would be the road junction at Sant' Adriano, 5 kms northeast of Marradi, which was guarded by the 650-m summit of Monte Casalino, held of course by the Germans. Capturing the town would open a second line of advance along the valley of the Marzeno River to the east of the Lamone.

Armour Stymied

The autumn downpours having resumed, A Squadron finally managed to get to Marradi during the night of October 1–2, and were immediately engaged in laying down directed fire on targets in the hills overlooking Sant' Adriano. Unfortunately, efforts to reconnoitre usable tank routes over the next few days proved fruitless. With the tanks reduced to playing "a spectators' game," Maj.-Gen. Russell had his infantry attack on their own. Even a visit to A Squadron's mess by Field Marshall Alexander and Lt.-Gen. Kirkman did little to raise the tankers' spirits—letting others do the fighting had never been their regiment's way. Though the weather gods remained unco-operative, A Squadron's goal remained getting at least a few tanks forward to support 19th Indian Brigade's attack on Monte Casalino.[33] Brig. Dobree's men had already captured the lower slopes, but efforts to follow up those gains had been stymied. A night patrol by the 3/8 Punjabs, which Capt. Quinn accompanied, did locate a possible route that infantry and armour could have jointly used to attack the massif from the rear, but only if the ground dried. Regardless, with field artillery reduced to a meagre twenty rounds per day, finding routes to move and supply tanks was a low priority.[34]

The Calgary Regiment's various units were now spread out over 50 kms of road, with only the two forward squadrons even in touch by radio. Richardson spent his days just trying to see all the scattered elements of his command and maintain some sense of cohesion. Years later, he recalled "the terrific problems that confronted us ... with very, very limited roads or trails that we could use [for movement or resupply] .... There was really no hope of what you might call tank warfare ... so we were ... a type of moving artillery ... and hoping for the best."[35]

Ten days of off-and-on attacks by Indian infantry failed to wrest Monte Casalino from the enemy. But as larger operations couldn't proceed until that part of the line had been cracked open, a major assault went in on October 17. After three days of savage fighting against diehards who refused capture, the Gurkhas obliged them, taking only five prisoners in clearing the summit as other Indian battalions secured the slopes. The attack had been aided by the enterprise of A Squadron, which had somehow managed to get two troops to a site where they could blast enfilading German defences on nearby Monte Martino. But for the most part the infantry had had to claw its way forward without close armour support, their heavy casualties bearing that out.[36]

Back into the Fray

"The closing stages of the "long night" of tank inactivity were taking place," the regimental war diary rejoiced on October 22.[37] Once again, the Germans—in this case the 578th Grenadier Regiment—were falling back. The 8th Indian Division was now advancing along two parallel axes toward its Sant' Adriano objective, Sword route, the main road north of Marradi through Brisighella, and to its east, Planet route, a lesser highway leading to Modigliana. Brig. Tom

Dobree's 19th Brigade (supported by Maj. Taylor's A Squadron), and Brig. Charles Boucher's 17th Brigade (supported by Maj. James' B Squadron), edged forward in fog and rain. Unlike the 8th's artillery, whose batteries were still short of shells, German gunners were unusually active, and the tanks paused to fire neutralizing HE salvoes at anything suspicious spotted in the surrounding hills.[38] Richardson ordered C Squadron forward all the way from Vicchio so it could be employed quickly if needed. But in the rain and slop, prospects of pressing more aggressively remained dim—some days visibility was so bad even tank shoots were impossible. But with only a single road in the divisional sector deemed fit for wheeled transport, the worst problems as usual were logistical, as evidenced by the two infantry brigades' getting nothing more than mule resupply some days.[39]

A Looming Winter

Recognizing that his forces had little more to give before ice and snow claimed the mountains, Gen. Clark finally called off the offensive on October 27. Simply to keep the Germans under a measure of pressure, active hostilities were to continue when nature permitted. Indeed, the weather, and not the German Army, was now "the most uncompromising foe of all,"[40] with the prospect of spending a second winter trapped in the Italian mountains depressing everyone.

November initially brought improvement neither in the weather nor in the cautious pace of the localized, intermittent advances. The frequency of German shelling increased, and tank positions appeared to be among the primary targets, a sort of back-handed compliment the regiment would happily have done without. On November 7 and 8 the good old days briefly returned, with B Squadron taking advantage of a short break in the wet, foggy weather to lob 600 HE shells onto German positions. Save for limited reliefs, most of the formations in the XIII British and II American Corps had been in the line continuously for over two months, under the most trying conditions of geography and steadily worsening weather; they were utterly worn out. But as Maj.-Gen. Russell emphasized over and over, "[officers and men] are being asked to make an all-out effort, as success here, even though it may not be spectacular, will directly contribute to far-reaching results elsewhere."[41] Of course he was right, but it was little solace to those serving under him. While the morale in Murphy's brigade remained positive overall, there was "a certain amount of bitterness" about the absence of home leave for the longest-serving men, Ottawa's handing of the Zombies (the home defence conscripts, a few thousand of whom were finally headed overseas), and the lack of information on the much-rumoured post-war programs for veterans.[42] After all they had been (and were) going through, the interrupted deliveries of imported beer must have seemed especially cruel. There was always Italian beer, but this could only be obtained if empty bottles were turned in, making these the most prized commodity in the brigade for a time.

With both routes snaking back and forth from one side of their respective valleys to the other, and repeatedly blocked, advances were measured in a few hundred metres of road. By November 18, however, several B Squadron troops had finally reached Modigliana and A Squadron were making progress on their route north of Sant' Adriano. As a captured German report observed, Indian and British infantry typically advanced along ridges parallel to the valley bottoms to which the armour and other motorized elements were bound. Apart from the difficulties of the terrain itself, the rifle companies had to subdue strongpoints that barred their advance. This was the role where the tank proved its worth. Registered shoots in support of the infantry were often just as much for morale as material assistance, though usually delivering both.[43]

By November 25, the westernmost corps of Eighth Army, on XIII British Corps' right flank, was investing Faenza and about to cut directly across the face of the 8th Indian Division's own advance, which effectively squeezed the latter out over the next few weeks, brigade by brigade. Richardson could see his regiment "would be out of business," and with the rest of Russell's division, go into reserve. The imminent prospect of warmer and drier accommodation and leaves to Florence raised spirits, but this was still one of the regiment's lowest points during the entire campaign.[44]

With the D-Day Dodgers in Sunny Italy

Allied soldiers serving in Italy—whether British, Commonwealth, or American—keenly felt others' disinterest in their campaign. It was bad enough before the Normandy landings, when the view back home was that Italy was just a tune-up that could excite only next of kin, but after D-Day things got much worse. With the bulk of the Allied forces pouring into North West Europe, public interest in Italian goings-on plummeted.[45] For the soldiers stuck there, anger turned to disillusion, and disillusion to cynicism, as epitomized in the improvised lyrics sung to the melody of the immensely popular (on both sides in the Mediterranean Theatre) German love song "Lili Marlene." The original version of "The D-Day Dodgers" was written by L/Sgt. Harry Pynn of the 78th British Infantry Division, but there were plenty of variations, some rather more colourful than others. However, the closing verse was common to all versions, and poignantly expressed the men's personal sense of abandonment and loss:

If you look round the mountains and through the mud and rain,
You'll see the rows of crosses, some which bear no name,
Heartbreak and toils and suffering gone,
The boys beneath, they linger on,
They were some of the D-Day Dodgers,
And they're still in Italy.

The Forgotten Among the Forgotten

Even among Canadian war correspondents, interest in Italy waned. Like many of the senior Canadian commanders, quite a few departed for England during the winter of 1943–44 to cover the Second Front, with Ross Munro and broadcaster Matthew Halton leading the exodus. Among the top tier, only the CBC's Peter Stursberg stayed on.[46] Censorship was a constant problem, and getting despatches cleared was a lot harder than in North West Europe. Most of the time, covering the Canadians in Italy meant I Canadian Corps fighting its way up the Adriatic Coast.[47] Separated by hundreds of kilometres from the main Canadian force, the 3,000 odd officers and men of 1st Canadian Armoured Brigade might as well have been fighting on Mars, or for that matter not fighting at all.

The first substantial reporting of the Calgary Regiment's experience in Italy consisted of a few detailed Canadian press reports on Motta and San Leonardo, with the first of these not appearing in the *Herald* until early May 1944.[48] Like most contemporary war reporting, the stories focused on individual acts of heroism and incorporated the names of as many soldiers and their home towns as possible.[49] The veritable flood of front-page coverage on the Gustav and Adolf Hitler Line operations was delayed less than a week, but it is doubtful there would have been near as much if the entire Canadian contingent hadn't been participants. Albertans would certainly have caught references to "tanks of a veteran formation" and "a western Canadian regiment [having] proved themselves" in fighting their way across the Gari and through Aquino.[50] But as the 1st Canadian Armoured Brigade battled their way north to the Arno, newspaper reports were hit and miss, and beyond the Arno, all but disappeared.[51]

The daily and weekly newspaper in Alberta still carried the bulk of the war news, but CBC radio's innovative on-site coverage, which was often delayed only a day or two before reaching Albertans' homes, was more intimate and immediate. Stursberg covered Honker and in several instances the pursuit to the Arno as well. Like all radio men, he had a knack for telling a vivid "picture story" while keeping the censors from "massacring it."[52] A recording made during the Lake Trasimene operations gives a good impression of this skill. He and Richardson, he told his unseen listeners, had watched:

> one of his squadrons [which] was supporting a British unit and from the hill top we could see the black beetles of the tanks on the bright green and yellow checker board of the countryside—the ancient hills and dales had lost none of their beauty through the passage of time.[53]

About a month later, as the regiment fought its way through the Chiana Valley, he conjured up an image of the incongruity of combat amidst such beauty:

> The lush Tuscan countryside with every village … turned into a fortress … our tanks had to shoot up the buildings to drive the snipers and machine gunners out … We've suffered losses—black hulks of knocked out tanks mar the beauty of these ancient hills …. But we're surging ahead now.[54]

In a second report that day, Stursberg reminded his listeners that while the three Canadian regiments "are crack troops, they're not as well-known as other Canadian units in Italy." But ask any British or Indian infantry and "they'll tell you how good they think these Canadian tanks are—they'll tell you alright—in fact they won't stop telling you."[55] The only other reporting of their exploits recounted the epic withdrawal from the snowbound Apennines at the end of December. Ironically the CBC had picked up that story from the NBC network's Fifth Army Radio program and a BBC report based on an article in the Canadian Army newspaper *Maple Leaf*.[56]

La Fine

By early December Russell's infantry, which he deemed utterly spent, continued to edge ahead in fits and starts, but the supporting armoured operations to all intents had ceased. Orders to begin dismantling Bailey bridges so they could be used elsewhere pointed to this becoming a permanent state of affairs.[57] What would have been a bitter moment was sugared somewhat by the Eighth Army commander's fulsome praise of the 8th Indian Division's performance during the entirety of the Gothic Line operations. Sharing McCreery's praise with his command, Russell pointed to the 17th Indian Brigade as being particularly deserving of recognition. In penning his own congratulations, Brig. Boucher made special mention of "the supporting arms whose efforts made this success possible at comparatively little cost to the infantry." Having taken pains to point out that "the pressure of tanks of B Squadron 14 CAR on the battlefield was always decisive," he then quite rightly added that "it was mainly due to the fine work of 7 Field Company Indian Engineers that [the tanks] were able to support the infantry throughout these operations."[58] Such formal acknowledgements were often embellished for morale-building purposes, but they were much appreciated by their Canadian recipients whose recent efforts had been pretty much a thankless trial.

Not being needed in the line, Lt.-Col. Richardson concentrated the bulk of his command in Marradi and nearby San Martino where they could at least resume a regular program of maintenance and training. Officers and men threw themselves into the task of improving their billets with all their usual Canadian ingenuity."[59] And leave of a sort resumed as well, with a three-day university course on Renaissance art in Florence attracting 130 officers and men, some no doubt more enthused in the subject than others.

Fireflies

During this period the regiment received its first Sherman Fireflies, an upgraded model of the tank equipped with the powerful 17-pounder (76-mm high velocity) anti-tank gun that was already seeing use in France against the more heavily armoured (and armed) Panthers and Tigers.[60] For now, the plan was to equip each of the three regiments in the 1st Armoured Brigade with a dozen Fireflies, fewer than half the number Richardson had personally recommended. Unfortunately what the new gun added in armour penetration, it lost when firing high explosive rounds, almost the tanks' sole work during the past six months. Consequently, each armoured regiment was also allotted six Shermans armed with the 105-mm howitzer. The remainder of their Sherman strength would still be equipped with the 75-mm dual-purpose gun which had proved its worth in the infantry support role.[61]

Stalemate, a Sad Parting, and a Merry Christmas

Behind the scenes, Generals Clark and McCreery and their staffs were endlessly debating how—or increasingly, if—to break through to Bologna and the Po Valley during the winter. As the year came to an end, Field Marshall Alexander finally intervened—they would go on the defensive and prepare for spring.[62]

Just a week earlier, word had come that the 8th Indian Division would soon be transferred to the far left flank of the American Fifth Army. The Indians "left without ceremony," the war diary lamented, but "better no farewell than a sad one." It had been a remarkable partnership, "unmarred by failures or differences," which had overcome cultural and language barriers.[63] The trust vested in the Calgary Regiment was real. When paired with other armour during their subsequent advance north, sepoys from the 1/5 Mahrattas pressed their brigadier, "Where are our own tanks?" And asked to choose a regiment for postwar affiliation, the Indian officers of the 3/8 Punjabs unanimously chose the 14th Canadian Armoured Regiment. These feelings were reciprocated. Asked by a war correspondent what it was like to fight with Indian troops, a young lieutenant had bluntly responded "we're happy as hell."[64] Years later, Stoney Richardson summed up his regiment's experience with the 8th Indian Division during the campaign north of the Arno River:

> We had all the confidence in the Indians and the Indians had great confidence in us. If this had not happened we certainly would not have been so successful in [that] terrible mountainous country ... It really boiled down to a battle of supply, food, ammunition and tough terrain. And, of course, the outstanding feature of the whole thing was the morale, the ambition, and the fighting spirit of our Calgary tanks as well as the Indian Division people that we were supporting.[65]

As the 1st Armoured Brigade's war diary touchingly acknowledged, "one of [our] greatest regrets in leaving Italy will be saying good bye to such a superb fighting machine whose men have never let us down and whose friendship we will never forget."[66]

On Christmas Eve, Richardson confided to his officers that Brig. Murphy had just informed him the brigade would soon withdraw to XIII British Corps' reserve area at San Donato near Florence for a long overdue period of rest and refitting. And long overdue it was, with the Calgary Regiment itself having been operationally committed for 346 of the past 482 days.[67] The 25th dawned clear and blanketed in white, but only the temperature was cold. Following British Army tradition, the Christmas meal, preceded by rum punch (more rum than punch), was served by the officers. It was truly a feast: roast chicken and lamb, creamed potatoes, peas, cauliflower, plum pudding with custard sauce, oranges, a chocolate bar, and a bottle of vermouth to top up the coffee for each trooper and NCO. Far from home and loved ones, in a war that was won but not yet over, the value of the regiment as family had never been more clearly displayed.

The Longest Day

On Boxing Day afternoon Richardson and two of his squadron commanders drove to 1st Brigade headquarters, where Murphy briefed them on their pending withdrawal. In one respect it was their good fortune since both sister regiments were fated to remain holed up in the frigid mountains for several more weeks.[68] But a winter withdrawal in mountainous country filled Murphy with dread. Early on December 28, the advance party set off, with the remaining elements to follow a day or two later—in total, almost 650 men as well as over 100 wheeled vehicles (all equipped with chains in anticipation of the worst) and seventy-odd tracked vehicles. Conditions were treacherous, especially the first thirty-odd kilometres to Borgo San Lorenzo. As the war diary described it:

> [The ordeal] commenced as A Sqn pulled out [at 0200] along rutted, frozen … roads towards Borgo …. Steel tracks, weighted down by 30 tons, refused to grip on the glazed surfaces. Tracks revolved without the tanks moving more than inches …. The wind was cutting, and [with only the drivers inside] frozen tank crews walked hour after hour through the night, frequently huddling around the exhaust while they crept yard by yard up to the mountain pass. By daybreak, the tail [of the convoy] was only a few miles below Marradi …. With daybreak came the hovering snow storm, making the road still more dangerous …. It was harrowing … to watch a vehicle slide ponderously and helplessly toward a four hundred foot drop, finally crashing heavily against the frail protective bank …. At the pass [Maj. James] organized Italian labour to repair and gravel the surfaces. Luck and steadfast driving got the first twenty tanks through by 1000 hours, [and] the rest followed by 1400 hours …. [I]t was dark many hours before the last tank reached San Donato—some 17 hrs after the start.[69]

The route covered roughly 120 kms, with only the first half of it hard going. But the tanks had still averaged barely 7 kph. Murphy considered their feat "one of the finest [the regiment] has performed and I bear in mind in saying so the outstanding work … performed in the face of the enemy."[70]

A Retrospective from Shangri-La

Exhausted men awoke on the last day of 1944 in another world, greeted by clear skies and comparatively balmy temperatures. The new billets offered steam heating, electric lighting and the unspeakable luxury of hot showers.[71] With their weeks-long ordeal in the winter-bound Apennines, the most inhospitable tank country imaginable, finally over, it was possible to look back at their achievements in 1944. The year's final war diary entry summed things up well:

The year's successes were out of proportion to the losses suffered, which is the most that any formation could wish for. The Calgary Regiment was fortunate in its leaders, fortunate in the actions it fought, and fortunate in its infantry and artillery associations. Yet successes were not undeserved, for it fought with considerable versatility, being by turns cautious, daring, slippery, or dogged, usually as the occasion demanded. It tried to follow the twin golden rules of never taking unnecessary chances, but if necessary risking everything rather than letting the infantry down.[72]

By early January the entire front had effectively shut down, with active patrolling by both sides the only belligerent activity, but they were a long way from any of that.[73] Anticipating their involvement in a breakthrough assault come spring, everyone worked hard to revive dormant armoured warfare skills. When they learned that the 4 Mahrattas,[74] the 8th Indian Division's anti-tank regiment, was going to give up their 17-pounders for American M10 tank destroyers, a Sherman derivative, some of the drivers volunteered to set up a training course for them.[75] Overall, their stay proved a pleasant, productive interlude. As the war diarist concluded with tongue firmly in his cheek, "such climate and scenery offer the long sought explanation of why Europeans winter in Italy."[76]

Off to the Senio

All good things must end, some more abruptly than others, and on January 24 Richardson received orders from brigade to close the training schools, cancel leave and get his command ready to transfer to the Adriatic sector. For Richardson's men the move would be almost a pleasure trip compared to what faced the 11th and 12th Regiments in extracting themselves from their frozen Apennine redoubts. Richardson soon grasped that they were going to relieve British armour supporting the 56th British Infantry Division who were holding a section of line along the Senio River immediately north of Faenza. Convinced they had been tabbed for something rather more dramatic, the disappointment was palpable as the news filtered down. The terrain greeting them a week later was bleak—flat farmland criss-crossed by ditches and canals, the odd blasted grove of trees, and everywhere mud. The remaining inhabitants were surprisingly congenial in spite of their pathetic circumstances. As Maj. Ritchie, the second-in-command, glumly noted, it was just going to be "more sitting, shooting, watching and waiting."[77]

Release from Purgatory

It had always been Ottawa's intention that the Canadian Army would be re-united when military circumstances permitted, and while the British agreed—they could hardly do otherwise—there was little sign this was imminent at the end of 1944. However, once it became clear the Americans were determined to win a decision in North West Europe, and transfer formations from Italy to achieve it, the log-jam broke. On February 5, the War Office informed Canadian Military Headquarters (London) that all Canadian units in Italy would soon transfer to that theatre. In fact, preliminary planning for Operation Goldflake was already complete.[78]

A Brief Taste of the Senio

However, all this lay in the regiment's future. By February 2 they had relieved their British predecessors and were adapting to a rather new style of fighting. The daylight hours were generally quiet, with the raiding and counter-raiding taking place at night. In the absence of much to shoot at during the day, fire support tasks also took place at night.[79] Given that the 56th's commander, Maj.-Gen. G. T. Whitfield, insisted he would not send his men into battle without tank support they could count on, and an assault across the Senio must come, the squadrons commenced training with their paired infantry battalions. They were shocked to discover that one of the 56th's brigades had had no systematic training in infantry-armour co-operation at all, which at least made the rifle companies receptive to what they were told.[80]

On February 10, Lt.-Col. Richardson was summoned to brigade headquarters for briefings, and unbeknownst to any of his officers, was soon winging his way to First Canadian Army headquarters in Belgium. In quick succession, contradictory orders landed on Maj. Ritchie's desk—to prepare to be relieved beginning February 18, and to be ready to support 56th British Division's attack on February 19 or 20! Wisely, the acting-CO gave priority to the former, because the attack would be put off.[81]

Operation Goldflake

About the same time, Murphy was finally permitted to brief his widely dispersed command—in addition to the Calgary Regiment near Forli on the Senio, both the Three Rivers Regiment and brigade headquarters were still well to the north in Borgo San Lorenzo, and the Ontario Regiment almost at Porto San Giorgio on the Adriatic. The news that they were packing up was, to say the least, well received, and the destination hardly mattered. Murphy and his staff feverishly set about co-ordinating the complex logistical arrangements to move three armoured regiments from one side of Italy to the other.[82] Four days later, Maj. Ritchie briefed his officers about their pending move to the vicinity of Leghorn. Tight security would require the removal of all unit indicators from both men and machines. Even casually discarding cigarette packages was prohibited. By early afternoon on February 26, the last of five trains ferrying the regiment's Shermans, Stuarts, and M3 half-tracks steamed out of Forli station on a circuitous 800-km rail route that would end at Harrods Camp, "a sprawling city of tents" built on a stretch of sandy flats on the outskirts of Pisa. On March 1, following a rather more direct road route through Florence and down the Arno valley, the wheeled vehicles and remaining personnel set off to join them.[83]

The camp seethed with rumours about where the various units were headed, so Ritchie made it official—Belgium.[84] D-Day Dodgers no more, morale soared. Of course there were regrets that the task for which they'd risked their lives—and their friends had died—would now be completed without them, but there was little nostalgia for Italy or the Italian Campaign as the war diary made abundantly clear:

> To leave poor Italy with its mud, destruction and ignorance of sanitation was, for most members of the Regiment, nothing short of a prison parole. Like a prison term, the chief properties of [our] recent existence ... had been boredom, inactivity and apparent lack of any future.[85]

Loading the regiment onto LSTs for the crossing to Marseille took two days. As the first convoy slipped away from the docks early on March 5, their naval escort hovering in the distance, it was as if Italy itself was saying *arrivederci*. In a postcard view, the sea was a mirror with the purple coastline set against a brilliant dawn sky. Unfortunately, the fine weather didn't hold, and the second and third convoys encountered heavy seas. A disaster was barely averted when one of the LST's threw a propeller and was left wallowing with a tank that had broken loose from its moorings sliding dangerously into the thin sides of the cargo hold. While the American crew watched on, having conspicuously doffed their boots just in case, Lt. George Thring and a few of his mates quickly managed to secure it.[86] All the LSTs were successfully unloaded at the Marseille docks on March 8 and immediately set off for a sprawling encampment 30 kms outside the city.[87] By late on the following afternoon, all the armour and their crews had entrained, steaming northward that very night. The remainder of the regiment drove off in their own jeeps and trucks, spending the nights at a series of American-run transit camps along the route.[88]

Vive la France

The picturesque Rhône Valley, largely untouched by war even after Dragoon and the subsequent push north by the American and Free French troops, offered a sharp contrast to the impoverished, battle-scarred villages and farms they had become used to (and so despised) in Italy. So did the paved, well-maintained highways. A large billboard proclaiming "Visit Sunny Italy—the Land of Sunshine and Art" elicited plenty of laughter as they drove past on their first morning.[89] The greatest trial was having to refuse the incessant offers of locals bent on selling them bread, eggs, and wine. Security protocols forbade it. As they passed through northern France and into Belgium, civilians "were increasingly hospitable ... with much waving of hands and smiles of encouragement, something that had been rarely seen in southern France and practically never in Italy."[90] Road weary from their 1,300-km journey, but in good spirits, the convoy pulled into their new home, the Belgian town of Dottignies (now Dottenijs) not far from Courtrai (now Kortrijk).

Dottignies

Nothing prepared the officers and men for the warmth of their reception in Dottignies, where they were billeted in civilian homes for the entirety of their three-week stay.[91] After greeting his men, Richardson informed the officers and RSM they would not be participating in upcoming British operations to cross the Rhine. That would at least permit the resumption of training and maintenance as well as limited leave to London, Paris, and Brussels. Squadrons would be reorganized to match theatre practice, each now comprising four troops of four tanks each, two 75-mm-gunned Shermans and two Fireflies.[92] Surely the most welcome announcement was that dances would be organized and the local pubs declared in-bounds from 1700 till 2200. Toward the end of the month the entire regiment paraded under an overcast sky for an inspection by Brig. Murphy in the town square. After speaking briefly, he placed a wreath at the town war memorial. The ceremony ended with the singing of "O Canada," "God Save the King," and the Belgian anthem, and was followed by a banquet and no less than four dances. Toward the end of their stay, all of the tank crews had an opportunity to practise their gunnery, which was particularly welcomed by crews converting to the Firefly. The range work took a rather novel form: the gunners simply pumped their allotted rounds into the German defences at Dunkirk, whose garrison had continued to hold out.[93] But as the officers and men revelled in their fine new surroundings, and enjoyed a break from combat, far to the east a very painful story was unfolding.

Der Brotmarsch

As the Nazi regime entered its death throes in early 1945, it was grimly determined to delay the liberation of the roughly quarter million Allied prisoners of war held in German camps. For those whose camps lay in the path of the advancing Red Army, it meant forced evacuation westward during an especially harsh winter. The treatment meted out to the columns of POWs depended greatly on the attitude of the guards escorting them and the civilians they encountered along their route. Planning was minimal, food and medical care scarce, and discipline arbitrary and sometimes cruel. Almost 80,000 prisoners of war—including the NCO and other rank members of the Calgary Regiment captured at Dieppe—suffered through this ordeal before being liberated in April by British, American, Free French and on rare occasions, Soviet forces.[94]

The majority of the Dieppe prisoners had been transferred from Stalag VIII-B (Lamsdorf) to Stalag II-D (Stargard) in January 1944. Generally they remembered conditions there being somewhat better, and that German reasonableness increased in lockstep with the prospects of Allied victory.[95] On January 23, Tpr. Forbes Morton penned a quick *kriegsgelangenenpost* note to his parents and siblings reassuring them that he was well, looking forward to his twenty-third birthday in five days' time, eagerly awaiting the arrival of his October next-of-kin parcel, and keen to get home and find a wife—though probably not in that order.[96] It would be the end of April before he could write them again, and it would be as a free man.

On the Road

For Tpr. Denis Scott, the ordeal began on February 5 when the commandant told the assembled prisoners that they had to gather their belongings and what food they could carry and prepare to start moving west in 24 hours. Scott and about 200 other POWs soon found themselves marching through the rubble-filled streets of the Baltic port of Stettin, all but disappearing in the sea of refugees—women, children and old men—carrying their few goods in wheelbarrows and baby carriages or piled atop carts, all wailing "Russky Kommen, Russky Kommen!" In miserable weather and stalked by hunger, they pressed on, trudging along backroads for several days before stopping for a night in some unheated barns and sheds, repeating that ritual for weeks. "We were ready to eat anything," Scott remembered. The prisoners' condition rapidly deteriorated, and dysentery was rife. After over five weeks on the road and utterly exhausted, they reached Stalag X-B near Bremerhaven. When a convoy of International Red Cross "White Trucks" arrived carrying food parcels, "it was better than Christmas," Scott remembered. But after a few days, they were ordered to move on, the SS needing the camp for inmates from Belsen concentration camp. What Scott saw the next morning as he and his comrades departed was forever seared in his memory:

> There were trucks and wagons loaded with bodies ..., they were piled high like so many broken dolls .... Those who could walk were crying and moaning and begging us for food [and] the goons with wooden clubs beat them mercilessly .... When we left down the same road we actually stepped over bodies ... [and] most of us were crying.[97]

Fortunately their column wasn't strafed, such friendly fire accidents being all too common, and with the British Army sweeping through the area, liberation was only days away.

Tpr. Don Craigie's group of prisoners left a few days after Scott's. They reached the outskirts of the port of Rostock just as Bomber Command was levelling the city, sheltering in a jail for a week after the senior officer among their guards warned them the locals would kill them if they showed themselves. On the march again, the men without great coats or proper boots suffered terribly from cold. Fed nothing but raw pork, the prisoners wolfed it down. But they would spend a week on a farm where the wife fed them as well as she could in return for work.[98] It was like that, with some civilians hurling abuse (and worse) at the haggard columns, and other instances where German refugees shared their last scraps of food.

The group of prisoners Tpr. J. D. White accompanied spent a month marching along a meandering route westward, trudging 20 kms or more each day. The men considered themselves fortunate that their guards were from the camp—perhaps familiarity would soften their treatment. Throughout the ordeal, they never laid sight on a Red Cross parcel, and the German ration was a loaf of rock-hard black bread each day, which half a dozen men shared. Occasionally they were able to barter some cigarettes for a bit of flour or a few turnips.[99] The prisoners had been sternly warned that scavengers would be shot, but constant hunger overcame any fears and men would slip away at night to try their luck.

Liberation

The Free French liberated Tpr. J. D. White's group, then trucked them to a nearby town and simply told them to live in any of the homes they wished and wait for the Americans. Not surprisingly, the local population were docile. After a few days mostly sleeping and eating, the Americans duly arrived and in short order, White and his mates were ferried back to England.[100] As for Tpr. Denis

Scott, the camp they had finally reached was liberated by Scottish soldiers on April 28. Thirteen days later he was in an English hospital, being thoroughly checked over, as were all the ex-POWs. He was almost 35 kgs lighter than the day he surrendered.[101] In the 60-odd days since he and a group of other Dieppe prisoners at a work camp had been given all of three hours to pack whatever food they could onto an improvised sledge before trudging off into the unknown, Tpr. Vern Richardson had trekked almost 750 kms. He had seen and endured his share of the misery. By the time they had reached Bavaria toward the end of April, their guards, who were now clearly worrying about their own fate, promised there would be no atrocities, a fate prisoners understandably feared—when the Americans arrived, they would simply hand them over. On May 1 they met up with a recce unit from an American armoured division, and the next day GIs escorted the now ex-POWs to a nearby village, divided them into groups of six, and told them to find a house and make themselves at home, but not be rough. Richardson and his chums tried to calm the terrified residents down, though not too much. During their two-day stay, he and his friends "liberated" all the food and anything else of value they came across. It wasn't long after that, crammed aboard American transports, they were ferried back to England.[102]

Not everyone's liberation experience was quite so painless. Tpr. Archie Anderson's group were freed by the Red Army. Worried they might be held for weeks, Anderson and a few others, including an American POW who spoke passable Russian, literally escaped from their liberators, finally managing to make contact with British paratroopers who treated them to "more sweet tea and stew than they could eat."[103] On VE Day they flew to England in the belly of a Lancaster bomber.

The Allied Plan

After the Allies had defeated the German Ardennes offensive (the Battle of the Bulge) in December 1944, their plans shifted to forcing the Rhine River and then encircling the Ruhr Basin. After the Americans had gotten across first, Operation Plunder, a major Anglo-Canadian thrust, followed in the Wesel area. Plunder opened the way to the whole of northern Germany as well as the final encirclement of the Ruhr, which Allied forces completed on April 1.

The first operation of the now reunited Canadian Army was carried out on April 2–3. It called for Lt.-Gen. Charles Foulkes' I Corps to evict the Germans from the Nijmegen-island sector, the stretch of land between Nijmegen on the Waal [Rhine] River, and Arnhem on the [Neder] Rijn River."[104] Bypassing the 85,000-strong German garrison of *Festung Holland* would have spared Canadian, British, and Polish soldiers' lives but have risked famine claiming many more lives and the enemy laying waste to the economy. Clearing the "island" was a necessary preliminary to crossing the Ijssel and Neder Rijn and capturing Arnhem, which in turn were prerequisites to clearing the remainder of the country. It was as part of that liberation offensive that the Calgary Regiment was now committed.[105]

Into Action Again

On the evening of April 3, Lt.-Col. Richardson received orders that his regiment would move into southern Holland. While the thought of being so close to the German frontier electrified everyone, their new surroundings, less than 10 kms behind the front lines, were a bleak sight, with all the nearby buildings badly damaged and littered with trash. On April 9 they were ferried by truck to the southern edge of the Reichswald Forest where they met up with their trainborne tanks. From there they followed a circuitous two-day approach that took them across the Waal at Nijmegen and up to the Rijn River where they would provide indirect fire support for Operation Anger, the 1st Canadian Division's assault on Arnhem.[106] By early on April 12 the last of the Shermans had taken up their firing positions. A sleepless day followed a sleepless night as HE shells—to the tune of 350 rounds per tank—were carefully unloaded and stacked, crews briefed and guns surveyed, all under the watchful eyes of 11th Field Regiment officers who would control the bombardment. At 2040, the silence was shattered as the barrels of three armoured, three field, and one medium artillery regiments erupted simultaneously. For two hours the fire was relentless. Then, after a brief respite, the fusillade resumed, reverting to on-demand fire until early morning when it tapered off for a time before commencing yet again. No one feeding the guns forgot that the lives of the infantry depended on their maximum effort. The 14th's war diarist tried to capture the experience:

> Who has ever forgotten the unnatural quiet after a night attack? There is only the occasional burst of [machine gun fire] in the distance … or an occasional shell. Bleary-eyed men crawl from a blanket or a turret after an hour's sleep, or refuse to wake at all for 0900 breakfast. There is little conversation and large indifference to everything, except to ask "How's the battle going?" "Haven't heard." Back in a gloomy room of half folded maps, cigarette butts, half eaten sandwiches, and unmade bedrolls and dirty cups, a telephone rings [with new no-fire lines]. Traced on the map, [they cut] out a third of Arnhem. Good news. 49 Division is well across the river and into the town. For us, it but remains to supply

all targets for the mopping up. The squadrons are very weary; but not so [weary] as the infantry.[107]

As darkness fell once more, Richardson arrived back from his London leave to reassume command from Maj. Ritchie. Around midnight, with its last defences cracking, and Arnhem "another weary milestone" on the victory road, his tanks, save C Squadron's, finally fell silent.[108]

Operations Re-framed

Follow-up plans were once more in flux. There were now hopes that negotiations with the German Army might substantially reduce casualties, both military and civilian (which proved to be the case). On April 13 Montgomery issued orders that the Canadian thrust into western Holland would proceed but more slowly. Although 1st Armoured Brigade's three tank regiments were ostensibly meant to hold the Neder Rijn, they ended up supporting offensive operations to the north and west, which in the following days liberated the entire central area of Holland. According to Intelligence there was now not a single German tank in the country, but there were anti-tank guns, the usual plethora of *panzerfausts* and *panzerschrecks*, and likely some *StuGs*, and of course plenty of anti-tank mines. For Canadian armour, as for Canadian infantry, these final engagements were filled with danger.[109]

Ede

Shortly after reaching their new harbour in the Zetten area, A and C Squadrons were ordered to return to Arnhem to join a push by the 49th (West Riding) Division's 147th Brigade westward along the north bank of the Neder Rijn to clear the enemy from the area around the towns of Ede and Wageningen. It would turn out to be the regiment's last significant attack of the war. Both squadrons were in place by the morning of April 16, occupying what had been a well-to-do residential area of the city before it had been pillaged. Richardson and his two squadron commanders, Majs. D. C. and R. R. Taylor, formulated a plan with the commanding officers of 11/Royal Scots Fusiliers and 1/Leicesters.[110] Ede, the first objective, was thought to be held by 200–300 members of the Dutch SS (in fact there were 150 Dutch SS as well as some German troops). A Squadron, with three rifle companies carried on their tanks, would dash straight into town and overwhelm the garrison, while C Squadron would outflank Ede and block any escape route.

Abruptly, around mid-afternoon, as plans were being finalized and before a proper recce had been carried out, the British and Canadian commanders were told to prepare to attack in two hours. Given Ede was 25 kms distant, this meant the assault would go in in fading light, leaving everyone shaking their heads. Still, there was an understandable confidence that their "superiority of equipment was so great that whatever methods were adopted, we would probably end up in Ede anyway."[111] Around 1730 they were on their way, a most satisfying display of Allied power in front of the hundreds of haggard German POWs who looked on disconsolately as the engines of dozens of Shermans coughed and then roared to life. But only twenty minutes later, L. S. Forest's lead tank was hit as it rounded a slow curve. It was dud, but before the Sherman could reverse, a second shot penetrated the frontal armour, killing the driver, Tpr. R. H. Hofer, badly wounding the co-driver and setting the tank alight. In the rapidly fading light, the force prudently hunkered down for the night.[112]

A new plan was hatched that called for C Squadron, screened by smoke, to overrun a dominating hill north of the road, then stay there to provide direct fire for A Squadron's follow-up frontal assault. Only two companies of the Royal Scots would participate in the latter, with the third, assisted by several troops of tanks, assigned to root out any anti-tank guns lurking in the woods between the start line and the farmland covering the final few kilometres into the town.

Launched at dawn, both the clearing operation and C Squadron's assault went like clockwork. Two hours later the main force moved off. They were met with heavy machine gun and rifle fire, and Richardson radioed his tanks to neutralize it—an order they executed with enthusiasm. As the advance finally closed in on the suspect factory buildings, a bombardment was laid down at almost point-blank range. Finally, a troop under C Squadron's Capt J. W. Rainey drove forward to ram gaping holes in the walls so several Wasps (universal carriers equipped with flame-throwing equipment) of the Royal Scots could drench the interiors with blazing fuel. Survivors who scrambled to escape found a hot welcome from the machine guns of Lt. Maltby's troop from A Squadron, which had used the commotion to slip around to the rear of the factory area. Many of those fleeing were cut down before they could surrender. Organized resistance collapsed, leaving the tanks and infantry to cautiously clear out the remainder of the town. In what was chiefly a tank show, deploying overwhelming firepower had guaranteed the attackers' casualties as well as losses among the civilians they were trying to liberate would be modest. Half of the defenders were killed or wounded, and corpses, many charred beyond recognition, lay about. No one in the regiment would have felt this butcher's bill was an unfair exchange at this—or any other—stage of the war, and for some it was overdue payback for German treachery at Aquino on 23 May 1944.

Once the firing ceased, the townsfolk scrambled from their basements and mobbed C Squadron, which had assembled in the town's main square. As the startled crewmen opened their hatches, they could not help but notice that "[the] faces were stamped with the mark of malnutrition or downright starvation." While the liberated did most of the celebrating, the majority of the liberators, "satisfied with a job done" but pretty worn out, tried to catch some sleep.[113]

A Sort of "Phony War"

The following day word came from brigade headquarters to retire to the Zetten area and resume assisting the Belgian Brigade as it slowly advanced westward, clearing the strip of territory between the Neder Rijn and the Waal. But further aggressive action by I Canadian Corps was soon suspended, no one in the British or Canadian high commands having any stomach for casualties at this stage of the war—a view certainly shared by all fighting units. Moreover, the Allies had agreed to a de facto ceasefire as part of their negotiations with German military and civil authorities in occupied Holland, which they hoped would spare further suffering by the population. The Calgary Regiment received its stand-down orders early on the evening of April 19, though they were allowed to respond to fire until a week later when Richardson passed on orders that, short of repelling an attack, all firing, even of small arms, was prohibited without brigade approval.[114] The prospect of general inactivity at least enabled the men to attack the maintenance backlog. Most crews were especially keen to weld on spare track links to thicken their turret and hull armour until some of the Shermans looked like they were moulting.[115] And there was also time for a bit of infantry-tank training with the recently raised Belgian units. Encamped in front of the Ochten canal, the cold, wet weather reminded most of their miserable few weeks on the Senio. Whenever they could, officers and men huddled in small groups around radio sets, hoping to hear the latest war news on the BBC. At least comrades were no longer dying, and as the war diary put it, "home was nearer to us all."[116]

Victory Won

By early May the front line had become very quiet. Having learned in Italy the need to deal with animal carcasses, Richardson quickly gave permission for their bulldozers to assist local farmers. Plans to resume organized sports were also well underway. Then, just before 2100 on the evening of May 4, word spread like wildfire that the BBC had announced the surrender of all German forces in the Netherlands, news confirmed within minutes by I Canadian Corps. Acting on Murphy's orders, Richardson authorized a special issue of rum for all troops and invited officers and many other ranks to the officers' mess to toast their regiment. The sky was lit up for hours with signal flares fired in impromptu celebration. As the night dragged on the euphoria subsided, most soldiers turning to more sombre thoughts about those who'd paid for this victory.[117] Appropriately, May 5 dawned sunny and warm but caution was still in order until it was certain all enemy units had received the news.

Plans now had to be hashed out to deal with the masses of German POWs who would soon have to be processed and disarmed, as well as to apprehend Dutch SS members. Any advance would be impossible until engineers, hopefully with Germans' co-operation, had cleared the countless mines and booby traps. And it was also clear that the movement of Dutch civilians would have to be controlled to prevent epidemics, if nothing else. Finally, troops were told they should intervene in popular acts of revenge against former collaborators before they became too ugly.[118]

On May 7, word reached the regiment that the morrow would officially be VE Day. The following afternoon, Lt.-Col. Richardson assembled as many of his officers and men as duties would spare to listen to Churchill's speech over the BBC.[119] Since most soldiers in Holland were still recovering from earlier celebrations, the local Dutch population had to compensate, which they surely did. In his personal message, Richardson reminded his officers and men that their impressive list of battle honours had exacted a bitter toll in lives, wounds and imprisonment, and "it is most appropriate that we ... consider what they sacrificed in order [to] celebrate this day." Surely no one needed to be reminded. He then asked them to bear in mind that their regiment's reputation would also rest on how they carried out their duties while awaiting repatriation. He hoped their return to their homes, loved ones and friends would happen quickly, and reminded them that "with the training and experiences you have all had in the years of war there is no doubt ... you will be able to make a real contribution to the country we all love and for which we have fought."[120]

The erstwhile enemy, initially remarkably uncontrite, soon found the co-operative spirit, which was welcome news. At first, it was "an eerie sensation to pass by trucks full of well-armed German soldiers, or to see them standing by their now idle flak guns."[121] But within days, the men got used to seeing them crammed into a tawdry array of horse-drawn wagons or marching in bedraggled groups, guarded by a mere handful of soldiers, some columns taking a couple of hours to pass. Dutch civilians paid no heed to the Germans' misfortune—they were more interested in chatting to Canadian soldiers and staring longingly at the field kitchens busy preparing the men's noon meal. While senior officers immersed themselves in preparing for their new prisoner of war responsibilities, most of the regiment were honing their mathematical skills calculating precisely how many points they'd accumulated under Ottawa's demobilization regulations announced in the latest issue of *Maple Leaf*.[122]

Demobilization Plans and the Veterans' Charter

The war years saw the recognition that the state, and especially the federal government, should play a major role in improving ordinary Canadians' lives. Some of this was the result of lessons absorbed from the Great Depression. But Ottawa's success in managing the war economy illustrated the good that might be accomplished if the state intervened in peace time. There was also a widespread feeling that Canada had not done right by its Great War veterans in reintegrating them into post-war society. Certainly by 1944 the King government, urged on by the progressives in caucus and the cadre of very able civil servants who had masterminded much of Ottawa's war effort, accepted that generous assistance to the nearly one million new veterans—the likes of education and job training programs, housing assistance, and cash grants like the wartime gratuity—were essential to creating a prosperous post-war Canada. The creation of the Department of Veterans Affairs in 1944 was tangible evidence of this commitment, even if it would always have a somewhat fraught relationship with its constituency, and similarly the Veterans Charter passed by parliament in the same year. The array of veterans' programs and initiatives were far from perfect, too often embodied traditional class biases (the DVA invariably treated officers and enlisted men differently), and certainly did not abandon the long-standing commitment to individual responsibility. But as historian Peter Neary has concluded:

> By 1945, Canada had a rehabilitation program in place for veterans that was comprehensive and purposeful, could be seen as honouring the obligation of the country to those who enlisted, was clearly explained to its intended beneficiaries in the mass-circulation pamphlet *Back to Civil Life*, and enjoyed broad public support.[123]

And, one might add, broad support among veterans themselves, young men who had given up so much of their youth to the Great Depression and the war. But the burning desire to get home ensured the government's promise of rapid demobilization along modified first-in-first-out lines, a system taking into account the years and type of service as well as family status and the Canadian economy's employment needs, had every bit as much appeal.

A Love Affair With Canada

Preparations were gotten in hand for the regiment's participation in the Canadian Army's victory parade scheduled for the Dutch capital of The Hague on May 21. Altogether, ten officers, sixty-six other ranks and thirty-two tanks took part. The Calgary Regiment's were the first Allied tanks the city's population had seen, and they were mobbed when they rolled into the central square late on the afternoon of May 20. Within an hour only a handful of unhappy troopers remained behind to guard the Shermans—"everyone else had already made many friends and was out visiting for the evening."[124] The parade itself proved a great success, though it barely managed to navigate streets jammed with throngs of grateful men, women, and children amidst a sea of union jacks, Dutch tri-colours, and orange streamers (for the Dutch royal family). Simply put, it was a day for Canadians—they were the toast of the town. A very different kind of parade three days later saw 7,000 German POWs held by the regiment march through the gates of Tiel camp at the start of their long trek back to Germany.[125] Thousands more followed in the succeeding days. Both armies had come a long way from Dieppe.

Farewells

On May 25, a tragic accident cost the regiment their last fatal casualty in Europe when a recce squadron Stuart escorting German prisoners rolled off a dyke road, crushing L/Cpl. J. P. Rowles. With the war over, his death seemed especially tragic, and a large number of officers and men attended his funeral.[126] Rowles, who had enlisted in December 1943 and had only been with the regiment a short time, left a widow and two small children. Within a few days, Richardson had written Bessie Rowles, explaining the circumstances of the accident and reassuring her, in the fashion of such letters, that her husband had been killed instantly. It would be the last of the many such letters he had composed.

At month's end, the regiment moved to a new harbour near Driebergen east of Utrecht, where the first repatriation draft—seventeen other ranks—said their goodbyes and set off for Canada.[127] After the swell of emotions surrounding the end of the war, the federal election on June 11 was rather an anti-climax, but the men still showed a lot of interest and voted in impressive numbers.[128] On June 8, all personnel and tanks from the three regiments assembled near Amersfoort to participate in a final march past for their brigadier. It culminated in a moving tribute to fallen comrades, the officers and men saluting and each tank lowering its cannon as the "Last Post" sounded. Brig. Murphy had chosen the Calgary Regiment to provide the guard of honour. Very pleased with their discipline and polish, Lt.-Col. Richardson ordered a special rum ration and seventy-five cigarettes for all ranks and declared June 9 a regimental holiday.[129]

In another demobilization milestone, over the four-day period starting June 16 all tanks—painted, cleaned, and greased to look like they had just rolled off the assembly line in Detroit or Schenectady—were turned in.[130]

Understandably, it was emotional experience for crews. That task done, it was time for the Calgary Round Up, a much-anticipated farewell party for other ranks. Unquestionably the highlight was the appearance of 186 suitable dance partners provided by the YMCA Hospitality Bureau in Amsterdam. The festivities went onto in the wee hours, with music provided by Holland's foremost pre-war dance band, *The Ramblers*. Even the notoriously fickle Dutch weather co-operated.[131]

Restlessness

In the weeks since VE Day, petty indiscipline and minor crime had increased noticeably, and while such was to be expected, it could not be allowed to get out of hand. Transgressions from dangerous driving on the bicycle-clogged country-roads to incidents, albeit isolated ones, of drunkenness, black-marketeering and looting began to sour relations. Warnings were backed up by severe punishments for offences against civilians.[132] Stoney Richardson remembered the orderly room becoming so jammed with men up on charge that a message had to be sent, though he certainly understood his men's frustration over not knowing when they'd be going home, and having nothing meaningful to do while it was sorted out. Fortunately, he embraced the view that a little more drill and a lot more sports and educational and training programs offered the best prospects for focusing the men's energy on worthier pursuits, and it seemed to work.[133] For some time small groups had been departing, either reposted or having volunteered for the Canadian Army Pacific Force. But the floodgates were opening, with three officers and fifty-five other ranks (including the RSM) departing on June 20, followed two days later by a further seven officers and sixty other ranks. As the war diary lamented, these marked "the start of the more serious disintegration of the regiment."[134] It was not just a question of friends being wrenched apart. The point system, fair though it was in principle, qualified many who were indispensable to the regiment's smooth functioning to leave first.[135]

Franeker

To everyone's disappointment, Driebergen was not going to be their final camp before returning to England and then home. That would be the village of Franeker, only a few kilometres from the North Sea coast in northern Holland. Untouched by any fighting, it offered excellent camp facilities, but the local population never warmed to their Canadian guests.[136] As July—and the repatriation process—dragged on, morale suffered accordingly. The uncertainty was especially hard on those with British wives (and children) who worried about how Ottawa was going to handle the moving of dependents to

Canada.[137] At least there were now many vocational and educational courses on offer, mostly taught by officers, and in part for lack of anything better to do, these were heavily enrolled.[138] With the good summer weather, various sports leagues flourished, the contests against teams from other regiments being especially hard-fought affairs. Sailing or swimming outings, or visits to some of the nearby communities where traditional Dutch dress and other customs were still in vogue proved popular, too.[139] But the overarching problem was clear and no one's fault—the Canadians didn't want to be in Holland anymore, and the Dutch, despite never forgetting Canadians' role in their liberation, had become just as keen to see them leave.[140]

A Fighting Regiment No More

In August, word reached all three armoured regiments that, barring shipping bottlenecks, repatriation would commence no later than the end of the year. Forty officers and men, all of whom had participated in the raid, were able to attend the third anniversary ceremonies at Dieppe. A few days earlier the last of the liquor supply confiscated from the German Army in May had been divided up amongst the squadrons with orders to see they consumed it—orders that were followed to the letter.[141] Just on its own, the adoption of the point system ensured there would be no returning of complete units to Canada. But the army also intended to cross-post as many soldiers as possible to units returning to soldiers' home military districts. For an armoured unit like the Calgary Regiment, which had drawn many officers and specialists from other parts of the country, this launched a second wave of departures toward the end of August, and with it another round of farewell parties.[142] Finally, on September 8, the log-jam broke. Richardson informed all ranks returning to Alberta that they would be moving to England on September 21 (subsequently pushed back to the 27th), with those bound for other parts of Canada heading off around the same time. Since the rumours had settled on early November, this was exciting news.[143] Preparations—from packing personal gear to medicals—consumed most of the last few days in Franeker. Right on schedule, their convoy pulled out and headed for Nijmegen where, after a brief layover, they boarded ships for England.[144] There were smiles all round that day.

Home at Last

Most of the Dieppe POWs reached England by mid-May, and all of them passed through No. 4 Canadian Army hospital in Aldershot. Apart from receiving medical treatment, the staff bent over backwards to cater to their needs. Those who were otherwise fit received new uniforms intended to make them feel like soldiers who had done their duty. They also got a portion of their back pay and some leave to enjoy it. But there were also efforts to prepare them for the dramatic changes they would confront in Canada.

Among the Canadian servicemen (and women) jostling to get home, it was the former POWs who were given the highest priority.[145] Tpr. John White crossed the Atlantic on the Île de France and then crossed the country in sleeper cars. Word always seemed to leak out that there were prisoner of war passengers on a train, and crowds would gather at every station to cheer. When he finally reached Calgary, his mom and dad were on the platform to greet him. Tpr. Don Craigie had been awestruck by the distant lights of London as he flew into Southampton. After being checked out and fattened up a bit at Aldershot, he and twenty other Dieppe POWs boarded the *Queen Mary* bound for New York. During their brief stopover before entraining for Montréal, they were treated to a Yankees baseball game, the US Army generously paying for all their beer and hotdogs. When their presence was announced on the public address system, the crowd stood *en masse* and cheered. Craigie reached Calgary on July 15 and was officially demobilized on Labour Day. Like so many others, he had only one thought—how his new life on "civvy" street would unfold.[146] What being a POW would mean over the long term remained to be seen, but *kriegies* would face their share of difficulties as the years passed.

The rest of the regiment came home somewhat later, many of them in smaller groups of Alberta veterans drawn from all three services. The biggest party, numbering about 250 and including Lt.-Col. Richardson, finally reached Calgary on December 1, where the large crowds gathered along 8th Avenue welcomed them home as they marched to the armoury.[147] Mewata was jammed with family members who witnessed the CO dismiss his men for the final time to loud cheering from all ranks. Among them was George Thring who had risen from the ranks to become a lieutenant and troop commander by war's end. Thring and his wife had become engaged in the autumn of 1939, but he could not afford an engagement ring until just before they got married during his Christmas 1941 leave. In April 1943, after many months of training, he finally went overseas, where he saw plenty of action. In a memoir, Thring described his homecoming:

> Dorothy, our two mothers and the other folks and relatives were told to meet us inside [so] we rushed [in] … What a thrill it was to hug Dorothy and our moms. Many [times] I never knew if I would be returning! … Dorothy had booked a suite in the Palliser Hotel. We invited the officers and wives to come too. Well, what happened next? Hard to believe but all the wives and families were seated around the perimeter of the suite—where [were] we? On

the floor in the centre of the room playing "craps." We had been together through such stressful times it had bonded us like family.

After the initial celebrations, the two went on a second honeymoon just so they could get to know one another again. "I knew I had changed drastically and thank goodness she hung in there."[148]

Conclusion

The Calgary Regiment's role in the Italian Campaign from the crossing of the Arno through to breaching the Gothic Line remains obscure. The general anonymity of the D-Day Dodgers supplies part of the explanation, but even more they suffer from the 1st Canadian Armoured Brigade's separation from the rest of the Canadian Army in Italy. Fighting under British command and supporting British and Indian troops has never endeared its story to the country's military history buffs or for that matter its military historians. At the same time a candid examination of their operations reveals plenty of courage and skill but only a modest military contribution, one that became progressively more modest the further the tanks penetrated into the heart of the Apennines.

The Army Historical Section's assessment of the fighting through central Italy—which we know closely reflected Stoney Richardson's own views—was that up to the Arno "our tanks had slowly and systematically helped their infantry forward from one position to another,"[149] and in light of this the strains large armoured formations placed on overstretched logistics was probably a fair trade-off. But once north of the Arno, and particularly of the Sieve, deteriorating weather, unforgiving terrain, and the near collapse of logistics emerged as a more formidable opponent than the German Army, with the result that opportunities for close infantry support and bombardment—the three regiments' bread and butter—simply faded away. By mid-December 1944 it was obvious even to the tank units that "our usefulness to the 8th Indian Division was ended."[150] From September onward, the Calgary Regiment had done its best. At least the nature (and for long periods, absence) of fighting had cost few casualties.

From an operational and not simply a national perspective the Calgary Regiment's extraction from northern Italy made sense, but it was the latter—national identity politics—that made it happen. Unfortunately, the timing meant they arrived in the North West European Theatre too late to play more than a brief role. After V-E Day, everyone simply wanted to get home, including their prisoner of war comrades. Several months of quasi-occupation duty in Holland was an anti-climax. By the time summer ended, a finely honed fighting machine had been dismantled. The men were soon on their way home, confident they had done their duty, and mostly full of hope. All carried memories of friends who would never see Canada again.

6.1 KOCR reservists participating in a training exercise at Camp Wainright. Their Sherman looks like it could have fought at Ede. While still adequate for the purpose in the summer of 1956, it was a far cry from the Centurions equipping the regular army. (KOCRA, P-600-10-0013)

6.2 Reservists from The King's Own Calgary Regiment train on the frozen prairie at Camp Wainwright during the winter of 1948–49. Coping with insufficient (and inadequate) equipment, the inevitable personnel turnover of part-time units, and the ill-defined defence goals of successive Canadian governments, the reserves struggled to maintain their relevancy during the post-World War II years. (KOCRA, P-600-10-0049)

6.3 Local reservists practise civil defence rescue techniques at the "Greggsville" training facility, c. 1965. They had built it themselves at Sarcee Camp only a few years earlier. (KOCRA, P-600-10-0136)

6.4 KOCR reservists proudly parade with their regimental guidon, Mewata Armoury, c. 1960. (KOCRA, P-600-10-0008)

6.5 Mewata Armoury, c. 1940–45. Completed in 1918, the complex has been central to the life of Calgary's militia and reserve units—including The King's Own Calgary Regiment and its predecessors—ever since. (Glenbow Archives, pa-3538-24)

The Cold War Years   *301*

6.6 Cpl. Nathan Hornburg, killed in action in Afghanistan, 24 September 2007. Thousands of reservists have volunteered to serve in peacekeeping, peace enforcement and other international missions, particularly since the end of the Cold War. The King's Own Calgary Regiment has provided more than its share. Unfortunately few Canadians are aware of the magnitude of the reserves' contribution. (KOCRA)

9

Neither Peace nor War

Whither the Militia?

The 14th Canadian Armoured Regiment (The Calgary Regiment) officially disbanded as an active unit of the Canadian Army on 15 December 1945, leaving the wartime reserve unit to soldier on. The regiment would henceforth operate as a reserve formation (the term militia having been officially dropped),[1] a status it retains three-quarters of a century later. Along with the rest of the militia, The Calgary Regiment had struggled just to survive during the interwar years. Without the Second World War, its withering away would hardly have been noticed. What would be their fate now?

It was not obvious in the immediate aftermath of World War II that there wouldn't be another *levée en masse* like those of 1914 and 1939, but it became clear soon enough.[2] How would Canada's part-time army units recast their role to remain relevant and justify their continued existence? In a country where the regular army struggled to be taken seriously and frequently led a parlous existence, the reserves could face bleak times. That The King's Own Calgary Regiment (as it would come to be known) not only survived but by reserve standards flourished in such an unpromising environment was a notable achievement. This chapter will primarily explore that story through 1960—the regiment's fiftieth anniversary.

The Militia Reborn

By 1947 the Canadian Army, a formidable force in the latter years of World War II, had all but disappeared. Its replacement, the Active and Reserve (i.e. militia) forces, "were small, under-funded and ill-equipped."[3] Indeed, by late 1947 their respective strengths were 14,000 and 20,000, respectively, which was well below 1939 levels. But as the Iron Curtain ominously descended across central Europe, Ottawa and most of the population began taking military preparedness more seriously. While the regular army benefited the most, restrictions on the recruitment and training of part-timers eased as well.

303

A New Regimental Title

In the spring of 1946, the reserve unit was redesignated the 14th Armoured Regiment (The Calgary Regiment), and then within a few months the 14th Armoured Regiment (King's Own Calgary Regiment), and finally The King's Own Calgary Regiment (14th Armoured Regiment). Facing the anonymity of "militia" existence for the foreseeable future, the adoption of "King's Own" in the title had been enthusiastically embraced by all of the officers. It was Lt.-Col. D. F. Rodgers' dogged efforts that carried the day. Crucially, he won the endorsement of the new governor general, Viscount Alexander, who was all too familiar with the regiment's performance in Italy and personally approached King George VI on its behalf. And he could also count on the fulsome support of The King's Own Royal Regiment which had been encouraging the change for years.[4]

Militia Training in the Early Cold War

For the regiment's members returning from overseas in 1945, the transition to reservist was straightforward, as they were simply asked whether they wished to continue as a regular, join the "militia"/reserves, or be demobilized outright. A fair number chose the second option. Thanks to stocks of tanks, trucks and jeeps left over from the war, training was armour-focused and was carried out at the Mewata Armoury as well as the regiment's outposts in central Alberta. These included A Squadron in Olds (with detachments in Didsbury, Carstairs and Bowden), B Squadron in Stettler (with detachments in Big Valley and Castor), and C Squadron in Innisfail (with detachments in Red Deer and Condor). There seemed to be plenty of young men (and the necessary cadre of veterans) in central Alberta keen to soldier part-time, and the regiment took advantage of its storied tradition in those areas.[5] As always with part-time soldiering, the prospect of earning some additional income was a definite attraction. The regulars' training area near Wainwright hosted summer (and winter) camps and the Sarcee facilities on the edge of the city could accommodate live-fire exercises.[6]

Recruiting in both urban and rural areas drew mostly young men in their late teens, accounting for 90 percent of the ranks in 1948. Turnover was high, with men frequently finding they lacked time to train given competing family, employment or other demands. For those who could stay on, retention seemed to depend on the amount of training with actual military hardware the regiment could offer. Here the regiment's eight Shermans, three Grizzlies, (a Canadian-built version) and single Stuart were priceless assets. Weekend exercises in basic armoured tactics were scheduled as often as could be arranged, and when possible involved other squadrons. And to gain publicity, the regiment became a fixture at "every community effort which they were able to lend their support to."[7] The few weeks of annual summer camp at Wainwright were always a highlight, with the regiment sending 100 members in 1951. That same year several dozen officers and other ranks were able to attend training courses offered by The Lord Strathcona's Horse either locally or at the Royal Canadian Armoured Corps (RCAC) School at Camp Borden, and numbers participated in the army's own training manoeuvres. During these early years, a steady stream of reservists also drifted off to serve with the regulars.[8] Fostering a strong regimental spirit with annual social events like the St. George's Day celebrations and Brides Dinner also helped to retain members, as did the periodic visits of military and other luminaries which did double duty by heightening the regiment's profile in the community.[9] A good example of the latter occurred in May 1948 when the Indian High Commissioner to Canada, the Hon. H. S. Malik, presented The King's Own Calgary Regiment with a traditional Mahratta warrior sword gifted by the 1/Mahratta Light Infantry (of the new Indian Army) for "their magnificent support" of its predecessors in the British Indian Army during the Italian Campaign. Dignitaries, members of The KOCR, veterans of the 14th Armoured, in addition to a large turnout of ordinary citizens, jammed Mewata Armoury for the event.[10]

Acknowledging the Prisoners of War

As the Army and newly established Department of Veterans Affairs (DVA) moved quickly to get the freed Dieppe prisoners of war back home, the difficulties these men would encounter over the coming years was underappreciated. Achieving official recognition of their involvement would entail a long struggle, not least with the DVA, an institution which too often behaved more as adversary than advocate.[11] The prisoners of the Great War received little sympathy from Canadians who felt such men, being spared the risks of combat, had had an easy time of it. It was different now, for both home front propaganda and the armed forces' own efforts had stressed that being captured was not dishonourable and POWs had continued to do their duty under trying circumstances. Despite the widespread good intentions, the sense that the country's 10,000 POWs—including the nearly 200 from the Calgary Regiment—were a group deserving of special attention was lost amid the hundreds of thousands of discharged servicemen (and service women) who all had their own just claims for assistance through the Veterans' Charter, pensions and other measures.

During the immediate post-war years, many ex-POWs had trouble fitting in and quit the former jobs they'd returned to. Many ex-prisoners of war felt they had to make up for lost time, and often became frustrated when it didn't happen. A majority were able to settle down, at least to society's satisfaction, but mostly they had to do it on their own. The serious medical problems rooted in the poor medical care, malnutrition, and callous treatment prisoners had suffered took years to emerge.[12] But there were slights the Dieppe prisoners had to endure that ate away at them. For example, Don Craigie always felt it was unfair that Ottawa awarded Dieppe POWs a combat bar for their WWII service medal but not the France–Germany (Campaign) Star.[13] And Al Wagstaff felt a stigma as a *kriegie* that he was never able to shake.[14] Similarly, the realization that their experience simply didn't measure up to the excitement experienced by comrades who'd spent the war fighting and liberating took its toll. This was true even within the otherwise comfortable surroundings of veterans' reunions. What did the Calgary Regiment's *kriegies* know of Motta, San Leonardo, The Gully, Operation Honker, or a host of obscure Italian villages and towns stretching north from Rome across the Arno and into the heart of the Apennines? But that *was* the war for most of the veterans who gathered around the bar to swap stories, only a relative handful of whom remembered Seaford or Worthing. Life in Lamsdorf or Stargard only held meaning to men who had been there where, as the unthinking (or insensitive) might point out, they had been cut off from the real war.

Less than ten years after the war ended, the struggle to obtain special disability and pension recognition for Canadian prisoners of war was well underway, and by 1952 Ottawa began acknowledging the Hong Kong veterans' collective claim. But for Dieppe prisoners, individual claims still remained the rule, and even these were only guaranteed if had been imprisoned by the SS or Gestapo, and not the German Army. Thane Campbell's appointment as chief war claims commissioner began to change attitudes. His report argued convincingly that every Nazi prisoner had suffered maltreatment and deserved a special payment, with additions for incidents such as shackling and forced marches.[15] Nevertheless, gaining pension justice remained a slog. When Hong Kong prisoners finally received collective supplements to their pensions (as distinct from lump-sum payments) in 1971, European Theatre prisoners pressed for similar recognition —namely the acceptance that their health problems were caused or aggravated by the conditions they had endured in German POW camps. Given the US had already accepted the principle, medical opinion in Canada and elsewhere endorsed it, and most Canadians were in sympathy, the federal government finally came onboard, though implementation of a fairer system would still take years.[16] But for the Dieppe prisoners it had been a long slog, and too many never lived to see their claims validated, though at least their widows and children would gain some benefit.

Fitting in

As the Regina *Leader-Post* had aptly put it, for the new generation of veterans, coming home meant "the end of one long march and the beginning of another," the former "strewn with memories" and the latter "shin[ing] bright with hope."[17] For most "vets," including the hundreds from the Calgary Regiment, the return to civilian life went remarkably smoothly, despite some initial stumbles over the first job or housing. Some knew exactly what they wanted to do, and set about doing it, but for others it wasn't so clear and they spent time, sometimes quite a bit of time, searching. A survey of Second War veterans completed by DVA in the summer of 1946 indicated 82 percent had already found work, the great majority within two months of their discharge. And in the long run most would enjoy a good life—it was not just the baby boomers who would flourish in post-war Canada, but their parents, too.[18]

But regardless of how their return to "civvy street" went, in 1945 they were all changed men from the ones who'd enlisted only a few short years earlier. The Veterans Charter and other legislation designed to assist the returning serviceman helped immensely. For those who had left a job to join one of the services, having a guaranteed job to return to was a godsend. And even more so, the smoothly managed transition of the war economy to a peacetime footing.[19] Returned men in 1919 could only have dreamed of any of this. Few marriages were strengthened by prolonged separation and very different experiences neither spouse ever fully appreciated. Wives and husbands just "weren't the same anymore"—a situation both had to accept.[20] Many of the regiment's personnel had only been married a short time before being separated, and almost had to start their marriages anew. There were children they hardly remembered (or were remembered by), and in the case of embarkation leave conceptions, hadn't seen at all. Whether married or unmarried, some had lost parents and siblings. Others were shocked to realize that the parents of pre-war friends and school chums actually resented them for surviving, when their own sons or brothers had not. Psychological stresses added to the burdens of a great many vets, as physical disabilities did for others.[21]

Dieppe POW Don Craigie had dreamed of using his wartime gratuity and a loan from the Veterans' Land Act to start farming but ended up accepting a temporary job as a butcher at Burns Meat Packing in Calgary just to put some money in his pocket. He met an army buddy there and through him, Marybelle, the chum's sister. The couple fell in love and were married in December 1946. Utilizing the veterans' hiring preference offered by the federal civil service, Craigie moved on to a job with the Department of Agriculture, where he built a successful career as a meat and livestock health inspector.[22] For his part, Fred

Ritchie experienced a kaleidoscope of conflicting emotions upon demobilization. He had spent over a year as the second-in-command of an armoured regiment, and before that, led a tank squadron. "Civvy street" was bound to be a shock:

> I remember the first day back at work [in Montréal] wearing a suit rather than the familiar uniform I'd worn for five years. I felt suddenly anonymous. I had been a junior salesman with Dominion Textile before the war and that was the job I went back to, even though it had no appeal for me [but] I had a growing family to feed.[23]

Like many combat veterans, finding out that those who'd enjoyed the comforts of the home front had little interest in hearing a veteran's experiences was disheartening. Nonetheless, capitalizing on his wartime administrative experience, Ritchie steadily advanced at Dominion Textile to become a regional sales manager. Still, the job was gruelling, and both he and his artist wife longed for a calmer and more fulfilling life. In the end he quit the company, and they packed up and moved to Naramata in the Okanagan, where he turned an orchard into a career and relished every minute of it.

The 50/14s

Founded immediately after demobilization in 1919, the 50th Battalion Veterans' Association thrived during the interwar years, both because it met veterans' needs and because most lived in or near Calgary and could readily participate if they chose. With the return of the 14th Armoured Regiment veterans, the now middle-aged 50th Battalion men appropriately renamed their group The 50/14 Veterans' Association, gaining new blood (and relevance), though it is worth noting that Second War veterans proved less likely to join the Legion or regimental associations, or attend reunions, than Great War veterans.[24] The membership of the 50/14s was informally divided into several groups. Among Great War veterans, there were two—the 434s or originals, men whose service numbers were drawn from the 50th Battalion's original allotment (434001–434999), and those who enlisted later in the war.[25] Among the latter, many strongly identified with their original battalions, like the 137th. For veterans of the Second War, it was those captured at Dieppe and the "D-Day Dodgers," with "originals" found in both groups.

By the 1960s age was beginning to thin the ranks of the 50th men. Lt.-Col. Mason, for instance, had passed away in 1966. But Great War veterans continued to dominate the executive of an organization that counted over 400 members, making it one of the most active regimental veterans associations in the country.[26] The reunion banquet was the yearly highlight. In 1964 it was held on August 15 at the Palliser Hotel. The program always repeated segments deeply meaningful to the veterans, included a speech to fallen comrades, a wreath ceremony, a minute of silence, and a guest speaker, who in in this case was Brig. Bradbrooke, the regiment's first CO after it went active. There was also plenty of group singing, mostly wartime favourites with lyrics suitably cleaned up for the spouses and other guests. And of course a dance followed the formalities.

By the mid-1970s the number of Great War veterans attending, mostly due to ill-health or retirement to warmer climes, had shrunk to a mere handful.[27] Yet the participation of WWII veterans had declined, too, despite being a generation younger. Moving the reunions to other centres where there were a significant number of regimental "vets" like Red Deer didn't help noticeably. Those committed to The 50/14 Veterans' Association, like those committed to the Royal Canadian Legion, had a hard time understanding why an organization that meant so much to them meant much less (or nothing at all) to others. The World War II veterans were also more widely scattered across the country. After the severe losses at Dieppe, the regional identity of the Calgary Regiment eroded steadily with reinforcements coming from everywhere, so that while Albertans always constituted a majority, by 1944–45 it was likely no more than a bare majority. Jim Quinn, who by the early 1990s was serving as a lieutenant general in the Canadian Forces, offered an intriguing perspective on why his generation of veterans might not have felt as drawn to the regimental association. As he viewed it, the nature of an independent tank regiment in the Anglo-Canadian system worked against the sense of regimental loyalty one would observe in an infantry regiment or even an armoured regiment that served in an armoured division. Tactically the former operated as three independent squadrons, often in quite separate actions, and it was inevitable that loyalty and identity would be less focused on the regiment.[28]

Assessing the vitality of The 50/14 Veterans' Association as the years passed is a "cup half-full, cup half-empty" situation. Active membership at the end of the century was 246, plus seven widows. There were no veterans of the 50th left—the last, D. C. Archer, having died in October 1994, aged ninety-six.[29] The 1998 reunion was held at the Red Deer Legion and by all accounts the 141 attendees had a fine time. As usual, music was provided by the regimental band. One of the highlights was a message Stoney Richardson had sent to his old comrades. There were toasts to the 50th Battalion, the 14th Armoured, and The King's Own Calgary Regiment, and of course to fallen comrades. And for the twenty-four members who had passed away during the previous year, a moment of silence. When a collection was taken for the Gurkha Relief Fund, wallets were opened wide and undoubtedly memories of grim fighting in the Apennines stirred.[30]

Remembering

As the veterans returned in 1945, their memories of the war and the role they had played in winning it were only too vivid, and the latter was certainly a source of pride. They missed fallen comrades but at least their lives lay in front of them, in most cases full of promise. Remembering the war in formal and informal ways would come later. From the start, however, the next of kin of the fallen were immersed in remembering. All mothers were awarded the Memorial (or Silver) Cross. Mrs. Emily Hofer, whose son Richard had been killed in Holland in road accident only three weeks before VE Day, had hers approved two months later. But such awards, or compassionate letters from commanding officers (Richardson wrote to the next of kin of every man he lost) stirred up memories, too. Trying to intercede with the Army bureaucracy on behalf of the father of Tpr. William Ferguson, who was killed on 25 November 1944, a local recruiting officer and reserve padre pointedly noted "this boy's parents have taken the loss of their son very hard and are exceedingly bitter and grieved at heart and now feel it most keenly when his old comrades are returning home."[31] Fortunately, the bureaucratic Gordian knot was cut for most next of kin by the end of 1945. But during the next few years there were periodic reminders of their loss as form letters describing the disinterments and reinterments arrived in the mail. To its credit, the Canadian Army did its best to convey to widows and parents the respectful nature of these stages, and tried to engage them, most notably by requesting personal phrases to be etched on the final gravestones, a tradition inherited from the First World War and much more commonly used by next of kin after 1945.[32] Normally, photographs of the permanent resting place were also sent to next of kin. It would be decades before most of these graves could be visited, so the pictures were welcome. The mother of Sgt. Alton Allison, who was killed near Aquino in May 1944 and finally interred at the Cassino Commonwealth War Graves Cemetery, received a photograph of her son's gravesite in the spring of 1948.[33] The parents of Tpr. W. M. Childress, who was killed in the San Leonardo fighting, wrote the army in 1948 that they soon hoped to visit the Moro River Cemetery "to pay our respect to our dear son [as] we can do no less than that." But they also wanted to explore the nearby battlefields where, thanks to information received from several of his comrades, they knew the exact spot where he had lost his life. The army responded adroitly, noting that it was "perhaps somewhat soon for relatives to visit overseas graves, permanent construction work and embellishment of the cemeteries not being very far advanced as yet [but] there are no objections to relatives visiting the graves of their loved ones."³⁴ Quite understandably, Mr. and Mrs. Childress, who had a modest farm in the High River district, vainly hoped there might be public funds to help defray the cost of their trip.

As the years passed, next of kin and their descendants would begin visiting the cemeteries and battlefields of both World Wars. But it would be several decades before visits by Second War veterans became regular occurrences, some organized by associations like the 50/14s, and others with the assistance of the DVA (more latterly Veterans Affairs Canada). The first major pilgrimages started in the 1960s, but they were to Holland, a theatre that didn't especially resonate with the 14th's veterans. Dieppe was an obvious magnet for them, and Vimy for the 50th Battalion survivors who could still manage such long trips. The fiftieth anniversary of the Battle of Vimy Ridge was the first venture where the federal government made a significant effort to enable numbers of veterans to attend at public expense. Vimy was worth celebrating—it had always been so—but Ottawa's largesse had more to with the rise of separatism and the severe strains it put on national unity. Commemoration of birth-of-a-nation events, no matter how artificially constructed, were in demand for reasons that overshadowed mere military significance. In 1977, the 50/14 executive put forward Percy Blain, a 50th Battalion scout sergeant in April 1917, to represent their Great War members on that occasion, a pattern that would be repeated for some years.³⁵

Remembering took other forms, and many fell closer to home. Beginning in 1960, Victor Wheeler, one of the 434s, began tracking down other battalion veterans with the intention of writing a combination history/memoir of his and his comrades' experiences. As he outlined to one of his contacts, his book was "not all going to be murderous fighting, bludgeoning, dying and running blood, horror scenes and the like," but rather would "have plenty of humour, good-natured fun, and banter, good times ... faith [and] hope." After all, "to write otherwise is not to honour those who did not come back with us [nor would it contribute much] to those who may read about your exploits and mine, and many thousands like us."³⁶ Wheeler completed the manuscript in 1975, only to be told by every publisher he approached that the story was too long and wouldn't draw sufficient interest. As military historian Norm Christie has caustically observed, "it was ... a travesty that the Canada of 1975 cared so little for the brave Canadians of 1914–1918."³⁷ Ultimately the Alberta Historical Resources Foundation along with the Alberta-North-West Territories command of the Royal Canadian Legion stepped forward. *The 50th Battalion in No Man's Land* reached bookstores in 1980, a year after Wheeler's death.

There were other instances of organized remembrance of the 50th's story, each providing an opportunity to educate a public that sorely needed educating. On 2 October 1967, in front of numerous dignitaries and a throng of citizens, a newly constructed bridge over the Elbow River was dedicated in honour of John Pattison, VC. Veterans of the 137th and 50th Battalions had proposed the idea,[38] and with the support of local Legion branches and Alderman Roy Farrin's yeoman efforts on council, they had prevailed.[39] That same year members of the 137th Battalion CEF Association erected a memorial honouring their unit. For both initiatives, The King's Own Calgary Regiment had given its wholehearted support.

How Soon Forgotten—Canadians' Amnesia About World War II

Perhaps it had to be expected, but the Second World War had hardly ended before the majority of the Canadian public firmly turned their backs on it, leaving it to the veterans and their organizations as well as reserve units to keep the story alive. Unfortunately, what did survive in the national consciousness was generally devoid of context. The best example of this was the Dieppe raid. Despite notable Canadian accomplishments in Normandy, Italy, the North Atlantic and the skies over Germany, it was Dieppe—invariably portrayed as pure bungling and slaughter—that emerged in the public mind as the centrepiece of the Canadian military effort. Apart from being historically inaccurate, the raid's participants were left understandably bitter at how their sacrifices could be so readily dismissed as pointless. At least remaining Great War veterans could draw solace from their war having given birth to the nation, or so a broad swathe of the public came to believe, with the Canadian Corps' victories, not its defeats, front and centre.[40]

Though Not Everyone Forgot

As the years passed, though, individual veterans of both conflicts—and through them their former comrades—were reminded of their impact as liberators. News of Wheeler's efforts to produce a history of the 50th Battalion somehow managed to reach a Flemish school master in the Passchendaele area. He wrote to Wheeler in 1971, reminding him of the orphan who had hung around their huts after the fighting had ended, and how the soldiers had fed and clothed him. Wheeler couldn't remember the youngster—such events had not been uncommon—but he was quite overwhelmed that the boy had never forgotten his and his mates' kindness.[41]

Sometimes the regiment's men were remembered not just by individuals they'd touched but whole communities. Such was the case with Ede in the Netherlands, whose liberation in April 1945 had been the 14th's final action. Advancing on the town with British infantry, Lt. Jack Forrest's C Squadron tank had been knocked out by an anti-tank round that killed Tpr. R. H. Hofer. To commemorate the 45th anniversary of their town's liberation, Ede's citizens, a majority of whom had not even been born in 1945, were determined to mark the event in some lasting way. Funds were raised to build a memorial honouring both the Royal Scots Fusiliers and the Calgary Regiment. It would include a Sherman painstakingly restored as Lt. John Davies' tank *Cougar* by members of the 8th Canadian Hussars stationed on NATO duty in West Germany. Davies, along with Dick Maltby, another veteran of the assault, and Lt.-Col. A. F. McIntosh, a former CO of The KOCR, represented the regiment at the dedication. Though the Dutch were known for never forgetting those who had freed them, the three men were overwhelmed by the gratitude they were shown.[42] Over the years, veterans travelling to Italy would receive equally heart-warming welcomes.

The Honorary Colonel Presents a Guidon

During the winter of 1957–58, Ottawa authorized all reserve regiments to acquire new regimental colours or (for armoured regiments) guidons. Since The KOCR's guidon would bear their battle honours, choosing theirs for World War II could no longer be put off. This task fell to the then commanding officer, Lt.-Col. A. F. McIntosh, and his second-in-command, Maj. Jack Hunter. It is not clear whether the surviving wartime commanding officers were consulted, as had been the case after World War I. The ten selected from DND's permitted list included Dieppe, San Leonardo, the Gustav Line, the Trasimene Line, Sicily 1943, Cassino II, the Liri Valley, Arezzo, Italy 1943–45 and North West Europe, 1942–45.[43] By rule, the entire regimental cap badge could not be emblazoned on the guidon, so it was decided to include the City of Calgary steer, the Big Horn ram, and the family crest of Gen. Frank Worthington, the father of Canadian armour.[44]

With the guidon's design fixed, it remained to decide who might present it. A royal tour was scheduled for the summer of 1959, and since Queen Elizabeth II had assumed the role of the regiment's colonel-in-chief after her father's death, it was arranged she would present the new guidon personally at the same Victoria ceremony where the regular army's 1/PPCLI received their new colours. Inevitably, the PPCLI ceremony took precedence, but in her address she praised both equally for their gallant service in two world wars, reminding them that:

> The battle honours which are emblazoned on your new Colours and Guidon commemorate this service, and will remind you, and those who come after you, of the spirit of loyalty and devotion which have marked your famous regiments. They will keep before you the memory and the example of your gallant dead. I entrust these new Colours to your keeping, confident that you will always preserve them in honour and uphold the great tradition of which they are the symbol.[45]

Despite the regiment's modest role in the ceremonies, it remained a great honour, not to mention a glamorous ritual of the sort reserve units, with their generally bland, underappreciated existence, understandably revelled in. More than anything, it stirred regimental pride and camaraderie.[46]

Whither the Army, Whither the Reserves?

In 1952 The KOCR's strength totalled an impressive 334 active officers and men, plus thirteen COTC officer cadets and six regular force NCOs permanently attached as trainers. Keenness was never a problem, but for many balancing reserve duty with employment and/or family responsibilities was. Calgary's (and Alberta's) economy was entering a boom period fuelled by the development of the oil and gas industry which, despite periodic "busts," would see employment prospects throughout the province soar over the coming decades. It was a mixed blessing for the reserves. For those who embraced part-time soldiering, training comprised basic and special-to-corps (i.e. armoured) work, but with the regiment spread out across central Alberta, co-ordinating this and maintaining a sense of regimental identity presented major challenges.[47] Still, it was a great morale booster to work with some actual (if dated) tanks even if maintaining them was becoming a growing burden.[48] The modest field training reserve units could undertake left commanding officers constantly seeking additional budget allotments so more of their men could participate. While the army's Western Command helped when it could, meal allowances had to be diverted to cover pay shortfalls, with the men bringing their own food. Even money for fuel had to be conjured out of mysterious regimental sources. It was shades of the 1920s and 30s for those old enough to remember. The 1954 review of the regiment's Calgary establishment approvingly noted that "the calibre of the man in the ranks was very satisfactory, the officers and NCOs are of good calibre and a good unit spirit was noticeable, [and] the standard of training appears to be good."[49] A year later, active strength was 290 all ranks, sixty-three of whom participated in the week-long reserve camp at Wainwright.

The footprint in central Alberta, however, was becoming worrisome. A Squadron in Olds was the exception, turning out 151 for their annual Remembrance church parade in 1954. But for C Squadron in Red Deer, which had several troops scattered in surrounding communities, the story was far less rosy, as was also true for B Squadron, based in Stettler and Coronation, where numbers had been falling rapidly.[50] Maj.-Gen. Chris Vokes, now the GOC Western Command, was convinced the wages and mobility of oil employment was at fault, and the reserves certainly couldn't fight that. He pointed to Stettler, with a population of 3,000, where there were only a dozen boys attending high school. At the same time the booming economy meant local businessmen, who were often officers, simply couldn't spare the time. No one had attended summer camp for two years, and at his most recent inspection only two officers and five other ranks had shown up. B Squadron was shifted to Calgary with the expectation that recruiting in a larger centre would be better—which turned out to be the case as 120 officers and men paraded at the following year's inspection. A single troop from C Squadron was transferred to Stettler to maintain some presence in the area.[51]

Some of the efforts to stir recruiting and keep the reserves in the public eye were quite imaginative, including raising a twelve-strong mounted group garbed in lancers' dress uniforms who could appear at all the regiment's public events. The newly appointed commanding officer, Lt.-Col. W. A. Howard, a rising star in Calgary legal circles, put the case directly to Maj.-Gen. Vokes:

> Realistically, it is not so much the matter of carrying on a tradition, but the very practical and immediate purpose of adding more color and zest to the Regiment in its appeal to the young people and as a very positive attraction and aid in recruiting. While naturally assistance from the Army would be most desirable, nevertheless we are prepared to carry the project.[52]

No fan of the reserves, Vokes passed the request on to Ottawa without a recommendation, merely observing that The KOCR had no cavalry tradition. Ottawa offered neither spare saddlery, uniforms nor funding, but Howard forged ahead anyway. When the mounted unit debuted in the spring of 1955, Calgary media gave it prominent coverage, but Vokes was furious, lashing out at the "polyglot uniforms" (the men were wearing their regular dress uniforms and black RCAC berets) and "flagrant disregard" for traditions.[53] Though highly popular with the public, which after all was the point, the experiment enjoyed a brief life. By 1956, the total strength of The KOCR stood at just over 300 men and while in gradual decline, it wasn't yet a cause for worry. The regiment's attendance at the Wainwright summer camp, always a bell-weather of Alberta reserve units' health, was a robust 121.[54]

While the reserves felt themselves successful, certainly given the constraints they faced, the army's senior command disagreed. When 27 Brigade, Canada's initial contribution to NATO, had been cobbled together in 1951 almost entirely from reservists, the army had been shocked to find they required as much training as raw recruits off the street, and hadn't forgotten.[55] By 1952, the chief of the general staff, Lt.-Gen. Guy Simonds, considered that due to administrative and training inefficiencies, the reserves were failing in their primary task—producing the combat-ready soldiers needed for any rapid expansion of the army. The existence of numerous understrength reserve units hampered overall training, recruitment and retention, and each deficiency fed the others in a vicious circle. Virtually all senior regular force officers shared Simonds' low opinion, including the CO of Western Command under whose administrative oversight The KOCR functioned. Not surprisingly, Vokes dismissed the reserves a "wasteful, top-heavy and outmoded organization" plagued with too many anemic units and a pathetic training record, and noted that it was high time to disband the numerous failing units.[56] Yet as Vokes lamented, "the great snag [in attempting to do so] with certain armoured and infantry units is that we run smack into ... the locally named [or ethnically based—namely Scottish, regiments], all of which have built up traditions in peace and war" and would command strong public and political support.[57]

The convictions of reserve inadequacy led to the 1954 Kennedy Report,[58] which outlined ways unit training could be improved and the whole enterprise made more cost effective. A smattering of modest but useful reforms followed. Chronically understrength units would be amalgamated, absorbed or simply shut down, but the regimental system would be retained. To supply the modest numbers of trained soldiers now expected by the army, basic training in the reserves would be extended to four years but given the steady turnover of part-timers in the ranks, this would produce fewer, not more, trained men. Moreover, senior reserve officers feared that accepting what amounted to inferior training standards would open the door for the army to provide inferior training equipment.[59] Even with the reforms mandated, DND's opinion remained fundamentally unchanged: the reserves would still operate with a bloated, inefficient organization and fail to train their men to a satisfactory standard.[60]

Speaking in the House of Commons in June 1956, the Liberal minister of national defence, Ralph Campney, made clear the federal government's view of what constituted Cold War military preparedness:

The fact is, today, [war] is far too complex and too technical a matter to be left to the amateurs—only professionally trained and experienced servicemen can cope quickly with the weapons and tactics of modern war. To meet our commitments ... we must provide forces in being, completely trained, equipped and immediately ready.[61]

Later in the year, Lt.-Gen. Charles Foulkes, chairman of the Chiefs of Staff committee, confirmed where DND stood, opining that "it is going to be increasingly difficult to justify ... expenditure ... on a force [for] which we cannot clearly demonstrate any need that appears very realistic."[62]

A New Task for the Reserves

In December 1956, Brig. W. A. B. Anderson was commissioned to conduct yet another study of the organization, namely, equipping and training of the Canadian reserves. NATO's adoption of massive (nuclear) retaliation in place of conventional force as its deterrent policy reinforced the forces-in-being view.[63] From Anderson's perspective—which also happened to be the army's—only a fraction of reservists would ever be sufficiently trained to reinforce regular units, with the remainder providing a partly-trained civil defence force to be deployed if Canada suffered an atomic attack.[64] Because this new role wouldn't require their being trained or equipped for operations in the field, the reserves' budget could be reduced. And so could the demands on the army for training assistance. On the other hand, the thinner the training regimen, the more likely the keenest men would drift away. And while the regimental structure would survive, the institution of the reserves would have to fundamentally change its identity.[65]

Released in early 1957, the Anderson Report was embraced by the army, which saw its role as fighting wars, not digging Canadian civilians out of radioactive rubble.[66] By and large the reserves' leadership accepted it, too, for despite some yawning questions, the recommendations at least gave their units a clear role, and hence justified their existence. However, the timing could not have been worse since in June 1957, after twenty-two years out of power, the Progressive Conservatives under John Diefenbaker won a minority government that only nine months later they turned into a smashing majority. The new defence minister, George Pearkes, had won a Victoria Cross in World War I, and neither he nor his colleagues had been consulted by the army on any of these policy changes. Pearkes was sympathetic to the reserves, but he also saw the wisdom of their proposed civil defence role. And like most federal politicians he wanted to avoid stirring up a political hornet's nest in the form of the "militia lobby."[67]

In 1958 the Conservative government made official its intention "to provide a trained nucleus [of] militia units capable of assisting Civil Defence Organizations in the event of a national disaster or emergency."[68] In other words, a nuclear World War III. At long last, here was a role for the reserve forces in sync with Ottawa's appreciation of Canada's military priorities. Senior army ranks were convinced that the reserves would resent their new mandate as insufficiently military, given, as one senior army officer put it dismissively, they were always "ready to lick their weight in wildcats."[69] Resentment there was, but not over the civil defence mandate per se, for the reserves/militia had a history not being consulted by the regulars and then being given roles without the resources to carry them out. There was, of course, inevitable disappointment among the junior officer and enlisted ranks over the obvious dilution of their traditional military role.

Training for Armageddon

During these tumultuous few years, the regiment, now formally called The King's Own Calgary Regiment (RCAC), managed to soldier on. By 1958, however, the presence in central Alberta had appreciably weakened. A lone troop of the now Calgary-based B Squadron remained in Olds and a much understrength C Squadron in either Red Deer or (one troop) Innisfail. A Squadron was now based entirely in Calgary. The combined strength at year's end amounted to thirty-two officers, eighty-two non-commissioned officers, and 132 men. However, it was a worrying sign that a mere eighteen had been able to attend the June camp at Wainwright. That year's St. George's Day celebration, which coincided with the annual inspection, saw 120 all ranks parade in the city.[70] In 1959, DND relocated The South Alberta Light Horse from Calgary (and its various outposts east of the city) to Medicine Hat, with The KOCR's A Squadron taking their place in Gleichen and Strathmore.[71] Concentrating The KOCR in Calgary and its immediate area, which it would now only have to share with the Calgary Highlanders, offered better recruiting prospects.

That same year, the Diefenbaker government formalized aiding the civil power in the aftermath of a nuclear war as the reserves' principal role. In fact it had been the regiment's guiding principle for a year, though Lt.-Col. McIntosh was quick to point out that armoured corps training had continued, albeit at a reduced pace. The KOCR's CO was putting an optimistic gloss on things, for starting in 1958, the infantry, armoured and artillery units comprising the bulk of the Canadian reserve forces no longer received instruction in their combat specialization from regular force personnel. With this change, the disheartening process of surrendering the bulk of their related military equipment had commenced.[72]

Greggsville

Training of reserve units for nuclear civil defence was in full swing by the summer of 1959, with countless strategies and syllabi arriving on CO's desks from Ottawa. Injured pride aside, the 280-odd officers and men of The KOCR did their duty. The week-long assembly at Camp Sarcee, which focused on national survival, attracted a single officer and four other ranks from the regiment, while a dozen other ranks were able to attend a course on bulldozer operations at Camp Chilliwack. In both instances, the attendees were to return as instructors.[73] Amid the whirlwind changes being imposed on everyone, Her Majesty's presentation of their new regimental guidon mentioned earlier was a welcome reminder of their proud roots.[74]

Although dark days lay ahead, the publicity their new mandate generated in Calgary initially proved a spur to recruiting (and retention). Parade strength rose to 357 in 1960, with seventeen officers and ninety-one other ranks participating at Wainwright and three officers completing the Militia Officers Staff Course. But the great achievement of Lt.-Col. I. H. Dearness' first year in command was undoubtedly the construction of Greggsville[75] on a parcel of unused land at Sarcee Camp. Through spring and early summer, numerous local reserve personnel volunteered their weekends and evenings to help construct the training site, with The KOCR providing the largest contingent. Its aging Shermans even provided the bulk of the motive power needed to drag various derelict structures into position. Once completed, Greggsville was suitably apocalyptic, with two streets of faux bombed buildings, each partly demolished so its interior replicated a rescue scenario, and the surrounding area littered with burned cars, trucks, and every sort of debris.[76] As a training facility it proved first rate, and the army could not complain about the cost, which was next to nothing.

Within a year, the reserves' role changed again when the Diefenbaker government de-emphasized the civil defence focus, partly because of the reserves' general unhappiness with it and partly because US/NATO doctrine shifted away from massive nuclear retaliation to a more flexible response that required a conventional warfare capability.[77] In 1963 voters put the Liberals, with their much-ballyhooed plans for armed forces unification, back into power. While the new regime trumpeted more effective, co-ordinated defence policies, it was the promise of considerable savings in the defence budget that worried the reserves. Under the new defence framework they would take up various roles augmenting the army's domestic role, of which aid to the civil power was but one. Talk of increasing the reserves' combat readiness was generally seen for what it was political posturing to calm the disgruntled (and still politically feared) "militia lobby." The reserves' authorized strength was cut almost by half, with cutbacks, amalgamations and outright disbandment of a number of units as well as the shuttering of armouries following. Finally, most telling of all, DND abolished all reserve headquarters, leaving command and administration to be handled by Army District Headquarters, with senior reserve officers henceforth acting as mere advisers.[78]

A Regimental Postscript

From the 1960s onward, along with the rest of the Canadian reserve units, The King's Own Calgary Regiment would endure arguably its greatest trials. As an informal history of the regiment written in 1985 noted sardonically, "the past twenty-five years ... have been noteworthy in terms of the Regiment surviving the several reorganizations of the Militia in Canada." [79] Indeed, repeated role changes and reduced budgets would do much harm. Nor was their situation helped by the apathy exhibited by the majority of the Canadian public toward matters military, particularly during the 1960s, 1970s and 1980s.[80] When Lt.-Col. L. A. Gilchrist assumed command in 1972, The KOCR's strength had plummeted to eleven officers and ninety-four other ranks, and two months later it stood at fifty-eight all ranks, this despite an intensive recruiting effort. This marked the nadir, but despite a gradual recovery, recruitment and parading numbers remained chronically low.[81] The problems historically plaguing militia/reserve units—members' inability to balance jobs/careers, education, and family commitments with part-time military service to the inevitable cost of the latter—were insoluble. This, along with shortages of modern equipment and unclear (and frankly often unappealing) roles, undermined training, morale, and recruitment and retention efforts.[82] The primary civil defence role faded away by 1965, with The KOCR reverting to armoured training with its aged (but much loved) Shermans until these were taken away two years later. Thereafter the role shifted to reconnaissance (using jeeps) and then, beginning in 1979, back to the armoured role, although in practice a mix of the two continued even after they acquired a handful of Cougar light armoured vehicles in 1981.[83]

The 1960s also saw the end of the regiment's scattered outposts, and its concentration in Calgary as A (operational) and B (training) Squadrons. In 1979 Ottawa substantially increased the authorized strength (from 157 to 226). Funding realities often prevented the regiment recruiting to the new ceiling (or carrying out desired training), though it did make it possible to add a headquarters squadron.[84] In 1981 negotiations between the Tsuut'ina Nation and DND culminated in the loss of the Sarcee training facilities, a major blow to all Southern Alberta's reserve units since live-fire and other critical field training now required them to use the regular army's facilities at Wainwright or Suffield.[85] Still, it was not all setbacks. From the 1970s onward the regiment took advantage of the opportunities for those of their officers and other ranks to fill "call-outs" (officially called augmentation) for the regular force. These included tours in UN peace-keeping operations or with the Canadian Army in Germany, as well as stints in Canada with The Lord Strathcona's Horse (Royal Canadians), the armoured school at Camp Borden or DND Headquarters in Ottawa.[86] As declining defence budgets squeezed the regular force, such opportunities steadily increased, especially in the post–Cold War years. Of course as was always true for part-time soldiers, only those who could temporarily free themselves from their other obligations were able to take up such opportunities.[87] Interestingly, despite the initial gap between reservists' and regulars' training, a gap regularly used to dismiss reservists' competence, the Canadian Forces admitted that after both groups completed three months of pre-deployment training, there was no observable difference in their efficiency. While it didn't eliminate the superior attitude of regulars, it had a positive impact on many. It was also brought home to the Canadian Forces that reservists brought skills that were otherwise in short supply. Impressively, during the 1990s, reservists made up one-sixth of the soldiers sent on overseas missions, and there was a comparable involvement in domestic deployments such as disaster relief, although sadly this received little public acknowledgement.[88] Among those keen to take up these opportunities were The KOCR's female officers and other ranks. The country's changing human rights framework required that the regular forces gradually open up the full gamut of opportunities to women. The reserves had followed suit in 1970, to their credit often showing more open-mindedness than their Canadian Forces peers when it came to integrating female personnel.[89]

While the regiment's annual reports during the late twentieth and early twenty-first centuries invariably commented that "there were no major changes in function, organization [or] equipment," the record in taking up augmentation roles was impressive.[90] For example, in 1988–89, ten members (out of a regimental strength of 145) participated in peace-keeping operations in Cyprus, while in 1994 twenty-two served in UN operations in the former Yugoslavia, with many others following as part of a succession of UN/NATO involvements there.[91] Since the governments of the day preferred it that way, few Canadians understood how frequently these so-called "peace enforcement" operations could and did degenerate into fighting. This was followed by Afghanistan where combat was the norm and the public knew it, and where several dozen KOCR members served with distinction as individual soldiers in regular units, but always proudly representing their home regiment. A few were badly wounded, including Cpl. Mark Fuchko, who lost both legs when the tank he was driving was blown up by a roadside IED in 2008. A year earlier, Cpl. Nathan Hornburg was killed by a Taliban mortar round as he tried to repair the damaged track of an armoured recovery vehicle, becoming the first member of the regiment to be killed in action since 1945. And there were other, more traditional peace-keeping and -monitoring operations, equally demanding if nominally less dangerous. Maj. Joseph Howard participated in two of these, first in 2000 as a military observer in the Republic of the Congo and subsequently in 2005 as part of Operation Safari in war-ravaged Sudan.[92] There's no question that the participants in these deployments made notable contributions to their country and humanity, but at the same the extended absence of some of the best officers and other ranks placed a heavy strain on the regiment whose strength—the band excluded—generally hovered between 100 and 150.[93]

Conclusion

The fifteen years following the end of the Second World War exhibited many parallels with as well as some significant differences from the regiment's interwar years experience. Although far from perfect, the demobilization of the new wave of veterans and their subsequent reintegration into civilian life was generally well planned and executed. The hundreds of men from the Calgary Regiment (along with their current and future families) benefited from this, as did the rest of the nation. Similarly, the sustained efforts of former Canadian POWs, including the 170-odd members of the regiment captured at Dieppe, eventually won pension justice for that group. The bonding of Second War veterans with their Great War predecessors in the 50/14 Association was as successful as could have reasonably been expected. Members quietly provided emotional comfort and material assistance to other veterans in need and devoted themselves to completing the memorialization of their own and their former comrades' achievements on the battlefields of two world wars. While there was little they could do to reverse the growing disinterest of post-war generations in their country's military history, they never ceased trying.

And what of the regiment itself? The post-war decade and a half principally covered in this account saw The King's Own Calgary Regiment quickly revert to reserve status. As bleak as funding and public esteem were during the interwar years, at least the militia had known its purpose—to mobilize as part of a major expeditionary force. Such clarity was lacking during the Cold War years. With both the regular army and government embracing a forces-in-being doctrine, there would be no mass mobilization in the nuclear age. Merely being the repositories of the country's military tradition and the army's supposed footprint in the community didn't justify diverting even modest resources to the reserves. From the 1950s onward, investigation followed investigation, with the recommendations mostly circling around perceived problems or gathering dust. Ottawa never came to grips with the simple truth that units comprised of part-time citizen soldiers by their very nature couldn't achieve a standard of readiness matching that of full-time professionals, no matter the organizational framework or level of funding. So the reserves slowly withered away through lack of resources, and then were blamed for their inadequate state. The adoption of the civil defence role—distinctly unmilitary and broadly unpopular within the reserves—sums up the woes of an institution in search of a purpose which ultimately would be decided by others.[94]

The officers and men of The King's Own Calgary Regiment quite literally soldiered on from 1945 through 1960, doing their best to play a series of poor hands dealt by Ottawa. All manner of sacrifices were made by citizens who chose to serve their country through part-time soldiering. Their achievement needs to be judged by the environment in which they had to do it—from the demands of their civilian lives to inadequate training infrastructure, parsimonious budgets, an inevitably strained relationship with the defence establishment, and public disinterest. In that light, they gave their best, which is all Canadians had any right to ask.

CONCLUSION

In the Service of Their Country

Any assessment of The KOCR has to distinguish between two distinct periods—the world wars and two extended intervals of peace. The 50th Battalion fought for twenty-seven months. Despite the BEF's improved infantry tactics and ever greater firepower superiority, the attritional nature of the conflict along with their opponent's fighting skill ensured heavy casualties right to the end. In the initial wave of enlistment the great numbers of men possessing some pre-war military training—including many with the 103rd Regiment—undoubtedly aided the battalion in becoming proficient enough to quickly enter combat and perform to an acceptable standard. The first few battles changed things completely as casualties mounted and few of the reinforcements had any pre-war experience of part-time soldiering. With officers the situation was different, as the pre-war military training which virtually all possessed was a major asset to the battalion and remained so.

In the 1930s the militia was a considerably reduced force from its pre-1914 predecessor, and their training far less thorough. A sizable proportion—though still a minority—of the officers and men who left Canada in 1941 with the 14th Canadian Armoured had a militia background, but this steadily declined thereafter. As during World War I, the strongest militia imprint was found among the officers—Stoney Richardson being a stellar example of a talented militia officer who excelled in the wartime army. Nevertheless, the Cinderella view of the militia—that during World War II it was an indispensable source of officer and NCO material for the overseas force—is exaggerated. After all, only a portion of the regiment's officers and NCOs were accepted for active service in 1941, with age, fitness and the lack of necessary qualifications for the armoured corps being the principal shortcomings. That said, a significant number of officers and NCOs had already resigned from the regiment to enlist in other Alberta militia units as these were mobilized.

When it came to actual time in combat, the armoured version of the regiment fought much less than its infantry counterpart had a quarter century earlier. The 50th missed the worst of Passchendaele, but otherwise basically slugged it out with the rest of the Corps and accumulated the butcher's bill to prove it. In contrast, many who served in the 14th Armoured returned home in 1945 because their fate had been to fight in Italy rather than face the merciless tank battles that played out in Normandy. The fighting in Italy produced its own savagery—one only need ponder Motta and San Leonardo/Vino Ridge—but as the campaign dragged on the obstacles tanks faced were more an unforgiving combination of topography and climate than the German Army. After May 1944 the men hardly saw an enemy tank and there was little in the way of mobile warfare, with the regiment reverting almost exclusively to the unglamorous but vital role of infantry support. Finally, the armoured troops had better prospects for survival than the infantry—in either war. A large proportion of the men in an armoured regiment did not serve at the sharp end—those who did, namely the tank crews, certainly put their lives on the line but were still much safer than the infantrymen on the other side of the armoured plate. They had learned that lesson at Dieppe.

The 50th also fought on the decisive front of its war, participating during The Hundred Days in battles that number among the most crucial ever fought by Canadian soldiers. In contrast, the 14th served in a secondary theatre, for the European war was going to be decided in North West Europe and on the Eastern Front. Understandably, that realization eventually took a toll on morale. Of course, armoured regiments and infantry battalions received their marching orders, they didn't write them. The 14th Armoured didn't pick Italy or Dieppe just as their predecessors didn't pick Lens or Amiens.

Despite these differences, both incarnations of the regiment were assembled from waves of volunteers, and ultimately learned their craft the hardest way, by doing and dying. Each unit was assembled from scratch in wartime, a process which the 14th effectively had to go through a second time. Once overseas, the latter was exposed to more and certainly better training. But when they entered action, both the 50th and 14th had shown their inexperience. From the commanding officers on down, there were the errors of rashness and inexperience—Aloof Trench and Motta come to mind. But there were splendid achievements, the products of solid execution and daring—one thinks of the Marquion Line and San Leonardo. And there were far more of the latter than the former. As ever in the chaos of war, sometimes success merely crowned good luck, but there were also times—as at the forcing of the Gari River—when sheer bad luck, not bad planning or flawed execution, exacted its blood price. And there were a few occasions—fortunately precious few—when officers and men were sacrificed in doomed operations—with Dieppe not the only, but certainly the worst, example. Lastly, in both wars they were blessed with excellent commanding officers who were personally brave, identified and trained able subordinates, prepared their men thoroughly, and earned their soldiers' respect. Here Page, Neroutsos and Richardson stand at the head, but Andrews would surely have joined them if he had not been killed at Dieppe. Junior officers and senior NCOs—most of them unknown today—also deserve respect for their roles in training, steadying and leading their men in action. Most tank crews were led by NCOs, as were most infantry platoons, given the heavy attrition of junior officers once the battle was underway.

While focusing on the experiences and accomplishments of a single regiment, this account has shown that in major operations the 50th and 14th never fought in isolation. Whether it was the three other infantry battalions in the 10th Brigade or the two sister regiments of the 1st Canadian Armoured Brigade, not to mention artillery, infantry, signals and engineering resources, Canadian, British and Indian, there was always a larger fighting team involved, one benefiting from a cast of able senior commanders and staff officers at brigade, divisional, and corps headquarters.

Throughout its first fifty years, the regiment viewed itself primarily as a fighting unit. This is understandable. Yet for most of that time Canada was at peace, and the regiment's responsibilities were confined to part-time soldiering. As we have seen, particularly post-1945, The King's Own Calgary Regiment, like the rest of the reserves, was an organization in search of a role. Their task was made more difficult by the public's embrace of the citizen soldier concept, which had been reinforced by the country's Second World War experience, and which seriously questioned the utility of part-time soldiering. Furthermore, the public's (and army's) embrace of the army-in-being paradigm rendered the relevance of the reserves all the more problematic. During the long years of peace, it was easy to find flaws in the overall institution as well as its constituent parts like The KOCR. But an unattainable standard of professionalism was applied to find them wanting, when it was the essence of such a force that it could not be professional.

The peacetime leadership of the Calgary Regiment could only respond to directives from higher authority, and certainly from 1919 onward they rarely (if ever) contributed to the formulation of directives set by (and for the benefit of) others. It was the responsibility of the army and the federal government to solve the problems of the militia/reserve forces, and this they consistently failed to do. In the end, the regiment's leadership attempted to function as best they could within the framework they were given.

Any fair judgment passed on The King's Own Calgary Regiment during its first fifty years must be a positive one. Though ill-prepared, in both world wars it served the cause of Canada and its allies with distinction. The regiment's ties with Calgary and the surrounding communities of central and southern

Alberta were much closer during wartime than the longer periods of peace, but even then it contributed to keeping alive the positive aspects of military culture and heritage in the larger civilian community. Furthermore, it managed to ensure there was a nucleus of military skill in being which could be (and was) drawn upon to meet the Canada's military and civil needs. In all respects, these were tasks well done.

NOTES

NOTES TO INTRODUCTION

1. Box B103-002 (Calgary Rifles) KOCR (RCAC) Museum Historical Overview, KOCRA.
2. Famously uttered by a Canadian diplomat at the League of Nations in 1927 to explain the lack of interest of his government and countrymen in the world's troubles.
3. Box B103-002 (Calgary Rifles) KOCR (RCAC) Museum Historical Overview, KOCRA.
4. At Dieppe and during the Italian Campaign, 14th Armoured Regiment personnel were awarded three DSOs, seven MCs, five MMs and a lone DCM. Box B103-002 (Calgary Rifles) KOCR (RCAC) Museum Historical Overview, KOCRA.
5. This was hard to avoid, for if the Canadian story was going to be told, Canadians had to tell it, British (in the case of both world wars) and American (in the case of WW II) historians showing little interest.

NOTES TO CHAPTER 1

1. Vance, *Maple Leaf Empire*, 21–30. On the culture of British imperialism and military duty inculcated in the World War soldiers as youngsters, see Moss, *Manliness and Militarism*.
2. Box B103-001 Calgary Rifles, folder 001 and box B103-002 Calgary Rifles, Historical Sketches 4, KOCRA.
3. Box B103-001 Calgary Rifles, folder 001, KOCRA. The 10th Battalion soon became an Alberta unit for reinforcement purposes.
4. Mason had earlier left the 103rd to become second-in-command of the 31st (South Alberta) Battalion.
5. Ottawa assigned the 50th enlistment numbers 434001 to 434999. Holding one of these marked you as an "original" and was a great source of pride after the war. *Calgary Daily Herald*, 29 December 1914, 1 and 21 January 1915, 10.
6. By mid-June 1915 the 50th and two other infantry battalions were training at Sarcee Camp, with a total of sixty rifles between them. By 1916 eleven infantry battalions were training there, and the camp expanded to accommodate 15,000 men. Cunniffe, *Scarlet, Riflegreen and Khaki*, 18, box B103-002 Calgary Rifles, KOCRA.
7. Cunniffe, *Scarlet, Riflegreen and Khaki*, 22, box B103-002, Calgary Rifles, KOCRA and A. Russell and W. Gadsden, box 15, tape 1, 50th Battalion interviews, RG 41 BIII1, LAC.
8. Box B50-010 50th Battalion, folder 003 Nominal Rolls and Other Personnel Lists, KOCRA. Most would reinforce the 10th Battalion which permitted the 50th, which only reached the front in August 1916, to claim Festubert as a battle honour. Similarly, it could claim Second Ypres because of the large number of 103rd Regiment men who'd

proceeded overseas with the 10th in 1914. Box B103-002 50th Battalion, Historical Sketches 4, KOCRA.

9   The nickname had been informally adopted by the men themselves, though some accounts refer to "Mason's Maulers." Probably both were used.

10 *Calgary Daily Herald*, 21 October 1915, 1. *Calgary Daily Herald*, 28 August 1915, 1; Box 11, file 139, Victor Wheeler Papers, M5614, GA; and A. Russell and W. Gadsden, box 15, tape 1, 50th Battalion interviews, RG41 BIII1, LAC.

11 David Argo to Mrs. Mae Argo, 26 October 1915, box B50-020 50th Battalion, folder Argo, David, KOCRA.

12 Including the two reinforcement drafts already sent overseas, 79 percent of the officers and men raised by the 50th Battalion in 1915 were British immigrants. Box B50-010, folder 003 Nominal Rolls and Other Personnel Lists, 50th Battalion, KOCRA. Such men were more likely to have some military experience, mostly in the part-time Territorial Army, and therefore deemed more desirable recruits. London also encouraged the many young Britons abroad to enlist in the Dominion forces. Overall, almost one-half of the men who served overseas in the CEF were British immigrants.

13 Box B103-002 50th Battalion, Historical Sketches 2 and 10, KOCRA; W. Gadsden and A Russell, box 15, tape 1, 50th Battalion, RG41 BIII1, LAC; and box 11, folder 139, Victor Wheeler Papers, M5614, GA.

14 Various training syllabi for weeks ending 26 February, 10 April and 3 June 1916, box 4217, folder 8-1, 50th Battalion, RG 9 III C 3, LAC.

15 Max Aitken to Robert Borden, 10 September 1916, E series, roll A-1765, Max Aitken/Lord Beaverbrook Papers, MG 27 IIG1, LAC. Jackson, *Empire on the Western Front*, chapter 1 and Simpkins, *Kitchener's Army*, Part II, chapters 6–12.

16 Jackson, *Empire on the Western Front*, chapter 1; Morton, *Peculiar Kind of Politics*, chapters 3 and 4; and Harris, *Canadian Brass*, chapter 6.

17 Box B50-010 50th Battalion, folder 003, KOCRA and nominal roll of officers and other ranks, 27 October 1915, box 79, 50th Battalion, RG 9 III B 3, LAC.

18 Andrew Munro to father, 5 November 1915, Andrew Munro Papers, IWM.

19 David Argo correspondence during the winter of 1915–16, box B50-020 50th Battalion, folder Argo, David, KOCRA.

20 David Argo to Mrs. Mae Argo, 13 and 16 May, 19 June and 8 and 23 July 1916, box B50-020 50th Battalion, folder Argo, David, KOCRA.

21 David Argo to Mrs. Mae Argo, 9 April 1916, box B50-020 50th Battalion, folder Argo, David, KOCRA. Morton, *Peculiar Kind of Politics*, chapters 3 and 4.

22 Brennan, "Major-General David Watson," 111–43 and Jackson, *Empire on the Western Front*, chapter 1.

23 Max Aitken to Sam Hughes, 4 May 1916, E series, roll A-1764, Aitken/Lord Beaverbrook Papers, MG 27 IIG1, LAC.

24 Gen. R. Wighan to Headquarters 4th Canadian Division, 7 June 1916, E series, roll A-1765, Max Aitken/Lord Beaverbrook Papers, MG 27 IIG1, LAC and diary 17 June and 14 and 20 July 1916, David Watson Papers, MG 30 E69, LAC. W. Allen, box 15, tape 1, 50th Battalion, RG 41 BIII1, LAC and Andrew Munro to father, 18 February and 16 April 1916, Andrew Munro Papers, IWM

25 David Argo to Mrs. Mae Argo, 23 July 1916, box B50-020 50th Battalion, folder Argo, David, KOCRA. In the CEF's practice "overseas" meant continental Europe, not the British Isles, which in itself reflects the imperial perspective of most Anglo-Canadians.
26 David Watson to Max Aitken, 10 August 1916, E series, roll A-1765, Max Aitken/Lord Beaverbrook Papers, MG 27 IIG1, LAC. David Argo to Mrs. Mae Argo, 23 July 1916, box B50-020 50th Battalion, folder Argo, David, KOCRA.
27 Box 11, folder 139, Wheeler Papers, M5614, GA.
28 Wheeler, *50th Battalion*, 101.
29 10, 12 and 13 August 1916, 50th Battalion WD, LAC.
30 18–21 August 1916, 50th Battalion WD, LAC. Wheeler, *50th Battalion*, 4–5 and R. Stephen and J. A. MacDonald, box 15, tape 1, 50th Battalion, RG 41 B III 1, LAC.
31 28 August 1916, 50th Battalion WD, LAC.
32 Wheeler, *50th Battalion*, 4–5.
33 21–23 September 1916, 50th Battalion WD, LAC. Diary 28 September 1916, David Watson Papers, MG 30 E69, LAC.
34 Wheeler, *50th Battalion*, 12.
35 Nicholson, *Canadian Expeditionary Force*, 160–67; Cook, *Sharp End*, chapters 31 and 33; and Gary Sheffield, *Somme*, chapters 1–3.
36 Wheeler, *50th Battalion*, 16.
37 14–17 October 1916, 50th Battalion WD, LAC and A. Russell and W. Gadsden, box 15, tape 1, 50th Battalion, RG 41 BIII1, LAC. Overcome by the strain, one officer intentionally wounded himself. Wheeler, *50th Battalion*, 20–21.
38 David Argo to Mrs. Mae Argo, 1 November 1916, box B50-020 50th Battalion, folder Argo, David, KOCRA. 20–22 October 1916, 50th Battalion WD, LAC and David Argo to Mrs. Mae Argo, 11 October 1916, box B50-020 50th Battalion, folder Argo, David, KOCRA. For obvious reasons, reliefs were carried out at night, which made navigating the warren of communication trenches all the more difficult.
39 David Argo to Mrs. Mae Argo, 1 November 1916, box B50-020 50th Battalion, folder Argo, David, KOCRA.
40 Nicholson, *Canadian Expeditionary Force*, 180–92.
41 26 October 1916, 50th Battalion WD, LAC.
42 Wheeler, *50th Battalion*, 22.
43 Wheeler, *50th Battalion*, 31 and Lt.-Col. Edward George Mason and Maj. Robert Berry Eaton, RG 150, Acc. 1992-93/166, LAC. See Brennan, "Good Men for a Hard Job" and "Completely worn out by service in France."
44 Wheeler, *50th Battalion*, 29.
45 R. Stephen and J. A. MacDonald, box 15, tape 1, 50th Battalion, RG 41 B III 1, LAC.
46 Wheeler, *50th Battalion*, 23.
47 Diary 2 November 1916, David Watson Papers, MG 30 E 69, LAC. On the soldiers' spirits, David Argo to Mrs. Mae Argo, 13 November 1916, box 50-020 50th Battalion, folder Argo, David, KOCRA.
48 G. W. L. Nicholson, *Canadian Expeditionary Force*, 194 and 196.
49 17 and 18 November 1916, 50th Battalion WD, LAC and W. Allen, box 15, tape 1, 50th Battalion, RG 41 B III 1, LAC.

50 Nicholson, *Canadian Expeditionary Force*, 196–97.
51 David Argo to Mrs. Mae Argo, 11 October 1916, box B50-020 50th Battalion, folder Argo, David, KOCRA.
52 David Argo to Mrs. Mae Argo, 26 October 1915, box B50-020 50th Battalion, folder Argo, David, KOCRA. David Argo to Mrs. Mae Argo, 1 and 13 November 1916, box B50-020 50th Battalion, folder Argo, David, KOCRA.
53 C. T. Hodge to Mrs. Mae Argo, 6 January 1917, box B50-020 50th Battalion, Argo, David folder, KOCRA.
54 Sydney Nightingale to Mrs. Jessie Nightingale, undated (April 1916), box B50-023 50th Battalion, Nightingale, Sydney folder, KOCRA.
55 Director of Records to Mrs. Jessie Nightingale, 1 June 1920, box B50-023 50th Battalion, Nightingale, Sydney folder, KOCRA. Proceedings for the Board of Pension Commissioners for Canada to Mrs. Jessie Nightingale, 1 March 1917 and Director of Records to Mrs. Jessie Nightingale, 17 December 1917, box B50-023 50th Battalion, Nightingale, Sydney folder, KOCRA. Established in 1917, the Imperial War Graves Commission undertook the reburial and perpetual care of the graves of the Empire's dead, a responsibility they also assumed for the World War II dead.
56 Andrew Munro to his father, 4 December 1916, Andrew Mason Munro Papers, IWM. Andrew Munro to his father, 14 December 1916, Andrew Mason Munro Papers, IWM. Letters mailed on leave in England only had to survive the random attention of post office censors. Runners carried messages back and forth between headquarters and front-line units, an extraordinarily dangerous assignment.
57 Andrew Munro to his father, 4 December 1916, Andrew Mason Munro Papers, IWM and Wheeler, *50th Battalion*, 80.
58 20, 21 and 23 November 1916, 50th Battalion WD, LAC.
59 D. G. L. Cunnington, box 15, tape 3, 50th Battalion, RG 41 BIII1, LAC; memorandum, undated, box B50-023 50th Battalion, Nichol, Angus folder, KOCRA; Horace Blake to Victor Wheeler, 26 January 1964, box 2, folder 13, Victor Wheeler Papers, M-5614, GA; and Marti, *For Home and Empire*, 73–74. On race and recruitment in the Canadian Expeditionary Force, see Walker, "Race and Recruitment in World War I, 1–26 and Marti, *For Home and Empire*, chapter 3.
60 13 December 1916, 50th Battalion WD, LAC.
61 7 January 1916, 50th Battalion WD, LAC. Maj. Eaton briefly returned to the battalion just before Vimy, but in October had been granted a three-month leave to Canada where he was retained for service. Medical boards show he suffered from prolonged exposure to cold and wet conditions as well as deafness attributable to shell fire. Maj. Robert Berry Eaton, personnel folder, RG 150 Acc. 1992–93/166, LAC and Robert Eaton to Lionel Page, 31 August 1917 and Lionel Page to Charles Hilliam, 1 September 1917, box 4215, folder 3-16, RG 9 III C 3, LAC.
62 Lt.-Col. Charles Benson Worsnop, personnel folder, RG 150 Acc. 1992–93/166, LAC and diary 18 April 1917, David Watson Papers, MG 30 E 64, LAC. During the last two years of the war, many experienced officers who for medical or other reasons couldn't cope with the strains of command were profitably employed in England in a training capacity. Stewart, *Embattled General*, chapters 5 and 6 and Desmond Morton, *Peculiar Kind of Politics*, chapters 6 and 8.

63   10 January 1916, 50th Battalion WD, LAC. The heavier a unit's casualties, the more freely gallantry awards tended to be handed out.

64   Various entries January 1917, 50th Battalion WD, LAC.

65   Nicholson, *Canadian Expeditionary Force*, 236–37 and 241–45.

66   On the emergence of new tactical doctrine in the Canadian Corps, see Rawling, *Surviving Trench Warfare*, chapters 4 and 5 and Brown, "Not Glamorous, But Effective," 421–44. In the British Army, see Griffith, *Battle Tactics on the Western Front*, chapters 4 and 6–8. The French Army had absorbed the same basic lessons independently, and earlier. Robert Doughty, *Pyrrhic Victory*, chapters 4 and 5. And on the merits of Byng, see Brennan, "Julian Byng and Leadership in the Canadian Corps," 87–104.

67   Diary 12 May 1916, David Watson Papers, MG 30 E 69, LAC.

68   Brennan, "Major-General David Watson," 111–43 and Geoffrey Jackson, *Empire on the Western Front*, 80–81. Diary 8 and 10 May 1916, David Watson Papers, MG 30 E 69, LAC and Brig.-Gens. William St. Pierre Hughes and Edward Hilliam, personnel folders, RG 150 Acc. 1992-93/166, LAC.

69   Cook, *Shock Troops*, 55–72.

70   3 February 1917, 50th Battalion WD, LAC. 4 February 1917, *Report by Capt. R. W. Read (G. 14-1)*, 10th Brigade WD, LAC.

71   On Canadian raiding, see Miedema, *Bayonets and Blobsticks*. The Mills bomb was a hand grenade, while Stokes bombs (shells for the Stokes mortar) were typically tossed into the entrances of German bunkers to kill or maim the occupants. Phosphorous grenades were also highly effective in clearing bunkers. In the dark, restricted confines of trenches, clubs, knives and hand-held bayonets facilitated speedy and (relatively) quiet executions.

72   Riddle and Mitchell, *The Military Cross Awarded to Members of the Canadian Expeditionary Force 1915–1921*, 241.

73   14 February 1917, 50th Battalion WD, LAC.

74   8 February 1917, *Proposed Minor Operation G. 12-3*, app. B2, 10th Brigade WD (February 1917), LAC. 9 February 1917, operation order S. 299 (Lt.-Col C.A. Sykes); 10 February 1917, G. 12-4; 10 February 1917, Order No. 100 (Lt.-Col. R. D. Davies); and 13 February 1917, *Full Report on Raid Carried Out By 10th Infantry Brigade Night of 12th–13th February 1917* (Lt.-Col. R. D. Davies), app. B2, 10th Brigade WD (February 1917), LAC. The tapes marked out the confines of the attack as well as the position of trenches, bunkers and other objectives on a 1:1 scale.

75   13 February 1917, 50th Battalion WD, LAC.

76   In fact German losses were 44 killed, 110 wounded, and 52 missing. Sheldon, *German Army on Vimy Ridge*, 234.

77   It is difficult to determine precise losses as there were seldom follow-up reports listing those subsequently dying of their wounds.

78   Sheldon, *German Army on Vimy Ridge*, 233. A German infantry regiment was comparable to an Anglo-Canadian brigade.

79   Four of the Canadians taken prisoner were wounded who had been left behind.

80   Sheldon, *German Army on Vimy Ridge*, 235.

81   The assessment was made on 27 February 1917. Sheldon, *German Army on Vimy Ridge*, 238.

82　Sheldon, *German Army on Vimy Ridge*, 237.
83　Sheldon, *German Army on Vimy Ridge*, 237-38.
84　10 March 1917, 50th Battalion WD, LAC. Tim Cook, "'A Proper Slaughter'," 7-23. The 50th Battalion were only observers of the carnage that day, but the men never forgot the sight of grinning German soldiers waving empty sandbags and daring them in broken English to come over and join their countrymen. R. Stephen and J. A. MacDonald, box 15, tape 1, 50th Battalion, RG 41 BIII1, LAC.
85　Wheeler, *50th Battalion*, 59 and 91 and Andrew Munro to father, 4 May 1917, Andrew Mason Munro Papers, IWM. S. Dyde, box 15, tape 1, 50th Battalion, RG 41 BIII1, LAC. Box B50-022 50th Battalion, folder Meeres, Edward, KOCRA. On the evolution of battalion command in the Canadian Corps, see Brennan, "Good Men for a Hard Job," *Canadian Army Journal*, 9-28. One of the unusual ways Page centred himself amidst the hell of the trenches was by writing beautifully illustrated letters to his young daughter and nieces.
86　18 March 1917, 50th Battalion WD, LAC. Costigan and Casewell had both served in the 103rd Regiment, while Svendsen had served in the British Army. Eveleigh had no military background before enlisting in the 50th. All but Costigan, the only one who was Canadian-born, had been lieutenants when the battalion left Canada.
87　Rawling, *Surviving Trench Warfare*, chapter 4 and Jackson, *Empire on the Western Front*, 87-90. During February and March the 50th Battalion's War Diary rarely mentions training activities along the lines outlined in the BEF's newly-introduced instructional documents SS143, *Instructions for the Training of Platoons for Offensive Action*, and SS144, *The Normal Formation for the Attack*. Given corps, division and brigade headquarters insisted they do so, and carried out unannounced inspections to confirm this, such training likely struck the diarist as too normal to be worth mentioning.
88　*Training Schedule*, 31 March 1917, box 4217, folder 8-1, 50th Battalion, RG 9 III C 3, LAC. Little more than a week before the Vimy Ridge attack, Page was shocked to learn from his officers that 191 of his men had never thrown a Mills bomb!
89　1-5 April 1917, 50th Battalion WD, LAC.
90　Diary 26 December 1916 and 4 and 5 January and 20 March 1917, David Watson Papers, MG 30 E 69, LAC. Watson, having obtained Gen. Byng's full support, had addressed the problems vigorously, appointing two new battalion commanders, including Page, and immediately after the battle, replacing a third. The 10th's new brigadier was also his doing.
91　NCOs from the 50th who had participated in February's raiding earned one DCM and eight MMs.
92　The remainder had been designated Left Out of Battle.
93　8 April 1917, 50th Battalion WD, LAC.
94　Sheldon, *German Army on Vimy* Ridge, 251-52. Sheldon, *German Army on Vimy Ridge*, 254-55 and 259-60.
95　Much of the artillery, particularly the medium and heavy batteries, was British.
96　Nicholson, *Canadian Expeditionary* Force, 258-59. Such counterattacks would be blunted mostly by artillery and machine gun barrages.
97　Nicholson, *Canadian Expeditionary* Force, 260-61.
98　A. Russell and W. Gadsden, box 15, tape 2, 50th Battalion, RG41 B III 1, LAC.

99 Wheeler, *50th Battalion*, 97. Cook, *Shock Troops*, 136–37.
100 10 April 1917, 50th Battalion WD, LAC. Eventually, the majority of the missing would be officially listed as killed in action, and of course many of the severely wounded would die as well. When at full strength, as it was on the 10 April, there were sixteen platoons in the battalion, four per company. Officer casualties had surpassed 50 percent, which was by no means unusual for the Western front.
101 9 and 10 April 1917, 50th Battalion WD, LAC. Nicholson, *Canadian Expeditionary Force*, 261.
102 Bagley and Duncan, *Legacy of Courage*, 30 and 32 and Box B50-010 50th Battalion, Gallantry Nominations (Vimy), KOCRA. Henry Pattison remembered the 137th being lined up on parade in February to draw a fifty-man reinforcement draft for the 50th Battalion and hearing his father's name called out. Given his age, John Pattison should have been sent to the Forestry Corps, but in less than an hour the men were off to France. H. J. Pattison, box 15, tape 1, 50th Battalion, RG 41 B III 1, LAC.
103 Sheldon, *German Army on Vimy Ridge*, 315–17.
104 12 April 1917, 50th Battalion WD, LAC. Sheldon, *German Army on Vimy Ridge*, 317 and Jackson, *Empire on the Western Front*, 95–96.
105 Wheeler, *50th Battalion*, 101. Cook, *Shock Troops*, 137–39 and Wheeler, *50th Battalion*, 100. On Canadians killing prisoners while trying to surrender, see Cook, "The Politics of Surrender," 637–66.
106 Wheeler, *50th Battalion*, 112.
107 Diary 17 March 1917, David Watson Papers, MG 30 E69, LAC. Wheeler, *50th Battalion*, 101.
108 Wheeler, *50th Battalion*, 103. 12–13 April 1917, 50th Battalion WD, LAC.
109 G. Jones and W. Sinclair, box 15, tape 2, 50th Battalion, RG 41 B III 1, v 15, 50th Battalion, LAC.
110 Wheeler, *50th Battalion*, 107.
111 15–22 April 1917, 50th Battalion WD, LAC.
112 Andrew Munro to father, undated (December 1916), Andrew Mason Munro Papers, IWM.
113 8 May 1917, 50th Battalion WD, LAC.
114 Nicholson, *Canadian Expeditionary Force*, 266–67.
115 Sometimes referred to as the First, Second and Third Battles of the Scarpe after the river winding through the battlefield.
116 Nicholson, *Canadian Expeditionary Force*, 266–79 and Sheffield, *Forgotten Victory*, 190–99. Together, the Scarpe operations were among the costliest battles fought by British Empire forces during the entire war, with the BEF (including the Canadians) suffering close to 170,000 casualties in a little over five weeks. On the French Army's operations, see Doughty, *Pyrrhic Victory*, chapter 7 and Greenhalgh, *French Army*, chapter 5.
117 Patrick Brennan, "Julian Byng," 87–104.

NOTES TO CHAPTER 2

1. 25 and 26 April 1917, 50th Battalion WD, LAC.
2. From 1 through 11 May the 50th Battalion spent nearly equal amounts of time in support (which was well within the range of German artillery) and the front line. Although it did not participate in any significant operations, it still suffered 194 casualties from enemy fire, including twenty-nine killed. 1–11 May 1917, 50th Battalion WD, LAC.
3. 28 April 1917, 50th Battalion WD, LAC.
4. Robert Forrest to Victor Wheeler, 20 April 1964, box 10, folder 132, Victor Wheeler Papers, M-5614, GA. Robert Forrest to Victor Wheeler, 26 January 1964, box 1, folder 12, Victor Wheeler Papers, M-5614, GA.
5. All manner of explanations have been offered for this, at the time and since. The simple truth is that these men had hunted for years to support themselves and their families. During the pre-war years, the Bureau of Indian Affairs had provided rifles and ammunition for this purpose but permitted nothing larger than .22 calibre. To kill a moose with a punch-less weapon meant getting very close and then making a "heart-shot" with the first round so that the animal would die quickly and not be lost in the bush. The author thanks Darren Keewatin for this insight. Like most snipers, Norwest worked with a spotter. For most of the war, it was Pvt. Oliver Payne.
6. Dempsey, "Henry Norwest," 786–87; *Calgary Herald*, 11 November 1989, C9 (Norwest article), box B50-022 50th Battalion, folder Meeres, Edward, KOCRA; box B50-010 50th Battalion, folder 50th Battalion gallantry nominations (Vimy), KOCRA; and Persil Blain to Victor Wheeler, 13 March 1964, box 2, folder 13, Victor Wheeler Papers, M-5614, GA. Norwest's wife died later in 1918, but neither she nor her children would have been eligible for a pension without giving up their Native status. Nor would Norwest, had he lived, have qualified for a grant of farmland under the Veterans Land Act. As a soldier of First Nations ancestry, a bit of land in the Warvillers Churchyard Extension Commonwealth War Graves Commission cemetery sufficed for the government (and people) of Canada. *Calgary Herald*, 11 November 1989, C9 (Norwest article), box B50-022 50th Battalion, folder Meeres, Edward, KOCRA.
7. Nicholson, *Canadian Expeditionary Force*, 279–80.
8. 30 April and 1 May 1917, 50th Battalion WD, LAC and box B50-024 50th Battalion, folder Pattison, John G., KOCRA.
9. Officers were also ordered to ensure canteens were filled to the brim but only with water. 31 May 1917, operational order no. 27 (Lt.-Col. Page), app. 1, 50th Battalion WD, LAC.
10. 1 and 2 June 1917, 50th Battalion WD, LAC. 31 May 1917, operational order no. 27 (Lt.-Col. Page), app. 1, 50th Battalion WD (June 1917), LAC.
11. Wheeler, *50th Battalion*, 114.
12. C. McDonald, box 15, tape 1, 50th Battalion, RG 41 B III 1, LAC.
13. 3 June 1917, 50th Battalion WD, LAC and Wheeler, *50th Battalion*, 117–19.
14. Maj. Dawson had been badly wounded, dying the following day. 3 Jun 1917, 50th Battalion WD, LAC.
15. Nicholson claimed the retreat occurred before the German counterattack, but the 50th Battalion war diary maintained it occurred during it, while the 10th Brigade account broadly reinforces the latter claim. Capt. E. H. Hill, intelligence report, 4 June 1917, app.

10, 10th Brigade WD (May 1917), LAC. 3 June 1917, 50th Battalion WD, LAC and Box B50-024 50th Battalion, folder Pattison, John, KOCRA.

16 3 June 1917, 50th Battalion WD, LAC. Prisoners, while valuable intelligence sources, were a drain on an attack since on a battlefield littered with weapons, they had to be escorted to rear under guard. Page's orders called for lightly wounded men to perform these duties whenever possible. It was common practice for prisoners to assist stretcher bearers in clearing the Canadian wounded, something most were eager to do since it endeared them to their captors, who would be less inclined to shoot them. 31 May 1917, operation order no. 27 (Lt.-Col. Page), app. 1, 50th Battalion WD (June 1917), LAC.

17 Diary 3 June 1917, David Watson Papers, MG 30 E 69, LAC. Wheeler, *50th Battalion*, 120–21.

18 3 June 1917, 50th Battalion WD, LAC.

19 Nicholson, *Canadian Expeditionary Force*, 280–81.

20 3 June 1917, 50th Battalion WD, LAC and box B50-024 50th Battalion, folder Pattison, John, KOCRA. First reported wounded, twenty-three-year-old Lt. George Ambery was the nephew of Lt.-Col. George Mason. His body was never found and he was eventually listed as killed in action. Ambery's mother was bereft, desperate to know what had happened to her son. A poignant correspondence ensued between a friend of hers and Lt.-Col. Page and Maj. Parry (who was a pre-war friend of the mother) in an effort to determine details of the lad's fate. To their credit, both men devoted considerable time to interviewing returning wounded, though to no avail. Mrs. Olive Parry to Lt.-Col. Page, 26 Aug 1917 and Maj. Parry to Mrs. Olive Parry, 7 Sep 1917, box 4214, folder 1-10, 50th Battalion, RG 9 III C 3, LAC

21 R. Stephen, box 15, tape 2, 50th Battalion, RG 41 B III 1, LAC.

22 Box B50-024 50th Battalion, folder Pattison, John, KOCRA.

23 Box B50-024 50th Battalion, folder Pattison, John, KOCRA. H. J. Pattison, box 15, tape 1, 50th Battalion, RG 41 B III 1, LAC.

24 Box B50-024 50th Battalion, folder Pattison, John, KOCRA. In January 1916, without forewarning his parents, Henry Pattison managed to enlist in the 82nd Battalion though he was only sixteen. This led his father to enlist two months later, but since the 82nd was full, he chose the 137th, and then arranged for his son to transfer. Father and son went to England with the 137th in August 1916, whereupon John revealed his son's real age, ensuring he would not be sent to the front until he turned eighteen. John Pattison joined the 50th Battalion with a draft of 285 men from the 137th on 5 February 1917, whereas his son Henry only reached the front in early September. Box B50-024 50th Battalion, folder Pattison, John, KOCRA. It is clear from his future service that Henry was kept out of most dangerous situations because his father had been killed. H. J. Pattison, box 15, tape 1, 50th Battalion, RG 41 B III 1, LAC.

25 Gen. Byng's reward for transforming the Canadian Corps into a first-class fighting unit was to replace Gen. Allenby as Third Army commander. The Borden government insisted Byng's replacement be a Canadian, and Currie had been the obvious choice.

26 Nicholson, *Canadian Expeditionary Force*, 281.

27 Wheeler, *50th Battalion*, 128. A "blighty" was a wound serious enough to get one hospitalized in England for a goodly time.

28 5–8 June 1917, 50th Battalion WD, LAC. Lt.-Col. Page was a dedicated promoter of his men participating in sports which fostered morale, teamwork, camaraderie, fitness,

and battalion identity, all of which were worthy goals. Of course competitions pitting officers against other ranks offered extra advantages on the morale front. 28 June 1917, 50th Battalion WD, LAC.

29 11 and 16 June 1917, 50th Battalion WD, LAC.
30 27 June 1917, 50th Battalion War Diary, LAC. Concert hall-style entertainment was much in demand by front-line troops who were, after all, civilians in uniform. Over thirty were formed in the CEF, with the 3rd Division's ensemble, *The Dumbells*, the most famous. The 4th Division's main group was *The Maple Leafs*. O'Neill, "The Canadian Concert Party in France."
31 Nicholson, *Canadian Expeditionary Force*, 282 and 284 and Delaney and Durflinger, eds., *Capturing Hill 70*, Introduction.
32 1–9 July 1917, 50th Battalion WD, LAC.
33 Diary 6 August 1917, David Watson Papers, MG 30 E 69, LAC.
34 Various entries July 1917, 50th Battalion WD, LAC. On the successful battalion schemes, see 29 and 31 July 1917, 50th Battalion WD, LAC. Diary 21 July 1917, David Watson Papers, MG 30 E 69, LAC.
35 Losses on the 15 August, almost all by 1st and 2nd Division units, totalled 1,056 killed and 2,432 wounded. Nicholson, *Canadian Expeditionary Force*, 290.
36 Nicholson, *Canadian Expeditionary Force*, 289. Nicholson, *Canadian Expeditionary Force*, 287–89.
37 Nicholson, *Canadian Expeditionary Force*, 289–92 and Delaney and Durflinger, eds., *Capturing Hill 70*, especially chapter 7 and Conclusion.
38 Jackson, *Empire on the Western Front*, 108–16 and Delaney and Durflinger, eds., *Capturing Hill 70*, 22–24.
39 17–19 August 1917, 50th Battalion WD, LAC.
40 Nicholson, *Canadian Expeditionary Force*, 293.
41 20 August 1917, 50th Battalion WD, LAC. Orders no. 49 and 50, apps. F and G, and *Report on Operations by 50th Canadian Battalion from August 17th to August 26th, 1917* (Lt.-Col. L. Page), app. J, 50th Battalion WD (August 1917), LAC.
42 *Report on Operations by 50th Canadian Battalion from August 17th to August 26th, 1917* (Lt.-Col. L. Page), app. J, 50th Battalion WD (August 1917), LAC.
43 G. Jones and W. Sinclair, box 15, tape 1, 50th Battalion, RG 41 B III 1, LAC.
44 21 August 1917, 50th Battalion WD and *Report on Operations by 50th Canadian Battalion from August 17th to August 26th, 1917* (Lt.-Col. L. Page), app. J, 50th Battalion WD (August 1917), LAC.
45 Nicholson, *Canadian Expeditionary Force*, 292–95 and 21 August 1917, 50th Battalion WD, LAC.
46 22 August 1917, 50th Battalion WD, LAC.
47 21 and 22 August 1917, 50th Battalion WD, LAC.
48 *Report on Operations by 50th Canadian Battalion from August 17th to August 26th, 1917* (Lt.-Col. L. Page), app. J, 50th Battalion WD (August 1917), LAC. Many of the men coming up were hardly in better shape. One of the replacements, Lt. X, had only just returned from a stint as liaison officer with 27th Battalion. Others soon noticed his mental state becoming more and more erratic as he wandered about carrying a rifle with the bayonet mounted and obsessed about how all the wounded were going to be

gotten out. Within hours Page sent him on to a company short of officers, and the next anyone knew he was found dead in a trench. Years later a veteran recounted that upon hearing the heavy Dutch accent of a sergeant named Roerick, and being convinced that he was a German infiltrator in a Canadian uniform, Lt. X had gone berserk and bayoneted the sergeant three times. Another soldier promptly shot the officer dead—he was subsequently listed as "killed in action." Fortunately, Roerick recovered, maintaining that he'd fired the fatal shot. Page's own view was that "the strain had proved too much for [the man] and that he ... was shot ... in self-defence." Lt.-Col. Page to Brig. Hilliam, 26 August 1917, box 4215, folder 5-4, 50th Battalion, RG 9 III C 3, LAC. W Allen, box 15, tape 1, 50th Battalion, RG 41 B III 1, LAC.

49   *Report on Operations by 50th Canadian Battalion from August 17th to August 26th, 1917* (Lt.-Col. L. Page), app. J and 25 August 1917, report to HQ 10th Cdn. Inf. Bde., Lt.-Col. L. F. Page, app. K, 50th Battalion WD (August 1917), LAC. Watson, who inspected parts of the 4th Division's operational area the following day, noted that "the numbers of bodies lying around must be enormous as the stench is perfectly awful." Diary 26 August 1917, David Watson Papers, MG 30 E 69, LAC.

50   Wheeler, *50th Battalion*, 142.

51   Box B50-024, folder Orritt, William, KOCRA.

52   For example, see Jackson, *Empire on the Western Front*, 116-18; Delaney and Durflinger, eds., *Capturing Hill 70*, 22-24; Delaney, "The Corps Nervous System in Action," 71-74; Brennan, "Major—General David Watson, 126-27; and Cook, *Shock Troops*, 301-07.

53   Quoted in translation in Cook, *Shock Troops*, 304-05. Nicholson, *Canadian Expeditionary Force*, 297.

54   S. Dyde, box 15, tape 2, 50th Battalion, RG 41 B III 1, LAC. Box B50-022 50th Battalion, folder Meeres, Edward, KOCRA, and Wheeler, *50th Battalion*, 123.

55   25 and 26 August 1917, 50th Battalion WD, LAC.

56   30 August 1917, 50th Battalion WD, LAC.

57   Training "over the tapes" referred to marking practice fields to real-life scale, with coloured tapes, stakes and pylons being used to indicate trenches, known defensive positions and so forth. When training for an attack, this enabled the officers and men to familiarize themselves with what they would actually encounter, not the least distances. At other times, the "battlefield" so created would simply match the maps and attack orders prepared for the exercise by staff officers.

58   Diary 17 September 1917, David Watson Papers, MG 30 E 69, LAC.

59   25 and 25 August 1917, 50th Battalion WD, LAC. The names of officers awarded the MC were always listed in the battalion war diary, the names of enlisted men earning the MM (the same award) only occasionally.

60   Riddle and Mitchell, *Distinguished Conduct Medal*, 33.

61   Nicholson, *Canadian Expeditionary Force*, 298-304 and Sheffield, *Forgotten Victory*, 204-16.

62   As cited in Nicholson, *Canadian Expeditionary Force*, 311.

63   Nicholson, *Canadian Expeditionary Force*, 304-11.

64   The 17 October entry quoted in Nicholson, *Canadian Expeditionary Force*, 313. Nicholson, *Canadian Expeditionary Force*, 311-12.

65 Nicholson, *Canadian Expeditionary Force*, 311–14 and Cook, *Shock Troops*, 316–21, 323 and 325.
66 Rawling, *Surviving Trench Warfare*, 144–45.
67 Jackson, *Empire on the Western Front*, 121–12; Foley, "The Other Side of the Wire," 155–78; Nicholson, *Canadian Expeditionary Force*, 316–18; and Tactical Conditions, box 3853, folder 69-3, RG 9 III C 1, LAC.
68 10 October 1917, 50th Battalion WD, LAC.
69 14 October 1917, 50th Battalion WD, LAC.
70 Pill boxes/block houses were also very useful for sheltering the wounded until they could be gotten safely to the rear. Sheldon, *German Army at Passchendaele*, 260.
71 Sheldon, *German Army at Passchendaele*, 277–78. Von Kuhl's report was based on a combination of German battlefield observation, captured documents, and the interrogation of prisoners of war.
72 Sheldon, *German Army at Passchendaele*, 279.
73 20 October 1917, 50th Battalion WD, LAC.
74 21 October 1917, 50th Battalion WD, LAC.
75 Jackson, *Empire on the Western Front*, 122–29 and Nicholson, *Canadian Expeditionary Force*, 318–19.
76 22 October 1917, 50th Battalion WD, LAC. Or as the 10th Brigade's diarist put it tersely: "Weather conditions unfavourable; ground conditions, roads and tracks in bad state. Area [has been] heavily shelled." 22 October 1917, 10th Brigade WD, LAC.
77 23 October 1917, 50th Battalion WD, LAC. 24 Oct 1917, 50th Battalion WD, LAC.
78 25 October 1917, Brig. E. Hilliam to Lt.-Col. L. Page, app. D1, 10th Brigade WD (October 1917), LAC.
79 Sheldon, *German Army at Passchendaele*, 258.
80 26 October 1917, Brig. E. Hilliam to Maj.-Gen. D. Watson, app. D1, 10th Brigade WD (October 1917), LAC.
81 Apart from the usual "fog of war," the battlefield had been extensively "smoked" as part of the artillery support, chiefly to blind German machine gunners. Sheldon, *German Army at Passchendaele*, 258. Command posts, both battalion and brigade, were completely in the dark on 26 October. Casualties among runners were very heavy, and every other method from pigeons to signal lamps and electronic methods failed. 1 November 1917, *10th Canadian Infantry Brigade: Report on Operations in the Passchendaele Sector, October 21st to 28th 1917*, app. D1, 10th Brigade WD (November 1917), LAC.
82 The 46th suffered 70 percent casualties, almost of all from the murderous machine gun fire they encountered. Sheldon, *German Army at Passchendaele*, 259. The Bavarian units facing the brunt of the Canadian attack on 26 October were virtually annihilated. Reinforcements reaching the front could find only "a few lads covered in filth from top to bottom." Sheldon, *German Army at Passchendaele*, 265.
83 26 October 1917, 10th Brigade WD, LAC and 1 November 1917, *10th Canadian Infantry Brigade: Report on Operations in the Passchendaele Sector, October 21st to 28th 1917*, app. D1, 10th Brigade WD (November 1917), LAC. 26 October 1917, 10th Brigade WD, LAC.

84   26 October 1917, Brig. E. Hilliam to Maj.-Gen. D. Watson, app. D1, 10th Brigade WD (October 1917), LAC. 46th Battalion casualties for 26 October numbered 375 killed, wounded and missing—for the 50th Battalion it was ninety-three. Among the wounded was Capt. Arthur T. Lowes, who was officially listed as suffering from "shell shock." 1 November 1917, *10th Canadian Infantry Brigade: Report on Operations in the Passchendaele Sector, October 21st to 28th 1917*, app. D1, 10th Brigade WD (November 1917), LAC.

85   Burgess won a DSO and Thorne a MC for their actions that day. Burgess' citation read: "when part of the front line began to be driven back by the enemy, he at once went forward, took command, and by his example and influence succeeded in holding the position. He exposed himself fearlessly to an intense artillery and machine gun barrage to steady the men and keep them in their position, and he reorganized and established the line and [held it until] relieved ..., undoubtedly sav[ing] a critical situation." Riddle and Mitchell, *Distinguished Service Order*, 15. Thorne's citation lauded him for "untiringly [going] from post to post [under intense artillery fire], encouraging his men and reorganizing the defences." Riddle and Mitchell, *Military Cross*, 331.

86   The assessment that confusion and an overrating of the threat they faced had contributed more to the 46th Battalion's falling back than the ferocity of the German counterattacks was the personal view of Lt.-Col. Page. *Report on Operations—46th Canadian Infantry Battalion, October 26th 1917* (Lt.-Col. H. Dawson) and *Report of Operations of 50th Canadian Inf. Bn. From Octr. 21st to Octr. 26th, 1917* (Lt.-Col. L. Page), app. D1, 10th Brigade WD, LAC. The 10th Brigade War Diary made no such judgments, nor did Hilliam's report to Watson. 26 October 1917, 50th Battalion WD, LAC and 26 October 1917, Brig. E. Hilliam to Maj.-Gen. D. Watson, app. D1, 10th Brigade WD (October 1917), LAC. In his own report, Lt.-Col. Dawson noted that the "withdrawal did not, however, stop at the intended line, but continued to near the jumping off point," and that "numerous men coming back from the front area [and passing near the battalion headquarters] were halted and turned about. [But] these men," he pointed out, "were carrying parties and stretcher parties" who should have fallen back but were now desperately needed to stiffen the front-line position. Sgt. Turner was stationed at the outpost line throughout and an eyewitness to the 46th Battalion's retreat. He argued years later that the men had fallen back exactly as everyone had been trained—there had been no panic, but he understood that farther back it might have seemed more disorderly. A. Turner, box 15, tape 2, 50th Battalion, RG 41 B III 1, LAC.

87   Riddle and Mitchell, *Distinguished Conduct Medal*, 49 and 220–21.

88   26 October 1917, 50th Battalion WD, LAC and *Report on Operations 1 Nov 1917*, box 4208, folder 1-10, RG 9 III C 3, LAC.

89   Riddle and Mitchell, *Distinguished Conduct Medal*, 191.

90   27 and 28 October 1917, 50th Battalion WD, LAC.

91   27 and 28 October 1917, 10th Brigade WD, LAC.

92   Nicholson, *Canadian Expeditionary Force*, 320–27.

93   29–31 October 1917, 50th Battalion WD, LAC.

94   In comparison the more heavily committed 46th and 85th Battalions had suffered 403 and 394 casualties, respectively.

95   Quoted in Sheldon, *German Army at Passchendaele*, 269.

96 Jackson, *Empire on the Western Front*, 212–13 and Brennan, "Major-General David Watson," 127. Hilliam was given command of the 44th (British) Brigade which he led until the armistice.
97 Ross J. F. Hayter, CEF Personnel, RG 150 Acc. 1992-93/166, LAC.
98 War Diary, 50th Btn, various entries Nov and Dec 1917.
99 RG 9 III C 3, v 4217, folder 8, file 1, *Programme of Training* (drafted by Page), 1 Dec 1917.
100 War Diary, 50th Btn, various entries Dec 1917.
101 17 December 1917, 50th Battalion WD, LAC. Morton, *Peculiar Kind of Politics*, 132–48.
102 24–25 December 1917, 50th Battalion WD, LAC.
103 30 December 1917, 50th Battalion WD, LAC. 29 and 31 December 1917, 50th Battalion WD, LAC.
104 The wounded totals are inflated because they included a sizable number of soldiers wounded more than once.
105 15–18 January 1918, 50th Battalion WD, LAC.
106 4 February 1918, 50th Battalion WD, LAC. See also 5–8 February 1918, 50th Battalion WD, LAC. While training could not be carried out when the battalion was in the trenches, the demands for work parties never ended.
107 There were nuanced differences between Canadian (and other Dominion) and British practices, but mostly of emphasis, not substance. After all, sameness was necessary so British and Dominion formations could operate as interchangeable parts of a single army. Factors other than training and tactical distinctions contributed to the marked efficiency of the Australian, Canadian and New Zealand forces on the battlefield during 1917–18.
108 5 March 1918, 50th Battalion WD, LAC. Various entries March 1918, 50th Battalion WD, LAC.
109 20 and 21 March 1918, 50th Battalion WD, LAC.
110 11 March 1918, 50th Battalion WD, LAC. Various entries March 1918, 50th Battalion WD, LAC.
111 The Germans basically used the terms *stosstruppen* (shock troops) and *sturmtruppen* (storm troops) interchangeably.
112 Nicholson, *Canadian Expeditionary Force*, 364–68.
113 Sheffield, *Forgotten Victory*, 221–33; Showalter, *Instrument of War*, 253–62; and Travers, *How the War Was Won*, 50–100.
114 Greenhalgh, *French Army*, chapter 7 and Doughty, *Pyrrhic Victory*, chapter 9.
115 17 July 1918, *50th Canadian Battalion—Defence Scheme—Willerval Section*, app. 10, 50th Battalion WD (July 1918), LAC. 26 July 1918, *50th Canadian Battalion Defence Scheme Arleux Section*, app. 8, 50th Battalion WD (July 1918), LAC.
116 McCrae, *Coalition Strategy*, chapter 5.
117 Nicholson, *Canadian Expeditionary Force*, 378–82. See also Brown, *Robert Laird Borden*, chapter 11; Morton, *Peculiar Kind of Politics*, 162–66; and Hyatt, *General Sir Arthur Currie*, 163–65.
118 30 April 1918, 10th Brigade WD, LAC.
119 British divisions, like their Australian counterparts (but unlike the New Zealand Division), were considerably understrength for the remainder of the war.

120 Various entries June 1918, 50th Battalion WD, LAC.
121 Undated (June 1918), Operational Order no. 110, Battalion Tactical Scheme—with Tanks, 50th Battalion WD (June 1918), app. B, LAC; Diary 19 June 1918, Box B50-024 50th Battalion, folder Oke, Charles, KOCRA; and Wheeler, *50th Battalion*, 222.
122 Page was again on the sick list, and Parry was acting commanding officer.
123 20 June 1918, 50th Battalion WD, LAC.
124 Wheeler, *50th Battalion*, 108.
125 Cook, *No Place To Run*. One quarter of all the shells fired by Canadian Corps artillery during the Hundred Days Campaign were gas shells, indicating how effective Currie and his staff considered gas to be as an offensive weapon. As for its effectiveness in defensive warfare, mustard gas, which could persist for several days, was widely employed to create a sort of chemical minefield in areas the understrength German Army lacked troops to defend. This paralyzed logistics since horses, unlike men, could not really be protected.
126 Andrew Munro to father, 11 January 1918, Andrew Munro Papers, Papers, IWM.
127 30 and 31 July 1918, 50th Battalion WD, LAC.
128 Entries for the last day of the month, March–July 1918, 10th Brigade WD, LAC.

NOTES TO CHAPTER 3

1 On Foch's strategy, see Doughty, *Pyrrhic Victory*, 474–75. On Soissons, see Greenhalgh, *French Army*, 312–21.
2 Diary 29 July 1918, David Watson Papers, MG 30 E 69, LAC.
3 Nicholson, *Canadian Expeditionary Force*, 386–90 and 390n. Messenger, *Day We Won the War*, chapters 2 and 3.
4 Fourth Army was allotted 324 heavy "fighting" (i.e. infantry support) tanks and 96 of the new, and slightly more mobile, Whippets. Of these 162 of the former were assigned to the Canadian Corps, 42 to each assaulting division and 36 to the 4th. Nicholson, *Canadian Expeditionary Force*, 393. The Battle of Amiens was the largest deployment of tanks by the BEF in the entire war.
5 Nicholson, *Canadian Expeditionary Force*, 386–91. It can be very misleading to use divisions in comparing the size of armies. The reorganization of the Canadian Corps earlier in 1918 left its divisions nominally 22,000 men strong, and with little action since Passchendaele, they were at full strength. In contrast, British divisions had been reduced by one quarter and nominally numbered 14,000 men, though even this was rarely met, shortages being especially pronounced in the infantry. In the absence of conscription, and having seen heavier recent fighting than the Canadians, Australian battalions were now often barely 450 men strong, about one-half the Canadian figure. The divisions of the French Army, still the largest fighting force on the Western Front, numbered about 10,000 men. Thus, with four out of the twenty-one divisions committed, the Canadian Corps was providing close to one-half of Fourth Army's attacking strength. Greenhalgh, *French Army*, 251–52; Hart, *Very British Victory*, 314–15; and Pedersen, *Anzacs*, 379.
6 2 and 3 August 1918, 50th Battalion WD, LAC and Diary 1 August 1918, David Watson Papers, MG 30 E69, LAC.

7   4 August 1918, 50th Battalion WD, LAC. Diary 4 August 1918, box B50-024 50th Battalion, folder Oke, Charles, KOCRA.
8   5 and 6 August 1918, 50th Battalion WD, LAC. Diary 6 August 1918, box B50-024 50th Battalion, folder Oke, Charles, KOCRA.
9   6 August 1918, 10th Brigade WD, LAC.
10 6 August 1918, 50th Battalion WD, LAC.
11 Not the same Dury as they would assault some weeks later at the Drocourt–Quéant Line.
12 Diary 7 August 1918, box B50-024 50th Battalion, folder Oke, Charles, KOCRA. Brigade issued the formal orders to all four battalions at 1400 on 7 August. 7 August 1918, *10th Canadian Infantry Brigade Order No. 146*, app., 10th Brigade WD (August 1918), LAC.
13 7 August 1918, 50th Battalion WD, LAC. 7 August 1918, *Instructions No. 1 50th Canadian Battalion*, app., 10th Infantry Brigade WD (August 1918), LAC.
14 8 August 1918, 50th Battalion WD, LAC and *10th Canadian Infantry Brigade Narrative of Operations: Battle of Amiens August 6th to 11th, 1918*, app. E, 10th Infantry Bde WD (August 1918), LAC. A. Turner, box 15, tape 3, 50th Battalion, RG 41 B III 1, LAC.
15 9 August 1918, 50th Battalion WD, LAC and Jackson, *Empire on the Western Front*, 220–24.
16 Nicholson, *Canadian Expeditionary Force*, 415. *10th Canadian Infantry Brigade Narrative of Operations: Battle of Amiens August 6th to 11th, 1918*, app. E, 10th Infantry Bde WD (August 1918), LAC.
17 Nicholson, *Canadian Expeditionary Force*, 398–400, 410–11 and 414. Nicholson hardly does credit to this 4,500-m deep barrier. The old French and German lines remained intact, including masses of barbed wire and numerous concrete machine gun emplacements, all now obscured by vegetation. The trenches could not even be seen until you stumbled upon them. *10th Canadian Infantry Brigade Narrative of Operations: Battle of Amiens August 6th to 11th, 1918*, app. E, 10th Infantry Bde WD (August 1918), LAC.
18 A. Turner, box 15, tape 3, 50th Battalion, RG 41 B III 1, LAC.
19 *10th Canadian Infantry Brigade Narrative of Operations: Battle of Amiens August 6th to 11th, 1918*, app. E, 10th Infantry Bde WD (August 1918), LAC.
20 The attrition of the British tanks was staggering. The slab-sided behemoths were slow, no faster than the infantry on foot, and were protected by armour that was only proof against machine-gun and rifle fire. German field guns firing over open sights from concealed positions easily knocked them out, as could large calibre anti-tank rifles from closer range. Moreover, they were mechanically unreliable and broke down with startling frequency. Of the 415 tanks that went into action on 8 August, only 145 were still "runners" the following morning and the precipitous decline continued. It meant the actual number of tanks crawling forward on the 10 August to support the 4th Division fell well short of the thirty-six nominally assigned. Hart, *Very British Victory*, 326–44. All this said, tanks were a godsend to the infantry on the battlefield, their machine gun and cannon fire suppressing or destroying machine gun nests and monopolizing the attention and firepower of an enemy who still saw tanks as THE THREAT, thus allowing the attacking infantry to manoeuvre. Their great bulk also made short work of crushing uncut barbed wire. Infantry-tank co-operation was

a necessity for the survival of both but it was a new art and there was little proper doctrine and had been even less training.

21   10 August 1918, 50th Battalion WD, LAC.

22   Infantry tank communication was rudimentary to say the least—the tank commander made use of a limited repertoire of flag signals—basically "coming back," "broken down—don't wait," and "all clear—come on." For their part, the infantry were to hold up a helmet on a bayonet to indicate "held up," then point a rifle in the direction of the problem. *Instructions No. 1 50th Canadian Battalion,* 7 Aug 1918, app., 50th Battalion WD (August 1918), LAC. To convey anything else required face-to-face communication and resulted in exposure to enemy fire. Visibility was so poor from a tank that it was common for their commanders to exit and direct the driver and gunners from outside. This was appallingly dangerous for the commander, but it at least facilitated communication with the infantry.

23   10 August 1918, 50th Battalion WD, LAC. Visiting the Fouquescourt battlefield two days later, Gen. Watson was shocked by the number of bloated and dismembered bodies lying about, both men and animals. Diary 12 August 1918, David Watson Papers, MG 30 E69, LAC. Victor Wheeler recalled that "the cloying odours of congealed blood and putrefied flesh were overpowering." Victor Wheeler, *50th Battalion,* 245.

24   The men had been warned the Huns poisoned wells, and that in the hot, dry weather surface water would likely be fetid. The latter certainly proved correct.

25   10 August 1918, 50th Battalion WD, LAC. 14 August 1918, *Operations of 50th Canadian Battalion from 10-8-18 to 13-8-18* (Lt.-Col. L. Page), app. 11, 50th Battalion WD (August 1918), LAC and *10th Canadian Infantry Brigade Narrative of Operations: Battle of Amiens August 6th to 11th, 1918,* app. E, 10th Brigade WD (August 1918), LAC; and Diary 10 August 1918, box B50-024 50th Battalion, folder Oke, Charles, KOCRA.

26   *10th Canadian Infantry Brigade Narrative of Operations: Battle of Amiens August 6th to 11th, 1918,* app. E, 10th Brigade WD (August 1918), LAC.

27   Riddle and Mitchell, *Military Cross,* 326. 10 August 1918, 50th Battalion WD, LAC. The redoubtable Brown would earn a MC twenty-three days later near Dury. Riddle and Mitchell, *Military Cross,* 39. Men nominated for gallantry awards had invariably earned them, but only a portion would be approved. Sometimes lesser recognition was substituted, sometimes nothing at all. In the end, extraordinary acts of heroism routinely went unacknowledged. Everyone understood this, and so should we.

28   Riddle and Mitchell, *Distinguished Conduct Medal,* 66.

29   Riddle and Mitchell, *Distinguished Conduct Medal,* 274. For Harrop see Riddle and Mitchell, *Distinguished Conduct Medal,* 108.

30   Box B50-022 50th Battalion, folder Harrop, R. A., KOCRA.

31   On Walsh and the stretcher bearers, see 14 August 1918, *Operations of 50th Canadian Battalion from 10-8-18 to 13-8-18* (Lt.-Col L. Page), app. 11, 50th Battalion WD (August 1918), LAC. Among them was thirty-eight-year-old Pvt. Harvey Thorne, the author's great-uncle. 10 August 1918, 50th Battalion WD, LAC.

32   Riddle and Mitchell, *Distinguished Service Order,* 80. Of course earlier in the day, when his battalion was pinned down in front of Fouquescourt, he showed that sometimes it's best if a battalion commander returns to his headquarters where he can be in touch with the larger battle, and delegate local authority to trusted subordinates.

33 10 August 1918, 50th Battalion WD, LAC. Obviously, the war diary could not go into detail about the nature of the wounds, but "wounded" is an unfortunately sanitized term. Some men would be quickly dabbed with iodine and bandaged and never leave the line, while others would return within a week or two. But there was horrific trauma, too—faces blown away, limbs hanging by shreds of flesh. There were injuries that would leave them disabled for the rest of their lives—if they recovered from them (and given the proximity of field hospitals and the remarkable skill of army surgeons in an era before blood transfusions and antibiotics, most would). Diary 15 August 1918, David Watson Papers, MG 30 E69, LAC.

34 For August 10 and 11 total casualties reached 252. 14 August 1918, *Operations of 50th Canadian Battalion from 10-8-18 to 13-8-18* (Lt.-Col. L. Page) app. 11, 50th Battalion WD (August 1918), LAC.

35 Nicholson, *Canadian Expeditionary Force*, 418; See also 417–18.

36 Diary 10 August 1918, box B50-024 50th Battalion, folder Oke, Charles, KOCRA.

37 Diary 14 and 15 August 1918, David Watson Papers, MG 30 E69, LAC. The latitude of the Amiens battlefield lies just south of Calgary.

38 *10th Canadian Infantry Brigade Narrative of Operations: Battle of Amiens August 6th to 11th, 1918*, app. E, 10th Brigade WD (1918), LAC. Diary 11 August 1918, box B50-024 50th Battalion, folder Oke, Charles, KOCRA.

39 14 August 1918, *Operations of 50th Canadian Battalion from 10-8-18 to 13-8-18* (Lt.-Col L. Page), app. 11, 50th Battalion WD (August 1918), LAC.

40 Despite the infiltration tactics employed by the *stosstruppen* units and their absolute avoidance of frontal assaults, it was not unusual to see ordinary German units continuing to advance *en masse* on a well-defended position, with predictable slaughter. Travers, *How the War Was Won*, 87.

41 11 August 1918, 50th Battalion WD, LAC and 14 August 1918, *Operations of 50th Canadian Battalion from 10-8-18 to 13-8-18* (Lt.-Col L. Page) app. 11, 50th Battalion WD, LAC.

42 14 August 1918, *Operations of 50th Canadian Battalion from 10-8-18 to 13-8-18* (Lt.-Col L. Page) app. 11, 50th Battalion WD, LAC.

43 11 August 1918, 50th Battalion WD, LAC.

44 14 August 1918, *Operations of 50th Canadian Battalion from 10-8-18 to 13-8-18* (Lt.-Col. L. Page), app. 11, 50th Battalion WD, LAC.

45 12 and 13 August 1918, 50th Battalion WD, LAC and diary 13 August 1918, box B50-024 50th Battalion, folder Oke, Charles, KOCRA.

46 Nicholson, *Canadian Expeditionary Force*, 422–27. 14–17 August 1918, 50th Battalion WD, LAC.

47 Nicholson, *Canadian Expeditionary Force*, 419.

48 Walter Sinclair, box 15, tape 1, 50th Battalion, RG 41 B III 1, LAC.

49 18 August 1918, 50th Battalion WD, LAC. Lt.-Col. Page penned a tribute to be inserted in the battalion war diary, but one which certainly reflected the cultural stereotypes of the day. Norwest "was a peculiar character. Very silent, very intent. As delighted as a child at his success and as grim as the avenging angel when on his work … His patience was colossal [and] no risks too great to take, as long as he was killing …. His Indian blood possibly helped him in his work, possibly inherited his patience and cunning from his hunting forbears …. His memory will be ever with us, his example an

inspiration." 18 August 1918, *A Tribute* (Lt.-Col. L. Page), app. 12, 50th Battalion WD (August 1918), LAC. 26 January 1964, Robert Forrest to Victor Wheeler; 4 June 1963, Harold Scott to Victor Wheeler; and 17 June 1968, Herbert Hogg to Victor Wheeler, 17 Jun 1968, box 10, folder 132, Victor Wheeler Papers, M-5614, GA; and Wheeler, *50th Battalion*, 241–42.

50   27 and 28 August 1918, 50th Battalion WD, LAC.
51   David Muirhead, CEF Personnel, RG 150 Acc. 1992-93/166, LAC. Pvt. David Paterson was likely one of the first conscripts to die with the 50th Battalion. Seriously wounded at Hallu, he died four days later. Paterson had farmed in the Nanton area. Dennis, *Reluctant Warriors*, 82. Diary 15 August 1918, David Watson Papers, MG 30 E69, LAC.
52   29 August 1918, 50th Battalion WD, LAC.
53   Wheeler, *50th Battalion*, 150–51. For a similar appraisal by a junior officer, see S. Dyde, box 15, tape 2, 50th Battalion, RG 41 B III 1, LAC.
54   Dennis, *Reluctant Warriors*, 210–11. See also 192–93, 196 and 238–39.
55   Dennis, *Reluctant Warriors*, 140, 208–10, 216–17 and 225.
56   30 and 31 August 1918, 50th Battalion WD, LAC.
57   31 August 1918, 50th Battalion WD, LAC and WD, 10th Bde, Sep 1918, Appendices, *10th Canadian Infantry Brigade Narrative of Operations Battle of Arras September 1st to 4th, 1918*, app., 10th Brigade WD (September 1918), LAC.
58   Sheffield, *Forgotten Victory*, 242–44 and Hart, *Very British Victory*, 364 and chapter 11.
59   The Hindenburg Line ran from the Arras area south to the River Aisne near Soissons. As the Germans' last prepared defensive position in northern France, its loss would be disastrous.
60   Nicholson, *Canadian Expeditionary Force*, 427–32 and Jackson, *Empire on the Western Front*, 226–27.
61   Nicholson, *Canadian Expeditionary Force*, 434.
62   *10th Canadian Infantry Brigade Narrative of Operations Battle of Arras September 1st to 4th, 1918*, app., 10th Infantry Brigade WD (September 1918), LAC.
63   Diary 29 August 1918, David Watson Papers, MG 30 E 69, LAC.
64   Nicholson, *Canadian Expeditionary Force*, 435.
65   1 September 1918, 50th Battalion War Diary, LAC. *10th Canadian Infantry Brigade Narrative of Operations Battle of Arras September 1st to 4th, 1918*, app., 10th Brigade WD (September 1918), LAC. Diary 1 September 1918, box B50-024 50th Battalion, folder Oke, Charles, KOCRA.
66   *10th Canadian Infantry Brigade Narrative of Operations Battle of Arras September 1st to 4th, 1918*, app., 10th Brigade WD (September 1918), LAC.
67   2 September 1918, 50th Battalion WD, LAC.
68   2 September 1918, 50th Battalion WD, LAC. Diary 2 September 1918, box B50-024 50th Battalion, folder Oke, Charles, LAC and Cook, *Shock Troops*, 488–92.
69   *10th Canadian Infantry Brigade Narrative of Operations Battle of Arras September 1st to 4th*, 1918, app, 10th Brigade WD (September 1918), LAC.
70   *10th Canadian Infantry Brigade Narrative of Operations Battle of Arras September 1st to 4th*, 1918, app, 10th Brigade WD (September 1918), LAC.
71   Diary 2 September 1918, box B50-024 50th Battalion, folder Oke, Charles, KOCRA.

72 2 September 1918, 50th Battalion WD, LAC.

73 2 September 1918, 50th Battalion WD, LAC. Lt. Brown and Lt. McConnell had immediately assumed command of the companies. On the awarding of MMs, see 9 October 1918, 50th Battalion WD, LAC. The thirty-two-year-old Arthur Batson had moved west from Newfoundland before the war. He had been promoted from the ranks in the 31st Battalion before being transferred to the 50th. One soldier remembered him as quiet and unassuming, a very religious man who was never without his bible, but an excellent officer whose presence always calmed his men. R. Stephen and J. A. MacDonald, box 15, tape 2, 50th Battalion, RG 41 B III 1, LAC. Riddle and Mitchell, *Distinguished Service Order*, 80.

74 *10th Canadian Infantry Brigade Narrative of Operations Battle of Arras September 1st to 4th, 1918*, app., 10th Brigade WD (September 1918), LAC; Diary 31 August 1918, box B50-024 50th Battalion, folder Oke, Charles, KOCR; and Cook, *Shock Troops*, 492.

75 2 September 1918, 50th Battalion WD, LAC. By this stage of the war, German manpower shortages were severe. By early October, one German corps, nominally comprising seven infantry divisions, had an infantry strength of less than 5,000 men, and there were regiments containing fewer than 200. As the Hundred Days Campaign wore on, many German divisions were basically notional, and remnants of companies, battalions, and even regiments, were cobbled together to form ad hoc units. The Allies were largely unaware of this, and continued to link smaller units identified when prisoners surrendered or dead were found on the battlefield to divisions that no longer existed but of which they had once been a part. This led to overestimations of the number of enemy they confronted. Unfortunately the same holds in many historical accounts. To compensate for their dearth of infantry, and in many instances, fading morale, front-line German units were liberally strengthened with machine gun squads—*Korsettenstangen* (corset stays). Beach, *Haig's Intelligence*, chapter 14; Boff, *Winning and Losing*, 45–49; Lloyd, *Hundred Days*, 102–03; and Showalter, *Instrument of War*, 268–69.

76 2 September 1918, 50th Battalion WD, LAC.

77 Nicholson, *Canadian Expeditionary Force*, 437–39 and Cook, *Shock Troops*, 492–96.

78 *10th Canadian Infantry Brigade Narrative of Operations Battle of Arras September 1st to 4th, 1918*, app., 10th Brigade WD (September 1918), LAC. Word of a twenty-four-hour postponement reached Hayter at 0430, but he had already issued his cancellation order. *10th Canadian Infantry Brigade Narrative of Operations Battle of Arras September 1st to 4th, 1918*, app., 10th Brigade WD (September 1918), LAC.

79 Dennis, *Reluctant Warriors*, 115.

80 Diary 2 September 1918, David Watson Papers, MG 30 E69, LAC.

81 *10th Canadian Infantry Brigade Narrative of Operations Battle of Arras September 1st to 4th, 1918*, app., 10th Brigade WD (September 1918), LAC.

82 3–6 September 1918, 50th Battalion WD, LAC.

83 15 September 1918, 50th Battalion WD, LAC. Various entries, 7–14 September 1918, 50th Battalion WD, LAC.

84 War Diary, 50th Btn, 16–18 Sep 1918. It was no longer unusual to see replacement officers with the ribbon of the MM or DCM pinned to their tunics, experienced NCOs who'd just graduated from officer training courses in England. All told the battalion received only 124 replacements during the little over three weeks between the D–Q Line and Canal du Nord battles, twenty officers and 104 other ranks, but also lost the

dozen men funnelled into the battalion after Amiens as emergency reinforcements. War Diary, 50th Btn, 6, 10 and 12 Sep 1918.
85   18 September 1918, 50th Battalion WD, LAC.
86   19–22 September 1918, 50th Battalion WD, LAC.
87   Diary, 26 September 1918, box B50-024 50th Battalion, folder Oke, Charles, KOCRA. Negotiation among soldiers before the LOB list was settled wasn't unusual. A single man might offer to change positions with a friend who had a wife and children back home. Depending on the circumstances, their CO might approve it.
88   26 September 1918, 50th Battalion WD, LAC and 25 September 1918, *50th Canadian Battalion Instructions BW9*, app., 50th Battalion WD (September 1918), LAC.
89   20 September 1918, *50th Canadian Battalion Instructions BW2*, app., 50th Battalion WD (September 1918), LAC.
90   Each company's fourth platoon had been temporarily dissolved to bring the others up to strength. 30 September 1918, *Report on Operations September 27th to September 29th, 1918 50th Canadian Battalion* (Lt.-Col. L. Page), app. 12, 50th Battalion WD (September 1918), LAC.
91   Nicholson, *Canadian Expeditionary Force*, 440–43 and Hart, *Very British Victory*, 438–39.
92   Riddle and Mitchell, eds., *Distinguished Conduct Medal*, 87.
93   *10th Canadian Infantry Brigade Narrative of Operations—Battles before Cambrai—Friday Sept. 27th to Sunday Sept. 29th 1918*, app. E, 10th Brigade WD (September 1918), LAC.
94   Diary 26 September 1918, box B50-024, folder Oke, Charles, KOCRA.
95   See Cook, "'More a Medicine than a Beverage,'" 6–22.
96   20 September 1918, *50th Canadian Battalion Instructions BW3*, app., 50th Battalion WD (September 1918), KOCRA and Diary 27 September 1918, box B50-024 50th Battalion, folder Oke, Charles, KOCRA.
97   Riddle and Mitchell, *Distinguished Conduct*, 272.
98   *10th Canadian Infantry Brigade Narrative of Operations—Battles before Cambrai—Friday Sept. 27th to Sunday Sept. 29th 1918*, app. E, 10th Brigade WD (September 1918), LAC.
99   30 September 1918, *Report on Operations September 27th to September 29th, 1918 50th Canadian Battalion* (Lt.-Col L. Page), app. 12, 50th Battalion WD (September 1918), LAC and Cook, *Shock Troops*, 512 and 516–17.
100 30 September 1918, *Report on Operations September 27th to September 29th, 1918 50th Canadian Battalion* (Lt.-Col L. Page), app. 12, 50th Battalion WD (September 1918), LAC and Nicholson, *Canadian Expeditionary Force*, 445–46. Officers designated LOB were, except in extreme emergencies, not called forward. But it was Canadian practice to assign a handful of junior officers to a battalion without assigning them to a company or platoon. These formed a reinforcement pool to be tapped during a battle. It was a practical, if sad, recognition that junior infantry officers suffered very high loss rates. Nominally company strengths were around 200 men.
101 30 September 1918, *Report on Operations September 27th to September 29th, 1918 50th Canadian Battalion* (Lt.-Col L. Page), app. 12, 50th Battalion WD (September 1918), LAC and *10th Canadian Infantry Brigade Narrative of Operations—Battles*

before Cambrai—Friday Sept. 27th to Sunday Sept. 29th 1918, app. E, 10th Brigade WD (September 1918), LAC.

102 *10th Canadian Infantry Brigade Narrative of Operations — Battles before Cambrai—Friday Sept. 27th to Sunday Sept. 29th 1918*, app. E, 10th Brigade WD (September 1918), LAC.

103 The intent was to assemble troops at the last minute so they'd be in position by 15 minutes before Zero-hour, preventing heavy casualties if German artillery bombarded the front line. The assembly positions were located about 50 m behind the jumping-off (that is, front) line. 27 September 1918, *50th Canadian Battalion Operation Order No. 137*, app., 50th Battalion WD (September 1918), LAC.

104 Nicholson, *Canadian Expeditionary Force*, 449 and 27 September 1918, *50th Canadian Battalion Operation Order No. 137*, app., 50th Battalion WD (September 1918), LAC.

105 Riddle and Mitchell, *Military Cross*, 304. Riddle and Mitchell, *Military Cross*, 148. 28 September 1918, 50th Battalion WD, LAC. Reflecting on lessons learned two days later, Page emphasized that "too much time cannot be spent in training officers in tactics. I think the success of the [Marcoing Line operation] is largely due to a platoon commander grasping the situation and outflanking the enemy." 30 September 1918, *Report on Operations September 27th to September 29th, 1918 50th Canadian Battalion* (Lt.-Col. L. Page), app. 12, 50th Battalion WD (September 1918), LAC. *10th Canadian Infantry Brigade Narrative of Operations—Battles before Cambrai—Friday Sept. 27th to Sunday Sept. 29th 1918*, app. E, 10th Brigade WD (September 1918), LAC.

106 28 September 1918, 50th Battalion WD, LAC.

107 Moving selected field artillery batteries into the combat zone greatly assisted the infantry in overcoming strong points, but casualties to the gunners and their draft horses were heavy.

108 Riddle and Mitchell, *Military Cross*, 249.

109 30 September 1918, *Report on Operations September 27th to September 29th, 1918 50th Canadian Battalion* (Lt.-Col. L. Page), app. 12, 50th Battalion WD (September 1918), LAC. *10th Canadian Infantry Brigade Narrative of Operations—Battles before Cambrai—Friday Sept. 27th to Sunday Sept. 29th 1918*, app. E, 10th Brigade WD (September 1918), LAC.

110 28 September 1918, 50th Battalion WD, LAC.

111 *10th Canadian Infantry Brigade Narrative of Operations—Battles before Cambrai—Friday Sept. 27th to Sunday Sept. 29th 1918*, app. E, 10th Brigade WD (September 1918), LAC.

112 28 September 1918, 50th Battalion WD, LAC and 30 September 1918, WD, *Report on Operations September 27th to September 29th, 1918*, 50th Canadian Battalion (Lt.-Col. L. Page), app. 12, 50th Battalion WD (September 1918), LAC. Capturing artillery pieces had been unheard of earlier, but was now routine, a tribute to the rapidity and depth of the advances as well as the sad state of the German Army's horse-power which forced gun crews to abandon their weapons. The fact many guns had not been spiked points to collapsing morale.

113 30 September 1918, *Report on Operations September 27th to September 29th, 1918*, 50th Canadian Battalion (Lt.-Col. L. Page), app. 12, 50th Battalion WD (September 1918), LAC. Dennis, *Reluctant Warriors*, 136. Bullet wounds were much less traumatic and far cleaner (i.e., did not draw soil into the wound), and hence less prone to infections

like tetanus and gas gangrene which along with blood loss were the major complicating factors in medical treatment.

114 30 September 1918, *Report on Operations September 27th to September 29th, 1918*, 50th Canadian Battalion (Lt.-Col. L. Page), app. 12, 50th Battalion WD (September 1918), LAC.

115 *10th Canadian Infantry Brigade Narrative of Operations—Battles before Cambrai—Friday Sept. 27th to Sunday Sept. 29th 1918*, app. E, 10th Brigade WD (September 1918), LAC.

116 Nicholson, *Canadian Expeditionary Force*, 448–53. To admit the rapidly deteriorating state of the German Army in no way denigrates Canadian success but does provide a fuller explanation of how that success was achieved.

117 29 and 30 September 1918, 50th Battalion WD, LAC. *10th Canadian Infantry Brigade Narrative of Operations—Battles before Cambrai—Friday Sept. 27th to Sunday Sept. 29th 1918*, app. E, 10th Brigade WD (September 1918), LAC.

118 This handful were the only reinforcements documented. Groups of returning wounded were not mentioned because they weren't deemed reinforcements. Such reinforcement numbers, if complete, meant that during the last month and half of the war the battalion was operating at no better than half its nominal fighting strength. 29 and 30 September 1918, 50th Battalion WD, LAC. *10th Canadian Infantry Brigade Narrative of Operations—Battles before Cambrai—Friday Sept. 27th to Sunday Sept. 29th 1918*, app. E, 10th Brigade WD (September 1918), LAC.

119 3 October 1918, 50th Battalion WD, LAC. For details on Cunnington's capture and subsequently months as a prisoner of war, see D. Cunnington, box 15, tape 2, 50th Battalion, RG 41 B III 1, LAC. The Germans captured only a handful of men from the 50th Battalion.

120 11 October 1918, 50th Battalion WD, LAC. Diary 11 October 1918, David Watson Papers, MG 30 E69, LAC.

121 Diary 1 November 1918, box B50-024 50th Battalion, folder Oke, Charles, KOCRA. Cook, *Shock Troops*, 554–55.

122 See for instance Wheeler's gruesome account in *50th Battalion*, 271.

123 45,000 casualties out of a fighting force of around 100,000 men.

124 Nicholson, *Canadian Expeditionary Force*, 465–70. Cook, *Shock Troops*, 554–55 and "Politics of Surrender," 637–66.

125 Quoted in Nicholson, *Canadian Expeditionary Force*, 475.

126 They were frequently hungry, too, as rations had been cut to help feed the refugees forced southward by the retreating Germans to further hamper the Allied pursuit.

127 A. Russell and W. Gadsden, box 15, tape 3 and A. Turner, box 15, tape 4, 50th Battalion, RG 41 B III 1, LAC.

128 Diary 19 October 1918, box B50-024 50th Battalion, folder Oke, Charles, KOCRA. Wheeler, *50th Battalion*, 271.

129 25 October 1918, *Report on Operations October 17th to October 22nd, 1918, 50th Canadian Inf. Battalion* (Lt.-Col. L. Page), app. 34, 10th Brigade WD (October 1918), LAC.

130 17 and 18 October 1918, 50th Battalion WD, LAC and 25 October 1918, *Report on Operations October 17th to October 22nd, 1918, 50th Canadian Inf. Battalion* (Lt.-Col. L. Page), app. 34, 10th Brigade WD (October 1918), LAC.
131 18 October 1918, 50th Battalion WD, LAC.
132 19 October 1918, 50th Battalion WD, LAC.
133 Wheeler, *50th Battalion*, 293.
134 The principal staff officer of a corps. Hayter's replacement was Brig. John Ross, an experienced, capable officer who had commanded the 5th Brigade for a year until badly wounded at Amiens.
135 27 October 1918, 50th Battalion WD, LAC. A serving officer in the BEF, the heir to the throne (and future King Edward VIII) was seconded to the Canadian Corps for a month during the latter stages of the war. 25 October 1918, 50th Battalion WD, LAC.
136 29 October 1918, 50th Battalion WD, LAC.
137 Nicholson, *Canadian Expeditionary Force*, 470–71.
138 First Army intelligence estimated five German divisions were deployed. Nicholson, *Canadian Expeditionary Force*, 471. Assessing enemy strength in any sector by counting divisions, particular in the last months of the war, was a mug's game. The defenders likely outnumbered the attackers but their firepower and morale didn't match the Canadians'.
139 Nicholson, *Canadian Expeditionary Force*, 471–72.
140 Marble, *British Artillery*, 242–45. McNaughton was Canada's most innovative and capable artillery officer. As counter-battery staff officer, he was in charge of the Corps' heavy artillery. The field artillery was nominally in the hands of Maj.-Gen. E. W. B. Morrison, but in practice directed by his able senior staff officer, Maj. Henry Crerar. Altogether during the Mont Houy operation the Canadian and British gunners fired close to 88,000 rounds, or over 1,900 tonnes of shells.
141 Wheeler, *50th Battalion*, 278.
142 *Report on Operations, October 27th to November 2nd, 1918—50th Battalion*, app. 4, 50th Battalion WD (November 1918), LAC and Cook, *Shock Troops*, 556–62.
143 13 November 1918, *Narrative of Operations Second Battle of Valenciennes November 1st, 1918* (Brig. J. M. Ross), app. C, 10th Brigade WD (November 1918), LAC.
144 Riddle and Mitchell, *Military Cross*, 308.
145 Box B50-022, folder Mayson, William, KOCRA.
146 Nicholson, *Canadian Expeditionary Force*, 471-74.
147 1 November 1918, 50th Battalion WD, LAC. 13 November 1918, *Narrative of Operations Second Battle of Valenciennes November 1st, 1918* (Brig. J. M. Ross), app. C, 10th Brigade WD (November 1918), LAC.
148 Among the others was Pvt. Charles Oke, whose diary has been frequently cited in this chapter. Diary 5 November 1918, box B50-024 50th Battalion, folder Oke, Charles, KOCRA. Temporary blindness frequently followed exposure to mustard gas.
149 There was no 4th Division presence at all, even Watson snubbed his invitation. Diary 7 November 1918, David Watson Papers, MG 30 E69, LAC. BEF rules forbade the identification of individual formations (including both Dominion corps) in official releases in order to deny the enemy that intelligence, ensuring that all advances, victories and so forth were announced as British. This became increasingly irritating to

the senior ranks of the Canadians Corps during the Hundred Days. In an army where one-third of the officers and half of the other ranks were British-born, a Canadian national pride was blossoming and demanding recognition. See Brennan, "The other battle," 251–65.

150 Diary 11 November 1918, David Watson Papers, MG 30 E69, LAC. The French anthem was followed by God Save the King and then O Canada.

151 A. Turner, box 15, tape 4, 50th Battalion, RG 41 B III 1, LAC. J. A. Macdonald, box 15, tape 2, 50th Battalion, RG 41 B III 1, LAC. For Turner 11 November was filled with tragedy. The mid-afternoon mail-call brought a delayed cable from home informing him that his 2½-year-old son had died a week earlier. Turner had married just before the war broke out and their first child had been born after he had gone overseas— Turner had never seen him.

152 Edgar Doxee to his mother, box B50-021 50th Battalion, folder Doxee, Edgar, KOCRA. Wheeler, *50th Battalion*, 286.

153 Wheeler, *50th Battalion*, 286.

154 Various entries November and December 1918 and 13 January 1919, 50th Battalion WD, LAC.

155 Morton and Wright, *Winning the Second Battle*, 111. Various entries January–March 1919, 50th Battalion WD, LAC and Dennis, *Reluctant Warriors*, 206–10 and 216–17.

156 27-30 April 1919, 10th Brigade WD, LAC. Various entries, April 1919, 10th Brigade WD, LAC. Morton, *Peculiar Kind of Politics*, chapter 9.

157 3-4 May 1919, 50th Battalion WD, LAC. By 9 May the barracks were all but empty. Page had every man's leave extended till 20 May. 10 May 1919, 50th Battalion WD, LAC. On the Victory Parade, see Wheeler, *50th Battalion*, 311.

158 26-28 May 1918, 50th Battalion WD, LAC.

159 *Calgary Daily Herald*, 5 June 1919, 1.

160 Wheeler, *50th Battalion*, 311.

161 *Calgary Daily Herald*, 20 December 1918, 17 and 1 February 1919, 15 and 18.

162 *Calgary Daily Herald*, 7 Jun 1919, 7 and 13–14.

163 *Calgary Daily Herald*, 5 Jun 1919, 1. This was fewer than the number leaving England, since returning soldiers were let off the train wherever they chose, and a fair number who'd suffered severe wounds had already come back. All told more than 70 "originals" survived the war. Under the command of Maj. Eveleigh, about a hundred men from the group that had crossed on the *Empress of Britain* actually reached Calgary on 8 June. Their welcome had been more subdued.

164 *Calgary Daily Herald*, 5 Jun 1919, 1. Returning veterans of the battalion had formed the 50th Club, though there were also civilians involved. The GWVA was the principal veterans' organization for other ranks, the officer-controlled Royal Canadian Legion absorbing it in 1925.

165 *Calgary Daily Herald*, 9 Jun 1918, 7.

166 *Calgary Daily Herald*, 9 Jun 1918, 7 and Wheeler, *50th Battalion*, 311.

167 Box B103-002 Calgary Rifles, *Historical Sketches 2*, KOCRA.

168 *Calgary Daily Herald*, 11 Jun 1919, 9.

169 Morton and Wright, *Winning the Second Battle*, chapters 1–4; Morton, *When Your Number's Up*, chapter 11; J. L. Granatstein, *Canada's Army*, 150–52; and Cook, *Shock*

Troops, chapters 38 and 39. On the emergence of government and other public efforts to support the families of serving soldiers during the war years, see Morton, *Fight or Pay*.

170 Wheeler, *50th Battalion*, 312.
171 *Calgary Daily Herald*, 7 Jun 1919, 14.
172 *Calgary Daily Herald*, 5 Jun 1919, 1 and box 1764, folder DHS 11-16, RG 24, DHH. The latter totals, like all of Canada's official casualty statistics for the Great War, were inflated by including the same individuals each time they were wounded.
173 *Calgary Daily Herald*, 5 Jun 1919, 1.
174 Jackson, *Empire on the Western Front*, 246–54.

NOTES TO CHAPTER 4

1 Granatstein, *Canada's Army*, 158. Granatstein, *Canada's Army*, 155–58.
2 Lt.-Col. L. Page to mayor, 18 February 1919, box TCR001 Calgary Regiment 1919–41, folder Regimental Colours Miscellaneous, 1919–35, KOCRA.
3 Granatstein, *Canada's Army*, 158–59. There was also the question of those numbered battalions that had been broken up for reinforcements in England, as veterans demanded they also be perpetuated. Ones raised by a pre-war militia regiment or whose men had mostly gone to a single front-line battalion were incorporated into the lineage of the post-war militia regiment associated with that battalion.
4 Box B103-002 Calgary Rifles, Historical Sketches 2.
5 Box B103-002 Calgary Rifles, Historical Sketches 10.
6 Box B103-002 Calgary Rifles, Historical Sketches 11 and *Report of Annual Inspection, 1921*, box 5888, folder HQ7-111-18, RG 24, LAC.
7 Box TCR001 Calgary Regiment 1919–41, folder Ephemera 1919–24, KOCRA and box B103-002, Calgary Rifles, Personnel, Historical Sketches 2.
8 Two other battalions of the Calgary Regiment were also formed, the 2nd and 3rd, commemorating the 89th and 137th CEF Battalions, respectively, but only the 1st Battalion would operate as a fully-fledged militia unit.
9 Box B103-002 Calgary Rifles, Historical Sketches 8 and 10, KOCRA.
10 Box B103-002 Calgary Rifles, Historical Sketches 11and Gen. J. MacBrien to Brig.-Gen. A. Bell (OC MD 13), 5 Apr 1923 and Brig.-Gen. A. Bell to deputy minister of Department of Militia, 10 April 1923, box 5888, folder HQ7-111-18, RG 24, LAC.
11 *Annual Inspection Report, 1923–4*, box 5888, folder HQ7-111-18, RG 24, LAC. 10 April 1923, Brig.-Gen. A. Bell to deputy minister Department of Militia and *Annual Inspection Report, 1922–3*, box 5888, folder HQ7-111-18, RG 24, LAC.
12 Lt.-Col. L. Page to mayor, 18 February 1919, box TCR001 Calgary Regiment 1919–41, folder Regimental Colours Miscellaneous, 1919–35, KOCRA. *Regimental Activities Annual Report, 1929,* box TCR001 Calgary Regiment 1919–41, folder 006, KOCRA and *Report 2nd Battalion Calgary Regiment, 2 February 1923—7 February 1924*, box TCR003 Calgary Regiment 1920–39, KOCRA.
13 Wood, *Militia Myths*, 267–68.
14 The commemoration of the 1918 Armistice was, during the early years, as much about celebrating victory as honouring the fallen. The R. B. Bennett government proclaimed it as Remembrance Day in 1931. Vance, *Death So Noble*, 16–17 and 211–19.

15 Box B103-002 Calgary Rifles, Historical Sketches 11.
16 Box B103-002 Calgary Rifles, Historical Sketches 11.
17 *1928 Annual Report,* box TCR001 Calgary Regiment 1919–41, folder 001, KOCRA.
18 Box B103-002 Calgary Rifles, Historical Sketches 11.
19 *Report 2nd Battalion Calgary Regiment, 2 February 1923–7 February 1924,* Box TCR003 Calgary Regiment 1920–39, folder, KOCRA. Box B103-002 Calgary Rifles, Historical Sketches 11 and *Report 1st Battalion Calgary Regiment,* box TCR003 Calgary Regiment 1920–39, KOCRA.
20 *Report 2nd Battalion Calgary Regiment, 2 February 1923–7 February 1924,* box TCR003 Calgary Regiment 1920–39, KOCRA.
21 *Report 1st Battalion Calgary Regiment, 5 March 1926–17 February 1927,* box TCR003 Calgary Regiment 1920–39, KOCRA.
22 Box TCR001 Calgary Regiment 1919–41, folder 001 Historical Record 1920–34, KOCRA. Box 103-002, Calgary Rifles, Historical Sketches 4, KOCRA and *Report 1st Battalion Calgary Regiment 1928,* box TCR003 Calgary Regiment 1920–39, KOCRA.
23 Box B103-002 Calgary Rifles, Historical Sketches 11, KOCRA. Granatstein, *Canada's Army,* 160–61.
24 *Regimental Activities Annual Report 1929,* box TCR001 Calgary Regt 1919–41, folder 006 Historical Record 1920–34, KOCRA.
25 Box B103-002 Calgary Rifles, Historical Sketches 10, KOCRA and *Report 1st Battalion Calgary Regiment 1929,* box TCR003 Calgary Regiment 1920–39, KOCRA, and Granatstein, *Canada's Army,* 160–61.
26 *Report 1st Battalion Calgary Regiment 27 February 1925–4 March 1926* and *1929,* box TCR003 Calgary Regiment 1920–39, KOCRA. The Calgary Regiment's financial situation suffered from the fact that the 103rd Regiment had existed only since 1910, and half of what it had managed to put away had gone to the Calgary Highlanders in 1924 when the post-war regiment's two battalions had effectively gone their separate ways.
27 A third militia regiment was included in the 24th Brigade—the Southern Alberta Regiment based in Lethbridge and Medicine Hat.
28 Various, box TCR003, Calgary Regiment, 1920–39, folder 002 Memos and Correspondence, 1926–28, KOCRA.
29 Box 103-002 Calgary Rifles, Historical Sketches 10, KOCRA.
30 Apart from manifesting imperial sentiments, it is unclear why the officers of the KORR were apparently equally keen. Box B50-021 50th Battalion, folder Cunnington, D.G. L., KOCRA and box TCR001 Calgary Regiment 1919–41, folder 001 Historical Record 1920–34, KOCRA.
31 Box TCR001 Calgary Regiment 1919–41, folder 001 Historical Record 1920–34, KOCRA.
32 *Report 1st Battalion Calgary Regiment 1929,* box TCR003 Calgary Regiment 1920–39, KOCRA and *Regimental Activities Annual Report 1929,* box TCR001 Calgary Regiment 1919–41, folder 006, KOCRA. On the return to deference for all things British, see Granatstein, *Canadian Army,* chapter 5 and Vance, *Maple Leaf Empire,* 133, 139 and 142–44.

33 Lt.-Col. Naysmith and Maj. Robie, the commanding officers of the Calgary Regiment's skeleton 2nd and 3rd Battalions, were added to represent the interests of the 89th and 137th Battalions, respectively.

34 Lt.-Col. D. J. MacDonald (MD 13) to OC 1/Calgary Regiment, 19 December 1927, box B50-021 50th Battalion, folder Cunnington, D. G. L., KOCRA. Box B50-021 50th Battalion, folder Cunnington, D. G. L., KOCRA and box B103-002 50th Battalion, Historical Sketches 10, KOCRA.

35 Report on 1st and 2nd Battalions Calgary Regiment, 8 February 1924–26 February 1925, box TCR003 Calgary Regiment 1920–39, KOCRA. Lt.-Col. L. A. Cavanaugh to J. Allen, 11 March 1935, box TCR001 Calgary Regiment 1919–41, folder 003 Documents and Correspondence 1930–38, KOCRA and Brig.-Gen. A. H. Bell to deputy minister of Department of Militia, 10 April 1923, box 5888, folder HQ7-111-18, RG 24, LAC.

36 Lt.-Col. L. A. Cavanaugh to J. Allen, 11 March 1935, box TCR001 Calgary Regiment 1919–41, folder 003 Documents and Correspondence 1930–38, KOCRA.

37 Foran, *Calgary*, 117–28.

38 Lt.-Col. E. Knight to OC MD 13, 6 October 1930 and Lt.-Col. E. Knight to Brig.-Gen. A. H. Bell, 23 Oct 1930, box TCR001 Calgary Regiment 1919–41, folder 010 Correspondence re: Proposal Regimental Re-designation, KOCRA. Cunnington's appointment as commander of 24th Brigade in 1930 marked the departure of the last of the officers who had helped found the Calgary Regiment in 1920. Box TCR003 Calgary Regiment 1920–39, folder The Calgary Regiment 1st Battalion Historical Record 1930, KOCRA.

39 Lt.-Col. E. Knight to CO King's Own Royal Regiment (Lancaster), 28 May 1930, box TCR001 Calgary Regiment 1919–1941, folder Documents and Correspondence 1930–38, KOCRA.

40 Box TCR001 Calgary Regiment 1919–41, folder 001 Historical Record 1920–34, KOCRA.

41 Box B103-002 Calgary Rifles, Historical Sketches 4 and *King's Own Calgary Regiment—Resume of History from 1910 to 1960*, KOCRA.

42 *Historical Record 1st Battalion Calgary Regiment 1931*, box TCR003 Calgary Regiment 1920–39, folder Historical Record 1920–39 and box B103-002 Calgary Rifles, Historical Sketches 12, KOCRA.

43 Box B103-002 Calgary Rifles, Historical Sketches 12, KOCRA.

44 Box B103-002 Calgary Rifles, Historical Sketches 12, KOCRA.

45 Granatstein, *Canada's Army*, 162.

46 Lt.-Col. L. Cavanaugh to O. N. Patrick, President Calgary Board of Trade, 30 June 1933, box TCR001 Calgary Regiment 1919–41, folder 013 Documents and Correspondence 1930–38, KOCRA. In selecting the military base project, the prime minister's long involvement in the Calgary militia scene no doubt was a factor.

47 A leaflet handed out at its rallies denounced "MILLION DOLLAR BARRACKS—MILLIONS FOR MILITARY PURPOSES—SOLDIERS—BARRACKS—GUNS—WAR—THIS IS FASCIST PREPARATION IN CANADA," Box B103-002 Calgary Rifles, Historical Sketches 12, KOCRA.

48 Box B103-002 Calgary Rifles, Historical Sketches 2 and *Calgary Daily Herald* clippings (undated), KOCRA. Lt.-Col. L. Cavanaugh to O. N. Patrick, President Calgary Board of Trade, 30 June 1933, box TCR001 Calgary Regiment 1919–41, folder 013 Documents

and Correspondence 1930–38, KOCRA and box B103-002 Calgary Rifles, Historical Sketches 12, KOCRA.
49 Granatstein, *Canada's Army*, 167.
50 The new militia structure included sixteen cavalry regiments, fifty-nine infantry battalions, twenty-seven machine gun battalions, six tank battalions and four armoured car regiments. The rise in the number of machine gun battalions and the creation of armoured car and tank units reflected changes being introduced in the British Army within which any Canadian expeditionary force would have to integrate. canadiansoldiers.com/organization/1936modernization.htm.
51 Quoted from Marteinson, ed., *We Stand on Guard*, 213.
52 Granatstein, *Canada's Army*, 171.
53 Box B103-002 Calgary Rifles, Historical Sketches 8, KOCRA and Lt.-Col. L. Cavanaugh to OC KORR (Lancaster), 1 April 1937, box TCR 001 Calgary Regiment, 1919–41, folder 010 Correspondence re: Proposed Regimental Re-designation, KOCRA. One of Cavanagh's concerns had been that the shift from infantry to armour might force an end the alliance with The King's Own Royal Regiment (Lancaster), but both parties were keen to maintain it. Lt.-Col. L. Cavanaugh to OC KORR (Lancaster), 1 April 1937, box TCR 001 Calgary Regiment, 1919–41, folder 010 Correspondence re: Proposed Regimental Re-designation, KOCRA.
54 Box B103-002 Calgary Rifles, Historical Sketches 12, KOCRA.
55 Lt.-Col. J. Packard, OC 2/KORR (Lancaster) to Lt.-Col. L. Cavanagh, 14 February 1937, box TCR001 Calgary Regiment 1919–41, folder 017, Documents and Correspondence 1930–38, KOCRA.
56 Lt.-Col. L. Kavanaugh to Lt.-Col. J. Packard, OC 2/KORR (Lancaster), 27 March 1937, box TCR001 Calgary Regiment 1919–41, folder 017, Documents and Correspondence 1930–38, KOCRA.
57 Box B103-002 Calgary Rifles, Historical Sketches 12, KOCRA.
58 Box B103-002 Calgary Rifles, Historical Sketches 12, KOCRA.
59 Box B103-002 Calgary Rifles, Historical Sketches 4 and 10, KOCRA.
60 Box B103-002 Calgary Rifles, Historical Sketches 4 and 12, KOCRA.
61 *Calgary Herald* clipping, 7 February 1959, box TCR014, Calgary Regiment, Personnel, J–Z, folder Jull, W. K., KOCRA.
62 This was intended to be an annual event for the militia tank units, and the group of officers and men headed to Camp Borden for eight days of instruction in mechanized tactics. The course ended the day before Britain declared war. Box B103-002 Calgary Rifles, Historical Sketches 12, KOCRA.
63 Box B103-002 Calgary Rifles, Historical Sketches 8, 10 and 12, KOCRA.
64 Box B103-002 Calgary Rifles, Historical Sketches 12, KOCRA.
65 Box B103-002 Calgary Rifles, Historical Sketches 4, 8, 10 and 12, KOCRA.
66 Box B103-002 Calgary Rifles, Historical Sketches 12, KOCRA.
67 From 1867 onward, the official term for the regular army was the Permanent Active Militia, though it was not commonly used. On 1 September 1939 the Canadian Active Service Force (CASF) was formed to serve overseas. Members of Permanent Active Militia had to re-enlist to serve in the CASF, though in most cases this was a mere formality. In late 1940 the CASF became the Canadian Army (Active), or just Canadian

Army in popular usage. The militia was officially termed the Non-permanent Active Militia until 1940 when for the duration of the war it became the Canadian Army (Reserve), though "militia" continued in wide use for part-time army units.

68   Stacey, *Six Years of War*, 35.

69   Few Anglo-Canadians would have cared whether or not Ottawa had exercised Canada's rights under the 1931 Statute of Westminster to declare war in its own right. After the country had torn itself apart during the First World War, it mattered to Ottawa that this did not appear to French and "New" Canadians as just another knee-jerk colonial response. The optics mattered. On militia attitudes, see also Vance, *Maple Leaf Empire*, 141.

70   The CASF was authorized on 1 September 1939 as the expeditionary force. As with the Regular Army, members of the NPAM had to volunteer specifically for the CASF to serve overseas.

71   8 and 12 August 1940, 14th Armoured Regiment WD, LAC.

72   *Calgary Herald*, 17 October 1939 and Box B103-002 Calgary Rifles, Historical Sketches 10 and 12 and *The King's Own Calgary Regiment—Resumé of History from 1910 to 1960*, Historical Sketches 4, KOCRA.

73   Box B103-002 Calgary Rifles, Historical Sketches 2 and 8, KOCRA and *Calgary Herald*, 6 June 1940, 10.

74   Box B103-002 Calgary Rifles, Historical Sketches 10, KOCRA and *Calgary Herald*, 21 June 1940, 12.

75   Box B103-002 Calgary Rifles, Historical Sketches 12, KOCRA. *Calgary Herald*, 31 August 1940, 13 and Pt. 1 Orders, 12 September 1940, 14th Armoured Regiment WD, app., LAC.

76   Box B103-002 Calgary Rifles, Historical Sketches 12.

77   Box B103-002 Calgary Rifles, Historical Sketches 10.

78   *Calgary Herald*, 13 August 1940 and box B103-002, Calgary Rifles, Historical Sketches 12.

79   Unnamed soldier, box TCR001 Calgary Regiment 1919–41, folder 014 Documents Calgary Regt (Tank) 1940–41, KOCRA. Unnamed soldier, box TCR001 Calgary Regiment 1919–41, folder 014 Documents Calgary Regt (Tank) 1940–41, KOCRA.

80   British armoured doctrine called for armoured brigades to comprise the tank component of armoured divisions that would carry out breakthrough operations, whereas army tank brigades would be attached to infantry divisions as needed for infantry support. The concept of the latter persisted through the war. Because it would have to be compatible with British formations it fought alongside, the Canadian Army embraced it as well.

81   On the big army plan see Granatstein, *Canada's War*, 208–10 and *Canada's Army*, 186–89 and Stacey, *Six Years of War*, chapter 3.

82   Box B103-002 Calgary Rifles, Historical Sketches 4, KOCRA. Box B103-002 Calgary Rifles, Historical Sketches 2, KOCRA.

83   15 February 1941, 14th Armoured Regiment WD, LAC. Box TCR001 Calgary Regiment 1919–41, folder 014 Documents Calgary Regt (Tank)—Responsibilities of NPAM (1940), KOCRA.

84 MD 13 HQ to Lt.-Col. Jull, 15 February 1941; MD 13 HQ to OC 14th Army Tank Battalion, 22 February 1941; and Canadian Armoured Corps to MD 2 HQ (re: Calgary Regiment), 18 February 1941, 14th Armoured Regiment WD (February 1941), app. 1, Mobilization—14th Army Tank Battalion, LAC.

85 *Calgary Herald*, 13 February 1941, 1 and 17 February 1941, 10. MD 13 HQ to Lt.-Col. W. Jull, 15 February 1941, 14th Armoured Regiment WD (February 1941), app. 1, Mobilization—14th Army Tank Battalion, LAC and box TCR002 Calgary Regiment 1938–46, W. K. Jull Collection, Unit Mobilization Scheme The Calgary Regiment (Tank) 1938–42, KOCRA. The reservoir of mechanically-savvy recruits was a lot shallower than generally believed as only one Prairie farm in three had a working tractor in 1939, and many urban working-class men had little or no experience with automobiles.

86 17 and 18 February 1941, 14th Armoured Regiment WD, LAC and box 14CAR001 14th Armoured Regiment, folder 001 Historical Sketch—Calgary Regiment Tank, KOCRA.

87 18 and 21 February 1941, 14th Armoured Regiment WD, KOCRA and *Calgary Herald*, 21 February 1941, 9. Most of the soldiers from the army training centres were training as infantrymen.

88 *Calgary Herald* clipping, 7 February 1959, box TCR014, Calgary Regiment, Personnel, J-Z, folder Jull, W. K., KOCRA and *Calgary Herald*, 21 February 1941, 9.

89 Department of National Defence to MD 13 HQ, 25 February 1941, 14th Armoured Regiment WD (February 1941), app. 1, LAC. Mechanical aptitude was considered to be "knowledge of the I[nternal] C[ombustion] engine sufficient to carry out normal operational maintenance." *Enlistment of Officers in the RCAC, 26 February 1941*, 14th Armoured Regiment WD (February 1941), app. 1, LAC.

90 Box 14CAR001 14th Armoured Regiment, folder Report 1941, KOCRA. Among the thirteen were Capts. C. E. Page, J. Begg and C. E. Turney, and Lts. F. T. Jenner and C. A. Richardson. Both Begg and Richardson would be future commanding officers. Box TCR003 Calgary Regiment 1920–39, folder Daily Orders, Pt. 2 (various annual lists of officers), KOCRA.

91 25, 27 and 28 February and 1 March 1941, 14th Armoured Regiment WD, LAC and *Calgary Herald*, 15 March 1941, 11. A further 40 infantry trainees from the Edmonton Regiment were taken on strength.

92 4, 5 and 13 March 1941, 14th Armoured Regiment WD, LAC and box 14CAR001 14th Armoured Regiment, folder Report 1941, KOCRA.

93 13 March 1941, 14th Armoured Regiment WD, LAC.

94 16 and 17 March 1941, 14th Armoured Regiment WD, LAC. Administrative Instructions no. 69, 12 March 1941 and Transportation Instruction, 13 March 1941, 14th Armoured Regiment WD (March 1941), app. 3, LAC.

95 Canadian Armoured Corps to MD 2 HQ (re: Calgary Regiment), 18 February 1941, 14th Armoured Regiment WD (February 1941), app. 1, LAC and *Calgary Herald*, 18 March 1941, 10.

96 *Calgary Herald*, 3 July 1942, 13 and 4 July 1942, 9.

97 Box B103-002 Calgary Rifles, Historical Sketches 2 and 4 and *The King's Own Calgary Regiment—Resumé of History from 1910 to 1960*, Historical Sketches 4, KOCRA and *Calgary Herald*, 22 March 1941, 11.

98   Box B103-002 Calgary Rifles, Historical Sketches 2, 8 and 10 and *The King's Own Calgary Regiment, Resume of History from 1910 to 1960*, Historical Sketches 4, KOCRA.
99   Box 14CAR001 14th Armoured Regiment, folder Report 1941, KOCRA.
100 *Calgary Herald*, 29 September, 3, 22 October, 7 and 3 December 1943, 7.
101 Box B103-002 Calgary Rifles, Historical Sketches 8 and box 14CAR001 14th Armoured Regiment, folder 001 Historical Sketch—Calgary Regiment Tank, KOCRA.
102 *Calgary Herald*, 18 March 1941, 10.
103 20 March 1941, 14th Armoured Regiment WD and 20 March 1941, 1st Armoured Brigade WD, LAC. 18 and 19 March 1941, 14th Armoured Regiment WD, LAC.
104 24 March 1941, 14th Armoured Regiment WD, LAC.
105 28 March 1941, 14th Armoured Regiment WD, LAC. There were 250-odd such machines at Borden, scrounged from American stores and slipped into Canada as scrap beginning in October 1940 to avoid US neutrality laws. Though little updated from the Great War-vintage Renault FT-17 tanks, the Canadian Armoured Corps felt fortunate to have them. Given the war situation there was no possibility of obtaining anything better from Britain as had been the pre-war plan.
106 For a thorough description of the training regimen, see Henry, "Tanks of Dieppe," 32–38.
107 4 and 10 April 1941, 14th Armoured Regiment WD and Pt. 1 Orders nos. 28 and 29, 10 April 1941, 14th Armoured Regiment WD (April 1941), app. 2, LAC.
108 23 April 1941, 14th Armoured Regiment WD, LAC.
109 28 April 1941, 14th Armoured Regiment WD, LAC. A Canadian-built version of the British Valentine infantry tank was chosen to equip the 1st Army Tank Brigade when it was formed in 1940. Some 1,400 were ultimately built. Fearing production delays, among other concerns, the army chose not to adopt it save for training purposes in Canada. Most of the 1,400 built went to the USSR where they gave yeoman service.
110 *Calgary Herald*, 16 April 1941, 16.
111 15–17 May 1941, 14th Armoured Regiment WD, LAC. On training, various entries May 1941, 14th Armoured Regiment WD, LAC.
112 *Evaluation of Brigade Exercise, 15–27 May 1941*, 1st Armoured Brigade WD (May 1941), app., LAC.
113 Circular no. 58, Maj. J. G. Andrews to officers commanding brigade units, 10 May 1941, 1st Armoured Brigade WD (May 1941), app., LAC.
114 27 May 1941, 14th Armoured Regiment WD, LAC. 22–26 May 1941, 14th Armoured Regiment WD, LAC.
115 29 and 30 May 1941, 14th Armoured Regiment WD, LAC. The length of embarkation leave varied by the distance a man needed to travel—in this case five days for those with local destinations and up to ten days for those with more distant ones, like Alberta. 4 and 9 June 1941, 14th Armoured Regiment WD, LAC.
116 Pt. 1 Order no. 66, 29 May 1941, 14th Armoured Regiment WD (May 1941), app., LAC.

NOTES TO CHAPTER 5

1. Box 14CAR-001 (14th Armoured Regiment), folder 001 Fred Bagley, *Priceless Sacrifice*, KOCRA.
2. 18 June 1941, 14th Armoured Regiment WD, LAC.
3. The advance party, about one-sixth of the battalion's strength, crossed in the same convoy but aboard another liner, HMTS *Britannic*. 20 June 1941, 14th Armoured Regiment WD, LAC. In May and June 1945 the same liner brought thousands of British war brides and their children to new homes in Canada.
4. 20 and 21 June 1941, 14th Armoured Regiment WD, LAC.
5. The *Pasteur* and other troopships converted from fast ocean liners usually made their crossings without escort. Less than a month after the sinking of the German battleship *Bismark*, fear of encountering large units of the *Kriegsmarine* remained high, not least among the *Pasteur's* passengers. 22 June 1941, box 14CAR (14th Armoured Regiment), L. G. Alexander Diaries, no. 1, 1 March 1941–5 February 1943, KOCRA.
6. Ship's standing orders (undated), app., 14th Armoured Regiment (June 1941), LAC.
7. 26 June 1941, box 14CAR (14th Armoured Regiment), L. G. Alexander Diaries, no. 1, 1 March 1941–5 February 1943, KOCRA.
8. 30 June 1941, 14th Armoured Regiment WD, LAC. Various entries 21–30 June 1941, 14th Armoured Regiment WD, LAC.
9. 1 July 1941, 14th Armoured Regiment WD, LAC.
10. 2 July 1941, 14th Armoured Regiment WD, LAC.
11. 3–5 July 1941, 14th Armoured Regiment WD, LAC.
12. 11 July 1941, 14th Armoured Regiment WD, LAC. The Matilda IIA* was a slow (perhaps 15 kph cross-country) but heavily armoured infantry tank with a 40-mm gun. Its best days were behind it.
13. 13 July 1941, 1st Armoured Brigade WD, LAC. 13 and 14 July 1941, 14th Armoured Regiment WD, LAC.
14. 29 August 1941, 14th Armoured Regiment WD, LAC. The authorized tank strength of an army tank battalion was constantly fluctuating but averaged around fifty machines. *Organization of an Army Tank Battalion* (undated), app. 2, 14th Armoured Regiment WD (August 1941), LAC.
15. 15, 17 and 20 July 1941, 14th Armoured Regiment WD, LAC.
16. 26 July 1941, 14th Armoured Regiment WD, LAC.
17. Summary of the month, 14th Armoured Regiment WD (July 1941), LAC.
18. 6 August 1941, 14th Armoured Regiment WD, LAC.
19. 16 August 1941, 14th Armoured Regiment WD, LAC. The fear of paratroop landings as a preliminary to wholesale invasion continued to dominate British (and hence Canadian) defensive planning. The still only partially equipped armoured units would man what tanks they had, with the rest of the men fighting as infantry. *Appreciation of Task "Canada" by Comd. I Cdn Army Tank Bde on 15 Jul 41*, app. 26, 1st Armoured Brigade WD (July 1941), LAC.
20. *Report on AJAX Exercise*, 16 August 1941, app. 3, 1st Armoured Brigade WD (August 1941), LAC.

21 *Appreciation of Training Programme 1 Cdn Tank Bde* (Brig. Worthington), 9 Jun 1941, app. 12, 1st Armoured Brigade WD (August 1941), LAC. The 11th and 12th were mobilized in 1939.

22 24 August 1941, 14th Armoured Regiment WD and summary of *Exercise Defence of Wiltshire No. 2*, app. 4, 14th Armoured Regiment WD (June 1941), LAC.

23 Pt. 1 orders, 23 August 1941, app. 2, 14th Armoured Regiment WD (August 1941), LAC. At least the rabbits appear to have been consumed, the war diary for 30 July referring to a rumour that "an illegal rabbit-pie was served to several officers in the sergeants' mess."

24 Pt. 1 orders, 9 August 1941, 14th Armoured Regiment WD (August 1941), LAC. 23 August 1941, 14th Armoured Regiment WD, LAC.

25 16 July 1941, Daily intelligence summary no. 7, app. 4, 14th Armoured Regiment WD (July 1941), LAC. Pt. 1 orders, 8 August 1941, app., 1st Armoured Brigade WD (August 1941), LAC.

26 Stacey and Wilson, *Half Million*, chapter 2.

27 Vance, *Maple Leaf Empire*, 179. See also 174–79.

28 Vance, *Maple Leaf Empire*, 179. See also 181–83.

29 Various entries 12 and 22–30 September 1941, 14th Armoured Regiment WD, LAC.

30 Pt. 1 orders no. 113, 21 October 1941, app., 14th Armoured Regiment WD (October 1941), LAC.

31 27–30 October and 3–4 November 1941, 14th Armoured Regiment WD, LAC.

32 9 October 1941, 14th Armoured Regiment WD, LAC.

33 21 October 1941, 14th Armoured Regiment WD and *Syllabus of Training*, week of 6–12 October 1941, app. 5, 14th Armoured Regiment WD (October 1941), LAC. Overall, equipment, including tanks, had been arriving in good quantity. *Progress Report, 28 September–4 October 1941*, 10 October 1941, app. 2, 1st Armoured Brigade WD (October 1941), LAC.

34 24 October 1941, 14th Armoured Regiment WD, LAC.

35 7 and 10 November 1941, 14th Armoured Regiment WD, LAC.

36 The planned replacement for both the Matilda II and Valentine infantry tanks, the Mk IV Churchill, was hastily introduced almost without testing in 1941, and plagued with mechanical faults. Early models included a rather unnerving warning from Vauxhall Motors: "Fighting vehicles are urgently required, and instructions have been received to proceed with the vehicle as it is rather than hold up production. All those things which we know are not as they should be will be put right." Eventually the kinks were ironed out and from 1943 onward the Churchill proved a very combat-worthy and adaptable tank. Those initially equipping the Calgary Regiment were Mk IIs. Heavily armoured (inspiring confidence in their crews), they weighed 36 tonnes as a result, and could make perhaps 25 kph on roads though considerably less cross-country. The main armament was the already inadequate 2-pounder (40-mm) which would eventually be replaced as one of *many* required upgrades. Churchill Tank, https://en.wikipedia.org/wiki/Churchill_tank. Churchill Infantry Tank Mk IV, www.tanks_encyclopedia.com/ww2/gb/A22_Churchill_Tank.php

37 19–20 November 1941, 14th Armoured Regiment WD, LAC.

38 Box 14CAR001 14th Armoured Regiment, folder 001 Stoney Richardson Conversations with Dick Maltby, August 1989, KOCRA. 28 November 1941, 14th Armoured Regiment WD, LAC.

39 8-11 December 1941, 14th Armoured Regiment WD, LAC and box 14CAR006 14th Armoured Regiment, folder Andrews, J. (biography 1961), KOCRA.
40 16-18 December 1941, 14th Armoured Regiment WD, LAC. A rear party, which had stayed behind to clean up the camp at Headley, reached Seaford on the 20th.
41 Box 14CAR001 14th Armoured Regiment, folder 00l, Stoney Richardson Conversations with Dick Maltby, August 1989, KOCRA.
42 *Training Schedule Week Ending 14 Feb 42*, undated, app. 7, 14th Armoured Regiment WD (February 1942), LAC.
43 12 February 1942, 14th Armoured Regiment WD, LAC. The sense that a German invasion of the British Isles was imminent extended beyond civilians. The Calgary Regiment's considered opinion was that "the likelihood of an invasion [is] very close." 1 March 1942, 14th Armoured Regiment WD, LAC.
44 14 March 1942, 14th Armoured Regiment WD, LAC. *Bn Trg Programme Week Ending 14 Mar 42*, 4 March 1942, app. 3, 14th Armoured Regiment WD (March 1942), LAC.
45 18 March 1942, 1st Armoured Brigade WD, LAC. *Progress Report to Canada*, 15 Mar 1942, app., 1st Armoured Brigade WD (March 1942), LAC.
46 6 April and 8 May 1942, 1st Armoured Brigade WD, LAC.
47 1, 2, 13 and 14 April 1942, 14th Armoured Regiment WD, LAC.
48 *Beaver III and IV Exercise Instruction No. 1*, 15 April 1942 (Lt.-Col. J. G. Andrews); *Notes on Beaver III*, 20 April 1942 (Lt.-Col. J. G. Andrews); and notes on Beaver III, 22 April 1942 (Lt.-Col. J. G. Andrews), app. 3, 14th Armoured Regiment WD, (April 1942), LAC.
49 23 April 1942, 14th Armoured Regiment WD, LAC. 19-23 April 1942, 14th Armoured Regiment WD, LAC.
50 24 and 25 April, 14th Armoured Regiment WD, LAC.
51 *General Notes on Beaver III—Lessons Learned within the Bn*, 27 April 1942 (Lt.-Col. J. G. Andrews, app. 3, 14th Armoured Regiment WD (April 1942), LAC.
52 *1st Cdn Army Tank Bde—Remarks of Chief Umpire (Exercise Beaver III)*, undated, app., 1st Armoured Brigade WD (April 1942), LAC.
53 *General Notes on 1 Cdn Corps Exercise Beaver III 19–24 Apr 1942*, app., 1st Armoured Brigade WD (May 1942), LAC. During the exercise all 139 Churchills in the brigade had driven over 200 kms, with 119 of them reported "off the road" at one time or other due to major or minor breakdowns. Henry, "The Tanks of Dieppe," n. 26, 53.
54 10-13 May 1942, 14th Armoured Regiment WD, LAC.
55 16 May 1942, 14th Armoured Regiment WD, LAC.
56 18 May 1942, 14th Armoured Regiment WD, LAC.
57 18 May 1942, box 14CAR, L. G. Alexander diaries, no. 1, 1 March 1941–5 February 1943, KOCRA.
58 English, *Monty and the Canadian Army*, 72–73. Henry, "Calgary Tanks at Dieppe," 61.
59 25 May 1942, 14th Armoured Regiment WD, LAC. 22-25 May 1942, 14th Armoured Regiment WD, LAC. 20 and 21 May 1942, 14th Armoured Regiment WD, LAC. As the training proceeded, the battalion had been receiving the latest version of the Churchill, armed with a 6-pounder (57-mm) gun and with various other improvements.
60 6 June 1942, 14th Armoured Regiment WD, LAC. 1–6 June 1942, 14th Armoured Regiment WD, LAC.

61 12 June 1942, 14th Armoured Regiment WD, LAC. 10, 11 and 15 June 1942, 14th Armoured Regiment WD, LAC.
62 Stacey, *Six Years of War*, 334.
63 13 June 1942, box 14CAR 14th Armoured Regiment, L. G. Alexander diaries, no. 1, 1 Mar 1941–5 Feb 1943, KOCRA.
64 Johnston, *Disaster of Dieppe*, 38.
65 21–24 June 1942, 14th Armoured Regiment WD, LAC. 25 and 26 June 1942, 14th Armoured Regiment WD, LAC.
66 Stacey, *Six Years of War*, 339.
67 3–6 July 1942, 14th Armoured Regiment WD, LAC.
68 7–8 July 1942, 14th Armoured Regiment WD, LAC; Johnston, *Disaster at Dieppe*, 40; and 9 and 14 July 1942, box 14CAR 14th Armoured Regiment, L. G. Alexander diaries, no. 1, 1 Mar 1941–5 Feb 1943, KOCRA.
69 14 and 18 July 1942, 14th Armoured Regiment WD, LAC.
70 Stacey, *Six Years of War*, 340. See also 335 and 340–45.
71 30 July 1942 and 1 and 2 and 5–12 August 1942, 14th Armoured Regiment WD, LAC.
72 *Report by Lieut JHB MacDonald re Operation against Dieppe—19 August 1942*, undated, app. 12, 1st Armoured Brigade WD (August 1942), LAC.
73 Box 14CAR001 14th Armoured Regiment, folder 001, Fred Bagley, *Priceless Sacrifice*, KOCRA. Initially produced as a training film promoting the "careless talk costs lives" message, *Next of Kin* was released commercially in Britain in 1942. In the film, a raid on a French port suffers heavy losses as a direct result of security lapses by some of the soldiers involved in the operation and the civilians with whom they mingle. All British and Commonwealth soldiers were shown the movie.
74 Pt. 1 Orders, no. 170, 17 Aug 1942, app. 1, 14th Armoured Regiment WD (August 1942), LAC and *Report by Lieut JHB MacDonald re Operation against Dieppe—19 August 1942*, undated, app. 12, 1st Armoured Brigade WD (August 1942), LAC. Later in his report, MacDonald recounted that while travelling in mid-July, he and another officer had stopped at a pub for supper, only to be regaled with most of the outline of Rutter by the owner who insisted he had received the information from a Canadian general. The fact remains, however, that German intelligence was much less well informed than the aforesaid publican, and certainly possessed nothing that compromised Jubilee.
75 16–18 August 1942, 14th Armoured Regiment WD, LAC and *Report by Lieut JHB MacDonald re Operation against Dieppe—19 August 1942*, undated, app. 12, 1st Armoured Brigade WD (August 1942), LAC. TLCs were a British design dating from 1940 and were made by both British and Americans shipyards in numerous variants. The American version was designated Landing Craft, Tank or LCT. The type used at Dieppe had a crew of twelve, a top speed of less than 10 knots, and could carry three heavy tanks. They were not armoured for contested landings.
76 Box 14CAR001 14th Armoured Regiment, folder 001, Fred Bagley, *Priceless Sacrifice*, KOCRA.
77 18 August 1942, 14th Armoured Regiment WD, LAC.
78 Box 14CAR001 14th Armoured Regiment, folder 001, Fred Bagley, *Priceless Sacrifice*, KOCRA.

79   Box 14CAR001 14th Armoured Regiment, folder 011, *Onward II*, 50/14 Veterans' Association (June 1991, Rev. Waldo Smith, *Our Padre's Story*, KOCRA.

80   Stacey, *Six Years of War*, 346–47. Controversies about the Dieppe raid abound in popular literature, but scholars have been more circumscribed. This account draws exclusively on the latter, and the documentary record, to flesh out the role and achievements of the Calgary Regiment. For further accounts, see Villa, *Unauthorized Action* and Whitaker and Whitaker, *Dieppe*.

81   Stacey, *Six Years of War*, 346–48 and 352.

82   Stacey, *Six Years of War*, 352–59 and *Report No. 9, Operation "Jubilee," Pt. III: Some Special Aspects*, 10 February 1944, box 6918, RG 24, LAC.

83   There are several well-researched and readable accounts of Canada's worst day in the war, starting with Stacey's *Six Years of War*, chapters 11 and 12 and Whitaker and Whitaker, *Dieppe*. A popular account is Zuehlke, *Tragedy at Dieppe*.

84   Stacey, *Six Years of War*, 375. See also 363–74 and 389.

85   Stacey, *Six Years of War*, 359, 363–86 and 388–89.

86   Only about half of the combat engineers scheduled to land with the tanks got ashore, and they suffered nearly 90 percent casualties. Whitaker and Whitaker, *Dieppe*, 252.

87   *Observations on the Dieppe Raid—19 Aug 42 by Major CB Van Straubenzee 12th Cdn Army Tank Regt, 25 Aug 1942*, app. 12, 1st Armoured Brigade WD (August 1942), LAC and Stacey, *Six Years of War*, 390–93. Ammunition resupply was of course impossible.

88   Page eventually was able to provide the most detailed report on the tanks' operations, assembled from his own experiences and thorough interviews of fellow officer prisoners, and smuggled home when he was repatriated in October 1943. Report no. 108, *Operation "Jubilee": The Raid on Dieppe, Sec 2: The Attack on the Main Beaches*, amendment 1, 26 November 1949, box 6918, RG 24, LAC.

89   Johnston, *Disaster of Dieppe*, 51. Johnston, *Disaster of Dieppe*, 46–59.

90   The main armament being modest, the shells were small, which meant a large number could be stowed—150 for the 2-pounders and 84 for the 6-pounders, plus 58 rounds for the 3-inch howitzers in the Mk Is. The Besa machine guns carried between 5,000 and 7,000 rounds in belts, depending on the Mark. Henry, "Tanks of Dieppe," app. 4, 167.

91   Box 14CAR—Personnel S-U (14th Armoured Regiment), folder Scott, Denis, POW memoir, KOCRA.

92   Report no. 108, *Operation "Jubilee": The Raid on Dieppe, Section 2: The Attack on the Main Beaches*, 10 February 1944, box 6918, RG24, LAC.

93   Box 14CAR-001 (14th Armoured Regiment), folder 001, Fred Bagley, *Priceless Sacrifice*, KOCRA. Report no. 108, *Operation "Jubilee": The Raid on Dieppe, Section 2: The Attack on the Main Beaches*, 10 February 1944, box 6918, RG24, LAC; box 14CAR-002 (14th Armoured Regiment), folder Alexander, A. (Dieppe diary), KOCRA; and Whitaker and Whitaker, *Dieppe*, 262.

94   19 August 1942, box 14CAR L. G. Alexander Diaries (14th Armoured Regiment), no. 1, 1 March 1941–5 February 1943, KOCRA; box 14CAR-002 (14th Armoured Regiment), folder Alexander, Laurence G. (Doc), Dieppe Diary, KOCRA; box 14CAR006—Personnel A (14th Armoured Regiment), folder Andrews, J., KOCRA; and box 14CAR-012 (14th Armoured Regiment), folder 001, Maj. C. P. Stacey, *Memorandum of Interviews with Major CE Page and Other Personnel Repatriated from Germany, 29 Oct 1943*, KOCRA. Lt.-Col. Andrews' name is inscribed on the Brookfield Memorial (for the

missing) near Woking, England. The eyewitness descriptions of what happened to TLC 8 during the second landing attempt are confused and even contradictory, reflecting the chaos of the moment, but they do convey the general outline of what happened.

95 19 August 1942, box 14CAR L. G. Alexander Diaries (14th Armoured Regiment), no. 1, 1 March 1941–5 February 1943, KOCRA.

96 *Calgary Herald*, 5 September 1942, 1.

97 16–18 August 1942, 14th Armoured Regiment WD, LAC and Lt. J. H. B. MacDonald, *Operation against Dieppe, August 1942* (undated) and Maj. C. B. Van Straubenzee (12th Armoured Regiment), *Observations on the Dieppe Raid*, 25 August 1942, app. 12, 1st Armoured Brigade WD (August 1942), LAC.

98 Box 14CAR-001 (14th Armoured Regiment), folder 011, *Onward II*, 50/14 Veterans Association (June 1991), (Rev.) Waldo Smith, *Our Padre's Story*, KOCRA.

99 16–18 August 1942, 14th Armoured Regiment WD, LAC and Lt. J. H. B. MacDonald, *Operation against Dieppe, August 1942* (undated), app. 12, 1st Armoured Brigade WD (August 1942), LAC. The barges were the lightly armoured (and much smaller) infantry landing craft. These were used during the later withdrawal attempts. They also suffered grievous losses.

100 19 August 1942, box 14CAR L. G. Alexander Diaries (14th Armoured Regiment), no. 1, 1 March 1941–5 February 1943, KOCRA and box 14CAR-002 (14th Armoured Regiment), folder Alexander, Laurence G. (Doc), Dieppe diary, KOCRA.

101 Box 14CAR-001 (14th Armoured Regiment), folder 001 Fred Bagley, *Priceless Sacrifice*, KOCRA.

102 Box 14CAR-001 (14th Armoured Regiment), folder 001 Fred Bagley, *Priceless Sacrifice*, KOCRA.

103 19 August 1942, box 14CAR—Personnel, O-P (14th Armoured Regiment), folder Pinder, Tom (POW diary 1942–43), KOCRA.

104 Box 14CAR-001 (14th Armoured Regiment), folder 001 Fred Bagley, *Priceless Sacrifice*, KOCRA.

105 Box 14CAR—Personnel S-U (14th Armoured Regiment), folder Scott, Denis (POW memoir), KOCRA.

106 Johnston, *Disaster of Dieppe*, 60–66.

107 That said, other tank crewmen were offered cigarettes by their captors and generally set at ease as to what at least their immediate fate would be. Box 14CAR—Personnel S-U (14th Armoured Regiment), folder Scott, Denis (POW memoir), KOCRA.

108 Box 14CAR—Personnel A (14th Armoured Regiment), folder Anderson, A. F., *A Story or Two as Remembered about Dieppe and Stalag VIII-B, 1942–1945*, KOCRA; box 14CAR-001 (14th Armoured Regiment), folder 001 Fred Bagley, *Priceless Sacrifice*, KOCRA; and box CAR14—Personnel C (14th Armoured Regiment), folder Craigie, Don, Fred Bagley, *Don Craigie and the Ordeal of Dieppe*, KOCRA.

109 19 August 1942, box 14CAR—Personnel Q-R (14th Armoured Regiment), folder Richardson, V, POW diary, KOCRA.

110 19 August 1942, box 14CAR—Personnel Q-R (14th Armoured Regiment), folder Richardson, V, POW diary, KOCRA.

111 Most of the partly dressed and bootless Canadian troops seen in German photographs had been preparing to swim out to evacuation boats.

112 19 August 1942, box 14CAR—Personnel Q-R (14th Armoured Regiment), folder Richardson, V, POW diary, KOCRA.
113 14CAR—Personnel G-H (14th Armoured Regiment), folder Ganshirt, J., War Claims Commission—Statement Concerning Claim for Maltreatment, KOCRA.
114 Box 14CAR—Personnel C (14th Armoured Regiment), folder Craigie, Don, Fred Bagley, *Don Craigie and the Ordeal of Dieppe*, KOCRA and box 14CAR—Personnel S-U (14th Armoured Regiment), folder Scott, Denis (POW memoir), KOCRA. Surviving records are confusing—it is not even clear the Calgary prisoners always moved together on the way to their POW camp. Some accounts say they stayed at the brickyard for two days, others for four or one, and so on.
115 The infamous German black bread prisoners received comprised rye and potato flour, a little wheat flour, wood fibre and meat. Apart from being rock hard, it was "sour, awful, but good enough when you were hungry." 19 August 1942, box 14CAR—Personnel Q-R (14th Armoured Regiment), folder Richardson, V., POW diary, KOCRA.
116 20 August 1942, box 14CAR—Personnel, O-P (14th Armoured Regiment), folder Pinder, Tom (POW diary 1942–3), KOCRA. 20 August 1942, box 14CAR—Personnel Q-R (14th Armoured Regiment), folder Richardson, V., POW diary, KOCRA.
117 21 August 1942, box 14CAR—Personnel Q-R (14th Armoured Regiment), folder Richardson, V., POW diary, KOCRA.
118 Box 14CAR-001 (14th Armoured Regiment), folder 011, *Onward II*, 50/14 Veterans Association (June 1991), Al Wagstaff, *Dieppe's Prisoners of War*, KOCRA. All memoirs and other accounts refer to Verneulles but the town may well have been Verneuil-sur-Seine.
119 Johnston, *Disaster of Dieppe*, 69–78. Box 14CAR—Personnel C (14th Armoured Regiment), folder Craigie, Don, Fred Bagley, *Don Craigie and the Ordeal of Dieppe*, KOCRA; and box 14CAR—Personnel S-U (14th Armoured Regiment), folder Scott, Denis (POW memoir), KOCRA. 14CAR—Personnel G-H (14th Armoured Regiment), folder Ganshirt, J., War Claims Commission—Statement Concerning Claim for Maltreatment, KOCRA and box 14CAR—Personnel S-U (14th Armoured Regiment), folder Scott, Denis (POW memoir), KOCRA.
120 Pt. 1 orders no. 176, 22 August 1942, app. 1, 14th Armoured Regiment WD (August 1942), LAC. 19–22 August 1942, 14th Armoured Regiment WD, LAC. A further 92 reached Seaford two days later.
121 Box 14CAR-001 (14th Armoured Regiment), folder 011, *Onward II*, 50/14 Veterans Association (June 1991), Rev. Waldo Smith, *Our Padre's Story*, KOCRA.
122 23 August 1942, 14th Armoured Regiment WD, LAC.
123 Box 14CAR001 (14th Armoured Regiment), folder 011, *Onward II*, 50/14 Veterans Association (June 1991), Rev. Waldo Smith, *Our Padre's Story*, KOCRA.
124 20 August 1942, 19 August 1942, box 14CAR L. G. Alexander Diaries (14th Armoured Regiment), no. 1, 1 March 1941–5 February 1943, KOCRA.
125 Box 14CAR-002 (14th Armoured Regiment), folder Alexander, A. (Dieppe diary), KOCRA.
126 Stacey, *Six Years of War*, 395. Report no. 83, *Preliminary Report on Operation "Jubilee,"* 19 September 1942, box 6918, RG 24, LAC.
127 Schmidlin to Crerar, 9 September 1942, app. 8, 1st Armoured Brigade WD (September 1942), LAC. Report no. 9, *Operation "Jubilee," Part III: Some special aspects*, 10 Feb

1944, box 6918, RG 24, LAC and Report no. 83, *Preliminary Report on "Jubilee,"* 19 September 1942, box 6918, RG 24, LAC and Vance, *Maple Leaf Empire*, 189–90.

128 Stacey, *Six Years of War*, 392. The preliminary appraisal by German intelligence officers had dismissed the fighting ability of the Canadian troops, noting especially a lack of initiative and that they had "surrendered in swarms." *Intelligence report on British landing at Dieppe* [trans.], 22 Aug 1942, box 6918, RG 24, LAC. But this judgment was overruled by senior officers of the 302nd Division who rightly noted that "the large number of casualties and wounded PW shows that the enemy put up a valiant fight [and] that in addition to the above whole units were captured is explained by the hopelessness of further resistance." 14CAR-012 (14th Armoured Regiment), folder 001, *Report of the Battle Experiences of the 302 German Inf Div* [trans.], KOCRA.

129 Stacey, *Six Years of War*, 398. Stacey, *Six Years of War*, 391.

130 *Intelligence Report on British landing at Dieppe* [trans.], 22 August 1944, box 6918, RG 24, LAC. Stacey, *Six Years of War*, 393.

131 Stacey, *Six Years of War*, 399–404.

132 Maj. C. B. Van Straubenzee (12th Armoured Regiment), *Observations on the Dieppe Raid*, 25 August 1942, app. 12, 1st Armoured Brigade WD (August 1942), LAC.

133 The Germans' examination concluded sixteen Churchills reached the promenade. Report no. 116, *Operation "Jubilee," Additional information from German sources*, 10 May 1944, box 6918, RG 24, LAC.

134 14CAR012 (14th Armoured Regiment), folder 001, Maj. C. P. Stacey, *Memorandum of Interviews with Major C. E. Page and Other Personnel Repatriated from Germany*, 29 Oct 1943, KOCRA.

135 14CAR012 (14th Armoured Regiment), folder 001, *Report of the Battle Experiences of the 302 German Inf Div* [trans.], KOCRA and Stacey, *Six Years of War*, 380.

136 Box 14CAR001 (14th Armoured Regiment), folder 011, *Onward II*, 50/14 Veterans Assoc. (June 1991), Hugh Henry, *The 14th Canadian Army Tank Regiment at Dieppe*, 68–69, KOCRA. Apart from Lt.-Col. Andrews, those killed included Trps. R. Cornelssen, P. Friesen, Thomas Gorman, E. C. Huscroft, V. F. Olliffe, Charles L. Provis, William D. P. Sawers, William Stewart, and M. F. Zima; L/Cpl. Dwight E. Welch; Sqdn. Sgt.-Maj. Alexander Tough; and Capt. D. G. Purdy. List of killed 14th Armoured Regiment, KOCRA.

137 Box 14CAR001 (14th Armoured Regiment), folder 011, *Onward II*, 50/14 Veterans Association (June 1991), Hugh Henry, *The 14th Canadian Army Tank Regiment at Dieppe*, 68–69; 19 August 1942, 14th Armoured Regiment WD, LAC; Stacey, *Six Years of War*, 380 and 389; and 19 August 1942, 14th Armoured Regiment WD, LAC.

138 Stacey, *Six Years of War*, 393.

139 Stacey, *Six Years of War*, 396.

140 *Calgary Herald*, 19 August 1942, 1.

141 *Calgary Herald*, 20 August 1942, 1 and 2.

142 *Calgary Herald*, 21 August 1942, 2.

143 *Calgary Herald*, 24 August 1942, 2.

144 Soldiers knew anything frank in a cable meant the cable would not be sent, so they self-censored, mentioning just their own fate, and often that of a few other comrades which could be passed on to their loved ones.

145 *Calgary Herald*, 24 August 1942, 1.
146 Balzer, *Information Front*, 112. The entire chapter 4 is pertinent and is appropriately entitled "'Sugaring the Pill': Selling Dieppe to Canadians."
147 *Calgary Herald*, 4 September 1942, 1 and 3. *Calgary Herald*, 5 September 1942, 1.
148 *Calgary Herald*, 19 September 1942, 1.
149 Box 14CAR001 (14th Armoured Regiment), folder 001 Fred Bagley, *Priceless Sacrifice*, KOCRA.
150 *Calgary Herald*, 18 and 21 December 1942, 1.
151 Capt. (Hon.) W. E. L. Smith to Mrs. Olliffe, 7 November 1942, box 26730, folder Victor Olliffe, RG 24, LAC.
152 Mr. F. and Mrs. H. L. Olliffe to Office of Records, Adj. Gen. Office, 13 March 1943, box 26730, folder Victor Olliffe, RG 24, LAC.
153 Telegram to Mrs. Olliffe, 15 April 1943, box 26730, folder Victor Olliffe, RG 24, LAC.
154 Office of Records, Adj. Gen. Office to Mrs. Olliffe, 11 Jun 1943, box 26730, folder Victor Olliffe, RG 24, LAC.
155 Maj. Hadley to British Red Cross (via Swiss Legation, Berlin), 4 September 1942, box 27307, folder Dwight Welch, RG 24, LAC.
156 Welch was reinterred in Holland in the Holten Commonwealth War Graves Cemetery in 1948. In a touching action, Canadian military authorities were approached later that year by a Dutch resident of Holten who informed them that he and his wife had adopted Welch's grave and would take care of it. He had enclosed a letter to the parents in the hope it would be sent on to them (which it was) "so that they might know that their son is not forgotten in a ... country far away, but that his life [has] a place in our hearts too." I. de Jong-Munsterman to Director of Records, 19 November 1948, box 27307, folder Dwight Welch, RG 24, LAC.
157 Lt. E. Bennett to family, undated, box 25643, folder Rhinard (Bobby) Cornelssen, RG 24, LAC.
158 Tpr. A. Johnson to Mrs. W. Johnson, 20 September 1942, box 25643, folder Rhinard (Bobby) Cornelssen, RG 24, LAC.
159 M. McIntyre to Miss J. Nabb, 28 September 1942, box 25643, folder Rhinard (Bobby) Cornelssen, RG 24, LAC. All of these excerpts were gleaned from Canadian Army censorship reports of prisoner of war mail.

NOTES TO CHAPTER 6

1 24 August 1942, 14th Armoured Regiment WD and *Nominal Roll of Officers on Strength, 14 and 21 August 1942*, 24 August 1942, app. 3, 14th Armoured Regiment WD (August 1942), LAC.
2 1–10 September 1942, 14th Armoured Regiment WD, LAC.
3 11 September and 9 November 1942, 14th Armoured Regiment WD, LAC.
4 Progress Report to Canada, 8, 16 and 23 October 1942, app. 5, 1st Armoured Brigade WD (October 1942), LAC.
5 Schmidlin to Crerar, 9 September 1942, app. 8, 1st Armoured Brigade WD (September 1942), LAC.

6   When Dr. Alexander received his MC from King George VI at a Buckingham Palace awards ceremony on 27 October, the King's comment was a terse "it was a dirty show, good work, congratulations." 27 October 1942, box 14CAR—Personnel (14th Armoured Regiment), folder L. G. Alexander diaries, no. 1, 1 March 1941–5 February 1943, KOCRA.

7   12 October 1942, 14th Armoured Regiment WD, LAC.

8   21, 22 and 30 October 1942, 14th Armoured Regiment WD, LAC.

9   1 November 1942, 14th Armoured Regiment WD, LAC. This had been achieved by stripping twenty-six Churchills from the British 36th Tank Brigade. *Progress Report to Canada*, 23 Oct 1942, app. 5, 1st Armoured Brigade WD (October 1942), LAC.

10   Pt. 1 orders, no. 909, 1 October 1942, app., 14th Armoured Regiment WD (October 1942), LAC.

11   27 and 28 November 1942, 14th Armoured Regiment WD, LAC.

12   Pt. 1 orders, no. 281, 24 December 1942, app., 14th Armoured Regiment WD (December 1942), LAC.

13   Pt. 1 orders, no. 273, 15 December 1942, app., 14th Armoured Regiment WD (December 1942), LAC. Pt. 1 orders, no. 278, 19 December 1942, app., 14th Armoured Regiment WD (December 1942), LAC. In January 1943 First Canadian Army discontinued pay stoppages and the publication of names in an effort to get soldiers suffering from venereal disease to seek prompt treatment. Pt. 1 orders, no. 8, 12 January 1943, app., 14th Armoured Regiment WD (January 1943), LAC.

14   Report to 1 Canadian Corps, 4 January 1943, app. 10, 1st Armoured Brigade WD (January 1943), LAC.

15   2, 5, 9 and 16 December 1942 and 20 January and 5 February 1943, 14th Armoured Regiment WD, LAC.

16   24 December 1942, 14th Armoured Regiment WD, LAC and G. Thring letter, 7 January 1999, box Capt. George Thring Papers, folder 50/14 Veterans Association, KOCRA. Given they had all but disappeared in England, chocolate bars were wonderful treats for the children.

17   25 and 26 December 1942, 14th Armoured Regiment WD, LAC.

18   28 December 1942, 14th Armoured Regiment WD, LAC. Troopers' pay was raised from $1.30 a day to $1.50, with the dependents monthly deduction rising from $20.00 to $23.00. Beyond this, additional dependents benefits were paid by the Government of Canada. Pt. 1 orders, no. 282, 26 December 1942, app., 14th Armoured Regiment WD (December 1942), LAC.

19   4–11, 18 and 22 January 1943, 14th Armoured Regiment WD, LAC.

20   25 February 1943, 14th Armoured Regiment WD, LAC.

21   Stacey, *Six Years of War*, 249–51 and 22 February 1943, 14th Armoured Regiment WD, LAC.

22   Granatstein, *Canada's Army*, 212–16 and 231.

23   1–12 March 1943, 14th Armoured Regiment WD, LAC. Their tanks consumed nearly 12,000 gallons of gasoline, and the wheeled vehicles another 40,000, an illustration of the demanding logistics of armoured warfare. 17 March 1943, 14th Armoured Regiment WD, LAC.

24   13 and 15 March 1943, 14th Armoured Regiment WD, LAC.

25   Comments—"Exercise Spartan," 15 March 1943, app., 14th Armoured Regiment WD, LAC.
26   18 March 1943, 14th Armoured Regiment WD, LAC. The Ram grew out of the need to acquire a cruiser tank for the Canadian Armoured Corps at a time when British tanks were in short supply. To speed production, the Ram was based on the American M3 General Lee design. While it proved adequate, the vast production of the superior M4 Sherman meant they were only used for training, where similarity to the Sherman—the latter, too, was based on the M3—was a distinct advantage. Eventually most were converted to Kangaroo armoured personnel carriers or Sexton self-propelled howitzers. http://tanks-encylopedia.com/ww2/canada/Ram-Cruiser-Tank/php
27   20 March 1943, box 14CAR—L. G. Alexander Diaries (14th Armoured Regiment), no. 2, 5 February 1943–20 May 1944, KOCRA. Box 14CAR001, folder 001, Stoney Richardson conversations with Dick Maltby, August 1989, KOCRA.
28   The commanding officer of the 15th (Scottish) Division, whose army tank brigade was the recipient of the Churchills, was so impressed by their running order that he wrote a fulsome letter of thanks to Gen. Crerar. Pt. 1 orders, no. 91, 19 April 1943 (Gen. Bullen-Smith to Crerar, 13 April 1943), app., 14th Armoured Regiment WD (April 1943), LAC. Brig. Wyman was pleased as punch. Wyman to Neroutsos, 17 April 1943, app., 14th Armoured Regiment WD (April 1943), LAC.
29   31 March and various entries 1–10 April 1943, 14th Armoured Regiment WD and *Range Practices—AFV Range*, 24 Mar 1943, app. 11, 14th Armoured Regiment WD (March 1943), LAC.
30   Henry, "Tanks of Dieppe," 128 and box 14CAR001, folder 001, Stoney Richardson conversations with Dick Maltby, August 1989, KOCRA. In the British regimental system which the Canadian Army adopted, this was always a potential problem. An outsider could be resented, at least initially, and his appointment was usually a sign that higher command thought the regiment needed shaking up, that none of the other officers were deemed sufficiently capable, or that factions ensured no internal appointment was broadly acceptable.
31   27 and 30 April 1943, 14th Armoured Regiment WD, LAC.
32   7 May 1943, box 14CAR L. G. Alexander Diaries (14th Armoured Regiment), no. 2, 15 February 1943–20 May 1944, KOCRA.
33   3 and 4 May 1943, 14th Armoured Regiment WD, LAC.
34   Tank Encyclopedia, http://tanks-encyclopedia.com/ww2/US/M4-Sherman.php and *Canadiansoldiers*, http://Canadiansoldiers.com/vehicles/tanks/Shermantanks/htm and Charles Prieur, *War Chronicles 1939–1945 Three Rivers Regiment (Tank)*, unpublished manuscript, http://www.12rbc.ca/upload/pdf/news/war-chronicles-anglais-28-02-6.pdf.
35   Box 14CAR001, folder 001, Stoney Richardson conversations with Dick Maltby, August 1989, KOCRA. On crews' initial view, box 14CAR—Personnel, C (14th Armoured Regiment), folder Cawsey, C., memoirs, KOCRA.
36   Nicholson, *Canadians in Italy, 1943–1945*, 3–8 and 20–26. Capturing the island would reopen the Mediterranean to Allied shipping while at the same time threaten the mainland of Italy with attack, undermine Italian morale, and potentially force the Germans to divert military resources to Italy's defence.
37   8 May 1943, 1st Armoured Brigade WD, LAC.

38   Various entries 4–10 May 1943, 14th Armoured Regiment WD, LAC and box 14CAR-001, folder 001, Stoney Richardson conversations with Dick Maltby, August 1989, KOCRA.
39   Various entries 11–22 May 1943, 14th Armoured Regiment WD, LAC and *Syllabus of Trg AFV Range Kirkcudbright*, 11 May 1943, app., 14th Armoured Regiment WD (May 1943), LAC.
40   The sealing was done with a plastic material. The goal was to have the tanks capable of wading in as much as 2 m of water.
41   26 May 1943, 14th Armoured Regiment WD, LAC.
42   Pt. 1 orders, no. 117, 22 May 1943, app., 14th Armoured Regiment WD (May 1943), LAC. When it came to lacking amenities for off duty hours, "Doc" Alexander dismissed Langholm as "even worse than [the] Salisbury Plain. Believe it or not." 18 June 1943, box 14CAR L. G. Alexander Diaries (14th Armoured Regiment), no. 2, 15 February 1943–20 May 1944, KOCRA.
43   Pt. 1 orders, no. 111, 14 May 1943, app., 14th Armoured Regiment WD (May 1943), LAC. Pt. 1 orders, no. 112, 15 May 1943, app., 14th Armoured Regiment War Diary (May 1943), LAC. The black beret identified soldiers as being armour and was a source of pride.
44   The assaulting forces, including the 12th Army Tank Battalion, sailed in a separate convoy.
45   1 July 1943, 14th Armoured Regiment WD, LAC. 17, 20 and 25 June 1943, 14th Armoured Regiment WD, LAC and *Memorandum On Trg On Board Ship*, 2 June 1943, app. 6, 1st Armoured Brigade WD (June 1943), LAC. The Landing Ship, Tank was about ten times the displacement of the LCT (Landing Craft, Tank), and could carry up to twenty-two 30-ton tanks. LSTs were ocean-going vessels capable of making up to 12 knots. Despite the irreverent sobriquet Large Slow Target bestowed by their crews, it was a robust ship that suffered relatively few losses considering the circumstances under which they were compelled to operate. "Landing Ship, Tank," http://www.en.wikipedia.org/wiki/Landing_Ship_Tank.
46   Various entries 1–7 and 8–9 July 1943, 14th Armoured Regiment WD, LAC.
47   *Memorandum on Trg on Board Ship*, 2 Jun 1943, app. 7, 1st Armoured Brigade WD (June 1943), LAC.
48   28 June and 1 and 5 July 1943, box 14CAR L. G. Alexander Diaries (14th Armoured Regiment), no. 2, 15 February 1943–20 May 1944, KOCRA.
49   10, 12 and 13 July 1943, 14th Armoured Regiment WD, LAC.
50   13 July 1943, 14th Armoured Regiment WD, LAC.
51   Nicholson, *Canadians in Italy*, 19–20.
52   15 and 16 July 1943, 14th Armoured Regiment WD, LAC.
53   All three men had to be evacuated to a military hospital in Algeria.
54   17–22 July 1943, 14th Armoured Regiment WD, LAC and 21 July 1943, box 14CAR L. G. Alexander Diaries (14th Armoured Regiment), no. 2, 15 February 1943–20 May 1944, KOCRA.
55   Box 14CAR002 Personnel, A (14th Armoured Regiment), folder Alexander, Laurence, Sicilian and Italian Campaign Notes, 14 July 1943, KOCRA. Sicily was the poorest part of Italy, and southern Italy one of the poorest areas of Europe.

56 23–25 July 1943, 14th Armoured Regiment WD, LAC.
57 Box 14CAR—Personnel C (14th Armoured Regiment), folder Cawsey, C., memoirs, KOCRA.
58 28 July 1943, 14th Armoured Regiment WD, LAC. 1 Canadian Army Tank Brigade Operational order no. 4, 27 July 1943, app. 5, 14th Armoured Regiment WD (July 1943), LAC. The 11th would subsequently see action during the first ten days of August supporting British attacks. Nicholson, *Canadians in Italy*, 167–68.
59 9 and 10 August 1943, 14th Armoured Regiment WD, LAC.
60 Box 14CAR-001, folder 001, Stoney Richardson conversations with Dick Maltby, August 1989, KOCRA. Box 14CAR002 Personnel, A (14th Armoured Regiment), folder Alexander, Laurence, Sicilian and Italian Campaign Notes, 14 July 1943, KOCRA.
61 *Calgary Herald*, 3 August 1943, 7.
62 *Calgary Herald*, 11 September 1943, 1.
63 11 August 1943, 14th Armoured Regiment WD, LAC.
64 Nicholson, *Canadians in Italy*, 88–164.
65 For its part, Wyman's command suffered twenty-two killed and eighty-three wounded, of which the Three Rivers Regiment suffered the greater portion—twenty-one killed and sixty-two wounded. The Calgary Regiment's losses totalled only eight wounded. These were casualties in action and did not include accidents.
66 Nicholson, *Canadians in Italy*, 180–202.
67 17 and 18 August 1943, box 14CAR L. G. Alexander Diaries (14th Armoured Regiment), no. 2, 15 February 1943–20 May 1944, KOCRA and box 14CAR-002 Personnel, A (14th Armoured Regiment), folder Alexander, Laurence, Sicilian and Italian Campaign Notes, 15 and 19 August 1943, KOCRA. 12, 15 and 19 August 1943, 14th Armoured Regiment WD, LAC.
68 31 August 1943, 14th Armoured Regiment WD, LAC.
69 1 and 2 September 1943, 14th Armoured Regiment WD, LAC.
70 3 and 4 September 1943, 14th Armoured Regiment WD, LAC, *1 Cdn Div Intelligence Summary*, no. 11, 4 September 1943, app., 14th Armoured Regiment WD (September 1943), LAC and Nicholson, *Canadians in Italy*, 202–09.
71 5 September 1943, box 14CAR L. G. Alexander Diaries (14th Armoured Regiment), no. 3, 21 May 1943–9 March 1945, KOCRA.
72 5 September 1943, 14th Armoured Regiment WD, LAC.
73 6–7 September 1943, box 14CAR L. G. Alexander Diaries (14th Armoured Regiment), no. 3, 21 May 1943–9 March 1945, KOCRA. On the second day a squadron of armoured cars from the Princess Louise Dragoon Guards linked up with Neroutsos' small battle group.
74 6 and 7 September 1943, 14th Armoured Regiment WD, LAC and Nicholson, *Canadians in Italy*, 209–10. On the difficulties the terrain of the Calabrian interior posed for vehicle movement, see *13 Corps Planning Intelligence Summary No. 3—Topographical Appreciation of Calabria*, 13 Aug 1943, app. 19, 1st Armoured Brigade WD (September 1943), LAC.
75 6–7, 8 and 10 September 1943, box 14CAR L. G. Alexander Diaries (14th Armoured Regiment), no. 3, 21 May 1943–9 March 1945, KOCRA and box 14CAR-002 Personnel, A (14th Armoured Regiment), folder Alexander, Laurence, Sicilian and Italian

Campaign Notes, 6 and 9 September 1943, KOCRA. 8 September 1943, 1st Armoured Brigade WD, LAC.

76 10 September 1943, box 14CAR L. G. Alexander Diaries (14th Armoured Regiment), no. 3, 21 May 1943–9 March 1945, KOCRA.

77 15 September 1943, box 14CAR L. G. Alexander Diaries (14th Armoured Regiment), no. 3, 21 May 1943–9 March 1945, KOCRA.

78 Box 14CAR002 Personnel, A (14th Armoured Regiment), folder Alexander, Laurence, Sicilian and Italian Campaign Notes, 9 September 1943, KOCRA.

79 Nicholson, *Canadians in Italy*, 220–21 and 12 September 1943, 14th Armoured Regiment WD, LAC.

80 17–22 and 2September 1943, 14th Armoured Regiment WD, LAC and Nicholson, *Canadians in Italy*, 224–28.

81 *Calgary Herald*, 29 September 1943, 1.

82 Various entries 23–30 September 1943, 14th Armoured Regiment WD, LAC.

83 Nicholson, *Canadians in Italy*, 235. 1 October 1943, 14th Armoured Regiment WD, LAC.

84 Box 14CAR016 Italy (14th Armoured Regiment), folder 007 Reimer, Peter, *The First Battle of Motta*, 1 October 1943 (memoir), KOCRA.

85 Nicholson, *Canadians in Italy*, 236. The fact that the Canadian Army was completely motorized gave it great mobility, in theory (and often in practice) a huge advantage against the only partially mechanized *Heer*. But it also tied lines of advance and logistical support to roads and their associated bridges and viaducts. This posed great difficulties in Italy where roads were generally of low quality, easily interdicted by demolitions, and invariably under observation by the enemy in the surrounding hills.

86 Box 14CAR002 Personnel, A (14th Armoured Regiment), folder Alexander, Laurence, Sicilian and Italian Campaign Notes, 1 October 1943, KOCRA.

87 Box 14CAR002 Personnel, A (14th Armoured Regiment), folder Alexander, Laurence, Sicilian and Italian Campaign Notes, 1 October 1943, KOCRA. 1 and 2 October 1943, 14th Armoured Regiment WD, LAC. The standard field artillery piece in the British (and Canadian) Army was the 25-pounder (88-mm) gun/howitzer which could provide plunging fire, something the Sherman's 75-mm cannon could not.

88 Box 14CAR002 Personnel, A (14th Armoured Regiment), folder Alexander, Laurence, Sicilian and Italian Campaign Notes, 1 October 1943, KOCRA. During the course of the battle, Calgary gunners managed to despatch two 88s at point-blank range as well as knock out a number of the (then) standard 50-mm and smaller 37-mm anti-tank pieces. The infamous Eighty-eight was an 88-mm anti-aircraft gun with the high muzzle velocity associated with such weapons and a longer killing range than any other German anti-tank gun. A Sherman's armour stood little chance against it and the crews knew it.

89 Box 14CAR016 Italy (14th Armoured Regiment), folder 007 Reimer, Peter, *The First Battle of Motta*, 1 October 1943 (memoir), KOCRA.

90 The thickest armour of any tank protected its front, the normal direction of advance, meaning any withdrawal entailed slowly backing up, a manoeuvre further complicated by the fact it had to be done all but blind if the commander's hatch was closed.

91 1 and 2 October 1943, 14th Armoured Regiment WD, LAC. Richardson was the commander of B Squadron, and Ritchie his second-in-command, but as could be the

case, in this instance the latter led the tanks into action while for the former remained at headquarters helping to direct the battle.

92   1 October 1943, box 14CAR L. G. Alexander Diaries (14th Armoured Regiment), no. 3, 21 May 1943–9 March 1945, KOCRA.

93   Nicholson, *Canadians in Italy*, 236 and 1 and 2 October 1943, 14th Armoured Regiment WD, LAC.

94   Box 14CAR-002 Personnel, A (14th Armoured Regiment), folder Alexander, Laurence, Sicilian and Italian Campaign Notes, 1 October 1943, KOCRA.

95   Box 14CAR-016 Italy (14th Armoured Regiment), folder 007 Reimer, Peter, *The First Battle of Motta*, 1 October 1943 (memoir), KOCRA and box 14CAR034 (14th Armoured Regiment)—Personnel C, folder Charbonneau, A., MC citation, KOCRA.

96   2 October 1943, 14th Armoured Regiment WD, LAC. 1 October 1943, 14th Armoured Regiment WD, LAC.

97   Within 72 hours of having suffered the losses, brigade forwarded six replacements from its reserve pool, a response German commanders could only dream of. 4 October 1943, 1st Armoured Brigade WD, LAC.

98   Box 14CAR—Personnel, S-U (14th Armoured Regiment), folder Underhill, F. D., MM citation, KOCRA.

99   2 October 1943, 14th Armoured Regiment WD, LAC. The killed in action included Cpl. Fennell, L/Cpl. Brothers, and Tprs. Baerr, Beisig, Cooper, French, Hourie, Lepp, Renaud and Rowley.

100 Quoted in Nicholson, *Canadians in Italy*, 237.

101 Box 14CAR George Thring Papers (14th Armoured Regiment), folder George Thring, *My Life's Story*, KOCRA.

102 3 October 1943, 14th Armoured Regiment WD, LAC.

103 Box 14CAR002 Personnel, A (14th Armoured Regiment), folder Alexander, Laurence, Sicilian and Italian Campaign Notes, 3 October 1943, KOCRA.

104 Box 14CAR002 Personnel, A (14th Armoured Regiment), folder Alexander, Laurence, Sicilian and Italian Campaign Notes, 4 October 1943, KOCRA.

105 4–6, 8 and 11–14 October 1943, 14th Armoured Regiment WD, LAC and various entries in October 1943 including 31 October, 1st Armoured Brigade WD, LAC. For the larger context of Canadian operations between Motta and Campobasso, see Nicholson, *Canadians in Italy*, 238–51.

106 15 and 17–19 October 1943, 14th Armoured Regiment WD, LAC. The Calgary Regiment had covered 650 kms in ten days without a single mechanical failure, a remarkable feat for tracked vehicles. 26 October 1943, 14th Armoured Regiment WD, LAC.

107 22 October and 2–4 November 1943, 14th Armoured Regiment WD, LAC; 1 November 1943, 1st Armoured Brigade WD, LAC; Pt. 2 orders, no. 11, 16 October 1943, 1st Armoured Brigade WD (October 1943), LAC; and Nicholson, *Canadians in Italy*, 250.

108 Pt. 2 orders, no. 9, 8 October 1943, 1st Armoured Brigade WD, LAC.

109 *Lessons Learned in Sicilian and Italian Campaign*, 1 November 1943, app. 6, 14th Armoured Regiment WD (October 1943), LAC.

110 *Lessons Learned in Sicilian and Italian Campaign (A Squadron)*, 30 October 1943, app. 6, 14th Armoured Regiment WD (October 1943), LAC. Maj E. A. C. "Ned" Amy had come over from the Ontarios after Trotter was killed.

Notes to Chapter 6   375

111 *Lessons Learned in Sicilian and Italian Campaign (B Squadron)*, 30 October 1943, app. 6, 14th Armoured Regiment WD (October 1943), LAC.

112 *CAC Training in England* (Lt.-Col. Neroutsos), 31 Oct 1943 and *CAC Training in England* (A, B and C Sqns.), 30 October 1943, app. 5, 14th Armoured Regiment WD (October 1943), LAC.

113 31 October and 1 November 1943, 1st Armoured Brigade WD, LAC.

114 Nicholson, *Canadians in Italy,* 264–74.

115 In August, 1st Army Tank Brigade had been officially renamed the 1st Armoured Brigade, and the 11th, 12th and 14th Army Tank Battalions the 11th, 12th and 14th Armoured Regiments, respectively. The full title of the 14th became 14th Armoured Regiment (The Calgary Regiment). The new nomenclature was only adopted in the field in November. Nicholson, *Canadians in Italy,* n. 276.

116 18–21 and 24 November 1943, 14th Armoured Regiment WD, LAC and 16 November 1943, 1st Armoured Brigade WD, LAC.

117 *Weekly Report to Commander 1 Cdn Corps*, 29 November 1943, 1st Armoured Brigade WD (November 1943), LAC. Experience in Sicily and on the mainland showed a major engine overhaul on Sherman Mk Vs had been required only after they'd covered 1,600–2,400 kms, depending on the terrain (soft ground and steep grades wreaked havoc on running gear, transmissions, and clutches) and the discipline the crews showed in completing daily maintenance. Engine overhauls were only possible, of course, if replacement engines were available. In fact, not a single Sherman in the 1st Armoured Brigade had suffered a major transmission failure, and engine failures at low mileages had been very rare. *Weekly Report to Commander 1 Cdn Corps*, 29 November 1943, 1st Armoured Brigade WD (November 1943), LAC. Richardson attributed the high tank reliability to the fact that "the maintenance and care of our equipment had been very, very well carried out." Box 14CAR001 (14th Armoured Regiment), folder 011, *Onward II*, 50/14 Veterans Association (June 1991), Lt.-Col. C. A. "Stoney" Richardson, *Stoney's Story*, 3, KOCRA. One of the inevitable consequences of the chronic parts shortages was the propensity of passing tank crews to strip damaged vehicles to build up a personal reserve of the most vital parts. But it reduced otherwise-repairable tanks "to nothing more than a bare hull," and such cannibalizing became a military offence. Brigade order no. 264, 28 December 1943, 1st Armoured Brigade WD (December 1943), LAC.

118 29–30 November and 2 and 5–6 December 1943, 14th Armoured Regiment WD, LAC.

119 Nicholson, *Canadians in Italy,* 288–301.

120 Box 14CAR001 (14th Armoured Regiment), folder 011, *Onward II*, 50/14 Veterans Association (June 1991), Maj. Ned Amy, *Love Those Shermans*, KOCRA.

121 The twenty-five-year-old Maj. Amy was carrying out his first operation with the Calgary Regiment, though he had considerable combat experience with the Ontarios. Donaldson, "Thunder in the Mountains," 66.

122 Both tanks were recovered by the Light Aid Detachment of the Royal Canadian Ordnance Corps. Numbering about two dozen men, one LAD was permanently attached to each armoured regiment and carried out recoveries of immobilized tanks, whether they were merely stuck, broken down mechanically, or damaged in action but deemed repairable. Their work was invaluable.

123 Even though the main road was obviously mined, it would have been suicide for engineers to attempt to clear it while under German fire. And the only way to stop the German fire was to take San Leonardo.

124 *Beyond the Sangro—An Account of the Operations of 1 CAB during December 1943, Report from OC 14 Cdn Armd Regt 9-20 Dec 1943*, Pt. III, Sec. 3, app. 40, 1st Armoured Brigade WD (February 1944), LAC.

125 Donaldson, "Thunder in the Mountains," 70–71 and Box 14CAR001 (14th Armoured Regiment), folder 011, *Onward II*, 50/14 Veterans Association (June 1991), Herb Knodel and Peter Reimer, *The Battle of San Leonardo—9 December 1943*, KOCRA.

126 Box 14CAR001 (14th Armoured Regiment), folder 011, *Onward II*, 50/14 Veterans Association (June 1991), Maj. Ned Amy, *Love Those Shermans*, KOCRA; Box 14CAR001 (14th Armoured Regiment), folder 011, *Onward II*, 50/14 Veterans Association (June 1991), Herb Knodel and Peter Reimer, *The Battle of San Leonardo—9 December 1943*, KOCRA; and Roy, *Seaforth Highlanders of Canada*, 247.

127 By the time Lt. Charbonneau's tank was pulled back later in the day, they had only five of thirty-five 500-round machine gun belts they'd set out with, a single HE round, and five AP rounds. "It had been a busy day," as Herb Knodel later recalled. Box 14CAR001 (14th Armoured Regiment), folder 011, *Onward II*, 50/14 Veterans Association (June 1991), Herb Knodel and Peter Reimer, *The Battle of San Leonardo—9 December 1943*, KOCRA.

128 Donaldson, "Thunder in the Mountains," 74.

129 Nominally, Panzer Grenadier Divisions had six infantry battalions and a tank battalion (usually self-propelled guns), as well as the usual field artillery and other supporting arms. Unlike the normal German infantry division, which relied mostly on horse-drawn transport, a panzer grenadier division was fully motorized. At full strength—which was rare in practice—it numbered some 10,000 men. "Panzergrenadier," https://en.wikipedia.org/wiki/Panzergrenadier.

130 The *Panzerkampfwagen* IV was by this time the most common German tank encountered. In combat effectiveness, it was roughly comparable to the Sherman. "Panzer IV," https://en.wikipedia.org/wiki/Panzer_IV.

131 Wyman issued the broad attack order, but it had fallen to Neroutsos to assemble the various elements on very short notice, and of course to Amy to execute the attack. For his superior command decisions at San Leonardo as well as his regiment's high level of training, Neroutsos was awarded the DSO. Box 14CAR Personnel, N (14th Armoured Regiment), folder Neroutsos, C, DSO citation, KOCRA.

132 Box 14CAR004 Personnel, A (14th Armoured Regiment), folder Amy, E., MC citation, KOCRA; Nicholson, *Canadians in Italy*, 295–305; and Zuehlke, *Ortona*, 137–41.

133 Roy, *Seaforth Highlanders of Canada*, 248.

134 9 December 1943, 14th Armoured Regiment WD, LAC; Donaldson, "Thunder in the Mountains," 79; and Nicholson, *Canadians in Italy*, 301–03. The killed in action included Sgt. A. J. Harrison, Cpl. W. C. Oaks, A/Cpl. P. M. Scott, and Tprs. C.A. Childress, R. A. Cole and A. G. Hurd. Altogether the regiment "lost" twenty-seven of its tanks though most had gotten stuck or broken down. But they couldn't contribute to the capture or defence of San Leonardo.

135 Box 14CAR George Thring Papers (14th Armoured Regiment), folder George Thring, *My Life's Story*, KOCRA.

136 "Battle Exhaustion," the official name adopted by the Canadian Army during World War II for the debilitating psychological effects of combat, was emerging as a major source of casualties by late 1943. More advanced (and effective) treatments were

emerging which commanders often, but not always, embraced. Copp and McAndrew, *Battle Exhaustion,* chapters 3–5.

137 10 December 1943, 14th Armoured Regiment WD, LAC.

138 Only about one-sixth of the 11th and 14th Regiment tanks towed to workshops during the period of heavy fighting in the first half of December had been knocked out (these were salvaged for spares); brigade tank workshops worked furiously to repair the others. 11 and 16 December 1943, 1st Armoured Brigade WD, LAC.

139 12 December 1943, 14th Armoured Regiment WD, LAC. 11 December 1943, 14th Armoured Regiment WD, LAC. The Germans wasted their manpower in these and many other counterattacks. The 90th Panzer Grenadier Division's CO was cashiered during the battle for his mishandling of the division. By the end of the fighting in and around Ortona, it had been reduced to little more than a husk. Nicholson, *Canadians in Italy,* 309–10.

140 They were Tprs. A. H. Ward and E. A. Anderson.

141 13–14 December 1943, 14th Armoured Regiment WD, LAC and Nicholson, *Canadians in Italy,* 304–10.

142 *Beyond the Sangro—An Account of the Operations of 1 CAB during December 1943, Report from OC 14 Cdn Armd Regt 9–20 Dec 1943,* Pt. III, Sec. 3, app. 40, 1st Armoured Brigade WD (February 1944), LAC and Box 14CAR001 (14th Armoured Regiment), folder 011, *Onward II,* 50/14 Veterans Association (June 1991), David Ewart, *Sadness and Bravery on "Vino Ridge,"* KOCRA.

143 13 December 1943, 1st Armoured Brigade WD, LAC; box 14CAR004 Personnel, G–H (14th Armoured Regiment), folder Halstead, C. R., MC citation, KOCRA; and Nicholson, *Canadians in Italy,* n. 315.

144 15 December 1943, 14th Armoured Regiment WD, LAC and Box 14CAR-001, folder 001, Stoney Richardson conversations with Dick Maltby, August 1989, KOCRA.

145 14 December 1943, 1st Armoured Brigade WD, LAC.

146 Box 14CAR001 (14th Armoured Regiment), folder 011, *Onward II,* 50/14 Veterans Association (June 1991), David Ewart, *Sadness and Bravery on "Vino Ridge,"* KOCRA.

147 The tankers, along with the infantrymen still holding the position, "undertook an in-depth study of the art of wine-tasting—an ample supply being at hand." The ridge had gotten its informal name from the numbers of wine vats located in the area. Box 14CAR001 (14th Armoured Regiment), folder 011, *Onward II,* 50/14 Veterans Association (June 1991), Herb Knodel and Peter Reimer, *The Battle of San Leonardo—9 December 1943,* KOCRA.

148 Nicholson, *Canadians in Italy,* 315–20.

149 1st Canadian Division report cited in Nicholson, *Canadians in Italy,* 318. On casualties, 31 December 1943, 14th Armoured Regiment WD, LAC.

150 Nicholson, *Canadians in Italy,* 321–33. The defenders in Ortona were mostly *Fallschirmjäger* of the 1st Parachute Division, who had also contested The Gully.

151 18–22 December 1943, 14th Armoured Regiment WD, LAC.

152 *Beyond the Sangro—An Account of the Operations of 1 CAB during December 1943, Report from OC 14 Cdn Armd Regt 9–20 Dec 1943,* Pt. III, Sec. 3, app. 40, 1st Armoured Brigade WD (February 1944), LAC.

153 *Beyond the Sangro—An Account of the Operations of 1 CAB during December 1943, Report from OC 14 Cdn Armd Regt 9-20 Dec 1943*, Pt. III, Sec. 3, app. 40, 1st Armoured Brigade WD (February 1944), LAC.

154 Donaldson, "Thunder in the Mountains," 81-83.

155 23 December 1943, 14th Armoured Regiment WD, LAC.

156 The Navy, Army and Air Force Institutes ran canteens and many other services for servicemen (and their families) both overseas and in Britain. Their focus was the other ranks.

157 24 December 1943, 14th Armoured Regiment WD, LAC. 25 and 27-29 December 1943, 14th Armoured Regiment WD, LAC.

158 27-31 December 1943, 14th Armoured Regiment WD, LAC and *Battle casualties of 1 Cdn Armd Bde, 10 Jul 43 to 3 Jan 44*, app., 1st Canadian Armoured Brigade WD (January 1944), LAC. The totals were twenty-five killed, seventy wounded and four missing in action. These were 38 percent of the brigade's casualties which, considering the 14th Regiment's reserve role in Sicily, attests to its being in the thick of the fight thereafter.

159 There are many personal accounts of Canadian veterans and their wartime experiences. But in contrast there is practically nothing on the experiences of parents, wives—including widows—or children, which has left a great gap in our understanding of the war and its impact on Canada.

160 Box 14CAR Personnel, S-U (14th Armoured Regiment), folder Slifka, L., letter to his wife, 3 June 1942, KOCRA.

161 Box 14CAR Personnel, Q-R (14th Armoured Regiment), folder Raskin, Elly, letter from his wife, 30 September 1943, KOCRA.

162 *Calgary Herald*, 20 April 1943, 1 and 3.

163 *Calgary Herald*, 30 April 1943, 12.

164 Interview with Donald Alexander, 22 January 2015.

165 *Calgary Herald*, 23 June 1941, 13 and Box 14CAR001 (14th Armoured Regiment), folder 011, *Onward II*, 50/14 Veterans Association (June 1991), Ellen Taylor, *The Ladies' Auxiliary*, KOCRA.

166 Box 14CAR001 (14th Armoured Regiment), folder 011, *Onward II*, 50/14 Veterans Association (June 1991), Ellen Taylor, *The Ladies' Auxiliary*, KOCRA; box 14CAR Personnel, Q-R (14th Armoured Regiment), folder L/Cpl. Hursh, S., KOCRA; and *Calgary Herald*, 24 April 1942, 7, 30 April 1943, 12 and 9 November 1943, 6.

167 Box 14CAR001 (14th Armoured Regiment), folder 011, *Onward II*, 50/14 Veterans Association (June 1991), Ellen Taylor, *The Ladies' Auxiliary*, KOCRA.

168 Vance, *Maple Leaf Empire*, 183.

169 Vance, *Maple Leaf Empire*, 186-87 and Stacey and Wilson, *Half Million*, 134-48. Once established, the Canadian Wives Bureau, which the army ran for all three services, saw to it that the over 40,000 wives and 20,000 children were well cared for and prepared, such as they could be, for the start of their new lives in Canada. Stacey and Wilson, *Half Million*, 141.

170 Padre N. E. L. Smith memo, 6 May 1943, box 27003, folder Philip Scott, RG 24, LAC. Various forms, Box 27003, folder Philip Scott, RG 24, LAC.

171 Estates Branch, Canadian Military HQ (London) to Mrs. Scott, 17 May 1944, box 27003, folder Philip Scott, RG 24, LAC.
172 Mrs. P. M. Scott to Director of Records, Adj. Gen. Branch, 17 January 1946 and DVA to Mrs. P. M. Scott, 1 February 1946, box 27003, folder Philip Scott, RG 24, LAC.
173 Canadian Red Cross, AB Div. to Directorate of Repatriation (Ottawa), 22 February 1945, box 27003, folder Philip Scott, RG 24, LAC.
174 Mrs. John Fahrner (Scott) to DVA, 18 July 1949, box 27003, folder Philip Scott, RG 24, LAC. Various forms and correspondence, box 27003, folder Philip Scott, RG 24, LAC.

NOTES TO CHAPTER 7

1   In January 1944, after the Sangro and Ortona operations, Field Marshal Montgomery had offered formal congratulations to all of his units. His cable to the Canadian tankers noted that "if you want a job done get the First Canadian Armoured Brigade." Box B103-002 (Calgary Rifles), Historical Sketches 8, KOCRA.
2   Nicholson, *Canadians in Italy,* 338–55.
3   1 January 1944, 14th Armoured Regiment WD, LAC and 3 January 1944, 1st Armoured Brigade WD, LAC. The attached component included medical personnel, sappers and other specialists, and of course the Light Aid Detachment.
4   7 January 1944, 14th Armoured Regiment WD, LAC.
5   8 and 30–31 January 1944, 14th Armoured Regiment WD, LAC and Nicholson, *Canadians in Italy,* 375–78.
6   23 February 1944, 14th Armoured Regiment WD, LAC and 27 February 1944, 1st Armoured Brigade WD, LAC. Wyman assumed command of the 2nd Armoured Brigade which was subsequently deployed to Normandy.
7   3 and 5 March 1944, 14th Armoured Regiment WD, LAC.
8   *Weekly Report on Operations, 1 Cdn Armd Bde, 6–12 Mar 1944,* app. 22 and *13–19 March 1944,* app. 23, 1st Armoured Brigade WD (March 1944), LAC. Drunkenness was becoming a concern within the regiment. Pt. 1 orders, N-26, 20 March 1944, 14th Armoured Regiment WD, LAC. Whether fairly or not, the Canadians were singled out as the worst miscreants at the main Eighth Army rest area at Bari. Pt. 1 Orders, No. 29, 8 Mar 1944, app. 1, 1st Armoured Brigade WD (March 1944), LAC.
9   23 March 1944, 14th Armoured Regiment WD, LAC; 31 March 1944, 14th Armoured Regiment WD, LAC; and Nicholson, *Canadians in Italy,* 384.
10 25 March 1944, 1st Armoured Brigade WD, LAC. Neroutsos had long considered lightly armoured, wheeled reconnaissance vehicles "absolutely useless" for the task. *Beyond the Sangro—An Account of the Operations of 1 CAB during December 1943, Report from OC 14 Cdn Armd Regt 9-20 Dec 1943,* Pt. III, Sec. 3, app. 40, 1st Armoured Brigade WD (February 1944), LAC.
11 Box 14CAR Personnel, V-Z (14th Armoured Regiment), folder White, John, Dieppe/POW memoir, KOCRA.
12 1 September 1942, box 14CAR—Personnel O-P (14th Armoured Regiment), folder Pinder, Tom, POW diary 1942-43, KOCRA; box 14CAR—Personnel C (14th Armoured Regiment), folder Craigie, Don, Fred Bagley, *Don Craigie and the Ordeal of Dieppe,* KOCRA; and box 14CAR—Personnel Q-R (14th Armoured Regiment), folder Richardson, C.V., POW diary (undated), KOCRA.

13   Box 14CAR—Personnel Q-R (14th Armoured Regiment), folder Richardson, C. V., POW diary (undated), KOCRA and box 14CAR—Personnel C (14th Armoured Regiment), folder Craigie, Don, Fred Bagley, *Don Craigie and the Ordeal of Dieppe*, KOCRA.

14   Box 14CAR—Personnel S-U (14th Armoured Regiment), folder Scott, Denis, POW memoir. In May the officers of the 2nd Division had taken an eleven-day course on how to evade capture, cope with capture and escape, but there was nothing on dealing with a long period of captivity. Vance, *Objects of Concern*, 101. It is unclear whether it was offered to Calgary Regiment's officers. Other ranks were totally unprepared.

15   10 April 1943, box 14CAR—Personnel O-P (14th Armoured Regiment), folder Pinder, Tom, POW diary 1942-43, KOCRA. Box 14CAR—Personnel, G-H (14th Armoured Regiment), folder Ganshirt, J., War Claims Commission, Statement Concerning Claim for Maltreatment, 29 April 1954, KOCRA.

16   Box 14CAR—Personnel S-U (14th Armoured Regiment), folder Scott, Denis, POW memoir, KOCRA; box 14CAR—Personnel C (14th Armoured Regiment), folder Craigie, Don, Fred Bagley, *Don Craigie and the Ordeal of Dieppe*, KOCRA; and box 14CAR-001 (14th Armoured Regiment), folder 011, *Onward II*, 50/14 Verarans Assoc. (June 1991), Al Wagstaff, *Dieppe's Prisoners of War*, KOCRA.

17   Box 14CAR—Personnel S-U (14th Armoured Regiment), folder Scott, Denis, POW memoir, KOCRA; box 14CAR-001 (14th Armoured Regiment), folder 011, *Onward II*, 50/14 Veterans Assoc. (June 1991), Al Wagstaff, *Dieppe's Prisoners of War*, KOCRA; box 14CAR—Personnel Q-R (14th Armoured Regiment), folder Richardson, C. V., POW diary (undated), KOCRA; and Vance, *Objects of Concern*, 145-47.

18   Various entries, box 14CAR—Personnel, O-P (14th Armoured Regiment), folder Page, C. E., POW diary, KOCRA. *Oflag* stood for *Offizierslager* whereas *Stalag* stood for *Stammlager*.

19   Vance, *Objects of Concern*, 103-04, 111-13 ff. and 120-25.

20   Box 14CAR—Personnel A-B (14th Armoured Regiment), folder Anderson, A. F., *A Story or Two as Remembered about Dieppe and Stalag VIII-B, 1942-1945*, KOCRA.

21   Vance, *Objects of Concern*, 149-50 and 156.

22   16 February 1943, box 14CAR—Personnel O-P (14th Armoured Regiment), folder Pinder, Tom, POW diary 1942-43, KOCRA. Box 14CAR-001 (14th Armoured Regiment), folder 011, *Onward II*, 50/14 Veterans Assoc. (June 1991), Al Wagstaff, *Dieppe's Prisoners of War*, KOCRA.

23   Vance, *Objects of Concern*, 149 ff.

24   Box 14CAR-001 (14th Armoured Regiment), folder 011, *Onward II*, 50/14 Veterans Assoc. (June 1991), Al Wagstaff, *Dieppe's Prisoners of War*, KOCRA.

25   *Calgary Herald*, 9 March 1943, 6 and 13 March 1945, 5 and box TCR002—W. K. Jull Papers, 1938-46 (Calgary Regiment), folder Correspondence and Ephemera, 1940-46, undated memorandum (late 1943), KOCRA.

26   Box 14CAR—Personnel C (14th Armoured Regiment), folder Craigie, Don, Fred Bagley, *Don Craigie and the Ordeal of Dieppe*, KOCRA; box 14CAR—Personnel S-U (14th Armoured Regiment), folder Scott, Denis, POW memoir, KOCRA; box 14CAR-001 (14th Armoured Regiment), folder 011, *Onward II*, 50/14 Veterans Assoc. (June 1991), Al Wagstaff, *Dieppe's Prisoners of War*, KOCRA and Vance, *Objects of Concern*, 139-45.

27 Box 14CAR-001 (14th Armoured Regiment), folder 011, *Onward II*, 50/14 Veterans Assoc. (June 1991), Al Wagstaff, *Dieppe's Prisoners of War*, KOCRA and Box 14CAR—Personnel C (14th Armoured Regiment), folder Craigie, Don, Fred Bagley, *Don Craigie and the Ordeal of Dieppe*, KOCRA.

28 21 November 1942, box 14CAR—Personnel O-P (14th Armoured Regiment), folder Pinder, Tom, POW diary 1942-43, KOCRA. There was always the opportunity to slip the true state of affairs past German censors by using coded phrases only the letter's recipient would understand, for instance by saying not to worry, they were as healthy or well-fed as uncle Fred, when Uncle Fred was notoriously lean or sickly.

29 M. Leithead to (sister) Mae, 4 July 1943, box 14CAR—Personnel I-L (14th Armoured Regiment), folder Leithead, M., collection of *Kriegsgelangenenpost*.

30 F. Morton to parents, 19 and 24 September and 8 October 1943, box 14CAR—Personnel M (14th Armoured Regiment), folder Morton, Forbes, *Kriegsgelangenenpost* and letters to parents, 1942-43, KOCRA.

31 M. Leithead to (sister) Mae, 9 January 1944, box 14CAR—Personnel I-L (14th Armoured Regiment), folder Leithead, M., collection of *Kriegsgelangenenpost*, KOCRA.

32 M. Leithead to (sister) Mae, various dates 1943-44, box 14CAR—Personnel I-L (14th Armoured Regiment), folder Leithead, M., collection of *Kriegsgelangenenpost*, KOCRA and various dates, box CAR14—Personnel M (14th Armoured Regiment), folder Morton, Forbes, *Kriegsgelangenenpost* and letters to parents, 1942-43, KOCRA. Very few letters to prisoners of war survive, for even if saved to reread (and reread), as was usually the case, most were lost in the chaos of the last months of the war.

33 Henry, "The Tanks of Dieppe," 121. Vance, *Objects of Concern*, 134-38.

34 15 April 1943, box 14CAR—Personnel O-P (14th Armoured Regiment), folder Pinder, Tom, POW diary 1942-43, KOCRA.

35 After reaching England on a POW medical repatriation in October 1943, Maj. C. E. Page confirmed the mellowing of the shackling protocols. Box 14CAR—Personnel Q-R (14th Armoured Regiment), folder Richardson, C. V., POW diary (undated), KOCRA; box 14CAR—Personnel C (14th Armoured Regiment), folder Craigie, Don, Fred Bagley, *Don Craigie and the Ordeal of Dieppe*, KOCRA; and box 14CAR—Personnel S-U (14th Armoured Regiment), folder Scott, Denis, POW memoir, KOCRA. On the Christmas celebrations, box 14CAR—George Thring Papers (14th Armoured Regiment), folder 50/14 Veterans Assoc., Thring letter 7 January 1999, KOCRA.

36 Box 14CAR—Personnel, V-T (14th Armoured Regiment), folder White, John, POW reminiscences, KOCRA. Box 14CAR—Personnel Q-R (14th Armoured Regiment), folder Richardson, C. V., POW diary (undated), KOCRA.

37 Box 14CAR—Personnel C (14th Armoured Regiment), folder Craigie, Don, Fred Bagley, *Don Craigie and the Ordeal of Dieppe*, KOCRA.

38 Box 14CAR—Personnel Q-R (14th Armoured Regiment), folder Richardson, C. V., POW diary (undated), KOCRA.

39 Vance, *Objects of Concern*, 157-61 and box 14CAR—Personnel S-U (14th Armoured Regiment), folder Scott, Denis, POW memoir, KOCRA.

40 Vance, *Objects of Concern*, 160 and box 14CAR—Personnel, N (14th Armoured Regiment), folder Nelson, Gus, POW reminiscences and MM citation, KOCRA. McMullen received the DCM.

41 14CAR—Personnel, I–L (14th Armoured Regiment), folder Johnston, Roy, POW memoir, KOCRA; box 14CAR—Personnel C (14th Armoured Regiment), folder Craigie, Don, Fred Bagley, *Don Craigie and the Ordeal of Dieppe*, KOCRA; box 14CAR—Personnel S–U (14th Armoured Regiment), folder Scott, Denis, POW memoir, KOCRA.

42 Box 14CAR—Personnel A–B (14th Armoured Regiment), folder Anderson, A. F., *A Story or Two as Remembered about Dieppe and Stalag VIII-B, 1942–1945*, KOCRA.

43 Nicholson, *Canadians in Italy*, 387–99.

44 Field Return of Officers, 7 April 1944 and Field Return of Other Ranks, 1 April 1944, 14th Armoured Regiment WD (April 1944), LAC and 27–29 March 1944, 14th Armoured Regiment WD, LAC.

45 Caron and Purves commanded the Three Rivers and Ontario Regiments, respectively.

46 8 April 1944, 1st Armoured Brigade WD, LAC and *Summary of Corps Commander's Address to Senior Officers of 13 Corps at Venafro, 8th April 1944*, app., 1st Armoured Brigade WD (May 1944), LAC.

47 1 May 1944, 1st Armoured Brigade WD, LAC. These were the Ontario and the Calgary Regiments—the Three Rivers Regiment was otherwise occupied.

48 *In the Liri Valley: An Account of Operations 1 Cdn Armd Bde Italy April–May 1944*, app. A, 1st Armoured Brigade WD (May 1944), LAC. The 14th Regiment and 8th Indian Division had already carried out some squadron-battalion training earlier in the year, so they were building on a sound base. Unfortunately not all of the infantry battalions had been able to participate. Training Instruction no. 1, 9 March 1944, 21st Indian Brigade WD (March 1944), box 18879, WO 169, TNA. Russell's confidence in the Calgary Regiment's capabilities survived a major friendly fire incident during a fire support operation in late February which had left two of his men killed and eleven wounded. 28 February 1944, 19th Indian Brigade WD, box 18871, WO 169, TNA.

49 11–13 April 1944, 14th Armoured Regiment WD, LAC and *In the Liri Valley: An Account of Operations 1 Cdn Armd Bde Italy April–May 1944*, app. A, 1st Armoured Brigade WD (May 1944), LAC. The Indian Army operated in Urdu and British officers in Indian units had to be fluent. A growing number of Indian officers could speak functional English (or better), but NCOs were rarely fluent, and sepoys generally knew no English at all. In Italy, each infantry brigade in the Indian Army retained the pre-war standard of one British battalion and two Indian ones. From commanding officer down, no one in the British battalions was expected to speak Urdu. Officers would inevitably pick enough up for basic communication *after* being posted to an Indian brigade.

50 16, 17, 25–27 and 28–30 April 1944, 14th Armoured Regiment WD, LAC; Pt. 1 orders, N-80, 20 April 1944, 14th Armoured Regiment WD (April 1944), LAC; 4 and 7 April 1944, 1st Armoured Brigade WD, LAC; and 19 April 1944, 17th Indian Brigade WD, box 18867, WO 169, TNA.

51 Training Instructions no. 2, 31 March 1944, 21st Indian Brigade WD (March 1944), box 18879, WO 169, TNA and 9 April 1944, 8th Indian Division WD, box 18796, WO 169, TNA.

52 Note no. 15 "Honker," 18 April 1944, 8th Indian Division WD (May 1944), box 18797, WO 169, TNA. 20 April 1944, 17th Indian Brigade WD, box 18867, WO 169, TNA and *17 Ind Inf Bde River Cross Exercise*, undated, 17th Indian Brigade WD (April 1944), box 18867, WO 169, TNA.

53 30 April 1944, 14th Armoured Regiment WD, LAC and 27 April 1944, 1st Armoured Brigade WD, LAC.

54 Various entries 1–10 May 1944, 14th Armoured Regiment WD, LAC and 1st Armoured Brigade WD, LAC and *In the Liri Valley: An Account of Operations 1 Cdn Armd Bde Italy April–May 1944*, app. A, 1st Armoured Brigade WD (May 1944), LAC. It was the same for the Indian units. 3 and 4 May 1944, 19th Indian Brigade WD, box 18871, WO 169, TNA.

55 7–8 May 1944, 14th Armoured Regiment WD, LAC and 7–9 May 1944, 19th Indian Brigade WD, box 18871, WO 169, TNA.

56 10 May 1944, 1st Armoured Brigade WD, LAC. *In the Liri Valley: An Account of Operations 1 Cdn Armd Bde Italy April–May 1944*, app. A, 1st Armoured Brigade WD (May 1944), LAC.

57 10 May 1944, 14th Armoured Regiment WD, LAC.

58 Deception measures were extensively employed in the days preceding the attack. The intent was not just to mask the build-up but to convince the Germans that the Allied line was actually being thinned. WD, 1st Arm 9 May 1944, 1st Armoured Brigade WD, LAC.

59 11 May 1944, 14th Armoured Regiment WD, LAC.

60 The Italians (and British) called the Garigliano north of Sant' Angelo the Rapido, and the south of there the Gari. The Americans called to both parts the Rapido, which still leads to confusion.

61 "Battle of the Rapido River," https://en.wikipedia.org/wiki/Battle_of_Rapido_River.

62 Nicholson, *Canadians in Italy*, 399–401.

63 Operational order no. 17, 3 May 1944, 8th Indian Division WD (May 1944), box 18797, WO 169, TNA.

64 Intelligence Summary no. 389, 8 May 1944, XIII British Corps WD (May 1944), box 339, WO 170, TNA. German tanks and to a lesser extent their self-propelled guns were similarly road-bound.

65 Pal, *Campaign in Italy*, 152–53.

66 12 May 1944, CBC War Correspondent Scripts 1944, no. 4, box 20, folder 10, Peter Stursberg Papers, MG31 D78, LAC.

67 Box 14CAR—Personnel, Q–R (14th Armoured Regiment), folder Quinn, James, reminiscences of the Gari River and the Hitler and Gustav Lines, KOCRA.

68 Box 14CAR—Personnel, Q–R (14th Armoured Regiment), folder Quinn, James, reminiscences of the Gari River and the Hitler and Gustav Lines, KOCRA.

69 Pal, *Campaign in Italy*, 158 and Report no. 158 (Army Historical Section), *Operations of the 1st Canadian Armoured Brigade in Italy May 1944 to February 1945*, Pt. 1, *The Gustav and Hitler Lines*, folder 148.22 B1 (D1), DHH.

70 12 May 1944, 1st Armoured Brigade WD, LAC. Throughout the battle, numbers of Canadian engineers were attached to the regiment, clearing mines, blowing paths through anti-tank obstacles, and assisting in tank recovery operations. One was killed and another wounded. *In the Liri Valley: An Account of Operations 1 Cdn Armd Bde Italy April–May 1944, Part III, Sec (b), Engineer Operations with Armoured Regiments May 1944*, app. A, 1st Armoured Brigade WD (May 1944), LAC.

71 Corps intelligence summary, no. 366, undated (May 1944), XIII British Corps WD (May 1944), box 339, WO 170, TNA. Box 14CAR—Personnel, Q–R (14th Armoured Regiment), folder Quinn, James, reminiscences of the Gari River and Hitler and Gustav Lines, KOCRA.

72 Director of Public Relations (War Department India), *One More River*, 21. Each battalion had been assigned 16 assault boats and three large rafts.

73 Battle Log C, 13 May 1944, 8th Indian Division WD (May 1944), box 18797, WO 169, TNA; *Summary of Enemy Reactions, Methods and Losses during the Battle of the Gari River, 11-16 May 1944*, app. 1, 19th Indian Brigade WD (May 1944), box 18871, WO 169, TNA; and Intelligence Summary, no. 392, 12 May 1944, XIII British Corps WD (May 1944), box 339, WO 170, TNA.

74 This, too, failed, and the battalion finally managed to establish a viable bridgehead on the night of 12–13 May. In one of the cruel ironies of war, some A Squadron tanks had passed by the Argylls' position but the tank carrying the radio set linked to the infantry hit a mine and along with the radio, was disabled. Pinned down, their efforts to attract the attention of the other tanks were unsuccessful.

75 Battle Log A, 20h00 11 May to 08h00 12 May, 1944, 8th Indian Division WD (May 1944), box 18797, WO 169, TNA; Operational Order no. 26, 9 May 1944, 19th Indian Brigade WD (May 1944), box 18871, WO 169, TNA; 11 and 12 May 1944, 19th Indian Brigade WD, box 18871, WO 169, TNA; *Summary of Enemy Reactions, Methods and Losses during the Battle of the Gari River, 11-16 May 1944*, app. 1, 19th Indian Brigade WD (May 1944), box 18871, WO 169; Corps Intelligence Summary, no. 392, 12 May 1944, XIII British Corps WD (May 1944), box 339, WO 170, TNA; and Pal, *Campaign in Italy*, 167–72.

76 Initially there were four bridges planned for the use of the armour supporting the 4th British Infantry Division's attack north of Sant' Angelo and the 8th Indian Infantry Division's to the south. *Plymouth's* addition turned out to be critical because the construction of *Cardiff*, the 8th Indian Division's second bridge, had to be abandoned. Further north, *Amazon* was not completed until May 13th (with very heavy engineer casualties in the process) and *London* not until the 14th. Only *Oxford* (and *Plymouth*) were operational on the morning of the attack.

77 Box 14CAR—Personnel, S–U (14th Armoured Regiment), folder Seymour, Ian, reminiscences of the Kingsmill bridge, KOCRA.

78 Battle Log A, 20h00 11 May to 08h00 12 May 1944, 8th Indian Division WD (May 1944), box 18797, WO 169, TNA.

79 Box 14CAR—Personnel, S–U (14th Armoured Regiment), folder Seymour, Ian, reminiscences of the Kingsmill bridge, KOCRA and Nicholson, *Canadians in Italy*, n. 403. Kingsmill was an officer in the Royal Canadian Electrical and Mechanical Engineers, permanently attached to the Calgary Regiment. 12 May 1944, 14th Armoured Regiment WD, LAC and 12 May 1944, 1st Armoured Brigade WD, LAC.

80 Instances like this where artillery promptly intervened was deemed critical to the successful advance of armour in "close" country. Co-ordination between British and Canadian field and medium batteries (the RA supplied most of the Indian Army's field artillery) and Murphy's brigade was first-rate during the May battles. 31 May 1944 (summary of May operations), 1st Armoured Brigade WD, LAC.

81 Given that the construction of the most northerly bridge had been abandoned at first light, reopening *Plymouth* was critical. Despite being wounded directing the repairs,

Capt. Kingsmill, who won the MC that day, and his men managed to reopen it to jeep and carrier traffic by early afternoon, greatly easing the logistical situation. Sometime later it was reopened to tanks. 12 May 1944, 1st Armoured Brigade WD, LAC. 12 May 1944, 19th Indian Brigade WD, box 18871, WO 169, TNA. Tony Kingsmill's bridging concept had the inestimable value of speed if everything else worked, and proved its merits on the Gari, despite the bad luck of being quickly knocked out by a fluke German artillery round. The disadvantages were the sheer unwieldiness of the carrier tank/bridge arrangement and the need for a long, straight run at the river over ground solid enough to support its weight. The circumstances encountered during the remainder of the war in Italy meant it was never attempted again. Box 14CAR035—Personnel, Q-R (14th Armoured Regiment), folder Quinn, James, reminiscences of the Gari River and Gustav and Hitler Lines, KOCRA.

82 Nearly half the tanks of the two assault squadrons of the Ontarios had already bogged down in the mud on the far side of *Oxford*. Most were operational by the following morning. *In the Liri Valley: An Account of Operations 1 Cdn Armd Bde Italy April–May 1944*, app. A, 1st Armoured Brigade WD (May 1944), LAC.

83 While some were German mines, most were American, strewn everywhere along the east bank after their bloody nose on the Rapido. Unfortunately when they withdrew, they failed to hand over maps of the minefields to the units relieving them.

84 Box 14CAR016—Italy Documents (14th Armoured Regiment), folder 001, Allan Cawsey to Bob Sharpe, undated, KOCRA. Some idea of the chaos resulting from tanks bogging down or losing a track to a mine—Maj. Bob Taylor, A Squadron's CO, fought in five different tanks that day, having lost his own in the mud and at various points, commandeered the other four. 18 May 1944, CBC War Correspondent Scripts 1944, no. 4, box 20, folder 10, Peter Stursberg Papers, MG31 D78, LAC.

85 Maj. Donald C. Taylor, for his repeated demonstrations of courage, tenacity and tactical sense while commanding C Squadron during the Honker operations, was awarded the MC.

86 Box 14CAR033—Personnel, C (14th Armoured Regiment), folder Cawsey, A., memoirs, KOCRA; 12 May 1944, 14th Armoured Regiment WD, LAC; and Nicholson, *Canadians in Italy*, 402–03.

87 Box 14CAR035—Personnel, Q-R (14th Armoured Regiment), folder Quinn, James, reminiscences of the Gari River and Gustav and Hitler Lines, KOCRA and box 14CAR033—Personnel, C (14th Armoured Regiment), folder Cawsey, A., memoirs, KOCRA. The following morning while Cawsey stood in his open hatch scanning for enemy troops with his binoculars, he was wounded by a mortar fragment and spent the next two months in hospital.

88 Box 14CAR035—Personnel, Q-R (14th Armoured Regiment), folder Quinn, James, reminiscences of the Gari River and Gustav and Hitler Lines, KOCRA. *In the Liri Valley: An Account of Operations 1 Cdn Armd Bde Italy April–May 1944*, app. A, 1st Armoured Brigade WD (May 1944), LAC.

89 12 May 1944, 1st Armoured Brigade WD, LAC.

90 Donaldson, "Thunder in the Mountains," 88. See also 101.

91 31 May 1944 (summary of May operations), 1st Armoured Brigade WD, LAC.

92 12 May 1944, 14th Armoured Regiment WD, LAC. 12 May 1944, 1st Armoured Brigade WD, LAC. 13 Corps Intelligence Summary, no. 392, 12 May 1944, XIII British Corps WD (May 1944), box 339, WO 170, TNA.

93   12 May 1944, 8th Indian Division WD, box 18797, WO 169, TNA.
94   Donaldson, "Thunder in the Mountains," 103 and Pal, *Campaign in Italy*, 175.
95   Pal, *Campaign in Italy*, 183.
96   12 May 1944, XIII Corps WD, box 339, WO 170, TNA.
97   21 Ind Inf Bde Planning Note no. 4, 8 May 1944, 21st Indian Brigade WD (May 1944), box 18879, WO 169, TNA.
98   In fact, this description characterized the great majority of the country where the Canadian and British forces would be attacking during May and into early June. Donaldson, "Thunder in the Mountains," 94.
99   13 May 1944, 8th Indian Division WD, box 18797, WO 169, TNA.
100 13 May 1944, 14th Armoured Regiment WD, LAC and Pal, *Campaign in Italy*, 176. Apart from their many killed, the German battalion's losses included 130 prisoners of war, and a great deal of equipment.
101 Nicholson, *Canadians in Italy*, 405.
102 Pal, *Campaign in Italy*, 176-77; WO 170, v 339, WD 13 Corps May 1944, 13 Corps Intelligence Summary no. 393, 13 May 1944, XIII British Corps WD (May 1944), box 339, WO 170, TNA and *Summary of Enemy Reactions, Methods and Losses during the Battle of the Gari River, 11-16 May 1944*, app. 1, 19th Indian Brigade WD (May 1944), box 18871, WO 169, TNA. The 115th Panzer Grenadier Regiment possessed upwards of thirty tanks and the same number of *StuGs* but these were never deployed in strength.
103 During one such resupply trip, Lt. J. Purslow was killed when his carrier struck a mine.
104 14 May 1944, 14th Armoured Regiment WD, LAC. 14 May 1944, 1st Armoured Brigade WD, LAC and *In the Liri Valley: An Account of Operations 1 Cdn Armd Bde Italy April-May 1944*, app. A, 1st Armoured Brigade WD (May 1944), LAC.
105 For his repeated displays of courage and exceptional leadership of B Squadron through the Honker fighting, Maj. Fred Ritchie was awarded the MC.
106 15 May 1944, 14th Armoured Regiment WD, LAC; *In the Liri Valley: An Account of Operations 1 Cdn Armd Bde Italy Apr-May 1944* app. A, 1st Armoured Brigade WD, LAC; *Summary of Enemy Reactions, Methods and Losses during the Battle of the Gari River, 11-16 May 1944*, app. 1, 19th Indian Brigade WD (May 1944), box 18871, WO 169, TNA; and Pal, *Campaign in Italy*, 182. It was an indication of the Germans' desperate reinforcement situation that the Pignataro garrison included seventy students and their instructors rushed into the line from a nearby mountain warfare course.
107 13 Corps Intelligence Summary no. 431 (trans. German document on Anglo-American fighting tactics in Italy, 26 May 44), app. B, XIII British Corps WD (August 1944), box 343, WO 170, TNA.
108 16 May 1944, 14th Armoured Regiment WD, LAC; 15 and 16 May 1944, 1st Armoured Brigade WD, LAC; and Nicholson, *Canadians in Italy*, 407 and 409-20.
109 17 and 18 May 1944, 14th Armoured Regiment WD, LAC.
110 18 May 1944, 14th Armoured Regiment WD, LAC. 18 May 1944, 1st Armoured Brigade WD, LAC and *In the Liri Valley: An Account of Operations 1 Cdn Armd Bde Italy April-May 1944*, app. A, 1st Armoured Brigade WD (May 1944), LAC; and box 14CAR035—Personnel, Q-R (14th Armoured Regiment), folder Quinn, James, reminiscences of the Gari River and Gustav and Hitler Lines, KOCRA.

111 Pal, *Campaign in Italy*, 185–87 and 13 Corps Intelligence Summary no. 386, 1 May 1944 and no. 399, 20 May 1944, XIII British Corps WD (May 1944), box 339, WO 170, TNA.

112 Box 14CAR035—Personnel, Q–R (14th Armoured Regiment), folder Quinn, James, reminiscences of the Gari River and Gustav and Hitler Lines, KOCRA.

113 Box 14CAR035—Personnel, Q–R (14th Armoured Regiment), folder Quinn, James, reminiscences of the Gari River and Gustav and Hitler Lines, KOCRA. 19 and 21 May 1944, 13 British Corps WD, box 339, WO 170 and 13 Corps Intelligence Summary no. 399, 20 May 1944, XIII British Corps WD (May 1944), box 339, WO 170, TNA.

114 20 May 1944, 14th Armoured Regiment WD, LAC. 19 May 1944, 1st Armoured Brigade WD, LAC and *In the Liri Valley: An Account of Operations 1 Cdn Armd Bde Italy April–May 1944*, app. A, 1st Armoured Brigade WD (May 1944), LAC. Years later, when asked to comment on the British planning in front of Aquino, Neroutsos pointedly noted that "there was some confusion and lack of liaison with the infantry commanders of the 78th Division who gave out somewhat contradictory orders." Box 14CAR—Personnel, N (14th Armoured Regiment), folder Neroutsos, C. H., correspondence with historian W. A. McAndrew, 24 May 1987, KOCRA.

115 Nicholson, *Canadians in Italy*, 411–12. 22 May 1944, 1st Armoured Brigade WD, LAC.

116 Box 14CAR035—Personnel, Q–R (14th Armoured Regiment), folder Quinn, James, reminiscences of the Gari River and Gustav and Hitler Lines, KOCRA. Lt. George Thring, only recently recuperated from his wounds at Vino Ridge, remembered his friend Al Beresford visiting him the previous night and handing him a parcel for his wife. Beresford had a premonition that he was going to be killed, and try though he might, Thring could not talk him out of it. Box 14CAR—George Thring Papers (14th Armoured Regiment), folder George Thring, *My Life's Story*, KOCRA.

117 Beresford, twenty-three, had grown up in Calgary and was one of the regiment's originals, having worked his way up from trooper. He left a widow, Winnie. A Montréaler, twenty-four-year-old Harry Lamb had married his English war bride Jean in 1943. He had transferred to the Calgary Regiment from the Ontarios only ten days before he was killed. Both men were interred in Cassino Commonwealth War Graves cemetery after the war.

118 22–24 May 1944, 14th Armoured Regiment WD, LAC and 24 May 1944, 1st Armoured Brigade WD, LAC and *In the Liri Valley: An Account of Operations 1 Cdn Armd Bde Italy April–May 1944*, app. A, 1st Armoured Brigade WD (May 1944), LAC. 23 May 1944, XIII British Corps WD (May 1944), box 339, WO 170, TNA.

119 25 and 26 May 1944, 14th Armoured Regiment WD, LAC and Nicholson, *Canadians in Italy*, 435–36. 25 May 1944, 1st Armoured Brigade WD, LAC.

120 13 Corps Intelligence Summary no. 402, 24 May 1944, XIII British Corps WD (May 1944), box 339, WO 170, TNA.

121 27–31 May and 1 June 1944, 14th Armoured Regiment WD, LAC.

122 *Battle Casualties for May 1944*, app., 14th Armoured Regiment WD (May 1944), LAC. At the time this included four men missing and presumed killed. *In the Liri Valley: An Account of Operations 1 Cdn Armd Bde Italy April–May 1944, Summary of Casualties 8–30 May 1944*, app. A, 1st Armoured Brigade WD (May 1944), LAC. The regiment had suffered twenty-nine killed or died of wounds and another seventy wounded in all of 1943. *Casualties by Regiment, 1943*, 1st Armoured Brigade WD (January 1944), LAC.

123 *In the Liri Valley: An Account of Operations 1 Cdn Armd Bde Italy April–May 1944*, Part V Sec (b), Report on 1 Cdn Arm Bde RCEME Operations 11-29 May, app. A, 1st Armoured Brigade WD (May 1944), LAC.

124 *In the Liri Valley: An Account of Operations 1 Cdn Armd Bde Italy April–May 1944*, app. A, 1st Armoured Brigade WD (May 1944), LAC. The 121,000 .30 calibre machine gun rounds fired pointed in the same direction. These ammunition expenditures covered the period 12-18 May.

125 Buckley, *British Armour*, 82, 97, 107 and 180-86. Box 14CAR033—Personnel, C (14th Armoured Regiment), folder Cawsey, A., memoirs, KOCRA.

126 Box 14CAR-001 (14th Armoured Regiment), folder 011, *Onward II*, 50/14 Vererans Assoc. (June 1991), Jim Quinn, *Some Regimental Notes*, KOCRA.

127 14CAR—Personnel, Q-R (14th Armoured Regiment), folder Ritchie, Fred, reminiscences, KOCRA.

128 Buckley, *British Armour*, 126-28 and 186-87.

129 Box 30510, folder Wilfred Beresford, R 112, LAC.

130 *In the Liri Valley: An Account of Operations 1 Cdn Armd Bde Italy April–May 1944*, app. A, 1st Armoured Brigade WD (May 1944), LAC.

131 Box 14CAR033—Personnel, C (14th Armoured Regiment), folder Cawsey, A., memoirs, KOCRA.

132 *Report on Operations—11 May 44 to 28 May 44*, undated, 1st Armoured Brigade WD (June 1945), LAC. *Points of Interest Noted on Recent Operations*, undated (late May 1944), app., 1st Armoured Brigade WD (June 1945), LAC.

133 8 Ind Div Training Instruction no. 7, Maj.-Gen. Russell, 30 July 1944, 8th Indian Division WD (August 1944), box 18798, WO 169, TNA.

134 Nicholson, *Canadians in Italy*, 442 and 447-51. The German Army's own estimates indicated that units engaged in the battles of the Gustav and Hitler Lines had typically lost between 50 and 90 percent of their manpower and heavy weapons. See also Nicholson, *Canadians in Italy*, 459.

135 Pt. 1 orders, no. 34, 6 April 1944, app. 7, 1st Armoured Brigade WD (April 1944), LAC. Allfrey's letter was dated 30 March 1944.

136 1 June 1944, 14th Armoured Regiment WD, LAC. 6 and 7 June 1944, 14th Armoured Regiment WD, LAC.

137 11 June 1944, 14th Armoured Regiment WD, LAC. 10 June 1944, 14th Armoured Regiment WD, LAC and 11 June 1944, 1st Armoured Brigade WD, LAC.

138 Box 14CAR033—Personnel, C (14th Armoured Regiment), folder Cawsey, A., memoirs, KOCRA and box 14CAR-001 (14th Armoured Regiment), folder 011, *Onward II*, 50/14 Veterans Assoc. (June 1991), Stoney Richardson, *Stoney's Story*, KOCRA. Richardson was always guarded with his views, but in an interview in 1989, when asked about the various commanders under whom he had served, he commented favourably and in depth about all of them but one. Box 14CAR001 (14th Armoured Regiment), folder Stoney Richardson, conversations with Dick Maltby, August 1989, KOCRA.

139 12 June 1944, 14th Armoured Regiment WD, LAC.

140 13 June 1944, 14th Armoured Regiment WD, LAC. 10 and 11 June 1944, 1st Armoured Brigade WD, LAC.

141 14 June 1944, 14th Armoured Regiment WD, LAC.

142 14 June 1944, 14th Armoured Regiment WD, LAC. 17-18 June 1944, 14th Armoured Regiment WD, LAC. The Ontario Regiment would support the 78th British Infantry Division during the Trasimene operations.

143 14CAR—Personnel, Q-R (14th Armoured Regiment), folder Ritchie, Fred, reminiscences, KOCRA.

144 Box 14CAR001 (14th Armoured Regiment), folder Stoney Richardson, conversations with Dick Maltby, August 1989, KOCRA. 19 June 1944, 14th Armoured Regiment WD, LAC.

145 Intelligence Summary no. 418, *Operational Order no. 324, 334 [German] Inf Div* (trans.), app. C, XIII British Corps WD (June 1944), box 341, WO 170, TNA and Nicholson, *Canadians in Italy*, 465-66.

146 Nicholson, *Canadians in Italy*, 466 and n., 466 and Pratt, *1 Canadian Armoured Brigade*, 54.

147 1 Cdn Armd Bde Intelligence Summary no. 104, app. A, 1st Armoured Brigade WD (June 1944), LAC. This was the translation of an appraisal of the situation made by Gen. Heidrich of the 1st Parachute Division on 25 May.

148 21-22 June 1944, 14th Armoured Regiment WD, LAC and Box 14CAR001 (14th Armoured Regiment), folder Stoney Richardson, conversations with Dick Maltby, August 1989, KOCRA.

149 23 June 1944, 14th Armoured Regiment WD, LAC and 22 and 24-28 June 1944, 1st Armoured Brigade WD, LAC.

150 1 Cdn Armoured Bde Intelligence Summary, no. 115 [up to 6 July 1944], app. 6, 14th Armoured Regiment WD (July 1944), LAC.

151 *Intelligence summary no. 423* [orders from Field Marshall Kesselring (trans.)], app. A, XIII British Corps WD (June 1944), box 341, WO 170, TNA.

152 Nicholson, *Canadians in Italy*, 467-69 and 28 and 29 June 1944, 1st Armoured Brigade WD, LAC.

153 1 Cdn Armoured Bde Intelligence Summary no. 114 (up to 3 July 1944), app. 6, 14th Armoured Regiment WD (July 1944), LAC.

154 29 June 1944, 14th Armoured Regiment WD, LAC.

155 Box 14CAR001 (14th Armoured Regiment), folder Stoney Richardson, conversations with Dick Maltby, August 1989, KOCRA and 14CAR—Personnel, Q-R (14th Armoured Regiment), folder Ritchie, Fred, reminiscences, KOCRA. Richardson emphasized the generous help of many local farmers when their rations were pinched. But in too many cases the soldiers were thoughtless. They should have realized that when civilians fled into the hills to escape the fighting, they simply left their livestock behind, hoping when they returned the animals, on which their livelihood depended, would still be there. It would never have been tolerated in France, Belgium or Holland, but officers generally looked the other way in Italy. See Vance, *Maple Leaf Empire*, 199.

156 29 June 1944, 14th Armoured Regiment WD, LAC.

157 Naturally, both Canadian tank units blamed the other for the foul-ups. Pratt, *1 Canadian Armoured Brigade*, 142.

158 Sitreps, undated, 12th British Brigade WD (July 1944), box 549, WO 170, TNA and Report no. 160, Historical Section, *Operations of the 1st Canadian Armoured Brigade in Italy May 1944 to February 1945, Pt. 2, 3 Jun-1 Sep 1944*, folder 148.22 B1 (D1), DHH. As embarrassing as they were, the attackers' woes didn't match the difficulties faced by

the terrified Italian villagers occupying these communities, huddling where they could while the fighting raged around them.

159 This was the first operable Panther (Panzer Mk V) the regiment had damaged in Italy, and probably the first they had engaged, despite crews seeing the formidable tanks (and even more formidable Tigers) everywhere.

160 30 June 1944, 14th Armoured Regiment WD, LAC. Nicholson, *Canadians in Italy*, 470-71 and 29 and 30 June 1944, 1st Armoured Brigade WD, LAC.

161 On German morale in the sector, as gauged from prisoners of war, see 1st Cdn Armoured Brigade Intelligence Summary No. 107, 16 Jun 1944, app. 1, 14th Armoured Regiment WD (June 1944), LAC.

162 1 July 1944, 14th Armoured Regiment WD, LAC.

163 1 July 1944, 14th Armoured Regiment WD, LAC.

164 Report no. 160, Historical Section, *Operations of the 1st Canadian Armoured Brigade in Italy May 1944 to February 1945*, Pt. 2, 3 Jun–1 Sep 1944, folder 148.22 B1 (D1), DHH. 2 July 1944, 14th Armoured Regiment WD, LAC; 2 July 1944, 1st Armoured Brigade WD, LAC and Nicholson, *Canadians in Italy*, 471. This bare description hardly does justice to Kreger's heroism. Though under mortar and machine gun fire, he exited his Stuart to personally inspect all three bridges, and in one case with two crewmates, Tprs. Nick Mitruk and Paddy O'Neill, held off German demolition parties with a Bren gun for half an hour while engineers were brought forward. Kreger won a DCM. *Calgary Herald*, 31 July 1944, 11.

165 *Calgary Tanks Keep Germans Running in Italy*, Calgary Herald, 25 Jul 1944, 1.

166 2 July 1944, 1st Armoured Brigade WD, LAC. The railhead for resupply was still Cassino, so thoroughly had Allied air power devastated the Italian rail net as well as port facilities north of Naples. Report no. 160, Historical Section, *Operations of the 1st Canadian Armoured Brigade in Italy May 1944 to February 1945*, Pt. 2, 3 Jun–1 Sep 1944, folder 148.22 B1 (D1), DHH.

167 12th Inf Bde Intm Summary no. 46, period 3–8 July, app., 14th Armoured Brigade WD (July 1944), LAC.

168 4 July 1944, 14th Armoured Regiment WD, LAC. 3 July 1944, 14th Armoured Regiment WD, LAC and Nicholson, *Canadians in Italy*, 471.

169 4 July 1944, 14th Armoured Regiment WD, LAC. 12th Inf Bde Intm Summary no. 46, period 3–8 July, app., 14th Armoured Brigade WD (July 1944), LAC.

170 The *Panzerfaust* was hastily improvised mid-war to give German infantry a simple but devastatingly effective close-in anti-tank and bunker-busting weapon. Its very limited range made it a suicide weapon against tanks which had infantry in close support. The *Panzerschreck* (colloquially, the *Ofenrohr* or "smokestack") was developed from and a more powerful version of the American-designed Bazooka, but as the name suggests, gave away its position when fired. Both weapons were used to ambush Allied tanks, usually from the side or rear where their armour was thinner. *Recoilless Anti-Tank Grenade* (undated), app. J, 1st Armoured Brigade WD (July 1944), LAC; Intelligence Summary no. 415, *Extracts from Various Reports on Weapons in Use by 1 Para Regt*, XIII British Corps WD (June 1944), box 341, WO 170, TNA; and *Morale in 356 [German] Inf Div*, 8th Indian Division Intelligence Summary no. 140, undated, app., 1st Armoured Brigade WD (August 1944), LAC.

171 5 July 1944, 14th Armoured Brigade WD, LAC. 12th Inf Bde Intel Summary no. 46, period 3-8 July, app., 14th Armoured Regiment WD (July 1944), LAC. Nicholson, *Canadians in Italy,* 472.

172 6 July 1944, 14th Armoured Regiment WD, LAC.

173 12th Inf Bde Intel Summary no. 46, period 3-8 July, app., 14th Armoured Regiment WD (July 1944), LAC. 12 Inf Bde Information Summary no. 46, 3-8 July 44, 12 British Brigade WD (July 1944), box 549, WO 170, TNA. Nicholson, *Canadians in Italy,* 472-73.

174 7 July 1944, 14th Armoured Regiment WD, LAC and 6 and 7 July 1944, 1st Armoured Brigade WD, LAC.

175 9 July 1944, 14th Armoured Regiment WD, LAC. 8 July 1944, 14th Armoured Regiment WD, LAC; 8 and 9 July 1944, 1st Armoured Brigade WD, LAC; and Box 14CAR001 (14th Armoured Regiment), folder Stoney Richardson, conversations with Dick Maltby, August 1989, KOCRA.

176 27 June 1944, CBC War Correspondent Scripts 1944, no. 2, box 20, folder 8, Peter Stursberg Papers, MG31 D78, LAC.

177 10 July 1944, 14th Armoured Regiment WD, LAC. On collaborating with partisans for the first time, see 4 July 1944, 14th Armoured Regiment WD and various other entries in early July and 4 July 1944, 1st Armoured Brigade WD, LAC. For many Canadian soldiers "the Italian [civilian] continues to be anything but popular," as an army censorship report noted with understatement. *Extracts from CMP Appreciation & Censorship Report No. 52 for Period 1-15 Sep 44 Inclusive,* app., 1st Armoured Brigade WD (June 1945), LAC. 14-21 August 1944, 19th Indian Brigade WD (August 1944), box 18871, WO 169, TNA.

178 For a very thorough examination, see 12 Inf Bde Information Summary no. 50, 15-17 July 1944, 12th British Brigade WD (July 1944), box 559, WO 170, TNA.

179 Nicholson, *Canadians in Italy,* 473 and 16 July 1944, 1st Armoured Brigade WD, LAC.

180 15-17 July 1944, 14th Armoured Regiment WD, LAC and 16 July 1944, 1st Armoured Brigade WD, LAC.

181 Nicholson, *Canadians in Italy,* 473.

182 16 July 1944, 1st Armoured Brigade WD, LAC.

183 8th Indian Division Training Instruction no. 7, 30 July 1944 (Maj.-Gen. Russell), 8th Indian Division WD (August 1944), box 18798, WO 169, TNA. This was another instance of the British Army following a dubious practice with inferior results for its combined arms operations. When possible, the US Army (and the Free French forces) followed the far more sensible approach of assigning individual independent tank battalions to the same infantry units so that familiarity was established.

184 18 July 1944, 14th Armoured Regiment WD, LAC. In fact, A Squadron was matched with 1/Argyll and Sutherland Highlanders, B Squadron with 6/13 Frontier Force Rifles and C Squadron with the 3/8 Punjabs, the exact pairings of May. 19 July 1944, 14th Armoured Regiment WD, LAC and 22 and 23 July 1944, 1st Armoured Brigade WD, LAC.

185 Maj. Fred Ritchie spoke for his fellow officers when he pointed to the professionalism and extensive combat experience the 8th Indian Division brought to their tasks, as well as the impressive quality of their staff officers, an area in which the Canadian Army was

still feeling its way. 14CAR—Personnel, Q-R (14th Armoured Regiment), folder Ritchie, Fred, reminiscences, KOCRA.
186 19 July 1944, 14th Armoured Regiment WD, LAC. In a message to Brig. Murphy, Maj.-Gen. Alfred Ward, the 4th Division's commanding officer, acknowledged the three regiments' "sterling work" and "splendid determination and fighting spirit." Nicholson, *Canadians in Italy*, 475.
187 Nicholson, *Canadians in Italy*, 473–75.
188 20–21 and 22 July 1944, 14th Armoured Regiment WD, LAC and Nicholson, *Canadians in Italy*, 475. C Squadron was temporarily assigned to 21st Indian Brigade, meaning all three squadrons would be committed to action simultaneously.
189 22 July 1944, 14th Armoured Regiment WD, LAC.
190 22 and 23 July 1944, 14th Armoured Regiment WD, LAC and Nicholson, *Canadians in Italy*, 476. Although the Indian Army's priority was building up its forces to fight the Japanese, the three divisions in Italy were not suffering from a shortage of Indian reinforcements, though once the men arrived in theatre, they had to spend additional time in mountain warfare training. That said, given the Indian Army's unique organization along ethnic and caste lines, there were often problems with having the right mix of reinforcements at hand. The far larger problem was reinforcing the British component—one-third of the infantry, most of the field artillery and many of the technical specialists in an Indian infantry division in theatre were British, and with the British Army desperately short of reinforcements of every description, units in Italy had a very low priority. Furthermore, for language reasons replacing British junior officers serving in Indian units was always a challenge, and combat losses from this cadre were inevitably high. Kavanaugh, *10th Indian Division*, chapter 4 and appendices 7 and 8.
191 24 July 1944, 14th Armoured Regiment WD, LAC. 24 July 1944, 1st Armoured Brigade WD, LAC.
192 25 and 28 July 1944, 14th Armoured Regiment WD, LAC. On the Germans' creativity with booby traps, see 1 Cdn Armoured Bde Intelligence Summary No. 114, covering period up to 3 July 1944, app. 6, 14th Armoured Regiment WD (July 1944), LAC.
193 Nicholson, *Canadians in Italy*, 476.
194 26 July 1944, 14th Armoured Regiment WD, LAC. 26 July 1944, 1st Armoured Brigade WD, LAC and 1 Cdn Armoured Bde Intelligence Summary No. 114, covering period up to 3 July 1944, app. 6, 14th Armoured Regiment WD (July 1944), LAC.
195 27–29 July 1944, 14th Armoured Regiment WD, LAC; 19 July 1944, 1st Armoured Brigade WD, LAC; and 27 and 28 1944, XIII British Corps WD (July 1944), box 342, WO 170, TNA.
196 31 July 1944, 14th Armoured Regiment WD, LAC.
197 9 August 1944, 14th Armoured Regiment WD, LAC. 2 and 8–11 August 1944, 14th Armoured Regiment WD, LAC and 6 August 1944, 1st Armoured Brigade WD, LAC.
198 Box 14CAR001 (14th Armoured Regiment), folder Stoney Richardson, conversations with Dick Maltby, August 1989, KOCRA.
199 The army's report on morale as gleaned from the censorship for the first two weeks of August highlighted growing problems in the 1st Armoured Brigade, noting that "the majority of personnel, ... both officers and men, clearly feel that a leave period is long overdue [given] the length of time they have been performing an operational role. All ranks state bluntly that they are tired, and need a rest." In the words of one anonymous

14th Regiment trooper: "Our boys are getting pretty sore. We are the only Canadian troops here not in the Canadian Corps and they have all been out on leave at rest camps a long time now. We ... are attached directly to a Limey Corps and believe me they sure work us. When the infantry we are working with go out, up come fresh ones and we keep going." *Appreciation and Censorship Report for Period 1-15 Aug 44 Incl.*, app., 1st Armoured Brigade WD (June 1945), LAC. The 1st Armoured Brigade men also shared the growing bitterness felt throughout the Canadian Army over the lack of a mandatory provision of home leave for the long-service men, some of whom had been overseas for over four years. The toll on their marriages was a particular concern. *Extracts from Appreciation and Censorship Report No. 49 for Period 16-31 July 44 Inclusive*, app., 1st Armoured Brigade WD (June 1945), LAC.

NOTES TO CHAPTER 8

1. 25 August 1944, 19th Indian Brigade WD (August 1944), box 188871, WO 169, TNA.
2. 17-18 August 1944, 14th Armoured Regiment WD, LAC and 11-12 and 19-21 August 1944, 1st Armoured Brigade WD, LAC.
3. 20 August 1944, 14th Armoured Regiment WD, LAC.
4. Pal, *Campaign in Italy*, 415.
5. 23 and 24 August 1944, 14th Armoured Regiment WD, LAC.
6. 25 August 1944, XIII British Corps WD, box 343, WO 170, TNA.
7. 26 August 1944, 14th Armoured Regiment WD, LAC. 25 August 1944, 14th Armoured Regiment WD, LAC and 25 and 26 August 1944, 1st Armoured Brigade WD, LAC. B Squadron crossed on 31 August with the remainder of 8th Indian Division's infantry.
8. These summits rose about 600 m above sea level, but from the valley bottoms they were formidable obstacles indeed and offered superb observation. The 356th Infantry Division had been badly mauled from the moment it had been inserted into action south of the Trasimene line. Much of its *Volksdeutsche* element (ethnic Germans born in Eastern Europe) had deserted, with the remainder transferred to the field artillery where suitable opportunities were more limited. Its infantry battalions were a combination of older men combed from the rear echelons and teenagers, predominately German-born. Save for the youngest, these soldiers were described as less fanatic (for the most part) than the parachutists, but capable fighters. Despite their six infantry battalions numbering only about 250 men each, they were now battle-hardened, ably lead, and liberally equipped with anti-tank weapons from *Panzerfausts* to 88s, along with *StuGs* and even a few tanks. Tactically it "had shown all the usual German skill." Intelligence Summary no. 444, Morale in 356 Inf Div, app., XIII British Corps WD (August 1944), box 343, WO 170, TNA.
9. 27 August 1944, 14th Armoured Regiment WD, LAC and 27 and 28 August 1944, 1st Armoured Brigade WD, LAC. 28 August 1944, 1st Armoured Brigade WD, LAC. Captured German documents expressed awe over the unrelenting volume, not to mention accuracy, of British artillery fire, whether supporting attacks or in the counter-battery role. 8th Ind Div Intelligence Summary no. 138, 1 August 1944, app., 1st Armoured Brigade WD (August 1944), LAC.
10. 31 August 1944, 14th Armoured Regiment WD, LAC; 1 September 1944, 1st Armoured Brigade WD, LAC; and *Report on Operations of 14 CAR (Calgary Regt) for Period 21 Jul to 30 Nov 44*, Capt, R. T. Currelly, 12 December 1944, folder 141.4 A1 4013 (D1), DHH.

Currelly was a historical officer, but the report was revised by Lt.-Col. Richardson, as was the practice.

11 1 September 1944, 14th Armoured Regiment WD, LAC. 30 August and 1 September 1944, 1st Armoured Brigade WD, LAC and Nicholson, *Canadians in Italy,* 485–86.

12 Nicholson, *Canadians in Italy,* 487–92.

13 As partisan activity increased, German reprisals against the civilian population were merciless. "Maximum severity" was the army's official policy, with large numbers of hostages taken and shot, and whole villages burned to the ground on mere suspicion of partisan sympathies. Italian Fascist militias also carried out reprisals. Operations against Partisans, order no. 2, I Parachute Corps, 20 July 1944 [trans.], app., 1st Armoured Brigade WD (August 1944), LAC.

14 1–5 and 7–8 September 1944, 14th Armoured Regiment WD, LAC and *Report on Operations of 14 CAR (Calgary Regt) for Period 21 Jul to 30 Nov 44,* Capt. R. T. Currelly, 12 December 1944, folder 141.4 A1 4013 (D1), DHH. Nicholson, *Canadians in Italy,* 531

15 10 September 1944, 14th Armoured Regiment WD, LAC.

16 Nicholson, *Canadians in Italy,* 597–98.

17 Nicholson, *Canadians in Italy,* 598.

18 Nicholson, *Canadians in Italy,* 598. Nicholson, *Canadians in Italy,* 495–97 and Director of Public Relations/War Department (India), *One More River,* 28.

19 *Operations of British, Indian and Dominion Forces in Italy—XIII Corps in Northern Apennines,* Part III: *The Campaign in the Northern Apennines (10 Aug 1944 to 1 Apr 1945),* Section G: *13 Corps in the Mountains,* undated (April 1945), 17, box 7520, WO 204, TNA and Nicholson, *Canadians in Italy,* 598–600.

20 12 September 1944, 14th Armoured Regiment WD, LAC and 11 and 12 September 1944, 1st Armoured Brigade WD, LAC.

21 13 September 1944, 14th Armoured Regiment WD, LAC. *Report on Gothic Line Positions Area M Veruca and M Citerna,* Capt. J. L. Whitton, B Sqn., 18 September 1944, app. 6, 14th Armoured Regiment WD (September 1944), LAC and 13 September 1944, 1st Armoured Brigade WD, LAC. British and Indian reports say much less about the fire support given by the tanks than the Calgary Regiment's war diary does, stressing that they aided the infantry when they could whereas the field artillery (and mortars) were there every day. Information log, 18 September 1944, XIII British Corps WD (September 1944), box 346, WO 170, TNA and Pal, *Campaign in Italy,* 433–34 and 514–20.

22 *Report on Operations of 14 CAR (Calgary Regt) for period 21 Jul to 30 Nov 1944,* app., 1st Armoured Brigade WD (June 1945), LAC.

23 18 September 1944, 17th Indian Brigade WD (September 1944), box 18867, WO 169, TNA.

24 Operational Instruction no. 18, 15 September 1944, app., XIII British Corps WD (September 1944), box 345, WO 170, TNA.

25 15 September 1944, 14th Armoured Regiment WD, LAC. 18 September 1944 and various other entries as well as Sitrep (situation reports) for September, 17th Indian Brigade WD (September 1944), box 18867, WO 169, TNA. The 25-pounder gun/howitzers could be towed into position by wheeled vehicles, conquering steeper grades and causing less damage to the roads, especially in muddy conditions.

26   13 and 16 September 1944, 14th Armoured Regiment WD, LAC; 15–18 September 1944, 1st Armoured Brigade WD, LAC; and Pal, *Campaign in Italy*, 435–36. Pal notes that the greater utility of towed artillery was anticipated.

27   Nicholson, *Canadians in Italy*, 600 and *13 Corps Intelligence Summary no. 462*, 17 Sep 1944, app., XIII British Corps WD (September 1944), box 345, WO 170, TNA. By this stage, most German battalions had from (rarely) 400 men to fewer than 100. The average was about 250, or less than a third of the average Indian battalion and less than half of the average British. 13 Corps Intelligence Summary no. 465, 25 September 1944, app., XIII British Corps WD (September 1944), box 345, WO 170, TNA.

28   Nicholson, *Canadians in Italy*, 601–02; 20 September 1944, 1st Armoured Brigade WD, LAC; and Director of Public Relations/War Department (India), *One More River*, 10 and 30.

29   17 and 18 September 1944, 14th Armoured Regiment WD, LAC. Richardson was soon off to Rome on a week's leave himself.

30   21 September 1944, 14th Armoured Regiment WD, LAC. 19–20 September 1944, 14th Armoured Regiment WD, LAC. 19 and 25 September 1944, 17th Indian Brigade WD (September 1944), box 18867, WO 169, TNA and *Operations of British, Indian and Dominion Forces in Italy—XIII Corps in Northern Apennines, Part III: The Campaign in the Northern Apennines (10 Aug 1944 to 1 Apr 1945)*, Section G: *13 Corps in the Mountains*, undated (April 1945), 26–27, box 7520, WO 204, TNA. When interrogated, German POWs listed severe weather, exhaustion, artillery fire which seemed to never end, and indifferent food as the major causes of their misery. For those facing Indian units, fear of being captured was always added to the list. Intelligence Review no. 31, 31 October 1944, 21st Indian Brigade WD (October 1944), box 18880, WO 169, TNA. "Spontaneous" retreats had become such a serious problem with some German units that Kesselring ordered soldiers withdrawing without authorization be shot on the spot. Intelligence Summary no. 468, 8 October 1944, XIII British Corps WD (October 1944), box 347, WO 170, TNA.

31   25 September 1944, 14th Armoured Regiment WD, LAC. 24 September 1944, 14th Armoured Regiment WD, LAC and WO 204, v 7520, *Operations of British, Indian and Dominion Forces in Italy—XIII Corps in Northern Apennines Part III: The Campaign in the Northern Apennines (10 Aug 1944 to 1 Apr 1945)*, Section G: *13 Corps in the Mountains* (undated April 1945), 57, box 7520, WO 204, TNA.

32   Nicholson, *Canadians in Italy*, 602–03; 26–29 September 1944, 14th Armoured Regiment WD, LAC; and 28 and 29 September 1944, 1st Armoured Brigade WD, LAC.

33   3–7 October 1944, 14th Armoured Regiment WD, LAC.

34   *Report on Operations of 14 CAR (Calgary Regt) for Period 21 Jul to 30 Nov 44*, Capt. R. T. Currelly, 12 December 1944, folder 141.4 A1 4013 (D1), DHH and Nicholson, *Canadians in Italy*, 603.

35   Box 14CAR001 (14th Armoured Regiment), folder Stoney Richardson, conversations with Dick Maltby, August 1989, KOCRA. 9–11 October 1944, 14th Armoured Regiment WD, LAC.

36   13 and 17–20 October 1944, 14th Armoured Regiment WD, LAC; various entries including 17–20 October 1944, 1st Armoured Brigade WD, LAC; and Box 14CAR001 (14th Armoured Regiment), folder Stoney Richardson, conversations with Dick Maltby, August 1989, KOCRA.

37   22 October 1944, 14th Armoured Regiment WD, LAC.

38 17 Ind Inf Bde Operational order no. 41, 22 Oct 1944, app., 14th Armoured Regiment WD (October 1944), LAC. 22 and 23 October 1944, 14th Armoured Regiment WD, LAC.

39 26–28 October 1944, 1st Armoured Brigade WD, LAC and *Report on Operations of 14 CAR (Calgary Regt) for period 21 Jul to 30 Nov 44*, Capt. R. T. Currelly, 12 December 1944, 1st Armoured Brigade WD (December 1944), LAC. *Operations of the 1st Canadian Armoured Brigade in Italy, May 1944 to February 1945*, Pt. 3, The Gothic Line, Historical Section, box 6920, RG 24, LAC; Nicholson, *Canadians in Italy*, 605 and 1 December 1944, 14th Armoured Regiment WD, LAC. Being dependent on mules was not as bad as having no mules to be dependent upon, which was the enemy's predicament. WO 169, v 18879, WD 21 Ind Bde Sep 1944, 21 Ind Inf Bde Intelligence Review no. 27, 15 Sep 1944, 21st Indian Brigade WD (September 1944), box 18879, WO 169, TNA.

40 Nicholson, *Canadians in Italy*, 605. 28 October and 1–5 November 1944, 14th Armoured Regiment WD, LAC.

41 WO 169, v 18799, WD 8 Ind Div Dec 1944, 8 Ind Div Planning Note no. 35, 8 December 1944, 8th Indian Division WD (December 1944), box 18799, WO 169, TNA.

42 18 November 1944, 1st Armoured Brigade WD, LAC. Indian soldiers were hardly in a better position when it came to leave, and censor reports revealed considerable dissatisfaction with British failures to deliver on earlier promises. Kavanagh, *10th Indian Division*, 121–38. Pt. 1 order no. N-75, 19 November 1944, app., 14th Armoured Regiment WD (November 1944), LAC.

43 21 November 1944, 14th Armoured Regiment WD, LAC. 10–18 November 1944, 14th Armoured Regiment WD, LAC; 13, 16 and 17 November 1944, 1st Armoured Brigade WD, LAC; and 8 Ind Div Intelligence Summary no. 164, 5 November 1944, app., 14th Armoured Regiment WD (November 1944), LAC.

44 27 and 30 November 1944, 14th Armoured Regiment WD, LAC. An indicator of declining morale over the previous weeks had been a marked rise in looting and other disciplinary offences throughout all Canadian units, and by officers as well as men. Pt. 1 order N-77, 23 November 1944, app., 14th Armoured Regiment WD (November 1944), LAC. Under orders himself, Richardson had everyone in his command read or hear read out Lt.-Gen. McCreery's message of 25 November where the Eighth Army's commander sternly denounced looting, often from abandoned homes and farms, pointing to the conditions of poverty and hunger endured by Italian peasants and villagers as a direct consequence of the fighting and to their willingness to shelter escaped prisoners as well as provide intelligence, both at the risk of their lives. Allied forces bore a moral responsibility to treat these people justly. Pt. 1 order N-81, 3 December 1944, app., 14th Armoured Regiment WD (December 1944), LAC.

45 Balzer, *Information Front*, 50–51.

46 Balzer, *Information Front*, 47. Balzer, *Information Front*, chapter 2.

47 Sweazey, "Broadcasting Canada's War." Balzer, *Information Front*, 47 and chapter 2.

48 *Calgary Herald*, 9 May 1944, 6.

49 These many references made it clear just how diverse the provinces of origin—and diluted the initial Alberta character of the regiment—had become after the heavy Dieppe losses.

50 *Calgary Herald*, 16 May 1944, 1. *Calgary Herald*, 18 May 1944, 1 and 3 and 25 May 1944, 1.

51 Calgary *Herald*, 25 July 1944, 1 and 31 July 1944, 11.
52 Stursberg to Bert Powley, 13 June 1944, War Correspondent—Italy CBC 1944—messages, box 20, folder 6, Peter Stursberg Papers, MG31 D78, LAC. Connor Sweazey generously shared this material from the Stursberg Papers.
53 24 June 1944, CBC War Correspondent Scripts 1944, no. 2, box 20, folder 8, Peter Stursberg Papers, MG31 D78, LAC.
54 6 July 1944, CBC War Correspondent Scripts 1944, no. 2, box 20, folder 8, Peter Stursberg Papers, MG31 D78, LAC.
55 6 July 1944, CBC War Correspondent Scripts 1944, no. 2, box 20, folder 8, Peter Stursberg Papers, MG31 D78, LAC.
56 19 July 1945, 14th Armoured Regiment WD, LAC and box 14CAR016—Italy (14th Armoured Regiment), folder 001, transcript of BBC report from Italy, 22 January 1945, KOCRA.
57 Nicholson, *Canadians in Italy,* 654–56. 10 December 1944, 1st Armoured Brigade WD, LAC. It was little wonder Russell's command were worn out—the division had been continually in action since 21 July, the Calgary Regiment being with them the whole time.
58 Operations—complimentary, no. 401/G, 29 November 1944, 17th Indian Brigade WD (November 1944), box 18867, WO 169, TNA.
59 12 December 1944, 14th Armoured Regiment WD, LAC. 10 and 13 December 1944, 14th Armoured Regiment WD, LAC and 8 December 1944, 1st Armoured Brigade WD, LAC. For the time being B Squadron remained in Modigliana, about 20 kms to the northwest, supporting the 1/5 Gurkhas.
60 *War Office Conferences—Standardization and Organization, 1 Nov 44*, app., 1st Armoured Brigade WD (June 1945), LAC. Buckley, *British Armour*, 96–97, 111 and 168–73. Given the 1st Armoured Brigade rarely faced anything more formidable than a *StuG*, inadequate numbers of Fireflies didn't have the consequences it did in France. Buckley, *British Armour*, 107–08.
61 The 17-pounder suffered from a poor HE round until late in the war. This necessitated keeping large numbers of regular Shermans in action. Buckley, *British Armour*, 176–77.
62 As quoted in Nicholson, *Canadians in Italy,* 643.
63 23 December 1944, 14th Armoured Regiment WD, LAC.
64 Director of Public Relations/War Department (India), *One More River,* 26.
65 Box 14CAR001 (14th Armoured Regiment), folder Stoney Richardson, conversations with Dick Maltby, August 1989, KOCRA. Indian units in Italy have never received their due credit. At the time, the British Army tended to consider them less battle-worthy than white troops. Racism definitely played a role. The presence of so many capable British officers, and complete British battalions, in the Indian brigades reassured the Canadians, but the officers and men of the 14th, all of whom had grown up in a society where racism was pervasive and acceptable, deserve credit for opening their eyes.
66 20 February 1945, 1st Armoured Brigade WD, LAC. In the aftermath of the Gari fighting, the Three Rivers Regiment accused the Indian battalions of being too eager to take to ground and stay there even when their tank support resumed its advance. This seems so out of character with the Calgary and Ontario Regiments' experience that it's hard to know what to make of it. Report no. 158, *Operations of the 1st Canadian*

Armoured Brigade in Italy May 1944 to February 1945, Pt. 1, *The Gustav and Hitler Lines*, Historical Section, folder 148.22 B1 (D1), DHH.

67   29 December 1944, 1st Armoured Brigade WD, LAC. 25 December 1944, 14th Armoured Regiment WD, LAC.

68   28 and 30 December 1944, 1st Armoured Brigade WD, LAC.

69   30 December 1944, 14th Armoured Regiment WD, LAC. During the most difficult stretches, several members of each crew had to walk ahead of their tank as guides. "This Trip Calgarys Sure to Remember," *Maple Leaf*, 16 January 1945, app., 14th Armoured Regiment WD (January 1945), LAC. About 55 kms from San Donato, the frozen, exhausted column had passed through the lines of the 11th Armoured where they had been greeted with hot tea and sandwiches, welcomed into warm billets and been refuelled—comrades true. 30 December 1944, 1st Armoured Brigade WD, LAC. The first 30 kms to Borgo San Lorenzo added 110 kms to the Shermans' odometers, some indication of the severe ice conditions. Box 14CAR016—Italy (14th Armoured Regiment), folder 001, transcript of report broadcast on *CBC News Roundup*, 22 January 1945, KOCRA. This was simply copied from a piece written by Lt. P. S. Millar, the regiment's intelligence officer, for *Maple Leaf*.

70   Pt. 1 orders, no. 1, Brig. W. C. Murphy to Lt.-Col. C. A. Richardson, 2 January 1945, app. A, 14th Armoured Regiment WD (January 1945), LAC.

71   31 December 1944, 14th Armoured Regiment WD, LAC.

72   31 December 1944, 14th Armoured Regiment WD, LAC. The casualties suffered in 1944 included twelve officers and twenty-one other ranks known to have been killed or died of their wounds, with five other ranks still listed as missing/presumed killed. Another twenty officers and 113 men had been wounded, one of the latter having been taken prisoner. All told, this constituted one-quarter of their nominal strength. 31 December 1944, 14th Armoured Regiment WD, LAC.

73   Nicholson, *Canadians in Italy*, 651–52.

74   Maj. B. W. Bill Malcolm, the author's father-in-law, served as one of their battery commanders throughout 1944.

75   Richardson to OC 4th Mahratta A/Tank Regiment, 22 January 1945, app., 14th Armoured Regiment WD (January 1945), LAC. 2, 6 and 10 January 1945, 1st Armoured Brigade WD, LAC. The M10 was also part of Canadian armoured regiments' vehicle establishment.

76   8 January 1945, 14th Armoured Regiment WD, LAC.

77   31 January 1945, 14th Armoured Regiment WD, LAC. 24, 26 and 29 January 1945, 14th Armoured Regiment, LAC and 23–25 January 1945, 1st Armoured Brigade WD, LAC.

78   Nicholson, *Canadians in Italy*, 656–63.

79   *Tanks in the Po Valley*, Maj. D. W. Davidson, undated (early February 1945), app. 6, 1st Armoured Brigade WD (February 1945), LAC.

80   1–7 February 1945, 14th Armoured Regiment WD, LAC. 31 January 1945, 1st Armoured Brigade WD, LAC.

81   20 February 1945, 14th Armoured Regiment WD, LAC. 15 and 16 February 1945, 14th Armoured Regiment WD, LAC and 14 February 1945, 1st Armoured Brigade WD, LAC.

82   18 February 1945, 1st Armoured Brigade WD, LAC.

83 22, 24–26 and 28 February 1945, 14th Armoured Regiment WD, LAC. On the strict security measures, 14 Cdn Arm Regt ADM Instr No. 1, 23 February 1945, app. 5, 14th Armoured Regiment WD (February 1945), LAC.
84 3 March 1945, 14th Armoured Regiment WD, LAC.
85 31 March 1945, 14th Armoured Regiment WD, LAC. The brigade war diary was rather less negative about the Italian experience, perhaps inevitably so given that while its headquarters personnel could appreciate the bigger picture and what had been achieved, they hadn't endured the miserable conditions that officers and men in fighting units had. 1 March 1945, 1st Armoured Brigade WD, LAC. 1–6 March 1945, 1st Armoured Brigade WD, LAC; and Nicholson, *Canadians in Italy,* 662–63.
86 Box 14CAR—George Thring Papers (14th Armoured Regiment), folder George Thring, *My Life's Story,* KOCRA.
87 6–8 March 1945, 14th Armoured Regiment WD, LAC.
88 9 and 10 March 1945, 14th Armoured Regiment WD, LAC.
89 10 March 1945, 14th Armoured Regiment WD, LAC. 14 March 1945, 14th Armoured Regiment WD, LAC.
90 Brig. Murphy's speech to his officers immediately upon their arrival in Belgium reinforced the new reality as to how the Canadian Army must now treat civilians. He reminded them that Belgians had been oppressed by the Nazis for four long years, and that many had resisted them and suffered greatly for doing so. "It was definitely laid down," the war diary emphasized, "that all personnel would be instructed as to the *change of atmosphere and attitude in this new theatre* [author's emphasis]." His points were well taken and no doubt sincere, but inadvertently confirm that the underlying sentiments on display in Italy were not just embraced by tank crewmen purloining pigs or squadron officers refusing to discipline them for it but were found farther up the chain of command. 16 March 1945, 1st Armoured Brigade WD, LAC.
91 15 March 1945, 14th Armoured Regiment WD, LAC. The rest of the brigade's units felt just as welcomed in the nearby communities where they stayed. 10 and 12 March 1945, 1st Armoured Brigade WD, LAC.
92 The establishment of the armoured regiments was now sixty-three tanks—thirty-one Shermans with 75-mm guns, eight with 105-mm howitzers and twenty-four Fireflies. 17 March 1945, 1st Armoured Brigade WD, LAC.
93 15, 17 and 28–29 March 1945, 14th Armoured Regiment WD, LAC and Pt. 1 orders no. 14, 16 March 1945, app., 14th Armoured Regiment WD (March 1945), LAC.
94 Vance, *Objects of Concern,* 176. Various reasons were and continue to be offered for this evacuation policy, including preserving the prisoners as bargaining chips, executing them later as reprisals for Allied war crimes (e.g. the bombing of German cities), or simply to be marched to death, reprisal by other means. The prisoners were part of the sea of German civilian refugees fleeing from Central and Eastern Europe during this same period. Almost no officer prisoners were involved in the marches, the Germans leaving them in their regular camps.
95 Box 14CAR—Personnel S–U (14th Armoured Regiment), folder Scott, Denis, *The March through Germany* (memoir), KOCRA and box 14CAR—Personnel C (14th Armoured Regiment), folder Craigie, Don, Fred Bagley, *Don Craigie and the Ordeal of Dieppe,* KOCRA.

96 Morton to parents, 23 January 1945, box 14CAR—Personnel M (14th Armoured Regiment), folder Morton, Forbes, *Kriegsgelangenenpost* and letters to his parents, 1942–45, KOCRA.

97 Box 14CAR—Personnel S–U (14th Armoured Regiment), folder Scott, Denis, *The March through Germany* (memoir), KOCRA. During the last months of the war, the International Red Cross, mostly through its Swedish organization, obtained the approval of the German government (and the co-operation of the Allied Powers) to operate convoys of trucks and buses which would bring succour to and in some cases remove from danger prisoners of war and civilian internees. The vehicles were painted white so as to be readily identified by prowling Allied ground attack aircraft.

98 Box 14CAR—Personnel C (14th Armoured Regiment), folder Craigie, Don, Fred Bagley, *Don Craigie and the Ordeal of Dieppe*, KOCRA.

99 Box 14CAR—Personnel V–Z (14th Armoured Regiment), folder White, John, Dieppe/POW memoir, KOCRA.

100 Box 14CAR—Personnel V–Z (14th Armoured Regiment), folder White, John, Dieppe/POW memoir, KOCRA.

101 Box 14CAR—Personnel S–U (14th Armoured Regiment), folder Scott, Denis, *The March through Germany* (memoir), KOCRA.

102 Box CAR14—Personnel Q–R (14th Armoured Regiment), folder Richardson, C. V., POW diary (undated), KOCRA.

103 Box 14CAR—Personnel A–B (14th Armoured Regiment), folder Anderson, A. F., *A Story or Two as Remembered about Dieppe and Stalag VIII-B, 1942–1945*, KOCRA.

104 8 April 1945, 14th Armoured Regiment WD, LAC. Stacey, *Victory Campaign*, 524, 534–44 and 564–68.

105 10 and 11 April 1945, 1st Armoured Brigade WD, LAC.

106 4, 7–8 and 10–11 April 1945, 14th Armoured Regiment WD, LAC and 8 and 9 April 1945, 1st Armoured Brigade WD, LAC.

107 12 April 1945, 14th Armoured Regiment WD, LAC.

108 14 April 1945, 14th Armoured Regiment WD, LAC. The first tanks of the Ontario Regiment had managed to get across the Neder Rijn on the morning of 13 April after which they provided close support for the British infantry investing the city. Stacey, *Victory Campaign*, 571.

109 Stacey, *Victory Campaign*, 572–81.

110 15 April 1945, 14th Armoured Regiment WD, LAC.

111 16 April 1945, 14th Armoured Regiment WD, LAC.

112 16 April 1945, 14th Armoured Regiment WD, LAC.

113 17 April 1945, 14th Armoured Regiment WD, LAC. *Descriptive account advance to Ede Apr 16/17 '45*, app. 8, 14th Armoured Regiment WD (April 1945), LAC and 17 April 1945, 1st Armoured Brigade WD, LAC.

114 17–20, 22–23 and 25–27 April 1945, 14th Armoured Regiment WD, LAC and various entries in late April and 1 May, 1st Armoured Brigade WD, LAC. On the cease fire and accompanying negotiations to liberate the remainder of Holland peacefully, see Stacey, *Victory Campaign*, 581–87.

115 20 April 1945, 14th Armoured Regiment WD, LAC. Crews were obsessed with the efficacy of this measure, although wartime tests confirmed it generally made no

difference at all. Anecdotally it did, and one could hardly blame men threatened daily with incineration for grasping at any expedient. 16 and 17 April 1945, 14th Armoured Regiment WD, LAC.

116 30 April 1945, 14th Armoured Regiment WD, LAC. Casualties for the month had been one killed and five wounded. 30 April 1945, 14th Armoured Regiment WD, LAC.

117 4 May 1945, 14th Armoured Regiment WD, LAC. 3 May and 4 May 1945, 14th Armoured Regiment WD, LAC. 1st Armoured Brigade WD, 1st Arm Bde, LAC.

118 5 and 6 May 1945, 14th Armoured Regiment WD, LAC and 1st Armoured Brigade WD, LAC. The disarming often saw personal weapons, especially Luger pistols, turn into souvenirs or items to barter with Dutch civilians. The Canadian Army immediately cracked down on both practices. Pt. 1 orders, no. 28, 8 May 1945, app., 14th Armoured Regiment WD (May 1945), LAC. One German soldier trying to pass himself off as a Dutch civilian picked the wrong checkpoint—Tpr. R. G. Brodeur recognized him as a co-worker on the Chrysler assembly line in Windsor immediately before the war. 30 May 1945, 14th Armoured Regiment WD, LAC.

119 8 May 1945, 14th Armoured Regiment WD, LAC. 7 May 1945, 14th Armoured Regiment WD, LAC.

120 *Commanding Officer's "VE Day" Message*, 8 May 1945, app., 1st Armoured Brigade WD (May 1945), LAC.

121 8 May 1945, 14th Armoured Regiment WD, LAC. 9, 11 and 16 May 1945, 14th Armoured Regiment WD, LAC. Until they reached the designated concentration areas German soldiers were not disarmed. Given the attitude of the Dutch underground this was probably a wise precaution. Both Murphy and Richardson accepted that the Belgian soldiers with whom they were now collaborating would also have settled scores. 8 May 1945, 1st Armoured Brigade WD, LAC.

122 11 and 12 May 1945, 14th Armoured Regiment WD, LAC.

123 Neary, *Civvy Street*, 281–82. Vance, *Maple Leaf Empire*, 212. For an analysis of the development, execution and legacy of programs for Canada's Second World War veterans, see also Neary and Granatstein, eds., *Veterans Charter*. The Family Allowance Act and the continuation of the Wartime Housing Corporation's activities into the immediate post-war years, although not designed for veterans per se, greatly benefited this community.

124 20 May 1945, 14th Armoured Regiment WD, LAC. 21 May 1945, 14th Armoured Regiment WD, LAC.

125 24 and 26 May 1945, 14th Armoured Regiment WD, LAC.

126 25 and 27 May 1945, 14th Armoured Regiment WD, LAC and Lt.-Col. Stoney Richardson to Elizabeth Rowse, 28 May 1945, 14CAR—Personnel Q–R (14th Armoured Regiment), folder Rowles, J. P., KOCRA.

127 31 May 1945, 14th Armoured Regiment WD, LAC.

128 1 June 1945, 14th Armoured Regiment WD, LAC. In the end, almost 80 percent of the officers and men cast ballots. 12 June 1945, 14th Armoured Regiment WD, LAC. Pt. 1 orders, no. 26, 2 May 1945 and Brigade orders, no. 71, 2 May 1945, app. 1, 14th Armoured Regiment WD (May 1945), LAC. In a shock to the government with its many veterans initiatives in place, the soldier vote went overwhelming for the CCF and cost Mackenzie King his own seat in Saskatchewan.

129 7-9 and 13 June 1945, 14th Armoured Regiment WD, LAC and undated entry, 1st Armoured Brigade WD (June 1945), LAC.

130 It was assumed most of the armoured fighting vehicles would be going to the Pacific, hence the emphasis on having them in top-notch running order. 15 May 1945, 1st Armoured Brigade WD, LAC. Amazingly, two Shermans issued to the regiment in Scotland made it through to VE Day. One was Maj. Bob Taylor's *Alberta*, and the other was *Calgary* which had been holed by an anti-tank gun during the Liri Valley fighting but subsequently repaired to serve as a recovery vehicle. Both had almost 5,000 kms to their credit when turned in. Box 14CAR001 (14th Armoured Regiment), folder 011, *Onward II*, 50/14 Veterans Assoc., (June 1991), Stoney Richardson, *Stoney's Story—Home at Last*, KOCRA.

131 16, 18 and 19 June 1945, 14th Armoured Regiment WD, LAC. As seemed to be the case everywhere in Holland, if local men were not invited to dances along with local women, the latter rarely showed up. 5 July 1945, 14th Armoured Regiment WD, LAC.

132 Pt. 1 orders, no. 48, 12 June 1945, app., 14th Armoured Regiment WD (June 1945), LAC; Pt. 1 orders, no. 41, 29 May 1945, app., 1st Armoured Brigade WD (May 1945), LAC: and Pt. 1 orders, no. 54, 13 June 1945, app., 1st Armoured Brigade WD (June 1945), LAC. VD infection rates were another complication when it came to relations with the locals. These had soared after the German surrender, despite soldiers being warned that their repatriation would be held back three months. By early July, the Calgary Regiment had the ignominious honour of having the second highest infection rate in the 5th Division, fourteen new cases having been reported during their first nine days at Franeker, though one suspects most of trouble had been gotten into while on leave in Amsterdam. The rate declined steadily during the remainder of the summer. 14 and 25 July 1945 and various entries in August 1945, 14th Armoured Regiment WD, LAC. As units demobilized, the regiment was formally attached for a time to the 5th Armoured Division.

133 13 and 14 June 1945, 14th Armoured Regiment WD, LAC; undated entries, 1st Armoured Brigade WD (June 1945), LAC; Stacey, *Victory Campaign*, 615–17; and Box 14CAR001 (14th Armoured Regiment), folder 011, *Onward II*, 50/14 Veterans Assoc., (June 1991), Stoney Richardson, *Stoney's Story—Holland*, KOCRA.

134 20 June 1945, 14th Armoured Regiment WD, LAC. 22 June 1945, 14th Armoured Regiment WD, LAC. Even with cross-posted replacements, the regiment's manpower had dropped by about 100 officers and men within a matter of weeks. Field Returns of Other Ranks, 6 July 1945 and Field Return of Officers, 20 July 1945, app., 14th Armoured Regiment WD (July 1945), LAC.

135 29 June 1945, 14th Armoured Regiment WD, LAC.

136 On the attitudes of the Franeker civilians, various entries e.g. 18 July 1945, 14th Armoured Regiment WD, LAC. The previous troops billeted there had not been popular, which didn't help matters. Box 14CAR001 (14th Armoured Regiment), folder 011, *Onward II*, 50/14 Veterans Assoc., (June 1991), Stoney Richardson, *Stoney's Story—Holland*, KOCRA.

137 7 and 17 July 1945, 14th Armoured Regiment WD, LAC and Pt. 1 orders, no. 64, 23 Jul 1945, app., 14th Armoured Regiment WD (July 1945), LAC.

138 Pt. 1 orders, no. 78, 30 August 1945, app., 14th Armoured Regiment WD (August 1945), LAC.

139 Various entries July and August 1945, 14th Armoured Regiment WD, LAC and Pt. 1 orders, no. 78, 30 August 1945, app., 14th Armoured Regiment WD (August 1945), LAC.

140 Granatstein, *Canada's Army*, 314.

141 9 August 1945, 14th Armoured Regiment WD, LAC. 6 August 1945, 14th Armoured Regiment WD, LAC.

142 18 August 1945, 14th Armoured Regiment WD, LAC. Most found themselves temporarily members of the Ontario Regiment or the 8th Reconnaissance Regiment (14th Canadian Hussars) which returned to Saskatchewan. Pt. 1 orders, no. 78, 30 August 1945, app., 14th Armoured Regiment WD (August 1945), LAC.

143 8 September 1945, 14th Armoured Regiment WD, LAC. 9 and 10 September 1945, 14th Armoured Regiment WD, LAC.

144 27–30 September 1945, 14th Armoured Regiment WD, LAC. The last entry for the war diary was 30 September 1945.

145 Vance, *Objects of Concern*, 222–23.

146 Box 14CAR—Personnel (14th Armoured Regiment), folder Craigie, Don, Fred Bagley, *Don Craigie and the Ordeal of Dieppe*, KOCRA and box 14CAR—Personnel V–Z (14th Armoured Regiment), folder White, John, Dieppe/POW memoir, KOCRA.

147 Box B103-002 (Calgary Rifles), KOCR (RCAC) Museum Historical Overview, KOCRA.

148 Box 14CAR—George Thring Papers (14th Armoured Regiment), folder George Thring, *My Life's Story*, KOCRA. Box 14CAR001 (14th Armoured Regiment), folder 011, *Onward II*, 50/14 Veterans Assoc., (June 1991), Stoney Richardson, *Stoney's Story— Home at Last*, KOCRA.

149 *Report on Operations of 14 CAR (Calgary Regt) for Period 21 Jul to 30 Nov 44*, R. T. Currelly, 12 December 1944, folder 141.4 A1 4013 (D1), DHH. The Historical Section's reports were reviewed and approved by senior officers, which for portions dealing with 14th Armoured Regiment operations meant Richardson and Murphy.

150 *Operations of the 1st Canadian Armoured Brigade in Italy, May 1944 to February 1945*, Pt. 3, *The Gothic Line*, Report no. 175, Historical Section, box 6920, RG 24, LAC. *Report on Operations of 14 CAR (Calgary Regt) for Period 21 Jul to 30 Nov 44*, R. T. Currelly, 12 December 1944, folder 141.4 A1 4013 (D1), DHH.

NOTES TO CHAPTER 9

1 While post-1945 "reserve" was the official term, the long familiar "militia" continued to be used for some time by the units themselves and of course by the public.

2 Granatstein, *Canada's Army*, 315.

3 Granatstein, *Canada's Army*, 311 and 316–17.

4 Brig. W. S. Macklin to 14 Armd Regt, 10 August 1946; Maj.-Gen. R. M. Luckock to Rodgers, 11 March 1946; Lt.-Col G. E. Leighton to Sect'y. DND, 21 January 1946; Adj. Gen. to MD 13, 3 May 1946; and MD 13 to Sect'y. DND, 10 May 1946, box 5888, folder HQ7-111-24, RG 24, LAC. One of the KORR (Lancaster's) battalions had become an armoured regiment during the war which made the ongoing ties of infantry and armour less of a mixed marriage. Rodgers had replaced Lt.-Col. Jull as commanding officer in September 1945. Stoney Richardson took over in 1946, serving as CO for three years.

5   Lt.-Col. J. T. Jenner to Maj.-Gen. M. H. S. Penhale (GOC, Western Command), 29 April 1950 and to Army HQ (Ottawa), 2 June 1950, folder 141.4A14019 (D1) 14th Armoured Regiment, DHH. C Squadron shifted to Red Deer in 1950.
6   Box B103-002 (Calgary Rifles), Historical Sketches 2 and 4, KOCRA; B103-002 (Calgary Rifles) KOCR (RCAC) Museum Historical Overview, KOCRA and *Annual Historical Report 1 Apr 1948–31 Mar 1949*, KOCRA
7   *KOCR Annual Report 1 Apr 1949–31 Mar 1950*, KOCRA.
8   *KOCR Annual Report 1 Apr 1948–31 Mar 1949*, KOCRA. Calgary counted seventeen officers and 140 other ranks, with the comparable figures for Olds being seven and sixty-two, Stettler seven and seventeen, and Innisfail nine and ninety-one, for a total strength of thirty-nine officers and 310 other ranks. By 1951 the overall strength had risen to forty-nine officers and 429 other ranks. *KOCR Annual Report 1 Apr 1948–31 Mar 1949*, KOCRA and *KOCR Annual Report 1 Apr 1950–31 Mar 1951*, KOCRA.
9   *KOCR Annual Report 1 Apr 1949–31 Mar 1950*, KOCRA.
10 Calgary *Herald*, 12 May 1948, 9 and 25 May 1948, 1.
11 Cook, *Fight for History*, 110.
12 Vance, *Objects of Concern*, 217–21 and 223–25.
13 While the French government took its time, there was still deep appreciation in 1998 when it issued certificates honouring all who had taken part in the Dieppe raid as participants in France's liberation. Box 14CAR—George Thring Papers (14th Armoured Regiment), folder 50/14 Veterans Assoc., Thring letter 7 January 1999, KOCRA.
14 Box 14CAR-001 (14th Armoured Regiment), folder 011, *Onward II*, 50/14 Veterans Assoc. (June 1991), Al Wagstaff, *Dieppe's Prisoners of War,* KOCR; box 14CAR—Personnel C (14th Armoured Regiment), folder Craigie, Don, Fred Bagley, *Don Craigie and the Ordeal of Dieppe*, KOCRA; and Vance, *Objects of Concern*, 100.
15 Vance, *Objects of Concern*, 237–41.
16 Vance, *Objects of Concern*, 241–42.
17 Cook, *Fight for History*, 49.
18 Cook, *Fight for History*, 104–05.
19 Of course thanks to the Great Depression many of the younger World War II veterans had no pre-war job to come back to.
20 Cook, *Fight for History*, 49. See also 49–69.
21 There were, of course, far too many widows, women who would have happily dealt with such problems.
22 Box 14CAR—Personnel C (14th Armoured Regiment), folder Craigie, Don, Fred Bagley, *Don Craigie and the Ordeal of Dieppe*, KOCRA.
23 Box 14CAR—Personnel Q–R (14th Armoured Regiment), folder Ritchie, F., memoir, KOCRA.
24 Less than one-quarter of the World War II veterans joined the Legion, despite its offer of comradeship and its sterling work advocating for their interests with Ottawa. Cook, *Fight for History*, 150.
25 Box B50-023 50th Infantry Battalion, folder Nicol, Angus, KOCRA.
26 This, too, paralleled the situation in the Legion, and for a time after the war was a source of frustration for many younger veterans. Cook, *Fight for History*, 152.

27 Bob Barnetson to Wheeler, 25 May 1963 and 28 March 1977, box 1, folder 10 and reunion program, 1964, box 8, folder 106, Victor Wheeler Papers, M5614, GA and *Calgary Herald*, 17 August 1964, 12. For a time there was a West Coast Association of the 50/14's with their own annual get-togethers in British Columbia.

28 Box 14CAR-001 (14th Armoured Regiment), folder 011, *Onward II*, 50/14 Veterans Assoc. (Jun 1991), Jim Quinn, *Some Regimental Notes*, KOCRA. Bob Barnetson to Wheeler, 8 January 1974, 25 January 1976 and 28 March 1977, box 1, folder 10, Victor Wheeler Papers, M-5614, GA. Generalizing across WWII veterans, historian Tim Cook speculates that the chief factors for those choosing not to join the Legion (and by extrapolation other like associations) were a determination to settle into civilian life and move on from the war. Cook, *Fight for History*, 103–04, 150 and 190.

29 Shafer Parker, "The last hero of Calgary's famous 50th," *Alberta Report*, 28 November 1994 in box B50-023 50th Battalion, folder Nicol, Angus, KOCRA.

30 Box 14CAR—George Thring Papers (14th Armoured Regiment), folder 50/14 Veterans Assoc., Thring letter 7 January 1999, KOCRA.

31 Rev. Capt. J. Graham to DND, 16 July 1945, box 25855, folder Ferguson, William, RG 24, LAC.

32 Dir. of Records/Adj. Gen. to Mrs. Orville Larson (wife), 7 August 1945, box 26317, folder Larson, Orville, RG 24, LAC.

33 Box 25320, folder Allison, Alton, RG 24, LAC. Dir. of Records/Adj. Gen. to Christopher Hofer, 20 July 1946, box 26122, folder Hofer, Richard, RG 24, LAC.

34 Dir. of War Service Records to W. M. Childress, 14 October 1948, box 25577, folder Childress, Charles, RG 24, LAC. W. M. Childress to DND, 5 October 1948, box 25577, folder Childress, Charles, RG 24, LAC.

35 Bob Barnetson to Wheeler, 28 March 1977, box 1, folder 10, Victor Wheeler Papers, M5614, GA. On "vet tourism," Cook, *Fight for History*, 213.

36 Wheeler to Cyril Baines, 7 September 1964, box 1, folder 9, Victor Wheeler Papers, M5614, LAC.

37 Christie, *Preface* in Wheeler, *50th Battalion*, iv.

38 Pattison had enlisted in the 137th and then been sent to the 50th as part of a reinforcement draft.

39 Box B50-024 50th Battalion, folder Pattison, John, excerpts from Fred Bagley, *John & Henry: The Pattisons*; Florence and Paul Swanson to Ald. Mark Tennant, 21 June 1967 and secretary, 50/14 Veterans' Assoc., 25 May 1967; R. I. Stirling (Legion) to Mayor Jack Leslie, 29 June 1967; and Mayor Jack Leslie to Bob Barnetson, 20 September 1967. Unfortunately Pattison's son John, who had served in the 50th himself and had a long career in the militia unit, reaching the rank of RSM and directing the band for years, had passed away shortly before the ceremony.

40 Cook, *Fight for History*, 4, 9–13, 179, 226–33, 348–49 and 422–23.

41 Wheeler to Percy Blain, 7 October 1971, box 1, folder 12, Victor Wheeler Papers, M-5614, GA.

42 Box 14CAR001 (14th Armoured Regiment), folder 011, *Onward II*, 50/14 Veterans Assoc. (Jun 1991), R. G. Maltby, *Ede Says "Thanks,"* KOCRA.

43 Box B103-002 (Calgary Rifles), Historical Sketches 2, J. B. Scott, *Regimental Honours*, 27 April 1988, KOCRA. Those which could have been chosen but were not included Motta

Montecorvino, The Gully, Pignataro, Aquino and the Advance to Florence. Given the 14th Canadian Armoured Regiment saw no combat in Sicily it was a dubious choice.

44   Box B103-002 (Calgary Rifles), Historical Sketches 2, J. B. Scott, *The Story of the Guidon*, 27 April 1988, KOCRA.
45   *Report of the Presentation of Colours by Her Majesty the Queen … 17 Jul 1959*, Annex 4, undated, folder 145.2P7 (D3), DHH.
46   Box B103-002 (Calgary Rifles), Historical Sketches 2, J. B. Scott, *The Story of the Guidon*, 27 April 1988, KOCRA.
47   *KOCR Annual Report, 1 Apr 1951–31 Mar 1952*, KOCRA.
48   Lt.-Col. M. R. Dare (GSO1 Western Command) to KOCR, 19 June 1951 and Lt.-Col. H. W. MacEwing to HQ Western Command, 15 July 1954, folder 141.4A14019 (D1) 14th Armoured Regiment, DHH. Lt.-Col. J. T. Jenner to Army HQ, Ottawa, 2 June 1950 and Lt.-Col. H. W. MacEwing to HQ Western Command, 11 June 1951, folder 141.4A14019 (D1) 14th Armoured Regiment, DHH.
49   *Inspection Reports KOCR January 1951–May 1957*, GOC Inspection of Western Command Militia 1954, 15 April 1954, folder 327.009 (D294) 14th Armoured Regiment, DHH. Lt.-Col. MacEwing to HQ Western Command, 16 January, 28 March, undated (early September), 13 September and 31 October 1951, folder 327.039 (D3) 14th Armoured Regiment—Corres., Syllabi, Trng Repts Jun 1950–Jan 1952, DHH.
50   Maj.-Gen. Vokes to Army HQ (Ottawa), 4 August 1954, folder 141.4A14019 (D1) 14th Armoured Regiment, DHH.
51   *KOCR Annual Report, 1 Jan 1955–31 Dec 1955*, KOCRA and Maj.-Gen. C. Vokes to Army HQ (Ottawa), 4 August 1954, folder 141.4A14019 (D1) 14th Armoured Regt., DHH.
52   Lt.-Col. W. A. Howard to HQ Western Command, 30 November 1954, folder 141.4A14019 (D1) 14 Armoured Regt., DHH. Lt.-Col. W. A. Howard to HQ Western Command, 21 January 1955 and Capt. Doug Smith (KOCR adj.) to HQ Western Command, 30 November 1954, folder 141.4A14019 (D1) 14 Armoured Regt., DHH.
53   Maj.-Gen. Vokes to KOCR, 26 April 1955, folder 141.4A14019 (D1) 14 Armoured Regiment, DHH. *Calgary Herald*, 4 April 1955, 12 and Col. J. S. Ross (Western Command) to KOCR, 25 March 1955 and Maj.-Gen. C. Vokes to Army HQ (Ottawa), undated (February 1955), folder 141.4A14019 (D1) 14th Armoured Regt., DHH.
54   *KOCR Annual Report*, 1 Jan 1956–31 Dec 1956, KOCRA and *Inspection Reports KOCR Jan 1951–May 1957, GOC inspection of Western Command militia 1956—KOCR*, 10 June 1956, folder 327.009 (D294), DHH.
55   Kasurak, *National Force*, 18 and 43.
56   Sherwin, "Total War to Total Force," 43; see also 44.
57   Kasurak, *National Force*, 42–43. Sherwin, "Total War to Total Force," 38.
58   After Maj.-Gen. Howard Kennedy, a retired militia officer who chaired the three-man panel.
59   Sherwin, "Total War to Total Force," 44–53. For example, regular armoured units would train on their new Centurion tanks, while reservists continued to toil on World War II-vintage Shermans and Stuarts.
60   Kasurak, *National Force*, 43–44. Sherwin, "Total War to Total Force," 26–28.
61   As quoted in Sherwin, "Total War to Total Force," 61.

62   Kasurak, *National Force*, 44.
63   Sherwin, "Total War to Total Force," 54–59.
64   Kasurak, *National Force*, 44–45.
65   Sherwin, "Total War to Total Force," 70–77 and Kasurak, *National Force*, 45.
66   Burtch, *Give Me Shelter*, 130–34 and 138–39.
67   Sherwin, "Total War to Total Force," 79–81.
68   Sherwin, "Total War to Total Force," 68; see also 64–68.
69   Quoted in Kasurak, *National Force*, 47; see also 46–48; Burtch, *Give Me Shelter*, 138–39, 150 and 153; and box B103-002 (Calgary Rifles), Historical Sketches 2 and 4, KOCRA.
70   *KOCR Annual Report, 1 Jan–31 Dec 1958*, KOCRA. Annual Historical Report, 1 Jan–31 Dec 1958 (including Maj.-Gen. J. V. Allard, vice chief of general staff, memo to Alberta reserve units, 15 September 1958), KOCRA.
71   *KOCR Annual Report, 1 Jan–31 Dec 1959* (including Maj.-Gen. J. V. Allard, vice chief of general staff, memo to Alberta reserve units, 2 March 1959), KOCRA and Box B103-002 (Calgary Rifles), Historical Sketches 2 and 4, KOCRA.
72   Box B103-002 (Calgary Rifles), Historical Sketch 4, KOCRA; Sherwin, "Total War to Total Force," 81–82; and Kasurak, *National Force*, 46.
73   *KOCR Annual Report, 1 Jan–31 Dec 1959*, KOCRA. Of the 283 on the rolls, 198 paraded in Calgary, Gleichen and Strathmore, but only 50 in Red Deer.
74   *KOCR Annual Report, 1 Jan–31 Dec 1959*, KOCRA.
75   The complex honoured Brig. H. T. R. Gregg, the commander of 22 Militia Group.
76   *KOCR Annual Report, 1 Jan–31 Dec 1960*, app. A, KOCRA.
77   Sherwin, "Total War to Total Force," 82–83 and 85–86.
78   Sherwin, "Total War to Total Force," 100; see also 85–100.
79   Box B103-002 (Calgary Rifles), Historical Sketch 4, KOCRA.
80   Cook, *Fight for History*, 202–05 and 214–15 and Sherwin, "Total War to Total Force," 101. By the mid-1960s, only about one-third of Canadians were wearing a poppy. Cook, *Fight for History*, 204–05.
81   *KOCR Annual Report, 1 Jan–31 Dec 1971, 1 Jan–31 Dec 1972* and *1 Jan–31 Dec 1974*, KOCRA. Between 1964 and 1970, the overall strength of the militia/reserve declined from almost 47,000 to just under 20,000. Sherwin, "Total War to Total Force," 100–01.
82   *KOCR Annual Report, 1974* and *1976*, and McDonald, *Canadian Armed Forces*, https://publications.gc.ca/collections/Collection-R/LoPBdP/BP/prb9911-e.htm. These remained an ongoing problem. Interview with Wyn van der Schee, 24 April 2010.
83   Box B103-002 (Calgary Rifles) KOCR (RCAC) Museum Historical Overview, KOCRA. The Cougar was the tank-training, reconnaissance and fire-support version of the LAV (Light Armoured Vehicle) I, a 10-ton 6-wheel vehicle equipped with a turret-mounted 76-mm cannon. AVGP (Wikipedia), https://en.wikipedia.org/wiki/AVGP.
84   Interview with Wyn van der Schee, 24 April 2010.
85   Box B103-002 (Calgary Rifles), Historical Sketches 2 and 4, KOCRA; box B103-002 (Calgary Rifles) KOCR (RCAC) Museum Historical Overview, KOCRA; and *KOCR Annual Report, 1 Jan–31 Dec 1979*, KOCRA.
86   Box B103-002 (Calgary Rifles), Historical Sketches 2 and 4, KOCRA.

87 It did not help that there was no legislation in Canada to protect reservists' jobs, unlike in the United Kingdom, Australia and New Zealand. McDonald, *Canadian Armed Forces*, https://publications.gc.ca/collections/Collection-R/LoPBdP/BP/prb9911-e.htm.
88 McDonald, *Canadian Armed Forces*, https://publications.gc.ca/collections/Collection-R/LoPBdP/BP/prb9911-e.htm. Interview with Joseph Howard, 18 December 2019. Deploying reservists in disaster relief earned the army public favour since the media rarely distinguished between the two groups and the army did little to clarify any misunderstandings. Deploying the reserves also cost next to nothing. The KOCR was deeply involved in flood abatement operations in Calgary in 2013. *KOCR Annual Report, 2013*, KOCRA.
89 Interviews with Wynn van der Schee, 24 April 2010; Pam Goebel, 23 September 2011; and Joseph Howard, 18 December 2019.
90 *KOCR Annual Report, 1990*, KOCRA.
91 Box B103-002 (Calgary Rifles) KOCR (RCAC) Museum Historical Overview, KOCRA and *KOCR Annual Report, 1997, 2000* and *2004*, KOCRA.
92 *KOCR Annual Report, 2000* and *2005*, KOCRA. Interviews with Mark Futchko, 5 December 2016 and Joseph Howard, 18 December 2019.
93 *KOCR Annual Report, 2011*, KOCRA.
94 Kasurak, *National Force*, 5 and 45–48 and Sherwin, "Total War to Total Force," iii and 110–14.

Bibliography
Research Sources Cited

Primary Sources

THE KING'S OWN CALGARY REGIMENT ARCHIVES (CALGARY)

50th Overseas Battalion, Boxes B50-010, B50-020, B50-021, B50-022, B50-023, B50-024 and B50-050

Calgary Rifles, Boxes B103-001 and B103-002

Calgary Regiment, 1919–41, Boxes TCR001 and TCR002

Calgary Regiment, 1920–39, Box TCR003

Calgary Regiment, 1938–46, Boxes TCR001 and TCR002

Calgary Regiment, Box TCR004

14th Armoured Regiment, Boxes 14CAR001, 14CAR002, 14CAR004, 14CAR006, 14CAR012, 14CAR014, 14CAR016, 14CAR033, 14CAR034 and 14CAR035

14th Armoured Regiment, Boxes 14CAR L. G. Alexander Diaries, Stoney Richardson Papers, George Thring Papers and Personnel Records

14th Armoured Regiment, KOCR Annual Reports, 1948–2013

Library and Archives Canada (Ottawa)

CBC Records, RG41 B III 1, box 15

Department of Militia and Defence, RG 9 III B 3, Box 79, RG 9 III C 3, Boxes 4214, 4215, 4216 and 4217

Department of National Defence, RG 24, Boxes 5888, 6918 and 6920

Second World War Personnel Files (KIA), RG 24, Boxes 25320, 25325, 25577, 25643, 25855, 26317, 26433, 26730, 27003, 27220 and 27307 and R112, Box 30510

CEF Personnel Files, RG 150 Acc. 1992–93/166, various folders

Max Aitken/Lord Beaverbrook Papers (MG 27 IIG1), E series, Rolls A-1764 and A-1765

Peter Stursberg Papers (MG31 D78), Box 20

David Watson Papers (MG 30 E69), Diaries

War Diaries, 50th Battalion, 1916–19 (online LAC)

War Diaries, 10th Brigade, 1916–19 (online LAC)

War Diaries, 14th Armoured Regiment, 1939–45 (online LAC)

War Diaries, 1st Armoured Brigade, 1941–45 (online LAC)

DIRECTORATE OF HISTORY AND HERITAGE (OTTAWA)
Folders 141.4 A1 4013 (D1), 141.4 A1 4019 (D1), 145.2 P7.009 (D3), 148.22; B1 (D1) and 327.039 (D3)

THE NATIONAL ARCHIVES (KEW)
War Diaries, 17th Indian Brigade (WO 169, Box 18867)

War Diaries, 19th Indian Brigade (WO 169, Box 18871)

War Diaries, 21st Indian Brigade (WO 169, Boxes 18879 and 18880)

War Diaries, 12th British Brigade (WO 170, Box 549)

War Diaries, 8th Indian Division (WO 169, Boxes 18796, 18797, 18798 and 18799)

War Diaries, XIII British Corps (WO 170, Boxes 339, 341, 342, 343, 345, 346 and 347) WO 204, Box 7520

GLENBOW ARCHIVES (CALGARY)
Victor Wheeler Papers, M-5614, Boxes 1, 2, 9, 10 and 11

IMPERIAL WAR MUSEUM (LONDON)
First World War Letters of Andrew Mason Munro

Newspapers
Calgary Daily Herald (various issues, 1914–19)

Calgary Herald (various issues, 1939–45)

Interviews
Donald Alexander in conversation with the author, 22 January 2015.

Mark Fuchko in conversation with the author, 5 December 2016.

Pam Goebel in conversation with the author, 23 September 2011.

Joe Howard in conversation with the author, 18 December 2019.

Wyn van der Schee in conversation with the author, 24 April 2010.

Secondary Sources

Bagley, Fred and, Harvey Daniel Duncan. *A Legacy of Courage: "Calgary's Own" 137th Overseas Battalion, CEF.* Calgary: Plug Street Books, 1993.

Balzer, Timothy. *The Information Front: The Canadian Army and News Management during the Second World War.* Vancouver: UBC Press, 2011.

Beach, Jim. *Haig's Intelligence: GHQ and the German Army, 1916-1918.* Cambridge, UK: Cambridge University Press, 2013.

Boff, Jonathan. *Winning and Losing on the Western Front: The British Third Army and the Defeat of Germany in 1918.* Cambridge, UK: Cambridge University Press, 2012.

Brennan, Patrick H. "'Completely worn out by service in France': Combat Stress and Breakdown among Senior Officers in the Canadian Corps." *Canadian Military History* 10, no. 2 (Spring 2009): 5–14.

Brennan, Patrick H. "Good Men for a Hard Job: Canadian Infantry Battalion Commanders on the Western Front." *Canadian Army Journal* 9, no. 1 (Spring 2006): 9–28.

Brennan, Patrick. "Julian Byng and Leadership in the Canadian Corps." In *Vimy Ridge: A Canadian Reassessment*, edited by Geoffrey Hayes et al, 87–104. Waterloo, ON: Wilfrid University Press, 2007.

Brennan, Patrick H. "Major-General David Watson: A Critical Appraisal of Canadian Generalship in the Great War." In *Great War Commands: Historical Perspectives on Canadian Army Leadership 1914-1918*, edited by Andrew Godefroy, 111–43. Kingston, ON: Canadian Defence Academy Press, 2010.

Brennan, Patrick H. "The Other Battle: Imperialist vs. Nationalist Sentiments among Senior Officers of the Canadian Corps." In *Rediscovering the British World: Proceedings of the Second British World Conference*, edited by R. D. Francis and Phillip, Buckner, 251–65. Calgary: University of Calgary Press, 2005.

Brennan, Patrick, and Thomas Leppard. "How the Lessons Were Learned: Senior Commanders and the Moulding of the Canadian Corps after the Somme." In *Canada and War: 1000-2000*, edited by Yves Tremblay, 135–43. Ottawa: Canadian War Museum, 2001.

Brown, Ian. "Not Glamorous, But Effective: The Canadian Corps and the Set-piece Attack, 1917-1918." *Journal of Military History* 58, no. 3 (July 1994): 421–44.

Brown, Robert Craig. *Robert Laird Borden: A Biography*, vol. 2, *1914-1937*. Toronto: University of Toronto Press, 1980.

Buckley, John. *British Armour in the Normandy Campaign 1944.* London: Frank Cass, 2004.

Burtch, Andrew. *Give Me Shelter: The Failure of Canada's Cold War Civil Defence.* Vancouver: UBC Press, 2012.

Cook, Tim. *The Fight for History: 75 Years of Forgetting, Remembering, and Remaking Canada's Second World War.* Toronto: Allen Lane, 2020.

Cook, Tim. "The Fire Plan: Gas, Guns, Machine Guns and Mortars." In *Capturing Hill 70: Canada's Forgotten Battle of the First World War*, edited by Douglas Delaney and Serge Marc Durflinger, 102–36. Vancouver: UBC Press, 2016.

Cook, Tim. "'More a Medicine that a Beverage': 'Demon Rum' and the Canadian Trench Soldier of the First World War." *Canadian Military History* 9, no. 1 (Winter 2000): 6–22.

Cook, Tim. *No Place to Run: The Canadian Corps and Gas Warfare in the First World War.* Vancouver: University of British Columbia Press, 1999.

Cook, Tim. "The Politics of Surrender: Canadian Soldiers and the Killing of Prisoners in the Great War." *Journal of Military History* 70, no. 3 (July 2006): 637–66.

Cook, Tim. "'A Proper Slaughter': The March 1917 Gas Raid at Vimy Ridge." *Canadian Military History*, 8, no. 2 (Spring 1999): 7–23.

Cook, Tim. *The Secret History of Soldiers: How Canadians Survived the Great War.* Toronto: Allen Lane, 2018.

Cook, Tim. *At the Sharp End: Canadians Fighting the Great War 1914–1916.* Toronto: Viking, 2007.

Cook, Tim. *Shock Troops: Canadians Fighting in the Great War, 1917–1918.* Toronto: Penguin, 2008.

Copp, Terry and McAndrew, Bill. *Battle Exhaustion: Soldiers and Psychiatrists in the Canadian Army, 1939–1945.* Montréal and Kingston: McGill-Queen's University Press, 1990.

Crerar, Duff. *Padres in No Man's Land.* Montréal and Kingston: McGill-Queen's University Press, 1995.

Cunniffe, Dick. *Scarlet, Riflegreen and Khaki: The Military in Calgary.* Calgary: Century Calgary Publications, 1975.

Delaney, Douglas, and Serge Durflinger, eds. *Capturing Hill 70: Canada's Forgotten Battle of the First World War.* Vancouver: University of British Columbia Press, 2016.

Delaney, Douglas. "The Corps Nervous System in Action: Commanders, Staffs and Battle Procedure." In *Capturing Hill 70: Canada's Forgotten Battle of the First World War*, edited by Douglas Delaney and Serge Durflinger, 51–77. Vancouver: University of British Columbia Press, 2016.

Dempsey, James. "Henry Norwest." *Dictionary of Canadian Biography*, Vol XIV (1911–1920), edited by Ramsay Cook, 786–87. Toronto: University of Toronto Press, 1998.

Dennis, Patrick. *Reluctant Warriors: Canadian Conscripts and the Great War.* Vancouver: UBC Press, 2017.

Director of Public Relations, War Department (India). *One More River: the Story of the Eighth Indian Division.* Bombay: H. W. Smith, 1946.

Doughty, Robert. *Pyrrhic Victory: French Strategy and Operations in the Great War.* Cambridge, MA: Harvard University Press, 2005.

English, John. *The Decline of Politics: The Conservatives and the Party System, 1901-20.* Toronto: University of Toronto Press, 1977.

English, John A. *Monty and the Canadian Army.* Toronto: University of Toronto Press, 2021.

Foley, Robert T. "The Other Side of the Wire: The German Army in 1917." In *1917: Tactics, Training and Technology,* edited by Peter Dennis and Jeffrey Grey, 155-78. Canberra: Chief of the Army's Military History Conference, 2007.

Foran, Max. *Calgary: An Illustrated History.* Toronto: James Lorimer, 1978.

Granatstein, J. L. *Canada's Army: Waging War and Keeping the Peace.* Toronto: University of Toronto Press, 2002.

Granatstein, J. L. *Canada's War: The Politics of the Mackenzie King Government, 1939-1945.* Toronto: University of Toronto Press, 1975.

Greenhalgh, Elizabeth. *The French Army and the First World War.* Cambridge, UK: Cambridge University Press, 2004.

Griffith, Paddy. *Battle Tactics on the Western Front: The British Army's Art of Attack 1916-18.* New Haven, CT: Yale University Press, 1994.

Harris, Stephen. *Canadian Brass: The Making of a Professional Army, 1860-1939.* Toronto: University of Toronto Press, 1988.

Hart, Peter. *1918: A Very British Victory.* London: Weidenfeld & Nicolson, 2008.

Henry, Hugh G. "The Canadian Tanks at Dieppe." *Canadian Military History,* 4 (1995), no. 1: 61-74.

Hyatt, AMJ. *General Sir Arthur Currie: A Military Biography.* Toronto: University of Toronto Press, 1987.

Jackson, Geoffrey. *The Empire on the Western Front: The British 62nd and Canadian 4th Divisions in Battle.* Vancouver: UBC Press, 2019.

Johnston, Roy. *The Disaster of Dieppe: A Wartime Autobiography.* Winnipeg: Universal Bindery, 1991.

Kasurak, Peter. *A National Force: The Evolution of Canada's Army, 1950-2000.* Vancouver: UBC Press, 2013.

Lloyd, Nick. *Hundred Days: The End of the Great War.* London: Viking, 2013.

Marble, Saunders. *British Artillery on the Western Front in the First World War.* Farnham, UK: Ashgate, 2013.

Marti, Steve. *For Home and Empire: Voluntary Mobilization in Australia, Canada, and New Zealand during the First World War.* Vancouver: UBC Press, 2019.

Marteinson, John, ed. *Stand on Guard.* Montréal: Ovale, 1992. http://canadiansoldiers.com/organization/1936 modernization.html.

Marteinson, John and McNorgan, Michael R., eds. *The Royal Canadian Armoured Corps: An Illustrated History.* Kitchener, ON: Royal Canadian Armoured Corps, 2000.

McCrae, Meighen. *Coalition Strategy and the End of the First World War: The Supreme War Council and War Planning, 1917–1918*. Cambridge, UK: Cambridge University Press, 2019.

McDonald, Corrine. *The Canadian Armed Forces: The Role of the Reserves*. Ottawa: Political and Social Affairs Division (DND), 1999. https://publications.gc.ca/collections/Collection-R/LoPBdP/BP/prb9911-e.htm

Messenger, Charles. *The Day We Won the War: The Turning Point at Amiens 8 August 1918*. London: Weidenfeld & Nicolson, 2008.

Miedema, Aaron Taylor. *Bayonets and Blobsticks: The Canadian Experience of Close Combat 1915–1918*. Kingston, ON: Legacy Books, 2011.

Morton, Desmond. *A Peculiar Kind of Politics: Canada's Overseas Ministry in the First World War*. Toronto: University of Toronto Press, 1982.

Morton, Desmond. *Fight or Pay: Soldiers' Families in the Great War*. Vancouver: UBC Press, 2004.

Morton, Desmond. *When Your Number's Up: The Canadian Soldier in the First World War*. Toronto: Random House, 1993.

Morton, Desmond with Copp, Terry. *Working People: An Illustrated History of Canadian Labour*. Ottawa: Deneau, 1981.

Morton, Desmond and Wright, Glenn. *Winning the Second Battle: Canadian Veterans and the Return to Civilian Life 1915–1930*. Toronto: University of Toronto Press, 1987.

Moss, Mark. *Manliness and Militarism: Educating Young Boys in Ontario for War*. Don Mills, ON: Oxford University Press, 2001.

Neary, Peter. *On to Civvy Street: Canada's Rehabilitation Program for Veterans of the Second World War*. Montréal and Kingston: McGill-Queen's University Press, 2011.

Neary, Peter and Granatstein, J. L., eds. *The Veterans Charter and Post–World War II Canada*. Montréal and Kingston: McGill-Queen's University Press, 1998.

Neiburg, Michael. *The Second Battle of the Marne*. Bloomington, IN: Indiana University Press, 2008.

Nicholson, G. W. L. *Canadian Expeditionary Force, 1914–1919*. Ottawa: Queen's Printer, 1964.

Nicholson, G. W. L. *The Canadians in Italy: 1943–1945*. Ottawa: Queen's Printer, 1967.

O'Neill, Patrick B. "The Canadian Concert Party in France." *Theatre Research in Canada/Recherches théâtrales au Canada* 4, no. 2 (Fall 1983). https://journals.lib.unb.ca/index.php/TRIC/article/view/7462/8521

Pal, Dharm. *The Campaign in Italy 1943–45. Official History of the Indian Armed Forces in the Second World War 1939–1945*, edited by Bisheshwar Prasad. Hyderabad, India: Combined Inter-Services Historical Section (India and Pakistan)/Orient Longmans, 1960.

Pedersen, Peter. *The Anzacs: Gallipoli to the Western Front*. Camberwell, UK: Penguin, 2007.

Prieur, Charles. *War Chronicles 1939–1945 Three Rivers Regiment (Tank)*. Unpublished manuscript, accessed 5 November 2024. https://www.12rbc.ca/wp-content/uploads/2021/11/War-Chronicles-Charles-Prieur-Anglais.pdf

Rawling, Bill. *Surviving Trench Warfare: Technology and the Canadian Corps, 1914–1918*. Toronto: University of Toronto Press, 1992.

Riddle, David, and Donald Mitchell. *The Distinguished Conduct Medal Awarded to Members of the Canadian Expeditionary Force 1914–1920*. Winnipeg: Kirkby-Marlton Press, 1991.

Riddle, David, and Donald Mitchell. *The Distinguished Service Order Awarded to Members of The Canadian Expeditionary Force and Canadians in the Royal Naval Air Service, the Royal Flying Corps and Royal Air Force, 1915–1920*. Winnipeg: Kirkby-Marlton Press, 1991.

Riddle, David, and Donald Mitchell. *The Military Cross Awarded to the Members of the Canadian Expeditionary Force, 1915–1921*. Winnipeg: Kirkby-Marlton Press, 1991.

Roy, Reginald. *The Seaforth Highlanders of Canada 1919/1965*. Vancouver: Evergreen Press, 1969.

Sheffield, Gary. *Forgotten Victory*. London: Review, 2002.

Sheffield, Gary. *The Somme*. London: Cassell, 2003.

Sheldon, Jack. *The German Army at Passchendaele*. Barnsley, UK: Pen & Sword Military, 2007.

Sheldon, Jack. *The German Army on Vimy Ridge 1914–1917*. Barnsley, UK: Pen & Sword, 2008.

Showalter, Dennis. *Instrument of War: The German Army 1914–18*. Oxford, UK: Osprey, 2016.

Simpkins, Peter. *Kitchener's Army: The Raising of the New Armies 1914–1916*. Manchester: Manchester University Press, 1988.

Stacey, Charles P. *Six Years of War: The Army in Canada, Britain and the Pacific*. Ottawa: Queen's Printer, 1966.

Stacey, Charles P. *The Victory Campaign: The Operations in North-West Europe, 1944–1945*. Ottawa: Queen's Printer, 1960.

Stacey, Charles P, and Barbara Wilson. *The Half Million: The Canadians in Britain, 1939–1946*. Toronto: University of Toronto Press, 1987.

Stewart, William. *The Embattled General: Sir Richard Turner and the First World War*. Montréal and Kingston: McGill-Queen's University Press, 2015.

Travers, Tim. *How the War Was Won: Factors that Led To Victory in World War One*. London: Routledge, 1992.

Vance, Jonathan F. *Death So Noble: Memory, Meaning and the First World War*. Vancouver: University of British Columbia Press, 1997.

Vance, Jonathan F. *Maple Leaf Empire: Canada, Britain and Two World Wars*. Don Mills, ON: Oxford University Press, 2012.

Vance, Jonathan. *Objects of Concern: Canadian Prisoners of War through the Twentieth Century*. Vancouver: University of British Columbia Press, 1994.

Villa, Brian Loring. *Unauthorized Action: Mountbatten and the Dieppe Raid*. Don Mills, ON: Oxford University Press, 1990.

Walker, James W. StG. "Race and Recruitment in World War I: Enlistment of Visible Minorities in the Canadian Expeditionary Force," *Canadian Historical Review* 70, no. 1 (March 1989): 1–26.

Wheeler, Victor. *The 50th Battalion in No Man's Land*. Ottawa: CEF Books, 2000.

Whitaker, Denis and Shelagh. *Dieppe: Tragedy to Triumph*. Toronto: McGraw-Hill Ryerson, 1992.

Wood, James. *Militia Myths: Ideas of the Canadian Citizen Soldier 1896–1921*. Vancouver: UBC Press, 2010.

Zuehlke, Mark. *Ortona*. Toronto: Stoddart, 1999.

Zuehlke, Mark. *Tragedy at Dieppe*. Vancouver: Douglas & McIntyre, 2012.

Theses and Dissertations

Donaldson, Keith. "Thunder in the Mountains: 1st Canadian Armoured Brigade in Italy, 1943–1944." Master's thesis, University of Calgary, 2008.

Henry, Hugh George. "The Tanks of Dieppe: The History of the Calgary Regiment (Tank), 1939 to August 19, 1942." Master's thesis, University of Victoria, 1991.

Kavanagh, Matthew. "The 10th Indian Division in the Italian Campaign, 1944–45: Training, Manpower and the Soldier's Experience." Master's thesis, University of Birmingham, 2014.

Pratt, William. "1 Canadian Armoured Brigade and the Battle of Lake Trasimene, 20–28 June 1944." Master's thesis, University of New Brunswick, 2010.

Sherwin, Tamara. "From Total War to Total Force: Civil-Military Relations and the Canadian Army Reserve (Militia), 1945–1995." Master's thesis, University of New Brunswick, 1997.

Sweazey, Connor. "Broadcasting Canada's War: How the Canadian Broadcasting Corporation Reported the Second World War." Master's thesis, University of Calgary, 2017.

Index

103rd Regiment (Calgary Rifles), 7–8, 10–12, 34, 61, 112, 117, 325, 329n4, 329n6, 329n8, 334n86, 357n53, 357n62, 380n1

A

Adolf Hitler Line, 209, 215, 224, 227, 237–238, 246, 275, 384n67, 384n68, 384n69, 385n71, 386, 386n87, 386n88, 387n110, 388n112, 388n113, 388n116, 389n134, 399
 German defences, 23, 46, 49, 81, 152, 181, 215, 227, 240, 260, 265, 272, 283
Alexander, Donald, 202–203
Alexander, Harold, 304
Alexander, Laurence "Doc," 134, 140, 149, 158, 162, 166, 168, 172, 176, 181, 184–186, 190, 202–203, 245, 266, 272, 277, 361n5, 365n94, 370n6
Allfrey, Charles, 245, 389n135
Allison, Alton, 171, 239, 310, 406n33
Aloof Trench, 43–47, 326
Ambery, George, 337n20
Amiens (Battle of), 1, 35, 37, 59, 65–66, 70–71, 73–74, 76, 79–83, 88, 96, 103, 117, 326, 343n4, 344n14, 344n16, 344n17, 344n19, 345n25, 345n26, 346n37, 346n38, 349, 352n134
Amy, Edward "Ned," 191, 194–196, 217, 375n110, 376n121, 377n131
Ancre, 17, 117
Anderson Report, 317
Anderson, A. F., 169
Anderson, Archie, 136, 172, 219, 223–224, 286
Anderson, Ole, 195
Anderson, William, 317
Andrews, John "Johnny," 138, 146–151, 154, 157–158, 165, 327, 365n94, 368n136
anti-military sentiments, 120-121
 in Calgary, 2, 12, 113, 118–119, 315
 in Canada, 4, 116, 120, 320–321, 356, 356n47, 409n87
anti-tank guns, 129, 145, 155, 163–164, 175, 182, 185–189, 191, 195–197, 208, 225, 227, 230, 233, 238–242, 251, 253–254, 260, 262, 267, 277, 280, 288–289, 313, 344n20, 374n88, 384n70, 391n170, 394n8, 403n130
17-pounder, 277, 280, 398n61
75-mm, 164, 176, 198, 232–233, 238, 241, 277, 283, 374n87, 400n92
8.8 cm, 190
Aquino, 209, 211, 238–241, 244–245, 250, 275, 289, 310, 388n114, 407
Archer, D. C., 309
Arezzo Line, 249, 253–256, 261, 313
Argo, David, 13, 17, 20, 61, 331n25, 331n38
Argo, Mae, 17, 20, 61, 331n25, 331n38
armistice, 54, 57, 69, 83, 100–101, 105, 114, 342n96, 354n14
Armstrong, William, 11–12, 61
Arnhem, 286–288
Arno River, 209, 215, 247, 249, 257–258, 260–261, 263, 265–266, 275, 278, 282, 297, 306
Arras, 22, 23, 33, 37, 55, 71, 81, 83, 90, 93, 103, 117, 347n59
Australian Corps, 51, 57, 71, 73–75, 342n107, 342n119, 343n5

B

Badicorte, 253
Batson, Arthur, 87, 348n73
battle exhaustion, 32, 215, 243, 377n136, 378. *See also* shell shock
battle honours, 112, 117, 291, 313–314
Beaton, J., 196
Begg, John, 109, 125, 127, 134, 140, 157–159, 162, 171–175, 202, 206, 359n90
Bennett, Edward, 136, 151, 169, 369n157
Bennett, R. B., 11, 112, 120, 123, 354n14
Beresford, Wilfred, 239, 244, 388n116, 388n117
big army plan, 127, 358n81
Bogert Force, 185
Borgo San Lorenzo, 267, 271, 279, 281, 399n69
Boucher, Charles, 273, 276

419

Bourlon Wood, 90–91, 95
Bowen, G. T., 22
Bradbrooke, Gerard, 128, 131, 143–144, 146, 309
Bramshott Camp, 13, 15, 68, 101–102
British Army WWI, 3, 6, 13, 17–20, 22–25, 31–35, 40, 42, 45–46, 48–50, 54–59, 66, 71, 73, 78, 83, 85–86, 90, 96, 98–99, 105, 116, 122, 130
   7th Brigade Tank Corps, 55
   British XVII Corps, 90
   British XXII Corps, 90
   First Army, 23, 33, 37, 41, 43, 56, 71, 81, 83, 90, 96–97, 352, 352n138
   Third Army, 90, 337n25
British Army WWII, 143–144, 146, 152–153, 163, 166, 171, 173–175, 177, 179, 181–183, 185, 194, 208, 211, 215–217, 219, 224, 226–227, 229–232, 234–235, 237–240, 243, 245, 247, 249–250, 252–257, 259–261, 265–267, 270–271, 273–274, 276, 278, 280–281, 283–286, 288, 290, 297, 313, 325, 327
   1/Argyll and Sutherland Highlanders Regiment, 230, 233, 235–237, 259–260, 392, 392n184
   1st British Infantry Division, 265, 270
   1/Leicester Regiment, 288
   1/Royal Fusiliers Regiment, 265
   1/Royal West Kent Regiment, 250–251, 253
   2/Lancashire Fusiliers Regiment, 239
   2/Royal Fusiliers Regiment, 250, 253, 255
   4th British Infantry Division, 85, 230, 234, 249, 252–253, 255–257, 385n76
   6/Black Watch Regiment, 253, 255
   6th British Armoured Division, 249, 255, 257
   11/Royal Scots Fusiliers Regiment, 288
   12th British Infantry Brigade, 249, 254, 390n158, 392n178
   28th British Infantry Brigade, 254
   56th British Infantry Division, 280–281
   78th British Infantry Division, 238, 274, 390n142
   98th (Self-Propelled) Field Artillery Regiment, 232, 257
   147th British Infantry Brigade, 288
   British XIII Corps, 181, 183, 224, 226–227, 229, 240, 249, 254, 257, 259, 261, 266–267, 271, 273–274, 278, 385n75, 387n102, 391n170, 394n8, 395n21, 395n24, 396n27, 396n30
   Eighth Army, 179, 186, 215–217, 224, 227, 237, 239–240, 245, 249, 261, 266–267, 274–276, 380n8, 397n44
Brooke, Alan, 177
Brown, F. A., 47

Brown, Percy, 78, 345n27, 348, 348n73
Buissy Switch, 83
Burgess, Walter, 52, 341n85
Burns, John, 122, 203
Burns, Patrick, 113, 116, 122
Butler, R. W., 198
Byng, Julian, 17, 23–24, 34, 41, 90, 114, 333n66, 334n90, 335n117, 337n25

C

Caix, 74
Calgary Highlanders, 2, 113–114, 116–118, 125, 318, 355n26
Calgary Regiment (14th Reserve Army Tank Battalion), 110, 128–129
Calgary Regiment (Tank) formation 1936, 121-22
   training, 123–124, 126
Cameron, D. F., 171
Camp Borden, 3, 122–123, 127, 129–130, 133, 141, 146, 202–203, 305, 321, 357, 357n62
Camp Wainwright, 299, 304–305, 314, 316, 318–319, 321
Campney, Ralph, 316
Campobasso, 186, 190–191, 208, 375n105
Canadian Active Service Force (CASF), 125, 357n67
Canadian Army in Italy, 3, 126, 180–181, 183–185, 189–192, 200, 213, 216, 244, 247–248, 255–256, 261, 263, 267, 274–276, 278, 280–283, 297, 304, 312, 326
Canadian Army Pacific Force, 294
Canadian Army post-WWII, 303, 310, 321
Canadian Army Reserve regiments
   Calgary Highlanders, 2, 113–114, 116–118, 125, 318, 355n26
   South Alberta Light Horse, 318
Canadian Army WWII, 144, 146, 164, 166, 168, 173–174, 177–178, 199, 202, 204, 206, 215, 256, 263, 276, 281, 286, 292, 294–295, 297, 303, 310, 321
   1st Canadian Armoured Brigade, 6, 192, 199, 224, 226–227, 235, 237, 245, 257, 259, 261, 275, 277–278, 288, 297, 327, 361n19, 362n33, 363n53, 364n74, 364n75, 370n14, 372n45, 373n74, 375n97, 375n105, 376n115, 376n117, 378n138, 379n158, 380n3, 380n6, 383n48, 383n49, 384n58, 384n70, 385n80, 386n82, 387n106, 387n110, 388n114, 388n122, 391n164, 391n166, 391n170, 392n177, 392n184, 393n199, 394n9, 395n13, 395n21, 397n39, 397n42, 398n60, 398n66, 399n69,

420   Index

400n85, 400n90, 400n91, 400n92, 402n118, 402n121, 403n130, 403n132
1st Canadian Army Tank Brigade, 127, 147, 174, 176–177, 183, 206, 215, 360n109, 376n115
1st Canadian Infantry Division, 6, 12, 177, 181, 189, 192, 224, 227, 235, 237, 257, 261, 275, 287, 297, 327, 379, 379n158, 384n69, 390n158, 391n164, 391n166, 397n39, 398n66, 404n150
2nd Canadian Infantry Brigade, 186, 190
2nd Canadian Infantry Division, 15, 51, 101, 150, 186, 190
2nd Field Artillery Regiment, 189
3rd Canadian Infantry Brigade, 17, 35, 183
5th Canadian Armoured Division, 147, 216, 239, 403n132
11th Armoured Regiment (Ontario Regiment), 26, 171, 238, 383n47, 399n69
11th Army Tank Battalion (Ontario Regiment), 127, 130, 141, 143, 151, 172, 178, 181–182, 190, 231, 239–240, 249, 254, 256, 260, 264–265, 271, 281, 375n110, 376n121, 383n45, 386n82, 388n117, 398n66
12th Armoured Regiment (Three Rivers Regiment), 280, 366n97, 368n132, 383n47
12th Army Tank Battalion (Three Rivers Regiment), 127, 173, 181, 199, 236, 251, 264, 281, 371n34, 373n65, 383n47, 398n66
14th Armoured Regiment (Calgary Regiment), 5, 192, 229, 262, 271, 304–305, 308–309, 326, 359n85, 359n89, 359n90, 359n91, 360n105, 360n109, 360n115, 361n3, 361n5, 361n14, 361n19, 362n23, 363n43, 363n59, 364n73, 364n74, 364n75 366n107, 367n114, 367n115, 368n128, 368n136, 370n6, 370n13, 370n18, 370n23, 371n26, 371n28, 372n45, 373n58, 373n74, 374n87, 374n88, 374n91, 376n117, 377n127, 377n131, 377n134, 378n139, 378n147, 379n158, 380n3, 380n8, 381n14, 382n28, 382n32, 382n35, 383n49, 385n79, 385n81, 386n84, 387n100, 387n106, 388n114, 388n116, 388n122, 389n138, 390n155, 391n164, 392n177, 392n184, 393n190, 394n7, 394n9, 395n21, 395n25, 396n30, 397n39, 397n42, 397n44, 398n65, 399n69, 399n72, 400n85, 401n97, 401n108, 401n114, 401n115, 402n118, 402n128, 403n130, 403n131, 403n132, 403n134, 403n136, 404n142, 404n149, 405n13, 406n28
14th Army Tank Battalion (Calgary Regiment), 127, 129, 132, 146, 149, 165, 170, 359n84, 359n85, 376n115
25th Armoured Delivery Regiment, 241

48th Highlanders of Canada, 198
Cameron Highlanders of Canada, 153, 223
Canadian I Corps, 191, 215, 227, 237, 239, 275, 290
Carleton and York Regiment, 184, 198
Essex Scottish Regiment, 153–155, 160
Fusiliers Mont-Royal, 141, 154
Hastings and Prince Edward Regiment, 216
Princess Patricia's Canadian Light Infantry Regiment, 115, 146, 197, 199, 313
Royal Canadian Dragoons, 186
Royal Canadian Regiment, 186–187, 189, 196
Royal Hamilton Light Infantry Regiment, 153, 157
Seaforth Highlanders of Canada, 128, 194, 377n126, 377n133
South Saskatchewan Regiment, 52, 153
Canadian Army WWII miscellaneous units:
61st Light Aid Detachment, 138, 252, 376n122, 380n3
Historical Branch, 269
No. 4 Canadian Army Hospital, 295
Canadian Expeditionary Force (CEF), 9–10, 12, 34, 37, 54, 81, 111–112, 202, 312, 330n12, 331n25, 332n59, 334n96, 335n116, 338n30, 338n35, 343n4, 343n5, 344n17, 347n51, 349n100, 351n116, 352n138, 354n8, 357n50
1st Division, 6, 12, 83, 90, 181–182, 189, 192, 224, 227, 235, 237, 257, 261, 275, 287, 297, 327, 379, 379n158, 384n69, 390n158, 391n164, 391n166, 397n39, 398n66, 404n150
2nd Division, 9, 15, 17, 42–43, 51, 101, 150, 163, 190, 338n35, 381n14
3rd Division, 17, 35, 51, 83, 183, 338n30
4th Division, 1, 18, 22, 24, 28, 30, 37, 40, 42–43, 46, 49, 51, 53, 59, 74, 79–80, 83, 85, 88, 92, 94–95, 98, 100–101, 105–106, 117–118, 251, 330n24, 338n30, 339n49, 344n20, 352n149, 393n186
6th Brigade, 45
10th Battalion, 10, 112, 117–118, 329n3, 329n8, 340, 340n81, 340n83, 341n84, 344n12, 344n14, 344n16, 344n17, 345, 345n25, 347, 347n57, 347n65, 348n78, 349n101, 350n105, 350n109, 351n117, 351n118
10th Brigade, 15, 24–26, 30–31, 33, 49–51, 53–54, 60, 67, 69, 75, 77, 87, 90–91, 95–96, 98, 100, 106, 251, 327, 336n15, 340n76, 340n81, 341n84, 341n86, 344n12, 348n74, 350n105, 351n118
11th Brigade, 18–19, 28, 30, 42, 74

Index   *421*

Canadian Expeditionary Force (CEF) (*continued*)
    12th Brigade, 18, 27–28, 30, 51, 74–75, 77, 80, 85, 88, 91–92, 94–95, 100
    27th Battalion, 43, 338n48
    44th Battalion, 17–18, 24–25, 30, 37–39, 69, 75, 77, 91
    46th Battalion, 19, 51–52, 60, 69, 75, 77, 80, 94, 341n84, 341n86
    47th Battalion, 15, 42, 45, 69, 86, 93, 95, 99
    50th Battalion, 1, 3, 5, 9–14, 18–20, 24–27, 30–32, 35, 40, 44–46, 49, 52–53, 55, 57, 59–61, 64, 69–71, 73–74, 77, 79, 81–82, 85, 90, 93–96, 99–100, 103–106, 108, 112–113, 116–117, 308–309, 311–312, 325, 329n8, 330n12, 331n25, 331n38, 332n55, 332n61, 334n84, 334n85, 334n86, 334n88, 335n100, 335n102, 335n105, 336n2, 336n6, 336n15, 337n16, 337n20, 337n24, 337n27, 337n28, 338n30, 338n34, 338n48, 339n49, 340n76, 341n84, 341n86, 342n106 343n121, 344n12, 345n22, 345n23, 345n27, 346n33, 346n49, 347n51, 348n73, 348n75, 349n87, 349n90, 349n100, 350n103, 350n105, 350n112, 350n113, 351n118, 351n119, 352n135, 352n148, 353n151, 353n157
        arrival in France, 42
        battle honours, 112, 117
        Japanese-Canadian soldiers, 21
    56th Battalion, 20, 61
    75th Battalion, 19, 26
    137th Battalion, 10, 21, 31, 64, 112, 312, 356n33
    Canadian Corps, 1–2, 17–18, 22–24, 28, 34–35, 41, 48, 51, 53, 56–59, 68, 71, 75, 79, 82–83, 87, 90, 96, 105–106, 333n66, 334n85, 337n25, 343n125, 343n4, 343n5, 352n135
Canadian media coverage (WWII), 165-166, 182, 185, 229, 255, 275-276
Canadian prisoners of war (POWs), 6, 26, 35, 39–40, 81, 92, 96, 108, 136–137, 159–165, 167, 169, 171, 203–204, 217–224, 284–286, 295–297, 305–307, 322, 333n79, 335n105, 351n119, 365n88, 365n91, 366n103, 366n105, 366n107, 366n109, 366n110, 367, 367n112, 367n114, 367n115, 367n116, 367n117, 367n118, 367n119, 369n159, 380n11, 380n12, 381n13, 381n14, 381n15, 381n16, 381n17, 381n18, 381n22, 381n24, 381n26, 382n27, 382n28, 382n32, 382n34, 382n35, 382n36, 382n38, 382n39, 383n41, 399n72, 400n94, 401n97, 401n99, 401n100, 401n102, 404n146, 405n14

Geneva Convention, 219, 222
    special pensions, 306, 322 (*see also* prisoners of war [Dieppe])
Canadian Red Cross, 219, 380n173. *See also* prisoners of war (Dieppe); Red Cross
Canadian soldiers' interaction with civilians:
    Belgian, 69, 283, 400n90
    British, 135, 144–145, 163, 173
    Dutch, 212, 291, 293–295, 369n156, 402n118, 403n131
    Italian, 184–185, 191
Canadian Wives Bureau, 379n169
Canadian Women's Army Corps, 246
Canal de l'Escaut, 90, 98
Canal de la Sensée, 90, 96–97
Canal du Nord (Battle of), 1, 67, 83, 85, 87–89, 95, 103, 108, 117, 348n84
Carnie, T. L., 157
Caron, Fernand, 225–226, 383n45
Casaglia Pass, 267, 269–270
Casewell, Lionel, 27, 30–31, 334n86
Castelfiorentino, 260
Cavanagh, L. A., 109, 120–122, 357, 357n53, 357n55
Cawsey, Alan, 233–234, 264, 386n84, 386n87
Charbonneau, A. J., 187–189, 195–196, 375n95, 377n127
Chemin des Dames, 22, 48
Childress, C. A., 195, 377n134
Churchill tank, 134, 136, 146, 148–149, 154–157, 163–164, 171–172, 174–175, 177, 217, 362n36, 363n53, 363n59, 368n133, 370n9, 371n28
Churchill, Winston, 264
Cider Crossroads, 197, 199
civil defense, 300, 317–320, 323
    reserves' role, 319
Clapperton, David "Dave", 134, 166, 182
Clark, Mark, 245, 273, 277
Clark, Mildred, 204–205. *See also* Scott, Mildred
Clarke, E. J., 52
Clouse, F. L., 94
Cold War, 302, 304, 316, 321–322
Cole, Elmer, 217
Cole, Victor, 18
Colville, J. H., 43
Commonwealth/Imperial War Graves Commission, 21, 332n55, 336n6
Corley, J. B., 77
Cornelssen, R. C. "Bobby", 136, 169, 368n136
Costigan, John, 27, 30, 334n86
Cote, J. O., 159

Court, Ted, 142, 151, 173, 187, 189
Craigie, Donald, 222, 285, 296, 306–307, 367n114, 382n35
Crerar, Henry, 145, 163, 216, 352n140, 371n28
Cunningham, Thomas, 159
Cunnington, Douglas, 96, 108, 115, 117, 119, 332n59, 351n119, 355, 355n30, 356n38
Currelly, R. T., 269, 394n10, 395, 395n14, 396n34, 397n39, 404n149, 404n150
Currie, Arthur, 41–42, 46, 48, 50, 54, 57, 59, 71, 73, 75, 81, 83, 85, 87–88, 90, 95, 97–98, 100, 342n117, 343n125
Curtin, Tom, 252
Cusack, G., 22

D

D-Day Dodgers, 3, 274–275, 282, 297, 308
Darroch, Rev. G. E., 264
Davies, R. D., 25, 69, 333n74
Davis, Charles, 87
Dawson, Herbert, 37, 52, 69, 336n14, 341n86
Dearness, I. H., 319
demobilization, 68, 102–104, 214, 291–293, 308, 322
  re-integrating into civilian life post-WWII, 307, 322–323
Department of Veterans Affairs/Veterans Affairs Canada, 206, 292, 305, 311
Diefenbaker Government, 318–319
  defence policies, 319
Diefenbaker, John, 317
Dieppe Raid (Operation Jubilee), 5, 132, 134, 140, 150, 152–153, 163, 165, 171, 174, 183, 203, 217, 312, 364n74, 365n80, 365n82, 365n87, 365n88, 367n127, 368n133, 405n13
  German defences, 23, 46, 49, 81, 152
Dixon, A. B., 78
Dobree, Thomas, 227, 231, 234, 237, 257, 272–273
Donabie, Robert, 187, 190
Dottignies, 211, 283
Douglas, Bryce, 156
Dowler, J. H., 87
Dowling, Ralph, 156
Doxsee, Earl, 100
Driebergen, 213, 293–294
Drocourt-Quéant Line (Battle of), 1, 83–86, 88, 117, 344n11, 348n74
Dyde, Henry, 94, 334n85, 339n54, 347n53

E

Eaton, Robert, 14, 18–19, 22, 27, 113, 331, 331n43, 332n61
Ede, 64, 212, 288–289, 298, 313, 401, 401n113, 406n42
Electrical Generating Station, 37–38, 62
  Callons Trench, 37–38, 40
Elliot, W. R., 19, 22
Elliott, C. G., 179
Elmes, Howard, 244
Elsa River, 259–260
Émerchicourt, 97
Empoli, 257, 260–261
Evans, W. L., 244
Eveleigh, Wesley, 27, 30, 77, 103, 334n86, 353n163
Ewart, David, 199, 378n142, 378n146
Exercise Spartan, 140, 174–175, 371n25

F

Faenza, 267, 271, 274, 280
Fahy, E. J., 22
Femmina Morta, 269–270
Ferguson, William, 310, 406n31
Festubert, 117, 329
Florence, 3, 21, 249, 254, 257, 261, 263, 267, 274, 277–278, 282, 406n39, 407
Foch, Ferdinand, 71, 83, 343n1
Foiano della Chiana, 252
Forest, L. S., 289
Forrest, Robert, 30, 336n4, 347
Foulkes, Charles, 286, 317
Fouquescourt, 75, 77, 81, 345, 345n23, 345n32
Fox, J. E., 91
Franeker, 294–295, 403n132, 403n136
Fraser, David, 92
Free French Army (*Corps Expéditionaire Française*) in Italy, 227, 238, 256, 283–285, 392n183
Freeman, Richard, 167
Fresnes-Rouvroy Line, 83
Fuchko, Mark, 322

G

Gabbiano, 251–252
Gari River, 138, 210, 215, 224, 226–227, 229, 231–232, 234–236, 244, 246, 384n60, 385n81, 386n87, 387n106, 388n116, 398n66
gas warfare, 26, 35, 44–45, 47, 55, 58, 85, 87, 91, 99–100, 343n125, 351, 352n148
Gentelles Wood, 74

Index   423

German Army (in Italy) WWII, 137, 152–153,
    159, 161, 164–165, 173, 177, 183, 185 187, 190,
    192, 199, 210, 215, 218–219, 221–222, 224,
    229, 235–238, 240, 247, 249–251, 253–256,
    259, 261, 263, 265–267, 269, 271–273, 286,
    288, 290–291, 295, 297, 306, 326
  1st Parachute (*Fallschirmjägers*) Division, 240,
    249–250, 378n150, 390n147
  2/576th *Panzergrenadier* Regiment, 236
  3rd *Panzergrenadier* Division, 260
  90th *Panzergrenadier* Division, 196–197,
    378n139
  115th *Panzergrenadier* Regiment, 233, 387,
    387n102
  302nd Infantry Division, 152
  334th Infantry Division, 249
  356th Infantry Division, 249, 264–265, 394n8
  578th Grenadier Regiment, 272
  715th Infantry Division, 264, 270
  735th Infantry Regiment, 265
  Herman Göring Panzer Division, 249
German Army WWI
  1st Bavarian Corps, 28
  5th Prussian Grenadier Guards Regiment, 31
  6th Army, 28
  11th Bavarian Division, 51
  11th Bavarian Regiment, 51
  16th Bavarian Division, 26
  18th Infantry Regiment, 30
  261st Infantry Regiment, 30
  Army Group Crown Prince Rupprecht, 28
Gilbert, Roy, 167
Gilchrist, L. A., 320
Glenn, Allan, 151, 155–158, 160
Gordon, William, 52
Gothic Line, 209, 247, 249, 256, 263, 267–268,
  270–271, 276, 297, 395, 395n21, 397n39
Graham, Howard, 189
Grant, William, 22, 78
Gray, G. F., 196, 265
Greenwell, George, 172
The Gully, 197, 199, 306, 378n150
Gustav Line, 209, 215, 224, 227, 228n65, 235,
  237–238, 246, 275, 313, 385n81, 388n116,
  389n134, 389n66. *See also* Operation Honker

H
Haase, Jack, 187
Haig, Douglas, 17–18, 48, 79, 88, 348n75
Hallu, 75, 77–78, 80, 108, 347n51
Halstead, Charles, 198, 378, 378n143
Halton, Matthew, 275

Harris, J. R., 85, 330n16
Harrison, A. J., 195, 377n134
Harrods Camp, 282
Harrop, R. A., 78, 345, 345n29, 345n30
Hayter, Ross, 54, 69, 73, 75, 77, 85–88, 90,
  93–96, 98, 348n78, 352n134
Heber-Percy, Algernon, 249–250, 252, 257
Helmer, Calvin, 158, 168, 172
Hill 70 (Battle of), 1, 42, 46, 117, 338n31,
  338n37, 339n52. *See also* Lens (Battle of)
Hilliam, Edward, 24, 37, 41–44, 46, 51, 54,
  332n61, 338n48, 341n84, 341n86, 342n96
Hindenburg Line, 22, 83, 85, 96, 347n59. *See
  also* Drocourt-Quéant Line (Battle of)
Hodge, C. T., 20, 44, 93–94, 332n53
Hodges, Alfred, 44, 93–94
Hodgkins, A. R., 22
Hofer, Emily, 310
Hofer, Richard, 289, 310, 313, 406n33
Holland, 212, 263, 286–288, 290–291, 294–295,
  297, 310–311, 369n156, 390n155, 401,
  401n114, 403n131, 403n133, 403n136
homecoming, 2, 102, 104, 214, 296
  50th Battalion 1919, 102
  Calgary Regiment 1945, 214
Hornburg, Nathan, 302, 322
Horne, Henry, 23, 33, 37, 41–42, 46, 49, 83, 90,
  95, 100
Horne, James, 166
Howard, Joseph, 322, 409n88, 409n89, 409n92
Howard, William, 315, 407n52
Howe, Frank, 166, 168
Hughes, Sam, 12–13, 330n23
Hughes, William St. Pierre, 24, 54, 333n68
Hundred Days Campaign, 59, 66, 69, 71, 97, 106,
  326, 343n125, 348n75, 353
Hunter, J. S., 226, 313
Hyde, R. E., 195

I
Indian Army in Italy, 215, 234, 270, 305,
  383n49, 385n80, 393n190
  1/5th Gurkha Rifles, 265, 270, 398n59
  1/5th Mahratta Regiment, 259, 269, 278
  3/8th Punjab Regiment, 230, 232–235, 272,
    278, 392n184
  6/13th Royal Frontier Force Rifles, 208,
    235–237
  8th Indian Division, 198, 225–227, 229–230,
    234–237, 256–257, 260–261, 263–267, 269,
    271–272, 274, 276–278, 280, 297, 383n48,
    383n52, 385n76, 391n170, 392n183, 392n185,
    394n7

17th Indian Brigade, 235, 264, 269, 271, 276, 395n25, 396n30
19th Indian Brigade, 225–227, 229, 235–236, 256, 264, 272, 383n48, 384n54, 385n81, 387n102, 387n106, 392n177
21st Indian Brigade, 236, 259, 264, 383n48, 383n51, 387n97, 393n188, 396n30, 397n39
Ironside, William, 46, 51

J

James, W. G., 85, 269, 273, 279
Jenkins, A. T., 22
Jenner, F. T., 171, 359n90
Johnson, Al, 169, 369n158
Johnson, Johnny, 197
Johnston, Roy, 155–156, 160, 223, 364
Jull, Walter, 109, 123, 126–130, 359n85, 404n4

K

Kaiserslacht, 56
Keegan, Herbert, 14, 25, 27, 55, 69, 77, 86
Keightley, Charles, 239–240
Kennedy Report, 316, 407n58
Kesselring, Albert, 247, 249, 251, 256, 263, 266–267, 390n151, 396n30
The King's Own Calgary Regiment, 1–2, 4–6, 31, 298–299, 301–305, 309, 312–316, 318–323, 325, 327, 329n4, 405n8, 408n81, 408n82, 408n83, 409n88
The King's Own Royal Lancaster Regiment, Territorial Army, 116, 118, 122, 357n53, 404n4
Kingsmill Bridge, 231, 385n77, 385n79. *See also* Plymouth Bridge
Kingsmill, Tony, 138, 231–232, 385, 385n79, 386
Kirkham, Norman, 167
Kirkman, Sidney, 224–225, 227, 234, 249, 257, 263, 265–266, 269, 272
Knibbs, P. V., 253
Knight, E. R., 119–120, 356n38
Knodel, M., 135, 196, 377n127, 378n147
Kreger, Lionel, 252, 391n164

L

Ladies auxiliary, 104–105, 114, 116, 200, 203–204, 219–220
Lamb, Harry, 388n117
Lamone River, 267, 271
Landing Ship Tank (LST), 178–179, 183, 282, 372n45
Langholm, 176, 178, 372n42

Langley, R. C., 244
Larke, Rev. A. E., 241
Lauzon, Adrien, 237
Leadley, P. G., 37–38
Leese, Oliver, 236–237, 239
Leghorn, 282
Lens (Battle of), 1, 35–37, 41–43, 45–47, 54, 56, 64, 117, 326. *See also* Aloof Trench
Leslie, Alexander, 252
Lipsett, Louis, 51
Liri Valley, 215, 224, 227, 236, 243, 313, 383n48, 383n49, 384n70, 386n82, 387n106, 388n114, 388n122, 389n124, 403n130
Lowes, Arthur, 22, 341n84
Luftwaffe, 152, 210, 226, 240
Lynch, Curly, 187

M

MacBrien, James, 54, 75, 87, 99, 354, 354n10
MacDonald, J. H. B., 151–152, 158, 364n72, 364n74, 364n75, 366n97, 366n99
machine gun, 19, 30–31, 37–39, 42, 44, 47, 49, 52–53, 75, 77–79, 83, 85–87, 90, 92–99, 115, 119, 121–124, 145, 153–156, 160, 169, 177, 187–190, 195, 197–198, 219, 225, 230, 232–233, 237–239, 255, 267, 287, 289, 334n96, 340n82, 341n85, 344, 344n17, 344n20, 348n75, 357n50, 365n90, 377n127, 389n124, 391n164
MG 08, 31, 75
Maestro della Chiana canal, 251
Maltby, Richard, 289, 313, 371n30, 389n138, 390n155, 396n36, 398n65
Marcoing Line, 90, 93–94, 350n105
Marquion Line, 67, 81, 90–91, 326
Marradi, 214, 271–272, 277, 279
Marshall, R. C., 102
Mason, Edward, 9, 11–15, 18, 61, 104, 117, 329n4, 330n9
Mason, Katharine, 104–105
Matilda IIA* tank, 142–143, 145, 361, 361n12, 362n36
Mayhew, Johnny, 159
Mayson, William, 99, 352n145
McCallum, H., 22
McCann, Henry, 156
McConnell, Samuel, 348, 348n73
McCreery, Richard, 276–277, 397n44
McIndoe, D. H., 134, 171
McIntosh, A. F., 313, 318
McIntyre, Michael, 166, 169, 369n159
McKittrick, Charles, 14

Index   425

McLean, George, 232
McLean, J. F., 197
McMullin, J. W., 244
McNaughton, Andrew, 99, 140, 145, 174–175, 352n140
McWithy, William, 233
Mewata Armoury, 114, 120, 122, 125–126, 129, 296, 301, 304–305
Military District (MD) 13, 115, 121–122, 126, 128, 130, 354n10, 356n34, 356n38, 359n84, 359n85, 359n89, 404, 404n4
Military Service Act, 81–83
Military Voters' Act, 54
militia (Calgary, pre-WWI)
  imperialist sentiments, 11
Millar, Perry, 247, 399n69
Miller, A. J., 171
Mœuvres, 67
Moncrief, C. W., 195
Monte Casalino, 271–272
Montespertoli, 260
Montgomery, Bernard, 149–150, 181, 185, 194, 288, 380n1
Monz, J. L., 181
Moore, Stuart, 80, 87
Morgan, D., 25, 195
Moro River, 194, 205, 310
Morrill, L., 53
Morrison, E. W. B., 352n140
Morton, Forbes, 284, 382n30, 382n32, 401n96
Motta Montecorvino, 134, 139, 186–190, 201, 206, 275, 306, 326, 375n105, 406n43
mountain warfare (Italy), 217, 266, 269, 387n106, 393n190
Mountbatten, Louis, 150
Muirhead, David, 81–82, 347n51
Munro, Andrew, 21, 59, 332n56, 334n85
Munro, Ross, 182, 185, 275
Murphy, William "Spud", 211, 216, 225–226, 234, 236, 238–240, 244–246, 249, 256, 273, 278–279, 281, 283, 290, 293, 385n80, 393n186, 400n90, 402n121, 404n149
Murray, Rev. William, 78, 94

N

Navy, Army and Air Force Institutes (NAAFI), 201, 240, 379n156
Neder Rijn River, 286–288, 290, 401n108
Nelson, Gus, 138, 222–223, 382n40
Neroutsos, Cyril, 175–176, 178–179, 183–184, 186–187, 189, 191–192, 196–197, 199–200, 205–206, 211, 217, 225–226, 229, 231–232, 236–237, 239–240, 244, 246, 327, 371n28, 373n73, 377n131, 380n10, 388n114
New Zealand 2nd Infantry Division, 194, 255, 260, 342n107, 342n119, 409n87
Newhaven, 147, 150–151, 159, 162
Nightingale, Jessie, 332n54, 332n55
Nightingale, Sydney, 20, 332n54
Nijmegen, 286–287, 295
Non-Permanent Active Militia, 112, 116, 121, 358
  1st Battalion Calgary Regiment, 112–113, 355n26, 355n32
  2nd Battalion Calgary Regiment, 112–114, 129
Norwest, Henry, 35, 37, 81, 336n5, 336n6, 346n49

O

Odlum, Victor, 42, 54, 87, 98
Oflag VII-B, 163, 219, 381n18. *See also* prisoners of war (Dieppe)
Oke, Charles, 73–74, 79–80, 85–86, 97, 344n12, 349n87, 352n148
Oliver, William, 78
Olliffe, Frederick, 167–168
Olliffe, Hilda, 168
Operation Ajax, 143, 361n20
Operation Anger, 287
Operation Baytown, 183–184
Operation Dragoon, 266, 283
Operation Goldflake, 281
Operation Honker, 226–227, 229, 241, 245, 256, 275, 386n85, 387n105
Operation Husky, 179. *See also* Sicily
Operation Jubilee, 150, 152–153, 163, 165, 364n74, 365n88. *See also* Dieppe Raid
Operation Rutter, 149–151, 174, 364n74
  cancellation, 150, 348n78
Orritt, William, 46, 339n51
Overyssche, 69, 101
Oxford Bridge, 231–233, 235, 385n76, 386n82

P

Page, C. E., 94, 155, 163–164, 246, 327, 359n90, 365n88, 365n94, 382n35
Page, Lionel, 26–27, 30–32, 37–47, 49–56, 59, 62–63, 69–70, 73–75, 77–78, 80–83, 85–86, 88, 90–96, 98, 100, 102–105, 112–113, 164, 332n61, 334n85, 334n88, 334n90, 336n9, 337n16, 337n20, 337n28, 338n48, 339n49, 341n86, 343n122, 346n49, 349n90, 349n100, 350n105, 350n112, 350n113, 353n157

426 Index

Palsson, Victor, 188
Panaccioni, 233–236
Panet, Éduard, 73
Panzer Mark IV, 196–197, 377n130
Panzerfaust, 253, 288, 391n170, 394n8
Panzerschreck, 253, 288, 391n170
Parry, J. R. L., 14–15, 45, 55, 57, 85, 337n20, 343n122
Passchendaele (Battle of), 1, 41, 43, 48–51, 53–54, 59, 63, 103, 117, 312, 325, 340n70, 340n71, 340n81, 340n82, 341n84, 343n5
Patterson, Pat, 156, 261
Pattison, Henry, 31, 40–41, 335n102, 337n24, 406n39. *See also* war memorials
Pattison, John, 10, 31, 40–41, 64, 103, 312, 335n102, 337n20, 337n24, 406n38, 406n39
Payne, Oliver, 81, 336n5
Pearkes, George, 317
Peronne Wood, 74
Petrignano, 250–251
Pignataro, 236–237, 387n106, 407
Pinder, Thomas, 152, 159, 220–221, 382n28
Plumer, Herbert, 48
Plymouth Bridge, 231–232, 235, 385n76, 385n81. *See also* Kingsmill Bridge
Polish Army in Italy, 152, 227, 229, 234, 237–238, 286
II Polish Corps, 227, 229, 234
Pontassieve, 264–265, 267
Potenza, 185
Prescott, Thomas, 100
Priest (self-propelled 25-pounder artillery), 264
prisoners of war (Dieppe), 3, 6, 132, 136–137, 159–162, 164–165, 167, 169, 171, 203–204, 217–224, 284–286, 295–297, 305–308, 322, 365n88, 366n109, 366n110, 367n112, 367n114, 367n115, 367n116, 367n117, 367n118, 381n16, 381n17, 381n18, 381n22, 381n24, 381n26, 382n27, 405n14. *See also* Red Cross
Canadian Prisoner of War Relatives Association, 220
communication with next of kin, 221, 284, 382n29, 382n30, 382n31, 382n32, 401n96
Der Brotmarsch (hunger march), 284
food concerns, 217, 219–221, 284–286
liberation, 285–286
POW camps, 137, 162, 169, 217–219, 221–223, 284, 286, 306, 366, 366n108, 381n20, 383n42, 401n103
shackling, 221–222, 306, 382n35
Purves, Robert, 171, 175, 187, 225–226, 383n45

Q

Quinn, James, 212, 229, 232–234, 237–239, 242, 272, 309, 385n81, 388n116, 406n28

R

Radcliffe, Percy, 23
Raillencourt, 93
Rainey, J. W., 289
Ralston, Layton, 145
Ram tank, 175
Rapido River, 227, 230, 235, 384n60, 384n61, 386n83
Raskin, Elly, 201
Raskin, Marjorie, 201
Rattray, C, 52
Rawlinson, Henry, 71, 79
Red Cross, 137, 167–169, 206, 218–222, 284–285, 369n155, 380n173, 401n97
Reggio Calabria, 184
Reynolds, B. A., 253
Rhône Valley, 283
Richardson, C. A. Stoney, 134, 146–147, 161, 182, 188, 191, 201, 226, 241, 247, 249–251, 253–257, 262–264, 267, 270, 272–274, 276–278, 280–281, 283, 287–291, 293–297, 309–310, 325, 327, 371n30, 374n91, 376n117, 389n138, 390n155, 397n44, 398n65, 399n75, 402n121, 403n130, 403n133, 403n136, 404n149
Richardson, Gordon, 216
Richardson, Vern, 161, 222, 286
Ritchie, Fred, 116, 187, 196, 239, 243, 246–247, 254, 257, 280–282, 288, 308, 374n91, 387n105, 390n155, 392n185
Roberts, Hamilton "Ham", 22, 140, 150, 154, 163–164
Rodgers, D. F., 304, 404n4
Rosenthal, H., 22
Ross, Duke, 189
Ross, John, 99, 352n134
Rocelx, 98
Rowles, James, 293, 402n126
Royal Canadian Legion, 309, 311, 353n164
royal visit (1939), 124
Rupprecht, Crown Prince, 26, 28, 48
Russell, Dudley, 225–226, 230–232, 235–237, 245, 256, 259, 265–266, 269–270, 272–274, 276, 383n48, 392n183, 398n57
Rutledge, A. H., 158

Index   427

S

Sains-les-Marquion, 90
San Donato, 278–279, 399n69
San Leonardo, 194–197, 199–200, 205–206, 216, 376n123, 377n125, 377n126, 377n127, 377n131, 377n134, 378n147
San Martino, 214, 277
San Pancrazio, 210, 253–255
Sangro River, 192, 194, 377n124, 378n142, 378n152, 379n153, 380n1, 380n10
Sarcee Camp, 7, 12–13, 105, 109–110, 115, 119, 122, 125–126, 300, 304, 319, 329n6
Scott, A. W., 43
Scott, Denis, 160, 218, 284–285, 366n107, 381n14, 382n35, 401n97
Scott, Mildred, 205. *See also* Clark, Mildred
Scott, Percy, 204–205
Seaford, 134–135, 146–148, 150–151, 162, 165, 171, 204, 306, 363n40, 367n120
Second Battle of Arras, 22–23, 33, 37, 71, 81, 83, 90, 93, 103, 117, 347n57, 347n59, 347n62, 347n65, 347n66, 347n69, 347n70, 348n74, 348n78, 348n81. *See also* Vimy Ridge (Battle of)
Senio River, 280–281, 290
Seymour, Ian, 232, 385n77, 385n79
Sharpe, Henry, 93–94
shell shock, 18, 341n84. *See also* battle exhaustion
Sherman tank, 176–177, 187–189, 191, 195–198, 207–211, 227, 232–233, 236–237, 239, 241–242, 244, 252, 262, 277, 280, 289, 298, 313, 371n26, 371n34, 374n87, 374n88, 376n117, 377n130
  Firefly variant, 211, 277, 283, 398n60, 400n92
Sicily, 176–177, 179, 181–183, 215, 217, 257, 313, 372n55, 373n60, 373n67, 373n75, 374, 374n78, 374n86, 374n87, 374n88, 375n94, 375n103, 375n104, 375n109, 375n110, 376n111, 376n117, 379n158, 407
Sieve River, 265–267, 269, 297
Simmonds, Guy, 184
Singleton, J. W., 181
Slade, Arthur, 87, 97, 99
Slifka, Lyman, 201, 379n160
Smethurst, Ken, 156
Smith, Rev. Waldo, 158
Somme (Battle of), 1, 15, 17–24, 54, 61, 91, 103, 331n35
  Desire Support Trench, 18–19, 22

South African Army in Italy, 252, 257, 260
  6th South African Armoured Division, 257
Spry, Daniel, 186–189
St. Martin, Vital, 250
Stalag II-D (Stargard), 223, 284. *See also* prisoners of war (Dieppe)
Stalag VIII-B (Lamsdorf), 162, 169, 217–218, 222, 284, 381n20, 383n42, 401n103. *See also* prisoners of war (Dieppe)
Stanton, A. G., 157
Stuart tank, 213, 217, 234, 241, 250, 262, 264, 282, 293, 304, 391n164, 407n59
StuG III assault gun, 233, 235, 237–238, 241–242, 249, 251–252, 254, 259–260, 288, 387n102, 394n8, 398n60
Stursberg, Peter, 229, 255, 275–276, 386n84
Svendsen, Olaf, 27, 30–31, 37, 39, 113–114, 117, 334n86
Swinton, J. W., 25
Szeler, Tony, 237

T

Tank Landing Craft (TLC), 136, 149, 151, 154, 156–159, 364, 364n75, 366
Taylor, Donald C., 134, 188, 233–234, 250, 273, 288, 386n85
Taylor, James, 43, 78
Taylor, Robert R., 134, 166, 171, 181, 214, 217, 232, 239, 288, 386n84, 403n130
Thorne, Albert, 52, 341n85
Thring, Dorothy, 139, 296
Thring, George, 139, 190, 197, 282, 296, 370, 370n16, 388n116, 405n13
Trasimene Line, 245, 247, 249, 276, 313, 390n142, 394n8
trench raiding, 24–28
Trotter, Debruce G., 134, 171, 185, 187, 375n110
Tufts, R. N., 87
Turney, T. A., 166
Tweed, Thomas, 77
Tweedy, Kenneth, 252

U

Underhill, Frank, 189, 375n98
US Army in Italy, 227, 230, 266–267, 271, 296, 384n60, 392n183
  US Fifth Army, 224, 245, 266, 277
  US II Corps, 267

V

Valenciennes (Battle of), 1, 96, 98–100, 103, 117, 352n143, 352n147
  Mont Houy, 98–99, 352n140
Valentine, George, 166
Valiano, 250–251
VE Day, 286, 291, 294, 310, 402n120, 403n130
Venafro, 217, 241, 383n46
Veterans Charter, 292, 307, 402n123
veterans' associations, 103, 105, 308–309, 365n79, 366n98, 367n118, 367n121, 367n123, 368n137, 370, 370n16, 376n117, 376n120, 377n125, 377n126, 377n127, 378n142, 378n146, 378n147, 379n165, 379n166, 379n167
  50th Battalion, 103, 105, 308, 311
  Calgary Regiment (50/14 Association), 308–309, 365n79, 366n98, 367n118, 367n121, 367n123, 368n137, 370, 370n16, 376n117, 376n120, 377n125, 377n126, 377n127, 378n142, 378n146, 378n147, 379n165, 379n166, 379n167
  veterans' reunions, 306, 308–309, 406n27
Vicchio, 269, 273
Vimy Ridge (Battle of), 1, 5, 11, 22–23, 25–29, 31–35, 37, 40, 47–48, 54–55, 59–60, 64, 68, 91–92, 103, 114, 117, 311, 332n61, 333n81, 334n88, 335n102, 336n6
  Hill 145, 26, 28, 30–31
  The Pimple, 25–26, 30–31, 37
Vino Ridge, 197, 199, 326, 378n142, 378n146, 388n116
Vokes, Christopher, 194, 198, 315–316, 407n50, 407n51, 407n53
von Fasbender, Karl Ritter, 28
von Kuhl, Hermann, 46, 340n71

W

Waal River, 286–287, 290
Wagstaff, Al, 156, 306
Wallace, Richard, 141, 157, 159
war brides, 103, 204–205, 361n3, 388n117. *See also* Canadian Wives Bureau
war memorials, 107, 114, 283, 313, 365n94
  137th Battalion, 312
  Pattison Bridge, 40–41
Ward, Alfred Dudley, 252, 393n186
Wasp, 289
Watkin, A. L., 92, 134
Watson, David, 14–15, 18–19, 21, 24, 26–27, 30, 32–33, 35, 39, 42–43, 46–47, 51, 54, 71, 77, 83, 85, 87, 90, 96, 98, 100, 332n62, 334n90, 339n49, 341n84, 341n86, 342n96, 345n23, 346n33, 347n51, 352n149, 353n150
Watson, W. G., 78
Webber, Norman, 87
Webster, Lester, 14–15
Weir, John, 44
Welch, Dwight, 169, 368n136, 369n155, 369n156
Wells, Alan, 232, 237
Westlake, Harry, 18
Wheeler, Victor, 15, 17, 21, 30, 32–33, 38–39, 46, 58, 82, 101, 103, 311–312, 345n23, 406n27
Whitaker, Denis, 157
White, J. D., 217, 222, 285, 296
Whitfield, G. T., 281
Whitton, J. L., 226, 395n21
Worsnop, Charles, 22, 24–26, 332n62
Worthing, 135, 172–173, 175–176, 204, 306
Worthington, Frank, 127–128, 130–131, 142–143, 145–147, 149, 313, 362n21
Wright, Joshua, 13, 19
Wyman, Robert, 140, 147–149, 163, 171, 173–174, 177–178, 192, 194, 216, 371n28, 373n65, 377n131, 380n6

www.ingramcontent.com/pod-product-compliance
Lightning Source LLC
LaVergne TN
LVHW070614010525
810121LV00002B/6